# THE STATE-BY-STATE GUIDE TO WOMEN'S LEGAL RIGHTS

# THE STATE-BY-STATE GUIDE TO WOMEN'S LEGAL RIGHTS

NOW Legal Defense and Education Fund
and Dr. Renée Cherow-O'Leary

**McGraw-Hill Book Company**

New York   St. Louis   San Francisco   Auckland   Bogotá
Hamburg   Johannesburg   London   Madrid   Mexico   Milan
Montreal   New Delhi   Panama   Paris   São Paulo   Singapore
Sydney   Tokyo   Toronto

1 2 3 4 5 6 7 8 9 D O C D O C 8 7 6

ISBN 0-07-047778-7 {PBK}
ISBN 0-07-047779-5 {H.C.}

LIBRARY OF CONGRESS CATALOGING-IN-PUBLICATION DATA

The state-by-state guide to women's legal rights.
  Bibliography: p.
  1. Women—Legal status, laws, etc.—United States—
States. I. Cherow-O'Leary, Renée. II. NOW Legal
Defense & Education Fund. III. Title.
KF478.Z95S73  1986        346.7301'34        86-2972
ISBN 0-07-047779-5        347.306134
ISBN 0-07-047778-7 (pbk.)

DISCLAIMER

This book is for informational purposes only and does not constitute legal services or representation. For specific legal advice, there is no substitute for consultation with a practicing attorney who possesses thorough and up-to-date knowledge of the law in your state or locality and who is informed about all the relevant details of your situation.

Despite every effort to ensure the accuracy of this book's contents, some errors may appear. Moreover, laws can change quite rapidly, and court interpretations of laws often vary. Therefore, no guarantee can be given as to the accuracy and completeness of any information provided in this guide. The authors hereby specifically disclaim any liability for loss incurred as a consequence of any material presented in this book.

# CONTENTS

# PREFACE

The history of twentieth-century America has yet to be written. But many contemporary observers of its social and political changes believe that transformation in the meaning of being female will be recorded as the most significant and powerful event in this century. And nowhere is the record of those changes more profound or revealing than in the federal and state laws which have been enacted or revised in the last two decades to reflect women's changing role in the United States. This book is a compendium of those changes.

Twenty years ago—almost 50 years after women won the right to vote—marriage in most states still meant a forfeiture by women of legal rights to person or property. The wealth acquired by a couple during their marriage, however large or small, legally belonged to the husband. A married woman had no legal protection against a husband who physically abused or raped her. A married woman could not obtain her own credit card, sign a mortgage, or negotiate a loan. With her legal identity merged into that of her husband, a married woman routinely assumed his name as well.

Today we are moving closer to the ideal of marriage as an economic partnership, with more and more states requiring, through judicial or legislative reform, recognition of a homemaker's noneconomic contributions in devising divorce settlements and custody arrangements. Marital rape is slowly being recognized as a crime against women. A woman's right to enter into financial transactions independently is well-established.

Twenty years ago nearly 80 percent of those pursuing degrees in education were women; 95 percent of all nursing students were women; 98 percent of all secretaries were women. By contrast, only 8 percent of law degrees and 5 percent of medical degrees were awarded to women. From college down through elementary schools, athletic programs were a male preserve. Typing and home economics classes were girls' clubs; electronics and science and "shop" were open only to boys.

With the passage of Title IX by Congress in 1972, prohibiting discrimination in education on the basis of sex, women's full integration into the educational process got underway. With each passing year the opportunities for girls and women to pursue educational, professional, and athletic goals comparable to those of boys and men have increased dramatically. While recent Supreme Court decisions place the gains of the last decade in jeopardy, women's pursuit of equality in the educational arena continues. The changes wrought in our schools and colleges are profound and far-reaching.

Twenty years ago, women's work experience was defined by lack of access to many trades and professions, extremely limited opportunities for advancement even in those job classifications to which they were permitted entry, extensive segregation into "women's" jobs, and a discriminatory wage scale. With roughly 43 percent of adult women in the paid labor force, 80 percent of them were clustered in only twenty job classifications, and women as a whole earned only 59 percent of a man's wage.

Today, evidence of the "feminization" of the work force can be seen throughout our economy. Changing social and economic patterns have brought millions of women into the work force in the last two decades. The passage of federal antidiscrimination laws like the Equal Pay Act of 1963 and Title VII of the Civil Rights Act of 1964 have substantially eliminated the most blatant barriers to women's participation in our economy. Certainly, discrimination remains: the wage gap between men and women has been closed only slightly, to 64 percent. More subtle forms of discrimination like sex harrassment and stereotypic attitudes about women's capabilities and proper role continue to contaminate decision making, particularly at higher levels of employment. But with the elimination of sex-segregated want ads in 1973—the daily reminder of the duality of our labor force—we removed the last vestige of blatant institutionalized discrimination from civilian employment.

The NOW Legal Defense and Education Fund, founded in 1971 by the National Organization for Women to affect and enforce the legal changes underway, has dedicated itself to this pursuit of legal, social, and economic equality for women. At the federal, state, and local level, in the courts, the legislatures, and the media, we have advocated broad-based institutional reforms designed to alter forever the legal landscape of women's rights and responsibilities. Through our efforts, and those of others like us, the laws which define women's place in our society have been almost completely rewritten. As the NOWLDEF stands midway between its own beginning and the beginning of the twenty-first century, we offer you this chronicle of sweeping legal revolution. We offer it as a tribute to all the heroines of the last 20 years whose commitment, tenacity, and courage have changed women's lives for all time. And we offer it as an investment in the girls and women of today in the hope that a knowledge of the law will empower them to live their lives to the fullest and to complete the struggle for equality for those who will come after.

Jackie Washington, President
Stephanie Clohesy, Executive Director 1979–1985
Marsha Levick, Legal Director
NOW Legal Defense and Education Fund

# ACKNOWLEDGMENTS FOR PART I

A book written by the mother of two young children, as this one is, depends not only on the sources required to produce the best text but also on the resources behind the scenes needed to give a writer that most precious commodity—time. I have been fortunate on both counts.

Thanks go to Stephanie Clohesy and Marsha Levick of the NOW Legal Defense and Education Fund and to their able staff for consistent support, thoroughness in research assistance, and clear answers to innumerable questions. Marsha's calm demeanor was soothing at critical moments in the writing. Stephanie encouraged me to attend the U.N. Decade for Women Conference in Nairobi, Kenya—an enriching experience which helped me link American legal process and global feminist issues in the book's final chapter, "Women in the Community."

I am grateful to Dan Weaver, my editor at McGraw-Hill, who was patient and resilient.

Over two summers, my husband took my son and daughter on innumerable trips to the homes of relatives and friends so that I would have unencumbered time to work. My love and thanks to the three of them—John, Kara, and David—for understanding and giving me the gift of silence. Thanks also to Dessie Hughes, who is my right arm and has been for almost 10 years. Finally, I want to thank Eli and Marianne Cherow for always believing in me and never stinting on love.

Renée Cherow-O'Leary

# ACKNOWLEDGMENTS FOR PART II

This guide would probably not have been written without the inspiration and imagination of Shana Alexander, who originally conceived of the idea for such a book and graciously invited NOW LDEF to assist her in this effort. I am therefore indebted to her for the idea and enormously grateful to her for subsequently giving the rights to develop the book to NOW LDEF. I thank as well Joy Harris of the Lantz Agency, who assisted and facilitated this transfer of rights.

A special thanks also to Stephanie Clohesy and Phyllis Segal, former executive director and legal director of LDEF, respectively, who knew a good idea when they saw one and gave the guide its initial push toward completion; to the past and present board members of LDEF, who supported the staff in this undertaking, and to Roxanne Conlin, in particular, who reviewed the final manuscript; and to Susan Blumenthal, who did all of the initial state-by-state research and took the first crack at writing the state law summaries.

For her work in developing the final outline for the state summaries and for overseeing the production of the first twelve states, I thank Noemi Bonilla, paralegal and now part-time law student. For joining the effort at a critical time and supervising the completion of the remaining thirty-eight states, and for her overall dedication, commitment, and persistence, I thank Marcelle Blanc.

For providing helpful editorial assistance, I thank Emily Spitzer and Sally Goldfarb, staff attorneys at LDEF, and Leslie Wolfe, director of our Project on Equal Education Rights. For their assistance with research, and last-minute cite checking, I thank Alison Wetherfield, Katrina Church, Linda Perlmuth, and Michele Cotton, LDEF interns.

I also thank the Helena Rubinstein Foundation, whose support of our law student internship program helped to fund the salaries of many of the interns who contributed to this guide. The views expressed in the book, however, are solely those of the authors and do not necessarily reflect the opinions of the Helena Rubinstein Foundation. Among the law student interns, a special thanks to Amy Lefkof, who consistently researched her assignments above and beyond our expectations. I thank also Bernice Hoffman, Timothy James, Cleo Cacoulides, Karima Lewis Blackwood, Linda Williams, Karamah Khashiur, Maria Tobia, Amy Pellman, Jacqueline Rayfield, Ursula Bischoff, Jean Collins, Robin Frankel, Sherri Rosenberg, Robin Bernstein, Kathleen S. Trainor, and Lisa Loscalzo.

For their monumental typing effort and good-humored attitude in the face of what must have seemed an endless task, I thank Veronica Scutaro-Weismann, Charlae Olaker, Patricia Young and Myra Simon.

Of course, none of the above people who contributed to the preparation of this book bears responsibility for its final content.

For their faith in this project and their patience and assistance in moving it towards completion, I thank Dan Weaver and Martha Cameron of McGraw-Hill.

Last but not least, I thank Renée Cherow-O'Leary, who undertook cheerfully and fearlessly to write the first five chapters of this book and who was a pleasure to work with throughout.

Marsha Levick

# Part 1

# AN OVERVIEW OF WOMEN'S LEGAL RIGHTS

# 1

# THE LEGAL PROCESS

*In an important sense legal rules are never clear and, if a rule had to be clear before it could be imposed, society would be impossible. The mechanism of law accepts differences of view and ambiguities of words. It provides for the participation of the community . . . by providing a forum for the discussion of policy. . . . The law makes it possible to take the first step.*

Edward H. Levi
*An Introduction to Legal Reasoning*

*Even when laws have been written down, they ought not always remain unaltered.*

Aristotle
*Politics, Book II*

Many people think about the law as a code of fixed rules and regulations, usually severe, which have a punitive aspect to them. If someone "lays down the law" to you, that person seems to be speaking the final word. Or we may have a biblical image that laws come down from a higher source and are written in stone.

Yet, even a cursory acquaintance with the law books shows that law is the result of an ever-changing process of individual and community concerns, political pressure, social mores, and interpretation of events in light of current expectations and social values. This is particularly evident when we examine U.S. laws that affect women. In the past decade these laws have undergone a transformation which parallels the changing roles women are now playing in society. But, despite progress, the law often lags behind general social practices. While the state-by-state laws do reflect many of the new dimensions of women's lives, there is still much more to do to bring the law into line with modern women's needs.

The great strength of the American legal system is that it is not stagnant and doctrinaire. It is a flexible but intricate web through which it is possible to find access at many different points. However, there is no access without demand for it. This book will provide a map through the web.

A famous passage of the U.S. Constitution states: "We hold these truths to be self-evident, that all men are created equal, that they are endowed by their Creator with certain inalienable rights, that among these are life, liberty, and the pursuit of happiness." Let us assume that the term *men* is used in its generic sense to include both men and women, but let us be aware that it did not mean this at the time it was written. The concept of *rights* embodied in the Constitution is inherent in all of our country's law.

The first ten Constitutional amendments are known as the Bill of Rights, and these set forth our basic guarantees: freedom of religion, speech, press and assembly; a speedy trial by jury; and protection against excessive bail, cruel and unusual punishment, unreasonable search and seizure, and self-incrimination. Other rights have been added over the years. These include the abolition of involuntary servitude in the Thirteenth Amendment, which ended slavery and paved the way for the critical Fourteenth Amendment, which guarantees due process and equal protection under the law for all citizens. Both of these were passed in the period immediately after the Civil War. But while the Fourteenth Amendment gave all male Negro citizens the right to vote, it did not enfranchise women of any race. The fight for women's suffrage lasted until 1920, when the Nineteenth Amendment to the Constitution was adopted guaranteeing that "the right of citizens of the United States to vote shall not be denied or abridged . . . on account of sex."

An amendment does not become a part of the Constitution unless it is ratified by the legislatures of three-fourths of the states or by constitutional conventions in three-fourths of them. A state can vote to reject an amendment and reconsider or adopt it later. But whether a state which has already ratified an amendment can nullify its vote is still unresolved. Three states—Idaho, Nebraska, and Tennessee—were in this position when the deadline for the ratification of the proposed federal equal rights amendment expired in 1982. Although the passage of the federal ERA failed, sixteen states have adopted state equal rights amendments. These state amendments prevent the enactment and enforcement of discriminatory laws based on gender. The states which have passed equal rights provisions are Alaska, Colorado, Connecticut, Hawaii, Illinois, Maryland, Massachusetts, Montana, New Hampshire, New Mexico, Pennsylvania, Texas, Utah, Virginia, Washington, and Wyoming.

The distinction between state and federal laws is an important one. Disputes arising under state or federal laws are decided in different court systems with some areas of overlapping responsibility. This book will explain in each chapter both the federal laws, whose guarantees are applicable in all states, and the separate state provisions for each category.

Courts at both the federal and state levels are organized in tiers, and decisions flow from the lower to the higher courts. A distinction between "lower" and "higher" courts in both federal and state court systems is that between *trial* and *appellate courts*. A case begins in the trial court; the facts are presented, and the law is then applied to these facts. Once a judge or jury has ascertained the facts presented by both sides, a decision is made and one party in the case "wins." If a party is dissatisfied with the results, it may seek review of the decision in a higher court, one that rules on what occurs in the lower court. This process is called an *appeal*. Each state organizes its own series of trial and appellate courts, and the number and names of these courts vary from state to state.

The federal court system is divided into twelve geographical circuits. Within each circuit there are trial courts, which are called *district courts*. The federal appellate court in each circuit is called the *court of appeals*. The court of appeals for a circuit only hears appeals from district courts which are located in that circuit. The highest appellate court is the United States Supreme Court, which reviews cases from the twelve federal circuits. The Supreme Court also hears appeals from the federal circuit, which reviews federal administrative decisions, for example, decisions of the Merit Systems Protection Board. In addition, a decision of the highest available state court may be brought before the Supreme Court in selected cases.

Along with these general courts, there are special courts which exclusively handle various types of problems, such as tax questions. Overall, the higher the court in the system, the more impact its decisions will have and the greater will be its influence. The U.S. Supreme Court, of course, is a key instrument of social change through the force of its decisions.

Appellate courts often review a case based on whether there was an error in applying the law or in *procedure*. Proper procedure is very important because it forms the basis of *enforcement* of any legal right. Without a strict observance of rules of legal practice, a court would not be able to carry on its business. Thus, although in special cases a person can act as his or her own attorney, in most life situations where major personal, professional, financial, or family decisions are going to be made, a lawyer ought to be consulted.

A lawyer or attorney is a person who has studied law, been admitted to the bar, and is expected to have sound moral character. In effect, an attorney is someone who acts as an agent for the client in legal matters. A client may be either a *plaintiff* or *defendant* in a case. The plaintiff brings the lawsuit; the defendant is the person, corporation, or entity against whom a civil lawsuit or criminal proceeding is brought. A *civil action* is a proceeding to enforce a legal right or recover money as payment for an injury or loss. *Criminal law* covers acts or omissions which are harmful to the public, and which are punishable by fine or imprisonment as a result. Crimes are classified as *felonies*, which are the most serious, *misdemeanors*, or *violations*, which are the least serious.

Once you decide you need a lawyer, you have to find one. There are several routes to finding a private lawyer. The best way is to talk to people in your community who have worked with a lawyer they trust. If you work for a company that has a lawyer on its staff, this person may be able to refer you to appropriate counsel (unless, of course, you are building a case against the company). Consider whether the lawyer you may choose works alone or is a member of a firm. Do not pay for a referral. You are entitled to get a few leads, to call for a free consultation, and "shop around." There are many different fee structures when you work with a private lawyer that you hire, so be sure to ask for a full outline of fees before any work is done. Ask your lawyer to provide you with a statement of actual or estimated charges in writing.

Other options for finding a lawyer include determining whether you are eligible for assistance from Legal Aid or from a public defender in criminal matters. Eligibility depends on where you live, the size of your family, and how much you earn. Contact your local bar association to find the names and locations of the free legal service organizations in your area.

If you have a problem involving a government service or government-regulated industry, you may be eligible to receive the assistance of a local, state, or federal lawyer from one of the government agencies. As a taxpayer, you are entitled to this advice. Your case may also be of interest to nonprofit organizations which specialize in lobbying or advocacy to remedy particular social problems. Such organizations might include the National Organization for Women, professional, health or civil rights groups, and others. Local chapters of these organizations are usually listed in the telephone book; if not, you can contact their national headquarters. You may get free representation if your case embodies key legal or legislative principles of interest to the group, but, more likely, you will get practical referral suggestions.

When a case is brought before a judge and jury by a lawyer, *evidence* is offered to persuade these evaluators of the existence of a fact. The rules of evidence are complex, but the purpose of evidence is to lead to the truth. The amount of evidence necessary to sway the case in your favor does not depend upon the quantity but on the *legal standard of proof* or the degree of persuasiveness required to establish proof. In criminal cases, this proof must be made evident "beyond a reasonable doubt." This is the most difficult standard of proof, because it is individual liberty which is at stake. Since civil actions usually involve money remedies rather than curtailment of the liberty of the offender (jail terms), civil cases can often be won on a lesser standard of proof, *preponderance of the evidence*, which means only a little more than 50 percent probability.

In presenting a case, lawyers make arguments to support their position; *judges* often rely on *precedent* as a basis for decision making. This means that past decisions are the guideposts for present ones. However, there are always precedent-breaking cases where judges at various levels decide that previous cases do not apply to present situations. When this happens, a whole new set of guidelines is then established. This is, of course, exactly the case in many of today's decisions in women's rights cases. As stated earlier, this is one way the law changes.

Once a case is decided, it is published in appropriate codifications of the law. You may find these in a law library with the help of a librarian. A basic rule in deciphering citations is to know that the first number refers to a volume in a series of books; the words or letters that follow abbreviate the title of the book; the second number after this signifies the page or section in the volume. After this, the abbreviated name of the court in which the case was held, the state where the court is located, and the year the case was decided are sometimes listed in parentheses. For example, in the citation *Rackin v. University of Pennsylvania*, 386 F. Supp. 992 (E.D. Pa. 1974), the first listing is the title of the case. It may be found in Volume 386 of the series of books called the *Federal Supplement* at page 992. The decision was issued by the U.S. District Court for the Eastern District of Pennsylvania in 1974. A law librarian is your best source of information about locating case documentation. Law libraries are located at law schools in your area. Your local librarian can help you, as can your local bar association.

Many people are intimidated by legal language. Every field has its professional jargon, but the law is notorious for its use of three complex words when one simple one might do. There has been some effort over the past few years, particularly in government agencies, to simplify legal language and make the meaning of a given law clearer to the average person. There are also readily available glossaries of legal terms which can define key items that are standard in legal documents. Because words and their interpretation are the currency of the law, everything is very carefully phrased. But this should not deter anyone from examining original cases to understand the background of their own situation. Essential phrases will reappear, and examples of actual cases, such as those which will appear in the pages of this book, can provide insight into the way the law works, not in theory but in practice.

In creating and enforcing women's legal rights, *legislatures* are at least as important as courts. The United States Congress, state legislatures, and local legislative bodies all have the power to make laws by proposing and passing legislation. Indeed, courts spend much of their time interpreting *statutes* that have been enacted by legislatures.

There is another major source of decision-making power that affects women's legal rights: *public administrative agencies*, which are bodies set up by federal, state, or local law to perform government or public functions. The main purpose of these agencies is to implement legislation by establishing rules, regulations and guidelines. Such agencies will often research the effects of a given law as it is applied, hold hearings, and make recommendations. These administrative bodies must make public disclosures about their decisions through public records and may issue guidelines and policy statements about the functions they regulate. Some agencies also have the power to adjudicate individual cases.

The regulations and decisions of an agency are not laws, but they have the force and effect of laws unless thrown out by a court. Public agencies are held in check through judicial review. However, a plaintiff often cannot request this review unless all channels of appeal offered by the agency have been exhausted. An example of an agency is the Equal Employment Opportunity Commission (EEOC), which is discussed in more detail in the "Employment" section of this book. This agency was established to administer the provisions of Title VII of the Civil Rights Act of 1964, which made it illegal to discriminate against women in their employment. State agencies such as the Motor Vehicles Bureau regulate and implement state rules about ownership and operation of motor vehicles in a given state. Agencies turn the provisions of the law into day-to-day practice.

After all this discussion of the legal process, we should be aware that there are other alternatives to *litigation* or contests in court. There is *arbitration*, which requires the parties to agree to refer the dispute to others whom they select and be bound by the decision. The general rule is that all persons or entities with the capacity to make contracts can submit issues which arise from contract disagreements to arbitration. There are also *mediation* centers to help clashing parties resolve their differences by having an independent person intervene and assist in reconciliation before the conflict escalates into a court case.

The legal process is not mysterious. It can be understood. But it is full of symbolism and ritual. Judges wear robes to cloak them in the honor of their position, to distinguish them as separate and elevated and objective. Proper form and procedure—rituals which some would call mere technicalities—are essential to the management of issues that would otherwise threaten the social fabric.

The words of the law must be transformed into institutions by which we order the complexities of our lives.

Women are more aware than ever about how to get things done within this system and how to use other pressures—publicity, demonstrations, lobbying, education, and negotiation, among them—to assert their claims. The rest of this book will show how the legal system in each state has dealt with the issues that affect women's lives—at home, at school, in the workplace, and in the community.

One final word: the goal of the legal system is not to be an end in itself. John Stuart Mill, the British philosopher, knew this when he wrote his famous treatise, *On the Subjection of Women*: "Laws would never be improved if there were not numerous persons whose moral sentiments were better than the existing laws."

# 2

# HOME AND FAMILY

*The pact that we made was the ordinary pact*
*of men & women in those days*
*I don't know who we thought we were . . .*
*Like everybody else, we thought of ourselves as special . . .*

Adrienne Rich
"From a Survivor," *Diving Into the Wreck*

Perhaps no aspect of human experience has been more idealized than marriage and family life. Women have been raised to believe that it is in the roles of wife and mother that we fulfill our deepest destiny. Yet, it is also true that domestic life has been a source of suffering for some women. With it came a lack of freedom, status as mere property, and physical exhaustion from hard work for which there was no pay and from childbearing beyond the limits a body could bear.

As women have won legal rights, our domestic lives have changed significantly. Statistics bear out the radical shifts in the nature of families over the past 15 years. According to the Census Bureau, the number of unmarried couples living together has more than tripled since 1970. There were 1.89 million unmarried households in 1983; about one in every twenty-five couples was unmarried. The Census Bureau reports that the proportion of 30- to 34-year-old women who had never married in 1980 was more than twice as high as in 1970. The median age for first marriage in 1983 was 25.4 years for men and 22.8 years for women.

Sex outside marriage is a fact of life and is casually depicted in all media. Single parenting is also a major factor in the new American family. Most single parents are divorced women. Some single women are choosing to have a child and raise it alone; some have chosen to adopt a child. Twenty-two percent of children under 18 lived with only one parent in 1983, up from 11.9 percent in 1970. One in ten teenagers gets pregnant each year. And although over 40 percent of all marriages end in divorce, remarriage is also on the upswing, forcing couples to deal with the complexities of stepparenting and new extended families.

In the area of reproductive freedom, religious strictures against abortion and a socially conservative mood in the country clash with legal decisions affirming a woman's right to choose. On the other hand, new biological breakthroughs in fetal monitoring and *in utero* surgery, as well as fundamentalist pressures to redefine a fetus as a legal "person," are creating ethical, legal, and moral dilemmas of major proportions.

9

Another major family issue, domestic violence, including rape, wife abuse, and child abuse, is emerging from shrouds of secrecy to command public attention and concern. The problems of "displaced homemakers," older women whose marriages have disintegrated and who do not have the training to enter the labor market, have also received publicity over the past several years. All of the issues we have mentioned have forced a reassessment of traditional family law.

The author Leo Tolstoy wrote in *Anna Karenina*: "Happy families are all alike; every unhappy family is unhappy in its own way." In this chapter, we will discuss those happy and unhappy occasions which mark family life and which require legal guidance.

# MARRIAGE

In American popular songs of several decades ago, "girls" who were the marrying kind were those men found to be docile, doll-like, and dreamy. The ideal woman was depicted as a helpmate who seemed to have no needs of her own. In fact, the image of a bride—a wife—as a child, a toy, or a pet is not an uncommon one. English common law, the ancient law of England on which American law is largely based, regarded husband and wife as one person—the husband. Under the early concept of "unity of the spouses," a married woman's legal identity effectively disappeared.

For a daughter, marriage was linked to a change of economic status from the control of her parents to domination by her husband. A woman might bring a dowry of money, goods, or property to the marriage, but she did not manage it. To be an unmarried woman meant being an outsider in adult society. Marriages were arranged to avoid this fate. Terms such as "old maid" and "spinster," which were in use until recently, emphasized the lot of a woman whose destiny was isolation, virginity, and dedication to domestic work.

In earlier periods, it was openly acknowledged that marriage was primarily an economic union. In our time, we consider the decision to wed to be based on a relatively modern concept for an age-old feeling: the couple is "in love." Love in the past was seen as a luxury, something which might grow as the couple started the tasks of daily living. But today, the worship of romantic love in our culture blinds us to the essential economic bonds of marriage. As one sardonic commentator put it, "We deny the importance of money during courtship, argue about money during marriage, and attempt to destroy each other financially during divorce."

Since modern marriage attempts to balance personal autonomy and emotion with financial and contractual obligations, there is a natural tension built into the system. If we consider a contemporary couple that chooses to marry, we can see what legal issues impinge on their lives as they move from the single to the wedded state.

The age of consent for marriage varies from state to state. A key factor is parental approval. In states such as Alabama, New Hampshire, Texas, and Utah, boys and girls can be wed as young as age 14. Without parental consent, marriage is not permitted until age 18 in most states. A woman generally may not marry her brother, half-brother, father, son, grandson, grandfather, great grandfather, uncle, or nephew. Parallel prohibitions exist for a man. Yet there are interesting exceptions. In Pennsylvania, there is no prohibition against marrying your great grandparent. In Wisconsin, a man can marry his first cousin as long as she is a female 55 years of age or older. Many states, but not all, forbid marrying in-laws.

Apart from incest taboos, there are other categories of restrictions on the right to marry. Bigamy and polygamy are illegal in all states. If a person wishes to remarry, any previous marriage must be terminated by annulment or divorce or by the death of the spouse. Homosexual marriage, while publicized for a while in the press, is not recognized legally anywhere in the United States. Twelve states expressly prohibit marriages between persons of the same sex. Other states merely declare that marriage is a personal relationship or civil contract between a male and female. Mental defects that also act as barriers to marriage are defined state by state and include a ban on marriage for those who are insane, imbeciles, or idiots as certified by tests, courts, or institutional commitment, primarily because these individuals are presumed to lack the capacity to understand what marriage is.

Legally, there are some obligatory procedures which a couple must perform before the wedding. While these formalities vary slightly from state to state, they usually include taking blood tests, obtaining a marriage license, and observing a waiting period of a few days in some states before the actual ceremony takes place. The last precaution is to prevent people from marrying casually, in jest, or under the influence of drugs or alcohol.

In addition, the primary purpose of the blood test is to reveal venereal disease, although other results, such as Rh factor incompatibility, may be uncovered as well. If the tests reveal communicable venereal disease, the clerk can refuse to issue the marriage license. Failure to comply with the health test does not make a marriage invalid, but if one party hides venereal disease from the other, it may provide that person with grounds for annulment.

Most licenses are valid for a period of 30 to 60 days. If the couple does not marry within that period, a new license must be obtained. Some states permit a 6-month period of validity for the license. Legal marriages in one state are accepted throughout the country. Most states have invalidated or placed limits on the recognition of common-law marriages, relationships entered into without a formal marriage ceremony but in which the couple lives together as husband and wife.

In etiquette books of an earlier period, a woman, once married, would be advised to assume her husband's name for all legal purposes. Today, multiple designations are possible and accepted. For example, Susan Smith married to John Jones may retain her birth name, hyphenate her birth name and husband's name as Susan Smith-Jones, or drop her birth name entirely to become Susan Jones. She and her husband may *both* change their names. No states currently require a woman to assume her husband's surname.

Since the use of names is such a personal preference, the only practical concern in this matter is to maintain consistency. This is important for credit purposes, when naming children, or to avoid social confusion. Your "legal name" is the name you use vis-à-vis the state in such documents as driver's license, car registration, and property deeds or when you are voting, holding public office, obtaining credit, applying for social security, filing income tax returns, or securing a passport. Changing your name to your husband's or deciding to revert to your birth name does not require formal court proceedings. However, you do need to amass identification in the name desired. This is harder to do for a married woman who has begun to use her husband's surname and then shifts back to her birth name.

"Home" is a word fraught with emotional associations. Folk wisdom says "home is where the heart is." But where the heart is, the body must follow. Legally, when a couple marries and establishes a home, they are also establishing a legal domicile. This is the place, geographically, where they live together and to which they expect to return. The law makes a distinction between a "domicile" and a "residence." The general rule has been that a wife must adopt the residence of her husband, and she cannot, without just cause, maintain a separate domicile. Today, however, most states recognize that wives may need to establish their own domiciles for various purposes, including voting, running for public office, jury service, taxation, and probate. Many states will now allow a married woman to establish her own domicile if she is living apart from her husband for "cause," and several will now allow her to do so for any reason at all. Practically speaking, where the person officially lives can make a large difference in income and obligations—eligibility for tuition fees at a state college, for example—so a woman's right to separate domicile, even if she is married, can be of critical importance.

Many sociologists have studied the way a couple chooses to share marital resources and organize time. The traditional specialization of male and female duties has been based, in general, on the fact that the wife's time is less expensive in terms of wages in the marketplace and the husband's time more "valuable" outside the home. Even when modern couples marry, it is often with the implicit understanding that after a time, or from the beginning, the wife may have full responsibility for running the home and for rearing the children. While today's typical couples frequently have a two-career marriage, there is still the important question of appropriate expectations for financial support of one spouse by the other.

In the majority of states, if a woman does not have any income of her own, she is theoretically dependent upon her husband's wage earning outside the home and on his generosity. In community property states, her husband's earnings would be considered joint property. Under the new Uniform Marital Property Act marriage is considered an economic partnership in which the roles of homemaker and breadwinner receive equal recognition. The unique focus of this act is that shared and vested ownership rights in the marital property "are in place at divorce or death" and do not have to be determined by court order or "transfer." Wisconsin was the first state to adopt a version of this act in 1984. Legislation to adopt the act is pending in several other states. The Uniform Marital Property Act recognizes that a wife's contributions, while not monetary, are certainly a significant economic factor. Studies indicate that if the services performed by a homemaker were calculated on the open market, they would be worth $46,000 a year.

Common law required that a husband support his wife. The wife, in exchange, had an obligation to provide her husband with her services and her company. The latter, called "consortium" legally, meant the physical, sexual, and psychological sharing known as "conjugal rights." Husband and wife had reciprocal, though very different, marital obligations.

Although this arrangement seemed satisfactory, in practice it has been a different story for many women. Courts have refused to enforce support during marriage, taking cover in the doctrine of "family privacy." Courts were willing to intervene only if there was a marital breakdown and the couple was living apart. So, if a husband refused to give his wife a penny for her own personal needs, she could not, as long as she continued to live with him, expect to obtain a court order to provide her with reasonable support money. The courts have stated as their rationale that they cannot intervene to supervise the day-to-day problems of husband and wife.

Common-law issues concerning support extended to the common-law expectation that a husband was obligated to pay the wife's debts for household "necessaries" and to pay the creditors who furnished these items to the wife. Enforcement of the "necessaries doctrine" has traditionally been the exclusive right of the creditors. Because of the burden of litigating to enforce this duty, most merchants were unwilling to extend credit to women for the purchase of necessaries and required that the husband give his prior approval, leaving a woman in the role of a dependent and supplicant. The new laws establishing a woman's right to obtain credit on her own will be discussed further under "Economic Equality" in Chapter 5 of this book.

Today, the common-law necessaries doctrine is on the books in only a handful of states: Georgia, Kentucky, Maryland, Ohio, Oklahoma, and South Carolina. A large number of other jurisdictions have gender-neutral provisions that hold both spouses liable for necessaries purchased by either of them or for family expenses associated with the education of the children. Twenty-six states have eliminated the common-law rule altogether and require both spouses to support each other. Several states provide that the wife must support her husband if he is in need or is unable, owing to infirmity, to support himself. Other states either impose a duty of support strictly on the husband or have no provisions at all. In community property states, family expenses are the debts of both, and they are to be paid for out of the community property.

Loss of the sexual companionship, company and the cooperation and affection of a husband or wife as a result of a physical injury to either person by a third party is known legally as the "loss of consortium." All but seven states permit a lawsuit against the third party for damages, but some states only permit the husband to sue for the loss.

Suits between husband and wife are more controversial. If one spouse physically injures the other, over a third of the states allow the injured spouse to sue the other. Yet many states adhere to the legal concept called "interspousal tort immunity," which simply means that spouses are barred from suing each other for damages. In an Illinois case, a wife was prohibited from suing her husband for injuries she sustained in a car accident caused by her husband's negligence while the couple was living together as husband and wife. The court ruled that the state had an interest in fostering marital harmony and preventing fraud and collusion. Differing treatment of spouses and nonspouses did not violate the doctrine of equal protection under the law because, the court said, the potential for fraud stemming from the marital relationship was great.

Another twist on the nature of the intimacy between husband and wife comes up in the issue of testimonial privilege and the confidentiality of the marital relationship. If one member of a couple committed a crime, should one be witness against the other? Their right of marital privacy presupposes a privilege of uninhibited communication. Without this, they could only confide in each other at their peril. However, under the laws of evidence, anyone called as a witness in a trial has a right as well as a duty to answer all relevant questions unless protected by special privilege. Eight states have statutes which hold that one spouse is incompetent to testify against the other in a criminal proceeding. Sixteen states provide a privilege against adverse spousal testimony. Nine other states and the District of Columbia hold that if the witness wants to testify against the spouse, that spouse has no right to object. The other seventeen states have completely abolished the right of a husband or wife to assert spousal privilege in criminal cases.

Love cannot be legislated. Couples who come together and decide upon marriage usually do so out of feeling, commitment, and aspirations for the future. These may or may not be fully articulated between them, but despite today's high divorce rate, it is still true that couples enter marriage with high hopes of permanence.

Yet, lifelong love matches have always been exceedingly rare. Today the pace of society, traditional American mobility, and new child-rearing patterns have brought more realism to the expectations of marriage partners.

As women and men have challenged the definitions of their roles in marriage, both personally and in the courts, the decision to adhere to a contract written and agreed to by both parties has become increasingly common. The desire to clarify what was expected between partners led to the making of contracts by couples planning to marry. In these prenuptial contracts, both parties agree on their rights and obligations in the marital relationship prior to entering into the marriage. The contract can be developed with or without a lawyer. Once the couple is married, state law still governs interpretations of these contracts.

States have increasingly recognized the validity of prenuptial and postnuptial agreements and have even begun to look upon them with favor, since they promote marital harmony by determining in advance rights and responsibilities in a practical way. By setting the terms to be followed in the event of a separation or divorce, as well as in the event of a spouse's death, these agreements minimize the involvement of the courts. About thirty states recognize prenuptial contracts as valid. In these states, the courts verify that the parties entered into the agreement voluntarily, that there was no attempt to get the better of one partner by deceitful means, and that the terms are basically fair.

Courts in Illinois, Iowa, and South Dakota have refused to enforce provisions of these agreements when one spouse was relieved of the responsibility to support the other. The fear here was that the impoverished spouse would become a public charge. In ten other states, statutes permit spouses to enter into contracts to determine their property distribution without permitting husbands and wives to alter their legal relationship in other ways.

# RIGHTS OF UNMARRIED COUPLES

**HETEROSEXUAL COUPLES:** The U.S. Census of 1980–1981 revealed that approximately 1.8 million heterosexual couples—about 4 percent of all couples—were living together in the United States without marriage. About 28 percent of all unmarried couples have one or more children present in the household; more than 4 million persons, including children, live in a household with two unmarried adults of the opposite sex. About half the individuals living together have been married previously.

Unmarried heterosexual couples are being drawn more fully into the mainstream of society. One sociologist in the *Journal of Marriage and the Family* writes: "The probability of unmarried cohabitation some time during the life course is far greater than data on current living arrangements might suggest. Living together is less an alternative lifestyle and more a normative phenomenon in American life."[1]

Unmarried couples have fewer legal rights than couples who are married. Because of the ambiguity of the law, couples who live together can begin to compensate for their lack of legal protection only by defining their living arrangements themselves through agreement. If there is any sharing of expenses or assets, any intention of permanence on the part of either cohabitant, any need to define expectations on the part of either cohabitant with regard to support, child care, property ownership, or inheritance, a contract in writing is recommended. However, a contract cannot assure the parties all the rights available to married couples. For example, in almost all states unmarried couples are not entitled to family plan insurance.

The agreement a couple drafts should resemble that of a business partnership and be as reasonable and comprehensive as possible. While not necessary, it is preferable to write it with the aid of legal counsel.

The Tenth National Conference on Women and the Law suggested the following topics in a panel on relationship contracts:

- *Money and budget*. Included are such issues as how to budget, payment of household and entertainment expenses, whether to make loans to each other, how to handle inheritance, life insurance, and personal estates, including naming an executor of a will.

- *Conflict resolution*. This includes how to go about settling disputes, what circumstances would put an end to the agreement, and what procedure to use to amend the agreement.

- *Home care*. This would include, for example, decoration of the home or access of the household to friends.

- *Relationship management*. This covers the roles each partner would take in the management of daily life, when one could change a domicile for career pur-

poses, child-rearing responsibilities, intention to marry, name change or retention, the need for privacy, what to do in the case of unwanted pregnancy,
and how each felt about sexual relations with others. Additional topics include
responsibility for pets and use of the family car.

Obviously no agreement can cover all issues! But even a few items on which
agreement is clear can be very reassuring as a legal foundation for a relationship.

Another difficult legal question for persons living together is the financial status
of the couple when one of the parties is receiving alimony. Many states—Alabama,
California, Connecticut, Georgia, New York, Oklahoma, Pennsylvania, Tennessee, and Utah, for example—reduce or terminate alimony payments if the recipient
is living with another person. Other states have determined the effects on a
case-by-case basis. An Ohio case said that a woman who was living with a lover
and partially supported by him showed a decreased financial need sufficient to
justify termination of her alimony.

In 1979, a new legal concept emerged which challenged previous financial
decisions for unmarried couples.[2] The case involved Hollywood actor Lee Marvin
and Michele Triola Marvin, his "live-in lover," as the tabloids labeled her. Ms.
Marvin adopted his name late in their 6-year relationship because, she said, she
was embarrassed to register at hotels in her own name when they traveled. When
the couple's relationship dissolved, she sued Lee Marvin for half of his property.
She claimed that she had given up a career as a singer, cared for Lee Marvin's
home, and provided meals and companionship.

There was no evidence in the *Marvin* case of any written contract to support
her claim. She was never party to a joint bank account, nor was any property
held jointly. All of the couple's assets had been purchased by Lee Marvin. California does not recognize common-law marriage, but the Supreme Court of California
said that a fair apportionment of property, even without a contract, can be determined if the property was accumulated through "mutual effort." This was not
proven in the *Marvin* case.

Instead, the court awarded Michele Triola Marvin $104,000 for "rehabilitation
purposes so that she may have the economic means to re-educate herself and
learn new, employable skills or to refurbish those used during her most recent
employment so she may return from her status as a companion of a movie star
to a separate, independent, but perhaps more prosaic existence." The term that
became popularized as the name for an award to an unmarried partner in an
established relationship is *palimony*.

What this case did was attach financial obligations for support to what had
previously been a relationship without any legal status. Although the circumstances
of the relationship had to be considered, it was a precedent-breaking event and
has influenced the presentation of other cases around the country. Recent palimony
decisions have been catalysts for the adoption of contracts by unmarried couples.
There is no guarantee, of course, of an outcome similar to the *Marvin* case.
Nevertheless, many states are establishing guidelines for its application.

Many states refuse to admit that the relationship of an unmarried heterosexual
couple can be "stable and significant." For example, in Iowa, a man was injured

in a motorcycle accident. Both of his legs were broken, and he was forced to spend 2 months in the hospital and 2 months in a body cast. His cohabitant of 8 years filed a claim against the driver of the car for loss of consortium. The court denied her suit saying that even though their relationship had all the characteristics of a real marriage, the couple did not have "the intent to be married." The court said it must favor the *de jure* family, the family under the law, as the basic unit of social order. On the other hand, a 1984 California ruling said that an unmarried cohabitant could sue for loss of consortium if the relationship is stable and significant.

**HOMOSEXUAL COUPLES:** Problems are compounded for gay and lesbian couples because they cannot marry even if they wish to. The view in all states is that marriage is, by definition, a union between a man and woman. This interpretation says that equal protection of the laws is not violated by a state's classification of persons authorized to marry. A Washington state case said that marriage exists as a protected institution because of its social value as the unit for propagation of the species. Same-sex marriage is exempt because the partners are physically incapable of bearing children.

Of the states mentioned previously that modify alimony when a recipient cohabits, all exclude homosexual relationships from consideration. So some states sweep gay and lesbian relationships under the rug by not even acknowledging that they exist, except in child custody cases, where they are almost never ignored. Some courts, in stereotypical fashion, conclude that a heterosexual home is preferable, even if both parents live as unmarried cohabitants.

In a 1980 New York case, a lesbian mother of three children sought to obtain custody from the children's father who, at the time, was living with a woman. There was evidence in the record that the father was a severe disciplinarian, and the children had been observed to be improperly clothed, dirty, and hungry. The court stated that the mother's homosexuality deserved comment: "Such sexual deviation does not *ipso facto* constitute unfitness for custody. However, it is a factor to be taken into account."[3] The children were left with their father, who was ordered to participate in counseling.

When gay or lesbian couples break up or when one partner dies, many property problems arise. In a landmark California case, *Conley v. Richardson*, a childless lesbian couple ended their relationship, and one partner was ordered to pay the other $100 a month temporary support.[4] The plaintiff's lawyers had based the case on the *Marvin* palimony decision. The couple also had a written agreement in addition to what the court called "the oral agreement implied by their living together." The case was the first application of the *Marvin* principle to a lesbian relationship. Again the state of California led the break from tradition.

In recent years, unmarried gay and lesbian couples have won other victories: the right to demand that their income be aggregated for a joint-mortgage application to determine creditworthiness in the District of Columbia; the right to adopt a child for a male gay couple in California. Yet, by and large, sexual preference law is evolving slowly, and no consistent pattern has yet emerged. Decisions are often influenced by social and religious custom, and the rights of gay and lesbian cohabitants are particularly influenced by community mores. Nevertheless, the courts will continue to be the battleground where these issues are decided.

# DIVORCE

Over 40 percent of all marriages in the United States end in divorce. While the decision to marry may often be based on purely sentimental reasons, the decision to divorce is fraught with economic choices. A woman who is contemplating or in the midst of a divorce must be aware that divorce, according to an extensive study of sex bias in the courts, can "portend long-term, deepening poverty for a large proportion of women and their custodial children."[5] A study undertaken at Stanford University has confirmed that, in general, a woman's standard of living falls by 73 percent in the year following a divorce, while a man's typically rises by 42 percent.[6]

A woman considering divorce, then, must focus on her present and future income needs and those of her family and find a lawyer or develop a structure for negotiating these demands in her own best interests. There are two main routes toward resolution of economic and custody issues raised in divorce. The first and most typical way is to find a lawyer and resolve your divorce through the court system. The second is divorce mediation.

Most husbands and wives have conflicting interests at the time of a decision to divorce. No matter how amicable the decision, each person ought to be represented by separate counsel. The costs of a divorce are primarily those incurred for the lawyer's time. Check to find a lawyer whose fees are within an acceptable range in your community. The payment of the wife's legal fees depends upon the wife's financial situation. If a woman qualifies for legal aid, and the local legal aid office handles divorces, there is typically no charge for the lawyer. If a woman has her own income, she may pay the attorney's fees herself or negotiate for reimbursement from her husband. If she is without income, the court may order the husband to pay some of the fees, though not necessarily all. As in any other attorney-client relationship, a woman may fire her lawyer if she feels she is not being represented adequately.

The second option for divorcing couples is divorce mediation. Divorce mediation is a relatively new way to resolve differences. It is a voluntary process in which a neutral third party, a mediator, helps the two participants reach a mutually acceptable agreement about their respective rights and responsibilities after divorce. Mediation is less formal than court proceedings. Even if the parties are represented by lawyers, it is unlikely that the attorneys will actively participate in the mediation itself. The mediator has no authority to impose a decision on the parties. The goal of mediation is the resolution of a specific set of issues. If the spouses resolve the issues in the divorce through a negotiated separation agreement or mediation before going to court, the divorce is considered "uncontested." In many jurisdictions, uncontested divorces are heard not by a judge but by a referee who reviews the agreement to make sure it is fair and voluntary. The referee also sets in motion the judicial process necessary to dissolve the marriage.

In some states, mediation is mandatory. California was the first state to have a court-ordered mediation program. Most of the mandatory mediation is directed to disputes concerning children and property issues. Florida, Michigan, and Arizona have family mediation programs that are backed by strong court policy. Since 1980 at least nineteen states have enacted laws regarding mediation to promote amicable settlement of disputes and mitigate the potential harm to the spouses and their children caused by the legal dissolution of the marriage.

Because mediation is a field that is so new, mediators are neither licensed nor regulated by any government agency. But as their ranks proliferate, a variety of groups, including the American Psychological Association, the American Arbitration Association, and the American Bar Association, are setting up voluntary standards for ethical practice. If you are considering mediation, be certain to inquire about the background of the mediators and the standards to which they adhere. As with many other services, perhaps the best way to find a good mediator is by word of mouth. Lawyers or therapists may also recommend mediators with whom they have worked. It is important to feel comfortable about your choice, so take the time to make a careful selection.

Whether couples choose to use the traditional legal system or mediation to redress grievances and resolve conflicts, the issues to be confronted remain the same: alimony, child custody, child support, and distribution of property. Each state has different laws regarding these key concerns. Here we will give an overview of commonly accepted practices.

The old distinction between annulment and divorce is no longer of much legal consequence. At one time, more grounds existed for obtaining an annulment than for securing a divorce. An annulment presupposes that no valid marriage ever took place because of some impediment to the validity of the marriage contract. One of the partners, for example, may have been under the legal age of consent. With the recent expansion of grounds for divorce, resorting to annulment is no longer necessary.

Perhaps the major change in divorce law is the change in grounds for divorce. In the past, a couple could only get a divorce if one proved the other was at fault in the marriage. Adultery, bigamy, and physical or mental cruelty were some key charges. Today in all states a couple can get a "no-fault" divorce. Often, all that must be shown is that there has been an "irretrievable breakdown" of the marriage. Other terms used are "irreconcilable differences" and "incompatibility." Some states also require that the parties live apart for a period of time. The length of time varies from state to state, but it is usually a year.

Theoretically, no-fault divorce means that couples can concentrate on settling the economic and custody issues arising from the dissolution of their marriage with as little blame between them as possible. Of course, there are still cases where the divorce is contested.

Many states permit a divorce decree to be entered if the husband and wife have been living apart. However, living apart does not only mean in separate residences but not cohabiting or having sexual relations for a specific length of time. In the District of Columbia, for example, the parties may live under the same roof as long as they "pursue separate lives and share neither bed nor board."

Because of these restrictions, sleeping with your husband after you have decided to get a divorce can be legally construed as a move toward reconciliation. This act could impinge on the divorce process in no-fault states. Cohabitation with another man or in a lesbian relationship is also a danger for a woman who wishes to retain custody of her children. Even though blame is not supposed to be an issue, the question of "fitness" or moral correctness still persists.

To obtain a divorce in a particular state, one must be a resident of that state. There are state-to-state variations in residency requirements. In addition, most states and the District of Columbia have statutory provisions for judicial separation. This permits a husband and wife to live apart while still retaining many of the legal rights and obligations of marriage—support duties and prohibitions on re-marriage, for example. Sometimes separation is a prelude to divorce. At other times, it serves as a way for unhappy couples who will not divorce for religious or other reasons to remove themselves from a painful situation.

Deciding which party will remain in the family home during a judicial separation is extremely important. A lawyer ought to be consulted. At the time of divorce, the court may award the home to either the husband or the wife or order the sale of the home and division of the proceeds.

Under early common law, wealth and possessions passed from father to son. All children were considered possessions of their fathers. Over the years, in American courts, the "tender-years doctrine" evolved which presumed that at the time of divorce children under the age of 7 ought usually to be awarded to the mother.

Recently, pressure on the courts to neutralize the sex bias in custody cases has led to decisions based on the legal concept of "the best interests of the child." In effect, the states have shifted their traditional emphasis from parents' rights to those of the child. Typical of the new approach is the custody provision of the recent Wisconsin divorce law. It reads:

> In making a custody determination, the court shall consider all facts in the best interest of the child and shall not prefer one potential custodian over the other on the basis of the sex of the custodian. The court shall consider reports of appropriate professionals where admitted into evidence when custody is contested. The court may consider the wishes of the child as to his or her custodian. The court shall consider the following factors in making the determination: (a) the wishes of the child's parent or parents as to custody (b) the interaction and interrelationship of the child with his or her parent or parents, siblings, and any other person who may significantly affect the child's best interest (c) the child's adjustment to the home, school, religion and community (d) the mental and physical health of the parties, the minor children and other persons living in a proposed custodial household (e) the availability of public or private child care services (f) such factors as the court may in each individual case determine to be relevant.[7]

The law's growing sensitivity to the rights, wishes, and feelings of children caught up in divorce proceedings has led to the passage of statutes in many states which permit the judge to appoint an attorney to represent the child in custody disputes.

Within the last 5 years, the option of joint custody has surfaced as a new alternative to traditional custody arrangements which awarded custody to only one parent. Most authorities agree that joint custody is only appropriate when both parents willingly accept the plan and are capable of joint decision making for the child's welfare. On the surface, joint custody seems to be a step forward, but many lawyers are uncertain about its usefulness. Usually, the term "custody" denotes both legal and physical custody. Legal custody is the right or authority of a parent to make decisions concerning the child's upbringing, including decisions about the child's residency, medical care, or education. The legal custodian can initiate legal action on behalf of the child. Physical custody is the right to physical possession of the child, to have the child live with the custodial parent. The physical custodian handles all the day-to-day responsibilities of child rearing. Since most mothers continue to have the child reside with them, joint custody creates a situation where the noncustodial parent has decision-making power without commensurate responsibility. Some feminists feel that joint custody interferes with the mother's "ability to make needed and timely decisions regarding the child's welfare."[8]

Nevertheless, in the past several years, more than half the states have passed joint-custody statutes. In some of these states, it is mandated that joint custody be given first consideration by the courts; in others, joint custody is presumed by law to be in the best interests of the child. In other words, joint custody is presumed to be appropriate for most cases. On the other hand, without a true willingness to work together, joint custody may merely serve to continue the arguments which led to the divorce.

Until recently, custody decrees in one state were often not effective beyond state borders. This led to such abuses as child snatching, litigation of the same custody issues in two or more states, conflicting custody decrees, and emotionally wrenching effects on everyone involved.

The Uniform Child Custody Jurisdiction Act was drafted in 1968 to rectify the problem of interstate removal of children by their parents. Every state but Massachusetts has adopted the act and Massachusetts has a similar statute. This act penalizes child abduction and requires that the court having "closest connection" and the most evidence regarding the "care, protection, training and personal relationship" of the child be the primary source of decisionmaking in the case. The act establishes a principle of "continuing jurisdiction," which recognizes that the state originally having jurisdiction over the custody dispute continues to do so even if the parents or children move. With some exceptions, a state may not modify another state's decree. In addition, laws in some states make child snatching by parents a crime with penalties analogous to penalties for kidnapping under federal law.

Grandparents' rights issues are emerging as a new element in custody cases. At present, grandparents' rights issues are generally being handled on a case-by-case basis, although some states have recently passed legislation establishing grandparents' rights to visitation. Grandparents around the country are bringing cases to the courts or into mediation for the right to maintain contact with their grandchildren. With the rising divorce rate, many parents with custody eliminate visits from the ex-spouse's parents, fearing that the grandparents will "poison" the children's minds by siding with the former partner.

In addition to crucial custody issues, at the heart of a divorce settlement is money. Marriage at its core is an economic as well as legal and emotional partnership. Each spouse contributes services of economic value to the family. These may be rendered outside the home as paid employment or inside the home as homemaking. As we stated earlier, a homemaker's services would cost an estimated $46,000 per year on an open market. But traditionally, these services have not been valued in the divorce courts.

Alimony, or maintenance, is money awarded to a spouse for household and personal expenses, work-related costs, training and educational expenses, and recreation. Traditionally, alimony used to be awarded until one of the parties died or the spouse receiving it remarried. Today, new standards are beginning to be applied to alimony. The key component is whether a woman is capable of supporting herself. Increasingly, states are viewing the goal of alimony as "rehabilitative." This limits alimony to a specific time period for the purpose of granting the spouse funds to acquire sufficient education or training to "find appropriate employment and secure that person's future earning capacity."[9] In those cases when a woman's earnings are greater than her husband's, a woman may be asked to pay alimony to a man.

The Uniform Marriage and Divorce Act of 1974, another model piece of legislation on which states can base their own laws, suggests the following considerations for developing guidelines for alimony awards: the financial resources of the party asking for maintenance; the time necessary to acquire education or training for appropriate employment; the standard of living during the marriage; the length of time the couple were married; the age, physical fitness, and emotional condition of the one who seeks support; the ability of the other partner to meet his or her own needs and still contribute to the former spouse's support.

Lately, it has become popular to think of alimony as oppressive to men or as an "unliberated" position for women. Yet, while rehabilitative alimony does recognize women's capacities for change, it is often unrealistic to assume that women will find a job, especially at entry level, to compensate them at their accustomed standard of living or even several steps below. This is especially true for older women whose primary role has been as homemaker and for women who have no independent income or means of support other than what is awarded by the court. These women, without adequate resources, often wind up in the cycle of poverty common to women after divorce.

To ease the problems for such women, many states have passed displaced homemaker laws. A typical displaced homemaker is a 35- to 64-year-old woman who has spent most of her adult life raising a family. Her husband may have died, become disabled, or been laid off, or she may be divorced. Estimates on the number of these women in the United States go as high as 30 million. The reason that so many homemakers are poor is that the services they have provided are unsalaried—and they are not eligible for health, disability, or unemployment insurance, pension, or social security benefits based on the work they have performed!

Child support is the other major financial award to a divorced woman. All parents are required by law to support their children. If a woman gains custody of the children through a divorce, the husband is usually mandated to contribute toward food, clothing, shelter, education, medicine, insurance, and other needs as the child matures. An award for child support can be changed depending upon a change in circumstances in either the father's or mother's life or to adjust for inflation if a cost of living increment is negotiated.

Until recently, the tender-years doctrine mandated that custody automatically go to the mother unless she was proved incompetent. Yet today, many fathers are seeking and gaining custody of their children. Most states now expressly forbid any preference in custody based solely on sex. In fact, of all the recent developments in divorce law, none is more dramatic than the willingness of many states to award divorcing parents joint custody of their children. In these arrangements, the amount of child support has to be negotiated carefully.

In some cases, men will ask for joint custody in order to pay less child support. Fathers sometimes argue that they should pay no support at all if they have the children half the time. Usually the father has more than half the income. If a father does not honor his part of the parenting responsibilities, a woman may end up taking a lesser financial settlement while having the major burden of child care. The woman is then left with *de facto* sole custody and only a fraction of the costs of support.

Unfortunately, the statistics on the failure of fathers to meet their support obligations are staggering. More than 90 percent of all children who live with one parent live with their mother and have a living, noncustodial parent from whom they are entitled to receive support payments. Yet, 41 percent of all custodial parents are awarded no child support from the father. Only one-half the mothers awarded child support receive the full amount. Contrary to popular belief, there is little relationship between the father's ability to pay child support and either the amount of the award or the extent of compliance with the order.

Once a husband has defaulted on payments, a woman can work through several different channels to enforce her rights depending on the circumstances. A 1975 law known as Title IV-D of the Social Security Act has as its purpose aiding women on public assistance to find absentee fathers. For a nominal fee, nonwelfare mothers may also use the locator service to find their husbands. The state can examine its own records and files, from such agencies as the motor vehicles bureau, or ask the federal government to assist through Internal Revenue Service or Social Security records. This program is slow to collect, but it is useful when a person cannot afford the services of an attorney or investigator.

In the summer of 1984, the lobbying of many women's groups paid off in congressional passage of a bill to strengthen efforts to collect child support from delinquent spouses. The Child Support Enforcement Amendments of 1984 amend Title IV-D of the Social Security Act. The legislation expands the child support enforcement program by requiring states, as a condition of receiving welfare payments from the federal government, to implement procedures for enforcing court orders for child support payments. This can include mandatory withholding of past-due amounts from wages when payments are more than a month overdue, imposition of liens on real and personal property, and use of a credit bureau to provide information about the parent's debts when the amount in arrears is over $1000. Delinquent parents may also be required to post bond or give another guarantee to secure payment of support.

While these provisions have been attached to state formulas for welfare payment, they do not only apply to women on welfare. The funding formula to administer the program is designed to encourage states to use the act for non-AFDC families. A linchpin of the act for all families is the guarantee that state income tax and federal income tax refunds can be offset, that is, not sent to the delinquent parent, but diverted to the parent entitled to receive back support. It is estimated that the refund offset provisions will affect some 800,000 taxpayers the first year and ultimately as many as 2 million. The Census Bureau estimates that over 2 million children were being cheated out of $4 billion annually in child support.

For a mother who is unwed, there is another approach to finding the father of the child for support purposes. The paternity laws of a given state provide a vehicle for determining who the father of a child is and what his obligations are to the child, the mother, and the state for child support. Women in these cases have to cooperate by bringing a paternity suit. In most states, courts can order blood tests to determine paternity. Today, these tests can determine paternity with 90 percent accuracy or better. If the results point to a particular man as the father, the court can direct the father to pay money for past care, for maintenance until the child is 18, or for other obligations. In Delaware, for example, the father of an illegitimate child is bound to pay the Department of Health and Social Services all charges it incurs for maintaining the child under the age of 18. Kentucky law unequivocally states that "the father of a child born out of wedlock, whether or not the child is born alive, is liable to the same extent as a father of a child born in wedlock for reasonable expense of the mother's pregnancy, confinement and for education, necessary support and funeral expenses of the child."[10] Kentucky, too, is one of the states where a paternity suit may be initiated not only upon complaint of the mother but of the child or any person or agency contributing to the support of the child. Under the new Child Support Enforcement Amendments of 1984, states are required to extend the statute of limitations for actions to determine paternity and to compel support until the child's eighteenth birthday. Generally, the husband of a woman who bears a child as a result of artificial insemination is considered the father of the child for support purposes if he agreed to the insemination in writing.

Another federal act, the Revised Uniform Reciprocal Enforcement of Support Act of 1968 (RURESA), can be used when a person who owes money is in one state and the person entitled to the money is in a different state. Thirty-five states have adopted the revised act, fourteen have it on the books in its pre-1968 form, and New York has written its own statute with many of the same provisions. Basically the act requires filing a petition in your home state court. This petition is sent to a court in the state of the defaulting parent. There is no fee for this procedure. Payments, when demanded, are made to a clerk of the court. If the parent refuses to pay, the order is enforced by a citation of contempt, and a jail sentence is possible for not obeying the order. This act is now strengthened by the provisions of the Child Support Enforcement Amendments of 1984.

Women should be aware that the Internal Revenue Service classifies alimony and child support differently for tax purposes. A husband can deduct alimony from his income for income tax purposes. He cannot deduct child support. Conversely, a wife must pay taxes on alimony. She does not have to pay taxes on child support. Thus, in bargaining for these two items in a divorce proceeding, it is best to keep them separate. Otherwise, it is possible to end up with a heavier tax burden than anticipated.

A final financial consideration in a divorce is the division of property between partners. Property includes all physical and financial possessions in the family: house, car, furnishings, land, stocks, bonds, business interests, and like objects. Some states include pension rights and the value of a professional education in the assessment of property.

The two traditional systems for property distribution are those of separate property states and community property states. There are eight community property states—Arizona, California, Idaho, Louisiana, Nevada, New Mexico, Texas, and Washington. Under the general theory of community property, both spouses share equally in property acquired by their joint efforts. Both during the marriage and at the divorce each spouse is recognized as an owner of the property acquired during the marriage. These states return to each partner what each owned separately before the marriage or that which was acquired by inheritance or gift. The rest is divided equally at divorce.

The majority of states have adhered to the concept of separate property. Under this common-law scheme, ownership was determined in accordance with who held legal title. Title belonged to the person whose name was on the books or who had paid for the item. Since title was usually in the husband's name, a wife often had few ownership rights. Any award of marital property to her was viewed as a gift rather than as her right.

In recent years, the rigidity of the separate property scheme has given way in most states to the adoption of the concept of "equitable distribution." Under these principles, the court is directed to make the distribution of property fair and equitable, without regard to who actually has "title" or ownership of the property. Equitable means "just" and not necessarily "equal." As in the new alimony provisions, criteria determining equitable distribution include length of marriage; age, health, and sources of income of each party; economic and noneconomic (that is, homemaking) contributions of each spouse; whether it is desirable for the custodial parent to work outside the home; and so forth. More than forty states—among them, Colorado, Illinois, Maryland, New Jersey, New York, Pennsylvania, and South Carolina—have introduced provisions to achieve these ends.

There has also been a recent trend toward increasing the types of property subject to distribution upon divorce. Many states now classify pensions and retirement benefits, at least the portion accrued during the marriage, as co-owned marital property. In 1983, Congress passed the Uniformed Services Former Spouses' Protection Act in 1983, which said that military retirement pay is a potentially divisible asset for property settlement in a divorce. In accordance with the laws of a given state, a court may award up to 50 percent of the retirement pay to the nonmilitary spouse provided the couple was married for at least 10 years during the qualified service period. Disability pay and personal injury awards are also considered in some states to be divisible marital property.

Some states also consider the value of a professional degree earned during the marriage to be part of marital property. For example, New York recently held in *O'Brien v. O'Brien* that the economic value of the husband's medical degree could be divided, and a portion awarded to his wife at the time of their divorce. However, most states, including California, have declined to treat the professional degree as marital property. Many of these states will consider the enhanced earning power of the degree holder in calculating the amount of alimony and property awards. Finally, some states, such as New Jersey, award "reimbursement alimony," which compensates the spouse for his or her economic contribution to the degree holder's education. In some cases, courts have begun to consider life insurance policies in the division of property and as part of alimony or as security for alimony or child support. The general rule is that the obligation to pay alimony and child support does not necessarily end at the death of the husband if the court mandates that a life insurance policy with the ex-wife and children as beneficiaries be maintained.

The Social Security Act, too, has been amended to provide some benefits to divorced spouses whose marriages had lasted at least 10 years. These will be discussed in more detail in the section of this chapter on "Elderly Women."

The dissolution of a marriage unravels the threads of a complex fabric of events. Procedures are complex and should be undertaken with the best advice possible. No-fault divorce provisions and lobbying pressures from women's groups are changing the way divorce is legislated in this country. Nevertheless, divorcing women must be prepared to envision and negotiate a plan which eases not only the emotional and financial stress of the moment but which provides a coherent basis for future security.

# REPRODUCTIVE FREEDOM

A woman's right to reproductive freedom—that is, access to contraceptives, the right to choose whether to carry a pregnancy to term, the right to voluntary sterilization—is a relatively modern right whose contours continue to be shaped primarily by the courts, rather than the state legislatures. The last 20 years have witnessed a steady stream of cases raising issues of reproductive freedom that have wended their way through the federal court system, many of them ending in the United States Supreme Court. By its decisions, the Supreme Court has essentially defined, characterized, shaped, and at times limited that freedom.

Today, 23 years after the Court first recognized that the constitutional right of privacy may serve to protect and insulate procreative decisions from state interference or regulation, it is once again being asked to review state abortion legislation deliberately designed to pierce that shield of privacy. Today, some antiabortion activists who decry the "violent destruction" of unborn fetuses do not hesitate to seek the violent destruction of abortion clinics, thus endangering lives. Today, biomedical and technological advances threaten to place women's reproductive freedom on a collision course with the effort to recognize rights in the unborn.

Women's struggle to win reproductive freedom has been hard-fought because, to feminists, the right and the ability to control our own destinies means nothing without the right and the ability to control our own bodies. It is a struggle which, sadly, continues.

Until the mid-1960s, many states banned the prescription, sale, and use of contraceptives. State statutes such as those of Connecticut could impose a fine of $50 or more or imprison persons—including married couples—who used "any drug, medicinal article, or instrument for the purpose of preventing conception" or who abetted their use.

In 1965 the Connecticut statute was challenged in *Griswold v. Connecticut*.[11] In striking down the statute, the U.S. Supreme Court held that statutes banning contraceptives violated the fundamental constitutional right of privacy of married couples and their physicians. "Would we allow the police to search the precincts of marital bedrooms for telltale signs of the use of contraceptives?" the Court asked. "The very idea is repulsive to the notions of privacy surrounding the marriage relationship."

Subsequently, in 1972, in *Eisenstadt v. Baird*, the Supreme Court extended the *Griswold* ruling to unmarried persons, declaring that a state statute denying unmarried persons access to contraceptives denied them their right to equal protection under the law, as guaranteed by the Fourteenth Amendment.[12] The Court agreed that "the choice to use contraceptives is made by an individual who, married or single, has the right to be free from unwarranted governmental intrusion into matters so fundamental . . . as the decision whether to bear or beget a child."

In a 1977 case, *Carey v. Population Services International*, the Court held that the right to privacy in connection with decisions affecting procreation extended to minors as well as adults.[13] State restrictions inhibiting minors' privacy rights were valid only if they served "a significant state interest" not present in the case of an adult. In striking down a New York state statute prohibiting minors' access to contraceptives, the Court also expressed considerable doubt about whether limiting access to contraceptives would actually discourage sexual activity among the young as the state contended.

In 1973, in *Roe v. Wade*, the Supreme Court issued its historic ruling that the constitutional right of privacy is broad enough to encompass a woman's decision to terminate her pregnancy.[14] Invalidating a Texas statute which imposed criminal sanctions on anyone performing an abortion—and which had been in effect for over 100 years—the Court's dramatic ruling legalized abortion, but did not extend to women an unqualified right to terminate a pregnancy.

Balancing individual liberties against the regulatory powers of the state, *Roe v. Wade* made abortion legal with several conditions. The state may not interfere with the decision of a woman and her doctor to terminate her pregnancy prior to the end of the woman's first trimester of pregnancy. (State regulations affecting first-trimester abortions that have no significant impact on a woman's exercise of her right were in subsequent cases upheld by the Court so long as the state can demonstrate that the regulations serve important state health objectives and do not interfere with the physician-patient relationship or the woman's choice between childbirth and abortion.)

After the first trimester and until the fetus becomes "viable," the state may only regulate the abortion procedure in order to preserve and protect maternal health. *Viability* is that point when the fetus is capable of survival outside the woman's body. *Roe* placed the point of viability as early as approximately 6 months, or the end of the second trimester. After viability, because the state then has a legitimate interest in protecting the potentiality of human life, the Court held that a state may prohibit abortions altogether, except those necessary to preserve the life or health of the mother.

*Roe v. Wade* unleashed a flurry of litigation and legislative activity in the years following its pronouncement. Around the country, legislators hastened to enact abortion legislation which might limit the new right; in turn, courts struggled to apply the *Roe* analysis to the seemingly endless number of challenges to these laws being brought before them.

Among the issues considered by the courts after *Roe* was the extent to which states could permit a third party to "veto" a women's decision to terminate her pregnancy by requiring spousal or parental consent before the abortion could be performed. Spousal consent requirements were struck down by the Supreme Court in 1976 in *Planned Parenthood v. Danforth*.[15] The Court wrote, "Since it is the woman who physically bears the child and who is the more directly and immediately affected by the pregnancy, as between the two (a woman and her spouse), the balance weighs in her favor." A few states do require *notification* of a married woman's husband, if his whereabouts are known.

Parental consent provisions have been more troubling for the Court. While deciding in *Danforth* that "the State does not have the constitutional authority to give a third party an absolute, and possibly arbitrary, veto over the decision of the physician and his patient to terminate the patient's pregnancy, regardless of the reason for withholding the consent," the Court has declined to exclude parents of minor children entirely from the abortion decision.

In a series of decisions beginning with *Bellotti v. Baird* in 1979, the Court has instead crafted a compromise between the fundamental right of minors to terminate their pregnancies and the legitimate interests of parents in overseeing decisions which affect the health and well-being of their minor children.[16] Adhering to its view expressed previously in *Danforth* that a third party may not be permitted to veto absolutely the woman's decision, the Supreme Court held in *Bellotti* that if a state elects to require a pregnant minor to obtain parental consent before seeking an abortion, the state must also establish an alternative judicial proceeding whereby a minor may obtain consent without involving her parents in the decision if she does not choose to. This proceeding would enable the minor to demonstrate that she is mature and well-informed enough to make her own abortion decision, in consultation with her physician and independent of her parents' wishes. An immature minor seeking to obtain an abortion without her parents' knowledge or consent would also be permitted, in this same proceeding, to convince the state court that the abortion was *in her best interests*. To be constitutional, the Court also required that the judicial consent procedure be conducted in a confidential manner and that it proceed expeditiously to avoid any undue delay which could increase the medical risks associated with the abortion procedure.

Since *Bellotti*, the Court has modified its views somewhat regarding minors' access to abortion by drawing further distinctions between "emancipated" and "unemancipated" minors, and also between consent and notification. In *H.L. v. Matheson*, decided by the Court in 1981, a Utah statute requiring a physician to "notify, if possible," parents of minor children obtaining an abortion was upheld by the Court insofar as its application was limited to unemancipated minors dependent upon their parents.[17] An "unemancipated" minor is one who is living with her parents and has "made no claim or showing as to her maturity" or independence from her parents. The Court drew a distinction between "notice" and "consent" requirements, viewing notice requirements as legitimate to serve considerations of family integrity, protect adolescents, and allow parents to supply medical and other information to the physician.

Most recently, in *City of Akron v. Akron Center for Reproductive Health*, decided in 1983, the Court struck down an Akron, Ohio, ordinance requiring all minors under the age of 15 to obtain parental or judicial consent before obtaining an abortion.[18] The Court adhered to the principles set forth in *Bellotti*, that all minors, regardless of their age, must be given the opportunity to demonstrate either that they are mature enough to make the abortion decision independently or that the abortion would be in their best interests, even in the absence of parental consent.

In addition to consent and notification requirements, states have sought to enact other burdensome regulations designed to place roadblocks in the way of the abortion decision, either by deliberately skewing the woman's decision in favor of childbirth or by making the procedure more expensive or difficult. These obstacles include detailed and lengthy informed consent requirements, and regulations dictating the number of physicians who must be in attendance at the abortion, as well as the types of services that must be performed.

Informed consent requirements have typically involved both the requirement that only a physician may describe the procedure and a detailed list of information which must be given to the women, including graphic and unproven descriptions of the fetus at various stages of pregnancy and such nonmedical information as alternatives to abortion, the availability of welfare, or the fact that the father may be liable to support the child.

In a set of decisions issued in 1983, the Supreme Court expressly rejected the idea that only physicians can provide abortion counseling, clearing the way for the nonmedical personnel in many abortion clinics who frequently perform this task.[19] The Court also declined to permit states to dictate the content of the information which women must be given, partly because such "canned scripts" interfere with a physician's responsibility to determine what degree and type of information is in the patient's best interest and partly because the script tends to weigh the decision impermissibly in favor of childbirth.

In the same cases the Court also struck down a 24-hour waiting period between the obtaining of informed consent and the abortion. The Court saw no evidence that the waiting period either promoted safety or informed consent. And in fact, because any delay in obtaining an abortion can actually increase the risks connected with the procedure, mandatory waiting periods can have the opposite effect. In many circumstances, because abortions may only be performed on certain days, or because of the location of the clinic or the personal schedule of the woman, the 24-hour waiting period may stretch into much more.

The constitutionality of regulations imposing restrictive building or zoning requirements which either dictate construction and equipment needs or exclude abortion clinics from business districts is more difficult to predict. The federal courts seem split on the issue for now, with some courts viewing such regulations as an unconstitutional interference with a woman's privacy right to obtain an abortion and the physician's and clinic's right to perform it, while other courts see these regulations as a legitimate exercise of the state's right to regulate health care and promote childbirth.

On the other hand, laws requiring that abortions after the first trimester may only be performed in hospitals have been struck down by the Supreme Court, again because of the absence of any evidence that these laws are health-related and because of the difficulty and expense which they may add to the procedure. However, if the definition of hospital includes licensed outpatient clinics, the regulation will be permitted to stand, since this is considered an appropriate way for the state to carry out its legitimate interest in women's health.

Finally, states have also sought to impose regulations specifically governing medical procedures for late abortions, when there is a greater likelihood that the fetus is viable. The requirement that a second physician be present during these abortions, without providing an exception for medical emergencies in which the delay associated with waiting for a second physician may endanger the woman's health, was struck down by the Supreme Court in 1983. Likewise, requiring doctors to use the abortion method least dangerous to the fetus, where that method would *increase* the health risks to the mother has been held impermissible because the requirement fails to make the women's health the first priority. Laws imposing liability on doctors for their failure to preserve the life of a viable fetus will be struck down if they fail to preclude liability where the doctor is without fault.

Right after the *Roe v. Wade* decision, medicaid funding of abortions (federally funded medical insurance for low-income persons) expanded dramatically until it was provided in most states. In 1976, for example, over 250,000 poor women obtained medicaid-financed abortions. Then, in 1977, the Supreme Court ruled in *Beal v. Doe* and *Maher v. Roe* that neither the Social Security Act nor the Constitution requires states to provide funding for abortions which do not threaten the life or the health of the woman.[20] Along with this change in mood from the Court and with more strongly organized pressure from the "New Right," a coalition of conservative interests, the United States Congress passed several versions of the Hyde amendment, named after the congressman who sponsored it. These amendments and the implementing regulations restrict medicaid funding for abortions unless the woman's life would be endangered if the pregnancy were carried to term or the pregnancy is the result of rape or incest, "when such rape or incest has been reported promptly to an official agency."

In 1980, in *Harris v. McRae*, the Court ruled that not even health reasons entitled a woman to public financial assistance for abortion and that states are not required to provide abortion funds which will not be reimbursed by the federal government.[21] The use of public monies for abortion, as it now stands, is a decision left up to the legislative bodies of the individual states. State courts in Connecticut, Hawaii, and Massachusetts have invalidated state-imposed funding restrictions because they violate their state constitutions; hence government funding of abortions is available in those states. To date, only Pennsylvania has upheld state-imposed funding restrictions. Other states providing funding have simply not been challenged. Check Part 2 of this book for the situation in each state.

Over the past decade, new medical techniques affecting a woman's reproductive capacity have been introduced. Some rely on new technologies such as laser surgery; others depend on what has been termed *noncoital collaborative reproduction*, which introduce third parties, such as surrogate mothers, into the decision to create a child.

Two techniques posing the greatest legal challenges to family law are in vitro fertilization (IVF) and embryo transfer. In vitro fertilization occurs when the woman's egg is extracted and fertilized by her partner's sperm in a glass dish and then implanted in the woman. This technique is mainly used when the woman's fallopian tubes are blocked. If either partner is infertile, the egg or the sperm may be from a different donor, or a donor egg and donor sperm may be implanted in the woman. This means that the genetic mother and the gestational mother are different women.

The most ethically and politically controversial aspect of IVF is the status of the embryo. Some opponents argue that a fertilized egg is a human being and failure to reimplant it should be considered murder. Their concerns are reflected in an Illinois statute which requires the physician who performs IVF to assume the care and custody of the embryo subject to penalties of child abuse should any harm befall it. Another legal complication may arise when the embryo is frozen for future use but the parents die. This recently happened in Australia. In late 1984, the Australian legislature ruled that such embryos could not be destroyed and called for an attempt to have them implanted in another woman, a surrogate mother. Questions about the inheritance rights of such a child to the dead parents' estate were also raised in this case.

Embryo transfer is the technique of moving a fertilized egg into a uterus— but not necessarily the uterus of the woman from whom the original egg was taken. This is what allows for the possibility of a surrogate mother. The process is currently unregulated. But the primary legal question it raises is, Who does the child belong to? Is the surrogate mother, who is generally paid a fee for her services, selling her baby? The sale of a baby is illegal in all states. If none of the parties want the child because it is born with a defect of some sort, who is responsible for it? If the surrogate mother decides to keep the child, is she entitled to custody? There is no uniform law on any of these questions—they are too new. Some in the medical profession are calling for the development of a model state law to define the identity of the legal mother and father of all children, including those born to other than their genetic parents, and a law that would outlaw the sale of human embryos. These unprecedented options challenge the interpretation discussed earlier in this chapter of the constitutional right to beget and bear a child.

Another legal and ethical question arises from a more established reproductive technique—artificial insemination. Here a woman is inseminated by her partner's sperm by artificial means. This technique is usually used when the male has a low sperm count. If the man is infertile or if there is a possibility that he may pass along a harmful genetic condition, the sperm of an anonymous donor can be used. As lifestyles change, questions of artificial insemination of single women and lesbians have been raised.

The legal term *heterologous insemination* means that a woman is inseminated in some fashion from a man other than her husband. Twenty-three states now have statutes regulating heterologous artificial insemination. Most of the statutes either explicitly or implicitly limit the procedure to married women. The Connecticut and Colorado statutes are the most comprehensive. Nevertheless, there have been challenges to the system. A 36-year-old divorced woman filed a lawsuit after she was rejected for artificial insemination in Michigan because she was unmarried. As a result, Wayne State University in Detroit agreed in 1980 to include unmarried women in their artificial insemination program.

A woman's right to be sterilized is also part of her reproductive rights. Voluntary sterilization is legal in all fifty states. Sterilization is an increasingly popular method of contraception in the United States among women in all socioeconomic groups, despite the fact that sterilization of men, vasectomy, is a safer medical procedure.

Some courts have upheld the right of sectarian hospitals to refuse to perform sterilizations on religious and moral grounds. But public hospitals are required to perform sterilization operations under the constitutional guarantee of equal protection under the law. This is so because other surgical procedures of equal complexity and with no greater burden on hospital staff are regularly performed.

There is controversy surrounding sterilization because low-income, minority, and institutionalized women have been coerced into sterilization: departments of social services have threatened to terminate pregnancy benefits or deny payment for prenatal care and delivery. Since the federal government funds 90 percent of the cost of sterilization under its medicaid and family planning programs, the Department of Health and Human Services issued clear regulations in 1978 to prevent these abuses of the system.

Under these regulations, sterilization is prohibited for anyone under 21 years of age. A person must be advised in his or her native language about the irreversibility of the procedure and of any risks. There is a mandatory 30-day waiting period after written consent is given. Sterilization cannot be a condition for the termination or continuance of any government benefits, and officials who make such threats may be fined or imprisoned. Also, consent may not be obtained just before or after a woman has an abortion or while a woman is in labor or under the influence of drugs or alcohol. A private patient may also be entitled to sue for negligence, battery, or violation of her constitutional rights concerning reproductive choice.[22]

Many women's groups feel that these regulations, while admirable in theory, are difficult to monitor and enforce. Reports of cases of sterilization abuse continue to surface periodically. In these cases, many factors play a role—racism, physician attitudes, and education about contraceptive options. The Social Security Act requires that states participating in the federal medicaid or Aid to Families with Dependent Children (AFDC) programs provide family planning services to all eligible individuals, married or unmarried, who are in those programs. A person must voluntarily request such services, but unfortunately, many women do not know they exist. The service provides contraceptives to sexually active minors. Federal law requires that medicaid pay for family planning services and supplies. Other federally funded family planning services are available. Before a woman chooses sterilization, she has the absolute right of informed consent. If a woman chooses sterilization, she needs access to proper treatment and facilities.

Modern changes in reproductive rights and techniques offer the hope that every child born in America will be a wanted child. Yet this goal seems a long way off.

# DOMESTIC VIOLENCE

The statistics are chilling. Police respond to more domestic disturbance calls than to all other serious crimes combined. Over 2 million American women are severely beaten in their own homes every year, according to the National Coalition Against Domestic Violence, a grass-roots organization based in Washington, D.C. Each year, almost 4000 women are killed—more than 10 women every day—by their spouse or partner as a result of domestic violence. The FBI says that one in four female murder victims is killed by her husband or her boyfriend. Twenty-five percent of abused women were victimized at least once a week, according to a 1982 Texas survey. In half of all families involving battered wives, children are battered as well.

For a long time, it was seen to be the husband's "right" to beat his wife.[23] After all, she was his property. And women who were battered and beaten had nowhere to go. In 1970 there was no such thing as a shelter for battered women. Today there are more than 700 shelters and a national movement based on the belief that women and their children are entitled to a safe environment free from violence and the fear of violence. As Susan Schecter, a social worker and author of *Women and Male Violence*, says: "Since 1975, the ongoing struggle of the battered women's movement has been to name the hidden and private violence in women's lives, declare it public, and provide safe havens and support."[24]

In addition to other physical abuse, much of the violence which women experience is sexual. The laws relating to rape in most states include what is commonly referred to as a "marital rape exemption." These laws usually define rape as "the forcible penetration of the body of a woman not the wife of the perpetrator." And while almost every state has passed some rape reform legislation within the criminal justice system, there has been a much greater reluctance to change laws concerning spousal rape.

Nevertheless, recognition of marital rape as a real problem for women is growing. The marital rape exemption was recently ruled unconstitutional in New York. New York State prosecuted its first case and sentenced the husband to a jail term. In many other states, a husband cannot be prosecuted. For unmarried couples, there is sometimes a cohabitant exemption, and there may be a "voluntary social companion" exemption which can apply to husbands, cohabitants, or even dates! Most states require that there have been past voluntary sexual relations between the defendant and victim for the exemption to apply. West Virginia, however, requires no past sexual activity. We discuss marital rape further in the "Rape" section in Chapter 5 of this book.

Although the incidence of physical abuse is extensive, there is another common form of abuse, which is psychological. Emotional and verbal abuse is at least as damaging as physical abuse. Battered women often cite psychological humiliation and isolation as their worst battering experiences. Many battered women are ignored, ridiculed, criticized, punished, threatened, and manipulated with lies and contradictions. Too often, the women become depressed and lose confidence in themselves. This perpetuates the battering syndrome.

Under most state laws, there are three legal strategies for dealing with abuse: divorce or legal separation from the abusive partner and any legal orders needed to protect the victim from further abuse; criminal prosecution of the abuser; and an order of protection which requires the abuser to stop the abuse, threats, and harassment. A judge issues the order of protection after the husband or male partner has been served with notice and a court hearing has been held. In theory, the abuser will be in contempt of court if he violates the order. He can be fined or jailed. Rarely is the abuser put in jail. A woman should carry such an order with her in a purse and leave a certified copy at the local police precinct, according to some legal advisers. If children are involved, the protective order may provide for custody, visitation, child support or payment of other expenses, and agreements as to living arrangements. Generally, in most states, it is not necessary to file for divorce in order to get an order of protection.[25]

In addition to the traditional remedies of divorce, separation, support, and protective orders, attorneys for battered women have developed some new approaches. These include damage actions against batterers and against police officers and appropriate alimony awards for the battered woman. Let us examine each approach.

A battered woman may be able to seek damages against the batterer in a civil lawsuit. This is monetary compensation which may cover medical bills; lost wages; loss of earning capacity; damage to property; pain and suffering; physical and psychological injury; permanent injuries; humiliation, shame, and punitive damages. As of 1983 nine states permitted victims to seek monetary compensation from the abuser for such items as loss of earnings, out-of-pocket expenses, or costs and attorney's fees. These states are Alaska, California, Illinois, Maine, Massachusetts, Mississippi, New Hampshire, New York, and New Jersey. If this legal route is taken, the victim must usually prove physical and emotional damage through the use of evidence beyond her own statements. This might include objects or weapons used, color photographs of injuries taken as soon after the assault as is practical, medical records, and, if the police were called, a police report. Sometimes in these cases, an expert witness with professional training who has had contact with the victim can testify.

Since the police are usually the first to learn of abuse cases and are often the only agency to deal with the problem, formal record keeping usually begins at that level. Currently, most police departments do not segregate records of domestic violence from other forms of assault. Since many calls for assistance do not result in legal action, meaningful statistical collection is rarely in a form permitting easy retrieval. Some states are beginning to remedy this problem by requiring the collection and maintenance of domestic abuse information by law enforcement agencies. Both Wisconsin and Iowa do this. Massachusetts requires police officers to furnish certain information to abuse victims, including an outline of possible civil and criminal options and some statement of the officer's duties in providing medical assistance and protection.

Nevertheless, the police are often reluctant to respond to domestic crimes or to arrest an abuser. If a woman files criminal charges and the husband pleads guilty, he is often placed on probation. Even employees of civil and family courts do not always give an abused woman a true picture of her situation. Some attorneys now have decided that it has become necessary to bring suit against these officials to compel them to perform their duty or to obtain damages for harm resulting from their failure to do so. This is a new strategy and can be discussed with your lawyer.

Another remedy for battered women comes from the changes in divorce laws. When women are viewed as only temporarily unable to support themselves, the courts are reluctant to order permanent alimony. Instead, there is *rehabilitative maintenance*, which is a sum designed to enable a woman to regain a useful and constructive role through education, training, and therapy and to prevent financial hardship on a woman during the rehabilitative process. If a battered woman will be receiving rehabilitative maintenance, the amount awarded should reflect at a minimum her need for such additional forms of training as assertiveness skills and for the restoration of her physical and mental health to a level that permits her again to function in the world without fear.

Abuse of women cuts across all class and economic levels. We hear more about domestic violence among the poor because they turn more often to public agencies for help. Middle- and upper-income families can conceal violence more easily because they can often afford greater privacy. However, now that the issue has come into public awareness, networks are forming to offer support. Some programs work strictly with abusive men, offering them counseling and self-help techniques to identify and change violent behavior patterns. Other organizations hoping to avert domestic violence against women and children have set up 24-hour hot lines. The telephone numbers provided by the National Coali-

tion Against Domestic Violence will refer callers to appropriate state agencies.
Those numbers preceded by an 800 area code are toll-free.

| | | | |
|---|---|---|---|
| Alabama | (205) 767-3076 | Montana | (406) 228-4435 |
| Alaska | (907) 586-3650 | Nebraska | (402) 345-6555 |
| Arizona | (602) 258-5344 | Nevada | (702) 358-4214 |
| Arkansas | (501) 741-6167 | New Hampshire | (800) 852-3311 |
| California | (213) 392-9874 | New Jersey | (800) 322-8092 |
| Colorado | (303) 394-2810 | New Mexico | (505) 526-2819 |
| Connecticut | (203) 524-5890 | New York | (800) 942-6906 |
| Delaware | (302) 571-2660 | North Carolina | (919) 889-6636 |
| District of Columbia | (202) 529-5991 | North Dakota | (701) 255-6240 |
| Florida | (800) 342-9152 | Ohio | (614) 221-1255 |
| Georgia | (912) 234-9999 | Oklahoma | (800) 522-7233 |
| Hawaii | none | Oregon | (503) 239-4486 |
| Idaho | (208) 334-2480 | Pennsylvania | (717) 652-9571 |
| Illinois | (800) 252-6561 | Puerto Rico | none |
| Indiana | (812) 334-8378 | Rhode Island | (401) 723-3051 |
| Iowa | (515) 288-1981 | South Carolina | (803) 765-9428 |
| Kansas | (800) 257-2255 | South Dakota | (605) 226-1212 |
| Kentucky | (606) 581-6282 | Tennessee | (615) 623-3125 |
| Louisiana | (504) 389-3001 | Texas | (512) 482-8200 |
| Maine | (207) 623-3569 | Utah | none |
| Maryland | (301) 268-4393 | Vermont | none |
| Massachusetts | (617) 426-8492 | Virginia | none |
| Michigan | (800) 292-3925 | Washington | (800) 562-6025 |
| Minnesota | (612) 646-6177 | West Virginia | (304) 645-6334 |
| Mississippi | (601) 436-3809 | Wisconsin | (608) 255-0539 |
| Missouri | (314) 531-9101 | Wyoming | (307) 856-0942 |

Some states have enacted only minimal legislation in the area of domestic
violence. Delaware, for example, has made no provision for the funding of shelters. In Illinois and Nevada temporary restraining orders only last for a maximum
of 30 days. South Carolina will only provide a restraining order pending a divorce
and has no data gathering, funding for shelters, or other provisions for victims
of domestic violence on its books. Nevertheless, there is a range of public benefits
to which a battered woman may be entitled. While the Reagan budget has deci-
mated many programs, a battered woman should be assured that there are still
several support structures to tide her over the initial trauma of leaving and help
her with her fears of total economic insolvency. Some of the programs she can
investigate are Supplemental Social Security Income, medicaid, Aid to Families
with Dependent Children, child support enforcement programs, government-
funded legal services, public housing programs, unemployment insurance, and
Title XX social services under the Social Security Act, which authorize federal

payments to the states for provision of social services directed, among other things, to "the goals of economic self-support, personal self-sufficiency, prevention or correction of neglect of children or adults and the preservation of families." Because government programs are constantly in a state of flux, it is best to check with your state's department of social services or support staff at shelters or within national organizations to obtain up-to-the-minute information. Private charitable services may also be available.

The rising concern about domestic violence is evident in a national report issued by the U.S. Department of Justice in September 1984. Former attorney general William French Smith created a nine-member panel headed by the Detroit chief of police to hear testimony from 1000 witnesses and experts in New York City, Detroit, Kansas City, Seattle, San Antonio, and Sacramento. The recommendations include:

- Adopting the attitude that family violence should be regarded as criminal
- Establishing arrest as the preferred method of immediately dealing with such a crime
- Giving the victim and the suspect a statement of the victim's rights
- Organizing special units to process family violence cases

In addition, the report recommended saving children from the emotional stress of testifying in person at abuse trials by presenting a child's testimony on videotape. The stated purpose of the attorney general in ordering this study was to focus federal attention and leadership on the domestic violence issue.

Still, there is more to be done. There are about 700 shelters for battered women in the United States which can serve about 91,000 women and 131,000 children. Owing to lack of space, about 264,000 persons are turned away. Many women, then, have to do the best they can to protect themselves. The Wisconsin Governor's Commission on the Status of Women offers useful advice to women who have been the victims of domestic violence:[26]

## *Things to Do at the Time of Attack and Immediately After*

- Protect your face, chest, and abdomen and do all you can to avoid intensifying his anger.
- Leave as soon as you can. Go to a neighbor or a friend and take your children with you. Not taking the children may result in custody problems later.
- If you are unable to leave without assistance, call the police. While they are unlikely to arrest the batterer, their intervention can give you a breathing space. They may even escort you to a friend's house or find you a place to spend the night.
- Document your injuries. Have them photographed while the injuries are most visible. You will need proof if you later decide to take legal action.

## *Things You Can Do Once the Crisis Is Over*

- Seriously reflect on your relationship with your husband or partner. Could your relationship be improved by counseling? Could you yourself benefit from counseling even if the batterer is not willing to seek professional help? Or, are you willing to continue to risk serious injury in the hope that the violent behavior will disappear on its own?

- If the police officers did not file charges against your husband or partner and you wish to press charges, you can complain directly to the district attorney. But statistics have shown that women who decide to continue to live with the batterer are very unlikely to follow through on their complaints.

- If you do decide to leave, don't threaten, just do it. Don't provoke an unnecessary confrontation.

- Remember that it's up to you to take the first step to change your life. No one else can do it for you.

As this chapter indicates, however, once a woman makes her decision, there are many sources to help her build a new life.


# ELDERLY WOMEN

When Simone de Beauvoir wrote her classic work on women, *The Second Sex*, in 1949, she said: "Woman is haunted by the horror of growing old . . . she is still relatively young when she loses the erotic attractiveness and fertility which, in the view of society and her own, provide the justification of her existence and her opportunity for happiness. With no future, she still has half her adult life to live."[27] De Beauvoir lamented the fact that a woman who had spent her life in a strictly domestic manner would, by the age of 35 or so, be "finished."

In the subsequent four decades, there has been an amazing growth in awareness about aging and a burgeoning sense of the potentialities of older women. Today a woman of 35 or 40 is seen to be in her prime, with both family and employment opportunities still ahead of her. The present life expectancy for an American woman is 77.1 years; the most rapidly growing segment of the elderly are those over age 75, of whom 65 percent are women. At a National Organization for Women symposium on the future of the family, Betty Friedan coined a term to express the unprecedented opportunities for vital living after the age of 50: she urged women to view those years as a "new third of life."

Other signs point to the changing view of aging in our society. Because of changes in birthrates, the population of the country as a whole is becoming proportionately older. The field of gerontology, an academic discipline which studies aging from multiple perspectives, is growing. And the images of deterioration, isolation, depression, and desperation that were considered "normal" for aging women are being challenged by many organizations serving elderly people.

Nevertheless, laws which affect elderly women have been slow to change, and the relationship of past legislative and social inequities to current problems is most acute among elderly women. Past discrimination in education and in the work force and the economic structures of traditional marriage have contributed to the economic plight of many elderly women. This past discrimination, combined with female longevity, condemns many of these women to live in poverty or in institutions where they receive impersonal care.

The average age of widowhood in the United States is 56. Only one woman in twelve dies before her husband. Because of this, many women begin to look for work for the first time between the ages of 50 and 59—when their spouse dies or becomes disabled. Mature women who are working are often concentrated in low-paying, dead-end jobs. A third of all widows live below poverty level and less than 10 percent receive pension survivor benefits.

A substantial proportion of the elderly live alone. Only 5 percent of men and women over the age of 65 live in nursing homes, but of these 75 percent are women. Almost half the women over 75 live alone. There are many reasons for this: some wish to live alone, some have no children, some do not want to live with children, and children who work may have no one at home to care for an aging parent. Directly or indirectly, the family is still the primary caretaker for the aged.

The problems of older women can lead to domestic tensions. The elderly may sometimes be the victims of physical assault, verbal and psychological abuse, neglect, overmedication, or financial abuse. Their caretakers are most likely to be daughters and daughters-in-law, who are expected to assume the caretaking role without adequate support. These women may be caring for dependent children at the same time. Stress is high in these situations for both young and old.

The laws which affect elderly women fall into three categories: economic distress and its remedies; avoidance of victimization by third parties; and age discrimination in employment. In this section we will focus on the first category. When an elderly woman becomes a widow, this is often the first time in her life that she finds herself responsible for her financial affairs. Elderly women ought to be aware that there are government programs at the federal, state, county, and city levels which can help; these include food stamps, homemaker services, medicaid and medicare payments for nursing services, meals on wheels, rent-subsidized housing, and others. Of course, federal budget cuts have made these sources less secure.

Many national and community groups lobby for the rights of the elderly and can direct you to local programs. The most active groups include the Gray Panthers, the American Association of Retired Persons, the National Council of Senior Citizens, the Older Women's League, and the women's law projects that are housed at numerous law schools around the country and deal with issues that affect elderly women.

The laws that define a widow's right to a share of her husband's property involve such issues as the probating of a will; options to disregard a will; and the rights of a woman whose husband dies without a will.

The laws of descent and distribution in each state cover the way property will be distributed if a person dies intestate, that is, without leaving a valid will. The right to inherit or share in the property or estate of a person who dies without a will depends primarily on your relationship to the person. A typical pattern of succession is: spouse, children, parents, brothers and sisters and their lineal descendants, grandparents and their lineal descendants. If none of these exist, then the next of kin or nearest blood relatives are the inheritors. If none of these can be found, then the property goes to the state.

In general, the law that applies in any given case is the law of the state where the deceased had his or her permanent residence. If the deceased owned property in another state, the law of that state usually governs the distribution of that property.

Most states have abolished the vestiges of the old common-law traditions which treated men and women differently. States that have not passed community property laws have passed statutes that give the surviving spouse an alternative to what has been provided for her in the will. This is called an elective share. It can give the spouse ownership of both real estate and personal property. States with this right of election determine the size of the share by a formula written into the laws of the state. These laws aim to protect a widow from receiving an inequitable share of her husband's property. Nevertheless, the elective share is not a panacea. It may guarantee as little as one-third of the estate. There are also time limits which differ in each state as to when a widow must file for her claim and in which court she must file. In general, this filing takes place in probate court.

Probate is the process by which the document known as a will is established to be valid and genuine. Probate is also regulated by state law. The probate court also has jurisdiction over the administration of an estate in such matters as collecting and settling debts and distributing assets. Until a will is probated, it has no legal effect.

Probate costs money and can be very time-consuming as well. This may force a widow to suffer financial hardship, since all assets from the person's estate are frozen until the probate is completed. To ease financial pressures, states have mandated differing family allowances to be paid to the family as quickly as possible. But all necessary papers for probate and a petition for a family allowance must be filed first. Until then, the family is responsible for meeting its own financial obligations. State laws vary on this and must be consulted. The allowances may be given for the support of minor children or to manage household expenses. Depending on the state, it is either given as a lump sum or in periodic installments.

One of the major sources of support for older Americans is social security. For more than 60 percent of elderly women, social security is the sole source of income. Yet women receive significantly lower benefits than men. The reasons for this stem from the origins of the social security system. It was designed during the 1930s to help workers employed in the paid labor force live out their lives with economic security and dignity. The program was organized to meet the needs of the typical family of fifty years ago—a wife who worked as a full-time homemaker and a wage-earning husband in a marriage that was ended upon the death of one of the spouses.

But this "typical" family is rare in today's society. Currently more than half of married women are employed in the paid labor force. Women are paid only

59 to 62 cents for every dollar a man is paid. If present trends continue, almost 40 percent of all marriages will end in divorce. What appeared to be an adequate or even generous system in the 1940s now works to victimize women in several ways. If a homemaker is divorced after less than ten years of marriage, she receives no benefits. If she is divorced after ten years of marriage, she must wait until her husband retires or dies before she can begin receiving benefits. If a homemaker is widowed before the age of 50, she cannot receive benefits until she reaches age 50 unless she is disabled or raising young children. If her children are grown, she cannot receive benefits until she turns 60. She will receive the full benefit to which she is entitled only if she waits until age 65 to begin collecting. As her husband's dependent, a widow receives only part of her deceased spouse's benefit because the law fails to recognize the non-wage-earning contributions to the family of a homemaker. There are also inequities in the way benefits are calculated for a couple with two incomes. These occur in the system's failure to award service credit for women who take leaves of absence from work for maternity or child rearing. The social security system needs to be reformed to guarantee economic justice for men and women.

On the other hand, the pension rights of women have recently taken a major turn for the better. As a result of the passage by Congress of the Retirement Equity Act of 1984, state courts can treat pensions as joint property in divorce proceedings. The court can also require pension plans to pay all or a portion of an employee's benefits to an "alternate payee" under a qualified domestic relations order. This can be a judgment, decree, or order that relates to the provision of child support, alimony payments, or marital property rights.

The Retirement Equity Act also expands pension coverage for women who return to work after child-rearing leaves and provides that breaks in service of up to 5 years will not affect benefit entitlements. Certain pension rights are guaranteed to homemakers whose spouses die before retirement. The bill also prevents an employee from waiving coverage for survivors without the written consent of the spouse. In the past many women who thought they would be "taken care of" were shocked to learn that their spouses had waived survivor benefits and never told them. The legislation also reduced the age from 25 to 21 for workers to begin to be enrolled in pension plans. This legislation is a victory for women, particularly elderly women.

The difficulties older women face may be alleviated by more legislation affecting the elderly as the U.S. population ages. It is predicted that 45 percent of the population will be over 65 by the year 2000. Many researchers in the health fields are optimistic that the diseases which plague older Americans will soon be overcome or reduced in severity. Research on the quality of life of the elderly reveals the most important element in life satisfaction is the continuation of meaningful social ties. Scientists at the University of California at Los Angeles found that the death rate among men and women with the fewest social connections was more than double the rate for men and triple for women. This research suggests that women who wish to flourish in old age keep active and connected to family, friends, and organizations.

The researchers also found that the intensity of stress is less important than how a person handles it. How elderly women feel about themselves and their potential can affect physical and emotional health. The attitude of Lydia Bragger, chairperson of the activist Gray Panthers' Media Watch Task Force, may indicate a starting point for self-confidence. She said at a recent conference: "This is a pioneering generation of old people. They are standing up, they are fighting. They have better health and better education. It is a good time to be old."

# 3

# EDUCATION

*It was in making education not only common to all, but in some sense compulsory on all, that the destiny of the free republics of America was practically settled.*

James Russell Lowell
*New England Two Centuries Ago*

Though Americans pride themselves on the universal public education which has been part of the foundation of our democracy, there is a parallel thread running through the fabric of American history which carries the idea that educating women is folly. At best, this theme suggests that education is merely a supplement to woman's real role as keeper of the domestic flame. Legislatures have always had to be convinced that public funding for the education of women would not ultimately be money wasted.

Women were scarce in colonial America. Most education was conducted at home where young girls were indirectly exposed to it. Women also helped men in the variety of trades they practiced. And when they became widows, women often continued the management of their family businesses.

The industrial revolution in the early 1800s transformed these work and education patterns by introducing machine-oriented production which took place in centralized factories. The relationship of men and women who had worked together in home-based trades was permanently changed. Caroline Bird, feminist author, writes of this:

> By 1830, it was not as easy as it had been in colonial times to become doctors, lawyers, storekeepers, innkeepers, or women of affairs. Young people were now educated outside the home and in formal schools and impersonal places of business from which women were excluded as a matter of course. Like the new wage worker in factories, the new capitalists went out to work but they left their wives behind them. The Industrial Revolution which created the working woman also created her more influential mirror image, the lady of leisure.[1]

Although many women of the poorer classes worked for low wages in the new factories, the role of "lady" quickly became the model for all women. In egalitarian America, says Bird, every girl could hope that marriage would bring her this status. To produce these "ladies," over 200 finishing schools were founded between 1820 and the Civil War. College education for women was generally opposed. It was feared that the stress of education would endanger a woman's delicate health and impair her future childbearing potential. Women in college classrooms might force the lowering of standards. They might distract men from their studies. And if they became too educated, they might lose their femininity altogether!

Obviously there were women who protested these restraints and who fought for the right of women to be educated in a more serious manner. Emma Willard, a great American educational leader, addressed the New York state legislature in 1819. She proposed a publicly financed "seminary," or college for women, and said the time had come to change the course of women's education.

Male education flourished, she avowed, because of the care lavished upon it by legislatures. Female institutions languished because the students who attended them paid for the privilege and the curriculum was not subject to any serious evaluation. The livelihoods of the "preceptresses" who ran these schools depended upon a continuous stream of impressionable young girls. These women were instructed according to easily visible turns of fashion rather than in more durable habits of learning.

Willard believed college-educated women would become the teachers of the next generation of young girls and that it was through the power of educated women that society would receive its "tone" as to manners and morals. Yet her appeal to the legislators, in the long run, was based on the fact that most women became mothers and the prosperity of the nation would be determined by the character of the citizens these mothers produced.

By the time of the Civil War, some of the changes Willard had pleaded for had come to pass, particularly in the participation of women in the teaching and nursing professions. Women were so cheap to hire as "schoolmarms" that public education of boys and girls through high school became more and more commonplace. Girls who were educated in college-oriented high schools wanted to go to college, and by the turn of the century, most of what we now know as the prestigious private women's colleges, the so-called Seven Sisters—Barnard, Vassar, Wellesley, Smith, Radcliffe, Mt. Holyoke, and Bryn Mawr—had been founded.

Also around the turn of the century, a new invention precipitated the flow of women workers into offices. The typewriter became widely used in offices in the 1880s, and women who demonstrated their use were then hired to operate them. Soon, "business schools" to train women in typewriting were opened all over the country. The invention of the telephone, too, offered women a chance to work as operators. Both of these jobs, unlike factory labor, were clean and respectable and enabled women to earn money and meet suitable "gentlemen."

Even though Emma Willard pleaded with the legislators to establish a public women's college, her definition of an appropriate curriculum was one suited to the female sex. Most of the subjects were preparation for an enlightened form of "housewifery" and others were described as "ornamental," including needlework, drawing, painting, elegant penmanship, and instruction in dancing and music. This curriculum would prepare a woman to serve her community intelligently by "regulating the internal concerns of her family." For almost 100 years after, the curriculum developed in a sex-segregated manner. Modern feminists recognized that changing these entrenched patterns of schooling was the key to changing the status of women. What girls were taught, in the early years particularly, influenced them for a lifetime. Educational equality had to be at the heart of reforming social attitudes.

# TITLE IX OF THE EDUCATION AMENDMENTS OF 1972

It wasn't until 1972 that Congress officially recognized that sex discrimination existed in the schools and passed laws designed to remedy these deep-seated practices. The principal laws now in place which address sex discrimination in schools include Title IX of the Education Amendments of 1972 and federal or state constitutional guarantees of equal protection or equal rights.

Title IX prohibits sex discrimination in any educational program or activity receiving federal financial assistance. Title IX was modeled after Title VI of the Civil Rights Act of 1964, which prohibits discrimination on the basis of race or national origin in programs receiving federal financial assistance. This connection has its historical roots in the post–Civil War era, when blacks and women fought together for educational opportunity.

All federal agencies which fund educational programs or activities are responsible for the enforcement of Title IX. But because of the number of agencies involved, the civil rights sections of the Department of Justice and the Department of Education are charged with the major responsibilities of enforcement.

Although Title IX was passed in 1972, regulations to implement it were not issued until July 1975. The delay in promulgating these regulations inhibited lawsuits under Title IX. Nevertheless, it now provides the firmest legal base for monitoring sex equity in education.

At the same time that Title IX was enacted, Congress amended both Title VII of the Civil Rights Act of 1964 and the Equal Pay Act (see Chapter 4) to protect educational personnel against discrimination in employment.

Under Title IX, each institution which receives federal funds must appoint one employee to coordinate compliance efforts and investigate complaints. Students and employees must be notified of the procedures and the designated person for investigation. An individual is not required to use this structure and may file a private law suit. Schools may also be sued directly without relying on federal enforcement procedures. Although it may be possible to recover attorney's fees and other costs, court litigation is much more expensive and the guidelines under Title IX are less clear for resolving private grievances in this way.

Anybody can file a complaint alleging that a federally financed educational institution is in violation of Title IX. You do not have to be a victim of discrimination yourself in order to file a complaint; parents, students, interested citizens and community groups may all request an investigation of possible violations.

No specific form is required. What is necessary is a letter stating that you believe violations exist and the reasons for your belief. If certain basic information is missing from the letter, you will receive a form to complete asking for more details. Letters must contain the following: the name and address of the school district, college, or other institution you believe is discriminating by sex; a general description of the person(s) suffering from that discrimination; the approximate date the discrimination occurred or indication that it is ongoing; your name, address, and, if possible, a telephone number where you can be reached during the day; enough information about the discrimination so that what happened is clear.

The Department of Education is the agency which investigates complaints under Title IX and determines whether funding will be terminated in a given school district. The Justice Department actually brings a suit to court. The letter which you write describing the discrimination should be sent to the director of the regional Office for Civil Rights of the Department of Education with jurisdiction over your state. The regional offices, their addresses, and their jurisdictions are listed in Appendix G.

The complaint should be filed within 180 days of the alleged discriminatory act, although in special cases this deadline may be extended. The identity of the person making the complaint must be kept confidential by all parties. However, even if the names are not revealed to the school directly, they are often apparent from questions asked by an investigator. Title IX does prohibit schools from intimidating, coercing, and interfering with or discriminating against an individual who files a complaint or assists in the enforcement of the law. But, in practice, filing can result in ostracism from the group. On the other hand, in many cases more than one woman has been subjected to discrimination in a school, and the complaint may be filed for several complainants.

With certain exceptions, Title IX bars sex discrimination in any academic, athletic, extracurricular, vocational, research, occupational training, or other educational program—public or private, preschool to postgraduate—operated by a school district, governing body, organization, or agency which receives or benefits from federal aid. Exempted from the provisions of this law are:

- Schools whose primary purpose is the training for the U.S. military services or the merchant marine
- Admissions policies of private undergraduate institutions
- Admissions policies of public undergraduate institutions which have traditionally had a policy of excluding members of one sex
- Practices in schools controlled by religious organizations whenever compliance with Title IX would contravene their religious beliefs
- Membership policies of the Girl Scouts and Boy Scouts, the YMCA and the YWCA, Campfire Girls and other single-sex, tax-exempt "youth service" organizations whose members are primarily under age 19
- University-based fraternities and sororities
- Activities relating to the American Legion's Boys State, Boys Nation, Girls State, and Girls Nation conferences
- Father-son or mother-daughter activities as long as opportunities for "reasonably comparable" activities are offered to students of both sexes

- Scholarships or other aid offered by colleges and universities to participants in single-sex pageants which reward the combination of personal appearance, poise, and talent.

Title IX is not only concerned with activities which are characteristic of higher education. It is also a guarantee in elementary and secondary schools that girls and boys will not be arbitrarily segregated on the basis of sex in classes and school activities. Such segregation might occur in physical education; extracurricular programs and athletics; occupational and vocational training, services, aids, or benefits such as counseling, coaching, or the selection of awards; rules of behavior such as dress codes; or disciplinary actions which treat boys and girls differently. Even exposure to stereotyped curriculum materials can have an effect on boys and girls, and Title IX has had an impact on textbook content. Title IX is also a mandate for sex equity in these areas:

- Opportunity for recruitment and admission of students to institutions of vocational education, professional education, graduate higher education, and public institutions of higher education, although coed education is not required
- Student housing
- Financial assistance
- Health insurance and benefits
- Toilet, locker room, and shower facilities
- Access to academic, extracurricular, research, occupational training, course offerings, or employment assistance to students
- Access to athletic programs
- Counseling and counseling materials
- Employment in education, including recruitment, compensation, job classification, fringe benefits, marital or parental status, advertising and pre-employment inquiries

To cover situations not specifically cited, there is a fail-safe provision in Title IX which states that it is prohibited to "limit any person in the enjoyment of any right, privilege, advantage or opportunity."

In February 1984, the Supreme Court decided a case which had been in litigation for 7 years: *Grove City College v. Bell*.[2] The case hinged on the meaning of the Title IX term "any program or activity receiving federal assistance." The Court decided on a narrow interpretation, which means that only the specific activity directly receiving federal funds is covered by Title IX, not the entire institution or school. In a session of Congress in June 1984, many voiced their concern that the entire legislative intent of Title IX could be jeopardized. One member raised the point that under the *Grove City College* ruling, women at federally assisted educational institutions could be denied participation in athletic or math programs, denied use of certain facilities, or even denied admission as long as those particular programs were not receiving federal aid.

There is legislation before Congress, the Civil Rights Restoration Act, to reinstate Title IX as the broad protection it was before *Grove City College*. And there is a decade of social, educational, and legislative precedent from which to draw models for the future. The states too have been active partners in developing programs to achieve educational equity. Fourteen states have enacted laws modeled on the federal Title IX: Alaska, California, Florida, Hawaii, Iowa, Maine, Massachusetts, Minnesota, Nebraska, New Jersey, Oregon, Rhode Island, Washington, and Wisconsin. Let us consider what has been accomplished.

Proper education in physical fitness, motor skills, and group skills has equal value for both sexes. Physical education is an established part of the elementary and secondary school curriculum and is a required course in some colleges. Under Title IX, schools can no longer offer separate courses for girls and boys in any part of the curriculum, including physical education. Elementary school physical education classes were to be integrated by July 1976, and secondary classes by July 1978. The intention of Title IX is not to bring boys and girls into the same gym and have them engage in totally separate activities but to ensure successful coeducational classes.

A school can choose to separate boys and girls during the playing of contact sports such as football, basketball, wrestling, boxing, rugby, and ice hockey. But students may not be separated during instruction in these sports. If a teacher wants to group students by ability, students must be tested individually and measured by an objective standard without regard to sex. They should be tested for each sport in which they are to be grouped by ability, since skills will vary from sport to sport. This kind of testing should not lead to sex-segregated groups. If any single standard constantly causes members of one sex to lose out, that standard cannot be used and an alternative standard must be developed.

Title IX's goal of coeducational physical education classes has been attacked on religious grounds. Parents from a variety of religious denominations have been concerned about the "immodest apparel" worn by students during class. Because many school districts require physical education, students who do not participate in the program may not graduate. In 1978 the Department of Health, Education, and Welfare published a policy interpretation which said that "students who demonstrate that their religion prohibits certain coeducational courses may be excused from such courses or offered them on a sex-segregated basis."

In addition, schools cannot set different graduation requirements in physical education for boys and girls. Nor can teachers be assigned to classes on the basis of sex rather than on qualifications. Except for locker room duty, teachers must be accessible to students of both sexes. However, according to a 1983 publication of the National Women's Law Center, the transition to mixed classes in physical education has not yet been completed. Parents can be an active force in accomplishing these goals by being certain that schools are moving toward compliance.

If media coverage and public enthusiasm are any indication, there seems to be a growing respect for women's sports. This was certainly true of the 1984 Olympic Games in Los Angeles. The figures for high school women's participation in sports show that in 1970 just under 300,000 women served on athletic teams sponsored by their schools. In recent years, over 2 million women participated.

Title IX regulations do not require that school athletic programs for girls be an exact duplicate of those already in place for boys. They were intended to encourage the development of alternative programs depending on the needs and interests of female students. In general, these major factors can indicate equity:

- A selection of sports and levels of competition that effectively accommodate the interests and abilities of members of both sexes
- The provision of equipment and supplies
- Scheduling of games and practice time
- Travel and per diem allowance
- Opportunity to receive coaching and academic tutoring
- Assignment and compensation of coaches and tutors
- Provision of locker rooms, practice, and field facilities
- Provision of medical services
- Provision of housing and dining facilities and services
- Publicity

Equal expenditures on boys' and girls' sports may not alone signal compliance, since different sports have different cost considerations. Because girls' and women's sports are still outside the economic mainstream, women students at the University of Washington have sued to have women's athletics receive funds equivalent to university expenditures on football.

Title IX, in fact, has been a good vehicle for the creation of more girls' teams because it definitely permits separate programs for each sex under defined circumstances. Though permanent separate-but-equal teams can set dangerous precedents, the National Women's Law Center documentation indicates that "separate teams for girls may be the critical force that moves school athletic programs forward and away from restricted and inferior programs for girls which have been so common."[3]

When girls have tried to move beyond female teams into all-male teams, the courts have been ambiguous in their support. In Yellow Springs, Ohio, for example, a girl won the right to play on the middle school boys' basketball team because the school district challenged the state interscholastic athletic association rules on coed teams in contact sports.

In another case, an 11-year-old sixth-grade girl, who was assessed by a professional basketball coach to have the skills of an eighth-grade boy and a tenth-grade girl, was not permitted to join the basketball team. Here the Court ruled that since Title IX does permit separate teams, "if the classification is reasonable . . . the general rule cannot be said to be unconstitutional simply because it appears arbitrary in an individual case."[4] While the status of these individual challenges is mixed, Title IX has served the purpose of more equitable athletic programs for female students.

**CURRICULUM:** Title IX regulations exclude textbooks and curricular materials on the grounds that mandating the content of these would violate the First Amendment right of free press and limit academic freedom to select classroom materials. Nevertheless, since the early 1970s, there has been a strong movement among women's groups to sensitize parents, teachers, and administrators to sexism in language, course content, and graphics. Since textbooks define much of what will or will not be taught in a classroom, children come to view them as a major source of information about the world. Over the past decade, publishers have adopted many of the guidelines outlined in the 1970s by The Feminist Press for nonsexist curricular materials:

• Portray girls as decision makers

• Show girls with determination, courage, and a willingness to stand up for what they believe

• Show girls participating in outdoor activities which require physical coordination and strength

• Show girls engaged in adventurous and exciting activities, even as mischief makers once in a while

• Portray girls cooperating with other girls in various adventures or creative situations; avoid stereotypes of girls competing with each other for male attention

• Show that girls who are not particularly attractive according to present-day standards can still lead active and interesting lives

• Show that girls who are smart, academically inclined, or leaders can still be popular among their peers, both male and female

• Show girls working toward a variety of career goals, including such "nontraditional" fields as science, electronics, computers, law, politics, economics

The Feminist Press suggests that teachers, especially those in elementary schools, where key attitudes are formed, ask themselves questions about their behavioral expectations for boys and girls; the way they express displeasure and affection to their students; and about classroom discussions, bulletin board depictions, and the like which reinforce stereotyped attitudes. Teachers are urged to be role models for nonsexist attitudes and to monitor their attitudes and verbal cues for sex-role behaviors or statements such as "big boys don't . . ." or "nice girls don't. . . ." The key strategy in all of this is to be open with students about the efforts to combat traditional sex-role expectations and to allow students to talk about the problem and find answers for themselves. These may come from library books such as biographies, which give children new role models, as well as from the formal curriculum.

New curriculum issues are now being raised by the increasing use of computers in our schools. Questions about equal access to computers for all students, as well as the sexist or racist nature of the software used, must be considered. The Project on Equal Education Rights (PEER) of the NOW Legal Defense and Education Fund has published several guides on computer equity.

In higher education, feminist critiques of every field from literature to science and social science have become an integral part of the university curriculum. Many colleges have women's studies programs, and there is a worldwide network of women scholars and researchers introducing a changed curriculum by forcing the restructuring of old intellectual categories and disciplinary boundaries.

Title IX regulations forbid the exclusion of a girl or boy from a class or activity because of sex and mandate against separate courses for boys and girls. This applies to traditionally "male" courses such as industrial arts, business, technical subjects, and economics and traditionally "female" courses such as typing, home economics, and dance. Some exceptions include sex education classes, which may be taught separately, music classes which rely on segregation by voice type, and physical education courses, which have already been discussed earlier in this chapter.

**EMPLOYMENT IN EDUCATION:** Although women are numerically well-represented in education, they have been systematically relegated to lower-paying, less-prestigious jobs. This is as true in elementary and secondary schools as it is in higher education. Women are seldom principals, provosts, or presidents. Nationally, women are less than 1 percent of school superintendents. Women are also discriminated against in nonprofessional categories such as janitorial jobs.

In 1982, the Supreme Court held in *North Haven Board of Education v. Bell* that Title IX's prohibition on sex discrimination is intended to apply to employment practices of educational institutions receiving federal funds.[5] This provision covers recruitment, advertising, and the application process; hiring, promotion, tenure, and the right of return from layoff; all compensation decisions; job assignments and lines of progression and advancement; collective bargaining agreements; leaves of absences, including those for pregnancy and childbirth, childcare, or care of other dependents; fringe benefits, whether or not administered by the institution; training and selection for professional meetings and sabbaticals; participation in employer-sponsored recreational programs; and any other terms or conditions of employment. An institution may ask the sex of a job applicant but may not ask the applicant's marital status. In general, individual employment complaints in educational institutions will not be resolved by the Equal Employment Opportunity Commission; rather, they will be investigated through Title IX procedures at the Department of Education. (Laws governing the employment of women are discussed more fully in Chapter 4 of this book.)

Sex discrimination in admissions is prohibited by Title IX in institutions of vocational, professional, and graduate higher education and in *public* institutions of undergraduate higher education. Private undergraduate colleges are exempt. Single-sex, publicly funded undergraduate colleges, including the Air Force Academy, the Naval Academy, the Coast Guard Academy, and the Merchant Marine Academy, had all been integrated by 1982, although in many of these institutions the number of women enrolled represents a token amount. Title IX stipulates that for all covered institutions, remedial efforts to correct past discriminatory practices in recruitment are necessary if present practices do not rectify imbalances in class composition. In large universities where separate divisions may have separate admissions criteria, discrimination may occur in one program but not be sufficient to establish evidence of a university-wide violation of Title IX.

One major exception is the Public Health Service Act which provides extensive federal support for individuals training in the fields of health and allied health professions. Most medical and dental schools, schools of pharmacy, optometry, podiatry, veterinary medicine, public health, nursing, and other health professions receive government funding under this program. Amendments to the Public Health Service Act and the Nurse Training Act prohibited sex discrimination by recipients of these funds. Any woman who wishes to raise discrimination in admissions issues at these institutions is protected by law.

The awarding of financial aid is often a key factor in any student's decision to attend a given college. Title IX recognizes this by forbidding the distribution of financial aid in a different manner for males and females or on the basis of different eligibility requirements. However, schools may administer sex-restricted scholarships and fellowships established by wills or trusts or by foreign governments. Schools may offer athletic scholarships on the basis of gender but must provide "reasonable opportunities for such awards to each sex." Title IX regulations specifically forbid discrimination against women by assuming that a wife's domicile is that of her husband if she lives elsewhere. It is *her* place of residence that is to be considered for determination of tuition fees.

Housing and on-campus residency rules have changed. On the basis of Title IX, university housing for men and women must be comparable on the whole. A university cannot allocate all of the new, inexpensive, or convenient housing to students of one sex. The same premises of equity apply to married student housing, particularly for married students of both sexes with nonstudent spouses.

Until the end of the 1960s, many colleges maintained separate curfews and reporting-in procedures (parietal rules) for female students living in dormitories. The prevailing approach toward women by university housing policies was to act *in loco parentis*, as a substitute parent.

Today, these parietal rules are illegal. Many dormitories are now coed, and women as well as men may live off campus if they choose.

**PREGNANCY AND MARITAL STATUS:** More than 1 million teenagers become pregnant each year. In teenage pregnancy, which of course involves both sexes, discrimination in education is most often directed against young women. More than half of all female dropouts leave school because of pregnancy, and 80 percent of those under 17 never complete high school. Teenage mothers are also less likely than other mothers to be working outside the home and more likely to receive Aid to Families with Dependent Children.

Formerly, pregnant teenagers were unwelcome in the schools. They dropped out even if they did not want to because they were barred from certain courses or expelled. Any discrimination because of pregnancy is a violation of Title IX.

A pregnant student may not be (1) required to attend a special school; (2) barred from any program, course, or extracurricular activity including physical education; (3) refused the opportunity to compete for awards, honors, elective office; or (4) required to leave school for a specified period before or after the birth of the child. Unless all students who have special conditions are required to bring notes from their doctors, a pregnant student must not be expected to produce such notes. Depending on the leave policy of the school district, the student must be reinstated to the status she had when the leave began. If the district has a program for homebound students, those services must be made available to pregnant students on the same basis as they are to other students.

Although many districts, especially in large urban areas, offer special courses in child care and related home and family issues for pregnant students, these courses cannot be required unless they are required of every student in the district. The decision to attend any special program for pregnant students must be voluntary. Bus services must also be provided to the pregnant student if they are provided to others. If an educational institution has students covered by any medical policies, those plans must treat pregnancy in the same manner as any other temporary disability.

Before the landmark case of *Cleveland Board of Education v. La Fleur*, decided by the Supreme Court in 1974, pregnant teachers were usually required to leave their teaching responsibilities 5 or 6 months before giving birth.[6] One New York school district required that a woman report her pregnancy to the school board within 10 days of conception. The result of these policies was that teachers forced to take unpaid leaves faced financial hardships and that these "breaks in service" constituted impediments to career advancement or movement into supervisory roles.

Title IX regulations expressly prohibit recipients of federal financial assistance from discriminating against any employee or applicant for employment on the basis of pregnancy. In the Cleveland case, the Supreme Court held that the school board's termination policies presumed that every pregnant teacher was incapable of performing her tasks at a certain stage of the pregnancy and violated the teacher's due process rights under the Fourteenth Amendment and the constitutional right to choose whether or not to bear children.

In a subsequent case involving the San Diego, California, Unified School District, it was decided that a mandatory leave date within 1 month of the expected date of delivery was not unreasonable to avoid disruption in the continuity of education should the teacher suddenly become unable to teach because of the onset of labor. Other court cases have considered whether a pregnant woman who had to leave at a specific date was eligible for unemployment benefits, and in 1975 struck down a Utah statute rendering pregnant women ineligible. For the most part, Title IX and subsequent cases have legislated in favor of pregnant women's rights, whether as students or teachers. (See also Chapter 4 for a discussion of the federal Pregnancy Discrimination Act of 1978.)

**STUDENT ACTIVITIES AND SERVICES:** At the elementary and secondary school level, Title IX forbids most school organizations from discriminating on the basis of sex. Only such widely known organizations and groups as the YMCA and YWCA, the Girl Scouts, Boy Scouts, and Camp Fire Girls were allowed to maintain separate organizations. Congress amended the law in 1976 to exempt certain large-scale programs such as Boys State, Boys Nation, Girls State, and Girls Nation. This amendment also permits schools to sponsor mother-daughter and father-son activities.

Extracurricular activities in a school provide important channels for student expression of leadership ability, artistic development, social and recreational life, and exposure to a range of programs and ideas unrelated to strict academics. On the campus, Title IX extends to most clubs, except for a specific exemption from coverage of all fraternities and sororities which are purely social in nature. Honor societies and student professional groups are not exempted.

Because social fraternities and sororities are exempted, the classification of a group as "social" has been a key factor in deciding whether or not a given group could continue to maintain sex-segregated memberships. Another issue is to what extent "significant financial assistance" is provided to the group by the federally funded university.

Another student service which becomes increasingly important as adults return to school to take college courses is the provision of child care. Neither Title IX nor subsequent amendments explicitly address this issue. Only one case, *De La Cruz v. Tormey*, has ever raised the question of whether an educational institution's failure to provide child care services was a violation of Title IX.[7]

In this 1978 case, a young woman with low income and child-rearing responsibilities alleged that the school's failure to provide child care restricted or denied the access of women students to existing programs and services and deprived them of equal educational opportunity. The court held that failure to provide child care *may* constitute unlawful sex discrimination under Title IX, but under the standard created in *De La Cruz*, plaintiffs in future cases must show that the lack of child care has had a "disproportionate impact" on women and impairs the value of existing educational opportunities. Although the particular institution which was challenged in the case did begin to construct a child care center on one of its campuses, on-campus child care is still rare.

Codes of behavior for male and female students must have the same penalties for violation, and copies of student handbooks and other policy documents about discipline must be consistent with sex-neutral codes. Regulations affecting grooming and appearance have been in litigation at the elementary and secondary levels of education. Title IX formerly prohibited discrimination in this area, but in 1981 these rules were withdrawn by the U.S. Department of Education. The reasons given were that (1) these issues were more properly resolved at the local level and (2) resources spent litigating these issues were better spent on "more substantive concerns." At the postsecondary level, appearance and dress codes were seen to be a violation of basic personal liberties and an arbitrary interference by the state.

## OTHER FEDERAL LAWS

In addition to Title IX, there are other federal laws that promote sex equity in education. The Women's Educational Equity Act of 1984 (Title IV of the Education Amendments of 1984), which revises and extends the Women's Educational Equity Act of 1974 (WEEA), provides federal grants to enable educational institutions and agencies to meet the requirements of Title IX; it also funds projects which seek to "provide educational equity for women and girls who suffer multiple discrimination, bias, or stereotyping based on sex and on race, ethnic origin, disability, or age." The new act requires that at least one grant or contract be awarded for each of the six authorized activities listed in the act: curricula, textbooks, and other educational materials; preservice and in-service training; research and development; guidance and counseling; programs for adult women; and vocational education, career education, physical education, and educational administration. The new WEEA also revamps the small-grants program by increasing the maximum grant award from $25,000 to $40,000. Also, Title IV of the Civil Rights Act of 1964, as amended in 1972, provides federal funds to support sex-equity efforts by state education agencies and establishes regional sex desegregation assistance centers to aid local school districts in implementing sex equity.

Vocational choices are often influenced by sex bias. As early as nursery school girls play "dress up" and boys play with trucks. Later, these same girls may be encouraged to study cosmetology, while the boys will be guided toward mechanics or engineering. Many girls limit their own opportunities because they and their parents often approach vocational education with a narrow vision of what is appropriate. Many schools reinforce these notions by barring girls from traditionally male fields through recruitment, admission, and counseling practices which are discriminatory.

Under Title IX, vocational schools and programs must end all sex-discriminatory policies or practices which have kept girls from pursuing any course of study offered by any public vocational education program which receives federal funds. The federal funding need not originate from the U.S. Department of Education nor must the institution receiving funds be a school. Vocational education programs receiving government funds may also be located in a nonprofit organization, a state or local government agency, a corporation, or a union.

Federal funding of vocational education began a decade earlier than the passage of Title IX. The Vocational Education Act of 1963 was a federal grant-in-aid program that allocated funds to state agencies, which in turn distributed the funds to local agencies. This act was significantly amended in 1976 to mandate greater spending for programs to overcome sex bias, sex stereotyping, and traditional limitations of women in the work force. The 1976 amendments required, among other goals, that each state (1) hire a full-time sex-equity coordinator and provide a minimum of $50,000 of its federal funds for sex-equity activities annually, (2) submit a 5-year state plan on the ways equal access to vocational opportunities would be implemented for persons of both sexes, and (3) hold public hearings on state education goals. The law mandated membership of women on state and national vocational education advisory councils, including minority women, knowledgeable about sex discrimination in employment and training.

Recognizing that home and family patterns were changing, the act also provided funds to train displaced homemakers, single heads of households, and women seeking nontraditional jobs. The act also permitted, but did not mandate, spending program funds for activities which extended access to vocational educaton for women. This included child care and counseling.

The 1976 amendments expired in 1984 and testimony before Congress in

1983 about the effects of the act were discouraging. The nation's vocational education system still remains largely sex-segregated today. In spite of the increasing economic needs of women, there is a greater proportion of women in low-paying and low-status jobs. Theresa Cusick, testifying on behalf of the National Coalition for Women and Girls in Education told Congress that "no institution has integrated women fully into its professional, managerial, technical and production jobs. Completing this process must be a major item on the national economic and social agenda over the remainder of the 1980's."[8]

A new law, the Carl D. Perkins Vocational Education Act, makes fundamental changes in federal vocational education policy. Most significantly, it requires states to spend 8.5 percent of their basic state grant on programs and services designed to aid single parents and homemakers. These include support services, such as child care and transportation, and grants to community-based organizations that provide services or training to homemakers and single parents. Another 3.5 percent of the basic grant is to be used for the sex-equity program. These funds can be used for three purposes: (1) for programs, services, and activities designed to eleiminate sex bias and stereotyping in secondary and postsecondary education; (2) for programs, services, and activities designed to enable girls and women aged 14 to 25 "to support themselves and their families"; and (3) for support services for girls and women aged 14 to 25 and for participants in programs designed to eliminate sex bias and stereotyping. Finally, each state is required to allocate $60,000 for a sex-equity coordinator who is responsible for administering the single-parents and homemaker program and the sex-equity program and for gathering, analyzing, and disseminating data on the effectiveness of vocational education programs in meeting the needs of women.

If there is one person at the local level who is instrumental in career choice, it is the school counselor. Counselors have many functions: they can help a student select and schedule classes; administer tests to measure student abilities, interests, and achievement; interpret those tests to students; and provide direction for further educational and vocational options. The counselor decides what material will be available in the school to guide career and educational choices and may be involved in providing job referrals and writing references.

Since the counselor is often the contact person between the student and the business world, it is critical that stereotypical counseling attitudes be eliminated. Title IX prohibits discrimination in counseling and guidance services and in the use of test materials to determine vocational interests. For example, in a widely used occupational-interest survey, scores are based on the degree of agreement between the student's response on the test and responses of satisfied people in particular occupations. If a female scores high in the skills needed to become a banker, she may be advised to become a bank clerk! Since there are so few female bankers, the option to "think big" may not occur even to the counselor.

Career choices for men and women are influenced by many environmental and cultural factors. These include conflicts between home and career demands and expectations of various ethnic and social-class groups. The National Institute for Education has published guidelines for fairness in career interest measurement. These guidelines urge counselors to assess their own biases first. Only then can advisors work toward changing attitudes which limit student aspirations.

Title IX's provisions guide sex-equity issues in all the states. Monitoring state compliance with the broad range of regulations discussed in this chapter can be done in a variety of ways. *Organizing for Change*, published by the Project on Equal Education Rights of the NOW Legal Defense and Education Fund, suggests the following strategies for change:

- Know your school system and how power is distributed.
- Ask who makes decisions about the kinds of changes you want to make, how and when decisions are made, and who influences decision makers.
- Consider ways potential support may be mobilized in your community for your goals.
- Meet the press and develop a community public relations campaign for changes you wish to effect in the schools.
- Decide on priorities and remember that a smaller issue which can give you a quick win at the start of a campaign can affect the way school people see your group.
- Consider alternative action strategies and a comfortable basic approach suitable to group members and your school district.
- Do a preliminary cost-benefit analysis and time analysis for each goal decided upon by your groups.

It is best, in most cases, to go through school channels and document your efforts carefully by getting written responses to your written requests. Comprehensive documentation is the key to building a suit.

To obtain a list of the sex-equity coordinators in each state, contact Sex Equity, Office of Vocational and Adult Education, U.S. Department of Education, 7th and D Streets, SW, Room 5128, Washington, DC 20202. The telephone number is (202) 245-8176.

## STATE LAWS

The discrepancies in state equal education laws are enormous. Fourteen states have enacted sex-equity laws modeled on the federal Title IX: Alaska, California, Florida, Hawaii, Iowa, Maine, Massachusetts, Minnesota, Nebraska, New Jersey, Oregon, Rhode Island, Washington, and Wisconsin. Other states, for example, Louisiana and West Virginia, do not have laws that specifically prohibit sex discrimination in education but do have laws that ban sex discrimination in public accommodations. These public accommodations laws may be interpreted to include public schools or public recreational facilities. Still other states, for example, New Hampshire, New Mexico, and Pennsylvania, have equal rights provisions in their state constitutions that may operate to prohibit sex discrimination in education. Several states have no provisions whatsoever for equal educational opportunities under state law.

Discrimination challenges have been more effective in those states that have equal rights amendments than at the federal level under Title IX. State ERAs interpret sex discrimination in a more stringent manner and are clearer and more consistent in their support of remedies. Thus, it is preferable to bring claims under state ERAs whenever possible.

Professional and public concern about the quality of education in the United States has initiated a new movement for educational reform. Government reports have charged that ours is "a nation at risk" because we will not sustain our position as a world leader if our educational shortcomings are not remedied.

The response to these criticisms has been strongest at the state level. The fall 1984 education supplement to *The New York Times* reports:

> Nine states—Mississippi, Arkansas, Florida, California, Tennessee, South Carolina, North Carolina, Texas and Maine—passed major legislation aimed at reform. Wisconsin, for example, will increase the salary scale of its teachers; Idaho will lengthen the school day; Ohio is strengthening its teacher certification test. . . . Fourteen states have enacted or approved performance based teacher incentives such as merit pay, career ladders . . . or plans for master teachers. . . . Forty-seven states were considering or had changed high school graduation requirements. . . . Twenty have improved the use of instructional time . . . and thirty have new professional development programs for teachers.[9]

Yet the education reform movement—at both the state and federal levels—has virtually ignored the educational needs of girls and women and has overlooked the improvements in education brought about by the educational equity movement of the past 20 years. Further, many conservative elements in the United States wish to dismantle mechanisms for broad social change such as those mandated by Title IX. The progress of sex equity in education will depend on vigilant women working to ensure that our daughters and granddaughters are not left behind, ignorant of the technological and professional skills an educated person will need in the twenty-first century.

# 4

# EMPLOYMENT

*Employers who insist they are looking to hire women . . . say they're defeated because qualified women either do not exist or do not apply. . . . "Qualified" turns out to be a magic word—like abracadabra it changes eggs into rabbits or makes coins disappear.*

Betty Lehan Harragan
*Games Mother Never Taught You*

The full-fledged entry of women into the labor market represents one of the most important social changes in the American economy. At the beginning of the twentieth century in the United States, women in the workplace were generally single women who had no family, no independent income, or no marital prospects. Married women whose husbands had low income or were unemployed also worked. Many of these working women were employed as servants or in other occupations which required domestic skills. For middle-class white women marriage virtually precluded employment at this time, since the need to work implied a fall in fortune or social status.

Families in this period were often large, and frequently three or even four generations were included in one household. These homes were self-contained units; family members were productively engaged in various forms of work needed to maintain the household. In 1900 many women lived on farms or in rural areas. These women also performed arduous tasks. However, unpaid labor such as this never figured into formal economic calculations.

Waves of immigrants were arriving on American shores at the turn of the century. Many of these men and women took jobs that were characterized by low wages, long hours, and unsafe and unsanitary working conditions. Muckraking journalists in the early 1900s exposed inequities in the workplace and eventually forced legal reforms. As conditions and social attitudes changed, women began to seek out employment.

According to a Rand Corporation study, a sharp increase in wages contributed to women's interest in work during this period.[1] Opportunities for "clean" clerical work increased, and a wage differentiation which had existed for married workers was eliminated. Married women's wages had been 30 percent lower than those of single women on the theory that a married woman would not need to work.

Coincident with these developments was a significant rise in attendance at and completion of high school by women. Three long-term trends also contributed to women's entry into the labor market: the change from an extended-family to a nuclear-family structure; the growing urbanization of the population; and a strong decrease in the birth rate. Starting in 1921, the U.S. birthrates decreased by over one-third. This decrease coincided with a decline in infant and child mortality and the gradual spread of birth control information. Not surprisingly, childbearing reached historic lows during the depression.

World War II has been credited with encouraging the first large-scale modern movement of women into the work force while men were serving in the military. The image of "Rosie the Riveter" has become part of the folklore of that war. Yet the Rand Corporation study points out that the war had a lasting effect on women with their childbearing years behind them. They continued to work after the war, while women of childbearing age were caught up in the "baby boom" of the postwar years. From 1947 to 1957 women moved to suburbia with their growing families, and family "togetherness" was emphasized. Though 1956 marked the change in the American economy from more blue-collar to more white-collar jobs—a move from the industrial to the service sector—most women remained at home.

Throughout the 1960s this process was reversed, as women immersed themselves in the social changes of this period. The participation of educated women in the marketplace increased rapidly. Many older women went back to school to equip themselves for work. By 1970 statistics showed that many women who were mothers of school-age and preschool children were entering the labor force. The rising number of two-income families was a key socioeconomic development of the 1970s. In the early 1980s, a record three out of every five married couples with families reported that both members were wage earners.

Today, working mothers comprise 58 percent of the women participating in the labor force. This figure is indicative not only of rising economic needs and aspirations but also of changing family structures: increasingly, women are raising children alone. Yet employers have made few concessions to the special needs of working mothers. The barriers that these women face often force them to choose between inflexible work structures or family values. Jobs that offer more flexibility usually pay less. Thus, women pay a toll in stress and loss of income.

Statistics show that more than half of all employed women fall into two occupational categories. The largest group is still clerical workers—stenographers, typists, secretaries. The second largest group is service workers—telephone operators, waitresses, hairdressers, food handlers, nurses, and child care personnel among others. Women's progress has been hindered by this widespread sex segregation in employment, which is often combined with lower pay, restrictive job qualifications, fewer opportunities for training or access, and a lack of day-care facilities, flextime schedules, or part-time work. Nevertheless, over the past two decades many laws which guarantee a woman's right to fair treatment in the marketplace have been passed at the local, state, and federal levels.

Every woman should know her rights under the employment laws and should check the provisions of any contracts, union regulations, and personnel policies that affect her. If a woman is discriminated against, it may be an isolated case; but it may also be part of a larger pattern affecting many women employed in the same setting. Litigation on behalf of many women against a single employer is known as a *class action lawsuit*. These suits proliferated in the 1970s and have been the basis of substantial changes in policies and procedures.

For employment practices to be considered fair, they must now meet the standards of federal and state laws and regulations. If a worker believes that these laws have been violated, he or she is entitled to initiate legal action.

# WAGES

The Fair Labor Standards Act (FLSA), which is generally known as the federal wage and hour law, was enacted originally in 1938 to establish a nationwide minimum wage for persons in certain employment categories. It also set standards for overtime and for the employment of children. In 1974, FLSA protection was extended to private household workers whose earnings constitute wages for social security purposes and who are employed a total of at least 8 hours a week. In 1980, a provision was enacted which stipulated that an employer can only consider tips as 40 percent of the minimum wage which must be paid. As of January 1, 1981, the minimum wage was set at $3.35 per hour.

Some workers, such as the handicapped, apprentices, and students, may be paid less under the law. Individuals in a professional, executive, or administrative capacity, some salespersons who are on the road, and employees engaged in municipal service professions such as fire prevention and sanitation are exempt from the provisions. So are baby-sitters who work on a casual basis, some farm workers, seasonal workers, and others. The Wage and Hour Division of the U.S. Department of Labor enforces this act. Federal employees are monitored by the Office of Personnel Management. Complaints are treated confidentially, and employees cannot be discriminated against or discharged for filing a complaint.

The Equal Pay Act of 1963 was the first federal law designed to prevent sex discrimination by forbidding unequal pay for women and men who work in the same establishment and whose jobs require equal skill, effort and responsibility. Each factor must be examined separately. Differences in wages based on seniority, merit systems, systems which measure earnings by quantity or quality of production, or differences based on any other factor *other than sex* are permitted. The work must be performed under similar working conditions. Employers may not reduce the wages of any employee to eliminate differences. Wages are interpreted to mean all employment-related payments, including overtime, uniforms, travel, and other fringe benefits.

The term *equal work* is difficult to interpret. The act requires that compared jobs be "substantially equal," not identical. Measuring the worth of a job, however, is a very complex task. Many of the systems now in effect which measure the skills and education required and assign points to different job characteristics are antiquated and do not reflect social and technological changes. The New York State job classification and compensation system, for example, was set up in 1937 and last revised in 1954. Many of these evaluation systems rely on stereotypes about the value of women's work and men's work, according higher points for heavy physical work and lower points for clerical skills.

In addition, state protective labor laws, passed in many states at the beginning of this century, regulated women's work, rendering it in effect unequal by preventing women from lifting heavy weights, working evening hours, or working before or after childbirth. A famous case at Bell Telephone involved a female worker who was denied a job change to switchman because the company claimed she would have to lift a 31-pound fire extinguisher. After several years of litigation, the woman won the job and back wages.[2]

Some states still have restrictive laws on their books, but most of these have been invalidated. Yet South Dakota's equal pay provision, for example, eliminates physical strength as a category on which men and women should be judged equally. This means men can be paid more for "heavy" work. Under the federal Equal Pay Act, men who perform infrequent physical exertion in a workplace cannot be paid more because this does not constitute substantial additional effort.

The Equal Employment Opportunity Commission enforces this act. To file a complaint, contact a local office of this agency. The EEOC will keep your name confidential. It is not necessary to go through state agencies governing fair employment practices first. You must bring the lawsuit within 2 years of the alleged act of discrimination (or 3 years if the violation was willful) and can collect back wages only for the 2 years prior to starting the lawsuit. So it is important not to waste time in filing. In a successful lawsuit you can win back wages plus the same amount as punishment for the company (double back wages) plus attorney's fees and court costs. The Equal Employment Opportunity Commission may also negotiate with an employer for appropriate raises in pay scales to correct the violation of the law.

## COMPARABLE WORTH

The newest development in the fight for equal pay has come in the form of a concept called *comparable worth* or *pay equity*. Despite the passage of the Equal Pay Act, all studies of women's wages show that the ratio of women's wages to those of men has remained static for years. Since 1960, women's wages have ranged from 57 percent to 65 percent of men's wages. A Rand Corporation study predicts that by the year 2000 women's wages will be only 74 percent of men's wages.[3] This continuing wage gap is not simply a result of unequal pay for equal work. It is a product of systematic discrimination against women workers exemplified by occupational segregation and the persistent underpayment of so-called women's work.

Comparable worth expands the idea of equal pay for equal work by theorizing that men and women whose jobs make equivalent demands on them and call for comparable skills, whether or not the job is the same, should be considered of comparable worth to the employer and paid accordingly. This concept was given impetus by a 1981 decision of the U.S. Supreme Court, *County of Washington v. Gunther*, which held that women employees could claim sex-based wage discrimination under Title VII of the 1964 Civil Rights Act, even though the jobs to be compared did not meet the equal work standard of the Equal Pay Act.[4]

Currently, there is a nationwide proliferation of job evaluation studies, principally at the state level, to ascertain comparability and identify patterns of discrimination. The newest systems use a complicated scoring system based on a mathematical formula that compares, for example, the amount of freedom an employee has to make decisions and the effect such decisions have on the organization as a whole. Other values such as knowledge and skills, amount of information or dexterity needed to perform the job, mental demands of decision making, accountability and the amount of supervision the job requires, and working conditions, such as whether the job is performed inside a building or outdoors, are considered. Other systems consider how much travel is required, whether the worker has control over spending money, or how varied the job is. Interviews with employees are required to develop these scales.

Comparable worth has been called "the civil rights issue of the 1980s." Opponents say enforcing comparable worth would disrupt the economy. Since the Supreme Court's 1981 decision in *Gunther*, several lawsuits have been filed to further establish the concept of sex-based wage discrimination within "dissimilar" job classifications. Key among these was *AFSCME v. State of Washington*, a suit filed on behalf of over 15,000 employees clustered in female-dominated jobs whose salaries averaged 20 to 30 percent less than men in similarly rated male-dominated jobs.[5]

*AFSCME* won at trial; the U.S. Court of Appeals for the Ninth Circuit reversed the trial judge. The Ninth Circuit held that since Washington's wage scale simply reflected the market, the state was not required to "reclassify jobs to remedy a situation it did not create." AFSCME and the state of Washington subsequently settled the lawsuit, providing for substantial pay increases for workers in female-dominated jobs. Other litigation is now going on around the country, and legislative initiatives at the state and local level designed to voluntarily remedy glaring inequities between men's and women's wages continue unabated.

At the federal level, the Federal Equitable Pay Act of 1985, under consideration by Congress, proposes reclassification of federal jobs to correct wage imbalances. The bill urges evaluation of federal jobs in order to develop a salary classification scheme based on the actual value of the work.

## EQUAL EMPLOYMENT OPPORTUNITY

Title VII of the Civil Rights Act of 1964 was a major legislative achievement to guarantee equal employment opportunity for women. It prohibits discrimination based on sex, race, color, religion, or national origin in hiring or firing; in wages or fringe benefits; in classifying, referring, assigning or promoting employees; in facilities; in training, retraining, or apprenticeships; or in any other terms, conditions, or privileges of employment. Homosexuality and transsexuality are not viewed as falling under the protection of Title VII.

The Equal Employment Opportunity Commission (EEOC) has responsibility for the enforcement of Title VII. If you feel that you have been discriminated against by your employer, you must file a complaint quickly—within 180 days of the action you are protesting. If your state has a fair employment practices law, as forty-two states do, your complaint may be sent to the state agency first.

If the state does not complete action on the complaint within 60 days, the EEOC may proceed to investigate the charge. When the EEOC has completed its investigation, it will give you a "right to sue" letter, which permits you to initiate a private suit in court if you wish to. You are entitled to ask the EEOC for a right to sue letter 180 days after you file your complaint, whether or not they have completed their investigation. You must have this letter before any action can be initiated in court, and once you receive the letter, you only have 90 days to file the court complaint that starts the lawsuit. A labor union is considered a person under Title VII and can file a charge on behalf of itself or one of its members.

Employers with fifteen employees or more are covered under Title VII. Charges may also be brought against a labor union, an employment agency, a joint labor-management committee, school boards, and state and local governments as long as they have fifteen employees or members. If you are a federal employee, the rules are somewhat different: within 30 days of the alleged discrimination, you must consult with an EEOC counselor in your agency or department, and the counselor will try to resolve the complaint informally. Once you receive a "right to sue" letter, you have only 30 days to file your complaint in court.

There is only one caveat under Title VII which permits job distinction by sex. This is when gender constitutes a "bona fide occupational qualification (BFOQ)" for a job. An example of this would be a job opening for a wetnurse. The sex of an employee is rarely a BFOQ, however, and protective labor laws as discussed earlier have been superseded. Women may no longer be excluded from applying for jobs as fire fighters or police officers, nor may a presumed customer preference for female airline flight attendants prohibit men from applying for these jobs.

Title VII also outlaws more subtle, seemingly sex-neutral, rules which have a discriminatory impact on women or other protected groups. For example, an employer may have height or weight standards for a particular job which, though officially sex-neutral, effectively preclude most women from qualifying for the job. Other practices, such as requiring that all employees be high school graduates, may discriminate against minorities. If an employer can show that there is a "business necessity" for these requirements, then the employer will not be in violation of Title VII.

Other federal laws that promote equal employment opportunities are executive orders, which are directives issued by the President to the executive branch of the government. These orders have the force and effect of law. Exec. Order No. 11246, amended by Exec. Order No. 11375, applies to any company or institution which has a contract for more than $10,000 with the federal government. These orders also apply to service and supply contractors who have fifty or more employees and a contract of $50,000 or more and to any financial institution which serves as a depository of government funds or as an agent for issuing and paying U.S. savings bonds and notes. Since 1978, construction contractors must also comply with these executive orders. In the construction industry, compliance includes such things as ensuring that work sites are free of harassment, assigning two or more women to each construction project when possible, providing written notification of employment opportunities to female recruitment sources and community organizations, notifying the government if union referral processes impede efforts to meet affirmative action obligations, and disseminating the equal employment opportunity policies in advertising and conspicuously throughout the company. These regulations are under the jurisdiction of the Secretary of Labor and are administered by the Office of Federal Contract Compliance Programs (OFCCP). Proposals have been offered over the past 5 years to streamline the system and revise procedures, but the basic structure is still in effect.

# SEXUAL HARASSMENT

There are many subtle forms of discrimination that can affect job performance, promotion, and advancement. One of the most prevalent types of pressure placed on women in the workplace is sexual harassment. Sexual harassment is an unlawful employment practice under Title VII of the Civil Rights Act of 1964. The EEOC "Guidelines on Discrimination Because of Sex" define this behavior as "unwelcome sexual advances, requests for sexual favors, and other verbal or physical conduct of a sexual nature when submission to such conduct is either explicitly or implicitly a term or condition of an individual's employment." Harassment occurs either when submission to or rejection of the sexual advances are the basis for employment decisions affecting that person or when the sexual overtures have the purpose or effect of unreasonably interfering with an individual's work performance by creating an intimidating, hostile, or offensive working environment. The guidelines don't actually require loss of specific job benefits to state a claim; it is enough if your ability to function effectively and productively at work is interfered with.

Generally, the courts have held that employers who violate Title VII are strictly responsible for their acts and for those of their supervisory employees. The lower courts have said that this is true in the case of sexual harassment as well. In other words, if you have been sexually harassed by your supervisor, your employer will be liable jointly for the discrimination, whether or not the employer knew the harassment was taking place. In *Meritor Savings Bank v. Vinson*, the Supreme Court will have its first opportunity to rule on whether or not employers can be held strictly liable for the sexual harassment of employees by their supervisors. When the harassment is committed by a co-worker other than your supervisor, an employer is typically required to have had prior knowledge of the occurrence in order to support a finding of liability against the employer. Such prior knowledge is also required when the harassment complained of was committed by a client or customer.

Many corporations are clamping down on sexual harassment because they fear litigation and are endeavoring to set up training programs for managers and employees to combat sexual harassment. Unfortunately, harassment is like rape, in that it is hard to prove, because so many incidents happen without other witnesses present. Yet, in various studies of harassment, the figures show that nearly half of all working women have been harassed at some point, with an overwhelming incidence in formerly all-male workplaces.

Perhaps the most important advice to anyone burdened by sexual harassment is that adequate documentation is important to substantiate claims. Although the courts have held that "a woman employee need not prove resistance to sexual overtures in order to establish a Title VII claim of sexual harassment," it is best to say no in very clear language. Otherwise a woman is open to the charge that she had invited sexual advances by provocative behavior.

If a verbal refusal does not work, inform management in writing of the problem and state that this behavior is a violation of Title VII. Keep a copy of all correspondence to and from management. Some advisers suggest that you keep a log of events and conversations as accurately as possible. Do not keep the log in your desk! Finally, talk to an affirmative action specialist in your company or file charges with the Equal Employment Opportunity Commission in your area. Friends and coworkers may be able to offer counsel or perspective on the issue, especially if other people in the workplace have been harassed. As with other Title VII litigation, strict time limits must be observed in the filing of a complaint.

In addition to Title VII remedies, women who have been harassed at work are increasingly looking to state remedies against the individual harasser and the employer. In many states, for example, women may bring tort actions for assault, intentional infliction of emotional distress, tortious interference with business relations, or wrongful discharge. Because this is a growing area of the law, be sure to consult with a lawyer to make sure that you pursue all available remedies if you feel that you have been harassed.

An interesting strategy to prevent further harassment is proposed by Dr. Mary Rowe, a labor economist at the Massachusetts Institute of Technology. She suggests that a direct letter to the harasser using very explicit references can be effective in stopping the behavior. It is necessary to keep a copy of the letter for your files. Here is a sample which can be adapted to suit the situation:

> Dear————:
> On (day, date, time), when I met you to discuss my marketing project, you asked me to come to your apartment that evening and said it would help the success of my project. Several times in the past few months when I talked to you in your office, you put your arm around me and rubbed my back. Once you tried to fondle my breast. Last week at an office party, you asked me to go to bed with you. I do not believe you can judge my job performance fairly under these circumstances. I want our relationship to be purely professional from now on.[6]

Rowe reports that the typical reaction from the harasser was no reaction. The harassment just stopped.

# COMPANY POLICY TOWARD PREGNANCY AND CHILDBIRTH

A company's policy toward pregnancy and childbirth can be critical to a woman. In 1978, Congress enacted the Pregnancy Discrimination Act, an amendment to Title VII, which states that employment discrimination based on pregnancy, childbirth, and related medical conditions such as abortion is illegal. Employers cannot refuse to employ a woman because of pregnancy or fire her, force her to go on leave at an arbitrary point during pregnancy, or deny her reinstatement rights. Nor can a woman lose accrued retirement benefits, accumulated seniority, or credit for previous service.

The thrust of the EEOC guidelines is that women affected by pregnancy and related conditions must be treated in the same manner as other applicants or employees—on the basis of their ability or inability to work. The law does not require an employer to provide a specific number of weeks for maternity leave, treat pregnant employees differently from others, or establish new medical, leave, or benefit programs where none currently exist. Yet if such plans are in effect, coverage for women must be provided on the same terms as for other temporary disabilities. On the other hand, a pregnant woman who is not disabled is not entitled to sick leave benefits. Pregnancy alone is not considered a sickness, and individual variations in the health and ability of a woman to work are an important factor in realistically dealing with pregnancy.

One of the difficulties with the Pregnancy Discrimination Act is that there is no *requirement* for either a paid or an unpaid maternity leave. If a woman takes a leave of absence, there is no built-in guarantee that she will have her job back when she wants to return to the company. One Columbia University professor has estimated that more than one-quarter of the women working at least 20 hours a week are employed by companies whose policies do not guarantee their return to the same or a comparable job after time off for childbirth. Even in larger companies which had informal policies of maternity leaves, the trend since 1978 has been to cut back the leave and adopt a "medical disability" approach. This limits the leave to what is strictly necessary from a medical point of view.

On the other hand, while Title VII does not require employers to provide any maternity leave, if they choose to do so voluntarily, the leave must be available on a sex-neutral basis. In other words, if a policy allows women to take time off to care for their newborns—in addition to a *disability* leave following delivery—the same policy must be made available to men as well.

New federal legislation, the Parental and Medical Leave Act, has recently been introduced in Congress. This legislation, if passed, would require all public and private employers with five or more employees to provide up to 4 months' unpaid *parental* leave, with job security on the worker's return, and up to 6 months' unpaid leave for medical disabilities, including pregnancy, also with job security on the worker's return.

A few states—Montana, California, and Massachusetts, for example—have enacted state laws which require employers to provide minimum maternity leave to pregnant workers. Because these laws single out pregnancy as a basis for providing disability benefits, the Montana and California laws are being challenged as being in conflict with the federal Pregnancy Discrimination Act. The Supreme Court is expected to resolve this issue soon.

As for abortions, employers with religious or moral objections are not required to help finance them under existing health plans unless the abortion is necessary to preserve the life of the mother. Medical complications which result from abortion do have to be covered by any existing health or disability plan.

Employers may not fire or refuse to hire a woman simply because she has exercised her right to have an abortion. Still, there is widespread prejudice in the country these days against abortion. Clinics are under attack and great political pressure is being placed on legislators to support so-called right to life positions. While this has not altered the legal guarantees of the Pregnancy Discrimination Act, attitudes and opinions are harder to control. Women, as always, must be vigilant in monitoring their rights in this area.

# AGE DISCRIMINATION

The American media perpetuate images of youth as the desired physical ideal to which we should all aspire. Very little is presented to us of the positive consequences of age: maturity and experience. Since "sex sells," older women in particular have been the targets of age discrimination in our society.

One law protecting older people's rights is the Age Discrimination in Employment Act of 1967. This act prohibits discrimination in employment on the basis of age for persons aged 40 to 70. There is no upper limit with respect to employment in the federal government. State and local governments have been covered by the act since 1974.

The ADEA, as the age discrimination law is called, applies not only to public employers but to private employers of twenty or more employees and employment agencies which serve covered employers. Labor unions which have twenty-five or more members are also covered. The act prohibits help wanted advertisements that indicate preference, limitation, specification, or discrimination based on age. For example, terms such as "girl Friday" or "recent grad" may not be used because they indicate exclusion because of age. Yet, as in Title VII, there is a distinction made for situations where age is a bona fide occupational qualification (BFOQ) in a given job. This could include modeling "junior" fashions, for example, or the requirement of a physical examination where very heavy work is essential.

Since January 1979, the law has prohibited the involuntary retirement of workers under the age of 70. Of course, a person may wish to retire earlier. However, certain senior executives and high-level policy-making employees may have to retire earlier if a company mandates this. These employees are not covered by ADEA. The act also does not forbid discharge from a job with good cause.

To file a complaint of age discrimination, a person must first go to a state agency dealing with fair employment practices. This state or local agency must have the authority to seek relief from the discriminatory practice or to institute court proceedings. While some courts have ruled that recourse to proceedings under state law, if any exist, is mandatory, the state remedies need not be exhausted for an action to be filed with the EEOC on the federal level. Once an action is filed by the EEOC to enforce the act, it terminates the right of the individual to sue on her own behalf. The EEOC first attempts to resolve the matter through conciliation and voluntary compliance. If this fails, the EEOC may bring suit.

# HANDICAPPED WORKERS

Handicapped workers are protected from discrimination by federal law under Sections 503 and 504 of the Rehabilitation Act of 1973, as amended in 1978. Section 503 says that federal contractors with contracts in excess of $2500 may not discriminate against persons with mental and physical handicaps. This provision is enforced by the Office of Federal Contract Compliance Programs. Section 504 forbids discrimination against handicapped individuals in programs or activities receiving federal funds.

If you believe that you are qualified to do a particular job and feel you have been discriminated against because of a handicap, contact the agency which funds the program or the state human rights agency or the Equal Employment Opportunity Commission for guidance.

Apart from formal procedures against discrimination, disabled women are beginning to form organizations to provide role models for each other as they enter the marketplace. A grant-funded program called the Networking Project for Disabled Women and Girls sponsored by the YWCA in New York City, for example, brought two generations of disabled women together to talk about the roads to professional success which many disabled women have taken.

Informal groups which build contacts among women can be a source of personal support and professional exchange. Conferences, alumni associations, and other work-related organizations can expand the horizons of all working women.

In addition to stipulations under federal law, many state laws include categories of persons who may receive preferential treatment in hiring which are specific to local needs. In Arizona, preferential treatment may be given to Indians living on or near a reservation. California allows employers to regulate employment of spouses who work in the same department or facility. Many states have veteran's preference clauses. In Hawaii, employment preference is also extended to the widows of soldiers killed in war, provided they have not remarried. In Illinois, the parent of a veteran may receive preferential consideration. The state agencies administering fair employment practices laws can give you details about preferential treatment provisions.

The laws which cover veteran's preference, in many cases, include special consideration for disabled war veterans. Arizona includes handicapped persons in general in that category. Other fair employment laws on the state level include handicapped persons in their protected categories, while some states include a clause which says "physical or mental handicap which does not preclude performance of employment."

# OCCUPATIONAL HEALTH AND SAFETY

A new concern to women in the workplace has emerged over the past 15 years as the country as a whole has become more conscious of occupational health and safety.

Workers who are injured on the job or who contract a disease directly connected with their occupation can seek relief under state workers' compensation laws. In most states, employers are required to cover employees with this protection and heavy penalties are assessed for failure to comply. Each state has its own law, so that regulations and procedures for filing and settling claims vary greatly. The state department of labor can be of help in solving these problems.

On a larger scale, however, the Occupational Safety and Health Act of 1970 requires employers to ensure safe and healthful working conditions and to maintain a workplace free from recognized dangers that would cause death or physical harm. To monitor these, the Occupational Safety and Health Administration (OSHA) of the U.S. Department of Labor established standards which require that safe conditions, practices, or methods are implemented to protect workers on the job. It is the employer's responsibility to become familiar with the standards, to put them into effect, and to assure that employees have available to them the personal facilities and protective equipment necessary for safety and health.

Employees have a right to request an inspection if they believe that hazardous conditions exist in their workplace or an immediate inspection if they believe they are in imminent danger. OSHA, the enforcement agency, must notify the employee in writing if it decides an inspection is unnecessary. Employees also have a right to examine employer information about job-related accidents, to participate in establishing standards, to have an authorized employee representative accompany an OSHA inspector on a tour, and to be advised by their employer of any hazards prohibited by law. Employees are protected from retaliation by an employer for initiating an OSHA investigation.

Several cities and states have enacted laws requiring employers to inform employees about toxic substances to which they are exposed at the work site. The National Labor Relations Board has also ruled that unions can request the names of chemicals and other substances the workers they represent are exposed to and must be given this information.

The potential health hazards of jobs where large numbers of women are employed include solvents, correction fluids, rubber cement, and ozone from copying machines for clerical workers; ionizing and nonionizing radiation from video display terminals; dust, skin irritants, and chemicals for textile and apparel workers; chemicals in hair, nail, and skin preparations for beauticians; heat, heavy lifting, and chemicals for laundry workers and dry cleaners; radiation and anesthetic gases for health and hospital workers; and flammable, explosive, toxic, or carcinogenic substances in all types of work environments.

Since 1974, the National Institute for Occupational Safety and Health, which conducts research on safety and health problems and develops criteria for the use of hazardous materials, has investigated reproductive hazards of work for women. As a result, some employers are now adopting policies which will exclude pregnant women and women of childbearing age from jobs involving exposure to potentially toxic substances because of possible fetal damage. Some women feel that these exclusionary policies are reminiscent of the old "protective labor laws," which operated more to deny women employment opportunities than to protect them from serious hazards. More importantly, if the goal of these policies is to provide employment free of hazards, women are rightfully asking whether *men* at risk are also receiving this treatment. Since men also have a role in reproduction, a substance with which a man comes in contact could also increase the risk of miscarriage and birth defects or cause sterility or impotency. Such one-sided attempts to protect against illegal, reproductive hazards may well be discriminatory under Title VII. If you feel you are being unfairly excluded from an employment opportunity based on this type of regulation, file a charge of discrimination with the EEOC. The current position of OSHA is to consider charges of reproductive hazards on a case-by-case basis rather than as a generic issue.

OSHA compliance officers favor speedy abatement of hazards rather than involvement in protracted legal disputes. The Occupational Safety and Health Review Commission is an independent body which rules on employer and employee appeals of OSHA citations, penalties, time periods for compliance, and abatement orders. If an employee is discharged or discriminated against for exercising her rights under the OSHA laws, a discrimination complaint can be filed within 30 days of the incident.

In the past 5 years, the states have also developed elaborate codes for safety education programs, protective equipment in the workplace, and public information about toxic substances on the job. Alaska and California have especially comprehensive statutes. Connecticut requires that employers post signs to inform employees of their health and safety rights. New employees must be told within the first month on the job "in informal and comprehensible language" about any dangers. If the information is not supplied within 5 working days of a request, employees can refuse to work with a substance without penalty until the information is provided. Illinois and other states require that employers keep extensive records of employee exposure to toxins. In the Illinois statute, "such sheets must be preserved for at least 10 years after the toxic substance is no longer present in the workplace." Because of the long-range effects of some carcinogens, for example, this data retention is important. Other states mandate that medical examinations shall be conducted on all employees free of charge, and an employee's physician can be informed of the results.

While some states are in the forefront of this type of legislation, others have no legislative provisions outside of federal regulations. Employees, then, must actively guard their health and be on the alert for violations.

# LABOR-MANAGEMENT LAWS

Once a person is hired for a job, issues will arise which affect the person's performance and opportunities. The National Labor Relations Act of 1935, as amended over the years, guarantees employees the right to organize, to bargain collectively, and to engage in strikes, picketing, and other organized activities for their mutual aid and protection. It also guarantees the right of any employee to refrain from these activities. The act makes it an unfair labor practice for employers to interfere with employees in the exercise of these rights, to discriminate against them in hiring, firing, or any term or condition of employment because they have engaged in activities protected by the act.

An employer cannot refuse to bargain with a union that has been recognized as the employees' bargaining agent. Although the act does not specifically prohibit discrimination on the basis of race, sex, national origin, or religion, it does impose on unions the duty to represent fairly all employees in the unit. Discrimination in this duty of fair representation is an unfair labor practice.

A number of states have enacted right-to-work laws that make it illegal to mandate union membership as a condition of employment, even though the employer has agreed with the union to do so. The states that do *not* have right-to-work laws are Alaska, Colorado, California, Connecticut, Delaware, Maine, Maryland, Massachusetts, Michigan, Minnesota, Missouri, Montana (which has a limited law preventing union interference with sole proprietors), New Hampshire, New Jersey, New Mexico, New York, Ohio, Oklahoma, Oregon, Pennsylvania, Rhode Island, Vermont, Washington, West Virginia, and Wisconsin. Once a person joins a union, that person is bound by the rights and duties outlined in its constitution. Title VII does apply to labor unions and may be used as a remedy for discrimination by them.

## STATE LAWS

In addition to the federal laws mentioned in this chapter, each state, the District of Columbia, and Puerto Rico have specific laws covering some aspects of women's employment. Some of the laws provide for fair employment practices which are similar to Title VII. Other states prohibit additional types of employment discrimination, such as discrimination because of sexual preference, arrest record, political affiliation, marital status, color blindness, unfavorable military discharge, and sickle cell trait. Increasingly, states are passing their own equal pay laws, as well as sponsoring job evaluation studies to promote pay equity, at least among public employees. Legislation regulating the employment of aliens has also been enacted by some states. The use of lie detectors and voice stress analyzers to obtain employment information is not allowed in some states. There are also differing approaches by the states to pregnancy benefits and age discrimination. State and local governments can place citizenship or residency requirements on those employees performing strictly governmental functions. The U.S. Supreme Court has ruled that a state can pursue judicial relief for their citizens who are discriminated against in employment opportunities in another state. Check Part 2 of this book and consult with an attorney to find out the state and local laws regulating employment in your area.

## JOB TRAINING AND PLACEMENT

Finding the right job is often a difficult process. Federal laws provide for services to assist job seekers. The U.S. Employment Service operates in partnership with state employment agencies to provide free counseling, testing, and job placement in major cities across the country. Many of these offices have job banks which maintain computerized lists of job vacancies in a particular geographic area. Through screening and referral services, the job service, which should be listed in the telephone directory under state government listings, can channel applicants into various training programs.

The National Apprenticeship Act sponsors federal-state partnerships to teach skilled trades and crafts through a combination of on-the-job training and classroom instruction. Apprentices are paid while they learn. A number of states provide information about these programs through apprenticeship information centers, which are generally operated by the state employment service.

For many years, the federal government funded employment and training programs for unemployed and disadvantaged workers. From 1974 to 1982, the Comprehensive Employment and Training Act (CETA) developed programs geared to local needs for these workers. In 1982 this program expired and was replaced by the Job Training Partnership Act (JTPA). These job training programs are planned and implemented under the joint control of local elected officials and private industry councils designated by the governor of each state. The state department of labor or job service should be able to provide information about these projects.

According to statistics gathered by the CETA programs, the number of women who could be classified as displaced homemakers was estimated at 4 million, or 7 out of every 100 women aged 22 to 64. These displaced homemakers were mostly divorced, separated, or widowed women who were currently not in the work force and either had never worked or had last worked 5 years before the survey. More than 80 percent were over 40 years old; 50 percent were 55 years and older. After many years of working in the home, these women now need to earn a living in the paid labor force. According to the Bureau of Labor Statistics, these women have completed fewer years of formal schooling than other women. They are more likely to be poor.

By the early 1980s, over twenty-eight states had passed some form of displaced homemaker legislation, some of it related to laws against domestic violence. There are also hundreds of nongovernmental programs operated by women's groups, educational institutions, and employment agencies to serve women who need guidance before entering the job market. Educational and vocational programs are under federal mandate to be nondiscriminatory under Title IX legislation, as we discussed in Chapter 3. Women can pursue educational options to improve their employment status knowing that they are covered under the law.

# FIRING AND UNEMPLOYMENT INSURANCE

For many reasons, employers or employees may decide to terminate an employment situation. Historically, employers have had the right to fire employees at will unless there was a written contract which protected against this. Courts in approximately forty states now recognize some exemptions to the common-law doctrine that nonunion employees can be fired arbitrarily.[7] In these states, employees who believe they have been fired unlawfully may be able to sue for "wrongful discharge." At least half the states protect workers from being fired for refusing to engage in illegal activity or refusing to testify in court. Some states and municipalities have laws which prohibit being discharged for serving on a jury, refusing to take lie detector tests, or filing any claims of discrimination. Under the federal laws we have discussed, the broad right to fire employees is of course modified where the firing is the result of illegal discrimination.

Because there have been more successful suits against companies' termination policies, many firms are setting up mechanisms within the company to resolve employee complaints. A labor law attorney from San Francisco urges employers to develop an appraisal system for employees which is candid and allows for early identification of problems and reasonable time to correct unsatisfactory performance. The majority of employees are fired for cause, such as excessive absenteeism, fighting in the workplace, incompetence, possession or use of intoxicating substances, insubordination, and negligence. Some employees will leave a job voluntarily.

When a woman leaves a job voluntarily, she is not entitled to receive unemployment insurance in most states. Unemployment compensation is supported by federal and state taxes paid exclusively by employers. It entitles employees who lose their jobs to collect a certain amount of money weekly for a limited period of time. Benefits are paid as a matter of right, not of need. Each state administers its own program and determines who is eligible, how much money a person will receive and how long benefits will be paid. To be eligible, a person must be unemployed, able to work, and available for and seeking work.

In 1976, amendments to the unemployment compensation law prohibited states from refusing benefits to women solely on the basis of pregnancy or recency of pregnancy. Thus, the presumption that a pregnant woman was incapable of work was overturned. Pregnant women who receive unemployment insurance do have to meet the general requirement of seeking work and being available for and able to work. The 1976 amendments also added coverage for certain farm workers, for most state and local government employees, and to private household workers who had been paid $1000 or more in a quarter of any calendar year. This entitled many more women to collect unemployment benefits than had previously received them.

Quitting "without good cause" and being fired for misconduct are the two reasons for denying unemployment compensation. But recently, women who have left jobs because of sexual harassment have won challenges and received unemployment. Also, while most states have disqualified workers for leaving a job for family reasons such as getting married, moving with a spouse, or child care problems, some states will pay benefits to persons who have to quit their jobs for "compelling" personal reasons. Decisions in these cases are made according to individual circumstances.

Another difficulty that women face is that, in most states, being available for work means for full-time work. A few states will consider persons who can only work part-time as available and eligible for unemployment insurance if they have been working part-time in an occupation where there is a substantial demand for workers.

# SOCIAL SECURITY AND PENSION LAWS

Almost all workers, according to the U.S. Department of Labor, are now covered by social security or by one of the over 500,000 separate pension plans provided by state and local governments and by private corporations. Some workers are covered by more than one of these plans.

To receive social security benefits, you must apply for them once you have retired. The amount you receive is based on your average earnings over a period of years. You can receive full retirement benefits at age 65 and reduced benefits as early as age 62. If you retire between age 62 and 65, there is a permanent reduction up to a maximum of 20 percent in the amount of your benefits, which is dependent on the number of retirement checks you would receive before you reach age 65. If you work past 65, you get a credit, which is added to the amount of your monthly benefit. You are also entitled to medicare, which is health insurance available to people eligible for social security.

When the original social security program was passed in 1935, payment formulas were based on patterns of lifelong marriages in which women were homemakers. Wives and widows were seen as dependents who needed protection. In recent years, women's groups and several members of Congress have argued that social security provisions are no longer equitable or adequate to meet the needs of the modern woman.

There are some problems built into the system. Social security rules now provide that a wage earner is entitled to a full benefit based on his or her earnings record. A spouse also gets a benefit equal to 50 percent of this sum. When the wage earner dies, a surviving spouse can collect the full benefit.

Today, more than half of all married women hold jobs. Social security taxes are also deducted from their pay. But too often women cannot collect on the benefits they themselves have earned. The reason is that women are usually paid less than men and often they take time out for family needs during their working lives. Typically, their benefits would be less than those to which they are entitled as the spouse of a worker. A woman is not allowed to collect both her own benefits and those she can receive as a spouse. Millions of women, therefore, get no return on the money they have contributed to social security from their paychecks.

An even greater irony is that if a woman does collect on the basis of her own earnings record, the spouse's benefit that her husband is entitled to (the social security rules are gender-neutral) cannot be paid either if the husband has been a wage earner on his own. The way the formula works out, a working husband and a working wife may collect less in social security than a working man with the same total income whose spouse was not employed.

A new plan has been proposed which would consider the marriage an equal partnership, whether or not both spouses are employed. Every year the earnings of both the husband and wife would be added together and divided equally to form a record of entitlement to social security. Each would keep whatever social security they had earned before marriage. If one partner dies, the other partner inherits the credits of the deceased spouse.

A U.S. government study of this proposal released in 1984 concluded that such a formula would reduce many people's benefits, would be expensive to put into effect, and would not fit into the current system unless there was a long transition period. Critics of the government study say it did not present a balanced assessment.

There have been some changes enacted in social security, however. Laws which were enacted in 1983 to amend the act change ages of retirement and percentages in the formulas for the 1990s and into the twenty-first century. These 1983 amendments also addressed issues affecting elderly men. They emerged from a case in which a widower had been denied social security survivor benefits because he failed to prove that he had received at least half his support from his wife. Surviving wives had no such dependency test. The Supreme Court found that this differing treatment of men and women was illegal discrimination in violation of the Constitution.

The 1983 amendments provide social security benefits to aged divorced husbands and to aged or disabled surviving divorced husbands and fathers who care for the children of their retired, disabled or deceased wives or former wives. The amendments also allow the continuation of benefits for surviving divorced spouses upon remarriage—if that marriage takes place after the age of first disability for benefits. The continuation of benefits for disabled widows and widowers and disabled surviving spouses is permitted upon remarriage if that marriage takes place after age 50 and after the onset of the disability.

The entire social security system is now under examination for possible reforms. Women who have questions about current programs and policies should contact their local social security office.

In addition to social security, many workers are covered by private pension plans from which they derive an income. Because of the concentration of women in low-wage occupations and in nonunionized industries, women are less likely than men to be covered by private pension plans. Sometimes women fail to meet the age and service requirements of the plan.

The Employee Retirement Income Security Act of 1974 (ERISA) was passed to protect workers and their beneficiaries who depend on benefits from private pension plans. The law requires the disclosure of pension plan provisions and financial information; establishes standards of conduct for trustees and administrators of these plans; and sets up funding, participation, vesting, and insurance requirements for the plans. The law prohibits discharging a worker in order to avoid paying a pension benefit. ERISA does not require employers to establish pension plans, nor does it specify benefit levels.

ERISA's vesting rules have been criticized because younger women who usually only work a short time before leaving for child-rearing responsibilities are more likely to forfeit their benefits. These forfeitures subsidize benefits for long-range employees, who are more likely to be men. Spouses of participants in private pension plans who have been homemakers often found their protection limited or nonexistent if their spouse rejects the survivor annuity provision. With the passage of the Retirement Equity Act by Congress in 1984, discussed more fully in Chapter 2 in the section on "Elderly Women," this has been changed, and the spouse must now consent. The Retirement Equity Act also lowered the age at which workers may be enrolled in pension plans—from 25 to 21, an amendment that more closely reflects the employment experience of women. Finally, and of particular importance, the act now requires employers to provide a service credit for women on maternity leave. No longer will women be completely denied retirement service credit for breaks in their employment history associated with childbearing.

In some states, pensions are considered to be property in a divorce settlement. A more detailed discussion of pension issues related to divorce may also be found in the section on "Elderly Women" in Chapter 2.

# PATTERNS OF EMPLOYMENT OF WOMEN IN THE FUTURE

In 1983, the Women's Research and Education Institute of the Congressional Caucus for Women's Issues published a pamphlet on women and work in the 1980s. The author of the study, Ray Marshall, was formerly Secretary of Labor under President Carter.

As the study showed, there are many reasons why women have entered the job market in such numbers: the mechanization of household work has given women more time; birthrates are declining; higher education for women is on the increase; and medical technologies have led to greater life expectancy, which means there are more older women in the marketplace. Not only do women work out of economic necessity, but a paid job has also become an important symbol of self-worth. Women more than ever are taking pride in their role in the labor force.

Of course, the questions affecting women's employment in the future are those that trouble the American economy as a whole:

- On the international scale, what will be the impact of multinational corporations, migration patterns, international competition, and changing rules of international trade?
- Will declining rates of growth in the American economy reduce the pressure for equal employment opportunity and affirmative action?
- Are women moving into positions of power in unions and in management?
- Will the move from a goods-producing to a service-oriented society be a boon for women workers?
- Can women obtain the mathematical and science education and the vocational training needed to keep them competitive in the growing fields of high technology?

The answers to these questions must be provided by many factors which are often out of any individual woman's control.

A 1984 report in *The New York Times* says "job discrimination is so deep and pervasive that it will be years before women begin to approach parity with male workers."[8] Catalyst, a New York research group, reports that only 8 of every 1000 women employed hold high-level executive, administrative, or managerial jobs. Women occupy only 3 percent of the 16,000 seats on the boards of directors of the 1000 largest corporations listed by *Fortune* magazine.

There is no way to predict the ebb and flow of our volatile economy. Both men and women can anticipate rapid changes in patterns of work over the decade. By respecting each other's quest for job security and satisfaction, we will more deeply understand what Sigmund Freud meant when he said there are two great needs in each person's life—the need to love and the need to work.

# 5

# WOMEN IN THE COMMUNITY

*An institution is the lengthened shadow of one man.*

Ralph Waldo Emerson
*Self-Reliance*

Women participate in the lives of their communities in many different roles—from consumer to holder of executive office. Yet underlying our daily activities are local, state, and federal laws which regulate our public lives. The routine transactions of entering into a contract, obtaining credit, purchasing insurance, joining the military or dealing with the criminal justice system have made women aware of the institutional shadows where male values have predominated. Many laws and regulations of the army, banks, insurance companies, and courts have evolved from the period when women were not expected to fully participate in the life of their communities. Over the past 15 years women have gained substantial new rights. Women are no longer content to be eclipsed by institutional prejudices. The challenges to these institutions have offered women new opportunities under the law.

## WOMEN AND THE CRIMINAL JUSTICE SYSTEM

As women have organized to share information and resources, the extent of crimes of violence against women has become known. Two crimes are shockingly frequent: rape and battering. According to FBI statistics, a man batters a woman in her home every 18 seconds. One of three women will be forced to have sex without her consent in her lifetime.

Before women mobilized to deal with these problems in their communities, the prevalent attitude of the police and the justice system was to blame the victim. Women were told that their dress was too provocative, that they should not go out at night or be alone and unprotected in certain places. If a woman subjected herself to these risks and "something happened," she deserved the consequences. She should have known better.

When a man beat his wife, it was his marital privilege. She was his property. When he forced her to have sex, she was, after all, obligated to perform her part of the marital bargain.

78

The past 15 years have produced substantial legislative reform which has shifted the focus of the rape and battering laws from the conduct of the victim to that of the offender. Instead of asking, "Did she resist? Did she consent?" the law now asks, "Did he use force, coercion, or threats in order to accomplish the act or badger the woman into submission?" It is the defendant, not the victim who is accused of the crime. The new laws have also revised punishment provisions to suit the severity of the crime.

Legislative reforms do not always mean, however, that women will report these crimes or wish to undergo whatever personal or family pressures are created by bringing a case to court. As the authors of the book *Our Bodies, Ourselves* put it: "We have no idea whether or not better laws deter men from assaulting women."[1] Nevertheless, while sexist attitudes still prevail in many cases, if a woman does decide to go to court, she will find that there is more public and judicial support than ever for prosecuting violence against women. There is also more hope of finding doctors, lawyers, police, and counselors who can deal sensitively with the problem. Legislative reform has enabled women to report violence, press charges, and appear as witnesses. This will increase the likelihood of convictions and ultimately free more women from fear.

# RAPE

*Rape* is the use of threats or violence to force a person to engage in sexual activity against her will. It has been estimated that ten times as many rapes occur as are reported. Rape is more likely to be committed by a person we know (acquaintance or marital rape) than by a stranger.

Today in most states rape laws are sex-neutral, allowing both men and women to prosecute or be charged with rape. Several states still limit the meaning of rape to sexual intercourse with a woman. No state requires proof that the rapist completed the sex act. Ejaculation is not required, only penetration, however slight. Since slight penetration is impossible to verify medically, proof has become a question of the woman's credibility.

For a rape victim to establish credibility, she has to overcome several stereotypical judgments about sexuality: that women are subconsciously excited by the idea of violent sex and subconsciously invite it; that women charge rape as revenge against lovers who reject them; that women who are not physically attractive are eager for any sexual experience and that men who rape them are really accommodating them; that only "nice girls" can be raped and that women who are sexually active are "asking for it"; and that women bring rape upon themselves by the clothes they wear, the hour they are out, the neighborhood they choose to walk in. These demeaning and utterly false assumptions force a woman to be on the defensive. Her integrity is at stake. This is why so many women feel vulnerable and confused about reporting rape. She is forced to prove her lack of complicity at a time when she is feeling overwhelmed by emotional trauma and violation.

In the past, in addition to proving that rape was committed by force or coercion, the victim was forced to prove that she resisted the attack "to the utmost" and that she did not consent to the intercourse. Since the testimony of the rape victim has been regarded as inherently untrustworthy, the prosecution was often required to offer corroboration of the victim's story. And the defense attorney was often permitted to probe deeply into the victim's past sexual conduct, no matter how long ago this conduct took place.

The "resistance to the utmost" standard placed women in a no-win situation. If a woman did not resist to her full capabilities, she risked not being able to prove the rape. If she did resist, she risked receiving serious bodily injury or death in addition to the act of sexual defilement itself. Many legislatures have come to recognize that a futile attempt at physical resistance may place the victim's life in jeopardy and states have abandoned the "utmost" standard. However, some reference to resistance still occurs in many state statutes such as those of Idaho, Kentucky, Mississippi, Alabama, Wyoming, and the District of Columbia. In other jurisdictions, such as Alaska, Ohio, Iowa, New Jersey, and Vermont, the outmoded concept of resistance has been abandoned altogether. This, in effect, permits the victims of rape the same option of protecting their lives as other felony victims.

These more progressive states have eliminated the requirement that a victim prove lack of consent. The very definition of rape implies that the victim was compelled to submit by physical force or threats which she believed would be carried out. Consent is a moot issue at this point. Most states have also removed the need for any corroboration besides the testimony of the victim herself. Yet some states still qualify this by saying that this testimony "must be convincing to the point that a rational fact finder could find the defendant guilty beyond a reasonable doubt" (Kentucky) or that the victim's testimony is sufficient "unless the testimony is inherently improbable or incredible" (Maine).

Current misconceptions about rape include the belief that sexual intercourse, even if unwanted, is not really rape unless the perpetrator is a total stranger. In some states, if the victim was a "voluntary social companion" of the accused, it reduced the charge to an offense of a lesser degree. Formerly, at the conclusion of a rape trial, the judge was required to caution the jury that the accusation of rape was "easy to make but difficult to prove." Special jury instructions for rape increasingly have met with disfavor. There is no need to scrutinize rape testimony any more closely than any other crime.

On the other hand, extensive media publicity in certain rape trials such as the gang rape of a 21-year-old woman in New Bedford, Massachusetts, in 1983 raise the specter of finding impartial juries and tests the privacy laws in certain states. Connecticut has a 1981 law on its books which says that police records of sexual assaults may identify the victim by a pseudonym to protect the privacy of sexual assault victims. Although the defendant must be told the real name, the victim's address or other identifying data need not be revealed publicly in court.

Prosecutors say that fewer rapes will be reported if victims think their names will be widely publicized. Women's groups feel that a major part of the trauma of a sexual attack is the fear of being socially stigmatized. Most states have statutes protecting identities in sensitive legal areas such as juvenile or family court situations. But the records of sexual assaults, including the original complaint as it appears on a police blotter, are publicly available. Most organizations follow a policy of not using the name of the victim.

**STATUTORY RAPE:** Rape statutes also legislate against sexual intercourse with victims whom the law views as incapable of giving valid consent. Persons who are underage, mentally defective or incapacitated, unconscious, under the influence of alcohol or drugs, or physically helpless are not assumed to be able to give reasoned consent to sexual intercourse. Their "willingness" does not constitute a defense against the charge that intercourse with such persons is a form of rape.

Statutory rape is the rape of a person below a certain age. In most states, the statutory age is somewhere between 12 and 16 years old. Typically, only men can be charged with statutory rape. In a challenge to California's statutory rape law by a young man who said it discriminated on the basis of sex, the U.S. Supreme Court upheld the law's male-only application because of the greater risks to young women, i.e., pregnancy, that might flow from unwanted intercourse.

Because of the high incidence of teenage sex, legislatures have begun to decriminalize sexual relations between similarly aged minors. But where there is a possibility of the use of overbearing psychological or physical pressure or where the victim cannot clearly be regarded as a peer of the initiator of the sex, statutory rape can be charged. Some legislatures, for example, Colorado, Connecticut, Florida, Iowa, New Mexico, New Jersey, North Carolina, South Carolina, and Wyoming, have become increasingly concerned about the possible coercion of a minor by a family member, guardian, custodian, or teacher of the victim and have enacted statutes specific to those situations.

Several states have permissible defenses available to defendants accused of statutory rape. In Indiana and Kentucky, for example, it is a defense if the accused believed that the victim was older than the statutory age of consent. This defense is also available in other states—Minnesota, Missouri, Montana, North Dakota, Ohio, Oregon, and West Virginia—but the defense is limited to cases involving older victims. New Jersey, on the other hand, does not allow this defense at all.

**MARITAL RAPE:** "The husband cannot be guilty of rape committed by himself upon his lawful wife," Sir Matthew Hale, a seventeenth-century English jurist wrote, "for by their mutual matrimonial consent and contract the wife hath given up herself in this kind unto her husband which she cannot retract."[2]

Many people do not consider a husband's forced sexual intercourse with his wife as rape. Until recently, in most states there was no such crime. In at least nine states—Alabama, Arkansas, Kansas, Montana, South Dakota, Texas, Vermont, Washington, and West Virginia—husbands are immune from marital-rape prosecutions. In twenty-six others, they can be convicted only in very narrow circumstances, generally when the partners are living apart under court order or legally separated. In twelve states, the exemption from prosecution for marital rape has been expanded to cover unmarried couples. A man who rapes the woman he is living with but to whom he is not legally married cannot be charged with rape in these jurisdictions.

In 1984, the state of New York struck down sections of the penal code that generally exempt men from prosecution for acts with their wives that would constitute rape or sodomy if done by a man to a woman other than his wife. The state concluded that by making a distinction between marital and nonmarital rape, the law violated constitutional guarantees of equal protection. The New York law also abandoned a provision under which only men could be convicted of forcible rape. While women rarely commit rape, there was no justification, in the court's opinion, to exempt them from criminal sanctions.

New York joins seventeen other states, including New Jersey, Connecticut, Florida, Wisconsin, and California, that have abolished the marital exemption in some or all cases. The ruling was hailed by women's groups as an important step in the effort to end violence against women.

**IF YOU HAVE BEEN RAPED:** A rape victim should be examined by a doctor as soon as possible, both for her own protection and because the findings may be needed as evidence if there is a trial. As much as you may wish to, do not shower but go directly to a hospital emergency room or police station.

To help overcome the emotional trauma of rape, rape crisis centers have been established throughout the country to advise and comfort rape victims and to offer help through the legal process and trial. A rape crisis center or the district attorney's office is the best source of immediate legal advice about steps you should take after a rape.

Although most states no longer have required time periods for reporting a rape, a few still require that rapes be reported within 3 to 6 months. While it is natural to be reluctant, anxious, and apprehensive, it is important for you to tell someone you trust who can help you cope with the medical and legal steps ahead.

Rape is a psychic as well as a physical assault. Several state supreme courts have recently considered whether expert testimony from mental health professionals is admissible evidence to substantiate the victim's claim of being raped. There is often a pattern of post-rape reaction, with symptoms that include fear of offender retaliation, fear of being raped again, fear of being home alone, fear of men in general, fear of being out alone, sleep disturbance, change in eating habits and sense of shame. This rape trauma syndrome, as it has been called, is not listed as a distinct psychiatric diagnosis. It is generally subsumed under the broader category of post-traumatic stress disorder.

Legal rules of evidence define an expert as "any person qualified by knowledge, skill, experience, training or education." In cases concerning child victims, prosecutors often introduce expert testimony concerning rape trauma syndrome to substantiate the child's credibility. When the rape victim is an adult, prosecutors have sought to show that the victim suffers from rape trauma syndrome to counter the defense that the woman consented or was a willing participant in the act.

The Supreme Court of Kansas has determined that the presence of rape trauma syndrome is detectable and reliable as evidence. However, the Minnesota Supreme Court argued that the scientific evaluation of rape trauma syndrome "has not reached the level of reliability that surpasses the quality of common sense evaluation present in jury deliberations." Nevertheless, a woman who is suffering from these symptoms should know that they are part of an adjustment period, a reorientation to the world after severe distress, and the occurrence of such emotions can be admitted as evidence in some courts. Of course, the pain these emotions generate is real and crippling. Many women join support groups to meet with other women and better understand the experience. The more comfort and support a woman can find after a rape, the more quickly a healing process can begin.

Not only can a rape victim bring criminal charges against her attacker, but she should consider suing the rapist for damages in a civil action as well. Twenty-nine states have held that a cause of action to recover damages can exist in a rape case. Many jurisdictions have also permitted suits against others, such as landlords and owners of hotels and supermarkets, who may have contributed to the occurrence. Idaho and Utah, for example, will allow a person to sue and recover damages. Ohio, Iowa, and Minnesota allow the victim to be reimbursed by the state for expenses incurred for medical examinations related to the rape prosecution. Check with your attorney about your state's policies.

Penalties for rape vary widely from state to state. Twenty-four states and the District of Columbia provide for life imprisonment as the maximum penalty for rape. Several states had allowed the imposition of the death penalty, but in 1977, the U.S. Supreme Court decided in *Coker v. Georgia* that the death penalty for rape constituted cruel and unusual punishment in violation of the Eighth Amendment of the Constitution.[3]

# BATTERED WOMEN AND SELF-DEFENSE

The number of women in the United States who are beaten and abused is staggering. According to recent statistics, 25 percent of American families have a history of battering women. The problem is compounded because the men who do the battering are those with whom women share their domestic lives, not strangers. These men are husbands, lovers, fathers, or the fathers of our children.

The National Institute of Mental Health, in a recent study, found that women are most often sent to the emergency room after having been battered by a man. A doctor and sociologist who reviewed the medical records of women who received treatment at the Yale–New Haven Hospital found that women are more likely to be beaten during pregnancy. Battered women are also 80 percent more likely to commit suicide than nonbattered women.

The majority of women who are battered are abused repeatedly by the same person. Often beatings increase in frequency and severity over time. Sometimes, out of desperation, women in these situations have killed their lovers or spouses. The basic legal question raised here is, What is a woman's right to self-defense?

Many women who have killed in self-defense are serving long-term jail sentences. A study by the superintendent of the women's division of the Cook County Department of Corrections found that 40 percent of women in the prison system convicted of murder or manslaughter were women who had killed continually abusive male partners.

In response to the growing awareness of domestic violence, many states and localities have developed specially trained police units to cope with cases of spouse abuse. Some estimates say that about 20 percent of the deaths and 40 percent of injuries suffered by police occur when they try to intervene in domestic disputes. Nevertheless, police are being taught through role playing how to defuse family fights by projecting a calm, mediating manner and, when an assault has already taken place, to be prepared to conduct an assault investigation.

Several states have modified their laws to make it easier to arrest wife batterers. Feminists argue that only a small percentage of those arrested are ever prosecuted because the charges are reduced to minor infractions of the law and suspended sentences are recommended to the court. Judges often impose light sentences or none at all. Thus, the injured wife who persists does not always receive the protection of having her husband jailed. While some feminist attorneys believe that only prompt and certain punishment will deter spouse abuse, others in the justice system feel that criminal prosecution is an act of last resort, that it is an act of desperation. Obviously, for some women, this kind of protection and relief is a necessity.

Some women who are frustrated by the criminal justice system take the law into their own hands. These are the women who kill in self-defense. In a well-publicized case in Lansing, Michigan, Francine Hughes claimed that years of physical abuse drove her to pour gasoline around the bed of her sleeping husband and light it. A jury acquitted her of murder on the ground of temporary insanity. This case was used as the basis of a television program in 1985 called *The Burning Bed*. The program received public attention and media coverage.

In recent years, the self-defense plea has become increasingly common in wife-husband murders where there is a history of battering. In many states, to prove self-defense the defendant has to show a reasonable apprehension of imminent danger of great bodily harm. Lawyers have used evidence of past beatings and threats to show "reasonable apprehension," even in cases where the husband's actions at the moment of the killing are inconclusive or negligible. Lawyers have also successfully argued that it is not an unreasonable response for a physically outmatched wife to resort to a lethal weapon such as a gun or a knife if a man comes at her with his fists.

Acceptance of the self-defense plea is not universal. A key element in many recent cases is whether or not the woman committing the crime suffered from *battered-woman syndrome*, a term which refers to a set of emotional patterns and behaviors that characterize women suffering from repeated abuse. The syndrome is comprised of three distinct phases. In the first, tension mounts between the woman and her partner and minor abuse occurs. More serious violence follows, and the woman experiences a sense of powerlessness to do anything to stop her husband. Psychologists describe a phenomenon called "learned helplessness," a condition in which the woman becomes psychologically locked into her situation because of economic dependence on the man, an abiding attachment to him, and the failure of the legal system to adequately respond to the problem. Finally, there is a temporary lull in the physical abuse inflicted on the battered woman, and she forgives her assailant, hoping that the abuse will not recur. At some point, it does. In recent years, this syndrome has become a recognized diagnosis by professionals.

In some states, expert testimony on the battered-woman syndrome is admissible in court to show a female defendant's fear of imminent danger at the time she killed her husband or lover. In others, it is not. In 1984, for example, the New Jersey Supreme Court held that expert testimony on the behavior of women who have been subjected to sustained abuse is admissible in court to help establish claims of self-defense in murder cases. High courts in the states of Washington, Maine, and Georgia had already upheld the use of such testimony. It has been rejected by the District of Columbia, Ohio, and Wyoming. In other states, such as Florida, the refusal to accept expert testimony has been reversed on appeal. As one lawyer wrote in a report to attorneys about the practice of representing women who defend themselves against physical or sexual assault: "You can't really assert self-defense until you feel you have a self to defend; that's what women are finally developing."

# PREMENSTRUAL SYNDROME AND THE COURTS

In the early 1980s, British courts set free two women charged with murder on the basis of a defense that premenstrual syndrome—primarily described as monthly severe and uncontrollable mood swings—prompted them to kill. In both cases the charge was reduced to manslaughter.

The PMS defense has caused a stir among women's groups. Most women experience some bodily changes and mood shifts prior to menstruating. However, many women feel that the PMS defense revives the old stereotype that because they menstruate women are "irrational," not responsible for their actions, and as such are victims of their biological nature.

According to medical experts, about 3 to 10 percent of menstruating women suffer changes of such severity that their lives are disrupted for a week or two every month. This distress is real and devastating: psychologically, they may be plagued by irritability, anxiety, tension, aggression, and other symptoms. Medical treatment can run the gamut from hormone therapy to suggested diet and exercise changes. There are also support groups that urge premenstrual sufferers to schedule their time to allow for greater relaxation and self-awareness during this period.

Because the symptoms and treatment are so diffuse, the PMS defense has not been used successfully in the United States. If PMS is potentially intrinsic to all women, then any woman may exhibit irrational behavior. Also there has not been a concerted effort among women's groups in the United States to get behind this issue. PMS may become a factor in U.S. courts if it is more clearly defined medically—and if it does not create a defense for women which forces us back into the Victorian premise that biology is destiny.

# PORNOGRAPHY

Violence against women can take another form: the graphic depiction of sexual and violent acts against women in books, magazines, and video and motion pictures.

In 1973, the Supreme Court in the case *Miller v. California*, abandoned all attempts to establish a nationwide standard for obscenity.[4] According to the current law, a work can only be banned if sexual depictions were "patently offensive" to "contemporary community standards" and if, as a whole, it lacked "serious literary, artistic, political or scientific value." This decision placed the greatest emphasis on local judgments.

In 1984 and 1985, some feminists, operating on the assumption that the causes of real violence against women could emanate from widespread media depictions of it, decided to fight back. A "model antipornography law" was drafted by attorney Catharine MacKinnon and writer and political activist Andrea Dworkin. In this document, pornography is described as:

> The graphical sexually explicit subordination of women through pictures and/ or words that also includes one or more of the following: (i) women are presented dehumanized as sexual objects, things or commodities or (ii) women are presented as sexual objects who enjoy pain and humiliation (iii) women are presented as sexual objects who experience sexual pleasure in being raped or (iv) women are presented as sexual objects tied up, bruised or physically hurt (v) women are presented in postures or positions of sexual submission, servility or display (vi) women's body parts—including but not limited to vaginas, breasts or buttocks—are exhibited such that women are reduced to those parts (vii) women are presented as whores by nature or (viii) women are presented being penetrated by objects or animals or (ix) women are presented in scenarios of degradation, injury, torture, shown as filthy or inferior, bleeding, bruised or hurt in a context that makes these conditions sexual.[5]

In a statement of policy which precedes the law, the authors declare that existing federal and state laws are inadequate to remedy the sex discrimination imposed on women by pornography. Pornography, say the authors, promotes bigotry and contempt for women and diminishes women's opportunities for equality. Pornography is also seen as contributing to rape, battering, child sexual abuse, prostitution, and other exploitation that women encounter.

Versions of this law have been introduced as city ordinances in Minneapolis, Indianapolis, and Los Angeles. Following its enactment in Indianapolis, the law was promptly challenged in *American Booksellers Assoc. v. Hudnut* as a violation of the First Amendment.[6] It was subsequently struck down by both the U.S. District Court and the Court of Appeals for the Sixth Circuit. The Supreme Court affirmed the decision of the Sixth Circuit. The discussions about pornography that have ensued have divided groups that have traditionally stood together and created surprising coalitions. While feminist groups see pornography statutes as emanating from the concerns about any form of violence against women, right-wing fundamentalist, evangelist groups who support antipornography legislation associate it with homosexuality, interracial sex, divorce, birth control, promiscuity, and the deterioration of the family.

Objections to antipornography statutes of any sort come from many women's groups of all persuasions. The key arguments raise issues of censorship and freedom of the press and whether images are actually the cause of violence against women. Other women feel this is a spurious issue when so many real needs of women are yet to be met. Also, the definition of pornography forces people to admit that what is erotic and even artistic to some people is pornographic to another person. Questions of personal freedom are involved.

Nevertheless, there is a growing body of research into the effects of pornography and greater public debate about its social consequences.

A *Newsweek* magazine poll shows that Americans are ambivalent about pornography: they want conventional erotica while they would like to suppress more extreme forms. The new dialogue about pornography will create greater public awareness of the issue, and this may influence the law in the future.

# WOMEN IN THE MILITARY

The military is the largest employer and educator in the nation. Policies which limit the number of women who can enter the services deny women opportunities for job training and education in technical occupations and crafts which are in high demand. Exclusion from the benefits of military service also means lost opportunities for college scholarships, veterans' education benefits, veterans' preference in government employment, and veterans' insurance and loan programs. These restrictive policies also limit women's access to job openings in the private sector where high pay is available for defense-related skills of former service members.

Recent research on employed women of all races shows that those who have served in the Armed Forces are almost twice as likely to earn salaries of $300 per week or better than those women who have not. Thus, limitations on women's participation in the military can, once again, perpetuate an earnings gap between men and women.

At the end of fiscal year 1984, 203,310 women, both officers and enlisted, served in the U.S. Armed Forces. This number comprised 9.5 percent of the active-duty force. The number of enlisted women in each of the services was: Army, 66,100; Navy, 42,258; Air Force, 55,335; Marines, 8577; Coast Guard, 2108. By the end of 1987, the Department of Defense expects to have over 221,788 women on active duty. This number would be slightly less than 10 percent of the overall force.

The Armed Forces Qualification Test is a written test used by all branches of the Armed Services to determine the enlistment eligibility of personnel. It consists of four subject areas and measures basic verbal and quantitative abilities. There are five categories of scores from highest to lowest. The services actively recruit persons who score in categories I, II, and III. Congress has limited recruitment of persons who score in category IV to 20 percent of enlistees. The services do not enlist category V. The Armed Forces Vocational Battery, a ten-part test, measures aptitude and determines eligibility to enter specific military occupations. Service standards are subject to change. Higher scores are required by some services for recruits in special categories, such as non-high school graduates, and for the more technical military jobs. Some services also require female enlistees to be high school graduates, though no similar requirement is imposed on male recruits.

In 1978, when the Women's Army Corps was abolished and full integration of women into the regular Army was mandated, a "combat exclusion policy" was developed. This policy barred women from assignment to "Infantry, Armor, Cannon Field Artillery, Combat Engineer, and Low Altitude Air Defense Artillery unit of battalion or smaller size." Women were also barred from all military occupational specialties which would be concentrated in such units. As a result of this policy, thirty-eight job categories were closed to women.

In 1981, the Army expanded its policy by creating a new category of activity—"direct combat"—and has since analyzed all job specialties and units to determine the relative probability of a soldier routinely engaging in such direct combat. As a result of this analysis twenty-three additional specialties were closed to women in 1982.

According to testimony before Congress by a member of the National Information Center on Women and the Military, the battlefield analysis on which these restrictions were based appeared to be premised on a static war plan with traditional World War II front-line fighting—in direct contradiction to scenarios upon which current battle strategies are being formed. In 1983, thirteen of the twenty-three specialties closed to women were reopened after it became clear that replacing skilled women in the affected fields was not going to be easy.

In the other services, there are two acts of Congress which limit the utilization of women. Female members of the Air Force, except nurses and other professionals, "may not be assigned to duty in aircraft engaged in combat missions." Women in the Navy cannot be permanently assigned to combat vessels.[7] The Coast Guard, on the other hand, has no restrictions on the assignment of women. This means that in a time of war Coast Guard women could be serving in virtually identical positions to those from which their Navy sisters are barred.

The conflict between the "protective" attitude of some of the regulations and the loss of opportunities for women as a result has created tensions for women in the military. Many women's groups representing thousands of women have publicly stated that true equality for women will come when they are seen to be able to accept the equal division of societal obligations and duties. The Army Audit Agency's 1982 Report on Enlisted Women in the Army accepted the fact that female soldiers will serve in battlefield areas, be expected to defend themselves and their units, and be exposed to the same risks of injury, death, and capture as their male counterparts. If women today are to be asked to face these risks, the full protection of the Constitution should be behind them.

Definitions of single parents are inconsistent within the military. A single parent can refer to a member having physical or legal dependents. In some cases, military policies differ on whether a single parent is an unmarried person with the physical or legal custody of a child or children. Single parents are often thought of as women, but in fact a recent study by the Women's Equity Action League shows that males make up 58 percent of the single parents in the Air Force, 57 percent in the Army, 66 percent in the Navy, and 92 percent in the Marine Corps!

The services disagree on whether single parents pose a readiness problem. Currently, the Army, Navy, Marines, and Coast Guard forbid the initial enlistment of single parents unless they give up legal custody of their dependents. If single parents attempt to regain legal custody of their children during initial enlistment, proceedings can be taken to separate them from the service, or they can be barred from reenlistment. Custody can be regained after reenlistment. The Air Force permits single parents to enlist as long as they transfer custody for the first period of basic training. Officers may enter the military as single parents. If a service member becomes a single parent after initial enlistment, he or she is allowed to remain in the service. All single parents are expected to be available to perform all duty assignments in the military though different services require a child care plan. In overseas tours, single parents can bring their children with them and are sometimes allowed a "humanitarian deferment or assignment" until housing and education problems are settled.

Single parents in all services are entitled to the same benefits as married parents including residence in married couples' housing and an increased housing allowance. Unfortunately, most military communities do not have adequate child care facilities for dependents.

The services have just begun to formulate and implement family planning programs. Birth control information and devices are available free of charge for military personnel. Sex education is sporadic. All service members who become pregnant after basic training are entitled to free prenatal and maternity care within military facilities. Service members who become pregnant can choose to leave the service, but they cannot be forced to leave. Pregnant members who have been educated or specially trained by the services are not automatically let go. Government-paid abortions are only permitted to save the life of the mother.

Pregnancy continues to be an easy-out option for young female enlistees who desire to leave the service. The military has not studied whether the problems of sexual harassment, underutilization or poor utilization of staff, and prejudice are incentives for young women to become pregnant.

The Tax Equity and Fiscal Responsibility Amendment (TEFRA) to the Social Security Act went into effect in October 1982. This amendment enables a former spouse of an active-duty service member to file for allotments from the member's monthly pay for overdue spouse and/or child support without having to pursue court proceedings. Upon receiving notification of the deduction, the military member has 30 days to receive legal consultation from the judge advocate of the service involved or from a designated legal officer.

The former spouse and dependent children will not receive the allotment until the military member has received this consultation unless there is a lapse of 30 days or more during which consultation has not been arranged. After 30 days, the former spouse will receive the involuntary allotment on the first end-of-the-month payday regardless of the member's failure to receive consultation.

The provisions of this amendment do not stipulate the terms of the support payments. They only ensure that the former spouse and dependent children will receive whatever support payments are set forth in the divorce decree.

The 1985 Defense Authorization Act includes provisions to expand medical, exchange, and commissary privileges for former spouses who meet the following criteria:

- Former spouses of both active-duty and retired personnel who were married at least 20 years during the member's active-duty service may receive care in military medical facilities or under the Civilian Health and Medical Program for the Uniformed Services. These spouses may also receive exchange and commissary privileges.

- Former spouses of both active-duty and retired personnel who were married at least 20 years, including 15 years during the member's active-duty service, are eligible for full military medical coverage if their divorce is final on April 1, 1985. These spouses are not eligible for exchange or commissary privileges.

- Former spouses of both active-duty and retired personnel who were married at least 20 years, including 15 years during the member's active-duty service, and will be divorced after April 1, 1985 will be eligible for 2 years of military medical care. After 2 years of coverage, former spouses would have the option of buying low-cost medical insurance provided by the Department of Defense.

- Former spouses having their own health insurance are not eligible for medical benefits. However, if they later lose civilian health insurance, they would become eligible for the military coverage.

- All medical, exchange, and commissary privileges terminate if the former spouse remarries.

The spouse and dependent minors of an active-duty member of the military services may continue to receive medical, commissary, and exchange privileges if they are separated and do not reside with the member. There is no length of marriage requirement for a separated spouse to receive medical, commissary, and exchange privileges.

To receive benefits under this legislation, the former spouse should contact the personnel divisions of the respective services. To enforce back payments of support, call the city or county district attorney's office and ask for either the Title IV-D program or the Office of Paternity and Child Support Enforcement. These agencies will serve as a liaison to the appropriate branches of the service.

If you need help locating your spouse or former spouse, write to the Women's Equity Action League, 1250 I Street NW, Suite 305, Washington, DC 20005. WEAL can provide a fact sheet with the addresses and phone numbers of the Worldwide Locator Service for active-duty personnel and the retirement offices for each service. WEAL is also the sponsor of the Women and the Military Project and is an excellent source of current information.

The Uniformed Services Former Spouses Protection Act, an amendment to Title IX of the Defense Authorization Act, went into effect in February 1983.

The provisions of this act state that:

- A share of military retired pay shall be awarded to a military spouse upon divorce

- The divorces that occur after June 26, 1981, in states that formerly divided military pensions can be reconsidered, and a share of the pension awarded to the former spouse

- Divorces that were final before June 26, 1981, cannot be reconsidered because of this legislation if the military retired pay was not considered property in the original divorce decree

Payments to a former spouse may not exceed 50 percent of the military member's disposable retired or retainer pay. Up to an additional 15 percent may be appropriated to honor orders for child support, alimony, and nonpayment of property settlement for other than retired pay. Payments continue for the lifetime of the retired military member unless otherwise specified in the court order. Current regulations do not ensure that payments will continue upon remarriage of the former spouse.

Medical, commissary, and exchange privileges effective January 1985 under the Defense Authorization Act are the same as those for former spouses of military members on active duty mentioned above.

The current regulations regarding survivor benefits for former spouses are confusing and provide protection for very few former spouses. Legislation is pending which would correct the ambiguities. A military member may elect a beneficiary under the Survivor Benefit Plan upon retirement. As of September 1982, a former spouse may be named. The military member must voluntarily name a former spouse as beneficiary. A court cannot order survivor benefit coverage for a former spouse.

To receive benefits under the amendments, a former spouse should contact Ex-Partners of Servicemen/Women for Equality (EXPOSE) for information concerning court orders and other documents, lawyers, and the laws of individual states. Their address is P.O. Box 11191, Alexandria, VA 22312.

It is not unconstitutional for the military to discharge members for homosexual conduct, nor is it unconstitutional to refuse to recruit homosexuals into the military. It is less clear, however, whether the military may discharge individuals who make statements regarding their own homosexuality without actually engaging in homosexual conduct while in the service. Discharge under these circumstances raises questions about protected speech under the First Amendment. The Supreme Court has yet to rule decisively on this issue.

Various counseling services give practical information on how to fight forced separation based on allegations of homosexual activity, how to voluntarily initiate and obtain an honorable discharge, and how to survive as a gay member of the military. A book entitled *Counseling Lesbian and Gay Service Members* is available from the National Lawyers Guild, Military Law Task Force, 1168 Union Street, Suite 400, San Diego, CA 92101. Another book, *Your Rights in the Military: A Survival Guide for Lesbians and Gay Men*, is available from the Midwest Committee on Military Counseling, 59 East Van Buren, Room 809, Chicago, IL 60605.

At present, the U.S. Armed Forces seek recruits on a voluntary basis. Although males of 18 are required to register, there is no mandatory draft.

In 1981, in the case of *Rostker v. Goldberg*, the U.S. Supreme Court upheld the constitutionality of an all-male draft.[8] The Court also held that because of the combat restrictions on women, men and women are not similiarly situated for purposes of the draft.

Public opinion on whether the draft should be reinstituted varies widely. Nevertheless, recent polls indicate that over half the nation favors the conscription of women in the event of a draft. Women are seeking equal rights and are willing to assume equal responsibilities in the defense of their country.

## ECONOMIC EQUALITY

Two decades ago, President Lyndon Johnson initiated a crusade to eliminate poverty in the United States. Programs such as food stamps, medicaid, Head Start, medicare, and the Job Corps grew out of this effort. Yet in studies of 5000 American families over a 15-year period, a University of Michigan sociologist estimates that one-quarter of the United States population fell below the poverty line at one time or another during the 1970s, even though the official poverty rate in any one year was never more than 12.6 percent of the population.

For many, these hard times were the result of temporary setbacks—illness, divorce, unemployment—that were eventually overcome. Other groups of poor in America come from layoffs in factories in the midwest and from the nation's homeless population, many of whom suffer serious mental illness. But those most likely to depend on welfare benefits for long periods include high-school dropouts, nonwhites, unwed mothers, mothers with many children, and women who had not earned any income before going on welfare. Households headed by the very old and the disabled also fall into this category.

There are now 3.6 million poor families with a female head of household. This figure is up 82 percent since 1960. Such households comprise nearly half of all poor families. A report by the Urban League on the state of black America states that 70 percent of all poor black children live in female-headed households. Another study found that, regardless of place of residence or parent's education or race, young people who lived with single mothers were more likely to drop out of school than those living in two-parent households. The poverty of these households is further compounded by the fact that working women tend to hold down jobs which pay less than men. A woman who has a full-time job at $3.35 per hour, the current minimum wage, receives a gross income of $7000. The minimum wage has remained the same since January 1981, while living costs over the past 5 years have risen 21 percent. These factors explain what is meant by the "feminization of poverty."

As we have seen earlier in this book in the section on employment, women have made inroads into the job market by means of both the equal employment opportunity laws and the newer concept of comparable worth. To measure tasks for comparability requires a complex evaluation system, but studies are underway in many states and municipalities. The goal, of course, is to eliminate the wage gap between men and women in employment, whether in the public or private sector.

Even women with professional degrees, who are, in greater numbers, moving up into positions of power in business, law, medicine, and academia, still find obstacles in their path. In New York City, for example, the nation's largest law center, women comprised 25 percent of the lawyers in 111 firms surveyed but only 5 percent of the partners.

The concept of economic equality that we will be discussing in this chapter has less to do, then, with the specifics of education or employment and more to do with entry and access to opportunities that further economic stability in a woman's life. A woman's right under the law to enter into contracts, obtain credit, buy equitable insurance policies, and have access to fair housing and public accommodations are the economic factors we will consider here.

**CONTRACTS:** Whether you wish to buy a car, sign a lease, or obtain a credit card, a contract is the formal agreement which states the rights and obligations between parties who enter the agreement. The age at which a person may legally enter into a contract varies from state to state. In general, minors cannot enter into a contract, although they can contract for certain medical services such as services to treat venereal disease, without parental consent. Abortion and sterilization are generally excluded from these provisions.

A written contract is a powerful legal instrument. In many states, verbal contracts are not enforceable if they deal with more than a certain amount of money or are negotiated for a long period of time. The terms of a written agreement in most cases may not be expanded or altered by verbal side agreements. Therefore, the terms of the contract should cover all possible considerations.

Before entering into any contract, a woman should know what guarantees and warranties are included in the agreement and what penalties will be lodged for violations of the contract. Be careful about the fine print. Contracts should also state under what circumstances they may be canceled.

It can be very important to check with a lawyer before entering into a contract which involves a large sum of money exchanged, a partnership agreement, employment which you accept or under which you hire others, and the like. A woman's right to enter into contracts on her own for such large-scale purchases as buying a house has been solidified in recent years.

**CREDIT:** Credit has become a functional substitute for cash in our economy. It is an absolute requirement for a person in today's society. Obtaining credit is based on the judgment of a bank, credit card issuer, credit union, or business that an individual is "creditworthy." This means that the person is worth risking the advance of money, goods, or services because that person has the ability to pay for them later. An individual who applies for credit is rated according to a set of criteria, such as current income, home ownership, job stability, education, and outstanding debt liability. Then the person is given a credit "rating" on which lenders base funding decisions.

In the late 1960s, the Consumer Credit Protection Act was passed. It is also known as the Truth in Lending Act. Under its Regulation Z, there are four major provisions. A creditor must tell you in writing how much the credit will cost you. Creditors must not advertise falsely about terms or rates. The act provides protection if you change your mind about certain credit situations, such as when it is possible to cancel a contract and with what penalties. Finally, Regulation Z requires that credit cards be issued only upon request rather than mailed indiscriminately to consumers. The rules of liability for the cardholder in case of theft or unauthorized use are also outlined.

Before 1974, there were no federal laws mandating equal credit opportunities for women. It was assumed that women were poor credit risks because they were not traditional breadwinners. With the enactment of the Equal Credit Opportunity Act of 1974 and its amendments of 1976, women had a legal guarantee of credit rights. Regulation B of the 1981 Federal Reserve Board addresses in detail all phases of the credit-granting process, the evaluation process, and the reporting of reasons when credit is denied. Practically speaking, the regulations establish that:

- A person cannot be refused credit just because she is a woman
- A woman cannot be refused credit just because she is single, married, separated, divorced, or widowed
- A woman cannot be refused credit because a creditor decides she is of childbearing age and, as a consequence, will not consider her income stable
- When a woman applies for her own credit and relies on her own income, financial information about her spouse or her spouse's signature can be required only under certain circumstances
- A woman can keep her own accounts and her own credit history if her marital status changes and can build a credit record under the name she chooses

When a person is denied credit, the creditor is required to notify the applicant within 30 days after any adverse action is taken, or within 90 days if the lender makes a counteroffer of different terms or arrangements which the applicant does not accept. If the creditor is asked to supply reasons for denial, the applicant must request such notification within 60 days of the adverse action. This places the burden of gaining information on the applicant. However, such information provides the applicant with a record of her credit history and the reasons for denial used by lending institutions; this will help her improve her credit rating and assert her rights.

Credit discrimination can result from practices which seem fair and neutral on the surface but whose effects fall more harshly on one group than another. For example, although a creditor is prohibited from asking an applicant's race, an applicant's immigration status may be asked, thereby alerting a creditor to information about the applicant's background. This type of treatment is called "disparate-effects discrimination." An example that women encounter occurs when a woman receives income from alimony, child support, or separate maintenance. A creditor may not ask whether an applicant's income is derived from these sources unless a woman wants to specify this income as proof of creditworthiness. If a woman only receives these payments sporadically, she may be denied credit because of another's history of irregular payment. If she withholds this information, she may be denied credit on the basis of insufficient income.

Reaction by creditors to changes in the composition and creditworthiness of the pool of credit applicants has come slowly. Regulation B, for example, prohibits consideration of the existence of a telephone listing in the applicant's name. It does not prohibit consideration of home ownership. One is much easier to change than the other, but this characteristic is the one prohibited from consideration. Thus, discrimination against women may occur because the standard criteria have not been truly modified to reflect their lives.

To sue successfully under the Equal Credit Opportunity Act, a woman must prove *intentional* discrimination. That is, she must prove that the creditor failed to comply with, or violated, the provisions of the act. Because different creditors with different risk capabilities may well have different methods of utilizing criteria to arrive at credit qualifications, a violation of the act can be difficult to prove.

Compliance with the ECOA is enforced by government agencies and through private litigation. Overall administrative enforcement of the act rests with the Federal Trade Commission, with limited authority delegated to eleven other federal agencies. With the 1976 amendments, a new section was added authorizing the U.S. attorney general to initiate proceedings if necessary to remedy a pattern of pervasive discrimination. Lawsuits must be initiated within 2 years of the alleged discriminatory act, or 3 years if the U.S. attorney general or other federal agency initiates proceedings.

There is no minimum amount of statutory recovery of damages under ECOA. Dollar amounts are especially important in discrimination cases because they represent a concrete penalty for inflicting damages. Some courts have held that mental distress, humiliation, and embarrassment are "actual damages" entitled to financial compensation even though no out-of-pocket loss resulted. Punitive damages are available under the act, as are court-ordered attorney's fees.

Despite these seeming safeguards, the ECOA has generated surprisingly little litigation. As of 1984, fewer than fifty cases have been reported under the statute in the decade since its enactment. Several of these cases have resulted in challenges to the "patterns and practices" of established creditors such as the Household Finance Corporation and Federated Department Stores. These cases against large creditors were brought by the Federal Trade Commission and the Department of Justice. Few suits litigated privately have resulted in a positive judgment. Generally, it is difficult for a consumer to bring suit without knowing the reasons for credit denial. As we have seen before, it is the applicant who must write for reasons for the denial within a fixed period of time. As a practical matter, few consumers take the time to request a written explanation. Also, individuals who are denied credit may be fearful of taking on the credit "establishment" for fear that alienating a creditor will prevent future credit.

To gain your rights, it is necessary to use the law. Request your own credit report if you have been denied credit. Assert your rights to a creditor in writing if you feel that you are the victim of discrimination. Inform the enforcing agencies, beginning with the attorney general's office in your state. If your own direct action produces no result, you may wish to consult a lawyer.

Credit is an important means of financial independence. Smart banks and lending institutions are beginning to cultivate women as a new market for their services. The combination of these two factors, buttressed by the law, makes this an opportune time for women to establish credit.

# FAIR INSURANCE PRACTICES LAWS

According to figures compiled by the National Organization for Women, women typically pay $16,000 more than men for a lifetime of auto, health, disability, and life insurance. Discrimination against women in the availability, terms, and coverage of insurance policies is a serious problem.

In 1983, Congress considered a nondiscrimination-in-insurance bill designed to prohibit all insurers from discriminating on the basis of race, color, religion, sex, or national origin in the terms, conditions, rates, benefits, or requirements of any insurance, annuity, or pension contract. Specifically, the use of any actuarial table based on these criteria would be forbidden as a means of distinguishing between insured persons. Merged-gender tables would be used to calculate rates and benefits. Rates could be increased or decreased to comply with this bill but benefits under existing contracts could not be decreased.

The insurance industry attempts to justify assessing individual risks on the basis of membership in a group (i.e., gender) rather than on individual characteristics. Yet the sex mortality differentials, for example, may reflect significantly different behavior patterns between men and women—smoking, drinking, military service, automobile driving frequency, and career pursuit—rather than an indirect criterion such as gender.

Underlying this bill has been the hope that the fragmentation of society for economic purposes into male and female categories would be eradicated. It was hoped that the bill would provide a catalyst for the development of new methods of risk classification. However, in early 1984 the bill was defeated.

In August 1984, NOW filed a $2 million lawsuit in an attempt to use the courts to prevent insurance companies from using sex as a basis for setting rates. Rates are determined from actuarial tables compiled by the insurance industry. The suit charges Mutual of Omaha with illegally overcharging women for health coverage. This suit was filed in the District of Columbia under a local law barring sex discrimination in public accommodations. The definition of public accommodation is very broad. The term usually refers to a physical facility but can include a widely based public service or an organization whose intent is to serve the public. NOW filed a similar suit against Metropolitan Life Insurance Company in New York in October 1985 and plans to bring other suits in states that have similar laws. Both the 1984 and the 1985 suits are still pending.

The McCarran-Ferguson Act of 1976 grants to the states primary responsibility for regulating the business of insurance. States do prohibit "unfair discrimination" in rate setting under their Unfair Trade Practices Acts, though rarely do they prohibit discrimination in premiums based on sex. Since challenges to the validity of sex-based actuarial tables have been questioned only recently, there is little state litigation on this matter.

The goal of insurance reform is to eliminate discriminatory practices in all areas of the industry—in health, life, disability, auto insurance and in pensions and annuities. A nondiscrimination-in-insurance bill can provide the proper incentives necessary for insurance companies to invest in research which will find actuarial criteria to replace sex-based classifications in this industry.

## HOUSING AND PUBLIC ACCOMMODATIONS

There are many sources of discrimination which women have faced in the rental, purchase, and financing of housing. Whether on the basis of race, sexual preference, familial and marital status, physical or mental disability, or age—or a combination of these—women have often been denied equal treatment. As mentioned earlier in this chapter, this discrimination has partially come from antiquated attitudes about women's ability to obtain credit for a mortgage or to pay a regular rent.

Every state has laws which govern fair housing practices. The provisions of the District of Columbia, for example, set forth the key principles covered in most other states:

> It is unlawful to refuse to sell, lease or rent real property because of sex, marital status, changes in marital status, pregnancy, race, religion, color or national origin or ancestry. This information cannot be asked for either orally or in writing by the owner of any housing accommodation. No person can make, print, publish or cause to be made, printed or published any notice, statement or advertisement that indicates preference, limitation or discrimination in the above categories.[9]

The District of Columbia also outlaws the practice of *redlining*, which is discrimination by banks or financial institutions on investment in real estate because of the location of the residence or business. Redlining is often a subtle form of racial discrimination. It is also illegal to require different terms for a transaction than would operate in the prevailing market or to represent that a property is not available when it is.

Maine statutes are similar:

> It is unlawful for any person, bank, mortgage company or other financial institution to discriminate in the terms, conditions and privileges related to obtaining financial assistance. Neither can any housing owner harass, evict or otherwise discriminate against any person in the sale or rental of housing when the owner's dominant purpose is retaliation against a person who has opposed unlawful practices, informed law enforcement agencies of practices believed to be unlawful, or testified or assisted in any proceeding. It is also unlawful for any person to aid, abet, incite, compel or coerce any of the discriminatory acts or practices which are declared unlawful.[10]

Maine also stipulates that a person on federal, state, or local public assistance cannot be refused housing solely because that person is a recipient of these subsidies. Other states and cities have special provisions applying to housing in their localities.

Tenants' rights organizations have arisen in every state to offer advice about legal tactics and local regulations affecting landlord-tenant relationships. Women should use these organizations as key sources of information and as advocates for the exercise of legal rights.

Under the law the term *public accommodations* means all places in a community which are available to the general public without special conditions or restrictions. These include public streets, sidewalks, and highways; public buildings such as libraries; public facilities such as hotels, motels, and rest rooms; public places of amusement such as theaters; public recreational resources such as parks and beaches; and all common and public modes of transportation whether by land, air, or sea.

In recent years, there has been an expansion of the definition of the term public accommodations. The questions regarding accommodations now hinge on who exactly comprise the public and on whether access to public accommodations is full and equal for all groups. Lawsuits in which these questions have been raised have focused on whether clubs and organizations which have discriminated against women are violating public-accommodations laws.

Most states now have laws which guarantee the blind, the deaf, the physically disabled, and other handicapped people the same right as the able-bodied to use public accommodations. In fact, guaranteeing this access has been the major thrust of activist groups for the handicapped over the past few years. But in the statutes of most states, there is no mention of equal membership privileges in civic organizations as a right of public accommodation.

The Supreme Court ruled in July 1984 that the all-male Jaycees organization, a national leadership group with local chapters, could be required to accept women as members under state public-accommodation laws which forbid discrimination. The Court left open the broader question of whether the membership policies of exclusive private clubs could be challenged on the same basis. However, Associate Justice William Brennan, Jr., stressed the "large and basically unselective nature" of the Jaycees.[11] This characterization of the Jaycees may serve to distinguish public organizations from traditional private clubs with small and highly selective memberships.

Public-accommodation laws are flexible and offer many possible interpretations. These laws may open the way to a broader conception of the relationship between sex equity and the public good.

## WOMEN AND POLITICAL ACTION

On November 6, 1984, more women candidates ran for election on a national level than ever before. Women campaigned for 65 seats in the House of Representatives, 10 Senate seats, 19 statewide offices, and 1756 state legislative positions. For the first time in the nation's history, a woman shared the ticket of the Democratic party—for vice president of the United States.

Although the expectation that women's issues would dominate the 1984 election did not come to pass, women's votes did make a difference. Millions of women registered to vote for the first time, and women turned out to vote at a higher rate than men in 1984. Politicians became aware of the concept of the "gender gap," reflecting the fact that women vote for issues of concern to them and that these issues are different from those of men. Gender gap issues of peace and economic justice are of deep concern to women, even though they did not elect a woman candidate to the vice presidency.

Some analysts say that the real legacy of Geraldine Ferraro's campaign for vice president will be measured in the way that women think about themselves and their leadership in the future. This includes not only today's women but the young girls who saw that a woman could run for one of the highest offices in the United States and were influenced by the historic change in the making. The mechanics of this change have evolved in the more than 15 years that women have taken an active role in the U.S. political process.

Women with an interest in public affairs have only recently seen elective office or professional government service as viable outlets for their energies. Historically, women have been the mainstays of public-interest groups such as the League of Women Voters whose work is civic in nature. Groups such as this extend across the country spanning a broad ideological spectrum. The incentives for membership in these groups include a commitment to certain public policy goals and the strong desire to have an influence on politics while operating as a private citizen.

An example of the range of groups participating in public affairs can be seen in the membership of the ad hoc Coalition on Women and the Budget, which has published an analysis of the effects of President Reagan's budget on women and children for the past 3 years. Endorsing organizations include the Alpha Kappa Alpha Sorority, Inc., the American Association of University Women, the American Nurses Association, Church Women United, Coalition of Labor Union Women, Disability Rights Education and Defense Fund, Girls Clubs of America, Mexican-American Women's National Association, National Black Child Development Institute, National Coalition Against Domestic Violence, the National Low-Income Housing Coalition, Older Women's League, Planned Parenthood Federation of America, Women's International League for Peace and Freedom, and others. This list can only begin to give an idea of the wide-ranging opportunities for women to participate in the organization which best expresses their interests and concerns.

The Coalition on Women and the Budget has come to the conclusion that the Reagan budget of $925.5 billion for fiscal year 1985 demands an "inequality of sacrifice" by American women. The social programs which women rely on, the group concluded, have not been able to provide the support women need because of severe budget cuts. Since fiscal and budgetary priorities affect women's lives, these areas are of great concern to women who wish to take an active role in the political decision making in their communities and on the national level.

American feminists in the past few years have also moved beyond consideration of the United States as an isolated nation into a recognition that women around the world can link together to solve problems. Sisterhood is global. The stimulus for much of this thinking began in 1975 when the United Nations declared a Decade for Women. Over this 10-year period women's issues were highlighted in countries all over the world and at three U.N. conferences. The first began the decade in 1975 and was held in Mexico City. The second was a mid-decade review held in 1980 in Copenhagen. And the third was held in the summer of 1985 in Nairobi, Kenya. The purpose of this final meeting was to assess the accomplishment of the goals which had been established and decide on directions for the year 2000.

In *Women: A World Survey*, a report written by an economist from Washington who surveyed international governments and organizations, women were found to be "disproportionately represented among the poor, the illiterate, the unemployed and the underemployed. They represent a very small minority at the centers of political power."[12] Women hold no more than 10 percent of the seats in all national legislatures. And, despite progress in many areas, changes in the status of women around the world have been "extremely uneven and, on the whole, modest" since World War II. According to the report, "there is no major field of activity and no country where women have attained equality with men." This, of course, includes the United States.

The major document to emerge from the Nairobi conference is called "The Forward-Looking Strategies."[13] It uses the three themes of the U.N. Decade for Women: equality, development, and peace. In addition, there are sections on areas of special concern and on international and regional cooperation. This comprehensive document sets forth a series of guidelines and recommendations for member nations of the U.N. to promote the advancement of women between now and the year 2000. The following is a summary of the strategies suggested under the major subject areas as compiled by the International Women's Tribune Center, an organization based in New York which provides technical assistance and training, information services, and international networking for women's groups.

- *Equality*: Legislative changes in the economic, social, political, and cultural spheres; power to be shared on equal terms with men; effective institutions and procedures to be established to monitor the situation of women; elimination of stereotypes through formal and informal educational channels, the media, nongovernmental institutions, political party platforms and executive action; the sharing of domestic responsibilities by all members of the family and the equal integration of women's informal and invisible economic contributions into the mainstream of society.

- *Development*: Women to participate in development as intellectuals, policy makers, and planners; women to fully participate in political processes and to have an equal share of power in guiding development efforts and in benefiting from them; initial emphasis to be placed on employment, health, and education; grass roots participatory processes and planning approaches to be instituted using local talent, expertise, and resources; mainstream programs and projects that are not transitory women's projects to be formulated and implemented. The development section of the document is divided into specific action areas: employment, health, education, food and agriculture, industry, trade, commercial services, science and technology, communications, housing, transport, energy, environment, and social services.

- *Peace*: Governments, the U.N. system, nongovernmental organizations, relevant institutions and individuals to strengthen women's participation in peace activities; women's role in independence movements to be commended and used as a basis for their full participation in the reconstruction of their countries, and in the creation of new, humane, and just social and political systems; the development and testing of nuclear weapons and the arms race as a whole to be stopped; peace education to be established for all members of society, and intensive efforts made to eliminate incitement to prejudice, hatred, bigotry, discrimination, injustice, public and domestic violence, war, and abuse of power in whatever form they appear; legal measures to be formulated to prevent violence and to assist women victims; national machinery to be established to deal with the question of violence against women within the family and society.[14]

The goals of the strategies for the year 2000 are to make the concerns of women, which have been in the background for so long, a part of national and international policy.

A forum on women, the law, and development was also held in Nairobi under the sponsorship of OEF International. While its main thrust was to serve the needs of third-world women, the recommendations affect all women in need of legal information and representation. As the report indicates, the nature of law in a given society is inextricably linked to the character of the state. Any understanding of law must be supplemented by political and economic analysis. Justice is in fact at the core of equality, peace, and development. Law can be changed to serve the cause of justice: if women unite to exercise and consolidate political power, the law will be forced to become more just.

And so we have come full circle in this book—back to the legal process and its relation to justice.

The feminist movement in the United States is but one example of women organizing to establish a new social order. In the past 15 years, American women have experienced a transformation in their lives and in their sense of the possibilities for themselves. In the next 15 years these gains can be consolidated and expanded to become part of national public and international policy.

As Ethel Klein, the author of *Gender Politics*, writes:

> The feminist movement is not likely to disappear in the course of the next decades. . . . Women have found a political voice. They have a new consciousness of their role as women and a new confidence in themselves as citizens. Consequently, gender politics will be a dominant theme in the formulation of public policy as we approach the twenty-first century and consider what kind of brave new world we want.[15]

# Part ②

# STATE-BY-STATE GUIDE

## HOW TO USE THIS GUIDE

The remaining part of this book is a compilation and summary of state laws affecting women. The guide is organized alphabetically by state. Within each state, the laws are organized according to four broad categories, corresponding to those in Part 1, Chapters 2 to 5: home and family, education, employment, and community life. Within each category the laws are further broken down. For example, under the main heading "Home and Family," you will find the subheadings "Marriage," "Dissolution of Marriage," "Domestic Violence," "Inheritance Rights," "Reproductive Rights," and "Unmarried Couples." These categories are further subdivided; for example, "Dissolution of Marriage" includes the subheads "Annulment," "Legal Separation," and "Divorce." Matters pertaining to state divorce laws—for example, residency requirements, grounds for divorce, and child custody—are discussed under the section on divorce.

At the back of the book are a collection of appendixes which list various factors that the states may take into account in deciding individual cases. They are:

- Appendix A: Divorce or Annulment
- Appendix B: Child Custody
- Appendix C: Joint or Shared Custody
- Appendix D: Child Support
- Appendix E: Spousal Support/Alimony
- Appendix F: Property Distribution

The appendixes should be used and read jointly with the state summaries.

For example, if you are a resident of Missouri and you are interested in finding out whether Missouri law permits spousal support awards and, if so, what factors the courts consider in deciding on such awards, you would first locate Missouri alphabetically in this guide. You would then look for the heading "Dissolution of Marriage"; under that, you would find the subheading "Divorce" and then "Spousal Support/Alimony." The summary under this last section states that in Missouri alimony can be awarded to either spouse; the factors that are considered in awarding alimony are listed in Appendix E.

Each state law summary also includes a reference to the statutory citation for the particular law. In the example just given, you would see that the statutory section of Missouri law governing spousal support is section 452.355 of Vernon's Annotated Missouri Statutes. The symbol § means "section." If you wish to look up the statutory section yourself, you should go to a local law library and ask the librarian to assist you.

In some of the summaries, you may also find a reference to a particular case addressing the question you are looking up. For example, again using Missouri, if you wanted to know whether Missouri permits women to sue their husbands under *civil law* for rape, you would find, in turning to that section of the guide, that Missouri does *not* permit such lawsuits and that the authority for this is the case of *Huff v. LaSieur*, 571 S.W.2d 654 (Mo. App. 1978). This case may be found in volume number 571 of West's Southwest 2d. Reporter at page 654. The case was decided in 1978 by the Missouri Court of Appeals. Again, check with your local law librarian for assistance in finding these case references. Also, review Chapter 1, "The Legal Process," which contains further discussion about how to read and find case citations.

For the most part, the following summaries concern only state statutes. They do not generally address additional legal rights which may arise from federal statutes, federal and state judicial decisions, federal and state administrative regulations, municipal ordinances, and other sources.

Remember, this guide is only a *starting point* for learning about your legal rights. Never rely exclusively on this guide for what the law is in your state; consult with a lawyer, or ask your local law librarian to help you find the statutory and case materials yourself. No guide of this nature can ever be completely up to date, since state (as well as federal) laws are always subject to change.

# ALABAMA

## Home and Family

## MARRIAGE

**AGE OF CONSENT:** A person 18 years of age or older may consent to marry. (§ 30-1-4)*

**CONSENT REQUIREMENT:** A person under 18 years of age who has not been previously married is required to have the written or oral consent of the parents or guardian. A $200 bond, payable to the state of Alabama, with the condition that it will be void if the marriage is not illegal, is also required. (§ 30-1-5)

**LICENSE REQUIREMENT:** A valid license issued by the judges of the several counties is required to solemnize the marriage. The license is valid for 30 days from the date of issuance. (§ 30-1-9)

**PROHIBITED MARRIAGES:** Marriage is prohibited between individuals related either legitimately or illegitimately by blood or adoption; between a stepchild and stepparent, while the marriage creating the relationship exists; or between an aunt, nephew, or niece of the whole or half blood. Incest is a Class C felony. (§ 13A-13-3)

## DISSOLUTION OF MARRIAGE

**ANNULMENT:** A marriage may be annulled if it is incestuous or if one of the parties to the marriage is under the age of 14 years. (§§ 30-1-3, -4)

  *Residency Requirement:* There is no relevant statutory provision.

**LEGAL SEPARATION:** The judge may grant a judgment of divorce from bed and board for cruelty by either party or for any cause which would justify a divorce if the party applying desires only a divorce from bed and board. (§ 30-2-30)

  *Residency Requirement:* There is no relevant statutory provision.

**DIVORCE**

  *Residency Requirement:* When one of the parties to the divorce is a nonresident, the party filing the complaint must have been a resident for 6 months before filing. (§ 30-2-5)

  *Grounds for Divorce:* Appendix A, factors 1, 2, 4, 6 (for 2 years, sentence 7 years or longer), 7, 8, 9 (5 years), 10, 11, 28 (1 year), 31 (on wife's petition, no support, 2 years), and 32, are grounds for divorce. (§§ 30-2-1 to -2)

  *Conciliation Requirement:* There is no relevant statutory provision.

  *Property Distribution:* There is no statutory provision for the division of property. Under case law, the division of property is left to the discretion of the trial court. The trial court may divide jointly owned real or personal property acquired during the marriage but has no authority to award the wife's separate property regardless of whether she acquired such property before or after the marriage. [*Foster v. Foster*, 365 So. 2d 1227 (Ala. Civ. App. 1978)] The division of property need not be equal; it must only be "equitable" according to the circumstances of the case. [*Beale v. Beale*, 371 So. 2d 931 (Ala. Civ. App. 1979)]

*Unless otherwise specified, all citation references are to the Code of Alabama (1975).

*Child Custody:* Upon granting a divorce, the court may award custody of the children to either parent, as may seem right and proper. Appendix B, factors 1 and 2 will be considered. But in cases of abandonment of the husband by the wife, the husband shall have the custody of the children after they are 7 years of age, if he is suitable. (§ 30-3-1) Joint custody may be awarded. [*Stephens v. Stephens*, 255 So. 2d 338 (Ala. Civ. App. 1971); *Simmons v. Simmons*, 422 So. 2d 799 (Ala. Civ. App. 1982)]

*Child Support:* Upon granting a divorce, the court may award child support. (§ 30-31-1) The primary responsibility for the support of minor children rests on the father. [*Percer v. Percer*, 370 So. 2d 308 (Ala. Civ. App.), *cert. denied*, 370 So. 2d 311 (Ala. 1979)] If he is unable, the mother can be compelled to contribute. [*Bd. of Trustees v. Caldwell*, 400 So. 2d 402 (Ala. 1981)]

*Spousal Support/Alimony:* The judge, at his discretion, may award an allowance to either spouse out of the estate of the other, excepting any property acquired before the marriage or by inheritance or gift, unless the judge finds that such property or income produced by such property has been regularly used for the common benefit of the parties during the marriage. Misconduct of either spouse may be considered. Alimony may be terminated if the recipient is "living openly or cohabitating with a member of the opposite sex." (§§ 30-2-51, -52, -55)

*Enforcement of Support Orders:* A court may at its discretion, upon the filing of a petition either by the person owed support, by the district attorney, or by a representative of the Department of Pensions and Security, and upon a finding that previously owed support payments are delinquent, issue an order directing an employer to withhold and pay over to the clerk of the court, out of income due or to become due at each pay period, an amount the court finds necessary. The court may at its discretion award attorney fees. (§§ 30-2-54, -3-60 *et seq.*) In addition, a criminal action may be brought against the person owing the duty of support. Failure to support is a Class A misdemeanor. (§§ 13A-13-4 to -5) In the case of application for public assistance on behalf of a needy child, the Department of Pensions and Security is empowered to bring an action to collect support owed. (§§ 38-10-4 *et seq.*) See also the Uniform Reciprocal Enforcement of Support Act, §§ 30-4-80 *et seq.*

*Spouse's Name:* An ex-wife may be enjoined from the use of the given name or initials of the ex-husband. (§ 30-2-11)

*Divorce by Affidavit or Summary Judgment:* There is no relevant statutory provision.

*Displaced Homemaker Laws:* The chancellor of postsecondary education is authorized to establish multipurpose programs at 2-year colleges to provide the necessary training, counseling, and services to enable displaced homemakers to experience economic security vital to productive lives. (§§ 16-60-240, *et seq.*)

# DOMESTIC VIOLENCE

**STATUTORY PROVISION:** The Protection from Abuse Act prohibits any person 19 years of age or older, or otherwise emancipated, from attempting to cause or intentionally, knowingly, or recklessly causing physical injury with or without a deadly weapon; placing by physical menace another in fear of imminent serious physical injury; or abusing children. (§§ 30-5-1 to -2)

**WHO IS PROTECTED?** Under the act, spouses, persons living in common-law marriage relationships, parents and children, or other persons related by blood or marriage are protected. (§ 30-5-2)

**RELIEF AVAILABLE:** Upon the filing of the petition, the court may grant a protection order which may include ordering the abuser to refrain from abuse; granting possession of the residence or household to the exclusion of the abuser, or allowing the abuser to provide suitable, alternative housing; or awarding temporary custody and/or establishing temporary visitation rights and reasonable support. Any protection order shall be for a period of time not to exceed 1 year. (§§ 30-5-5, -7)

**MARITAL RAPE:** Husbands and cohabitants cannot be charged with rape. [§ 13A-6-60(4)]

**CIVIL LAWSUIT FOR RAPE OR ASSAULT:** There is no case directly on point. However, in *Johnson v. Johnson*, 201 Ala. 41 (1917), the court stated that a wife could not recover damages from her husband for assault.

**CHILD ABUSE:** The Alabama Child Abuse Act prohibits any "responsible person" (defined as a child's natural parent, stepparent, adoptive parent, legal guardian or custodian, or any other person who has permanent or temporary custody or responsibility for the supervision of a child) from torturing, willfully abusing, cruelly beating, or otherwise willfully maltreating any child under 18 years of age. Upon conviction, any individual violating the act may be punished by imprisonment for no less than 1 year nor more than 10 years. (§§ 26-15-1 to -4)

*Notification Requirement:* All health care workers, school teachers and officials, social workers, day care workers, law enforcement officials, or any other person called upon to render aid or medical assistance to any child is required to report any suspected case of abuse to the Department of Pensions and Security. (§§ 26-14-2 *et seq.*)

# INHERITANCE RIGHTS

**FAILURE TO MAKE A WILL:** If there are no other heirs, the surviving spouse is entitled to the entire estate; if the decedent is survived by parent(s) and there are no other heirs, the surviving spouse is entitled to $100,000 in value plus one-half of the balance of the estate; if the decedent is survived by one or more descendants who are not also the surviving spouse's descendants, the surviving spouse is entitled to one-half of the estate; if there are descendants who are also the surviving spouse's descendants, the surviving spouse is entitled to $50,000 in value plus one-half of the balance of the estate. If the estate is located in two or more states, the surviving spouse's share shall not exceed in the aggregate the allowable amounts. (§ 43-8-41)

**FAILURE TO PROVIDE BY WILL:** If the testator fails to provide by will for the surviving spouse who married the testator after the execution of the will, the omitted spouse shall receive the same share of the estate he or she would have received if there had been no will, *unless* it appears from the will that the omission was intentional or unless the testator provided for the spouse by transfer outside the will. (§ 43-8-90)

**CHILDREN BORN OUT OF WEDLOCK:** A child born out of wedlock may inherit if paternity is established before the death of the father or thereafter by clear and convincing proof. (§ 43-8-48)

**HOMESTEAD, PERSONAL, AND FAMILY ALLOWANCES:** The surviving spouse is entitled to a homestead allowance of $6000 in addition to any share passing to the surviving spouse by will. If there is no surviving spouse, each minor child and each dependent child is entitled to the allowance divided by the number of minor and dependent children. In addition, the surviving spouse is entitled to receive property of a value not exceeding $3500 in household furniture, automobiles, furnishings, appliances, and personal effects. In addition, the surviving spouse and minor children whom the decedent was required to support are entitled to a reasonable allowance out of the estate during the period of administration, which may not continue for longer than 1 year if the estate is inadequate. (§§ 43-8-110 to -112)

**OPTION TO DISREGARD THE WILL:** The surviving spouse has a right to take an elective share of the estate. A petition to take an elective share must be made within 6 months after the date of the decedent's will. The elective share shall be all of the estate reduced by the value of the surviving spouse's separate estate, or it shall be one-third of the estate of the deceased, whichever is less. If the surviving spouse lives outside Alabama, the right to take an elective share is governed by the law of the decedent's domicile at death. (§ 43-8-70)

# REPRODUCTIVE RIGHTS
## Abortion
*Statutory Provisions:* The existing statute which prohibits abortions unless necessary to preserve the woman's life or health (§ 13A-13-7) is unconstitutional pursuant to the U.S. Supreme Court's decisions in *Roe v. Wade*, 410 U.S. 113 (1973) and *City of Akron v. Akron Center for Reproductive Health*. 462 U.S. 416 (1983).

**BIRTH CONTROL:** There is no relevant statutory provision.

**STERILIZATION:** There is no relevant statutory provision.

# UNMARRIED COUPLES
**COMMON-LAW MARRIAGE:** Although there is no relevant statutory provision, the court has held that common-law marriages are valid. Three elements are necessary in order for a common-law marriage to constitute a valid marriage under the law: capacity to enter into marriage, present agreement or consent to be husband and wife, and consummation. See *Piel v. Brown*, 361 So. 2d (Ala. 1978).

**COHABITAL RELATIONSHIPS:** In *Albae v. Harvin*, 30 So. 2d 459 (Ala. 1947), the court affirmed a decree establishing a resulting trust of two parcels of land in favor of the complainant, and held that the complainant was entitled in equity to have the title to the property vested in her, where the testimony showed that although title to the property was taken in the name of a man with whom the complainant was living, the complainant paid the entire purchase price of the property with her own money and obligated herself to pay the down payment and all future installments.

## CHILDREN
*Custody:* The order of the court establishing a child's paternity may make appropriate provisions for the custody of the child. (§ 26-17-14)
*Legitimation Proceedings:* A child born out of wedlock may be legitimated by the marriage of the parents and recognition of the child by the father. In addition, the father of the child may legitimate the child and render the child capable of inheriting the *father's estate* as if born in wedlock by filing a notice of declaration of legitimation in writing, attested by two witnesses. (§§ 26-11-1 *et seq.*)
*Paternity Proceedings:* An action to determine the existence of the father and child relationship may be brought in juvenile court by the child, the mother, or a personal representative of the child; by the public authority chargeable by law with

support of the child; by the personal representative or a parent of the mother if the mother has died; by a man alleged or alleging to be the father; or by the personal representative or a parent of the alleged father. (§§ 12-15-31, 26-17-10) The action may be brought within 5 years of the child's birth. (§ 26-17-6)

*Obligations of the Putative Father:* Once paternity has been established, the court shall determine support payments. In determining the amount for support, the court shall consider the needs of the child and the ability of the parents to support. The court may direct the father to pay the reasonable expenses of the mother's pregnancy and confinement. (§ 26-17-15)

# Education

## STATUTORY PROVISION

There is no relevant statutory provision. However, it should be noted that if federal funds are involved, federal law, Title IX of the Education Amendments of 1972, Pub. L. No. 92-318, 20 U.S.C. §§ 1681–1686, may apply.

# Employment

## EQUAL PAY LAWS

There is no relevant statutory provision. However, it should be noted that federal law, the Equal Pay Act of 1963, 29 U.S.C. § 201 *et seq.*, may apply.

## FAIR EMPLOYMENT LAWS

There is no relevant statutory provision. However, an employer with more than fifteen employees is prohibited from discriminating on the basis of sex by federal law, Title VII of the Civil Rights Act of 1964, 42 U.S.C. §§ 2000e *et seq*.

## GOVERNMENT CONTRACTORS AND SUBCONTRACTORS

There is no relevant statutory provision. However, it should be noted that if federal funds are involved, federal law, Exec. Order No. 11246, 3 C.F.R. 339, *reprinted in* 42 U.S.C. § 60-1-2, may apply.

## STATE EMPLOYEE LAWS

There is no relevant statutory provision.

## VETERAN'S PREFERENCE

All veterans who have been honorably discharged from the military shall have five points added to entrance examination scores for civil service. All disabled veterans shall have ten points added. Veterans also have preference in retention. (§ 36-26-15)

# Community Life

## CREDIT

There is no relevant statutory provision. However, it should be noted that federal law, the Equal Credit Opportunity Act of 1977, 12 C.F.R. § 202, may apply.

## HOUSING

There is no relevant statutory provision.

## INSURANCE

Unfair discrimination in life, annuity, and disability insurance is prohibited. No person shall make or permit unfair discrimination between individuals of the same class and equal expectation of life in rates charged for any contract of life insurance or life annuity, or in the dividends or other benefits payable, or in any other terms and conditions of such contract. This includes unfair discrimination between the amount of premium, policy fees, or rates charged for any contract of disability insurance, or in the benefits payable thereunder, or in any of the terms and conditions of such contract or in any other manner whatever. (§ 27-12-11)

**ENFORCEMENT:** The Commissioner of Insurance is responsible for the enforcement of this provision. The commissioner is empowered to conduct examinations and investigations to determine whether any person has violated the provision. (§ 27-2-7)

## PUBLIC ACCOMMODATIONS

There is no relevant statutory provision.

# ALASKA

## Home and Family

## MARRIAGE

**AGE OF CONSENT:** A person 18 years of age or older may consent to marry. (§ 25.05.011)*

**CONSENT REQUIREMENT:** A person 16 years of age will be issued a marriage license with parental consent. A superior judge may grant permission for a person under 14 years of age to marry with or without parental consent. (§ 25.05.171)

**LICENSE REQUIREMENT:** One of the parties to a prospective marriage must file with the licensing office an application for a license at least 3 days before the date of issuance. (§§ 25.05.171, .091) Before a license is issued, each party must file a premarital certificate from a licensed physician. (§ 25.05.101) The license issued is valid for 3 months from the date of issuance. (§ 25.05.121)

**PROHIBITED MARRIAGES:** Marriage is prohibited if either party has a husband or a wife living, or if the parties are more closely related to each other than the fourth degree of consanguinity, whether of the whole blood or half blood, computed according to the rules of the civil law. (§ 25.05.021)

## DISSOLUTION OF MARRIAGE

**ANNULMENT:** Appendix A, factors 14, 33, 34, and 35, are grounds for annulment. (§ 25.24.030) Children born of an annuled marriage are legitimate. (§§ 25.05.051, .061)

*Residency Requirement:* If the party seeking the annulment is a resident of the state, the action may be brought at any time. If the marriage was not solemnized in the state and the action is brought to annul a marriage with a resident of the state, the action can be brought at any time. A member of the armed forces must have resided in the state for 1 year to satisfy the residency requirement. (§§ 25.24.080, .090, .100)

**LEGAL SEPARATION:** There is no relevant statutory provision.

**DIVORCE**

*Residency Requirement:* Although the person filing for divorce must be a resident, no time limit requirement is specified. (§ 25.24.080)

*Grounds for Divorce:* Appendix A, factors 1, 4, 8, 9, 14, 15, 16 (1 year), 17, 18, and 25, are grounds for divorce. (§ 25.24.050)

*Conciliation Requirement:* Either party in a divorce action may request mediation. When no request is made, the court may at any time order the parties to submit to mediation if it determines that mediation may result in a more satisfactory settlement between the parties. (§ 25.24.060)

*Property Distribution:* Joint or separate property acquired during the marriage shall be divided in a "just" manner without regard to fault. If equity requires, the court may divide real or personal property acquired before the marriage. [§ 25.24.160(4)(6)]

*Unless otherwise specified, all citation references are to the Alaska Statutes (1962).

*Child Custody:* The court will determine custody with the best interests of the child in mind. Appendix B, factors 3, 4, 6, 7, 8, and 9, will be considered. Neither parent is entitled to preference. (§ 25.24.150) Shared custody may be awarded if the court determines it is in the child's best interest. In determining whether to award shared custody, the court shall consider the child's needs and education, including any special needs that may be better met by one parent; any findings of a neutral mediator; and the optimal time for the child to be with each parent. The court shall also consider Appendix C, factors 4, 5, 8, 10 (any history of violence), 13, 14 (stability), and 15. (§ 25.20.090)

*Child Support:* Either or both parents may be required to make child support payments. [§ 25.24.160(2)] The court shall consider the need for support, the ability of both parents to pay, the extent to which the parents supported the child before divorce, and the ability of the parents to pay after separation and divorce. (§ 47.23.060)

*Spousal Support/Alimony:* The court may award an amount of money for maintenance to either party, in gross or in installments, as may be "just" and necessary, without regard to fault. [§ 25.24.160(3)]

*Enforcement of Support Orders:* Where a parent or parents are ordered to pay child support and fail to do so, the court may order either parent or both to assign a portion of their salary or wages to pay for the support, maintenance, nurture, and education of minor children. The court may require either or both parties to arrange with their employer for an automatic payroll deduction. If the employer agrees, the installment is to be forwarded by the employer to the clerk of the superior court for the benefit of the spouse or minor children to whom a duty of support is owed. A defaulting party may be found in contempt of court for failure to obey a support order and imprisoned until the support order is obeyed. [§§ 9.50.010(5), 9.50.050, 25.24.160] See also the Uniform Reciprocal Enforcement of Support Act, §§ 25.25.010 *et seq.*

*Spouse's Name:* The court may provide in the judgment for divorce to change the name of either party. [§ 25.24.160(7)]

*Divorce by Affidavit or Summary Judgment:* There is no relevant statutory provision.

*Displaced Homemaker Laws:* A displaced homemaker is defined as a person who has worked as a homemaker; who has provided unsalaried services for the family for a period of at least 3 years; who faces a significant reduction in family income because of divorce, death, separation, desertion, or disability; and who has encountered difficulties finding employment. The state has established multipurpose service centers to assist displaced homemakers. (§§ 47.90.010 to .070)

# DOMESTIC VIOLENCE

**STATUTORY PROVISION:** Under the act, domestic violence is defined as a crime, including homicide, assault and reckless endangerment, kidnapping and custodial interference, sexual offenses, and robbery, extortion, and coercion. (§§ 25.35.060)

**WHO IS PROTECTED?** Spouses, ex spouses, persons who live together, or persons who formerly lived together are protected. (§ 25.35.060)

**RELIEF AVAILABLE:** A victim of domestic violence may ask the court for injunctive relief restraining the infliction of further violence. An order of protection may be issued. The court may award custody of minor children and may order the abuser to leave the home, stop communicating directly or indirectly with the victim, pay support, or enter into counseling. The order may be in effect for a period not to exceed 90 days. This relief does not include any civil or criminal remedies available to the victim. (§§ 25.35.010, .020)

**MARITAL RAPE:** A wife may not charge her husband with rape unless they are living apart or the rape results in physical injury. (§ 11.41.445)

**CIVIL LAWSUIT FOR RAPE OR ASSAULT:** There is no case directly relating to rape. However, in *Drickensen v Drickensen*, 546 P. 2d 162 (Alaska 1976), the court held that family members may bring tort actions against other family members.

**CHILD ABUSE:** The Child Protection Act protects children whose health may be adversely affected through the infliction, by other than accidental means, of harm through physical abuse or neglect or sexual abuse or sexual exploitation. (§ 47.17.010)
    *Notification Requirement:* Persons who in their professional capacities have reason to believe that a child has suffered harm as a result of abuse or neglect are required to immediately report the same to the Department of Social Service or to a peace officer. A person who is required to report a case of child abuse and who willingly or knowingly fails to report it is guilty of a Class B misdemeanor. (§§ 47.17.020, .068)

# INHERITANCE RIGHTS

**FAILURE TO MAKE A WILL:** If there are no other heirs, the surviving spouse is entitled to the entire estate. If the decedent is survived by parent(s) or descendants who are also the surviving spouse's descendants, the surviving spouse is entitled to $50,000 and one-half of the estate. If the decedent is survived by one or more descendants who are not also the surviving spouse's descendants, the surviving spouse is entitled to one-half of the estate. (§ 13.11.010)

**FAILURE TO PROVIDE BY WILL:** If the testator fails to provide by will for the surviving spouse who married the testator after the execution of the will, the omitted spouse shall receive the same share he or she would have received if the spouse died without a will, *unless* the omission was intentional or the testator provided for the spouse outside the will and the intentions were that the provision be in place of a will provision. (§§ 13.11.110)

**CHILDREN BORN OUT OF WEDLOCK:** A child born out of wedlock may inherit through the father if the child has been legitimated. (§ 25.20.050)

**HOMESTEAD, PERSONAL, AND FAMILY ALLOWANCES:** A surviving spouse is entitled to a homestead allowance of $12,000; to a personal property allowance not exceeding $3500 in excess of any security therein in household furniture, automobiles, furnishings, appliances, and personal effects; or if there is not $3500 worth of personal property, then to other assets of the estate to the extent necessary to make up the $3500 value. (§§ 13.11.125, 13.11.130) In addition, the surviving spouse and minor children and children who were in fact being supported by the decedent are entitled to a reasonable allowance during the period of administration, which allowance may not continue for longer than 1 year if the estate is inadequate. (§ 13.11.135)

**OPTION TO DISREGARD THE WILL:** The surviving spouse may elect to take one-third of the "augmented estate" (the estate reduced by various stated expenses including allowance) within 6 months after the publication of notice to auditors for filing claims which arose before the death of the decedent, if the decedent lived in Alaska. If the decedent did not live in Alaska, the right of the spouse to elect a share of the property located in Alaska is governed by the laws of the state the decedent resided in. If the spouse does elect to take a statutory share, the spouse need not renounce the share he or she would have received under the will or if the decedent did not make a will. (§§ 13.11.070 to .095)

# REPRODUCTIVE RIGHTS
## ABORTION

*Statutory Provisions:* Abortions must be performed by a licensed physician and in a hospital or other facility approved for the purpose by the Department of Health and Welfare or in a hospital operated by the federal government or a federal agency. The requirement that abortions be performed in licensed facilities, even during the first trimester, is unconstitutional under *Doe v. Bolton*, 410 U.S. 179 (1973). Neither a hospital nor an individual may be required to perform or participate in an abortion. (§ 18.16.010)

*Residency Requirement:* The woman must be domiciled or physically present in Alaska for 30 days prior to the abortion. This requirement is unconstitutional under *Doe v. Bolton*, 410 U.S. 179 (1973).

*Consent Requirement:* An unmarried minor under 18 must have the consent of a parent or guardian before she can obtain an abortion. (§ 18.16.010) However, the statute is unconstitutional under *Planned Parenthood of Central Missouri v. Danforth*. 428 U.S. 52 (1976), unless the minor is provided with alternative means of securing the needed authorizations for an abortion. [*Belloti v. Baird*, 428 U.S. 132 (1976)]

**BIRTH CONTROL:** There is no relevant statutory provision.

**STERILIZATION:** There is no relevant statutory provision.

# UNMARRIED COUPLES

**COMMON-LAW MARRIAGE:** A common-law marriage is not valid in Alaska. See *Edwards v. Franke*, 364 P.2d 60 (Alaska 1961).

**COHABITAL RELATIONSHIPS:** In general, the courts have refused to treat cohabiting couples as if they were married upon termination of the relationship. See *Sugg. v. Morris*, 392 P.2d 313 (Alaska 1964); *Hill v. Ames*, 606 P.2d 388 (Alaska 1980). But see *Levar v. Elkins*, 604 P.2d 602 (Alaska 1980), where the court allowed a woman who had lived with a man for 20 years to recover $15,000 in return for services rendered as a housewife and caretaker of his children on the basis of his promise to provide for her for the rest of her life.

## CHILDREN

*Custody:* Either parent may be granted custody of a child born out of wedlock. (§ 25.20.060)

*Legitimation Proceedings:* A child born out of wedlock is legitimated if the father subsequently married the mother; or acknowledged in writing the paternity of the child; or is adjudged to be the father by a superior court, upon sufficient evidence which may include the alleged father's conduct and bearing toward the child, either by word or by act. (§ 25.20.050)

*Paternity Proceedings:* An action to determine paternity may be brought at any time by the Child Support Enforcement Agency on behalf of minor children, the mother, or the legal custodian. (§ 47.23.040)

*Obligations of the Putative Father:* The court may order either or both parents to pay the amount necessary for the support, maintenance, nurture, and education of the child. (§ 47.23.060)

# Education

## STATUTORY PROVISION

Discrimination on the basis of sex is prohibited in any education program or activity receiving federal or state funds. (§ 14.18.101)

## AREAS COVERED

The state law prohibits discrimination on the basis of sex in employment; in counseling and guidance programs; in recreation and athletic activities; in course offerings; in textbooks and instructional materials; and in scholarships, loans, and grants. The provision specifically prohibits discrimination on the basis of sex by the state university. (§§ 14.18.010 to .060, 14.43.135, 14.43.315)

**ENFORCEMENT:** The Board of Education is required to establish affirmative action programs to be implemented by all school districts. If the board finds the measures taken under the programs are ineffective, after a finding of noncompliance, it is required to withhold state funds. (§§ 14.18.070, .090) In addition, a victim of discrimination on the basis of sex may file a complaint with the Board of Education. A victim of discrimination in postsecondary education may also bring suit in the superior court for civil damages. (§ 14.18.100)

# Employment

## EQUAL PAY LAWS

It is unlawful for an employer to discriminate between the sexes in the payment of wages or to employ a female in an occupation at a salary or wage rate less than that paid to a male employee for work of comparable character or for work in the same operation, business, or locality. [§ 18.80.220(5)]

## FAIR EMPLOYMENT LAWS

Employers are prohibited from refusing employment or from discriminating in compensation, terms, conditions, or privileges of employment on the basis of sex, marital status, pregnancy, or parenthood. Labor organizations are prohibited from excluding or expelling from membership or discriminating in any way against their members or an employer or employee on the basis of sex, marital status, parenthood, or pregnancy. (§§ 18.80.200, .220)

# GOVERNMENT CONTRACTORS AND SUBCONTRACTORS

Contracts must contain provisions barring discrimination or differential treatment on the basis of sex. (Governor's Code of Fair Practices by State Agencies, art. II, issued August 11, 1967)

# STATE EMPLOYEE LAWS

Discrimination in recruitment, appointment, assignment, and promotion of state employees is prohibited. (Governor's Code of Fair Practices by State Agencies, art. I, issued August 11, 1967)

**ENFORCEMENT:** The Alaska Commission on Human Rights is responsible for the enforcement of all provisions prohibiting discrimination in employment. An individual who has been the victim of discrimination may file a complaint with the commission. (§ 18.80.100) The commission shall informally investigate, and if it finds that discrimination has occurred, it shall immediately try to eliminate the discrimination by conference, conciliation, and persuasion. (§ 80.80.110)

# VETERAN'S PREFERENCE

Five points are to be added to the passing scores of veterans applying for public employment under the merit system examination; ten points are to be added for disabled veterans.

# Community Life

# CREDIT

Discrimination in credit and financing practices on the basis of sex, pregnancy, parenthood, or marital status is prohibited. (§§ 18.80.200, .210, .250)

**ENFORCEMENT:** A person who has been discriminated against in credit, housing or public accommodations on account of sex or marital status may file a complaint with the Alaska Commission on Human Rights. (§ 18.80.100) The commission shall informally investigate, and if it finds that discrimination has occurred, it shall immediately try to eliminate the discrimination by conference, conciliation, and persuasion (§ 18.80.110)

# HOUSING

Discrimination in the sale, lease, or rental of property on the basis of sex, pregnancy, parenthood, or marital status is prohibited. (§ § 18.80.200, .210, .240)

**ENFORCEMENT:** See "Credit."

# INSURANCE

Unfair discrimination between individuals of the same class and equal life expectation in the rates charged for life insurance or annuity, or in the dividends or other benefits payable thereon, or in any other terms or conditions of the contract is prohibited. This includes both unfair discrimination between individuals of the same class and of essentially the same hazard in the amount of premium and policy fees charged for disability insurance and unfair discrimination for property, casualty, or transportation insurance and for the services covered under a group disability policy. (§ 21.36.090)

**ENFORCEMENT:** The director of insurance, on his or her own motion or on complaint of a person, may conduct an investigation to determine whether a prohibited discriminatory practice has occurred. If there are grounds to believe such a practice has actually occurred, the director may initiate the appropriate proceedings to resolve the issue. (§ 21.36.320)

# PUBLIC ACCOMMODATIONS

It is unlawful for the owner, lessee, manager, agent, or employee of a public accommodation to discriminate on the basis of sex, pregnancy, parenthood, or marital status in offering services. (§§ 18.80.200. .230)

**ENFORCEMENT:** See "Credit."

# ARIZONA

## Home and Family

## MARRIAGE

**AGE OF CONSENT:** A person 18 years of age or older may consent to marry. (§ 25-102)*

**CONSENT REQUIREMENT:** Persons under 18 may not marry without the consent of a parent or guardian *and* the approval of a superior court judge in the state. (§ 25-102)

**LICENSE REQUIREMENT:** In order to obtain a license to marry, the parties must file with the clerk of the superior court an oath declaring their names and ages, their places of residence, and their relationship. (§ 25-101)

**PROHIBITED MARRIAGES:** Marriages between parents and children, including grandparents and grandchildren of every degree; between brothers and sisters of the half or the whole blood; between uncles and nieces, between aunts and nephews; and between first cousins are prohibited and void. (§ 25-101)

## DISSOLUTION OF MARRIAGE

**ANNULMENT:** A marriage may be annulled by a superior court judge on any ground constituting an impediment which renders the marriage void. The court to the extent that it has jurisdiction to do so shall establish the rights and obligations of the parties with respect to children in the same manner as in a divorce. (§§ 25-301, 26-302) See "Divorce."

*Residency Requirement:* See "Divorce."

**LEGAL SEPARATION:** Irretrievable breakdown is the only grounds for legal separation. [§ 25-313A(3)]

*Residency Requirement:* In order to obtain a decree of legal separation, one of the parties must have been domiciled in the state, or if in the armed forces, stationed in the state, at the time the action is commenced. [§ 25-313A(1)]

### DIVORCE

*Residency Requirement:* One of the parties to the divorce action must have been domiciled, or if in the military, been present, in the state for 90 days before the commencement of the action. (§ 25-312)

*Grounds for Divorce:* Irretrievable breakdown is the only ground for divorce. [§ 25-312(3)]

*Conciliation Requirement:* Either party to an annulment, legal separation or divorce may petition the court for purposes of preserving the marriage by effecting a conciliation between the parties or for amicable settlement of the controversy so as to avoid further litigation. (§ 25-381.09 *et seq.*)

*Property Distribution:* Marital property is distributed equitably regardless of marital misconduct; each spouse's sole and separate property is awarded to that spouse. (§ 25-318)

*Unless otherwise specified, all citation references are to the Arizona Revised Statutes Annotated (1956).

118

*Child Custody:* In awarding custody the court considers the best interests of the child and factors 5, 9, 10, 11, 12, 13, and 14, listed in Appendix B. (§ 25-332A) Although there is no applicable statute regarding joint or shared custody, the courts have awarded joint custody where they find it to be in the best interests of the child. See *In re Winn*, 63 P.2d 198 (Ariz. 1936); *Henning v. Henning*, 362 P.2d 124 (Ariz. 1961)

*Child Support:* Appendix D, factors 1, 3, 4, 5, 6, and 16, are considered. (§ 25-320A)

*Spousal Support/Alimony:* Appendix E, factors 1, 2, 3, 4, 5, 6, 7, 8, 10, 13, 14, 15, and 16, are considered. (§ 25-319)

*Enforcement of Support Orders:* The county attorney may represent any party seeking to establish or enforce a duty of child support. In addition, the person owed child support may petition the court to hold the person owing support in contempt of court. Any person convicted of contempt of court is guilty of a Class 3 misdemeanor, punishable by a jail sentence (§§ 12-863-01, -2456) If an individual is in arrears for an amount equal to at least 1 month of child support or alimony, the person or agency owed support may petition the court to order the person owing support to assign a portion of that person's periodic earnings to the person owed support. In addition, the court may order support payments be made to the clerk of the superior court for remittance to the person entitled to support. Any support order may also be enforced by execution, attachment, garnishment, levy, appointment of a receiver, provisional remedies, or any such other form of relief provided by law as an enforcement remedy for civil judgments. An affidavit regarding all payments due should be filed with the clerk of the superior court along with the order of support. In addition, a person owed alimony may also petition the court to hold the person owing support in contempt of court. (§§ 12-864, 25-323, -323.01) See also the Revised Uniform Reciprocal Enforcement of Support Act of 1968, §§ 12-1651 *et seq*.

*Spouse's Name:* Upon the wife's request, the court shall order that her former name be restored. (§ 25-325C)

*Divorce by Affidavit or Summary Judgment:* There is no relevant statutory provision.

*Displaced Homemaker Laws:* There is no relevant statutory provision.

# DOMESTIC VIOLENCE

**STATUTORY PROVISION:** The law prohibits recklessly endangering another person with a substantial risk of imminent death or physical injury; threatening or intimidating another by word or conduct; intentionally or recklessly causing physical assault and injury or aggravated assault; interfering with the custody of a minor child; unlawfully imprisoning, kidnapping, or restraining another person; recklessly defacing or damaging property of another; or engaging in disorderly conduct with the intent to disturb another. (§ 13-3601)

**WHO IS PROTECTED?** The statute protects spouses and ex-spouses and persons related to each other by consanguinity or affinity to the second degree. (§ 13-3601)

**RELIEF AVAILABLE:** A peace officer may, with or without a warrant, arrest a person if probable cause exists that domestic violence has been committed and the person arrested has committed the offense. Other relief available to the victim of domestic violence includes an order of protection, an injunction, emergency telephone numbers for the local police, agency, and telephone numbers for emergency services provided by the local community. (§§ 13-3601B; -3601D)

**MARITAL RAPE:** A woman may charge her husband with rape only if they are living apart. (§ 13-1401)

**CIVIL LAWSUIT FOR RAPE OR ASSAULT:** There are no cases directly on point. However, in *Huebner v. Deuchle*, 514 P.2d 460 (Ariz. 1974), the court held that civil suits between spouses for intentional torts are permitted only after the parties have been divorced.

**CHILD ABUSE:** Child abuse is defined as any impairment which imperils a child's health or welfare and includes bruising, bleeding, failure to thrive, malnutrition, burns, internal injuries; and physical injury which creates a reasonable risk of death or causes serious or permanent disfigurement or impairment of health or loss of the function of any body organ or limbs. (§ 13-3623)

> *Notification Requirement:* All health care professionals, school personnel, social workers, peace officers, parents or any persons having responsibility for the care or treatment of children who have reasonable grounds to believe that a minor is or has been the victim of injury, sexual molestation, death, or physical neglect which appears to have been inflicted by other than accidental means must report this information immediately to a peace officer or to the protective services of the state Department of Economic Security. Failure to report is a Class 2 misdemeanor. (§ 13-3620)

# INHERITANCE RIGHTS

**FAILURE TO MAKE A WILL:** A surviving spouse is entitled to the entire intestate estate, which consists of the decedent's separate property and the decedent's one-half share of the marital property if the decedent left no issue or if issues are also the surviving spouse's issues. However, if the deceased left one or more issues who are not also the surviving spouse's issues, then the surviving spouse is only entitled to one-half of the deceased spouse's separate property and to none of the deceased spouse's one-half share of the marital property. (§ 14-2102)

**FAILURE TO PROVIDE BY WILL:** If a testator fails to provide by will for his or her surviving spouse who married the testator after the execution of the will, the omitted spouse will receive the same share of the estate as he or she would have received if the decedent had left no will unless it appears from the will that the omission was intentional or that the testator made other provisions for the surviving spouse outside the will. (§ 14-2301)

**CHILDREN BORN OUT OF WEDLOCK:** There is no statute entitling illegitimate children to inherit from their father where the father died without making a will. However, where a state court had ordered the deceased father to contribute to his illegitimate child's support and the father was supporting the child at time of his death, this was sufficient to establish the child's paternity and the child's right to claim a share in the father's intestate estate. See *Trible v. Gordon*, 430 U.S. 762 (1977).

**HOMESTEAD, PERSONAL, AND FAMILY ALLOWANCES:** A surviving spouse of a decedent who was domiciled in the state is entitled to $6000 in lieu of any homestead exemption the decedent may have had during his or her lifetime plus furniture, cars, appliances, and personal effects up to $3500 in value. These exemptions are subtracted from any share passing by will to the surviving spouse unless the will provides otherwise. (§§ 14-2401, -2402) In addition, the surviving spouse and dependent children are entitled to reasonable support during the period of administration of the will. If the estate is inadequate to meet claims against it, support payments may not continue for more than a year. The family allowance has priority over all claims except expenses of administration and homestead exemption; the allowance is in addition to any share or benefit passing by intestate succession but it must be subtracted from any share passing by will unless the will provides otherwise. (§ 14-2403)

**OPTION TO DISREGARD THE WILL:** There is no relevant statutory provision.

# REPRODUCTIVE RIGHTS

## ABORTION

*Statutory Provisions:* Existing statutes prohibit abortion unless necessary to save a woman's life. (§§ 13-3603 *et seq*.) However, these provisions are unconstitutional under *Roe v. Wade*, 410 U.S. 113 (1973), *Doe v. Bolton*, 410 U.S. 179 (1973), and *Nelson v. Planned Parenthood Center of Tuscon*, 505 P.2d 580 (Ariz. Ct. App. 1973). Existing statute which prohibits advertising of abortion or contraceptive services is unconstitutional under *Bigelow v. Virginia*, 421 U.S. 809 (1975) and *Carey v. Population Services International*, 431 U.S. 678 (1977). Only abortions necessary to save the life of the woman may be performed at hospitals under the jurisdiction of the Board of Regents, *i.e.*, teaching hospitals. (§ 15-730) This statute was upheld as constitutional in *Roe v. Arizona Board of Regents*, 549 P.2d 150 (Ariz. Sup. Ct. 1976). A hospital is not required to perform abortions, and all persons have the right to refuse to participate in abortions on moral or religious grounds. (§ 36-2151) If an abortion is performed and the fetus is delivered alive, the attending doctor has a duty to use all available means to preserve the life of the fetus; violation of this duty is a felony. (§§ 36-2301, -2303)

*Consent Requirement:* There is no relevant statutory provision. However, before an unmarried or unemancipated minor can obtain an abortion, notification must be given to her parent or legal guardian at least 24 hours prior to the performance of the abortion; or, the parent or legal guardian must provide the attending physician with a written, signed statement acknowledging receipt of such notification. This requirement is waived if the parent or legal guardian cannot be contacted; if the minor seeking the abortion has obtained a judicial order allowing the abortion without parental notification; or if the continuation of the pregnancy poses an immediate threat and grave risk to the life of the minor and the attending physician so certifies in writing. (§ 36-2152)

*State Funding:* Public funds cannot be used for the payment of an abortion unless the abortion is necessary to save the life of the woman having the abortion. (§ 35-196.02)

**BIRTH CONTROL:** There is no relevant statutory provision.

**STERILIZATION:** There is no relevant statutory provision.

# UNMARRIED COUPLES

**COMMON-LAW MARRIAGE:** Common-law marriages are void. (§ 25-111) Although Arizona does not recognize common-law marriages, it will, however, accord to a common-law marriage entered into in another state, where such a marriage is valid, the same legal significance as if the marriage had been legally entered into in Arizona. [*Grant v. Superior Court in and for Pima County*, 555 P.2d 895 (Ariz. 1976)]

**COHABITAL RELATIONSHIPS:** In *Cook v. Cook*, 691 P.2d 664 (Ariz. 1984), the Arizona Supreme Court held that a "partnership agreement" by cohabitants to share property is enforceable. In *Lee v. Lee*, 12 F.L.R. 467 (February 11, 1986), the Arizona Supreme Court extended the *Cook* ruling to include implied contracts between unmarried cohabitants where homemaking services are the only contribution of one party. However, the court limited its ruling in *Lee* to property that is *jointly titled*.

## CHILDREN

*Custody:* There is no statutory provision relating to the custody of children born out of wedlock.

*Legitimation Proceedings:* A child born out of wedlock is legitimate as if born in lawful wedlock. (§ 8-601)

*Paternity Proceedings:* An action to determine the paternity of a child born out of wedlock may be brought by the county attorney in the name of the state or by the mother, guardian, or a best friend of the child. The court may order the mother, child, and putative father to undergo blood- and tissue-type tests. [§§ 12-846, -847(c)]

*Obligations of the Putative Father:* If the defendant admits that he is the child's father or if the court finds him to be the father, the court shall direct the amount which the father must pay for the past care and support of the child, for expenses incurred by the mother during her confinement, for future support of the child, and for attorney fees and costs. (§ 12-849)

# Education

## STATUTORY PROVISION

There is no relevant statutory provision However, it should be noted that if federal funds are involved, federal law, Title IX of the Education Amendments of 1972, Pub. L. No. 92-318, 20 U.S.C. §§ 1681–1686, may apply. In addition, if state funds are involved or if the state is involved in certain circumstances, then the state constitution protects individuals from sex discrimination. (Ariz. Const. art 11, § 6)

# Employment

## EQUAL PAY LAWS

It is unlawful for an employer to pay any employee a lower rate of salary than the rate paid to an employee of the opposite sex who is employed in the same establishment and producing the same quantity and quality of work. However, wage differentials are not unlawful if they are based on such factors as seniority, skill, difference in shift or time of day worked, or other good faith factors other than sex. (§ 23-341)

**ENFORCEMENT:** Any person who believes he or she has been discriminated against in wages on the basis of sex may file a complaint with the Industrial Commission of Arizona. The commission shall take all steps necessary to enforce the payment of any wages found to be due to the employee. If the employee receives less than the wage to which the employee is entitled, the employee may recover the balance in a civil action, together with the costs of the suit, notwithstanding any agreement to work for a lesser wage. Such an action must be brought within 6 months of the date of the alleged violation. (§ 23-341)

# FAIR EMPLOYMENT LAWS

The Arizona Fair Employment Practices Law applies to employers of fifteen or more employees, employment agencies, and labor organizations. The law prohibits any employer from refusing to hire or from discriminating in compensation, terms, conditions, or privileges of employment on the basis of sex. The law prohibits a labor organization from excluding or expelling from membership or discriminating in any way against its members and an employment agency from refusing to refer an applicant for employment on account of the applicant's sex. (§§ 41-1461, -1463)

**ENFORCEMENT:** Any person who believes he or she has been unlawfully discriminated against on the basis of sex must file a charge with the Arizona Division of Human Rights within 180 days after the unlawful discrimination has occurred. (§ 41-1481)

# GOVERNMENT CONTRACTORS AND SUBCONTRACTORS

The Governor's Exec. Order No. 75-5, issued on April 28, 1975, prohibits contractors and subcontractors doing business with the state and its political subdivisions from discriminating against their employees on the basis of sex and other protected characteristics.

**ENFORCEMENT:** The Civil Rights Division of the Department of Law is charged with the enforcement of Exec. Order No. 75-5. The division investigates complaints by employees or prospective employees of government contractors or subcontractors which allege discrimination contrary to the provision of Exec. Order No. 75-5, Part 11A.

# STATE EMPLOYEE LAWS

Exec. Order No. 83-5 prohibits discrimination by state employers on the basis of sex and other protected classifications. It covers hiring, placement, upgrading, transfer, or demotion; treatment; rates of pay or other forms of compensation; training; layoff, termination or reinstatement; and state service examinations. (Exec. Order No. 83-5, issued August 31, 1983; State Fair Employment Practice Laws, No. 484, 453–436)

**ENFORCEMENT:** Those who feel they have been discriminated against in state employment should contact the Governor's Office of Affirmative Action.

# VETERAN'S PREFERENCE

Ten points are added to the passing scores of qualified veterans who take the civil service examination, and five points are added to the passing scores of spouses of veterans who died as a result of a service connected disability. (§ 38-492)

# Community Life

## CREDIT

There is no relevant statutory provision. However, it should be noted that the federal Equal Credit Opportunity Act of 1977, 12 C.F.R. § 202 may apply.

## HOUSING

There is no relevant statutory provision. However, a mortgage guaranty insurance company may not discriminate in the issuance or extension of mortgage guaranty insurance on the basis of the applicant's sex or marital status. (§ 20-1548) In addition, federal law, Title VIII of the Civil Rights Act of 1968, 42 U.S.C. §§ 3601–3619, and Exec. Order No. 11063, 3 C.F.R. 652 (1962), *reprinted in* 42 U.S.C. § 1982, as amended by Exec. Order No. 12259, 3 C.F.R. 307 (1981), *reprinted in* 42 U.S.C. § 3608, may apply.

**ENFORCEMENT:** See "Insurance."

## INSURANCE

It is unlawful to discriminate between individuals of the same class and equal expectation of life in the rates charged for life insurance or annuity contracts or between individuals of the same class and essentially the same hazard in the amount of premium, policy fees, or rates charged for disability insurance, or the benefits payable under these contracts, or in any other term or condition. It is also unlawful to discriminate in other kinds of insurance between insureds or subjects of insurance who have substantially similar risk or exposure factors or expense elements, in the terms or conditions of the insurance contract or in the rate or amount of premium charged. (§ 20-448)

**ENFORCEMENT:** The director of insurance has the power and authority to investigate insurance matters for possible violations of this provision. (§ 20-142)

## PUBLIC ACCOMMODATIONS

There is no relevant statutory provision.

# ARKANSAS

## Home and Family

## MARRIAGE

**AGE OF CONSENT:** A person 18 years of age or older may consent to marry. (§ 55-102)*

**CONSENT REQUIREMENT:** Parental consent or consent of guardian is required to marry if the male is 17 and the female is 16. (§ 55-102)

**LICENSE REQUIREMENT:** A notice of intention to wed, valid for 1 year after issuance and signed by both applicants, must be filed with the county clerk together with payment of the prescribed fee. In addition, a bond of $100 must be posted, which bond becomes void after the marriage has taken place. (§§ 55-207, -213)

**PROHIBITED MARRIAGES:** Marriages between a parent and child, between grandparents and grandchildren, between brothers and sisters of the half blood as well as the whole blood, betweem uncles and nieces, between aunts and nephews, and between first cousins are incestuous and void. (§ 55-103) Bigamous marriages are also void. (§ 55-108)

## DISSOLUTION OF MARRIAGE

**ANNULMENT:** Appendix A, factors 32, 33, 35, and 36, are grounds for annulment. (§ 55-106) Children born of an annulled marriage are legitimate. See *Evatt v. Miller*, 169 S.W. 817 (Ark. 1914)
   *Residency Requirement:* There is no relevant statutory provision.

**LEGAL SEPARATION:** Appendix A, factors 3, 4, 9 (with factor 30 for 3 years), 15, 16 (for 1 year), 17 (with factor 20), 18, 25 (1 year), 27, 28 (3 years) and 48 are grounds for legal separation. (§ 34-1202)
   *Residency Requirement:* There is no relevant statutory provision.

### DIVORCE
   *Residency Requirement:* Each party must reside in the state for 60 days in order to commence a divorce action and for 3 months before a final decree will be issued. (§ 34-1208.1)
   *Grounds for Divorce:* See "Legal Separation."
   *Conciliation Requirement:* There is no relevant statutory provision.
   *Property Distribution:* All property acquired during the marriage is divided equally between the spouses. However, if the court finds such a distribution unfair it will consider factors 1, 5, 6, 7, 8, 9, 10, 11 and 12, listed in Appendix F. Where grounds for divorce are 3 years' voluntary separation, fault may be considered. (§ 34-1214)
   *Child Custody:* The court considers the circumstances of the parties and the nature of the case in arriving at a reasonable custody award. (§ 34-1211) Although there is no statutory provision for joint or shared custody, the courts have awarded joint custody where they find it to be in the best interests of the child. See *Childers v.*

*Unless otherwise noted, all citation references are to the Arkansas Statutes Annotated (1947).

*O'Neal*, 476 S.W.2d 799 (Ark. 1972); *Drewry v. Drewry*, 622 S.W.2d 206 (Ark. Ct. App. 1981)

**Child Support:** The court considers the circumstances of the parties and the nature of the case in arriving at a reasonable amount of child support. (§ 34-1211)

**Spousal Support/Alimony:** Alimony or support may be granted to either party in fixed installments for a specified period of time and subject to contingencies such as the death of either party or remarriage of the receiving party. Where grounds for divorce are 3 years' voluntary separation, fault may be considered. (§ 34-1211)

**Enforcement of Support Orders:** Support orders are enforceable by means of sequestration of either party's property or property of his or her sureties or by equitable garnishment or contempt proceedings. (§ 34-1212) See also the Revised Uniform Reciprocal Enforcement of Support Act of 1968, §§ 34-2401 *et seq*.

**Spouse's Name:** The court may restore to the wife the name she bore before the marriage. (§ 34-1216)

**Divorce by Affidavit or Summary Judgment:** There is no relevant statutory provision.

**Displaced Homemaker Laws:** The Arkansas Equal Opportunity for Displaced Homemakers Act has established multipurpose service centers for homemakers who have worked for a substantial number of years in the home providing unpaid household services for family members. These centers provide counseling, training and employment references to those who were once dependent on another's income but who are no longer supported by that income or those who were once dependent on federal assistance but are no longer eligible for that assistance. Additional services include counseling on health care, financial, educational, nutritional, and legal matters. (§§ 81-630 to -636)

# DOMESTIC VIOLENCE

**STATUTORY PROVISION:** Battery and assault of one's wife are prohibited. (§§ 41-1653 to -1659)

**WHO IS PROTECTED?** The statute extends its protection to wives only. (§§ 41-1656 to -1659)

**RELIEF AVAILABLE:** The statute does not contain any provisions for relief. However, it is presumed that in the absence of specific relief within the statute, a battered wife could resort to relief provided for analogous crimes under criminal law.

**MARITAL RAPE:** A wife may not charge her husband with rape. However, the husband can be convicted as an accomplice if he helps another to rape his wife. (§ 41-1802)

**CIVIL LAWSUIT FOR RAPE OR ASSAULT:** There is no case directly on point. However, in *Leach v. Leach*, 300 S.W.2d 15 (Ark. 1957), the court held that a wife may sue her husband in tort.

**CHILD ABUSE:** The act prohibits any intentional physical or mental injury, sexual abuse, or exploitation inflicted on a child. (§ 42-807)

**Notification Requirement:** Persons who in their professional capacities have reasonable cause to believe that a child has been subjected to abuse, sexual abuse, or neglect are required to immediately report their observations to the Department of Social Services or to a peace officer. (§ 42-808) A person who is required to report a case of child abuse and knowingly fails to do so is subject to civil and/or criminal liability. (§ 42-816)

# INHERITANCE RIGHTS

**FAILURE TO MAKE A WILL:** The surviving spouse is entitled to the entire estate if the parties were married for 3 years or more and the decedent left no children or grandchildren, to one-half of the estate if the parties were married less than 3 years and the decedent left no children or grandchildren, and to nothing if the parties were married less than 3 years and the decedent left children or grandchildren. [§ 61-149(b)]

**FAILURE TO PROVIDE BY WILL:** When a person dies leaving a surviving spouse and a child or children, the surviving spouse is entitled to one-third of all lands owned by the deceased spouse during the marriage for the duration of his or her life and to an absolute one-third interest in all property other than land including bonds, bills, notes, and money received from the sale of timber, oil, gas, or other mineral leases or other mineral sales unless these properties had been legally relinquished by the surviving spouse. (§§ 61-201 to 204) If there are no children or debts, the surviving spouse is entitled to one-half of the deceased spouse's lands and to one-half of all property other than land. If there are debts, then the fractional share is reduced to one-third of the lands and personal property. (§ 61-206) The right of a surviving spouse to her legal share in her husband's lands is not affected if the husband had, during his lifetime, sold or encumbered the lands without his wife's consent. (§§ 61-207 to -208)

**CHILDREN BORN OUT OF WEDLOCK:** Children born out of wedlock may inherit both real property (land) and personal property from their mother or her blood kin. However, such children can only inherit from their father or his blood kin if they commence an action or assert a claim against the father's estate within 180 days of the father's death *and* one of the following has occurred: (1) a court of competent jurisdiction has determined the legitimacy or paternity of the child, or (2) the father has made a written acknowledgment of paternity, or (3) the father has willingly signed the child's birth certificate, or (4) the mother and father married before the child's birth, or (5) the mother and father attempted to marry each other before the birth of the child although the attempted marriage could be or is declared invalid, or (6) the father was supporting the child pursuant to a written voluntary promise or by a court order. [§ 61-141(d)]

**HOMESTEAD, PERSONAL, AND FAMILY ALLOWANCES:** A surviving wife is entitled to a rural homestead allowance of up to 160 acres of land worth up to $2500. However, regardless of value, the homestead cannot be reduced to fewer than 80 acres. Urban homestead allowance can consist of up to 1 acre of land and be worth up to $2500. However, regardless of value, the urban homestead cannot be reduced to less than one-fourth of an acre. (Ark. Const. art. 9, § 4) A surviving spouse and minor children of the decedent are entitled to receive support payments of up to $500 for 2 months after the decedent's death. The surviving spouse is also entitled to $2000, but only to $1000 if the decedent left debts. The surviving spouse may keep items of personal property, such as furniture, as are reasonably necessary for the continued occupancy of the family dwelling provided the parties lived together at the time of the decedent's death. [§62-2501(b)] A surviving spouse may remain in the house of the deceased spouse for 2 months without having to pay rent. (§ 62-2501.1)

**OPTION TO DISREGARD THE WILL:** A surviving spouse may choose to take against the will if he or she had been married to the decedent for more than 1 year. In addition to homestead rights and statutory allowances, the surviving spouse is entitled to dower or courtesy in the real estate and personal property of the deceased spouse as if the deceased had died without making a will. If the deceased left no descendants, the surviving spouse is also entitled to any residue left after all taxes and estate debts are paid. (§ 60-501)

# REPRODUCTIVE RIGHTS
## ABORTION

*Statutory Provisions:* Abortions can be performed by physicians licensed by the state. (§ 41-2561) Existing statutes prohibit abortion except to preserve the woman's life or health, require the written certification of three doctors justifying the need for the abortion, and require that all abortions be performed in hospitals. (§§ 41-2553, -2557, -2558, -2560) However, under *Smith v. Bentley*, 493 F. Supp. 916 (E.D. Ark. 1980), these statutes have been declared unconstitutional. If the fetus is viable, the attending physician must certify in writing that the abortion is necessary to preserve the life or health of the woman and indicate the medical reasons for the abortion and the probable health consequences to the woman if the abortion is not performed. These prerequisites do not apply to a minor whose pregnancy resulted from rape or incest. If the abortion results in a live birth, a second physician must be present to take charge of the infant and take all reasonable steps, in keeping with good medical practice, to preserve the life and health of the infant. (§ 41-2565)

*Consent Requirements:* The written consent of the woman is required. Existing statutes which require parental consent in the case of a minor and spousal consent in the case of a married woman have been declared unconstitutional under *Smith v. Bentley*.

*Residency Requirement:* A woman must have resided in the state for 4 months immediately before the abortion. (§ 41-2556) However, this provision has been declared unconstitutional under *Smith v. Bentley*.

**BIRTH CONTROL:** All medically acceptable contraceptive procedures, supplies, and information are available through "legally recognized channels" to every person regardless of sex, race, age, income, number of children, marital status, citizenship, or motive. Medically acceptable contraceptive invormation may be disseminated in state and county health and welfare departments, medical facilities, institutions of higher learning, and other state agencies. Private institutions, doctors, pharmacists, and paramedics are not obligated to provide contraceptive procedures, supplies, or information if they object on religious or moral grounds. [§§ 82-3104(a), (d), (e)] The statute which prohibits the display or advertising of contraceptives is unconstitutional under *Bigelow v. Virginia*, 421 U.S. 809 (1975) and *Carey v. Population Services International*, 431 U.S. 678 (1977).

**STERILIZATION:** Any person 18 years or older or any person under 18 who is legally married may request and consent to voluntary sterilization. Persons who are mentally incompetent may be sterilized involuntarily. [§§ 59-501, -502, 82-3104(b)]

# UNMARRIED COUPLES

**COMMON-LAW MARRIAGE:** Common-law marriage is not valid in Arkansas. (§ 55-201)

**COHABITAL RELATIONSHIPS:** Arkansas does not recognize property rights arising out of a cohabital relationship when the relationship ends. See *Higgins v. Higgins*, 516 S.W.2d 390 (Ark. 1974), where a woman was denied a share in the estate of the man with whom she had lived although the couple had lived together for many years, had traveled extensively together through states which recognize common-law marriage, and had held themselves out as husband and wife.

## CHILDREN

*Custody:* Once paternity has been established, either the mother or father may petition the court in the county where the child resides for custody of that child. The parent seeking custody must show that he or she is fit to raise the child; that he or she is capable of assuming responsibilities toward the child by providing care, supervision, protection, and financial support; and that it is in the best interests of the child to award custody to the parent seeking it. (§ 34-718)

*Legitimation Proceedings:* A child born out of wedlock is legitimated if the parents lived together before the child's birth and married and the marriage is later declared void, or if the parents married after the child's birth, or if the child was conceived following the artificial insemination of a married woman with the consent of her husband. [§§ 61-141(a) to (c)]

*Paternity Proceedings:* The mother or the putative father may bring an action to determine paternity within 3 years of the child's birth. (§ 34-213, -702, -716) Whenever relevant to the prosecution or defense of the action, blood tests may be ordered by the court and are admissible as evidence. (§ 34-705.1)

*Obligations of the Putative Father:* Once paternity is established, the court can order the father to pay for the mother's confinement and other costs incurred in the prosecution of the paternity action. The court may, at the mother's request, order the father to pay the mother a sum of not less than $10 per month for the child's support until the child reaches 18 and to post a penal bond in the sum of $500 as security for the monthly payments. Failure to pay the monthly support payments may subject the father to imprisonment. (§ 34-706)

# Education

## STATUTORY PROVISION

There is no relevant statutory provision. However, it should be noted that if federal funds are involved, federal law, Title IX of the Education Amendments of 1972, Pub. L. No. 92-318, 20 U.S.C. 1681–1686, may apply.

# Employment

## EQUAL PAY LAWS

Employers are required to pay equal wages for equal services regardless of the employee's sex. In addition it is unlawful to discriminate between the sexes in wages paid for comparable work. However, wage differentials are permitted if such differentials are based on seniority, experience, training, skill, ability, differences in duties or services performed, or differences in shift or time of day worked or any other reasonable differentiation not based on sex. (§ 81-333, -624)

> **ENFORCEMENT:** An employee who has been discriminated against in the payment of wages can, within 2 years of the occurrence of the alleged discriminatory act, sue the employer alone or with other employees who have been similarly discriminated against. The employee can recover any unpaid wages, liquidated damages, and reasonable attorney fees plus court costs. Alternatively, the employee may request the director of the Department of Labor to take an assignment of the employee's wage claim in trust for the employee, and the Director may take any legal action against the employer to collect the claim. (§ 81-626)

## FAIR EMPLOYMENT LAWS

There is no relevant statutory provision. However, an employer with fifteen or more employees is prohibited from discriminating on the basis of sex by Title VII of the Civil Rights Act of 1964, 42 U.S.C. §§ 2000e *et seq*.

## GOVERNMENT CONTRACTORS AND SUBCONTRACTORS

There is no relevant statutory provision. However, it should be noted that if federal funds are involved, federal law, Exec. Order No. 11246, 3 C.F.R. 339, *reprinted* in 42 U.S.C. 2000e app. at 1232, 41 C.F.R. 60-1.2, may apply.

## STATE EMPLOYEE LAWS

There is no relevant statutory provision.

## VETERAN'S PREFERENCE

The employment of veterans and their wives or widows is preferred in the civil service. Accordingly, five points are added to the civil service examination passing scores of veterans and their widows; ten points are added o the passing scores of disabled veterans and their wives. (§ 12-2319)

# Community Life

## CREDIT

It is unlawful for a creditor or credit card issuer to discriminate between equally qualified individuals solely on the basis of sex or marital status with respect to the approval or denial of credit in any consumer credit sale, open end credit plan, or consumer loan or in the issuance, renewal or denial of a credit card. (§ 70-925)

> **ENFORCEMENT:** A person who has been discriminated against in credit on account of sex or marital status may bring an action against the creditor within 1 year

of the occurrence of the discriminatory act. Any creditor or credit card issuer who is successfully sued for violation of this law may be fined up to $500 and be liable for reasonable attorney fees and costs in an action to enforce a judgment rendered against such creditor or credit card issuer. (§ 70-927)

# HOUSING

There is no relevant statutory provision. However, federal law, Title VIII of the Civil Rights Act of 1968, 42 U.S.C. §§ 3601–3619, and Exec. Order No. 11063, 3 C.F.R. 652, *reprinted in* 42 U.S.C. § 1982, as amended by Exec. Order No. 12259, 3 C.F.R. 307 (1981), *reprinted in* 42 U.S.C. § 3608, may apply.

# INSURANCE

It is unlawful to discriminate between individuals of the same class and equal expectation of life in rates charged for life insurance or annuity contracts or rates charged for accident or health insurance. It is equally unlawful to cancel or refuse to renew a policy or to limit the amount of coverage because of the geographic location of the risk, or to refuse to insure an individual solely on the basis of sex. [§ 66-3005(7)]

**ENFORCEMENT:** Upon receipt of a complaint alleging an unfair discriminatory practice, the Commissioner of Insurance has the power to investigate the charges alleged in the complaint. If they are proved to be true, the commissioner may order the insurer complained against to cease and desist from engaging in the discriminatory practice. The commissioner may also impose a monetary fine and may also either suspend or revoke the insurer's license if the insurer knew or should have known that he or she was violating the law. (§ 66-3008)

# PUBLIC ACCOMMODATIONS

There is no relevant statutory provision.

# CALIFORNIA

## Home and Family

### MARRIAGE

**AGE OF CONSENT:** A person 18 years or older may consent to marry. [§ 4101(a)]*

**CONSENT REQUIREMENT:** A person under 18 years of age may marry with the written consent of the parent(s) or guardian; an order of the superior court granting permission; and proof that the parties have participated in premarital counseling, if the court deems such counseling necessary. [§ 4101(b), (c)]

**LICENSE REQUIREMENT:** A license issued by the county clerk is required. Before the issuance of said license, a health certificate from a licensed physician must be filed with the clerk issuing the license. (§§ 4201, 4300) The health certificate requirement may be waived by a judge of the superior court in the county in which the license is to be issued. (§ 4306) An unmarried man and an unmarried woman, not minors, who have been cohabiting as husband and wife may, without obtaining a license, be married by any person authorized to solemnize a marriage. An authorization for the performance of such a marriage may be issued by the county clerk, the clerk of the court or a judge in private chambers upon the personal appearance of the parties to be married and payment of the required fees. Said authorization is valid for 90 days from the date of issuance and can only be used in the county in which it was issued. (§ 4306)

**PROHIBITED MARRIAGES:** Marriages between parents and children, ancestors and descendants of every degree, between brothers and sisters of the whole or half blood, between uncles and nieces, and between aunts and nephews are incestuous and void. (§ 4400) Bigamous and polygamous marriages are also void. (§ 4401)

### DISSOLUTION OF MARRIAGE

**ANNULMENT:** Appendix A, factors 19, 32, 33, 34, and 35, are grounds for annulment. (§ 4425)

*Residency Requirement:* There is no relevant statutory provision.

**LEGAL SEPARATION:** Appendix A, factors 22 and 40, are grounds for legal separation. (§ 4506)

*Residency Requirement:* There is no relevant statutory provision.

**DIVORCE**

*Residency Requirement:* A party filing for divorce must have been a resident of the state for 6 months and a resident of the county where the action is filed for 3 months. (§ 4530)

*Grounds for Divorce:* Appendix A, factors 22 and 40, are grounds for divorce. (§ 4506)

*Conciliation Requirement:* When parties seek a divorce or legal separation on grounds of irremediable breakdown of the marriage and it appears to the court

*Unless otherwise specified, all citation references are to West's Annotated California Code (1980).

that there is a reasonable possibility of a reconciliation, the court will stay the proceedings for 30 days. If no reconciliation is achieved at the end of this 30-day period, either person may move for divorce or legal separation. (§ 4508)

**Property Distribution:** Unless the parties agree otherwise, community property and quasi-community property are divided equally between the parties. When economic circumstances warrant, the court may award any asset to one party on such conditions as it deems proper to effect a substantially equal distribution of property. (§ 4800) Community contributions to the education or training of a party that substantially increases or enhances that party's earning capacity are reimbursable to the community. (§ 4800.3)

**Child Custody:** Custody will be awarded according to the best interests of the child in the following order of preference: to both parents jointly, to either parent, to the person in whose home the child has been living, or to any other person deemed by the court suitable to provide adequate and proper care and guidance for the child. The court will consider Appendix B, factors 6, 9 and 13; the child's health, safety, and welfare; any history of child abuse; and the nature and amount of contact with both parents. (§§ 4600, 4600.5, 4608)

**Child Support:** The court may order either or both parents to pay an amount necessary for the support, maintenance, and education of the child. Upon a showing of good cause, the court may order the parent(s) required to make the payments of support to give reasonable security for such support payments. (§ 4700) The court may order the payment of support during the pendency of custody and support proceedings. (§ 4357)

**Spousal Support/Alimony:** The court may award support to either party in any amount and for any period of time as the court deems just and reasonable. In making the award the court considers factors 1, 2, 3, 4, 8, 9, 10, 11, 13, and 14, listed in Appendix E. (§ 4801) During the pendency of proceedings for divorce, separation, or annulment, the court may order support or maintenance of either party. (§ 4455) Cohabitation of the supported party with a member of the opposite sex creates a rebuttable presumption of a decreased need for support based upon a determination of changed circumstances. (§ 4801.5)

**Enforcement of Support Orders:** Support orders may be enforced against a spouse or former spouse by the court by means of execution, by the appointment of a receiver, by contempt or by other means. (Cal. Civ. Proc. Code §§ 680.365, 681.010 *et seq.*) All property of the debtor spouse can be reached under a money judgment. (§ 695.010) Enforcement of judgment does not limit the right of a spouse to sue the defaulting spouse. (§ 683.050) In determining the amount of support due the court considers factors 3, 4, 5, 6, 7, 11, and 12, listed in Appendix E. (§§ 242, 246) See also the Revised Uniform Reciprocal Enforcement of Support Act of 1968, Cal. Civ. Proc. Code §§ 1650 *et seq.*

**Spouse's Name:** Upon the request of the wife the court shall restore her birth name or the name which she bore before the marriage. Such request is not to be denied because the wife has custody of a minor child who bears a different name. (§ 4457) This statute forbids discrimination by trade or business people against married women who choose to use their birth or former name. (§ 4457)

**Divorce by Affidavit or Summary Judgment:** A marriage of 5 years or less may be summarily dissolved if either party has met the state's residency requirement; there is an irremediable breakdown of the marriage due to irreconcilable differences; there are no children born of or adopted during the marriage, and the wife is not pregnant; neither party owns real property; there are no unpaid debts exceeding

$4000 incurred during the marriage; the total value of community property is less than $12,000 and neither party has separate property exceeding $12,000; the parties have executed an agreement regarding the division of their assets and the assumption of their liabilities and have executed any documents or given proof of any transfers necessary to effectuate the agreement; the parties waive any rights to spousal support; upon the entry of the final divorce judgment the parties waive their right to appeal or move for a new trial; the parties have read and understand the summary dissolution brochure; and the parties desire that the marriage be dissolved. (§ 4550)

*Displaced Homemaker Laws:* California repealed its displaced homemaker laws as of July 1, 1980.

# DOMESTIC VIOLENCE

**STATUTORY PROVISION:** The act prohibits a family or household member member from intentionally or recklessly causing or attempting to cause bodily injury or placing another family or household member in reasonable apprehension of imminent serious bodily injury to himself, herself, or another. (Cal. Civ Proc. Code § 542)

**WHO IS PROTECTED?** The act protects a spouse, a former spouse, or any other adult person who regularly resides in the household and has sexual relations with another family member or any household member residing in the household, or who within the last 6 months regularly resides in the household during which time he or she had sexual relations with another family member or household member presently residing in the household. (Cal. Welf. & Inst. Code. § 18291, § 542; Cal. Penal Code § 273.5)

**RELIEF AVAILABLE:** A victim of domestic violence can obtain the following relief: temporary restraining orders (§ 545); temporary custody and child support orders; orders providing monetary compensation, including restitution for lost wages, medical care and temporary housing expenses incurred as a result of the abuse; orders temporarily excluding the defendant from the dwelling; orders requiring either party to participate in counseling; and orders providing for the payment of attorney fees to the prevailing party. (§§ 547, 4359) In addition, pursuant to the Domestic Violence Centers Act, the following services are provided to victims of domestic violence: shelter; food; housing facilities; psychological support and peer counseling; referrals to community services; emergency transportation; arrangements for school-age children to continue their education during their stay at the shelter; medical care and legal assistance; counseling on re-education; marriage, family and employment training; housing referrals and other available social services. (Cal. Welf. & Inst. Code §§ 18294, 18295)

**MARITAL RAPE:** A woman may charge her husband with rape, but no arrest will be made unless the rape has been reported to a peace officer having the power to arrest or to the district attorney of the county within 90 days after the act occurred. (Cal. Penal Code §§ 262, 264)

**CIVIL LAWSUIT FOR RAPE OR ASSAULT:** There is no case law directly on point. However, one spouse may sue the other in tort where the tort is intentional. [*Self v. Self*, 376 P.2d 65 (Cal. 1962)]

**CHILD ABUSE:** The act prohibits any physical injury inflicted by other than accidental means on a child by another person, including sexual abuse of a child or any act or omission such as the willful cruelty to or the unjustifiable punishment of a child or corporal punishment or injury. (Cal. Penal Code §§ 273a, 273d, 11165)

*Notification Requirement:* Any child care custodian, medical practitioner, non-medical practitioner, or employee of a child protective agency who has knowledge of abuse, or in his or her professional capacity observes a child who he or she knows or reasonably suspects has been the victim of child abuse, must report the suspected abuse to a child protective agency immediately or as soon as possible by telephone and prepare and send a written report of the suspected abuse within 36 hours of receiving the information concerning the incident. Failure to report an incidence of child abuse is a misdemeanor. (Cal. Penal Code § 11172)

# INHERITANCE RIGHTS

The following are applicable to estates of decedents dying on or after January 1, 1985.

**FAILURE TO MAKE A WILL:** The surviving spouse is entitled to all the community property and all the quasi-community property. As to separate property, the surviving spouse is entitled to all if the decedent left no issue, parent, siblings or issue of deceased siblings; to one-half of the separate property if the decedent left one child or issue of a deceased child or if the decedent left no issue but a parent or parents or their issue; to one-third if the decedent left more than one child or one child and the issue of one or more deceased children or if the decedent left issue of two or more deceased children. (Cal. Prob. Code § 6400)

**FAILURE TO PROVIDE BY WILL:** If a testator fails to provide by will for his or her surviving spouse who married the testator after the execution of the will, the omitted spouse will receive one-half of each the community property and quasi-community property that belonged to the testator and a share in the separate property of the testator equal in value to that which the spouse would have received if the testator had died intestate, but in no event is this share to be more than one-half the value of the separate property in the estate (Cal. Prob. Code § 6560) unless the omission was intentional, or the testator provided for the spouse by transfer outside the will, or the surviving spouse made a valid agreement waiving the right to share in the testator's estate. (Cal. Prob. Code § 6561)

**CHILDREN BORN OUT OF WEDLOCK:** A child born out of wedlock is the legitimate heir of the mother. However, such a child can only inherit from the father where the father failed to make a will, if after the child's birth, the father and the child's natural mother married, or attempted to marry each other by a marriage solemnized in apparent compliance with the law, although the attempted marriage is or could be declared invalid; or with his consent, he was named the child's father on the child's birth certificate; or the father was obligated to support the child under a written voluntary promise or by court order; or he received the child into his home and openly held out the child as his natural child. (§§ 7003, 7004)

**HOMESTEAD, PERSONAL, AND FAMILY ALLOWANCES:** Until an inventory is filed and for a period of 60 days thereafter, the decedent's surviving spouse and minor children are entitled to remain in possession of the family dwelling, the wearing apparel, the household furniture, and other property of the decedent, exempt from the enforcement of a money judgment. (Cal Prob. Code § 6500) During the administration of the estate, the court may set apart a probate homestead for the use of the surviving spouse and the minor children of the decedent. (Cal. Prob. Code §§ 6520, 6521) The probate homestead can only be set apart for a limited period and in no case beyond the lifetime of the surviving spouse, or as to a child, beyond the child's minority. (Cal. Prob. Code § 6524) Any property of the decedent set apart as a probate homestead is liable for claims against the estate of the decedent, subject to the probate homestead rights. (Cal. Prob. Code § 6526) In addition, the surviving spouse and decedent's minor children are entitled to a reasonable family allowance out of the estate as is necessary for their maintenance during the administration of the estate. (Cal. Prob. Code § 6540) The family allowance terminates at the settlement of the estate or, if the estate is insolvent, no later than 1 year after the granting of letters testamentary. (Cal. Prob. Code § 6543)

**OPTION TO DISREGARD THE WILL:** If a married person domiciled in another state dies and leaves a valid will disposing of real property in California, and if the real property is not community property of the decedent and the surviving spouse, the surviving spouse has the same right to elect to take a portion of, or an interest in, such property against the will of the decedent as though the property were situated in the decedent's domicile at death. (Cal. Prob. Code § 120) The surviving spouse may waive his or her right to take community or quasi-community property against the decedent's will. [Cal. Prob. Code § 141(a) (7)]

# REPRODUCTIVE RIGHTS
## ABORTION

*Statutory Provisions:* The Cal. Health & Safety Code § 25951, a state criminal statute which prohibits abortion unless necessary to preserve the physical or mental health of a woman, is unconstitutional under *Roe v. Wade*. 410 U.S. 113 (1973) and *Connecticut v. Menillo*, 423 U.S. 9 (1975). The provision which requires an abortion to be performed in a hospital and with the prior approval of a hospital committee composed of two or more doctors (Cal. Health & Safety Code §§ 25951–25953) is unconstitutional under *Akron v. Akron Center for Reproductive Health*. 462 U.S. 416 (1983) and *Planned Parenthood Ass'n v Ashcroft*, 462 U.S. 4 (1983). However, a state can require that a second-trimester abortion be performed in a licensed clinic, *Simopoulous v. Virginia*, 462 U.S. 506 (1983). The fundamental right to privacy of procreative choice also extends to the mentally incompetent. [*Conservatorship of the Person of Valerie N.*, 199 Cal. Rptr 478 (1984)] Any pregnant female confined in a juvenile facility, detention facility, or state prison must be permitted to obtain an abortion if she wants one. (Cal. Welf. & Inst. Code §§ 220, 1773; Cal. Penal Code §§ 3405, 4028) A nonprofit hospital or other facility operated by a religious organization is not required to perform abortions. All medical employees have a right to refuse to participate in abortions on the basis of moral, ethical, or religious grounds. (Cal. Health & Safety Code § 25955) An infant prematurely born alive in the course of an abortion has the right to obtain medical treatment. (Cal. Health & Safety Code § 25955.9) Performing or soliciting an illegal abortion is a crime. (Cal. Penal Code §§ 274–276) Cal. Penal Code § 274 restricting abortions was found valid in its entirety in *People v. Barksdale*, 503 P.2d 257 (1973).

*Consent Requirement:* An unmarried minor may consent to receive hospital, surgical, and medical care in the treatment and/or prevention of pregnancy without parental consent. (Cal. Civ. Code § 34.5) However, a state may constitutionally require that notice be given to the parents of an unemancipated or immature minor before an abortion is performed. [*H.L. v. Matheson*, 450 U.S. 398 (1981)] However, parents cannot have absolute veto power over the decision of a mature minor to terminate her pregnancy. [*Belloti v. Baird* 428 U.S. 132 (1976); *Akron v. Akron Center for Reproductive Health* 462 U.S. 416 (1983)]

*Reporting Requirement:* The Department of Health shall establish and maintain a system for reporting therapeutic abortions. The reporting system must not require, permit, or include the identification by name of any person undergoing an abortion. (Cal. Health & Safety Code § 25955.5)

*State Funding:* The decision to have an abortion is a fundamental right of privacy in procreative choice and is not grounds for loss of privileges and immunities, including the receipt of public benefits. (Cal. Health & Safety Code § 259553) See also the *Committee to Defend Reproductive Rights v. Meyers*, 625 P.2d 779 (Calif. 1981).

**BIRTH CONTROL:** Hospital, medical, and surgical care related to the prevention of pregnancy may be furnished to any unmarried minor without parental consent. (Cal. Civ. Code § 34.5) County health officers must prepare a list of family planning clinics located in each county for distribution to all hospitals, to all doctors who request copies, and to all persons applying for a marriage license. (Cal. Health & Safety Code §§ 463, 464; Cal. Gov't Code § 26808) Family planning services shall be offered on a sliding fee schedule for all eligible person regardless of marital status, age, or parenthood; only the consent of the person receiving these services is required. (Cal. Welf. & Inst. Code §§ 14501, 14503) Upon request, any person confined in a state or local juvenile facility or state prison must be allowed to continue using birth control measures and to obtain information and education regarding prescription birth control measures; he or she must also be offered family planning services at least 60 days prior to the scheduled release date (Cal. Welf. & Inst. Code §§ 221, 1753.7; Cal. Penal Code §§ 3409, 4023.5)

**STERILIZATION:** Hospitals, clinics, or health facilities may nor require a person seeking sterilization for contraceptive purposes to meet any special nonmedical qualifications not imposed on individuals seeking other types of operations. (Cal. Health & Safety Code §§ 1232, 1258, 1459, 32138.10) A person's decision to be sterilized shall not be grounds for the loss of any privileges or immunities to which the person would otherwise be entitled, including the receipt of public benefits. (Cal. Health & Safety Code § 25955.3) A minor may not consent to sterilization without the consent of his or her parents or guardian. (Cal. Civ. Code § 34.5) Doctors performing voluntary, nonemergency sterilization upon medical recipients will not be paid for their services unless the patient has signed a document evidencing informed consent. (Cal. Welf. & Inst. Code § 14191) Insurance policies or plans which provide for payment of all or part of the cost of sterilization operations may impose disclaimers which exclude, reduce, or limit payments based on the individual's reason for desiring sterilization. [Cal. Health & Safety Code § 1373(b); Cal. Ins. Code §§ 10120, 10121; 1512(j)]

# UNMARRIED COUPLES

**COMMON-LAW MARRIAGE:** Common-law marriages are not valid in California. The state, however, will recognize such marriages validly entered into in states which recognize them. [§ 4100); *Tatum v. Tatum*, 241 F.2d 401 (1957)]

**COHABITAL RELATIONSHIPS:** In *Marvin v. Marvin*, 557 P.2d 106 (Cal. 1976), the California Supreme Court held that agreements between cohabiting adults with respect to their earnings and property rights were valid and would be upheld. The court indicated that express agreements are enforceable unless they explicitly rest on the provision of sexual services as consideration for the contract, and that in the absence of an express contract, a court should inquire into the conduct of the parties to determine whether relief could be granted under other theories for the reasonable value of household services less the reasonable value of support received under other theories. Such theories might include an implied contract or implied agreement of partnership or joint venture, a tacit understanding between the parties, equitable principles of constructive or resulting trust, or *quantum meruit*.

## CHILDREN

*Custody:* There is no relevant statutory provision.

*Legitimation Proceedings:* The parent-child relationship extends equally to every child and to every parent, regardless of marital status. See Uniform Parentage Act, §§ 7000 *et seq.*

*Paternity Proceedings:* A child, the natural mother, the presumed father, an interested party, or the district attorney may bring an action for the purpose of declaring the existence of the father and child relationship at any time. (§ 7006) Under the Uniform Act on Blood Tests to Determine Paternity, the court may order the mother, child, and alleged father to submit to blood tests. (Cal. Evid. Code § 892)

*Obligations of the Putative Father:* Once paternity is established, the court may order the father to pay for the support of the child, to furnish a bond or other security for the payment of the judgment and to pay for the reasonable expenses of the mother's pregnancy and confinement. The father may also be required to pay his proportionate share of fees and costs of the action. (§ 7010; 7011)

# Education

## STATUTORY PROVISION

All persons, regardless of their sex, are entitled to equal rights and opportunities in the educational institutions of the state. Discrimination in employment among students and nonstudents and among academic and nonacademic personnel on the basis of sex is prohibited, including the denial of employment or the exclusion of a person from a program or activity because of potential parental, family, or marital status or pregnancy or related conditions. (Cal. Educ. Code §§ 40, 230, 45021; Cal. Lab. Code 1420.2; Cal. Gov't Code § 12943) Sexual harassment in the California education system is also prohibited. (Cal. Educ. Code § 212.5)

## AREAS COVERED

The California education equity laws prohibit discrimination in educational materials and curricula, in school sponsored activities which reflect adversely upon persons because of sex, in educational and career counseling, and in athletics. (Cal. Educ. Code 40, 41, §§ 51500, 51501, 66016)

**ENFORCEMENT:** Discrimination in schools or community colleges should be reported to the governing board of the relevant school or community college district. (Cal. Educ. Code 6, §§ 260, 262)

# Employment

## EQUAL PAY LAWS

It is unlawful for an employer to discriminate on the basis of sex in wages paid for equal work. However, wage differentials are allowed if they are based on factors other than sex. [Cal. Lab. Code § 1197.5(a)]

**ENFORCEMENT:** The equal pay laws are enforced by the California Division of Labor Standards Enforcement. An employee who has been discriminated against in wages on the basis of sex may either file a complaint with the division or within 2 years bring a civil action for the recovery of such wages [Cal. Lab. Code § 1197.5(c),(e),(g)], or within 3 years bring a civil action for the recovery of wages if the violation was willful. [Cal. Lab. Code 1197.5(h)]

# FAIR EMPLOYMENT LAWS

Discrimination in employment on the basis of sex and other characteristics is prohibited. This applies to the state of California, its political and civil subdivisions, employers of five or more persons, employment agencies, and labor organizations. An employer may not treat a female employee who is affected by pregnancy, childbirth, or related medical conditions differently than other employees who are similar in their ability or inability to work or refuse a female employee disabled by these conditions a leave for a reasonable period up to 4 months. (Cal. Gov't Code §§ 12920, 12926; Fair Employment and Housing Act) An unemployed worker is ineligible for benefits if he or she left employment without good cause. Good cause for leaving is defined to include any illness or injury resulting from pregnancy, childbirth, or related medical condition. [Cal. Unemp. Ins. Code §§ 1256; 2626(a)]

**ENFORCEMENT:** The California Department of Fair Employment and Housing is charged with the enforcement of the law. Any person who has been the victim of an unlawful employment practice may file a verified complaint with the department within 1 year of the occurrence of the alleged discriminatory practice. (Cal. Gov't. Code 12960)

# GOVERNMENT CONTRACTORS AND SUBCONTRACTORS

Any employer who contracts to provide goods and services to the state is subject to the nondiscrimination requirements of the fair employment practices laws. (Cal. Gov't Code § 12990)

**ENFORCEMENT:** See "Fair Employment Laws."

# STATE EMPLOYEE LAWS

State employees are protected by the state's Fair Employment and Housing Act. [Cal. Gov't Code § 12926(c)] In addition, discrimination in state employment on the basis of the individual's sexual preference is prohibited under Exec. Order No. B-54-79, effective April 4, 1979.

**ENFORCEMENT:** See "Fair Employment Laws."

# VETERAN'S PREFERENCE

On the civil service exams, fifteen points are added to the passing scores of disabled veterans, and ten points are added to the passing scores of all other veterans, their widows or widowers and spouses of 100 percent disabled veterans. (Cal. Gov't Code § 18973)

# Community Life

## CREDIT

No person may be denied credit in his or her own name or offered credit on less favorable terms on the basis of marital status. Credit reporting agencies must file all credit information received after January 1, 1977 under the names of each person or spouse holding joint credit accounts in a manner which would enable either person or spouse to gain access automatically to the credit history without having to list or refer to the name of the other person. (§ 1812.30)

**ENFORCEMENT:** A person who has been discriminated against in credit on account of marital status may bring a civil action within 2 years of the occurrence of the alleged discriminatory act. (§ 1812.31, .32)

## HOUSING

It is unlawful for the owner of any housing accommodation to discriminate against any person or for any person to publish or print any notice or advertisement with respect to the sale or rental of a housing accommodation that indicates any preference, limitation or discrimination on the bases of sex and marital status. (Cal. Gov't Code §§ 12955, 51)

**ENFORCEMENT:** A person who has been discriminated against in housing on account of sex may either file a complaint with the Fair Employment and Housing Commission within 60 days of the occurrence of the alleged discriminatory act (Cal. Gov't Code § 12980) or file a civil action within 3 years of the occurrence of the alleged discriminatory act. [Cal. Civ. Code § 52; Cal. Div. Proc. Code § 338(1)]

## INSURANCE

It is unlawful for an insurer to fail or refuse to accept an application from, or to cancel or refuse to issue a policy of insurance to, any person because of that person's sex or marital status. Nor shall the sex of the applicant for insurance constitute a condition or risk for which a higher rate, premium, or charge may be required by the insurer. [Cal. Ins. Code §§ 679.71, 790.03(f)]

**ENFORCEMENT:** The Commissioner of Insurance has the power to examine and investigate all charges of discriminatory practices in the insurance industry. (Ann. Cal. Ins. Code §§ 790.04, .05)

## PUBLIC ACCOMMODATIONS

The Unruh Civil Rights Act provides equal access to public accommodations to all persons regardless of sex. (Cal. Civ. Code § 51)

**ENFORCEMENT:** Any person who has been discriminated against in the full enjoyment of a public accommodation on the basis of sex may bring a civil action in an appropriate court within 3 years of the occurrence of the alleged discriminatory act. [Cal. Civ. Code § 52; Cal. Civ. Proc. Code § 338(1)]

# COLORADO

## Home and Family

## MARRIAGE

**AGE OF CONSENT:** A person 18 years of age or older may consent to marry. [§ 14-2-106(I)]*

**CONSENT REQUIREMENT:** A person over the age of 16 but under 18 years of age may enter into marriage with the consent of both parents or the guardian, or if the parents are not living together, then the parent who has legal custody or with whom the child is living or the juvenile court may consent. If the child is under 16 years of age, then the consent of both parents, or the guardian, or if the parents are living apart the parent who has legal custody or with whom the child is living *and* the consent of the juvenile court are necessary. [§§ 14-2-106(1)(a)(I), -2-108]

**LICENSE REQUIREMENT:** When a marriage application has been completed and signed by both parties and at least one of the parties appears before the county clerk and pays a license fee, the license clerk shall issue a license to marry and a marriage certificate. Before a license is issued, each applicant shall file a certificate from a licensed physician. The license issued shall not be valid for more than 30 days. [§§ 14-2-106(2)(a) to (g), -2-107]

**PROHIBITED MARRIAGES:** Marriages that are prohibited are bigamous marriages; marriages between ancestors and descendants or between brothers and sisters, whether the relationship is by the half or the whole blood or by adoption; marriages between uncles and nieces and nieces or aunts and nephews, whether by half or whole blood, *except* if permitted by established customs of aboriginal cultures. (§§ 14-2-110)

## DISSOLUTION OF MARRIAGE

**ANNULMENT:** Appendix A, factors 19, 24, 32, 33, 35, 36, 37, and 38, are grounds for annulment. Children born of an annulled marriage are legitimate. [§§ 14-10-111, -111(4)]

*Residency Requirement:* If the marriage was not performed in the state, the residency requirement is 30 days. Otherwise, there is no residency requirement.

**LEGAL SEPARATION:** If the marriage is irretrievably broken, the parties may file for legal separation. (§ 14-10-106)

*Residency Requirement:* A person wishing to file for legal separation must be a resident for 90 days. (§ 14-10-106)

**DIVORCE**

*Residency Requirement:* See "Legal Separation."

*Grounds for Divorce:* If the marriage is irretrievably broken, the parties may file for divorce, (§ 14-10-106)

*Conciliation Requirement:* At the request of either party or the attorneys for the parties, or at the discretion of the court, the court may appoint a marriage counselor in any pending divorce or legal separation. The court shall not require either of the parties to submit to counseling. (§ 14-12-106)

*Unless otherwise specified, all citation references are to the Colorado Revised Statutes (1973).

*Property Distribution:* Property acquired during the marriage will be divided without regard to fault in such proportions as the court deems just after considering factors 1, 2, 3, and 4, listed in Appendix F. (§ 14-10-113)

*Child Custody:* Custody will be determined in the best interests of the child. The court will consider Appendix B, factors 5, 9, 10, 11, 12, 13, 14, and 15. (§ 14-10-124) Joint shared custody may be awarded upon motion of both parents. The court will consider factors 1, 2, 3, 4, and 5, listed in Appendix C. (§ 14-10-123)

*Child Support:* The court may order either or both parents to pay an amount reasonable or necessary, without regard to marital fault, after considering all relevant factors including Appendix D, factors 1, 2, 3, 4, and 5. (§ 14-10-115)

*Spousal Support/Alimony:* The court may award support to either party for such amounts and for such periods of time as the court deems just. The court will consider Appendix E, factors 2, 3, 4, 5, 6, 13, 14, and 18. (§ 14-10-114)

*Enforcement of Support Orders:* As part of any support action in which child support is ordered, the court shall order that a wage assignment be executed. The wage assignment may either be activated immediately upon agreement of the parties or held by the court until the clerk of the court is notified that 20 days have passed, since a payment was due under a support order. (§ 14-14-107) See also the Uniform Reciprocal Enforcement Support Act, §§ 14-5-101 *et seq*.

*Spouse's Name:* There is no relevant statutory provision.

*Divorce by Affidavit or Summary Judgment:* A divorce may be granted upon the affidavit of either or both parties if there are no minor children and the wife is not pregnant or if both spouses are represented by counsel and have entered into a separation agreement granting custody and child support and there are no disputes and there is no marital property or the spouses have agreed on the division of the marital property. (§ 14-10-120.3)

*Displaced Homemaker Laws:* The act establishes multipurpose service centers for individuals who have been homemakers for a substantial number of years, who have been dependent on the income of other family members, and who have lost that income. (§§ 8-15.5-102 *et seq*.)

# DOMESTIC VIOLENCE

**STATUTORY PROVISION:** Domestic violence is defined as any act or threatened act of violence committed by an adult or emancipated minor. (§ 14-2-101)

**WHO IS PROTECTED?** The act applies to any adult or emancipated minor who is a current or former relation or who is living in the same home. (§ 14-4-101)

**RELIEF AVAILABLE:** Restraining protection orders may be obtained from the county and district courts. Emergency protection orders can be issued by telephone at all times when the courts are otherwise closed. An emergency protection order may include restraining a party from threatening, molesting, or injuring any other party or minor children; excluding a party from the family home or from the home of another party; and awarding temporary custody. (§§ 14-4-102, -103)

**MARITAL RAPE:** A woman may not charge her husband with rape unless they are living apart. (§ 18-3-409)

**CHILD ABUSE:** Any person who intentionally, knowingly, or negligently causes or permits a child under 16 to be placed in a situation that may endanger the child's life or health; or to be abandoned, tortured, cruelly confined, or punished; or to be deprived of necessary food, clothing, or shelter is guilty of a crime. (§§ 18-6-401, 19-10-103)

*Notification Requirement:* Doctors, dentists, nurses, and others called upon to render aid to children must report suspected cases of child abuse. (§ 19-10-104)

# INHERITANCE RIGHTS

**FAILURE TO MAKE A WILL:** The surviving spouse is entitled to the entire estate if there are no other heirs, or to $25,000 and one-half of the estate if the decedent left one or more children or grandchildren who are not also the surviving spouse's children or grandchildren. (§ 15-11-102)

**FAILURE TO PROVIDE BY WILL:** If a testator fails to provide by will for the surviving spouse who married the testator after the execution of the will, the omitted spouse shall receive the same share he or she would have received if the spouse had died without a will *unless* it appears from the will that the omission was intentional or that the testator provided for the spouse by transfer outside the will. (§ 15-11-301)

**HOMESTEAD, PERSONAL, AND FAMILY ALLOWANCES:** A surviving spouse is entitled to a homestead exemption not exceeding $20,000, which may consist of a house and lot or lots of a farm consisting of any number of acres, free from claims of creditors. (§§ 38-41-201 to -211) In addition, the surviving spouse is entitled to an exempt property allowance of $7500 and a reasonable family allowance during the period of administration of the will. (§§ 15-11-402 to -405)

**OPTION TO DISREGARD THE WILL:** The surviving spouse may choose to disregard the will and is entitled to one-half of the "augmented" estate. The augmented estate is the estate reduced by funeral and administration expenses, exempt property allowance, family allowance, and enforceable claims, to which is added the value of transferred property within 6 months after the first publication of notice to filing claims which arose before the death of the decedent or within the year of the date of death, whichever time limitation first expires; however, the time limitation shall not expire before the expiration of 6 months following the submission of a will to probate. The right to disregard the will may be waived in writing. Disregarding the will will not affect the surviving spouse's right to the homestead exemption or family allowance. (§§ 15-11-202, -203 to 207)

# REPRODUCTIVE RIGHTS
## ABORTION

*Statutory Provisions:* Provisions of the existing abortion statute, which limit the circumstances under which a woman may obtain an abortion, require that an abortion be performed in a licensed hospital, and require the approval of a special hospital board composed of three doctors were held unconstitutional in *People v. Norton*, 507 P.2d 862 (Colo. 1973). Any person who performs an illegal abortion is guilty of a felony. (§ 18-6-102) No hospital is required to perform an abortion, and all persons have the right to refuse to participate in an abortion on moral or religious grounds. (§ 18-6-104)

*Informed Consent:* There is no relevant statutory provision.

*Parental Consent:* The provision of the existing abortion statute which requires parental consent in the case of a minor [§ 18-6-101(1)], was held unconstitutional in *Foe v. Vanderhoof*, 389 F. Supp. 947 (D. Col. 1975).

*Spousal Consent:* The provision of the existing statute, § 18-6-101(1), which requires the husband's consent in the case of a married woman is unconstitutional under *Planned Parenthood of Central Missouri v. Danforth*, 428 U.S. 52 (1976).

**BIRTH CONTROL:** All medically acceptable contraceptive procedures, supplies, and information must be readily and practically available to every person, regardless of sex, race, age, income, number of children, marital status, citizenship, or motive. No hospital, clinic, medical center, pharmacy, or state agency may promote any policy which interferes with a doctor or patient desiring any medically acceptable contraceptive procedures, supplies, or information. Medically acceptable contraceptive information may be disseminated by state and county health and welfare departments, medical facilities at institutions of higher learning, state agencies, and schools. (§ 25-6-102) A doctor may furnish birth control procedures, supplies, and information to any minor who is pregnant, a parent, married, or who has the consent of his or her parent, or who has been referred by another doctor, clergy, family planning clinic, institution of higher learning, or state agency, or who requests and is in need of birth control. (§ 13-22-105) The state or county may provide family planning and birth control services to every parent who is a public assistance recipient and to every other parent or married person who might want these services; fees may be charged for these services. The refusal of any person to accept family planning and birth control services cannot affect that person's right to receive public assistance or any other public benefit. (§§ 25-6-202, -204, -205)

**STERILIZATION:** A hospital, clinic, medical center, or institution may not subject any person seeking sterilization to any standard or requirement other than referral to a doctor. A doctor may sterilize any person over 18 who requests and consents to the procedure. An unmarried minor under 18 may not be sterilized without the consent of the parent or guardian. (§ 25-6-102) A mentally retarded person over 18 who has given consent may be sterilized; consent to sterilization must not be made a condition for release from an institution or a condition for the exercise of any right, privilege, or freedom. (§ 27-10.5-128, -132)

# UNMARRIED COUPLES

**COMMON-LAW MARRIAGE:** Common-law marriages are valid in Colorado. The factors which will be considered as establishing a common-law marriage are mutual intent and general reputation among acquaintances as husband and wife. [*Graham v. Graham*, 274 P.2d 605 (Colo. 1954); *Dexter v. Dexter*, 484 P.2d 805 (Colo. App. 1971)] The evidence concerning a common-law marriage should be clear, consistent, positive, and convincing. [*Employers Mut. Liability Ins. Co. of Wisconsin v. Industrial Commission*, 345 P.2d 901 (Colo. 1951)]

**COHABITAL RELATIONSHIPS:** There is no relevant case law on the rights of cohabiting couples.

## CHILDREN

*Custody:* There is no statute governing the custody of children born out of wedlock.

*Legitimation Proceedings:* A child born out of wedlock is legitimated if the mother and father have married or attempted to marry and the attempted marriage is later declared void and the father has acknowledged paternity of the child in writing with the court or registrar of vital statistics; if the father has consented to be named as the child's father on the child's birth certificate; if he is obligated to support the child under a written voluntary promise or by court order; if while the child is still a minor, the father receives the child into his home and openly holds out the child as his natural child; if the father acknowledges the paternity of the child in a writing with the court or registrar of vital statistics; or if blood tests have been administered and the results show that the alleged father is not excluded as the probable father and that the probability is 97 percent or higher. (§ 19-6-105)

*Paternity Proceedings:* A child, the natural mother, a man "presumed" to be the father, or any interested party may bring an action to determine the existence or nonexistence of the parent and child relationship. An action to determine the paternity of the father may not be brought later than 3 years after the birth of the child or 3 years after July 1, 1977, whichever is later. However, an action brought by or on behalf of a child whose paternity has not been determined is not barred until 3 years after the child reaches the age of majority. (§§ 19-6-107, -108)

*Obligations of the Putative Father:* The court may make provisions for the support of the child, visitation privileges, or any other matter in the best interests of the child. In determining the amount of support, the court shall consider all relevant facts including factors 6, 7, 8, 9, 10, 11, 12, 13, and 14, listed in Appendix D. (§ 19-6-116)

# Education

## STATUTORY PROVISION

There is no relevant statutory provision. But note that the definition of places of public accommodations includes "educational institution." See "Public Accommodations." Also, the Colorado equal rights amendment prohibits the denial or abridgement of equality of rights under the law on account of sex. (Colo. Const. art 2, § 29)

## AREAS COVERED

Library resources and instructional materials to public and nonpublic schools from federal grants are to be made available by the local board of education without discrimination on the basis of sex or other protected classes. [§ 22-32-110(1)(dd)].

**ENFORCEMENT:** The local board of education should be contacted if a person perceives a violation of this provision. (§ 22-32-110)

# Employment

## EQUAL PAY LAWS

It is unlawful to discriminate in the amount or rate of wages paid on the basis of sex. (§ 8-5-102)

**ENFORCEMENT:** A person who has been discriminated against in the payment of wages on account of sex may file a written complaint with the Director of the Division of Labor within 1 year of the alleged discriminatory act for the recovery of any unpaid wages. (§ 8-5-103)

# FAIR EMPLOYMENT LAWS

Discriminatory or unfair employment practices on the basis of sex are prohibited. The law covers employers, employment agencies, and labor organizations and includes the state of Colorado or any political subdivision, commission, department, institutions, or school district thereof. (§ 24-34-403)

**ENFORCEMENT:** The Colorado Human Rights Commission enforces the provision. A charge of discrimination shall be filed within 6 months after the date of occurrence.

# GOVERNMENT CONTRACTORS AND SUBCONTRACTORS

Government contractors and subcontractors are prohibited from discriminating on the basis of sex. (§ 8-17-101)

**ENFORCEMENT:** A contractor who discriminates on the basis of sex is guilty of a misdemeanor and if convicted may be liable for a fine of not more than $500 or imprisonment for not more than a year or both.

# STATE EMPLOYEE LAWS

State employment is covered under the Fair Employment Law. Discrimination in state employment is further prohibited under rules promulgated by the Colorado Department of Personnel, 4 Code of Colo. Regs. § 801-1, effective October 1, 1979, amended October 19, 1982.

# VETERAN'S PREFERENCE

On civil service exams for state employment, five points are added to the passing scores of veterans and their widows, and ten points are added to the passing scores of disabled veterans. Veterans are also given preference in employment as firefighters. [Colo. Const., art. XII Section 15(1)(b)(c)(d); § 31-30-210]

# UNEMPLOYMENT COMPENSATION

Employees who leave their job because of personal harassment not related to the performance of their job are eligible to receive benefits. Benefits are available to employees unable to work for health reasons, including pregnancy. Reduced benefits may be available to employees who leave work to marry or to move with another person. [§§ 8-73-108 (4)(0), -108(4)(b); -108(5)(c)(d)]

# Community Life

## CREDIT

Discrimination on the basis of sex is prohibited in consumer sales and in leases or loans by sellers, lessors, or lendors whose total original unpaid balances arising from said transactions are more than $1 million. (§ 5-1-109)

**ENFORCEMENT:** A person who has been discriminated against in a credit transaction on account of sex has the right to take court action to recover actual damages and exemplary damages in addition to reasonable attorney fees and the costs of the action. (§§ 5-1-203; 5-5-206)

## HOUSING

It is unlawful for any owner or person having the right to transfer, sell, rent, or lease any housing, or any agent of such person, to refuse to show, sell, transfer, rent, or lease, or otherwise to deny or withhold from any person such housing, or to discriminate in the terms, conditions, or privileges pertaining to any housing or the transfer, sale, rental, lease, or furnishing of facilities or services in connection with any housing on the basis of sex or marital status. However, it is not illegal to lease premises only to members of one sex. It is unlawful for any person to whom application is made for financial assistance for the acquisition, construction, rehabilitation, repair, or maintenance of any housing to discriminate in the terms, conditions, or privileges relating to the obtaining or use of financial assistance on the basis of sex or marital status. (§ 24-34-504)

**ENFORCEMENT:** Any person who has been the victim of discrimination in housing should file a complaint within 90 days of the discriminatory act with the Colorado Civil Rights Commission. (§ 24-34-504)

## INSURANCE

Discrimination is prohibited between individuals of the same class and equal expectation of life in rates charged for life insurance or annuity contracts or between individuals of the same class or essentially the same hazard in the amount of premium policy fees or rates charged for any contract of insurance, in the benefits payable under these contracts. It is also unlawful to make or permit to be made any classification solely on the basis of sex or marital status, unless such classification is for the purpose of issuing family units or is justified by actuarial statistics. [§§ 10-3-1104 (I)(f), (II), (III)]

**ENFORCEMENT:** Any person who has been the victim of discrimination in insurance should contact the Commissioner of Insurance, who is empowered to examine and investigate any person violating the provision. (§ 10-3-1106)

## PUBLIC ACCOMMODATIONS

It is unlawful for any person, directly or indirectly, to refuse, withhold from, or deny the full and equal enjoyment of the goods, services, facilities, privileges, advantages, or accommodations of a place of public accommodation, or to publish or post a written notice or advertisement that the patronage of an individual is unwelcome or undesirable at a place of public accommodation, on the basis of sex or marital status. However, it is not unlawful for a person to restrict admission to a place of public accommodation to individuals of one sex if such restriction has a bona fide relationship to the goods, services, facilities, privileges, advantages, or accommodations of the place of public accommodation. (§ 24-34-601)

**ENFORCEMENT:** A person who has been discriminated against in the use or enjoyment of a place of public accommodation on account of sex may either file a complaint with the Colorado Civil Rights Commission within 60 days after the alleged discriminatory act occurred or bring an action in any court of competent jurisdiction for the recovery from the defendant of a sum of not less than $50 nor more than $500. (§§ 24-34-306, -602, -604)

# CONNECTICUT

## Home and Family

## MARRIAGE

**AGE OF CONSENT:** A person 18 years or older may consent to marry. (§ 46b-30)*

**CONSENT REQUIREMENT:** Persons under 18 years of age may marry with parental consent or consent of the judge of probate; persons under 16 years of age may marry only with the consent of the judge of probate. (§ 46n-30)

**LICENSE REQUIREMENT:** A marriage license issued by the registrar for the town in which the marriage is to be celebrated is required. The license will not be issued unless a premarital certificate signed by a licensed physician has been filed with the registrar. There is a 4-day waiting period governing the issuance of marriage licenses. The license if valid for 65 days. (§§ 46b-24 to -27)

**PROHIBITED MARRIAGES:** Marriage between a man and his mother, grandmother, daughter, granddaughter, sister, aunt, niece, stepmother, or stepdaughter and between a woman and her father, grandfather, son, grandson, brother, uncle, nephew, stepfather, or stepson are incestuous and prohibited. (§ 46b-21) Any child born by a void or voidable marriage is legitimate. (§ 46b-60)

## DISSOLUTION OF MARRIAGE

**ANNULMENT:** If a marriage is prohibited or voidable, it will be annuled either under the laws of Connecticut or under the laws of the state in which the marriage was performed. (§ 46b-40)

*Residency Requirement:* There is no relevant statutory provision.

**LEGAL SEPARATION:** Appendix A, factors 1 (with factor 28), 2, 4, 6, 9, (for a total of 5 years), 16 (with factor 48 for 1 year), 17, 24, 25, and 27 (involving violation of conjugal duty), are grounds for legal separation. (§ 46b-40)

*Residency Requirement:* There is no relevant statutory provision.

**DIVORCE**

*Residency Requirement:* There is no residency requirement if one of the parties was a resident of the state at the time of the marriage and returned with the intention of remaining permanently, or if the grounds for divorce arose in the state; otherwise, the requirement is 1 year. [§ 46b-44(c)]

*Grounds for Divorce:* See "Legal Separation."

*Conciliation Requirement:* Either spouse or the attorney for minor children of the marriage may submit a request for conciliation to the clerk of the court. (§ 46b-53)

*Property Distribution:* The court may assign to either spouse all or any part of the estate of the other. Fault is one of the factors considered in the division of property. Factors 1, 5, 6, 7, 8, 9, 10, 11, and 28, listed in Appendix F, will be considered. (§ 46b-81)

*Unless otherwise specified, all citation references are to the Connecticut General Statutes Annotated (West 1958).

*Child Custody:* The court considers the best interests of the child in awarding custody and may award joint custody or sole custody to either parent or to a third party. The court will consider the wishes of the child if the child is of sufficient age and capable of forming an intelligent choice. The court will also consider the causes for the dissolution of the marriage if such causes are relevant to a determination of the best interests of the child. (§ 46b-56)

*Child Support:* Parents must support their children according to their respective abilities. In determining the amount of child support to be awarded, factors 1, 7, 8, 9, 10, 11, 12, 13, 14, 15, 16, and 18, listed in Appendix D, are considered. (§ 46b-84)

*Spousal Support/Alimony:* Alimony can be awarded to either spouse. In determining whether to award alimony, the causes for the dissolution of the marriage and any distribution of property are considered. Other factors considered are 1, 4, 13, 14, 15, and 16, listed in Appendix E. [§§ 46b-82, -83)] Alimony or support may be set aside, altered, or modified upon a substantial change of circumstances of either party. (§ 46b-86)

*Enforcement of Support Orders:* Whenever a spouse fails to make support payments, the dependent spouse may apply to the court for an order directing that support payments be withheld from the paycheck of the defaulting spouse. The overdue support is withheld from any amount in excess of the first $70 of the defaulting spouse's disposable income per week. Additionally, upon an order of the court, child support payments can be satisfied out of unemployment compensation benefits received by the party in default. A dependent spouse or child who seeks an execution against the spouse or parent owing the support is not precluded from pursuing other remedies, such as contempt orders, to enforce or punish the failure to obey a support order. (Conn. Pub. Acts 83-400) The defaulting spouse may be imprisoned for the contempt and liable for the costs of the contempt proceeding. (§ 46b-87) See also the Uniform Reciprocal Enforcement of Support Act, §§ 46b-180 *et seq*.

*Spouse's Name:* Upon the request of the wife, the court shall restore her former or birth name. (§ 46b-65)

*Divorce by Affidavit or Summary Judgment:* There is no relevant statutory provision.

*Displaced Homemaker Laws:* The Displaced Homemakers Transitional Assistance Act authorizes the labor commissioners to provide assistance to those women over 35 who formerly depended on another's income and who can no longer depend on that support. Services provided include vocational counseling and education, job training and placement, assistance with child care, and financial management counseling. (Conn. Pub. Acts 83-371)

# DOMESTIC VIOLENCE

**STATUTORY PROVISION:** Domestic violence is defined as a threat of present physical pain or injury by a spouse of either sex. (§§ 46b-15, -38)

**WHO IS PROTECTED?** The law protects spouses, former spouses, dependent children, and household and family members. (§§ 46b-15, -38)

**RELIEF AVAILABLE:** A victim of domestic violence can obtain orders of protection from the court. Such orders may enjoin the abusing spouse from restraining the abused person in any way; assaulting, molesting, sexually assaulting, or attacking the applicant; or entering the family dwelling or dwelling of the applicant. Protective orders are valid for 90 days and may be extended by the court. The Department of Human Resources is directed to establish shelters for the victims of domestic abuse. (§§ 46b-15, 46b-38, 17-31K)

**MARITAL RAPE:** A wife may charge her husband with rape. (§ 53a-71)

**CIVIL LAWSUIT FOR RAPE OR ASSAULT:** There are no cases directly on point. However, in *Maislin v. Lawton*, 314 A.2d 783 (Conn. 1983), the court held that a wife may sue her husband at common law.

**CHILD ABUSE:** The act protects children from physical injuries, malnutrition, sexual abuses, deprivation of necessities, cruel punishment, or emotional maltreatment. (§ 46b-120)

> *Notification Requirement:* Any health care professional, any school official, social worker, police officer, member of the clergy or mental health professional or any person paid for caring for children in a day care center who has reasonable cause to suspect that a child under 18 is abused or neglected must report such abuse or neglect immediately to the Commissioner of Children and Youth Services. (§§ 17-38a, b)

# INHERITANCE RIGHTS

**FAILURE TO MAKE A WILL:** The surviving spouse is entitled to the entire estate if the decedent left no heirs; to $50,000 and three-fourths of the balance of the estate if the decedent is survived by parents; to $50,000 and one-half of the balance of the estate if the decedent is survived by children or grandchildren who are also the surviving spouse's children or grandchildren; and to one-half of the estate if the decedent is survived by one or more children or grandchildren who are not also the surviving spouse's children or grandchildren. (§ 45-273a)

**FAILURE TO PROVIDE BY WILL:** If the testator fails to provide by will for the surviving spouse, he or she is entitled to a life interest in one-third of all the personal and real property owned by the decedent at death. (§ 45-273a)

**CHILDREN BORN OUT OF WEDLOCK:** A child born out of wedlock is the legitimate child of the mother and inherits from her. However, such a child can only inherit from the father if the father has been adjudicated the father of such a child by a court of competent jurisdiction or if the father has acknowledged paternity of the child under oath and in writing. [§ 45-274(b)]

**HOMESTEAD, PERSONAL, AND FAMILY ALLOWANCES:** The surviving spouse may be granted a reasonable amount of support and use of the family car during the administration of the estate. The decedent's family is allowed to remain in the family home until the estate is settled. If the decedent's personal estate is insufficient to pay the decedent's debts, the court may give household goods and other exempt personal property to the surviving spouse. (§§ 45-250 to -252, -273a)

**OPTION TO DISREGARD THE WILL:** The surviving spouse may reject the will and take instead a life interest in one-third of all the decedent's personal and real property. (§ 45-273a)

# REPRODUCTIVE RIGHTS

## ABORTION

> *Statutory Provisions:* Existing statutes prohibit all abortions, all attempts at abortion, and all aid, advice, and encouragement to bring about abortion unless necessary

to preserve the mother's life and require an abortion to be performed in a licensed hospital. (§§ 53-29 *et seq.*) These provisions were held unconstitutional in *Abele v. Markel*, 369 F. Supp. 807 (D. Conn. 1973). However, the constitutionality of this statute was upheld as applied to nonphysicians in *Connecticut v. Menillo*, 423 U.S. 9 (1975), and in *State v. Menillo*, 368 A.2d 136 (Conn. 1976).

*State Funding:*   State medicaid funding for abortions is restricted to those abortions necessary to preserve the life of the woman. (§ 17-134a; Policy 275, Chap. 3, Man. Vol. 3) This provision was declared unconstitutional in *Doe v. Maher* (No. 196874, Conn. Super. Ct., April 9, 1986).

**BIRTH CONTROL:**   There is no relevant statutory provision.

**STERILIZATION:**   No person may be sterilized unless he or she is 18 or older and has given informed consent, in writing, to sterilization. Sterilization of a person who is unable to give informed consent or who is under guardianship or conservatorship may be permitted only if a court finds that sterilization is in the person's best interests. (§ 45-78q) Sterilization for contraceptive purposes may only be performed by licensed doctors after the patient has given legal consent to the procedure. (§ 19-66b)

# UNMARRIED COUPLES

**COMMON-LAW MARRIAGE:**   Common-law marriages are not recognized by the state [*State ex rel. Felson et al. v. Allen*, 29 A.2d 306 (Conn. 1942)], nor are they accorded validity [*Hames v. Hames*, 316 A.2d 379 (Conn. 1972)].

**COHABITAL RELATIONSHIPS:**   In *Dosek v. Dosek*, 4 FLR 2828 (Conn. Super. Ct. 1978), the court held that agreements between cohabiting couples were valid and would be upheld. In *Dosek*, the couple had lived together for over 7 years, had agreed to combine their income for the purpose of living together as a family unit, and, in the event of separation, had agreed to divide their assets equally. The court held that the agreement was enforceable as a valid contract and that legal and equitable remedies were available to enforce that contract. In addition, a showing that a former spouse receiving alimony is living with another person may result in modification, suspension, reduction, or termination of alimony if the living arrangements cause such a change of circumstances as to alter the financial needs of the party. (§ 46b-86)

**CHILDREN**

*Custody:*   Once the parental rights of the father of a child born out of wedlock have been established, the father's rights and responsibilities are equivalent to those of the mother including custody, visitation, and support. (§§ 45-43, 46b-172a)

*Legitimation Proceedings:*   A child born out of wedlock is legitimate if the parents marry each other after the birth of the child, or if the father has been adjudicated to be the child's father by a court of competent jurisdiction, or if the father has acknowledged under oath and in writing to be the child's father. (§ 45-274)

*Paternity Proceedings:*   Proceedings to establish the paternity of a child born or conceived out of lawful wedlock, including a child born to or conceived by a married woman but begotten by a man other than her husband, may be brought by the mother or expectant mother or by the alleged father in the superior court for the geographic area in which either the mother or the putative father resides within 3 years of the child's birth. (§§ 46b-160, -172a) Upon request of either party, the court may order the parties to submit to blood tests to determine paternity. (§ 46b-168)

*Obligations of the Putative Father:*   Once paternity has been determined, the court will charge the father with the support and maintenance of the child, with the assistance of the mother if she is able, and will order him to pay a certain weekly sum to the mother until the child attains the age of 18. The court will also order the father to pay for the mother's confinement and the costs incurred for the support and maintenance of the child up to the time the paternity judgment is rendered. Executions and earnings assignments are available in paternity proceedings. (§§ 46b-171, -178)

# Education

## STATUTORY PROVISION

There is no comprehensive education equity act. However, § 10-15(c) provides that public schools are required to admit all children regardless of sex and all children have an equal opportunity to participate in the activities, programs, and courses offered. In addition, discrimination on the basis of sex in all state-conducted educational counseling, vocational guidance, and apprenticeship and on-the-job training programs is prohibited. (§ 46a-75) Also, local and regional school boards may not discriminate on the basis of sex or marital status in the employment of teachers in the public schools or in the determination of their salaries. (§ 10-153)

**ENFORCEMENT:** Persons who believe they have been discriminated against on the basis of sex in educational opportunities may, within 180 days of the occurrence of the alleged discriminatory act, by themselves or their attorney, file a complaint with the Connecticut Commission on Human Rights. Such persons may also petition the superior court for appropriate relief. (§ 46a-99)

# Employment

## EQUAL PAY LAWS

It is unlawful to discriminate in the amount of compensation paid to any employee solely on the basis of sex except that wage differentials may be based on such factors as length of service or merit rating. (§ 31-75)

**ENFORCEMENT:** An employer who violates the provisions of the equal pay law is liable to the employee for the difference between the wages owed and the wages paid. The employee may sue the employer to recover such wages, but the action must be brought within 1 year of the alleged violation. (§ 31-76)

## FAIR EMPLOYMENT LAWS

The state's fair employment practice law applies to the state of Connecticut, its political and civil subdivisions, all employers of three or more employees, labor organizations, and employment agencies. It prohibits discrimination based on sex and marital status in hire, discharge, compensation, terms, privileges, and conditions of employment, including sexual harassment. It makes unlawful the termination of a woman's employment or the denial of reasonable leave of absence, disability, or benefits because of pregnancy. In addition, it prohibits inquiring into an employee's or applicant's childbearing plans unless such information is directly related to workplace exposure to hazardous substances, and prohibits requiring an employee to submit to sterilization as a condition of employment. An employer is required to take reasonable measures to protect employees from exposure to hazards identified. [§§ 46a-51 (17), -60(a)(1) to (a)(10)]

**ENFORCEMENT:** The Connecticut Commission on Human Rights and Opportunities is charged with the enforcement of the fair employment practice law. Any person claiming to be aggrieved by an alleged discriminatory practice may file a complaint with the commission within 180 days of the occurrence of the alleged discriminatory act. (§ 46a-82)

## GOVERNMENT CONTRACTORS AND SUBCONTRACTORS

Any employer who contracts to provide goods and services to the state must agree not to discriminate on the basis of sex or marital status. (§§ 4-114a, 46a-71)

**ENFORCEMENT:** An employee of, or applicant for, employment with a government contractor or subcontractor who has been discriminated against on the basis of sex or marital status may file a complaint with the Commission on Human Rights within 180 days of the occurrence of the alleged discriminatory act. (§ 46a-82)

## STATE EMPLOYEE LAWS

Employment discrimination by state officials and supervisory personnel is prohibited. State employees also have the benefit of the fair employment practice law. [§§ 46a-70(a), -51(10)]

**ENFORCEMENT:** See "Fair Employment Laws."

## VETERAN'S PREFERENCE

On civil service examinations, five points are added to the passing scores of veterans; ten points are added to the passing scores of disabled veterans. (§ 7-415)

# Community Life

## CREDIT

It is unlawful for a creditor to discriminate against any person over 18 on the basis of sex and marital status. (§ 46a-66)

**ENFORCEMENT:** A person who has been discriminated against in credit on the basis of sex may *either* file a complaint with the Commission on Human Rights within 180 days of the occurrence of the alleged discriminatory act *or* bring an action against the creditor within 1 year of the violation. (§§ 46a-82, -98)

## HOUSING

Discrimination on the basis of sex and marital status is prohibited in public housing projects, other types of publicly assisted housing, any housing accommodation, commercial property, building lots, and mobile home parks, except that discrimination is permitted by the owner of a two-family home in which the owner or members of his or her family reside or by an owner who wishes to rent a room or rooms in the house where the owner or members of his or her family reside. An organization or association may rent sleeping accommodations exclusively to persons of one sex. It is not unlawful to deny housing accommodations to a man and a woman who are unrelated by blood or who are not married to each other. (§§ 46a-64, -64) The Connecticut Housing Finance Authority may not finance housing accommodations in which occupants are discriminated against on the basis of sex. (§ 8-265c)

**ENFORCEMENT:** A person who has been discriminated against in housing on the basis of sex may file a complaint with the Commission on Human Rights within 180 days of the occurrence of the alleged discriminatory act. (§ 46a-82)

# INSURANCE

There is no relevant statutory provision.

# PUBLIC ACCOMMODATIONS

Discrimination by the owners or operators of places of public accommodation, resort, or amusement on the basis of sex and marital status is prohibited. (§§ 46a-63, -64)

**ENFORCEMENT:** See "Housing."

# DELAWARE

## Home and Family

## MARRIAGE

**AGE OF CONSENT:** A male 18 years or older, and a female 16 years or older, may enter into a valid marriage. [Tit. 13, § 123(a)]*

**CONSENT REQUIREMENT:** Females under 18 years of age may not marry without parental or guardian consent. However, any person under the legal age may marry if he or she acknowledges under oath that he or she is the parent or prospective parent of a child. [Tit. 13, 123(b), (f)]

**LICENSE REQUIREMENT:** Persons wishing to marry must obtain a license valid for 30 days from the date of issuance. If one or both of the parents are residents of the state, they must obtain the license at least 24 hours before the ceremony. If neither party resides in the state, they must obtain the license at least 96 hours before the ceremony. (Tit. 13, § 107)

**PROHIBITED MARRIAGES:** Marriages between a person and his or her ancestor, descendant, brother, sister, uncle, aunt, niece, nephew or first cousin are incestuous and prohibited. [Tit. 13, § 1506(c)] Also prohibited are marriage to a person who is of unsound mind; marriage to a patient in a mental hospital unless the patient files a certificate signed by the superintendent of the mental hospital that such a person is fit to marry; marriage to one suffering a venereal disease unknown to the other party; marriage to a habitual drunkard or confirmed drug addict; marriage to a divorced person unless a certified copy of the divorce decree is inspected by the clerk of the court; marriage to a person on probation or on parole unless such person files with the clerk of the court a written consent to the proposed marriage signed by the probation officer or parole officer; and marriage between paupers. (Tit. 13, § 101) Children of void or voidable marriages are legitimate. (Tit. 13, § 105)

## DISSOLUTION OF MARRIAGE

**ANNULMENT:** Factors 32, 33, 35, 36, and 37, listed in Appendix A, are grounds for annulment. Prohibited marriages as listed above may also be annulled. (Tit. 13, § 1506)

*Residency Requirement:* There is no relevant statutory provision.

**LEGAL SEPARATION:** There is no relevant statutory provision.

**DIVORCE**

*Residency Requirement:* There is a 6-month residency requirement to obtain a divorce in Delaware. (Tit. 13, § 1504)

*Grounds for Divorce:* Irretrievable breakdown constitutes grounds for divorce. See Appendix A, factors 23, 28, 29, and 30. (Tit. 13, § 1505)

*Conciliation Requirement:* In contested cases, the court may either rule on the petition for divorce or stay the proceedings for a period of 60 days so that the parties may seek counseling. (Tit. 13, § 1517)

*Unless otherwise specified, all citation references are to the Delaware Code Annotated (Revised 1974).

*Property Distribution:* Marital property is divided equitably between the parties without regard to fault. In making such a division the court considers factors 1, 2, 3, 5 to 12, 17, 20, 21, 22, and 25, listed in Appendix F. (Tit. 13, § 1513)

*Child Custody:* Child custody is awarded according to the best interests of the child. Appendix B, factors 5, 10, 11, 12, 13, 14, and 15, are considered. (Tit. 13, § 722)

*Child Support:* The duty to support a child rests equally on both parents. In determining the amount of support due the court considers the overall position and factors 1, 3, 7, 9, 10, 12, 16, and 18, listed in Appendix D. (Tit. 13, §§ 501, 514, 701)

*Spousal Support/Alimony:* The court may award temporary alimony to either spouse during the pendency of the action; alimony to a spouse after a decree dissolving an irretrievably broken marriage due to mental illness; or alimony to a dependent spouse but such alimony is not to last for longer than 2 years after the marriage dissolution unless the parties were married for more than 20 years. In determining the amount of alimony to be awarded, Appendix E, factors 2, 3, 4, 5, 6, 12, 13, 14, and 18, will be considered. (Tit. 13, § 1512) Cohabitation with a member of the opposite sex consitutes a substantial change of circumstances which will justify either the modification or termination of alimony. (Tit. 13, § 1519)

*Enforcement of Support Orders:* A spouse to whom support is owed has the right to enforce the support order in family court. [Tit. 13, § 1519(c)] The court may order a person under a duty of support to pay reasonable support for the child and/or spouse through the court or the Bureau of Child Support Enforcement or directly to the spouse or ex-spouse or custodian of the child. (Tit. 13, § 950) Where no wage-withholding order is currently in effect, the income of the party owing support will be attached automatically upon the filing of a verified notice by the party awarded support that payment is in default 7 working days. [Tit. 13, § 513(b)(2)] If the party owing support fails to file an affidavit opposing the attachment within 10 days of the filing of the notice, the attachment will take effect immediately. If an affidavit of opposition is filed within 10 days, the court shall make a final determination regarding the attachment within 45 days. [Tit. 13, § 513(b)(3)] Withholding of income shall remain in effect for as long as the order of support upon which it is based or any modification of that order. [Tit. 13, § 513(b)(11)] See also the Uniform Reciprocal Enforcement of Support Act, Tit. 13, § 601.

*Spouse's Name:* The wife may resume her birth or former name. (Tit. 13, § 1514)

*Divorce by Affidavit or Summary Judgment: There is no relevant statutory provision.*

*Displaced Homemaker Laws:* The coordinator of the Displaced Homemakers Program is required to provide job counseling, training, placement services, education, and health services to displaced homemakers, and to undertake research for the creation of new jobs making maximum use of skills developed from homemaking experience. (Tit. 31, §§ 1301 *et seq.* )

# DOMESTIC VIOLENCE

**STATUTORY PROVISION:** Under the act, conduct by a family member against another family member which imperils the family relationship is prohibited. [Tit. 10, § 921(6)]

**WHO IS PROTECTED?** Persons protected by the domestic violence laws include husband and wife, a man and woman cohabiting in a home in which there is a child of either or both, a custodian and child, or any group of persons related by blood or marriage who are residing in one home under one head. [Tit. 10, § 901(9)]

**RELIEF AVAILABLE:** A victim may petition the family court for an order of protection. During an action for divorce or annulment, the court may grant an injunction enjoining either party from disturbing the peace of or molesting the other. Arrests without a warrant are allowed in cases where an officer has reasonable ground to believe that the person to be arrested has committed a crime. [Tit. 10, §§ 901(9), 902, 921(6), 925(15), 950(5); Tit. 11, § 1904; Tit. 13, §§ 513(8), 1509, 1510]

**MARITAL RAPE:** Spouses living together and cohabitors cannot be charged with rape. [Tit. 11, § 772(b)]

**CIVIL LAWSUIT FOR RAPE OR ASSAULT:** There is no relevant case on point, but a spouse may not sue the other for tort. [*Alfree v. Alfree*, 410 A.2d 161 (Del. 1979)]

**CHILD ABUSE:** Child abuse and neglect are defined as any intentional physical injury or an injury which results in a mental or emotional condition brought about by negligent treatment, sexual abuse, maltreatment, nontreatment, exploitation or abandonment of a child under 18. (Tit. 16, § 902)

  *Notification Requirement:* All health care professionals, school employers, social workers, psychologists, medical examiners, or other persons who know or reasonably suspect child abuse or neglect must report it to the Division of Child Protective Services of the Department of Services For Children Youth, and their Families. (Tit. 16, §§ 903, 904)

# INHERITANCE RIGHTS

**FAILURE TO MAKE A WILL:** The surviving spouse is entitled to the entire estate if the decedent left no other heirs; to $50,000 and one-half of the balance of the personal estate, plus a life estate in all real estate, if the decedent is survived by his or her parents or one or more of his or her children or grandchildren who are also the spouse's children or grandchildren; or to one-half of the personal estate, plus a life interest in all real estate, if the decedent is survived by one or more children or grandchildren who are not also the spouse's children or grandchildren. (Tit. 12, § 502)

**FAILURE TO PROVIDE BY WILL:** If the decedent's will was executed before the marriage and the decedent has not made provision for his or her spouse by will or otherwise, the surviving spouse is entitled to the same share in the estate as if the decedent died without making a will. (Tit. 12, § 321)

**CHILDREN BORN OUT OF WEDLOCK:** A child born out of wedlock may inherit through the mother only. If the child has been legitimated or the paternity of the father has been judicially determined before the father's death or has been established after his death by a preponderance of the evidence, a child born out of wedlock may inherit through the father. However, even though his paternity has been established, the father or his kindred cannot inherit from the child unless the father has openly treated the child as his own and has supported the child. (Tit. 12, § 512)

**HOMESTEAD, PERSONAL, AND FAMILY ALLOWANCES:** Within 9 months from the date of death or 6 months from the date of the granting of the letters testamentary or of administration, whichever is the shorter period, the surviving spouse must notify the Register of Wills in writing of his or her demand that a sum, not exceeding $2000, be set aside out of the proceeds of the decedent's estate as a family allowance. This does not affect any other rights to which the surviving spouse is entitled. (Tit. 12, § 2308)

**OPTION TO DISREGARD THE WILL:** If the decedent was domiciled in Delaware, the surviving spouse may elect to take $20,000 or one-third of his or her statutory share, whichever is less, less the amount of all transfers to the spouse; if the decedent was not a Delaware domiciliary, the right of the spouse to take a share of property located in Delaware is governed by the laws of the state in which the decedent was domiciled at death. If the spouse does elect to take his or her statutory share, he or she need not renounce that share under the will or through intestate succession. The spouse is entitled to a family allowance whether or not he or she elects to take the statutory share. (Tit. 12, §§ 901, 907)

# REPRODUCTIVE RIGHTS
## ABORTION

*Statutory Provisions:* Existing statutes limit the circumstances under which an abortion may be performed; require an abortion to be performed in a hospital; require that an abortion be approved by two doctors and a hospital review authority; establish a 120-day residency requirement before an abortion may be performed; and make performing, assisting, advising, or procuring an abortion a crime. (Tit. 11, §§ 651, 653, 654; Tit. 24, §§ 1766, 1790, 1793) However, these statutes have been held unconstitutional under *Delaware Women's Health Organization, Inc. v. Wier*, 441 F. Supp. 497 (D.Del. 1977). The refusal to submit to an abortion must not be grounds for loss of any privileges or immunities, including the receipt of public benefits. No hospital or person is required to perform or participate in an abortion. (Tit. 24, § 1791) When an abortion or attempted abortion results in a live birth, the person(s) performing the abortion must exercise the same degree of medical skill, care, and diligence which would be rendered to a child born as a result of a normal birth. (Tit. 24, § 1795)

*Informed Consent:* Informed consent consists of a written statement in which the woman acknowledges that she voluntarily consents to the abortion and that she has been advised about the procedure to be used, the probable effects of the abortion, the stage of fetal development, the risks involved, and the reasonable alternatives to abortion. Informed consent of the woman is required unless the abortion is necessary to save her life.

*Parental Consent:* Existing statutes require parental consent in the case of an unmarried minor under 18. [Tit. 13, § 703; Tit. 24, § 1790(b)(3)] These statutes have been held to be unconstitutional by *Delaware Women's Health Organization, Inc. v. Weir*, 441 F. Supp. 497 (D.Del. 1977).

*Spousal Consent:* There is no relevant statutory provision.

*Mandatory Waiting Period:* A waiting period of 24 hours is required unless the woman's life is in danger. (Tit. 24, § 1794)

**BIRTH CONTROL:** A minor over 12 who claims to be pregnant or exposed to the chance of becoming pregnant may give written consent for any diagnostic, preventive, lawful therapeutic procedures, medical or surgical care, and treatment except abortion. Parental consent is not required. A doctor may either provide or withhold from the parents of a minor the information as to the diagnosis, therapeutic procedures, care, and treatment rendered to the minor. However, parents must be notified of an intention to perform an operation upon a minor. (Tit. 13, § 708)

**STERILIZATION:** There are no relevant statutory provisions regarding voluntary sterilization. Existing statutes provide for involuntary sterilization of persons who are institutionalized because of mental retardation, mental illness, or epilepsy or of persons who are habitual criminals convicted of at least three felonies where the criminality is caused by mental abnormality or mental disease. (Tit. 16, §§ 5701, 5703)

# UNMARRIED COUPLES

## COMMON-LAW MARRIAGE: Common-law marriages are not valid in Delaware. [*Berdikas v. Berdikas*, 178 A.2d 468 (Del. 1962)]

## COHABITAL RELATIONSHIPS: There is no case directly on point, but see *Siple v. Corbett*, 447 A.2d 1184 (Del. 1982), where the court held that contracts founded upon consideration for romantic involvement including sexual favors are void and unenforceable.

## CHILDREN

*Custody:* Once paternity is established, the court may make appropriate provisions for the custody of the child. (Tit. 13, § 812)

*Legitimation Proceedings:* A child born out of wedlock is legitimated if the child's parents are or have been married and the child is born during the marriage; attempted to marry before the child's birth, even though the attempted marriage is later declared void; attempted to marry after the child's birth, and the father has acknowledged his paternity of the child under oath in a writing filed with the clerk of the family court, and with his consent he is named the father on the child's birth certificate; or he is obligated to support the child under a written agreement or a court order, or while the child is a minor he receives the child in his home and openly holds the child out as his natural child for a reasonable period of time; or if he acknowledges his paternity under oath in a writing filed with the clerk of the family court. (Tit. 13, § 804)

*Paternity Proceedings:* Any interested party, including the child or a guardian, the mother, or if deceased, her representative, an appropriate public agency, or the alleged father, may bring an action to determine the father and child relationship. (Tit. 13, § 805) The court may order the parties to submit to blood tests to determine the paternity of the child. [Tit. 13, § 810(e)] An action to determine the paternity may be brought until the child reaches the age of majority. (Tit. 13, § 806)

*Obligations of the Putative Father:* The duty to support a child under 18 years of age, whether born in or out of wedlock, rests equally upon both parents. (Tit. 13, § 501) The putative father owes a duty of support to the woman pregnant with a child conceived out of wedlock. This duty of support may include the mother's prenatal and postnatal medical and confinement expenses and any other relief the court believes reasonable. (Tit. 13, § 503)

# Education

# STATUTORY PROVISION

There is no relevant statutory provision. However, it should be noted that if federal funds are involved, federal law, Title IX of the Education Amendments of 1972, Pub. L. No. 92-318, 20 U.S.C. §§ 1681–1686, may apply.

# Employment

## EQUAL PAY LAWS

It is unlawful for an employer to discriminate in wages because of an employee's sex except where the differential is based on seniority, merit, or a system which measures earnings by quantity or quality of production or any other factor other than sex. (Tit. 19, § 1107A)

> **ENFORCEMENT:** A party who has been discriminated against on the basis of sex in the payment of wages may bring a civil action for the unpaid wages and liquidated damages within 1 year of the alleged discriminatory act. (Tit. 10, § 8111; Tit. 19, § 1113)

## FAIR EMPLOYMENT LAWS

The law applies to the state of Delaware; its political subdivisions; employers of four or more employees; employment agencies; labor organizations; and religious, fraternal, charitable, and sectarian corporations and associations supported in whole or in part by government monies and employing four or more persons within the state. The law prohibits an employer from refusing to hire or discriminating in compensation or terms, conditions, or privileges of employment; or labor organizations from excluding or expelling any person from membership; or an employment agency from refusing to refer for employment any person on account of that person's sex. (Tit. 19, §§ 710, 711)

> **ENFORCEMENT:** The Delaware Department of Labor is charged with the enforcement of the fair employment law. Any person who has been the victim of a discriminatory employment practice may file a charge with the Delaware Department of Labor within 90 days of the alleged unlawful employment practice or 120 days after its discovery, whichever is later. (Tit. 19, § 712)

## GOVERNMENT CONTRACTORS AND SUBCONTRACTORS

Government contractors and subcontractors who contract to provide goods and services to the state and whose contracts do not exceed $25,000 must agree not to discriminate against their employees or applicants for employment on the basis of sex. (Tit. 29, § 6920)

> **ENFORCEMENT:** See "Fair Employment Laws."

## STATE EMPLOYEE LAWS

State employees are covered by the fair employment law and by Exec. Order No. 9, issued July 15, 1960. [Tit. 19, § 710(2)]

## VETERAN'S PREFERENCE

The unmarried widows of veterans have five points added to their passing civil service examination scores; ten points are added to the passing scores of the unmarried widows of disabled veterans. (Tit. 29, § 5923)

# Community Life

## CREDIT

It is unlawful to deny a loan or other financial assistance on the basis of sex or marital status to a person applying for such a loan for the purpose of purchasing, constructing, improving, repairing or maintaining a dwelling, or discriminate in the fixing of the amount, interest rate, duration, or other terms or conditions of such loan or other financial assistance. [Tit. 6, § 4603(7)]

**ENFORCEMENT:** A person who has been discriminated against in credit on the basis of sex and marital status may file a complaint with the state Human Relations Commission within 180 days of the occurrence of the alleged discriminatory act. (Tit. 6, § 4605)

## HOUSING

It is unlawful to refuse to sell or rent a dwelling offered to the public to any person on account of that person's sex or marital status. Discriminatory advertisements are also prohibited. Dwellings owned and operated by a religious or nonprofit organization are exempted from the law's coverage. Also exempted are rooms or units in dwellings containing living quarters occupied or intended to be occupied by no more than four families living independently of each other, if the owner of the dwelling maintains and occupies one of these units as his or her residence. (Tit. 6, §§ 4603, 4604)

**ENFORCEMENT:** See "Credit."

## INSURANCE

Discrimination between individuals of the same class and equal expectation of life in the rates charged for any contract of life insurance or of life annuity, or in the dividends or other benefits payable thereon, or in any other of the terms and conditions of such contract is prohibited. Also prohibited is discrimination between individuals of the same class and of essentially the same hazard in the amount of premium, policy fees, or rates charged for any policy or contract of accident or health insurance, or in the benefits payable thereunder, or in any of the terms or conditions of such contract, or in any other matter whatever. [Tit. 6, § 4603(7)]

**ENFORCEMENT:** The Commissioner of Insurance has the power to examine and investigate all charges of discriminatory practices. If there is a finding that a prohibited discriminatory practice has occurred, the commissioner may order the insurer to cease and desist from engaging in the practice and may impose a monetary fine, revoke or suspend the insurer's license, or grant any other relief which is just and reasonable. (Tit. 18, § 2308)

## PUBLIC ACCOMMODATIONS

The owner, lessee, manager, superintendent, agent, or employee of any place of public accommodation is prohibited from denying access to such facilities on the basis of sex or marital status. (Tit. 6, § 4504)

**ENFORCEMENT:** A person who has been discriminated against in public accommodations on account of sex or marital status may by himself or herself or by attorney file a complaint with the Human Relations Commission within 90 days after the occurrence of the alleged discriminatory act. (Tit. 6, § 4506)

# DISTRICT OF COLUMBIA

## Home and Family

## MARRIAGE

**AGE OF CONSENT:** A person 16 years of age or older may consent to marry. (§ 30-103)*

**CONSENT REQUIREMENT:** Persons who are under 18 years of age and who have not been previously married may not marry without the consent of a parent or guardian. (§ 30-111)

**LICENSE REQUIREMENT:** In order to obtain a license to marry, the parties must state under oath on a printed application their names, the names of their parents or guardians if the parties are underage, whether they were previously married, and whether and in what degree they are related. (§ 30-110) After the application has been submitted, there is a 3-day waiting period before the license may be issued. (§ 30-109) No application for a marriage license will be received without a physician's statement that the applicant has submitted to a laboratory blood test within the previous 30 days and does not have infectious syphilis. (§ 30-117) A judge of the superior court may waive certain license provisions for reasons of public policy or physical condition of either of the applicants. (§ 30-118)

**PROHIBITED MARRIAGES:** Marriages between a person and a grandparent, grandparent's spouse, spouse's grandparent, aunt, uncle, parent or stepparent, spouse's parent, child, child's spouse, sibling, sibling's child, sibling's child's spouse or spouse's child's child are prohibited and null and void. [§ 30-101(1), (2)] Bigamous marriages are likewise prohibited. [§ 30-101(3)]

## DISSOLUTION OF MARRIAGE

**ANNULMENT:** Grounds for annulment are factors 19, 32, 33, 34, 35, 36, and 38, listed in Appendix A. (§§ 16-903, -904)
    *Residency Requirement:* If the marriage was performed outside the District of Columbia, one of the parties must be a bona fide resident at the time the action is commenced. Otherwise no residency requirements apply. (§ 16-902)

**LEGAL SEPARATION:** Factors 4, 17, 28, and 31, listed in Appendix A, are grounds for a separation from bed and board. [§ 16-904(b)]
    *Residency Requirement:* One of the parties to the marriage must have been a bona fide resident for at least 6 months preceding the commencement of the action. Members of the armed forces are deemed to reside in the District for purposes of this requirement if they reside there for a continuous period of 6 months during their period of military service. (§ 16-902)

**DIVORCE**
    *Residency Requirement:* See "Legal Separation."
    *Grounds for Divorce:* Appendix A, factors 28 and 31, are grounds for divorce. [§§ 16-904(a), -905(b), -906]

*Unless otherwise specified, all citation references are to District of Columbia Code (1967).

*Conciliation Requirement:* There is no relevant statutory provision.

*Property Distribution:* Upon annulment or divorce, in the absence of a valid agreement or decree of legal separation disposing the property of the spouses, the court shall assign to each party his or her separate property acquired before the marriage or acquired during the marriage by gift or inheritance, plus any increase in such property or property acquired in exchange for such property. [§ 16-910(a)] All other property accumulated during the marriage, regardless of how title is held, shall be distributed in an equitable, just, and reasonable manner, considering all relevant factors including, but not limited to, 1, 5, 6, 7, 8, 9, 10, 11, 17, 20, 21, 25, and 29, listed in Appendix F. [§ 16-910(b)]

*Child Custody:* During an action for divorce or annulment, the court may determine who shall have custody of minor children pending the proceedings, according to their best interests and without conclusive regard to the sex or sexual orientation, race, color, national origin, or political affiliations of either party. Appendix B, factors 6, 10, 11, 12, and 14, shall be considered, as well as all other relevant factors. [§ 16-911(a)(5)] In determining the custody and care of minor children following a decree of divorce, the same criteria will apply. [§ 16-914(a)] There is no relevant statutory provision for joint or shared custody.

*Child Support:* The court may decree that any parent pay reasonable sums periodically for the support and maintenance of his or her child or children. (§ 16-916) During a divorce or annulment action, the court may require one spouse to pay the other for the support of the children in that other spouse's care. (§ 16-911) There is no statutory provision setting out factors to be considered in setting support.

*Spousal Support/Alimony:* The court may require either spouse to pay alimony to the other, upon granting of a divorce, if it seems just and proper. (§§ 16-912, -913) During the pendency of an action for divorce or annulment, the court may order one spouse to pay alimony to the other. [§ 16-911(a)(1)] There is no statutory provision setting out factors to be considered in setting support. Whenever a spouse fails or refuses to maintain his or her needy spouse, although able to do so, the court may, upon application and a showing of genuine need, decree that that spouse shall pay reasonable sums periodically for the support of the needy spouse. [§ 16-916(a)]

*Enforcement of Support Orders:* The court may enforce support, maintenance and alimony orders by attachment, garnishment, and/or imprisonment for disobedience. (§§ 16-911, -912, -916) The court may enjoin any disposition of a spouse's property to avoid collection of the allowances required, order a party in arrears to assign part of his or her income to the person entitled to receive the payments, and order that payments be made to the clerk of the court for remittance to the person entitled to receive the payments. (§ 16-911) Income tax refunds of people who are in arrears with court-ordered child support payments may be intercepted. [§ 47-1812.11 (4)] See also Uniform Reciprocal Enforcement of Support Act §§ 30-301 *et seq.*

*Spouse's Name:* Upon the request of a party who assumed a new name upon marriage, the court shall state in the decree of divorce either the birth name or other previous name which the party desires to use. (§ 16-915)

*Divorce by Affidavit or Summary Judgment:* There is no relevant statutory provision.

*Displaced Homemaker Laws:* There is no relevant statutory provision.

# DOMESTIC VIOLENCE

**STATUTORY PROVISION:** Upon the complaint of any person of criminal conduct if it appears that the conduct involves an "intrafamily offense," the U.S. attorney shall notify the Director of Social Services, who may investigate the matter. [§ 16-1002)(a)] Intrafamily offenses are acts, punishable as a criminal offense, committed by an offender against a person to whom the offender is related by blood, through legal custody, by marriage, or by having a child in common, or with whom the offender has shared a residence within the last year, and who is or was in a close relationship with the offender which renders application of the law regarding intrafamily offenses appropriate. (§ 16-1001)

**WHO IS PROTECTED?** See "Statutory Provision."

**RELIEF AVAILABLE:** The U.S. attorney may refer the matter to the director of the Department of Social Services, who may investigate and make appropriate recommendations. The U.S. attorney may also file a criminal charge and consult the Department of Social Services for appropriate recommendations for conditions of release. The U.S. attorney may alternatively refer the matter to the Corporation Counsel for the filing of a petition for civil protection in the family division of the superior court. (§ 16-1002) Also, the Corporation Counsel, or a complainant acting on his or her own initiative, may file a petition for civil protection in the family division. (§ 16-1003) Following a hearing, the court may issue a protective order directing the party to refrain from the conduct committed, or threatened, and to keep the peace; requiring the party to participate in psychiatric or medical treatment or counseling programs; directing the party to avoid the presence of the family member endangered; directing the party to vacate or not enter the victim's dwelling; directing the party to relinquish possession or use of certain personal property owned by the victim; awarding temporary custody of a minor child of the parties; providing for visitation rights with appropriate restrictions to protect the victim's safety; awarding court costs and attorney fees; ordering the police to take such action as the family division deems necessary to enforce its orders; and/or directing the party to perform or refrain from other actions as may be appropriate to the effective resolution of the matter. [§ 16-1005(c)] Temporary protection orders of not more than 14 days' duration may be issued upon the filing of the petition and before the hearing. [§ 16-1004(c)]

**MARITAL RAPE:** A woman may charge her husband with rape. (§ 22-2801)

**CIVIL LAWSUIT FOR RAPE OR ASSAULT:** Spouses may sue each other for the infliction of personal injury. (§ 30-201)

**CHILD ABUSE:** In addition to intrafamily offenses, it is a misdemeanor, punishable by a $250 fine or 2 years in prison or both, to torture, cruelly beat, abuse, or otherwise willfully maltreat any child under the age of 18 years or, for a person having the custody and care of a child under the age of 14 years, to expose the child in any place with the intent of abandoning the child. (§ 22-901) Any parent or guardian of sufficient financial ability who refuses or neglects to provide for any child under 14 is guilty of a misdemeanor and subject to a $100 fine or imprisonment in the workhouse for not more than 3 months, or both. (§ 22-902)

> *Notification Requirement:* Any physician, psychologist, medical examiner, dentist, chiropractor, registered nurse, licensed practical nurse, person involved in the care and treatment of patients, law enforcement officer, school official, teacher, social service worker, day care worker, and mental health professional who, in his

or her professional or official capacity, knows or has reasonable cause to suspect that a child has been or is in immediate danger of being mentally or physically abused or neglected shall report such knowledge or suspicion to either the metropolitan police or the Child Protective Services Division of the Department of Human Services. Any other person may make such a report. (§ 2-1352) The police generally have primary responsibility for the initial investigation of alleged child abuse. (§ 6-2104) The Child Protective Services Division maintains a register of cases of abused children. (§§ 6-2111 to -2119)

# INHERITANCE RIGHTS

**FAILURE TO MAKE A WILL:** A surviving spouse is entitled to the whole estate if the decedent leaves no child, parent, grandchild, sibling, or child of a sibling (§ 19-302); to one-half the estate when the decedent leaves no child or descendant, but does leave a parent, sibling, or child of a sibling (§ 19-304); and to one-third when the decedent leaves a child or a descendant of a child. (§ 19-303)

**FAILURE TO PROVIDE BY WILL:** Where the decedent has not made a devise or bequest to the spouse, or nothing passes by a purported devise or bequest, the surviving spouse is entitled to a legal share of the real and personal estate of the deceased spouse without filing a written renunciation, or the surviving spouse may elect to take dower. (§ 19-113) Dower entitles the surviving spouse to one-third of the lands owned by the deceased spouse at any time during the marriage. (§ 19-102)

**CHILDREN BORN OUT OF WEDLOCK:** Children born out of wedlock and their heirs may inherit from their mother, or from their father if parenthood has been established, or from each other or from the heirs of each other, as though they were born in lawful wedlock, and the mother and such father and their respective heirs may inherit from such children. (§ 19-316)

**HOMESTEAD, PERSONAL, AND FAMILY ALLOWANCES:** A surviving spouse is entitled to a $10,000 allowance out of the personal estate of the decedent for his or her personal use and that of the minor children. The allowance is paid in money or in specific property at its fair value, at the spouse's election, and is exempt from all debts and obligations of the decedent except funeral expenses not exceeding $750. When there is no surviving spouse, the surviving minor children are entitled to the allowance. The allowance is in addition to the spouse's and children's shares of the estate. (§ 19-101) The widow of a deceased man, where the marriage was made before November 29, 1957, or the surviving spouse of a decedent who died after March 15, 1962 is entitled to dower and may remain in the chief dwelling house of the decedent 40 days after the death without being liable for rent. The surviving spouse may in the meantime have reasonable sustenance out of the decedent's estate. [§ 19-102(a)]

**OPTION TO DISREGARD THE WILL:** Within 6 months after the will of the decedent is admitted to probate, the surviving spouse may file a written renunciation in the probate court renouncing all claim to any devise or bequest made under the deceased spouse's will, and may elect to take his or her legal share of the real and personal estate of the decedent, or, in lieu of the legal share of the real estate, to take dower in all the real estate to which the right of dower is applicable. The time for renunciation may be extended. A valid antenuptial or postnuptial agreement determines the surviving spouse's rights in the estate of the deceased spouse, but a spouse may accept the benefits of a devise or bequest made by the decedent. (§ 19-113)

# REPRODUCTIVE RIGHTS

**ABORTION:** A person procuring, producing, or attempting to procure or produce an abortion or miscarriage, unless necessary for the preservation of the mother's life or health and under the direction of a competent licensed practitioner of medicine, is liable for imprisonment of 1 to 10 years. (§ 22-201) However, this statute appears unconstitutional in light of the United States Supreme Court decision in *Roe v. Wade*, 410 U.S. 113 (1973).

**BIRTH CONTROL:** There is no relevant statutory provision.

**STERILIZATION:** No resident of a skilled or intermediate care or community residential facility may be sterilized by an employee or at the direction or under the authorization of an employee of such a facility. (§ 6-1968)

# UNMARRIED COUPLES

**COMMON-LAW MARRIAGE:** Common-law marriages are recognized. To establish a common-law marriage, there must be an express mutual present intent to be husband and wife, followed by good faith cohabitation. [*Johnson v. Young*, 372 A.2d 992 (App. D.C., 1977)]

**COHABITAL RELATIONSHIPS:** Cohabitants have the legal right to hold property jointly and to give or bequeath such property to each other without regard to the limitations imposed upon them by their nonmarital status. See *Coleman v. Jackson*, 286 F.2d 98 (D.C. Cir.), *cert. denied*, 366 U.S. 933 (1960).

## CHILDREN

*Custody:* There is no relevant statutory provision distinguishing children born out of wedlock for custody purposes.

*Legitimation Proceedings:* A child born out of wedlock is the legitimate child of the father and mother and the legitimate relative of their relatives by blood or adoption. (§ 16-908) A child's relationship to the father is established by proving he is the father by a preponderance of the evidence. (§ 16-909) Once established, the parent-child relationship exists for all rights, privileges, duties, and obligations under the laws of the District of Columbia. (§ 16-907)

*Paternity Proceedings:* Any individual may bring a civil action over which the court has jurisdiction for determining parentage. (§ 16-2341) Proceedings to establish parentage may be instituted after 4 months of pregnancy or at any time until the child's twenty-first birthday. (§ 16-2342) The family division of the superior court has exclusive jurisdiction over paternity proceedings. [§ 11-1101(11)] The court may require the child, mother, or an alleged parent to submit to medical, blood, or tissue-grouping tests. (§ 16-2343)

*Obligations of the Putative Father:* The natural parents of a child born out of wedlock have the duty to support that child while he or she is a minor. Parenthood is established either by judicial process or by acknowledgment by the alleged parent. (§ 30-320)

# Education

# STATUTORY PROVISION

It is an unlawful discriminatory practice for an educational institution to deny, restrict, abridge or condition the use of or access to any of its facilities and services to any person otherwise qualified, on the basis of sex, marital status, sexual orientation, family responsibilities, or source of income. (§ 1-2520)

## AREAS COVERED

There is an exception for religious and political organizations. (§ 1-2503) The sex discrimination provision does not apply to private undergraduate colleges or any private preschool or elementary or secondary school, except where such a college offers a course not available elsewhere in the District. (§ 1-2521) It is unlawful to assign different salaries to male and female teachers employed in the same grade of school and performing like duties. (§ 31-1001)

**ENFORCEMENT:** See "Community Life: Housing."

# Employment

## EQUAL PAY LAWS

See "Fair Employment Laws."

## FAIR EMPLOYMENT LAWS

It is unlawful for any employer, labor organization, or employment agency to discriminate on the basis of sex, marital status, sexual orientation or family responsibilities by failing or refusing to hire; by discharging or discriminating with respect to compensation, terms, conditions, or privileges of employment, including promotion; by excluding or expelling an individual from membership in a labor organization; by refusing to recruit or refer for employment, or by indicating a preference for a particular sex in advertisement for employment. (§§ 1-2502, -2512) Employers employing a parent, spouse, child, or domestic servant are exempted from the law's coverage. There are exceptions for business necessity and religious or political organizations. (§ 1-2503)

**ENFORCEMENT:** See "Community Life: Housing."

## GOVERNMENT CONTRACTORS AND SUBCONTRACTORS

Government contractors and subcontractors must agree not to discriminate against protected classes in employment; they must maximize the opportunities of minority business enterprises and recruit female and minority workers. (Commissioner's Order No. 73-51, issued February 28, 1973)

**ENFORCEMENT:** There is no relevant statutory provision.

## STATE EMPLOYEE LAWS

Every government agency is required to develop a detailed affirmative action plan in pursuit of full representation of all groups in the work force, including women. (§ 1-

507) In addition, no benefit program may be denied to any District employee on the basis of sex. (§ 1-607.7) Sexual harassment of D.C. employees is prohibited as a form of sex discrimination. (Mayor's Order No. 79-89, effective May 24, 1979)

**ENFORCEMENT:** Government agency employees may file grievances and appeals with the Office of Employee Appeals. (§§ 1-606.1 to .5, 1-617.1 to .3)

# VETERAN'S PREFERENCE

Five points are added to the employment register for any person who has served on active duty in the armed forces for more than 180 consecutive days and who has been honorably separated from the service. A disabled veteran receives an additional five points. The spouse or widow or widower of a veteran receives the same preference as is available in the federal service. (§ 1-607.3)

# Community Life

# CREDIT

Credit information bureaus, financial institutions, and the credit facilities of stores and businesses are included in the definition of public accommodations. [§ 1-2502(24)] See "Public Accommodations."

**ENFORCEMENT:** See "Housing."

# HOUSING

It is unlawful to discriminate in transactions involving real estate, including provision of repairs and real estate financing, on the basis of sex, marital status, sexual orientation, family responsibilities, source of income, or the presence of children. (§ 1-2515) The law does not apply to rental or leasing of housing accommodations where the owner or members of the owner's family occupy one of the living units and the number of units falls below certain limits. (§ 1-2518) There is an exception for religious and political organizations. (§ 1-2503)

**ENFORCEMENT:** Any person or organization, whether or not an aggrieved party, may file a complaint with the Office of Human Rights, including a complaint of general discrimination unrelated to a specific person or instance. The complaint generally must be filed within 1 year of the occurrence of, or the discovery of, the unlawful discriminatory practice. A person may also sue in court for damages and other appropriate remedies, unless he or she has filed an Office of Human Rights complaint which has not been dismissed or withdrawn. A person may not file a complaint if he or she maintains a court suit regarding the same act. Upon filing of a complaint, the Office of Human Rights shall investigate, attempt to eliminate discriminatory practice by conciliation, certify where appropriate that injunctive relief is warranted, and schedule a hearing. The final order may include the extension of full, equal, and unsegregated accommodations to all persons and the payment of compensatory damages to the aggrieved party. (§ 1-2541 to 2557)

# INSURANCE

No life insurance corporation may make or permit discrimination between individuals of the same class or life expectancy. (§ 35-520) Insurance companies are included in the definition of public accommodations. [§ 1-2502(24)] No insurer may fail or refuse to issue, renew, or cancel a policy of motor vehicle insurance on the basis of sex, marital status, sexual orientation, or family responsibilities. (§ 1-2533)

> **ENFORCEMENT:** The Superintendent of Insurance has supervision of all matters pertaining to insurance and insurance companies and must see that the laws relating to insurance or insurance companies are faithfully executed. (§§ 35-101, -102) In instances where a company has failed or refused to comply with the antidiscrimination provisions, the superintendent has the power to revoke or suspend the company's certificate of authority to transact business. (§ 35-405) After investigation, the superintendent may order the removal of any discrimination in fire, casualty, and marine insurance revealed during the investigation. (§ 35-1533) See also "Housing."

# PUBLIC ACCOMMODATIONS

It is an unlawful discriminatory practice to deny full and equal enjoyment of the goods, services, facilities, privileges, advantages, and accommodations of any place of public accommodations on the basis of sex, marital status, sexual orientation, family responsibilities, or source of income or business. (§ 1-2519) "Place of public accommodation" is defined very broadly to include a wide variety of establishments. There is an exception for *distinctly private* institutions, clubs, and places of accommodation. [§ 1-2502(24)]

> **ENFORCEMENT:** See "Housing."

# FLORIDA

## Home and Family

## MARRIAGE

**AGE OF CONSENT:** A person 18 years or older may consent to marry. (§ 741.04)*

**CONSENT REQUIREMENT:** Persons under 18 but at least 16 years of age can marry with the consent of their parents or guardian. But no such consent is required when both parents are deceased or when the minor has been previously married or when the minors are the parents of a child or are expecting a child. (§ 741.0405)

**LICENSE REQUIREMENT:** Before a license to marry is granted, the parties must file with the county clerk an affidavit stating their true and correct ages and a health certificate from a licensed physician. The license is valid for 30 days from the date of issuance. (§§ 741.04, .041, .051)

**PROHIBITED MARRIAGES:** Bigamous and incestuous marriages are prohibited. An incestuous marriage is a marriage between two persons related by lineal consanguinity or a marriage between a person and his sister, aunt, or niece; or her brother, uncle, or nephew. Persons entering into either a bigamous or an incestuous marriage are guilty of a felony in the third degree. (§§ 741.21; 826.01, .03, .04)

## DISSOLUTION OF MARRIAGE

**ANNULMENT:** There is no relevant statutory provision.

**LEGAL SEPARATION:** There is no relevant statutory provision.

**DIVORCE**

*Residency Requirement:* The party filing for divorce must have resided 6 months in the state prior to such filing. (§ 61.021)

*Grounds for Divorce:* Appendix A, factors 2 and 40, are grounds for divorce. (§ 61.052)

*Conciliation Requirement:* When there are minor children of the marriage or when one of the spouses denies that the marriage is irretrievably broken, the court may either order the parties to seek marriage therapy or encourage the parties themselves to effect a conciliation. (§ 61.052)

*Property Distribution:* There is no statute governing the division of marital property. The courts have held that a divorce destroys an estate by the entirety and converts the husband and wife into tenants in common as if they had never married. [*Dotter v. Dotter*, 147 So. 2d 209 (Fla. Dist. Ct. App. 1962)] If the parties so request, the court will grant an equitable distribution of marital assets, considering factors 1, 5, 6, 8, 11, 13, 14, and 15, listed in Appendix F. [*Tronconi v. Tronconi*, 425 So. 2d 547 (Fla. Dist. Ct. App. 1982)]

*Child Custody:* Child custody is awarded according to the best interests of the child and according to the Uniform Child Custody Jurisdiction Act.

---

*Unless otherwise specified, all citation references are to the Florida Statutes Annotated (West 1941).

[§ 61.13(2)(b)(1)] The father and mother are given equal consideration. Shared parental custody may be awarded by the court if it is in the best interests of the child. The court considers evidence of spouse abuse as evidence of detriment to the child. If the court finds that spouse abuse has recurred between the parties, it may award sole custody to the abused spouse and make such arrangements for visitation as will best protect the child and abused spouse from further harm. The court will also consider factors 1, 4, 6, 7, 8, 9, 11, 12, 13, 16, 17 (as a family unit), and 23, listed in Appendix B. [§§ 61.13(2)(b)(1), (3)]

*Child Support:* At any time during a proceeding for a dissolution of a marriage, the court may order either or both parents to pay such support as is equitable from the circumstances and nature of the case. [§ 61.13(1)]

*Spousal Support/Alimony:* The court may grant rehabilitative or permanent alimony to either party in periodic or lump-sum payments or both. In cases of adultery, the court may consider the circumstances surrounding the adultery in determining whether alimony shall be awarded and the amount of alimony, if any, to be awarded. Other factors considered by the court in determining alimony are 2, 3, 4, 8, 10, 11, 13, and 14, listed in Appendix E. (§61.08)

*Enforcement of Support Orders:* A judgment for the payment of alimony or child support may be enforced by a chancery court of the state. The chancery court may award costs and expenses and reasonable attorney fees incurred in the course of the enforcement proceeding. (§ 61.17) The court is empowered to direct the payment of alimony or child support ordered on or after January 1, 1985, to be made directly to the appropriate central governmental depository within the circuit. (§§ 61.08, .13, 181) See also Revised Uniform Reciprocal Enforcement of Support Act of 1968, §§ 88.011 *et seq.*

*Spouse's Name:* There is no relevant statutory provision.

*Divorce by Affidavit or Summary Judgment:* There is no relevant provision.

*Displaced Homemaker Laws:* The Department of Health and Rehabilitation Services is required to establish and maintain multipurpose service programs to provide necessary training, counseling and other related services to displaced homemakers so that they may enjoy the independence and economic security vital to a productive life. (§ 410.30)

# DOMESTIC VIOLENCE

**STATUTORY PROVISION:** The act defines spousal abuse to include assault, battery, and criminal sexual conduct against one's spouse. (§ 415.602)

**WHO IS PROTECTED?** Spouses and ex-spouses are protected under the act. (§ 415.602)

**RELIEF AVAILABLE:** A victim of spousal abuse who has filed a complaint with the police and who files a petition alleging spousal abuse with the court may obtain an injunction for protection from the court. (§ 741.30) The warrantless arrest of a spouse committing spousal abuse is permissible under certain circumstances. (§ 901.155) The Department of Health and Rehabilitative Services is required by law to establish, certify and fund spouse abuse centers and to carry on educational and informational programs on spouse abuse. (§ 415.603) Any law enforcement officer who investigates an alleged incident of spouse abuse must advise the person subject to the abuse of the availability of a spouse abuse center from which he or she may receive services. The law enforcement officer must give the victim immediate notice of the legal rights and remedies available on a standard form developed and distributed by the Florida Department of Law Enforcement. (§§ 415.606; 901.155)

**MARITAL RAPE:** A woman may charge her husband with rape. (§ 794.011)

**CIVIL LAWSUIT FOR RAPE OR ASSAULT:** There are no cases directly on point. The established law and policy of the state is that spouses may not sue each other. [*Orefice v. Albert*, 237 So. 2d 142 (Fla. 1970)]

**CHILD ABUSE:** Child abuse or neglect is defined as harm or threatened harm to a child's physical or mental health or welfare by the acts or omissions of the parent or other person responsible for the child's welfare. Harm and threatened harm include physical or mental injury sustained as a result of excessive corporal punishment; sexual battery; child prostitution; abandonment; failure to supervise; and failure to provide adequate food, clothing, shelter or health care. (§ 415.503)

*Notification Requirement:* Health care professionals, teachers, social workers, day care workers, and residential or institutional workers must report suspected cases of child abuse to the Department of Health and Rehabilitative Services. (§415.504) A person required to report a case of suspected child abuse or neglect who knowingly and willfully fails to do so is guilty of a misdemeanor in the second degree. (§ 415.513)

# INHERITANCE RIGHTS

**FAILURE TO MAKE A WILL:** The surviving spouse is entitled to the entire estate if the deceased spouse left no descendants, to $20,000 plus one-half of the balance of the estate if the decedent left lineal descendants who are also the spouse's descendants, or to one-half of the estate if the decedent left one or more descendants who are not also the spouse's descendants. (§ 731.102)

**FAILURE TO PROVIDE BY WILL:** If the testator fails to provide by will for the surviving spouse who married the testator after the execution of the will, the surviving spouse is entitled to a share of the estate equal in value to that which the surviving spouse would have received had the testator died without making a will, unless it appears from the will that the omission was intentional, or the testator provided for the surviving spouse outside the will, or the surviving spouse waived inheritance rights in a prenuptial agreement. (§ 732.301)

**CHILDREN BORN OUT OF WEDLOCK:** A child born out of wedlock is legitimated and is the heir of the father and members of the father's family if the child's parents married before or after the child's birth, even though the attempted marriage is declared void; if the paternity of the father is judicially established before or after the father's death; or if the paternity of the father is acknowledged in writing by the father. [§ 732.108(2)]

**HOMESTEAD, PERSONAL, AND FAMILY ALLOWANCES:** The surviving spouse is entitled to receive reasonable support during administration of the estate, not to exceed $6000; this allowance has priority over almost all claims except administrative costs, funeral costs, and last illness costs and is in addition to any share or benefit passing to a spouse by intestate succession, statutory share, or will (unless otherwise provided). (§ 732.403) The surviving spouse is also entitled to take a life interest in homestead, which then passes to the children upon the death of the surviving spouse. (§§ 732.401, .4015) The homestead is exempt from forced sale or the imposition of any lien except liens for the payment of taxes, an existing mortgage, improvement and repair and labor performed on the realty. (Fla. Const. art. 10, § 4) The surviving spouse of a decedent domiciled in Florida is also entitled to the decedent's car and household furnishings up to $10,000 and to the decedent's personal effects up to $1000, unless these effects are specifically disposed of in the will; these rights to exempt property have priority over all claims except a perfected security interest in any item of property; these rights are in addition to any share or benefit passing to the spouse by will (unless provided otherwise), by intestate succession, or by statutory share. (§ 732.402)

**OPTION TO DISREGARD THE WILL:** The surviving spouse of a decedent domiciled in Florida may reject the will and take 30 percent of the fair market value of all the decedent's property except for real property not located in Florida, and after deducting from the total value of the assets all valid claims against the estate paid or payable from the estate and all mortgages, liens, or security interests on the assets. If the decedent was not a Florida domiciliary, the spouse is not entitled to take a statutory share of the property located in Florida. (§§ 732.201, .205 to .207)

# REPRODUCTIVE RIGHTS

## ABORTION

*Statutory Provisions:* All abortions must be performed by a licensed medical or osteopathic physician. Pregnancy may not be terminated in the third trimester unless two physicians certify in writing that the abortion is necessary to preserve the life and health of the mother or that, owing to a medical emergency, the procedure was necessary to preserve the life of the mother and another physician was unavailable. (§ 390.001) Hospitals, health care facilities, and medical personnel are not required to perform or participate in abortions. [§ 390.001(8)]

*Informed Consent:* The physician must obtain the written informed consent of the pregnant woman or, in the case of a person who is mentally incompetent, the written consent of her court-appointed guardian. [§ 390.001(4)]

*Parental Consent:* In the case of an unmarried minor, the physician must obtain her written consent and the written consent of her parent, custodian, or legal guardian. If the minor indicates that she is mature enough to give her informed consent, or based on the fact that the parent has unreasonably withheld consent, or based on fear of physical or emotional abuse if the minor seeks parental consent, the physician may rely on an order from the circuit court authorizing the abortion. [§ 390.001(4)(b)]

*Spousal Consent:* The husband shall be given notice of the termination of the pregnancy and an opportunity to consult with the wife concerning the procedure. The physician may rely on the written statement of the husband or on that of the wife that such notice was given. If the husband and wife are separated or estranged, provisions for notice are not required. [§ 390.001(4)(a)]

*Reporting Requirements:* Both the physician who performs the abortion and the director of any medical facility in which a pregnancy is terminated shall maintain a record of such procedures, including the date the procedure was performed, the reason, and the length of the pregnancy at the time of the abortion. A copy of the record is filed with the Department of Health and Rehabilitative Services. The records are privileged information, and the name of the pregnant woman shall not be revealed except upon a court order. (§ 390.002)

**BIRTH CONTROL:** The Department of Health and Rehabilitative Services shall implement a comprehensive family planning program to include education and counseling; prescription of all medically recognized methods of contraception; medical evaluation; treatment of physical complications other than pregnancy resulting from the use of contraceptive methods; provision of services at locations and times readily available to the population served; and emphasis and stress on service to postpartum mothers. Fees are based on the cost of the service and the ability to pay. Maternal health and contraceptive information and services of a nonsurgical nature may be rendered to any minor so long as the minor is married, is a parent, is pregnant, has the consent of the parent or guardian, or may, in the opinion of the physician, suffer from health hazards if such services are not provided. Medical personnel are not obligated to give family planning services. (§ 381.382)

**STERILIZATION:** There is no relevant statutory provision.

# UNMARRIED COUPLES

**COMMON-LAW MARRIAGE:** A common-law marriage is not valid if entered into after January 1, 1986. (§ 741.211)

**COHABITAL RELATIONSHIPS:** The courts have allowed the enforcement of an express contract to support by parties who have cohabited where there had been lawful consideration other than an express or implied agreement regarding sexual relations. [*Poe v. Estate of Levy*, 411 So. 2d 253 (Fla. Dist. Ct. App. 1982)] Cohabitation with a member of the opposite sex is not grounds for the termination of alimony. [*Sheffield v. Sheffield*, 310 So. 2d 410, 413 (Fla. Dist. Ct. App. 1975)]

## CHILDREN

*Custody:* Child custody is awarded according to the best interests of the child and according to the Uniform Custody Jurisdiction Act. The father and mother are given equal consideration. [§ 61.13(2)(b)(1)] See also *Johnson v. Knight*, 424 So. 2d 166 (Fla. App. 1983), which holds that the natural father of a child born out of wedlock is a fit and proper person to have custody of the child.

*Legitimation Proceedings:* A child born out of wedlock is legitimated if the natural parents married before or after the birth of the child even though the attempted marriage is void, or the paternity of the father is established by an adjudication before or after the death of the father or the paternity of the father is acknowledged in writing by the father. (§ 732.108)

*Paternity Proceedings:* Any woman who is pregnant or has delivered a child may bring a paternity action in the circuit court in chancery within 4 years of the child's birth. [§§ 95.1(3)(b); 742.011]

*Obligations of the Putative Father:* If paternity is established, the court can order the father to pay to the complainant, her guardian or other person responsible for the child, sums sufficient to pay reasonable attorney fees and expenses incident to the birth of the child as well as a fixed monthly sum for the support of the child until it reaches its 18th birthday. (§§ 742.031, .041)

# Education

# STATUTORY PROVISION

The Florida Educational Equity Act prohibits an educational institution that receives federal or state financial assistance from discriminating against students or public education employees on the basis of sex or marital status. (§ 228.083)

## AREAS COVERED

Discrimination in guidance, counseling, financial assistance, educational programs and course offerings, recreational and athletic activities, and employment is prohibited. (§ 228.083)

**ENFORCEMENT:** The Office of Equal Educational Opportunity of the Department of Education is required to develop plains for the implementation of the act. [§ 228.083(8)] A person who has been discriminated against in violation of the act has a right of action for such equitable relief as the court may determine. The court may also award reasonable attorney fees and court costs to the prevailing party. [§ 228.083(10)]

# Employment

## EQUAL PAY LAWS

It is unlawful for an employer who employs two or more employees to discriminate on the basis of sex in wages paid to employees who, under similar circumstances, perform equal work requiring equal skill, effort and responsibility, except that wage discrimination is allowed if based on factors other than sex. [§§ 448.07(2), 725.07(1)]

**ENFORCEMENT:** A person who has been discriminated against in the payment of wages on account of sex may bring a civil action against the employer within 6 months after termination of employment. The court may award the prevailing party costs of the action and reasonable attorney fees. [§ 448.07(3)]

## FAIR EMPLOYMENT LAWS

The Florida Human Rights Act prohibits discrimination in employment on the basis of sex or marital status by any employer of fifteen or more employees, employment agency, labor organization, the state, or any governmental entity or agency. The act covers refusing to hire or discriminating in the terms, conditions, or privileges of employment; limiting, segregating, or classifying employees or applicants for employment; excluding or expelling from membership of a labor organization except where the discrimination occurs as the result of a bona fide occupational qualification or a bona fide seniority, employee benefit, or merit system. (§§ 742.031, .041; 760.02, .10)

**ENFORCEMENT:** An individual who has been discriminated against in violation of the Human Rights Act may file a complaint with the Florida Commission on Human Rights within 180 days of the occurrence of the alleged violation. If the commission fails to either conciliate or take final action on the complaint within 180 days, the complainant may bring a civil action. If the complainant prevails, the commission or court is empowered to award back pay (but not for more than two years before the filing of the complaint with the commission), reasonable attorney fees and other affirmative relief. [§§ 760.10(10) to .10(14)]

## GOVERNMENT CONTRACTORS AND SUBCONTRACTORS

There is no relevant statutory provision. However, it should be noted that if federal funds are involved, Exec. Order No. 11246, 3 C.F.R. 339, *reprinted in* 42 U.S.C. § 2000e app. at 1232, 41 C.F.R. § 60-1.2, may apply.

# STATE EMPLOYEE LAWS

Employment discrimination by both state and local governments on the basis of sex and marital status is prohibited. (§§ 110.105; 760.02) Sexual harassment in state employment is prohibited by Exec. Order No. 80-69, effective June 25, 1981.

**ENFORCEMENT:** See "Fair Employment Laws."

# VETERAN'S PREFERENCE

Five points are added to the civil service exam passing scores of veterans and their widows; ten points to the passing scores of disabled veterans and spouses of permanently and totally disabled veterans. (§§ 295.07, .08)

# Community Life

# CREDIT

It is unlawful to discriminate in the areas of credit and financing practices on the basis of sex or marital status. (§ 725.07)

**ENFORCEMENT:** A person who has been discriminated against in credit and financing on the basis of sex or marital status may bring a civil action within 4 years of the occurrence of the alleged discriminatory act. [§§ 95.11(f); 725.07]

# HOUSING

Discrimination in the sale or rental of housing on the basis of sex is prohibited. The printing or publication of sexually discriminatory advertisements with respect to the sale or rental of housing is also prohibited. (§ 760.23) Discrimination based on sex in the financing of loans for the purpose of purchasing, constructing, repairing or maintaining a dwelling is prohibited. (§ 760.25) These antidiscrimination statutes do not apply to the sale or rental of a single-family home by its owner if the house is sold or rented without the services of a real estate broker or without advertising the sale or rental. Nor do these restrictions apply to rooms or apartment buildings with four or fewer units if the owner actually resides in one of the apartments. (§ 760.29)

**ENFORCEMENT:** Any person who has been injured by a discriminatory housing practice may file a complaint with the Florida Commission on Human Relations within 180 days after the alleged discriminatory housing practice occurred. (§ 760.34)

# INSURANCE

Discrimination is prohibited between individuals of the same class and equal expectation of life in the rates charged for life insurance or annuity contracts or between individuals of the same class and essentially the same hazard in the amount of premium, policy, fees, or rates charged for accident, disability or health insurance, in the benefits payable under these contracts, or in any other term or condition of these contracts. It is unlawful to refuse to insure or refuse to continue to insure any individual or risk solely on the grounds of sex or marital status. [§§ 621.9541(g), (x)]

**ENFORCEMENT:** The Florida Department of Insurance has the power to examine and investigate all charges of discrimination in the insurance industry. If it determines that a discriminatory practice has occurred, it may issue an order requiring the insurer to cease and desist from engaging in such practice or it may either suspend or revoke the insurer's license or grant other appropriate relief. (§ 626.9581)

# PUBLIC ACCOMMODATIONS

The operator of a public lodging or food service establishment may not refuse any person admission, accommodation or service on the basis of sex. (§§ 509.092, .141, .142)

**ENFORCEMENT:** A person who has been discriminated against in public accommodations on account of sex may bring a civil action within 4 years of the occurrence of the alleged discriminatory act. [§ 95.11(f)]

# GEORGIA

## Home and Family

## MARRIAGE

**AGE OF CONSENT:** A person over 16 years of age may marry without parental consent. If there is proof of pregnancy or both applicants are the parents of a living child born out of wedlock, they may marry regardless of age.(§ 19-3-2)*

**CONSENT REQUIREMENT:** Parental consent is required if either party is under 16 years of age. Parental consent means the consent of both parents if they are living together; the consent of the parent with legal custody if the parents are divorced or separated; the consent of either parent if they are living together but one is unavailable because he or she is ill or because physical presence is impossible; or the consent of the legal guardian. (§ 19-3-37)

**LICENSE REQUIREMENT:** A license, issued by the judge of the probate court or by the judge's clerk, is required. An application for a license to be filed in the office of the judge of the probate court is required. Each person who applies for a license is required to present a physician's certificate. (§§ 19-3-30, -33 to -35, -40)

**PROHIBITED MARRIAGES:** Bigamous marriages are prohibited. Marriages between father and daughter or stepdaughter; mother and son or stepson; brother and sister of the whole or half blood; grandparent and grandchild; aunt and nephew; or uncle and niece are prohibited. (§§ 19-3-2, -3)

## DISSOLUTION OF MARRIAGE

**ANNULMENT:** Factors 19, 33, 35, 36, and 38, listed in Appendix A, are grounds for annulment. The code also provides that any child born before the marriage is annuled shall be legitimate while at the same time prohibiting annulments in instances where children are born or are to be born. In cases of minors or mental incompetents, a guardian may file for annulment on their behalf. (§§ 19-3-5, -4-1, -4-4) The Georgia Supreme Court has denied annulments in instances where children are involved; parties to such marriage must file for divorce. See *Wallace v. Wallace*, 145 S.E.2d 546 (Ga. 1975). In addition, where grounds for annulment and divorce overlap, the court may only permit a divorce as a remedy. See *Johnson v. Johnson*, 157 S.E. 689 (Ga. 1931).

    *Residency Requirement:* There is no relevant statutory provision.

**LEGAL SEPARATION:** There is no relevant statutory provision.

**DIVORCE**

    *Residency Requirement:* A person filing for divorce must be a resident for 6 months before filing. A nonresident may file for divorce against any person who has been a resident for 6 months. (§ 19-5-2)

    *Grounds for Divorce:* Factors 2, 3, 4, 6 (with 39), 8, 9 (with 30), 16, 17 (with 20), 25, 33, 36, and 38, listed in Appendix A, are grounds for divorce. No divorce shall be granted if there has been collusion, if the party complaining has consented

---

*Unless otherwise specified, all citation references are to the Code of Georgia Annotaged (1981).

to the behavior complained of, if both parties are guilty of like conduct, or if there has been voluntary condonation and cohabitation subsequent to the acts complained of. (§§ 19-5-3, -4)

*Conciliation Requirement:* There is no relevant statutory provision.

*Property Distribution:* The court will dispose of the property equitably. (§ 19-5-13) Note that in *Stokes v. Stokes*, 273 S.E.2d 169 (1980), the Georgia Supreme Court acknowledged that "equitable division of property" provides a basis for the award to one spouse of real or personal property titled in the name of the other spouse.

*Child Custody:* The party not in default in divorce shall be entitled to custody. However, the court may, in the exercise of its discretion, consider all the circumstances of the parties, including the best interest of the child, and change the custody award. A child who has reached the age of 14 may select the parent with whom he or she desires to live. The selection shall be controlling unless the parent is determined unfit. (§§ 19-9-1, -3) See also the Georgia Child Custody Intrastate Jurisdiction Act of 1978, §§ 19-9-20 *et seq.*, and the Uniform Child Custody Jurisdiction Act, §§ 19-9-40 *et seq.*

*Child Support:* Both parents are jointly liable to provide for the maintenance, protection, and education of the minor children. (§ 19-7-2) In the final divorce order, the court shall specify in what amount and from which party the child support payments will be made. Child support payments may be modified in the event of changed circumstances. (§§ 19-6-15, -17) Children are entitled to support commensurate with their proven customary needs, and the parent's financial ability to provide shall be considered. [*Harrison v. Harrison*, 209 S.E.2d 607 (Ga. 1974)] Although the court may only impose support until children reach the age of majority, if, under an agreement incorporated into the divorce decree, the father is responsible for meeting the educational needs of children past the age of majority, the agreement will be upheld. [*McClain v. McClain*, 221 S.E.2d 561 (Ga. 1975)]

*Spousal Support/Alimony:* Permanent or temporary alimony may be awarded to either spouse, in accordance with the needs of the party and the ability of the other party to pay, except in cases where the separation was caused by that party's adultery or desertion. In determining the amount of alimony, factors 1, 2, 3, 4, 8, 9, 10, 13, and 14, listed in Appendix F, are considered. All alimony will terminate upon remarriage of the party to whom the obligation is owed *unless* otherwise provided. Alimony is subject to revision upon a showing of change in income and financial status of the party from whom the obligation is owed. (§§ 19-6-1 *et seq.*)

*Enforcement of Support Orders:* A criminal or civil action may be brought in order to enforce alimony or child support payments. In addition, under the Child Support Recovery Act, the Department of Human Resources is authorized to bring an action on behalf of children to recover child support payments owed. (§§ 19-6-16, 19-11-1 *et seq.*) See also the Uniform Reciprocal Enforcement of Support Act, §§ 19-11-1 *et seq.*

*Spouse's Name:* In the final judgment of divorce, if requested in pleadings, the judge shall specify and restore to the party the name so prayed for in the pleadings. (§§ 19-5-12, -16)

*Divorce by Affidavit or Summary Judgment:* There is no relevant statutory provision.

*Displaced Homemaker Laws:* There is no relevant statutory provision.

# DOMESTIC VIOLENCE

**STATUTORY PROVISION:** The statute covers any felony, battery, assault, criminal damage to property, unlawful restraint, or criminal trespass. It excludes reasonable discipline administered by a parent to a child in the form of corporal punishment, restraint, or detention. [§§ 19-13-1(1), (2)]

**WHO IS PROTECTED?** The statute protects spouses, parents, and children or other persons related by blood or affinity and living in the same household. (§ 19-13-1)

**RELIEF AVAILABLE:** An individual who has been the victim of domestic violence may file a petition with the superior court seeking relief. The fee for filing such a petition is $16. The court may grant any protective order directing a person to refrain from such acts; grant a spouse possession of the residence or household and exclude the other spouse; require a party to provide suitable alternative housing; award temporary custody and establish temporary visitation; order eviction of a party from the residence and order assistance to the victim in returning to it, or order assistance in retrieving personal property if eviction has not been ordered; order either party to make child support payments; order either party to make spousal support payments; provide for possession of personal property of the parties; order a party to refrain from harassing or interfering with the other; award costs and attorney fees; order either party to receive appropriate psychiatric or psychological services; or include any additional protectons or provisions as deemed necessary. Any such orders shall not remain in effect for more than 6 months. (§ 19-13-4)

**MARITAL RAPE:** A wife may not charge her husband with rape. (§ 16-6-3)

**CIVIL LAWSUIT FOR RAPE OR ASSAULT:** There is no relevant case on point. However, in *Taylor v. Vezzani*, 135 S.E.2d 522 (Ga. 1964), the court held that a wife cannot sue her husband for torts.

**CHILD ABUSE:** Children are protected under § 19-13-1. In addition, cruelty against children is prohibited by § 16-5-70.

> *Notification Requirement:* As designated by the Department of Human Resources, all health care workers, school personnel, child care personnel, day care personnel, or law enforcement personnel must report to the child welfare agency providing protective services if they have reasonable cause to believe that a minor has had physical injury or injuries inflicted by a parent or caretaker by other than accidental means, or has been neglected or exploited by a parent or caretaker, or has been sexually assaulted or sexually exploited. (§ 19-7-5)

# INHERITANCE RIGHTS

**FAILURE TO MAKE A WILL:** The surviving spouse is entitled to the entire estate if there are no surviving children; to a share equal to that of each child if there are one to five children; or to one-fifth of the estate if there are more than five children. (§ 53-4-2)

**FAILURE TO PROVIDE BY WILL:** The testator may leave the entire estate to strangers, to the exclusion of the spouse and children. In such a case, the will should be closely scrutinized, and upon the slightest evidence of aberration of intellect, collusion, fraud, undue influence, or unfair dealing, probate should be refused. Note that marriage, divorce, or the birth of a child subsequent to the making of the will, in which no provision is made in contemplation of the event, results in the revocation of the will. (§§ 53-2-9, -76)

**CHILDREN BORN OUT OF WEDLOCK:** An illegitimate child may inherit as if legitimate from and through the mother or any other maternal kin. The child may not inherit from or through the father or any potential kin *unless*, during the lifetime of the father and after the conception of the child, the court has entered an order declaring the child to be legitimate or has otherwise entered an order establishing the father of the child. (§ 53-4-4)

**HOMESTEAD, PERSONAL, AND FAMILY ALLOWANCES:** The surviving spouse and minor children shall be entitled to a year's support, either in property or in money, to be estimated according to the circumstances and standing of the family. Application for support shall be filed within 3 years from the date of death. The amount set apart for the family shall in no event be less than $1600 if the estate is of that value, and if the estate does not exceed $1600, excluding household goods and furnishings, the whole estate shall be set apart for the support and maintenance of the surviving spouse and children. In addition, a sufficient amount of the household furniture is to be set apart for the use of the surviving children. When an estate is to be kept together for more than 12 months and there are no debts to pay, the surviving spouse and minor children shall have a year's support for each subsequent year. If the decedent has provided by will for the surviving spouse in lieu of a year's support, the surviving spouse must make an election. In addition, real estate and/or personal property up to $5000 may be exempted from levy and sale. (§§ 44-13-1, 53-5-2 *et seq.*)

**OPTION TO DISREGARD THE WILL:** There is no statutory provision allowing a surviving spouse to disregard the will. However, a surviving spouse taking under the will, who has a claim adverse to the will, shall be required to elect to claim under the will or against it. In addition, if the decedent has bequeathed property which belongs to the surviving spouse and has also given a benefit to the surviving spouse, the surviving spouse may elect to take either under the will or against the will. (§§ 53-2-111, -112)

# REPRODUCTIVE RIGHTS

## ABORTION

*Statutory Provisions:* Abortions may be performed by a licensed physician. Abortions are illegal after the first trimester unless they are performed in a licensed hospital or health facility licensed to perform abortions by the Department of Human Resources. Abortions after the second trimester are illegal unless three physicians certify that the abortion is necessary to preserve the life or health of the woman. If the product of the abortion is capable of meaningful or sustained life, medical aid must be available and rendered. (§ 26-1202) Criminal abortion is punishable by imprisonment of not less than 1 year and not more than 10 years in prison. (§ 26-1201) Hospitals, health care facilities, and medical personnel who object on moral or religiious grounds are not required to perform or participate in abortions. *Consent Requirements:* There is no relevant statutory provision. *Reporting Requirements:* Within 10 days of performing the abortion, the physician shall file with the Department of Human Resources a certificate of abortion containing whatever statistical data that the department requires and that is consistent with preserving the privacy of the woman. The hospital or other licensed health facility records shall be available to the district attorney of the judicial circuit in which the hospital or health facility is located. [§ 26-1202(d)] A person who fails to maintain these records within the time set forth is guilty of a misdemeanor. (§ 26-1203)

**BIRTH CONTROL:** Family planning services include distribution of literature, counseling, interviews with trained personnel, and referral to licensed physicians of local health departments for consultations, tests, examination, medical treatment, and prescriptions regarding birth control, infertility, and family planning methods and procedures, as well as the distribution of rythmn charts, drugs, medical preparations, contraceptive devices, and similar products. [§ 99-3102(b)] No person shall be denied public assistance, public health services, or other public benefits because of his or her refusal to accept family planning services. (§ 99-3105) Medical personnel with moral or religious objections are not obligated to give family planning services, and such refusal to do so shall not be grounds for any disciplinary action. (§ 99-3106)

**STERILIZATION:** A physician acting in collaboration or consultation with at least one other physician may perform a sterilization procedure on a person 18 years of over, or on a married person under 18 years, provided that a request in writing is made by such a person, and by his or her spouse if married and such spouse can be found after reasonable effort, and provided that a full and reasonable explanation is given by the physician as to the meaning and consequence of such an operation. (§ 84-932) Persons who are mentally retarded or brain-damaged or both may be sterilized under certain conditions. A petition must be filed by one or both parents, the legal guardian, or the next of kin of such a person. The Commissioner of Human Resources, the county director of any board of health or department of family planning may also file a petition with the signature of the parents or guardian. Upon the finding by two court-appointed physicians that the person's condition is irreversible or incurable, the court will approve the sterilization procedure. (§ 84-933) Medical personnel who object to the procedure on moral or religious grounds are not obligated to participate in the procedure. (§ 84-935.2)

**WRONGFUL BIRTH ACTION:** In *Blash v. Glisson*, 173 Ga. App. 104, 325 S.E.2d 607 (1984), it was held that the cost of raising the child cannot be recovered. Recoverable damages include expenses for unsuccessful medical procedures which led to conception or pregnancy and for pain and suffering, medical complications, costs of delivery, lost wages, and loss of consortium.

# UNMARRIED COUPLES

**COMMON-LAW MARRIAGE:** Common-law marriage is valid in Georgia. Three essential elements are necessary in order for a common-law marriage to exist: the parties must be able to contract; there must be an actual contract; and there must be consummation according to law. Existence of the marriage contract may be shown by such evidence as cohabitation as husband and wife, holding themselves out to the world as such, and repute in the vicinity and among neighbors and visitors that they are such, and all such facts as usually accompany the marriage relationship. In addition, the evidence presented must show a present mutual intent to marry; an agreement to marry in the future is not sufficient. The burden of proving the validity of a common-law marriage is on the one stating that there is a common-law marriage. [*Brown v. Brown*, 215 S.E.2d (Ga. 1975)]

**COHABITAL RELATIONSHIPS:** In *Rehak v. Mathis*, 238 S.E.2d 81 (Ga. 1977), the Georgia Supreme Court refused to allow a woman who cohabited with a man for 18 years to recover for homemaker's services and her share of the jointly purchased house, noting that the parties were unmarried and the woman had admitted cohabitation. The court stated that a court of law will not lend its aid to either party to a contract founded upon an illegal or immoral consideration.

## CHILDREN

*Custody:* Only the mother is entitled to custody, unless the child has been legitimated. (§ 19-7-25)

*Legitimation Proceedings:* Upon marriage of the mother and the reputed father, an illegitimate child is rendered legitimate and the child shall immediately take the surname of the father. The father of an illegitimate child may legitimate the child by filing a petition for legitimation with the court declaring the child to be legitimate and capable of inheriting from the father. (§§ 19-7-20 to -23)

*Paternity Proceedings:* A petition to establish paternity may be brought by the child, the mother, the alleged father, or any relative in whose care the child has been placed. The Department of Human Resources may bring an action for the benefit of any child receiving public assistance. (§ 19-7-43)

*Obligations of the Putative Father:* Both parents are responsible for providing for the maintenance, protection, and education of the child until his or her majority. (§ 19-7-24) Once paternity has been established, the court shall issue an order establishing child support, visitation privileges, or any other matter in the best interest of the child. (§§ 19-7-49, -51) The same remedies and procedures apply for enforcement and modification of visitation and child support as apply to such orders arising in the case of divorce.

# Education

## STATUTORY PROVISION

There is no relevant statutory provision. However, it should be noted that if federal funds are involved, Title IX of the Education Amendments of 1972, Pub. L. No. 92-318, 20 U.S.C. §§ 1681–1686, may apply.

# Employment

## EQUAL PAY LAWS

Any employer of ten or more employees is prohibited from discriminating on the basis of sex in wages paid to employees who perform equal work requiring equal skills, effort, and responsibility, under similar working conditions. Wage differentials are not prohibited if they are based on a seniority system, merit system, or quantity or quality of production or any factor other than sex. (§ 34-5-3) In addition, the state of Georgia has declared the practice of discriminating on the basis of sex by paying wages to employees of one sex at a lesser rate than the rate paid employees of the opposite sex for comparable work in jobs which require the same or essentially the same knowledge, skill, effort, and responsibility to be against public policy. (§ 34-5-1)

>   **ENFORCEMENT:** The Commissioner of Labor of the state of Georgia has the authority to eliminate unlawful pay practices by informal methods. In addition, an aggrieved employee may bring court action within 1 year after the violation. Any employer found to have violated the law is liable for unpaid wages. (§§ 34-5-2, -5)

## FAIR EMPLOYMENT LAWS

There is no relevant statutory provision. However, an employer with more than fifteen employees is prohibited from discriminating on the basis of sex by federal law, Title VII of the Civil Rights Act of 1964, 42 U.S.C. §§ 2000e *et seq.*

## GOVERNMENT CONTRACTORS AND SUBCONTRACTORS

There is no relevant statutory provision. However, it should be noted that if federal funds are involved, Exec. Order No. 11246, 3 C.F.R. 339, *reprinted in* 42 U.S.C. § 2000e app. at 1232, 41 C.F.R. § 60-1.2, may apply.

## STATE EMPLOYEE LAWS

Departments or agencies employing fifteen or more employees may not discriminate in hire, discharge, compensation, terms, conditions, or privileges of employment because of an employee's sex. [§ 45-19-22(5)]

>   **ENFORCEMENT:** The Office of Fair Employment Practices is responsible for enforcement of this provision.

## VETERAN'S PREFERENCE

Five points are added to the passing civil service exam scores of veterans; ten points are added to the passing scores of disabled veterans. (§§ 45-2-21, -22)

# Community Life

## CREDIT

Banks, lending companies, financial institutions, retail installment sellers, and persons extending credit may not discriminate on the basis of sex or marital status. (§ 7-6-1)

>   **ENFORCEMENT:** Anyone who feels they have been the victim of discrimination may bring an action for damages in any court of competent jurisdiction. (§ 7-6-2)

## HOUSING

It is unlawful for any owner, financial institution, insurance company, real estate broker, real estate salesperson, or agent to refuse to sell, purchase, rent, lease, or otherwise withhold any housing accommodation; to discriminate in the conditions or privileges of the sale, purchase, rental, lease, or furnishing of facilities, insurance coverage, or service in connection with any housing accommodation; to refuse to receive or transmit any bona fide offer to sell, purchase, rent, or lease any housing accommodation; to refuse to negotiate for sale, purchase, rental, or lease of any housing accommodation; to represent that any housing accommodation is unavailable for inspection, sale, purchase, rental, or lease when it is available; or to intimidate or harass any person in the occupancy, ownership, or leasing of any housing accommodation on the basis of sex, race, color, religion, or national origin. However, these provisions do not apply to any person who sells or offers to sell a housing accommodation who does not use the services of a real estate broker or salesperson and who is not in the business of building, buying, or selling housing accommodations; nor do they apply to the rental or lease of housing units in a house in which the owner or members of his or her family reside. It is unlawful for any owner, financial institution, insurance company, or agent to deny to any person casualty or mortgage insurance coverage, a loan, or other financial assistance for the purchase, construction, improvement, repair, or maintenance of a housing accommodation, or to discriminate, directly or indirectly, in coverage, cost, amount, interest rate, duration, or other terms or conditions of a loan or financial assistance on the basis of sex, race, color, religion, or national origin. (§§ 8-3-202, -206)

**ENFORCEMENT:** Any person who has been the victim of discrimination in housing may file a civil action in any court having jurisdiction over the defendant within 180 days after the act. The court may grant any relief it deems appropriate and may award actual damages and not more than $1000 in punitive damages, together with the court costs and reasonable attorney's fees, if the victim wins the suit, provided the victim is not financially able to pay. (§ 8-3-207)

# INSURANCE

Discrimination is prohibited between individuals of the same class, same policy amount, and equal expectation of life in the rates charged for life insurance or annuity contracts or between individuals of the same class and essentially the same hazard in the amount of premium, policy fees, or rates charged for accident or sickness insurance, in the benefits payable under these contracts, or in any other term or condition of these contracts. [§ 33-6-4(8)(A)] Every group policy or group insurance contract which provides major medical coverage and which includes maternity benefits must include coverage for complications arising out of pregnancy. (§ 33-24-24)

**ENFORCEMENT:** The Commissioner of Insurance has the power to examine and investigate all charges of discrimination in the insurance industry. If it has been determined that a discriminatory practice has occurred, the commissioner may issue an order requiring the insurer to cease and desist from engaging in such practice or may either suspend or revoke the insurer's license or grant other appropriate relief. (§§ 33-6-6, -8)

# PUBLIC ACCOMMODATIONS

There is no relevant statutory provision.

# HAWAII

## Home and Family

## MARRIAGE

**AGE OF CONSENT:** A person 18 years or older may consent to marry. (§ 572-1)*

**CONSENT REQUIREMENT:** A person under the age of 18 may marry with parental or guardian consent. If under 16, approval of the family court of the circuit within which the minor resides is required. (§§ 572-1, -2)

**LICENSE REQUIREMENT:** A person wishing to marry must apply personally for a marriage license, which is valid for 30 days from the date of issuance. The female applicant for a marriage license must show proof of immunization against rubella. (§§ 572-6, -7)

**PROHIBITED MARRIAGES:** Marriages between ancestors and descendants of any degree whatsoever, brother and sister of the half or whole blood, uncle and niece, or aunt and nephew, whether the relationship is legitimate or illegitimate are incestuous and void. (§§ 572-1, 580-21) Children born of void marriages are legitimate. (§ 580-27)

## DISSOLUTION OF MARRIAGE

**ANNULMENT:** Appendix A, factors 19, 35, 36, 38, and 41, are grounds for annulment. (§ 580-21)

*Residency Requirement:* See "Legal Separation."

**LEGAL SEPARATION:** Where the marriage is temporarily disrupted, a legal separation may be granted by the court for a period not to exceed 2 years. (§ 580-71)

*Residency Requirement:* A person filing for annulment, separation, or divorce must have been domiciled or physically present in the state for a continuous period of at least 3 months. (§ 580-1)

### DIVORCE

*Residency Requirement:* See "Legal Separation." However, no decree of absolute divorce will be granted unless either party has been domiciled or physically present in the state for a continuous period of at least 6 months. (§ 580-1)

*Grounds for Divorce:* Appendix A, factors 2, 13, and 31, are grounds for divorce. (§ 580-41)

*Conciliation Requirement:* When a divorce is sought on grounds of irretrievable breakdown of the marriage and one of the parties denies under oath that the marriage is irretrievably broken, the court may make a finding on the issue and stay the proceedings for not more than 60 days and advise the parties to seek counseling in an attempt to effect a reconciliation. (§ 580-42)

*Property Distribution:* The court will distribute the property of the parties, whether community, joint or separate, in a just and equitable manner. Factors 18, 24, and 25, and 26, listed in Appendix F, will be considered. (§ 580-47)

*Unless otherwise specified, all citation references are to the Hawaii Revised Statutes (1968).

*Child Custody:* Child custody may be awarded to either or both parents according to the best interests of the child, and to the wishes of the child if the child is of sufficient age and capacity to form an intelligent choice. Upon the request of either parent, joint custody may be awarded at the discretion of the court. The court may, upon the request of either parent, direct that an investigation be conducted to assist it in making a reasonable determination of the best interests of the child. (§§ 571-46, -46.1)

*Child Support:* The court may compel either or both parents to provide for the support, maintenance, and education of the child in a just and equitable manner. (§ 580-47)

*Spousal Support/Alimony:* The court may compel either party to provide for the support and maintenance of the other as is just and equitable. Support may be for an indefinite period or for a specific duration of time so as to allow a party to become self-supporting. Factors 3, 4, 5, 6, 8, 9, 10, 13, 14, 15, 16, and 17, listed in Appendix E, will be considered. (§ 580-47) Alimony shall be terminated upon remarriage unless the final decree or order provides otherwise. (§ 580-51)

*Enforcement of Support Orders:* A person who is under a duty to support his or her minor children or spouse and who fails to pay such support may be found in contempt of court for such failure to pay. The court may make an order assigning any amounts due to the spouse or minor children from that person's wages, salary, or other income for the benefit of the spouse or minor children. (§ 571-52) In addition, under the Uniform Desertion and Nonsupport Act, absence for a continuous period of 3 months or over of any spouse or parent who fails to make suitable provision for support establishes prima facie evidence of desertion and willful neglect, and where a third party owes money to the spouse or parent owing support, the court may order the money applied to the maintenance or support. (§ 575-2) See also the Uniform Reciprocal Enforcement of Support Act, §§ 576-1 *et seq.*

*Spouse's Name:* If she so requests, the wife may resume her former name after divorce. [§ 574-5(B)]

*Divorce by Affidavit or Summary Judgment:* There is no relevant statutory provision.

*Displaced Homemaker Laws:* There is no relevant statutory provision.

# DOMESTIC VIOLENCE

**STATUTORY PROVISION:** Physical harm, bodily injury, assault or the threat of imminent physical harm, bodily injury, or assault by family or household members is prohibited. [§ 586-1(1)]

**WHO IS PROTECTED?** The statute protects spouses, former spouses, parents, children, persons related by consanguinity and persons residing or formerly residing in the same dwelling. [§ 586-1(2)]

**RELIEF AVAILABLE:** A victim of domestic abuse may petition the family court for an order of protection or a temporary restraining order to restrain either party from threatening or physically abusing the other. A temporary restraining order is valid for 30 days and may be extended for up to 180 days at the court's discretion. [§§ 571-14(c), 586-3 to -5] A police officer may make a warrantless arrest of the abusing spouse whether the spouse abuse occurs within or without the officer's presence. If the officer has reasonable grounds to believe that there is a probable danger of spouse abuse, the officer may lawfully order the abusing spouse to leave the premises for a cooling-off period of 3 hours; if the spouse refuses to comply or returns to the premises before the expiration of 3 hours, the officer may arrest the spouse without a warrant. In addition, an abused spouse may petition the court to issue a warrant for the arrest of the abusing spouse. The police, in investigating any complaint of spouse abuse, may, upon request, transport the victim to a hospital or a safe shelter. (§ 709-906)

**MARITAL RAPE:** A woman cannot charge her husband with rape while they are living together. (§§ 709-730 to -732)

**CIVIL LAWSUIT FOR RAPE OR ASSAULT:** There are no relevant cases, but note that a married woman may not sue her husband. (§ 573-5)

**CHILD ABUSE:** Physical injury, psychological abuse and neglect, sexual abuse, negligent treatment, or maltreatment of a child under 18 by a parent, legal guardian, or person responsible for the child's care is prohibited. (§ 350-1)

> *Notification Requirement:* All health care professionals including pharmacists and psychologists; public and private school personnel; employees of institutions providing social, medical, and mental health services; employees and officers of law enforcement agencies and day care centers; and medical examiners or coroners who know or have reason to believe that a child has been abused or neglected or is threatened with neglect or abuse must promptly report the matter orally to the Department of Social Services and Housing or to the police department. Failure to report an incident of child abuse or neglect is a petty misdemeanor. (§§ 350-1.1, -7)

# INHERITANCE RIGHTS

**DOWER SHARE:** A surviving widow is entitled to a life interest in one-third of all the lands owned by her husband during the marriage and before July 1, 1977, that are not included in the husband's net estate which is subject to her statutory share. (§ 533-1)

**FAILURE TO MAKE A WILL:** The surviving spouse is entitled to the entire estate if there is no surviving issue or parent, or to one-half of the estate if there are surviving parents or issue. (§ 560-2-102)

**FAILURE TO PROVIDE BY WILL:** If a testator fails to provide by will for the surviving spouse who married the testator after the execution of the will, the omitted spouse will receive the same share of the estate he or she would have received if the decedent had left no will, unless it appears from the will that the omission was intentional or that the testator provided for the spouse outside the will. (§ 560-2-301)

**CHILDREN BORN OUT OF WEDLOCK:** A child born out of wedlock can inherit from the father if the child has been legitimated. (§ 584-4)

**HOMESTEAD, PERSONAL, AND FAMILY ALLOWANCES:** The surviving spouse of a decedent who was domiciled in the state is entitled to a homestead allowance of $5000, which may be taken in cash or property. This allowance has priority over all claims except administrative and funeral costs and the family allowance, and is in addition to any share or benefit passing by will, intestate succession, or statutory share. (§ 560-2-401) In addition, the surviving spouse and minor child are entitled to a reasonable allowance in money to be paid out of the estate for their maintenance during the period of administration. This allowance may not continue for more than 1 year if the estate is inadequate to discharge its debts. (§ 560-2-403)

**OPTION TO DISREGARD THE WILL:** If the decedent was domiciled in Hawaii, the surviving spouse may reject the will and take a statutory share of one-third of the net estate; if the decedent was not a Hawaii domiciliary, the spouse's right to a statutory share of property located in Hawaii is governed by the laws of Hawaii; if the decedent was not a Hawaii domiciliary, the spouse's right to a share of property located outside the state is governed by the laws of the state where the decedent was domiciled at death. (§ 560:2-201)

# REPRODUCTIVE RIGHTS
## ABORTION
*Statutory Provisions:* Abortions of a nonviable fetus may be performed by a licensed physician or surgeon, or by a licensed osteopathic physician and surgeon, in a hospital licensed by the Department of Health or operated by the federal government or any of its agencies. The attorney general of Hawaii has stated, in accordance with *Roe v. Wade*, 410 U.S. 113, that the requirement that abortions be performed in a hospital may not be enforced during the first trimester of pregnancy. [Op. Att'y Gen. No. 74-17 (1974)] Any hospital or person may refuse to participate or perform an abortion. [§ 453-16(d)] The Board of Medical Examiners may revoke, limit, or suspend any license to practice medicine and surgery if the holder procures or aids or abets in procuring a criminal abortion. (§ 453-8)
*Consent Requirements:* There is no relevant statutory provision.
*Reporting Requirements:* Within 1 month from the performance of an abortion a report shall be filed with the Department of Health in Honolulu or in the district in which the abortion was performed by the person performing the abortion. (§ 338-9)
*Residency Requirement:* A woman wishing an abortion is required to be domiciled or physically present in the state for at least 90 days immediately preceding such abortion. [§ 453-16(a)(3)] The attorney general has stated that the residency requirement is unconstitutional and invalid. [Op. Att'y Gen. No. 74-17 (1974)]

## BIRTH CONTROL
*Consent Requirements:* A minor between the ages of 14 and 17 who claims to be pregnant or to be afflicted with a venereal disease or who is seeking family planning services may consent to medical care and services. (§ 577A-2) Public and private hospitals, clinics, or physicians may, at the discretion of the treating physician, inform the spouse, parent, or custodian or guardian of any minor patient of the provision of medical care and services after consulting with the minor patient. (§ 577A-3) Medical care and services shall not include surgery or any treatment to induce abortion. (§ 577A-1)
*Family Planning Programs:* The Department of Health or its authorized agents shall furnish to each applicant for a marriage license information relating to population stabilization, family planning and birth control. (§ 572-5)

**STERILIZATION:** There is no relevant statutory provision.

# UNMARRIED COUPLES
**COMMON-LAW MARRIAGE:** Common-law marriages are not valid. (§ 572-1)

**COHABITAL RELATIONSHIPS:** In *Kienitz v. Sager*, 40 Haw. 1 (1953), the court held that a woman who believed she was legally married, when legally she was not, could recover a share of the property accumulated by her joint efforts and those of the man with whom she had lived in the honest belief that she was his wife. However, such a rule would not apply to persons who had cohabited and who, therefore, had no reasonable basis for such a belief and who were not innocent parties.

## CHILDREN

*Custody:* There is no relevant statutory provision.

*Legitimation Proceedings:* A child born out of wedlock may become legitimate upon the marriage of the parents; or upon the voluntary, written acknowledgment of paternity by the father and mother; or upon establishment of the parent and child relationship. Once legitimated, the child is entitled to the same rights as those enjoyed by a child born in wedlock and may adopt the surname requested by the parents, or if the parents cannot agree, the surname specified by the court to be in the best interest of the child. Upon legitimation, the child or the parents may request the issuance of a new birth certificate. [§§ 338-1(7), -21]

*Paternity Proceedings:* An action to determine paternity can be brought by the child or the child's personal representative; the natural mother or her personal representative; the alleged father, or if the father has died, his personal representative; or the Department of Social Services and Housing. (§ 584-6) A paternity action when brought by someone other than the child, must be brought within 3 years of the child's birth; if brought by the child, the action must be brought within 3 years after the child reaches the age of majority. (§ 584-7)

*Obligations of the Putative Father:* Upon a determination of paternity, the court may direct the appropriate party to pay for the support of the child, and the father may be ordered to reimburse the mother for the reasonable costs of her pregnancy and confinement. (§§ 584-15, -17)

# Education

## STATUTORY PROVISION

The Hawaii Constitution contains an equal rights amendment which prohibits sex discrimination by the local or state government and by school districts. (Hawaii Const. art. 1, § 3) In addition, it is the public policy of the state that no one shall be excluded from participation, be denied the benefits of, or be subjected to discrimination on the basis of sex under any educational or recreational program or activity receiving state or county funds or utilizing state or county facilities. (§ 296-60)

# Employment

## EQUAL PAY LAWS

It is unlawful for an employer to discriminate between the sexes in the payment of wages except that variations in pay are permissible for differences in seniority, duties or services performed or differences in shifts of time of day worked or hours of work. (§ 387-4)

**ENFORCEMENT:** A person who has been discriminated against in the payment of wages on account of sex may file a complaint with the Director of Labor and Industrial

Relations or may bring a civil action within 2 years of the alleged underpayment in any court of competent jurisdiction for the recovery of any amounts of unpaid wages. (§§ 387-12, 657-7)

# FAIR EMPLOYMENT LAWS

The Fair Employment Practices Law applies to the state, its political and civil subdivisions, employers employing one or more employees, employment agencies, and labor organizations. It prohibits an employer from refusing to hire or discriminating in compensation, terms, conditions or privileges of employment on the basis of sex or marital status; it prohibits an employment agency from refusing to refer for employment on the basis of sex or marital status; and it prohibits a labor organization from excluding or expelling applicants or members from membership on the basis of sex or marital status. (§§ 378-1, -2)

> **ENFORCEMENT:**  The Hawaii Department of Labor and Industrial Relations enforces the Fair Employment Practices Law. An individual claiming to be aggrieved by an alleged unlawful discriminatory practice may file a verified complaint with the department within 90 days of the occurrence of the alleged unlawful discriminatory practice. (§ 378-4)

# GOVERNMENT CONTRACTORS AND SUBCONTRACTORS

There is no relevant statutory provision.

# STATE EMPLOYEE LAWS

See "Fair Employment Laws." In addition, state employees may not be suspended, demoted or dismissed on account of their sex or marital status. (§§ 76-44, 378-1)

# VETERAN'S PREFERENCE

The civil service gives preference to the employment of veterans, disabled veterans and their spouses, and veterans' widows who have not remarried. (§ 76-103)

# Community Life

# CREDIT

The Fair Credit Extension Act prohibits discrimination in any credit transaction on the basis of marital status. (§ 477E-3)

> **ENFORCEMENT:**  Any individual who is a victim of discrimination in the granting of credit on the basis of marital status may bring a civil action in court within 1 year of the occurrence of the violation. In any successful action, the court may award attorney fees in addition to the cost of the action and damages. (§ 477E-4)

# HOUSING

Discrimination in the sale, lease, or rental of real property on the basis of sex or marital status is prohibited. The prohibition does not apply to the rental of a housing accommodation in a two-family house in which the lessor or members of his or her family reside or to the rental of rooms in a house in which the lessor or members of his or her family reside. (§§ 515-3, -4) In addition, it is unlawful to discriminate against an applicant for financial assistance in connection with the purchase, construction, or repair of real property on the basis of sex. (§§ 515-5)

**ENFORCEMENT:** Any individual who has been the victim of discrimination in housing may file a written complaint with the Department of Regulatory Agencies within 90 days of the occurrence of the alleged discriminatory act. (§§ 515-9 *et seq.*)

# INSURANCE

Discrimination between individuals of the same class and equal expectation of life in the rates charged for any contract of life insurance or of life annuity or in the dividends or other benefits payable under these contracts or policies is prohibited. Also prohibited is discrimination in favor of particular individuals or persons, or between insured or subjects of insurance having substantially like insuring risk and exposure factors or expense elements, in the terms or conditions of any insurance contract, or in the rate or amount of premium charged, or in the benefits payable, or in any other rights or privileges accruing under the contract. In addition, refusing to insure or continue to insure or limiting the amount of coverage available to an individual because of sex or marital status is prohibited. [§ 431-643)(7)] No motor vehicle insurance may base any standard or rating plan upon the sex or marital status of the applicant. (§ 294-33)

**ENFORCEMENT:** The Commissioner of Insurance examines and investigates all charges of prohibited discriminatory or unfair practices in the insurance industry. If, after a hearing, the commissioner determines that a party has engaged in such practices, the commissioner may issue a cease and desist order enjoining that party from further engaging in those practices. The commissioner may also impose monetary fines or either suspend or revoke the person's license if that person knew or should have known that he or she was violating the law. (§§ 431-644 to -646)

# PUBLIC ACCOMMODATIONS

There is no relevant statutory provision.

# IDAHO

## Home and Family

## MARRIAGE

**AGE OF CONSENT:** An unmarried person over 18 years of age, not otherwise disqualified, may consent to marry. (§ 32-202)*

**CONSENT REQUIREMENT:** A person under 18 years of age and over 16 years of age may marry with written parental consent. Anyone under 16 years of age may marry with written parental consent and upon order of the court. (§ 32-202)

**LICENSE REQUIREMENT:** A marriage license to be issued by the county recorder is required. Before the issuance of the license, a medical certificate, the form for which is to be provided by the Department of Health and Welfare, is required. (§§ 32-403, -412, -413)

**PROHIBITED MARRIAGES:** Marriages between parents and children, between ancestors and descendants of every degree, between brothers and sisters of the half as well as the whole blood, and between uncles and nieces or aunts and nephews are incestuous and void from the beginning whether the relationship is legitimate or illegitimate. (§ 32-205) Marriages between first cousins are prohibited. (§ 32-206) Children of void or prohibited marriages are legitimate unless the wife was pregnant with the child of a man other than the husband. (§ 32-503)

## DISSOLUTION OF MARRIAGE

**ANNULMENT:** Appendix A, factors 19, 32 to 35, are grounds for an annulment. (§ 32-501)

**LEGAL SEPARATION:** There is no relevant statutory provision. But when married persons have lived separate and apart without cohabitation for a period of 5 years, either party may sue for divorce upon proof of continuous living separate and apart. (32-610)

### DIVORCE

*Residency Requirement:* The party seeking the divorce must be a resident of the state for 6 full weeks before the commencement of the action. (32-701)

*Grounds for Divorce:* Appendix A, factors 4, 9, 15, 16, 17, 22, 25, and 31, are grounds for divorce. (§§ 32-603 to -610)

*Property Distribution:* Unless there are compelling reasons, the court shall divide the community property substantially equally. The court will consider but will not be limited by factors 5, 6 to 10, 16, 18, 19, and 21, listed in Appendix F. (§ 32-712)

*Child Custody:* In an action for divorce, the court may give such direction for the custody, care, and education of the children as may seem necessary or proper in the best interests of the children. The court shall consider all relevant factors including factors 5, 10, 12, 14, and 24, listed in Appendix B. (§ 32-717) Joint

*Unless otherwise specified, all citation references are to the Idaho Code (1977).

physical custody or joint legal custody or both, may be awarded. Absent a preponderance of the evidence, there is a presumption that joint custody is in the best interests of the child. (32-717B) See also the Uniform Child Custody Jurisdiction Act, §§ 31-1101 to -1126.

*Child Support:* The court may order either or both parents to pay an amount reasonable or necessary for the support of the child without regard to marital misconduct, after considering all relevant factors including factors 1, 3, 4, and 5, listed in Appendix D. (§ 32-706) Upon a showing of a substantial and material change of circumstances, child support may be modified. (§ 32-709)

*Spousal Support/Alimony:* The court may award maintenance to the innocent spouse after considering factors 2, 4, 5, 6, 12, 13, and 14, listed in Appendix E. The award shall be in such an amount and for such time as the court deems just. (§ 32-705)

*Enforcement of Support Orders:* Support payments may be ordered paid to the clerk of the court which enters the order. The clerk shall notify the prosecuting attorney of any failure to comply, and the prosecuting attorney shall be responsible for enforcement. (§ 32-710A) Execution or garnishment against earnings or unemployment benefits is also available for collecting delinquent child support obligations. (§ 11-103)

*Spouse's Name:* There is no relevant statutory provision.

*Divorce by Affidavit or Summary Judgment:* There is no relevant statutory provision.

*Displaced Homemaker Laws:* The Equal Opportunity for Displaced Homemakers Act recognizes the increased number of persons who, having fulfilled the role of homemaker, find themselves displaced because of divorce, death or disability of a spouse, or other loss of annual income. The act coordinates efforts by state and local public agencies in cooperation with private agencies to assist displaced homemakers. (§§ 39-5001 to -5009)

# DOMESTIC VIOLENCE

**STATUTORY PROVISION:** The infliction of physical injury on, sexual abuse of, forced imprisonment of, threat of forced imprisonment of a family or household member is prohibited. (§ 39-5202)

**WHO IS PROTECTED?** All persons who are related by blood or by marriage or who reside with, or have resided with, have been married to the person committing domestic violence are protected. (§ 39-5202)

**RELIEF AVAILABLE:** A police officer can make a warrantless arrest when, at the scene of a domestic disturbance, there is reasonable cause to believe, based upon physical evidence observed by that officer or statements made in his or her presence, that the person arrested has committed an assault or battery. [§ 19-603(b)] In addition, the Idaho Council on Domestic Violence regulates and funds domestic violence projects which must provide a safe house or refuge to the victims of domestic violence in addition to offering legal, psychological, medical, and vocational services. (§ 39-5210)

**MARITAL RAPE:** A spouse who has initiated legal proceedings for divorce or legal separation or who has been voluntarily living apart for 180 days or more may charge his or her spouse with rape. (§ 18-6107) However, the existence of the marital relationship between the victim and the accused is an affirmative defense which must be put at issue by the accused. [*State v. Huggin*, 665 P.2d 1053 (Idaho 1983)]

**CIVIL LAWSUIT FOR RAPE OR ASSAULT:** There is no relevant case law.

**CHILD ABUSE:** Any person who willfully causes or permits any child to suffer, or who inflicts unjustifiable physical pain or mental suffering upon a child, or who willfully causes or permits the child to be injured or places the child in a situation in which the health of the child is endangered, is guilty of a crime. (§ 18-1501)

> *Notification Requirement:* All health care professionals, school teachers, day care personnel, social workers, coroners, or other persons who have reasonable cause to believe that a child under 18 years of age has been abused, abandoned, or neglected or who observe the child being subjected to conditions which would reasonably result in abuse, abandonment, or neglect shall report such circumstances within 24 hours to the proper law enforcement agency or to the Department of Health and Welfare. (§ 16-1619)

# INHERITANCE RIGHTS

**FAILURE TO MAKE A WILL:** The surviving spouse is entitled to all the decedent's share of the community property, and all the separate property if there is no child or grandchild or surviving parent; to the first $50,000 and one-half the balance if the decedent left surviving parents or one or more children or grandchildren; or to one-half the estate if the decedent left one or more children or grandchildren who are not the spouse's children or grandchildren. (§ 15-2-102)

**FAILURE TO PROVIDE BY WILL:** A spouse who married the testator after the will was executed and was not provided for in the will shall receive his or her share as if the spouse had died without a will, unless it appears that the omission was intentional or that the surviving spouse was otherwise provided for. (§ 15-2-301)

**CHILDREN BORN OUT OF WEDLOCK:** A child born out of wedlock is the legitimate heir of the mother. If paternity has been established before the death of the father or is established thereafter by clear and convincing proof, the child may inherit through the father. However, the father or his relatives may not inherit through the child born out of wedlock unless the father has openly treated the child as his and has not refused to support the child. In addition, if the natural parents married after the birth of the child, even when the attempted marriage is void, the child born out of wedlock may also inherit through the father. (§ 15-2-109)

**HOMESTEAD, PERSONAL, AND FAMILY ALLOWANCES:** The head of the family may select a homestead worth up to $25,000 during his or her lifetime. Where no homestead has been selected and set aside, a surviving spouse is entitled to a homestead allowance of $4000 or of $10,000 if there are dependent children living with the spouse. (§ 15-2-401) However, the existence of a homestead set up during a spouse's lifetime is not a prerequisite for a surviving spouse claiming a homestead allowance under this statute. [*Shaw v. Bowman*, 609 P.2d 663 (Idaho 1980)] In addition to the homestead, the surviving spouse is entitled to an exempt property allowance from the estate of a value not exceeding $3500 in excess of any security interest in household furniture, automobiles, furnishings, appliances, and personal effects. (§ 15-2-402) In addition, the surviving spouse and minor children whom the decedent was obligated to support, and children who were being supported by the decedent, are entitled to a reasonable family allowance for their maintenance during the period of administration of the estate not to exceed 1 year. (§ 15-2-403) The homestead, property and family allowance are exempt and have priority over all claims against the estate and are in addition to any benefits passing under the will, unless otherwise provided. (§ 15-2-401)

**OPTION TO DISREGARD THE WILL:** The surviving spouse may elect to take one-half of the "augmented quasi-community property estate" and need not renounce his or her share under the will or through intestate succession, nor will the option to take the elective share affect the surviving spouse's right to the homestead, except as to the property and family allowances, unless otherwise provided for by provisions under the will which the surviving spouse has not renounced. (§§ 15-2-203, -206)

# REPRODUCTIVE RIGHTS
## ABORTION

*Statutory Provisions:* Abortions are strictly regulated by statute. Existing law provides that, except as expressly permitted, the performance of abortions is a felony punishable by fine or imprisonment or both. (§ 18-606) Abortions that are legal and not subject to legal sanctions are first-trimester abortions, which are performed after consultation between the doctor and patient and which, based on the judgment of the doctor, are found appropriate after considering certain matters such as physical, emotional, psychological and familiar factors; the possibility of a defective child; the fact that the pregnancy may have resulted from rape, incest or other felonious intercourse (which is presumed if the patient is under 16); or any other factors which the doctor thinks appropriate. First-trimester abortions may be performed in either a hospital, a clinic, or a doctor's office, provided these facilities are properly staffed and there is an acute care hospital in reasonable proximity. [§ 18-608(1)] Second-trimester abortions are subject to the same conditions as first-trimester abortions except that they must be performed in a hospital. [§ 18-608(2)] Third-trimester, or postviability, abortions are also subject to the above-mentioned conditions. However, in addition, they may be performed only if, in the doctor's opinion, corroborated by a like opinion of a consulting doctor, such an abortion is necessary to save the mother's life or, if the abortion were not performed, the pregnancy would terminate in the birth of a fetus unable to survive. Doctors performing abortions must use all available medical skills to preserve the life of a viable fetus. [§ 18-608(3)] Hospitals are not required to perform abortions, and all persons have the right to refuse to participate in abortions on personal, religious, or ethical grounds. (§ 18-612)

*Informed Consent:* The informed consent of the woman is required before the performance of an abortion. In order to assure that the woman's consent is truly informed, the Department of Health and Welfare makes available to the woman, at the expense of the doctor or hospital providing the abortion, easily understood printed material describing services available including adoption services; descriptions of the physical characteristics of a normal fetus accompanied by scientifically verified pictures depicting the fetus at various stages of development and descriptions of the abortion procedures. (§ 18-609)

*Parental Consent:* There is no relevant statutory provision. However, if the pregnant patient is unmarried and under 18 or is unemancipated, the doctor must, if possible, notify the parents or legal guardian of the pregnant patient at least 24 hours before the performance of the abortion. [§ 18-609(6)]

*Spousal Consent:* There is no relevant statutory provision.

*Health Insurance Regulations:* As of July 1, 1983, all health maintenance organization policies, contracts, or plans (§ 41-3934); all disability insurance policies (§ 41-2142); and all blanket or group disability insurance policies, contracts, or plans are to exclude coverage of elective abortions unless the exclusion is waived by the payment of a premium. Availability of this coverage is at the option of the insurance carrier. (§ 41-221DA)

*Reporting Requirements:* Attending doctors must report each abortion they perform within 15 days after the end of each reporting month to the Bureau of Vital Statistics; the report may not contain any information which would identify the woman. (§ 39-361)

*State Funding:* Funds available to the Department of Health and Welfare cannot be used to pay for abortions unless two consulting physicians recommend the abortion as necessary to save the life or health of the mother or unless the pregnancy is a result of a rape or incest as determined by the courts. [§ 56-209(c)]

**BIRTH CONTROL:** Doctors and registered health care providers may prescribe and supply contraceptive information and supplies to any person who is sufficiently intelligent and mature to understand the nature and significance of birth control information and devices. (§ 18-603) Wholesalers and manufacturers of contraceptives and prophylactics must register annually with the Board of Pharmacy and provide a list of all the products and brands of prophylactics and contraceptives they intend to sell in the state. (§ 39-801)

**STERILIZATION:** There is no relevant statutory provision regarding voluntary sterilization. Statutes provide for involuntary sterilization of persons who are irreversibly and incurably mentally incompetent because of mental retardation, organic retardation, or both. (§§ 39-3901 *et seq.* )

# UNMARRIED COUPLES

**COMMON-LAW MARRIAGE:** Common-law marriage is valid in Idaho. [*Freiburghaus v. Freiburghaus*, 651 P.2d 944 (Idaho Ct. App. 1982)]

**COHABITAL RELATIONSHIPS:** There is no relevant statutory provision. Relevant case law, however, holds that in the absence of either an agreement to pool earnings, a partnership, a joint venture, or circumstances sufficient to establish a constructive trust, neither a man nor a woman cohabiting with knowledge of the illegal nature of the relationship acquires, by reason of such cohabitation alone, any rights in the accumulations of the other during the period of their illegal relationship. [*Cargill v. Hancock*, 444 P.2d 421 (Idaho 1968)]

## CHILDREN

*Custody:* There is no relevant statutory provision.

*Legitimation Proceedings:* A child born out of wedlock becomes legitimate if the father and mother subsequently marry; if the father, from the time of the child's birth, publicly acknowledges the child as his own; if the father receives the child into his family (with the consent of his wife, if married) or otherwise treats the child as if the child were legitimate, or if the father legally adopts the child. (§§ 16-1510, 32-1006)

*Paternity Proceedings:* Proceedings to establish paternity may be brought by the mother, the child's guardian, any other person standing in a paternal relationship with the child, the child's next of kin, or the state of Idaho on behalf of a child receiving state aid. (§ 7-1110) This action may be brought only after the birth of the child and must be brought before the child reaches 18. (§ 7-1107)

*Obligations of Putative Father:* Each parent is liable for the necessary support and education of the child and for the child's funeral expenses. An order of support or a judicially approved settlement made before the parent's death is enforceable against the estate of a deceased parent. Once paternity has been established, the court will direct the father to pay a fair and reasonable sum for the support and education of the child until the child reaches 18. However, if the child continues his or her formal education beyond the age of 18, the court may, at its discretion, order continuation of support until the child reaches 21. (§ 7-1121) The court may also direct the father to reimburse the amounts paid in support of the child before the order of filiation, funeral expenses if the child has died, and all necessary expenses connected with the mother's pregnancy and confinement. (§ 7-1121)

# Education

## STATUTORY PROVISION

Discrimination on the basis of sex by an educational institution in the terms, conditions and privileges of the institution is prohibited. Educational institutions include all public and private schools and colleges. [§§ 67-5902(10), -5909(6)]

## AREAS COVERED

Areas covered include admissions; terms; conditions; privileges; primary, secondary, and higher educational institutions; written oral inquiries; admission records; publishing; advertisements; quotas; and educational opportunities. [§§ 67-5902(10), -5909(6)]

**ENFORCEMENT:** See "Housing."

# Employment

## EQUAL PAY LAWS

It is unlawful to pay any employee at a wage rate less than the rate paid to another employee of the opposite sex in the same establishment for work requiring equal skill, effort, and responsibility. Wage differentials are not prohibited if based on seniority or merit systems which do not discriminate on the basis of sex. [§§ 44-1702(1), 67-5909(1)]

**ENFORCEMENT:** See "Housing." In addition, an action to recover unpaid wages may be maintained in any court of competent jurisdiction by any employee. The court shall award attorney's fees and costs. (§ 44-1704) Also, the director of the Department of Labor is authorized to eliminate unlawful pay practices by informal methods and to supervise payment of wages owed to an employee. (§ 44-1703)

## FAIR EMPLOYMENT LAWS

The Fair Employment Practices Law applies to the state of Idaho, its political and civil subdivisions, employers of ten or more employees, labor organizations and employment agencies. It prohibits an employer from refusing to hire, to discharge or otherwise to discriminate against an individual on the basis of sex with respect to the terms, privileges and conditions of employment; it prohibits a labor organization from excluding or expelling from membership or from refusing to refer an individual for employment; and for an employment agency to refuse to refer an individual for employment on account of the individual's sex and from printing or publishing advertisements for employment indicating a preference for a particular sex. (§ 67-5909) However, this prohibition does not apply to religious corporations, associations, or societies with respect to employment of individuals in connection with religious activities; or to situations where sex is a bona fide occupational qualification reasonably necessary to the normal operation of the business; or to bona fide seniority systems. [§ 67-5910(1)]

> **ENFORCEMENT:** Employment discrimination is a misdemeanor punishable by imprisonment in a county jail for a period not exceeding 6 months or a fine of $300 or both. (§§ 18-113, -7303) See also "Housing."

## GOVERNMENT CONTRACTORS AND SUBCONTRACTORS

Government contractors and subcontractors are covered by the Fair Employment Practices Law. [§ 67-5902(6)]

> **ENFORCEMENT:** See "Housing."

## STATE EMPLOYEE LAWS

State employees are covered under the Fair Employment Practices Law. [§ 67-5902(6)(b)] Exec. Order No. 78-4, issued October 17, 1978, requires that state employees be recruited, appointed, assigned, and promoted solely on the basis of merit.

> **ENFORCEMENT:** See "Housing."

## VETERAN'S PREFERENCE

Five points are added to the passing civil service exam scores of any war veterans and also to the passing scores of their widows as long as they remain unmarried. Likewise, ten points are added to the passing scores of disabled war veterans, to their widows as long as they remain unmarried, and to the wives of disabled war veterans who are physically unable to work. This preference applies only to initial employment and not to promotions. (§ 65-506)

# Community Life

## CREDIT

There is no relevant statutory provision. However, the federal Equal Credit Opportunity Act of 1977, 12 C.F.R. § 202, may apply.

## HOUSING

It is unlawful for an owner, a real estate broker or salesperson, or any other person to refuse to engage in or negotiate any real estate transaction; or to discriminate in the terms, conditions, privileges, or furnishings of facilities or services in connection with a real estate transaction; or to represent property as not available when it is, or to solicit or advertise in a way which would indicate an intent to discriminate on the basis of sex. [§ 67-5909(7)] This provision does not apply to the rental of a unit in a two-family house or to the rental of rooms in a house in which the lessor or member of his or her family resides. [§ 67-5910(5)] It is further unlawful for a person to discriminate against an applicant for financial assistance in connection with a real estate transaction or for rehabilitation, repair or maintenance of real property. [§ 67-5909(8)]

**ENFORCEMENT:** Any persons who believe they have been unlawfully discriminated against may file a complaint within 2 years of the occurrence of the alleged discriminatory act with the Human Rights Commission. (§§ 67-5908, -5909) The commission will attempt to resolve the problem informally. If conciliation fails, the commission may file a civil action seeking appropriate relief within 1 year of the occurrence of the discriminatory act. (§§ 67-5907, -5908) In addition, the person so discriminated against may file a civil action in the district court on his or her own behalf not more than 2 years after the occurrence of the alleged discriminatory act. (§ 67-5908)

# INSURANCE

Discrimination is prohibited between individuals of the same class and equal expectation of life in rates charged for life insurance or annuity contracts or between individuals of the same class and essentially the same hazard in the amount of premium, policy fees, or rates charged for disability insurance, or in the benefits payable under these contracts, or in any other terms or conditions of these contracts. (§ 41-1313)

**ENFORCEMENT:** An aggrieved person may, upon a written demand, obtain a hearing with the Director of Insurance within 30 days of receipt of the demand. (§ 41-232) Upon the failure or refusal of the director to hold a hearing, or within 30 days after a hearing has been held, an appeal may be taken to the district court of the third judicial district by filing with the clerk a petition for review of the director's order or action. (§§ 41-241, -242)

# PUBLIC ACCOMMODATIONS

It is unlawful for any person to deny the full and equal enjoyment of the goods, services, facilities, privileges, advantages and accommodations of a place of public accommodation because of sex, or to publish or post a notice or advertisement that the patronage of an individual is unwelcome or undesirable on the basis of sex. [§ 67-5909(5)] This provision does not apply to private clubs or accommodations except to the extent that those accommodations are made available to the public. [§ 67-5910(3)]

**ENFORCEMENT:** See "Housing."

# ILLINOIS

## Home and Family

## MARRIAGE

**AGE OF CONSENT:** A person 18 years of age or older may consent to marry. [ch. 40 § 203(1)]*

**CONSENT REQUIREMENT:** A person 16 years of age or older may marry with parental or guardian consent or judicial approval. [ch. 40 § 203(1)]

**LICENSE REQUIREMENT:** Persons intending to marry must obtain a license from the county clerk. The license is issued upon furnishing satisfactory proof that the parties are of age and have undergone a premarital medical examination and that the marriage is not prohibited. (ch. 40 §§ 203, 204) However, regardless of the results of the premarital test, the county clerk is empowered to issue a marriage license to a woman who is pregnant at the time of the application or to a woman who has given birth to an out-of-wedlock child who is alive at the time of the application. (ch. 40 § 205)

**PROHIBITED MARRIAGES:** Bigamous marriages are prohibited. Marriages between an ancestor and a descendant, a brother and a sister (whether by the half or whole blood or by adoption), an uncle and a niece, an aunt and a nephew (whether by the half or whole blood), or first cousins, except for marriages between first cousins 50 years of age or older, are incestuous and void. Children born of void or prohibited marriages are legitimate. (ch. 40 §§ 212, 303)

## DISSOLUTION OF MARRIAGE

**ANNULMENT:** Appendix A, factors 19, 32, 33, 34, 35, 37, and 38, are grounds for annulment. (ch. 40 § 301)
   *Residency Requirement:* There is no relevant statutory provision.

**LEGAL SEPARATION:** Any person living separate and apart from his or her spouse, without fault, may obtain a legal separation with provisions for reasonable support and maintenance while the parties live apart. (ch. 40 § 402)
   *Residency Requirement:* There is no relevant statutory provision.

**DIVORCE**
   *Residency Requirement:* A party seeking a divorce must have been a resident of the state for 90 days before the commencement of the action. (ch. 40 § 401)
   *Grounds for Divorce:* Appendix A, factors 2 (with 22 and 31), 3, 4, 8, 15, 16, 17, 19, 20, 32, and 43, are grounds for divorce. (ch. 40 § 401)
   *Conciliation Requirement:* If the court concludes that there is a prospect of reconciliation, it may, at the request of either party or on its own motion, order a conciliation conference. (ch. 40 § 404)

---

*Unless otherwise specified, citation references are to Smith-Hurd Illinois Annotated Statutes (1934).

*Property Distribution:* Marital property is distributed by the court without regard to fault in just proportions. Appendix F, factors 1, 2, 3, 5 to 12, 16, 17, 21, and 25, will be considered. (ch. 40 § 503)

*Child Custody:* Custody is awarded according to the best interests of the child. Appendix B, factors 5, 10, 11, 12, 14, and 22, will be considered. Upon the application of either or both parents or upon its own motion, the court may award joint custody. (ch. 40 §§ 602, 603.1, 610)

*Child Support:* The court may order either or both parents to pay a reasonable and necessary amount for the support of their children without regard to marital misconduct. In making the award, the court will consider factors 1 through 5, listed in Appendix D. (ch. 40 § 505)

*Spousal Support/Alimony:* The court may award maintenance to either spouse in such amounts and for such periods of time as it deems just, without regard to marital misconduct, only if it finds that the spouse seeking maintenance lacks sufficient resources to provide for his or her reasonable needs and is unable to work or is otherwise without sufficient income. The court will consider all relevant factors, including factors 1 through 6, 12, and 18, listed in Appendix E. (ch. 40 § 504)

*Enforcement of Support Orders:* Failure of either parent to comply with a support order is punishable as in other cases of contempt. In addition, after a parent has been found to be in contempt, he or she may be placed on probation or sentenced to periodic imprisonment for a period of up to 6 months. The court may also order part or all of the earnings of a parent during a sentence of periodic imprisonment paid to the clerk of the circuit court or to the parent or guardian having custody. The court may enforce a judgment of maintenance by ordering the sequestration of marital property. Wage withholding orders are also available against a defaulting party owing a duty to support a minor child or a spouse. [ch. 40 §§ 503(h), 504(c), 505, 706.1] See also the Revised Uniform Reciprocal Enforcement of Support Act of 1968, ch. 68 §§ 101 *et seq.*

*Spouse's Name:* There is no relevant statutory provision.

*Divorce by Affidavit or Summary Judgment:* There is no relevant statutory provision.

*Displaced Homemaker Laws:* The Director of Commerce and Community Affairs is empowered to designate multipurpose service centers operated by community nonprofit agencies for displaced homemakers. These centers provide a myriad of services which include counseling, training and referral services that provide the displaced homemaker opportunities to become gainfully employed and independent. In addition, the centers attempt to identify community needs and seek funding for new public- and private-sector jobs and develop plans to include more displaced homemakers in existing training and placement programs. (ch. 23 §§ 3451 *et seq.*)

# DOMESTIC VIOLENCE

**STATUTORY PROVISION:** Striking, threatening, harassing or interfering with the personal liberty of any family or household member by any other family or household member is prohibited. Reasonable discipline of a minor child is permitted. (ch. 40 § 2301.3)

**WHO IS PROTECTED?** The law protects spouses, former spouses, individuals sharing a common household, parents and children, and persons related by blood or marriage. (ch. 40 § 2301.3)

**RELIEF AVAILABLE:** A police officer may, with or without a warrant, arrest a person where there is probable cause to believe that the person has committed or is committing an act of domestic violence and the offender and the victim are family or household members. The offense does not have to occur in the presence of the police officer. (ch. 40 § 2303) Other relief available to the victim of domestic violence includes orders of protection, injunctions, emergency relief, and shelter. (ch. 38 § 111.8; ch. 40 §§ 501, 2302, 2303, 2401)

**MARITAL RAPE:** A husband can not be charged with the rape of his wife. [ch. 38 § 12-8(c)]

**CIVIL LAWSUIT FOR RAPE OR ASSAULT:** There are no cases directly on point. However, with the exception of intentional torts, a woman may not sue her husband for torts committed during the marriage. (ch 40 § 1001)

**CHILD ABUSE:** Inflicting, causing to be inflicted, allowing to be inflicted, or creating substantial risk of physical injury which could cause or would likely cause death, disfigurement, impairment of physical or emotional health, or loss or impairment of bodily function to a child, by any means other than by accident is prohibited. (ch. 23 § 2354)

> *Notification Requirement:* All health care professionals, coroners, medical examiners, school personnel, truant officers, social workers, nursery school or day care center personnel, police officers, and psychologists are required to report all suspected cases of child abuse or neglect to the Department of Children and Family Services. In addition, any other person who has reasonable cause to believe that a child may be neglected or abused must make a report. All reported cases must be investigated within 24 hours. (ch. 23 § 2054)

# INHERITANCE RIGHTS

**FAILURE TO MAKE A WILL:** The surviving spouse is entitled to the entire estate of the deceased if he or she left no descendants; or to one-half of the estate if the deceased left descendant(s). (ch. 110½ § 2-1)

**FAILURE TO PROVIDE BY WILL:** The surviving spouse is entitled to an award of not less than $10,000 unless the testator expressly provides for the surviving spouse in the will and the surviving spouse does not renounce the will. (ch. 110½ § 15-1)

**CHILDREN BORN OUT OF WEDLOCK:** A child born out of wedlock is the heir of the mother and her kin. However, the child is heir to the father only if the father has acknowledged paternity or if during the father's lifetime or after his death, the father has been adjudged to be the father of the child. (ch. 110½ § 2-2)

**HOMESTEAD, PERSONAL, AND FAMILY ALLOWANCES:** The surviving spouse is entitled to a homestead allowance of up to $7500 in value. Such homestead allowance is exempt from all creditors' liens and judgment sales for the payment of the decedent's debts. (ch. 110 § 12-901) During the period of time in which the estate is being administered by the state, the surviving spouse is entitled to reasonable support of not less than $10,000, plus $2000 for each child for a period of 9 months, except where the will of the deceased spouse expressly specifies that the provisions in the will are in lieu of this award and the surviving spouse does not renounce the will. This allowance is exempt from all creditors' liens and judgments. (ch. 110½ § 15-1)

**OPTION TO DISREGARD THE WILL:** The surviving spouse may reject the will and take one-half of the deceased spouse's estate if the deceased spouse left no descendants or one-third of the estate if the deceased left descendants. (ch. 110½ § 2-8)

# REPRODUCTIVE RIGHTS

## ABORTION

*Statutory Provisions:* An abortion may only be performed by a physician if a physician has determined that the abortion is necessary. (ch. 38 § 81-23.1) Elective abortions may be performed by licensed physicians in abortion clinics, which must be licensed by the Department of Public Health. (ch. 111 § 4433; ch. 111½ § 157-8.4) When the fetus is viable, an abortion cannot be performed unless, in the medical judgment of the attending or referring physician, based on the particular facts of the case, the abortion is necessary to preserve the life or health of the mother. The physician must so certify in writing on a form prescribed by the Department of Public Health. (ch. 68 § 81-25) Unless a medical emergency exists, no abortion can be performed when the fetus is viable unless there is in attendance a physician other than the one performing the abortion who shall take control of and provide immediate medical care to any child born alive. The physician must use the method of abortion most likely to preserve the life of the viable fetus. (ch. 38 § 81-26) This provision was held unconstitutional in *Charles v. Daley*, 749 F.2d 452 (7th Cir. 1984). An appeal is pending before the U.S. Supreme Court. (*Diamond v. Charles*, 84-1379). No physicians, hospitals, or their employees who conscientiously object to abortions are required to perform or participate in abortions. (ch. 38 § 81-33)

*Informed Consent:* Before undergoing an abortion, the pregnant woman must certify in writing that her consent is informed and freely given. (ch. 38 § 81-23)

*Parental Consent:* There is no relevant statutory provision. However, abortions cannot be performed on unemancipated minors or incompetents unless both parents or the legal guardian of the minor or incompetent person are given at least 24 hours actual notice. If the minor or incompetent objects to notice being given to her parents or legal guardian, she may, on her own behalf or by her next friend, petition the circuit court of the county of her residence, or the county where the abortion is to be performed, for a waiver of the notice requirement. (ch. 38 § 81-64)

*Spousal Consent:* There is no relevant statutory provision.

*Health Insurance Regulations:* The noncontributory portion of state group health insurance programs covering state employees may not be applied toward abortions, induced miscarriages or induced premature births unless, in the opinion of the physician, such procedures are necessary to preserve the life or health of the woman or to produce a viable child. (ch. 127 § 526)

*Reporting Requirements:* Each abortion must be reported to the Department of Public Health no later than 10 days following the end of the month in which the abortion was performed. The report must include personal information about the patient, such as her age, race, marital status, and prior pregnancies, but it must not identify the abortee by name. The report also includes the identity of the physician, the place and date of the abortion, any ensuing complications, and the patient identification number. (ch. 38 § 81-30)

*State Funding:* State fundings for abortions are unavailable unless the abortion is necessary to preserve the life or health of the mother or unborn child. (ch. 23 §§ 5-5, 6-1)

**BIRTH CONTROL:** Doctors licensed to practice in the state may give birth control services and information to a minor who is either married, pregnant, or a parent or who has parental or guardian consent, or who is referred for such services by a physician, member of the clergy, or a planned parenthood agency. Where failure to provide the minor with such services would create a serious health hazard, doctors may also provide services and information. Doctors were required to describe certain drugs and contraceptives as "abortifacients." [ch. 38 §§ 81-20(10), -31(d)] These provisions were declared unconstitutional in *Charles v. Daley*, 749 F.2d 452 (7th Cir. 1984). An appeal is pending before the U.S. Supreme Court. (*Diamond v. Charles*, 84-1379) (ch. 11½ § 4651)

**STERILIZATION:** There is no relevant statutory provision.

## UNMARRIED COUPLES

**COMMON-LAW MARRIAGE:** Common-law marriages entered into after 1905 are invalid. However, such marriages entered into in a state where they are valid are legal. (ch. 40 § 21) See *Peirce v. Peirce*, 39 N.E.2d 990 (Ill. 1942).

**COHABITAL RELATIONSHIPS:** Cohabitation violates public policy. Therefore contracts, either expressed or implied, between knowingly unmarried cohabitants are not valid or enforceable. [*Hewitt v. Hewitt*, 394 N.E.2d 1204 (Ill. 1979)]

### CHILDREN

*Custody:* There is no relevant statutory provision.

*Legitimation Proceedings:* Children born out of wedlock are legitimate if the father has acknowledged paternity or if, during the father's lifetime or after his death, he has been adjudicated to be the father of the child. Legitimation can be proved by an authenticated copy of the holding of a court of competent jurisdiction or by clear and convincing evidence. A child whose parents intermarry and who is acknowledged by the father is legitimate. (ch. 110½ § 2-2)

*Paternity Proceedings:* An action to determine paternity may be brought by the child, the mother, a pregnant woman, any person or public official who has custody of or is providing or has provided financial support to the child, or a man presumed or alleging himself to be the father of the child or expected child. An action brought by or on behalf of the child must be brought no later than 2 years after the child reaches the age of majority. However if brought on behalf of the child by a public agency, it must be brought within 2 years after such agency has stopped providing assistance to the child. An action brought on behalf of any other person must be brought within 2 years after the birth of the child. [ch. 40 § 2508(8)]

*Obligations of the Putative Father:* The parents of a child born out of wedlock are obliged to support that child regardless of their marital status. (ch. 40 § 2503) Once the father and child relationship is established, the court may order the father to pay for the reasonable expenses incurred by the mother during her pregnancy, confinement and recovery. [ch. 40 2514(a)]

# Education

# STATUTORY PROVISION

The Illinois Constitution contains an equal rights provision which prohibits sex discrimination by the state and local government and by school districts. (Ill. Const. art 1, § 18)

School boards may not discriminate in the assignment of students. (ch. 122 § 18-12) Professional and occupational schools accredited by the state may not discriminate in admissions. (ch. 127 § 60) Medical, dental, or nursing schools that discriminate in admissions or use of their facilities may not receive state aid. (ch. 111½ § 822)

## AREAS COVERED

The areas covered include educational materials and curricula (Implementing Guidelines of State Board of Education, § 7.1), athletics (ch. 122 §§ 27-1, 34-18, 103-26), and sexual harassment of students in higher education. (ch. 68 §§ 5A-101, -102)

**ENFORCEMENT:** A person who is seeking employment with the Board of Education and who is discriminated against on the basis of sex can recover monetary damages of at least $500 from the discriminating party. (ch. 122 § 24-4) Students and others alleging discrimination on the basis of sex may file a written charge with the Illinois Department of Human Services within 180 days of the occurrence of the alleged discriminatory act. (ch. 68 § 7-102)

# Employment

## EQUAL PAY LAWS

It is unlawful for an employer to discriminate on the basis of sex in wages paid to employees for the same or substantially similar work requiring equal skill, effort and responsibility under similar working conditions. [ch. 48 § 1004(b)] Wage differentials are permitted if based on seniority, experience, training, skill, ability, difference in duties performed or difference in availability for other work or any other reasonable classifications except those based on sex. (ch. 48 § 4a)

**ENFORCEMENT:** An employee who has been paid less than the wage to which he or she is entitled may bring a civil action to recover the amount of all underpayments together with punitive damages, the costs of the action and reasonable attorney's fees. Such an action must be brought within 3 years of the date of the underpayment. (ch. 48 § 1012; ch. 68 § 2-104)

## FAIR EMPLOYMENT LAWS

The law applies to the state, its political and civil subdivisions, employers employing fifteen or more employees, employment agencies, and labor organizations. It prohibits discrimination in hire, recruitment, referral for employment, selection of apprentices, discharge, discipline, tenure or any other terms or conditions of employment on the basis of marital status or sex. [ch. 29 § 17(1); ch. 68 § 2-102] However, this prohibition does not apply where a valid merit or seniority system exists, sex is a bona fide occupational qualification, or the applicant or his or her relative is hired under veteran's preference or on the basis of the results of professionally validated ability tests. Employees do not include domestic servants in private homes, elected public officials or their immediate personal staff, or persons designated as evaluees or trainees in a vocational rehabilitation facility certified under federal law. (ch. 68 § 2-101)

**ENFORCEMENT:** The Illinois Department of Human Rights receives, investigates, conciliates, settles, or dismisses charges of discriminatory practices brought before it. A charge must be in writing, under oath or affirmation, and must be filed within 180 days of the occurrence of the alleged discriminatory practice. The charge may be made either by the aggrieved party or by the department itself. (ch. 68 § 7-102)

## GOVERNMENT CONTRACTORS AND SUBCONTRACTORS

Every party to a public contract must refrain from unlawful discrimination in employment and take affirmative action to assure equality of employment opportunities and to eliminate the effects of past discrimination. (ch. 68 § 2-105) No person shall be unlawfully discriminated against in connection with the contracting for or performance of any work or service of any kind by, for, or on behalf of the state or any of its political subdivisions. (ch. 29 § 17) No contractor, subcontractor, or contractor's agent may discriminate against or intimidate any employee hired for the benefit of the state or its political subdivisions on the basis of sex. The state may withhold a $5 penalty for each person and calendar day that an employee is discriminated against or intimidated from the amount payable to the contractor by the state or any municipal corporation. (ch. 29 § 20)

**ENFORCEMENT:** Anyone who violates this law is guilty of a petty offense and the aggrieved person may bring an action in the circuit court in the county in which either party resides. (ch. 29 §§ 21, 22) A person who aids, abets, incites or otherwise participates in the discriminatory act is also liable. (ch. 29 §§ 21, 22)

## STATE EMPLOYEE LAWS

State employees are covered by the Fair Employment Act. [ch. 68 §§ 2-101, -105(B)] Sexual harassment in public employment is prohibited by Exec. Order No. 80-1, January 24, 1980.

**ENFORCEMENT:** See "Fair Employment Laws."

## VETERAN'S PREFERENCE

Five points are added to the passing civil service examination scores of able-bodied veterans, and ten points to the passing scores of veterans receiving compensation from the Veterans Administration. In addition, ten points are added to the passing scores of the spouse or one parent of a veteran who suffered a war or service-connected death or disability. (ch. 15 § 431)

# Community Life

## CREDIT

It is unlawful for a lending institution to deny a loan or vary its terms without having considered all of the regular and dependable income of each person who would be liable for repayment, or to use lending standards that have no economic basis and that constitute unlawful discrimination. (ch. 68 § 4-102) It is unlawful for institutions offering credit cards to the public to refuse to issue a credit card on the basis of unlawful discrimination and to fail to inform the applicant, upon request, of the reason for the rejection of his or her application. (ch. 68 § 4-103)

**ENFORCEMENT:** The Illinois Department of Human Rights receives, investigates, conciliates, settles or dismisses charges of discriminatory practices. A charge must be in writing, under oath or affirmation, within 180 days of the occurrence of the alleged discriminatory practice. It may be made either by the party injured or by the department itself. (ch. 68 § 7-102) Furthermore, any person who has been discriminated against by a financial institution may bring an action in the circuit court of the county in which the financial institution is located within 2 years of the occurrence of the alleged discriminatory act for actual damages. (ch. 17 § 885; ch. 110 § 13-202)

# HOUSING

It is unlawful for any person engaging in real estate transactions to discriminate on the basis of sex or marital status. (ch. 68 § 3-102) This provision does not apply to the sale of a single-family home by its owner, to the rental of rooms or housing accommodations in a building with fewer than five apartments in which the lessor or his or her family lives, or to the rental of rooms in a housing accommodation for members of one sex only. (ch. 68 § 3-106) It is unlawful for any financial institution to deny or vary any of the services normally offered in connection with real estate mortgages or to use lending standards that have no economic basis and are discriminatory. (ch. 17 § 853)

**ENFORCEMENT:** See "Credit."

# INSURANCE

It is unlawful for an insurer to discriminate between individuals or risks of the same class or of essentially the same hazards or to charge any rate for the insurance of a motor vehicle which requires a higher premium because of the person's sex. (ch. 73 § 103)

**ENFORCEMENT:** The Director of Insurance has the power to examine and investigate insurance practices in order to determine their fairness or unfairness. (ch. 73 § 1032; Ins. Code § 425)

# PUBLIC ACCOMMODATIONS

It is unlawful for any person to deny or refuse to another the full and equal enjoyment of facilities and services of any place of public accommodation, or to publish, circulate, display, or mail any written communication which the operator knows will have the effect of denying the use of any of the facilities of the place of public accommodation, because of sex or marital status. (ch. 68 §§ 5-102, -103) This law does not apply to private clubs, facilities distinctly private (restrooms, shower rooms, health clubs), or to facilities which restrict the rental of rooms to individuals of one sex where the exemption is based on bona fide considerations of public policy. (ch. 68 § 5-103)

**ENFORCEMENT:** The Illinois Department of Human Rights investigates all charges of discriminatory practices in the area of public accommodations. A written charge, made under oath or affirmation, must be filed with the department within 180 days of the occurrence of the alleged discriminatory act. (ch. 68 § 7-102)

# INDIANA

## Home and Family

## MARRIAGE

**AGE OF CONSENT:** A person 18 years or older may consent to marry. (§ 31-7-1-5)*

**CONSENT REQUIREMENT:** Individuals who are at least 17 years of age may marry with the written consent of a parent or guardian, signed and verified in the presence of the clerk of the circuit court. (§§ 31-7-1-6, -2) Individuals under 18 may also petition the judge of the circuit or superior court of their county of residence to authorize the clerk of the court to issue a marriage license. (§ 31-7-2-3) Individuals under 17 may also marry if the following circumstances are met: the female is at least 15 years old and either pregnant or a mother; the male is the putative father of the child; both the male and the female have the written consent of their parents or guardians; and a judge of the circuit, superior, or county court of the residence of one of the parties authorizes the clerk of the cirucit court to issue a marriage license. (§ 31-7-1-7)

**LICENSE REQUIREMENT:** Persons intending to marry must obtain a license from the clerk of the circuit court of the county in which either or both of the parties reside. If the parties are nonresidents of the state, they must obtain the license from the clerk of the circuit court in which the marriage ceremony is to be performed. There is a 3-day waiting period for the issuance of the license, which is valid for 60 days from the date of issuance. (§§ 31-7-3-1 *et seq.*) Individuals may petition the circuit or superior court to issue the marriage license when they apply for it. [§ 31-7-3-9(b)] A premarital examination is required before the license is issued. (§ 31-7-4) A marriage license may not be issued if either party is of unsound mind, is under the influence of alcohol or narcotics, or has a transmissable disease. (§ 31-7-3-10)

**PROHIBITED MARRIAGES:** Bigamous marriages and marriages to insane or idiotic persons are void. (§ 31-7-6) Marriages between first cousins 65 years of age or older, entered into after September 1, 1977, are valid; otherwise, marriages between individuals more closely related than second cousins are prohibited. (§ 31-7-1-3) No legal proceedings are required to declare the nullity of a marriage prohibited by law. Children of void marriages entered into in good faith are legitimate. [*Light v. Lane*, 41 Ind. 539 (1973); § 31-7-8]

## DISSOLUTION OF MARRIAGE

**ANNULMENT:** Factors 33, 35, and 36, listed in Appendix A, are grounds for annulment. (§ 31-1-7-6)

*Residency Requirement:* There is no relevant statutory provision.

---

*Unless otherwise specified, all citation references are to Burns Indiana Statutes Annotated Code Edition (1971).

**LEGAL SEPARATION:** A legal separation may be obtained upon a finding by a court that conditions in, or circumstances of, the marriage render it currently intolerable for both parties to live together. (§ 31-1-11.5-3)

*Residency Requirement:* One of the parties must have resided in the state for 6 months and in the county for 3 months immediately preceding the filing of an action for legal separation. (§ 31-1-11.5-6)

## DIVORCE

*Residency Requirement:* See "Legal Separation."

*Grounds for Divorce:* Factors 2, 3, 15, and 40, listed in Appendix A, are grounds for divorce. (§ 31-1-11.5-3)

*Conciliation Requirement:* If the court finds that there is a reasonable possibility of a reconciliation between the parties, it may stay the divorce proceedings and order that the parties seek a reconciliation through available counseling. (§ 31-1-11.5-8)

*Property Distribution:* The court will divide all the property, whether jointly or separately owned or acquired before or after the marriage, in a just and reasonable manner. Factors 1, 3, 4, 18, 22, and 29, listed in Appendix F, are considered. (§ 31-1-11.5-11) However, if there is little or no marital property, the court may award either spouse a money judgment as a reimbursement for the financial contribution made by one spouse toward the higher education of the other. (§ 31-1-11.5-11)

*Child Custody:* Custody will be determined in the best interests of the child. Factors 2, 5, 10, 11, 12, and 14, listed in Appendix B, will be considered. [§ 31-1-11.5-21(a)] Joint legal custody may be awarded if the court determines it to be in the best interests of the child. Factors 4, 10, 14, 16, 17, and 18, listed in Appendix C, will be considered. [§ 31-1-11.5-21(f)]

*Child Support:* The court may order either or both parents to pay any reasonable amount for the support of a child without regard to marital misconduct after considering factors 2, 3, 4, and 5, listed in Appendix D. (§ 31-1-11.5-12)

*Spousal Support/Alimony:* The court will award maintenance to spouses who are physically or mentally incapacitated to the extent that they are unable to support themselves. [§ 31-1-11.5-11(e)(1)] Maintenance will also be awarded to a spouse having custody of a physically or mentally incapacitated child if the custodial parent must forego employment to care for the child. [§ 31-1-11.5-11(e)(2)] The court may also grant rehabilitative maintenance to a spouse for a period of 2 years after the divorce is granted and, in doing so, considers factors 2, 8, 11, 16, and 19, listed in Appendix E. [§ 31-1-11.5-11(e)(3)]

*Enforcement of Support Orders:* Upon an application to the court for the enforcement of a support order, the court may either enter a judgment against the person owing the support, requiring that person to pay all unpaid obligations, or order the person to make an assignment of his or her wages or salary to the person entitled to receive the support. The court may also impose a lien on real estate for failure to pay support. (§§ 31-1-11.5-13, -6-6.1-16) Support orders may also be enforced through contempt proceedings or any other remedy available for the enforcement of a court order. (§ 31-1-11.5-17) See also the Uniform Reciprocal Enforcement of Support Act, §§ 31-2-1-1 *et seq.*

*Spouse's Name:* Upon the wife's request, the court shall order that her former name be restored. (§ 31-1-11.5-18)

*Divorce by Affidavit or Summary Judgment:* There is no relevant statutory provision.

*Displaced Homemaker Laws:* There is no relevant statutory provision.

# DOMESTIC VIOLENCE

**STATUTORY PROVISION:** Assault by a spouse or former spouse or being placed in fear of imminent serious bodily injury by a spouse or former spouse is prohibited. (§ 4-23-17.5-7)

**WHO IS PROTECTED?** The statute protects spouses and former spouses. (§ 4-23-17.5-7)

**RELIEF AVAILABLE:** A victim of domestic violence may petition the court for a temporary order of protection. (§ 34-4-5.1-2) The court may order the abuser to refrain from abusing, harassing, or disturbing the peace of the other, or to move out of the marital residence as long as he or she is not the sole owner or lessor of the residence. The court may order either or both parties to pay maintenance and/or child support and to receive counseling or participate in a domestic violence education program. (§ 34-4-5.1-5) A permanent order of protection will only be granted if the parties are married and there is no divorce or legal separation action pending. (§ 34-45.1-3) In addition, state funded domestic violence prevention and treatment programs have been established which provide emergency shelter, a 24-hour telephone system to provide crisis assistance, emergency transportation, information referral, and victim advocacy services in the areas of health care, family counseling, job training, legal assistance, and counseling for dependent children. (§ 4-23-17.5-6)

**MARITAL RAPE:** A woman may charge her husband with rape only if a petition for divorce or legal separation or protective order is pending and the spouses are living apart. (§ 35-42-4-1)

**CIVIL LAWSUIT FOR RAPE OR ASSAULT:** No cases directly on point. However, the courts have held that spouses may sue each other for torts. [*Brooks v. Robinson*, 284 N.E.2d 794 (Ind. 1972)]

**CHILD ABUSE:** Under the Child Abuse Act, a child who is the victim of neglect or abuse will be deemed to be "in need of services" and may be taken into custody by any law enforcement officer, probation officer, or caseworker acting with probable cause, if it appears that the child's physical or mental condition will be seriously impaired or endangered and there is no reasonable opportunity to obtain an order of the court. (§§ 31-6-4-3, -6-4-4, -6-11 *et seq.*)

*Notification Requirement:* All health care professionals and any individuals who have reason to believe that a child is a victim of abuse or neglect must make an immediate oral report to the local child protection service or law enforcement agent. (§ 31-6-11-3) A person who knowingly fails to report an incident of child abuse or neglect is guilty of a Class B misdemeanor. (§ 31-6-11-20)

# INHERITANCE RIGHTS

**FAILURE TO MAKE A WILL:** The surviving spouse is entitled to the entire estate if the decedent is not survived by any other heirs; to one-third if the decedent left two or more children, one or more children and the child of a deceased child, or the children of two or more deceased children; to one-half if the decedent left one child or the children of a deceased child; to three-quarters if the decedent is survived by his or her parents. If the surviving spouse is a second or subsequent spouse who did not have children with the decedent and the decedent is survived by children or grandchildren from a prior marriage, the spouse is entitled to a share of the personal property as provided in the preceding sentence and to a life interest in one-third of the lands owned by the decedent. (§ 29-1-2-1)

**FAILURE TO PROVIDE BY WILL:** There is no relevant statutory provision.

**CHILDREN BORN OUT OF WEDLOCK:** A child born out of wedlock is the legitimate heir of the mother and her kin. However, such a child can only inherit from the father if the paternity of the child was established by law during the father's lifetime or if the father marries the mother of the child and acknowledges the child as his own. (§ 29-1-2-7)

**HOMESTEAD, PERSONAL, AND FAMILY ALLOWANCES:** The surviving spouse of a decedent domiciled in Indiana is entitled to an allowance of $8500 out of the decedent's personal property or, if the personal property is insufficient, out of the real property. This allowance may be paid after the administrative and funeral expenses are paid. (§ 29-1-4-1)

**OPTION TO DISREGARD THE WILL:** The surviving spouse may elect to take against the will and is entitled to receive one-third of the net personal and real estate; if the surviving spouse is a second or subsequent spouse who did not have children with the decedent and the decedent is survived by children or grandchildren from a prior marriage, the spouse is entitled to receive one-third of the net personal estate and a life interest in one-third of the decedent's land. If the value of the property left to the spouse in the will is less than the amount the spouse would receive by electing to take against the will, the spouse may elect to retain any and all specific bequests given in the will and receive the balance in cash or property. (§ 29-1-3-1)

# REPRODUCTIVE RIGHTS
## ABORTION

*Statutory Provisions:* It is the public policy of the state to prefer childbirth over abortion. (§ 16-10-3-4) All abortions must be performed by a licensed physician. During the first trimester, abortions will be permitted for reasons "based upon the pregnant woman's physician's professional medical judgment." [§ 35-1-58.5-2(1)] After the first trimester, all abortions must be performed in a hospital or an ambulatory outpatient surgical center licensed by the state. [§§ 16-10-1-6, -7; 35-1-58.5-2(2)] After viability, abortions may be performed if the physician certifies in writing that it is necessary to prevent substantial permanent impairment of the life or physical health of the woman. In addition, they must be performed in a hospital having premature impairment birth intensive care units and in the presence of a second physician. Physicians are required to take all reasonable steps to preserve the life and health of a viable fetus. [§§ 35-1-58.5-2(3), -58.5-7] Private or religious hospitals are not required to permit the use of their facilities for the performance of abortions. Any physician, employee, or staff member of any facility where an abortion may be performed may refuse to take part in an abortion on ethical, moral or religious grounds. [§ 35-58.5-2(1)]

*Informed Consent:* The informed consent of the woman is required unless the abortion is necessary to preserve her life. [§§ 35-1-58.5-1(f), -58.5-2]

*Parental Consent:* The written consent of the parents of an unemancipated minor under the age of 18 is required. However, a minor may, through her physician, petition the juvenile court for a waiver of the parental consent requirement. The court considers the concerns expressed by the minor or her physician in determining whether she is mature enough to make the abortion decision independently or whether the abortion is in her best interest. The court may appoint free legal counsel to represent the minor in the waiver proceedings. Where the waiver of parental consent is denied, the minor or her physician is entitled to an expedited appeal of the adverse decision. All juvenile court and appellate court records are confidential. (§ 35-1-58.5-2.5)

*Spousal Consent:* There is no relevant statutory provision.

*Reporting Requirements:* Doctors performing abortions must file forms developed by the Board of Health containing the age of the woman, the place the abortion is performed, the name and address of the doctor, the name of the father if known, the procedure employed, the medical reason for any abortion performed after viability, information as to whether the fetus was delivered alive, and records of all maternal deaths occurring within the health facility where the abortion was performed; these forms must be submitted to the board twice a year. (§ 35-1-58.5-5)

*State Funding:* State funding of abortions is restricted and will be provided only where the abortion is necessary to preserve the life of the woman. (§ 16-10-3-3)

**BIRTH CONTROL:** There is no relevant statutory provision.

**STERILIZATION:** There is no relevant statutory provision.

# UNMARRIED COUPLES

**COMMON-LAW MARRIAGE:** Common-law marriages entered into after January 1, 1958, are void. (§ 31-7-6-5)

**COHABITAL RELATIONSHIPS:** The courts have held that oral agreements between cohabitants are valid and enforceable. [*Glasgo v. Glasgo*, 410 N.E.2d (Ind. 1980)]

## CHILDREN

*Custody:* Custody is awarded according to the best interest of the child. In making the award, the court considers all relevant factors including factors 2, 5, 10, 11, 12, and 14, listed in Appendix B. (§ 31-6-6.1-11)

*Legitimation Proceedings:* The mother, a man alleging to be the child's biological father, or the child may bring a paternity action at any time. (§ 31-6-6.1-6) The court may order all the parties to undergo blood tests if necessary for a determination of paternity. (§ 31-6-6.1-7) A man is presumed to be the child's biological father if he and the child's biological mother are or have been married and the child is born within 300 days of the marriage's dissolution; or if he and the child's biological mother attempted to marry each other in a marriage in apparent compliance with the law even though the marriage is void or voidable, and the child is born during the attempted marriage or within 300 days of the attempted marriage's dissolution; or if, after the child's birth, he and the biological mother marry or attempt to marry in apparent compliance with the law, even though the marriage is void or voidable, and he acknowledged his paternity in writing filed with the registrar of vital statistics. (§ 31-6-6.1-9)

*Obligations of the Putative Father:* Once paternity has been established, the court may order either or both parents to support the child after considering all relevant factors including factors 2, 3, 4, and 5, listed in Appendix D. (§ 31-6-6.1-13)

# Education

## STATUTORY PROVISION

It is the public policy of the state to provide equal, nonsegregated, nondiscriminatory education opportunities and facilities to all, regardless of sex. (§§ 20-8.1-2-2, 22-9-1-2) Every discriminatory practice relating to education is unlawful. [§ 22-9-1-1(1)]

**ENFORCEMENT:** See "Community Life: Credit."

# Employment

## EQUAL PAY LAWS

It is unlawful to discriminate on the basis of sex in wages paid to employees doing work requiring equal skill, effort, and responsibility under similar working conditions. (§ 22-2-2-4)

**ENFORCEMENT:** An employee who has been discriminated against in wages on account of sex may bring an action in the circuit or superior court within 3 years of the occurrence of the alleged discriminatory act. (§ 22-2-2-9)

## FAIR EMPLOYMENT LAWS

The Fair Employment Practices Law applies to the state of Indiana and its political and civil subdivisions, employers who employ six or more employees, labor organizations, and employment agencies. (§§ 22-9-2-2, -1-3) The statute does not specify the proscribed discriminatory practices and declares that equal employment opportunity is a civil right. [§ 22-9-1-2(a)] Sexual harassment in state employment is prohibited by Exec. Order No. 6-82, effective February 26, 1982.

**ENFORCEMENT:** A person who has been discriminated against in employment on account of sex may file a complaint with the Indiana Civil Rights Commission within 90 days of the occurrence of the alleged discriminatory practices [§§ 1-2-5(c), 22-9-13(o)]

## GOVERNMENT CONTRACTORS AND SUBCONTRACTORS

Government contractors and subcontractors must agree not to discriminate against employees or applicants for employment on account of their sex. (§ 22-9-1-10)

**ENFORCEMENT:** See "Fair Employment Laws."

## STATE EMPLOYEE LAWS

State employees are covered under the Fair Employment Practices Law. [§ 22-9-1-3(h)]

**ENFORCEMENT:** See "Fair Employment Laws."

# VETERAN'S PREFERENCE

Ten points are added to the passing civil service examination scores of disabled veterans, their spouses, and the surviving spouses of deceased veterans; five points are added to the passing scores of able-bodied veterans, and two points to the passing scores of peacetime veterans. [§§ 4-15-1-18(c) to (e)]

# Community Life

## CREDIT

Discrimination in the extension of credit is prohibited. [§ 22-9-1-3(1)]

**ENFORCEMENT:** A person who has been discriminated against in credit on the basis of sex may file a complaint with the Indiana Civil Rights Commission within 90 days of the occurrence of the alleged discriminatory act. [§§ 1-2-5(c), 22-9-13(o)]

## HOUSING

It is unlawful to discriminate against any person in the acquisition, through purchase or rental, of real property, including housing, on the basis of sex. [§ 22-9-1-2(a)] It is unlawful to intentionally deny services, goods or facilities of public housing on the basis of sex. (§ 35-46-2-1)

**ENFORCEMENT:** See "Credit."

## INSURANCE

Discrimination is prohibited between individuals of the same class and equal expectation of life in rates charged for life insurance or annuity contracts or between individuals of the same class and essentially the same hazard in the amount of premium, policy fees, or rates charged for accident or health insurance, in the benefits payable under these contracts, or in any other terms or conditions of these contracts. [§ 27-4-1-4(7)]

**ENFORCEMENT:** The Commissioner of Insurance examines and investigates all charges of discriminatory practices in the insurance industry. If after holding a hearing, the commissioner determines that a discriminatory practice has occurred, the commissioner may also order the insurer to cease and desist from engaging in the discriminatory practice and impose a monetary fine or suspend or revoke the insurer's license. (§ 27-4-1-6)

## PUBLIC ACCOMMODATIONS

It is unlawful to deny access to places of public accommodations on the basis of sex. (§ 22-9-1-2)

**ENFORCEMENT:** See "Credit."

# IOWA

## Home and Family

## MARRIAGE

**AGE OF CONSENT:** A person 18 years of age or older may consent to marry. (§ 595.2)*

**CONSENT REQUIREMENT:** A minor 16 or 17 years of age may marry with parental or guardian consent and the approval of the district judge. (§ 595.2)

**LICENSE REQUIREMENT:** Persons wishing to marry must first obtain a license from the clerk of the district court. (§ 595.3) The license is issued 3 days from the date of application and is valid for 20 days thereafter. (§§ 595.3, 596.7) A premarital physical examination is required before a marriage license is issued. (§ 596.1) However, regardless of the results of the premarital examination, the clerk of the district court is authorized to issue a marriage license to the parties to a proposed marriage if the woman is pregnant at the time of the application. (§ 596.4)

**PROHIBITED MARRIAGES:** Marriages between parents and children or children's spouses; grandparents and grandchildren or grandchildren's spouses; brothers and sisters; and first cousins are incestuous and void. Bigamous marriages are also void, but if the parties live together after the death or divorce of the former spouse, the marriage is valid. (§ 595.19) Children born of void marriages are legitimate. (§§ 595.18, 598.31)

## DISSOLUTION OF MARRIAGE

**ANNULMENT:** See factors 19, 32, 35, and 38, listed in Appendix A. (§ 598.29)
   *Residency Requirement:* There is no relevant statutory provision.

**LEGAL SEPARATION:** Legal separation or separate maintenance will be granted if there has been a breakdown of the marriage relationship to the extent that the legitimate objects of matrimony have been destroyed and there remains no reasonable likelihood that the marriage can be preserved. (§§ 598.5, .17)
   *Residency Requirement:* There is no residency requirement if the defendant is a resident of the state and was personally served; otherwise, there is a 1-year residency requirement. (§ 598.6)

**DIVORCE**
   *Residency Requirement:* See "Legal Separation."
   *Grounds for Divorce:* See "Legal Separation."
   *Conciliation Requirement:* If either spouse so requests, or on its own motion, the court may require the parties to participate in conciliation procedures for a period of 60 days from the issuance of the order of conciliation. (§ 598.16)
   *Property Distribution:* Upon every judgment of annulment, divorce or separate maintenance the court divides the property of the parties and transfers title of the property accordingly. The court may protect and promote the best interests of chil-

---

*Unless otherwise specified, all citation references are to the Iowa Code Annotated (West 1946).

dren of the parties by setting aside a portion of the property of the parties in a separate fund or conservatorship for the support, maintenance, education, and general welfare of the minor children. The court divides all property or gifts received by one party equitably between the parties after considering factors 1, 2, 5, 6, 9, 10, 12, 14, 15, 16, 18, 21, and 25, listed in Appendix F. (§ 598.21)

*Child Custody:* Insofar as is reasonable and in the best interests of the child, the court shall award custody, including liberal visitation rights where appropriate, which will encourage the parents to share the rights and responsibilities of raising the child, and which will afford the child an opportunity for the maximum continuing physical and emotional contact with both parents, unless direct physical or significant emotional harm to the child is likely to result from such contact. If either parent so requests, the court will consider granting joint custody if it is in the best interests of the child. In doing so, the court considers factors 1, 2, 4, 10, 13, 19, and 20, listed in Appendix C. The court also considers whether the psychological and emotional needs and development of the child will suffer because of lack of active contact with both parents. (§ 598.41)

*Child Support:* Upon every judgment of annulment, divorce, or separate maintenance, the court may order either or both parents to pay an amount reasonable and necessary for the support of the child. Consideration is given to the child's need for close contact with both parents and recognition of joint parental responsibility for the welfare of the minor child. In any order requiring payments for support of a minor child, the court considers factors 1, 3, 4, 5, 22, 23, 24, and 25, listed in Appendix D. (§ 598.21)

*Spousal Support/Alimony:* Upon every judgment of annulment, divorce, or separate maintenance, the court may grant an order requiring support payments to either party for a limited or indefinite length of time after considering factors 2, 3, 4, 6, 10, 12, 13, 14, 15, 16, 17, 18, 19, and 21, listed in Appendix E. (§ 598.21)

*Enforcement of Support Orders:* When a person owing a duty of support fails to pay child support, the court may order that person to make an assignment of his or her wages, periodic earnings, or trust income to the clerk of the court for the use of the person to whom a duty of support is owed. (§ 598.22) Contempt proceedings are also available to enforce support orders. (§ 598.23-24) See also the Uniform Support of Dependents Law, §§ 252A.1 *et seq.*

*Spouse's Name:* Upon obtaining a divorce, a woman may change her name to her former or birth name. (§ 674.13)

*Divorce by Affidavit or Summary Judgment:* There is no relevant statutory provision.

*Displaced Homemaker Laws:* The law provides services to displaced homemakers including job counseling specifically designed for persons entering or reentering the job market after a number of years as a homemaker. (§§ 241.1 to .6)

# DOMESTIC VIOLENCE

**STATUTORY PROVISION:** Assault of one family member by another is prohibited. (§ 236.2)

**WHO IS PROTECTED?** The law protects spouses, persons cohabitating, parents, or other persons related by consanguinity or affinity, except children under 18. (§ 236.2)

**RELIEF AVAILABLE:** A victim of domestic abuse may obtain protective orders; emergency orders; temporary orders restraining the defendant from further abusing the plaintiff; orders granting exclusive possession of the family residence to the plaintiff; orders granting temporary custody, support, and maintenance for the plaintiff and minor children; and orders requiring the parties to seek counseling. (§§ 236.5, .6) Police intervention is available to prevent further abuse and to assist the abused person in obtaining medical treatment and necessary transportation to the nearest medical facility. (§ 236.12)

**MARITAL RAPE:** A woman can charge her husband with first- or second-degree rape. However, husbands and cohabitors can be charged with third-degree rape only if the parties are living apart at the time. (§§ 709.2 to .4)

**CIVIL LAWSUIT FOR RAPE OR ASSAULT:** There is no case on point. However, in *Cimijotti v. Paulsen*, 230 F. Supp. 39 (D.C. Iowa), *aff'd*, 340 F.2d 613 (1964), the court held that spouses may not sue each other for torts.

**CHILD ABUSE:** Intentional physical injury or sexual abuse of a child under 18 and failure to provide a child with the necessaries of life are prohibited. (§ 232.68)

*Notification Requirement:* All health care practitioners, social workers, psychologists, school employees, and day care center personnel who reasonably believe that a child is being abused must report such abuse within 24 hours of learning of the abuse to the Department of Human Services. (§§ 232.69, .70) Any person who knowingly and willfully fails to report an incidence of child abuse is guilty of a simple misdemeanor and may be civilly liable for the damages caused by such failure to report. (§ 232.75)

# INHERITANCE RIGHTS

**FAILURE TO MAKE A WILL:** If the decedent is survived by children or grandchildren, the surviving spouse is entitled to receive one-third of all land, all of exempt personal property, and one-third of all other personal property; if these properties together are worth less than $50,000, the spouse is entitled to additional real and personal property until this amount is reached. If the decedent is not survived by children or grandchildren, the surviving spouse is entitled to receive one-half of all lands, all of exempt personal property, and one-half of all other personal property (minimum of $50,000), and one-half the balance of the estate. (§§ 633.211, .212)

**FAILURE TO PROVIDE BY WILL:** When the decedent spouse dies without having made a will or otherwise fails to provide for the surviving spouse in the will, the surviving spouse may, in lieu of his or her share in the real property owned by the decedent at any time during their marriage, elect to occupy the homestead or marital home for life. (§ 633.240)

**CHILDREN BORN OUT OF WEDLOCK:** A child born out of wedlock may inherit from the mother. (§ 633.221) But such a child can only inherit from the father when paternity is proved during the father's lifetime or when the child has been recognized by the father as his own in writing. (§ 633.222)

**HOMESTEAD, PERSONAL, AND FAMILY ALLOWANCES:** The surviving spouse is entitled to receive reasonable support for 1 year; the allowance may include additional amounts for the support of dependents who live with the spouse. (§ 633.374) Where the decedent died without having made a will or where the surviving spouse rejects the will, the surviving spouse may elect to occupy the homestead for life instead of taking his or her share of the decedent's real property. (§ 633.240)

**OPTION TO DISREGARD THE WILL:** The surviving spouse may reject the will and take one-third of all lands owned by the decedent during the marriage, all exempt property, and one-third of all other personal property. (§ 633.238)

# REPRODUCTIVE RIGHTS
## ABORTION

*Statutory Provisions:* All abortions must be performed by licensed physicians, surgeons, or osteopathic surgeons. Any person who intentionally performs an abortion after the end of the second trimester of the pregnancy, unless it is performed by a licensed physician or surgeon to preserve the life or health of the woman, commits a felony. (§ 707.7) When the abortion results in a live fetus, the doctor performing the abortion must use all available professional skill, care, and diligence to preserve the fetus's life and health. (§ 707.10) A person who intentionally kills a viable fetus aborted alive is guilty of a felony. (§ 707.9) Private hospitals are not required to perform abortions, and all persons have the right to refuse to participate in abortions on religious, moral, or ethical grounds. (§§ 146.1, .2)

*Consent Requirement:* It is a felony to terminate a pregnancy without the patient's consent in the course of a felony or felonious assault. It is also a felony, of a lesser degree, to terminate a pregnancy intentionally without the woman's consent, unless the abortion is performed by a physician and the woman is in such condition that she cannot give her consent and the abortion is performed to save the life or health of the woman or fetus. (§ 707.8) The state attorney general has stated that neither a minor's parent or guardian may veto the physician-patient decision to terminate the minor's pregnancy. The minor's informed consent is sufficient to terminate a pregnancy during the first 12 weeks. [Op. Atty. Gen. No. 76-1-14 (July 15, 1976)]

*Health Insurance Regulations:* Health insurance programs provided by employers may exclude coverage of elective abortions, except where the life of the mother would be endangered if the fetus were carried to term or where medical complications have arisen from an abortion. (§ 610A.13)

**BIRTH CONTROL:** The Department of Social Services has authority to provide, pay for, and offer family planning and birth control services to every parent or married person who is a public welfare recipient. The refusal of any person to accept family planning and birth control services must not affect the right of the person to receive public assistance or any other public benefit. (§§ 234.21, .24)

**STERILIZATION:** There is no relevant statutory provision. However, the attorney general has stated that a physician may perform a sterilization operation upon a competent consenting adult requesting it. [Op. Atty. Gen. No. 35 (1932)]

# UNMARRIED COUPLES

**COMMON-LAW MARRIAGE:** Common-law marriage is valid in Iowa. [§ 595.11; *In re Marriage of Grother*, 242 N.W.2d 1 (Iowa 1976)] A party claiming the existence of a common-law marriage must prove all elements of such a marriage by a preponderance of clear, consistent, and convincing evidence. [*State v. Ware*, 338 N.W.2d 70 (Iowa 1983)] The elements of a common-law marriage include cohabitation, an intent to be married, and the parties holding themselves out to others as husband and wife. [*In re Estate of Dallman*, 228 N.W.2d 187 (Iowa 1975)]

**COHABITAL RELATIONSHIPS:** There is no case on point.

## CHILDREN

*Custody:* The mother of a child born out of wedlock has sole custody of the child unless the court orders otherwise where the child's paternity has not been acknowledged or the child has not been adopted. If a judgment of paternity is entered, the father may petition for rights of visitation or custody in an equity proceeding separate from any action to establish paternity. (§ 675.40)

*Legitimation Proceedings:* A child born out of wedlock is legitimated when its paternity is proved during the father's lifetime, or when the child has been recognized by the father as his own and such recognition was general and notorious or else in writing. (§ 633.22)

*Paternity Proceedings:* Paternity proceedings may be brought by the mother or other interested person, or by the child welfare authority if the child is likely to become a public charge. If the mother dies or becomes disabled, proceedings may be brought by the child acting through a guardian or next friend. (§ 675.8) The proceedings may be brought during the mother's pregnancy or any time after the child's birth. (§ 675.9) The court may, on its own motion and upon the request of a party, require the child, the mother, and the alleged father to undergo blood tests to establish paternity. (§ 675.41)

*Obligations of the Putative Father:* The parents of a child born out of wedlock owe the child necessary maintenance, education, and support. The father is additionally liable for the expense of the mother's pregnancy and confinement. (§§ 765.1, .26)

# Education

## STATUTORY PROVISION

Educational institutions may not discriminate on the basis of sex in any program or activity. This includes pregnancy and related conditions and the actual or potential parental, family, or marital status of a person. (§ 601A.9)

## AREAS COVERED

Areas covered include academic, extracurricular, research, occupational training, intramural, and interscholastic athletic programs and employment. (§ 601A.9)

**ENFORCEMENT:** See "Credit."

# Employment

## EQUAL PAY LAWS

Although Iowa has no equal pay act, the Iowa Civil Rights Commission has adopted rules prohibiting sex-based wage differentials. (Rules of the Iowa Civil Rights Commission, § 3.8) State employees are to be compensated for their work on the basis of comparable worth. (§ 79.18)

**ENFORCEMENT:** See "Credit."

# FAIR EMPLOYMENT LAWS

The Fair Employment Practices Law applies to the state, its political and civil subdivisions, employers of four or more employees, labor organizations, and employment agencies. It prohibits an employer from refusing to hire or from discriminating in compensation, terms, conditions, or privileges of employment on the basis of sex; a labor organization from excluding or expelling from membership or discriminating in any way against its members; or an employment agency from refusing to refer an applicant for employment on account of sex. (§ 601A.6)

**ENFORCEMENT:** See "Credit."

# GOVERNMENT CONTRACTORS AND SUBCONTRACTORS

Contractors and subcontractors must agree not to discriminate in employment on the basis of sex. [Rules of the Iowa Civil Rights Commission, § 2.15(6)]

**ENFORCEMENT:** See "Credit."

# STATE EMPLOYEE LAWS

State employees are covered by the Fair Employment Practices Law. [§ 601A.2(5)] In addition, employment discrimination in the executive branch is prohibited by Exec. Order No. 15, effective April 2, 1973. Discrimination based on sex in the merit system is also prohibited. (§ 19A.18)

**ENFORCEMENT:** See "Credit."

# VETERAN'S PREFERENCE

Five points are added to the passing civil service examination scores of veterans; ten points are added to the passing scores of disabled veterans. [§ 19A.9(21)]

# Community Life

# CREDIT

It is unlawful for any creditor to refuse to enter into a consumer credit transaction or impose finance charges or other terms or conditions more onerous than those regularly extended by that creditor to consumers of similar economic backgrounds on the basis of sex or marital status. [§§ 601A.10(1), (2)] It is unlawful for any creditor to refuse to offer credit, life insurance, or health and accident insurance on the basis of sex or marital status. [§ 601A.10(3)]

**ENFORCEMENT:** Complaints may be filed with the Iowa Civil Rights Commission within 180 days of the occurrence of the alleged discriminatory practice.

[§§ 601A.15(1), (12)] The complainant may also bring an action in the district court provided that he or she has timely filed a complaint with the Civil Rights Commission and the complaint has been on file with the commission for at least 120 days and the commission has issued a release to the complainant. [§ 601A.16(1)] The action must be commenced within 90 days after the issuance of the release of the commission. [§ 601A.16(3)] See Iowa Session Laws 1984, vol. 3, p. 98.

# HOUSING

Discrimination in real estate transactions on the basis of sex is prohibited. (§ 601A.8) However, the antidiscrimination laws do not apply to the rental or leasing of a two-family house in which the owner or members of his or her family reside, to the rental or leasing of less than six rooms in a single house in which the owner or members of his or her family reside, to the rental or leasing of a housing accommodation in which residents of both sexes must share a common bathroom facility on the same floor of the building, or to restrictions based on sex in the rental or leasing of housing accommodations by nonprofit corporations. (§ 601A.12)

**ENFORCEMENT:** See "Credit."

# INSURANCE

Discrimination is prohibited between individuals of the same class and equal expectation of life in the rates charged for life insurance or annuity contracts or between individuals of the same class and essentially the same hazard in the amount of premium, policy fees, or rates charged for any other contract of insurance, in the benefits payable under these contracts, or in any other term or condition of these contracts. [§ 507B.4(7)]

**ENFORCEMENT:** The Commissioner of Insurance has the power to examine and investigate all charges of discriminatory practices in the insurance industry. (§ 507B.3) If the charges are found to be true upon investigation, the commissioner may issue an order requiring the insurer to cease and desist from engaging in the discriminatory practice and may also impose a monetary fine or suspend or revoke the insurer's license if the insurer knew or reasonably should have known that he or she was violating the law. (§ 507B.7)

# PUBLIC ACCOMMODATIONS

It is unlawful for any owner, lessee, sublessee, proprietor, manager, superintendent, agent, or employee of any public accommodation to refuse or deny accommodations, advantages, facilities, services, or privileges or otherwise to discriminate or to advertise directly or indirectly that the patronage of an individual is unwelcome or objectionable on the basis of sex. (§ 601A.7)

**ENFORCEMENT:** See "Credit."

# KANSAS

## Home and Family

## MARRIAGE

**AGE OF CONSENT:** A person 18 years of age or older may consent to marry. (§ 23-106)*

**CONSENT REQUIREMENT:** Persons under 18 may marry with parental or guardian consent and approval of the district judge. (§ 23-106)

**LICENSE REQUIREMENT:** Persons wishing to marry must first obtain a marriage license from either a clerk or a judge of the district court. The license is issued 3 days from the date of application. (§ 23-106)

**PROHIBITED MARRIAGES:** All marriages between parents and children, including grandparents and grandchildren of any degree, between brothers and sisters of the half as well as the whole blood; and between uncles and nieces, aunts and nephews, and first cousins are incestuous and void. (§ 23-102) Children born of void marriages are legitimate. (§ 23-124)

## DISSOLUTION OF MARRIAGE

**ANNULMENT:** Factors 10, 19, 33, 38, and 45, listed in Appendix A, are grounds for annulment. (§ 60-1602)

*Residency Requirement:* There is no relevant statutory provision.

**LEGAL SEPARATION:** Grounds for Legal separation include factors 1, 43, and 46, listed in Appendix A. (§ 60-1601)

*Residency Requirement:* There is no relevant statutory provision.

### DIVORCE

*Residency Requirement:* Either party must have resided in the state for 60 days immediately preceding the filing of the action. (§ 60-1603)

*Grounds for Divorce:* See "Legal Separation."

*Conciliation Requirement:* The court, on its own motion or upon a motion of either party, may require the parties to seek marriage counseling if marriage counseling services are available within the judicial district where the action is being heard. [§ 60-1608(c)].

*Property Distribution:* The court divides the real and personal property of the parties, whether owned by either spouse before marriage, acquired by either spouse in the spouse's own right after marriage, or acquired by the spouses' joint efforts, by (1) dividing the property in kind; (2) awarding the property or part of the property to one of the spouses and requiring the other to pay a just and proper sum; or (3) ordering a sale of the property under conditions prescribed by the court, and dividing the proceeds of the sale. In making the division of property the court considers factors 2, 5, 6, 15, 21, 22, 26, and 29, listed in Appendix F. [§ 60-1610(b)]

*Child Custody:* If the parents have previously entered into a written agreement regarding the custody of their minor children, the court will approve this agreement

*Unless otherwise specified, all citation references are to the Kansas Statutes Annotated (1964).

if it finds it to be in the best interests of the children. Where no such agreement exists, the court determines custody in accordance with the best interests of the child by considering the length of time and circumstances in which the child has been under the actual care of someone other than a parent, and factors 5, 10, 11, and 14, listed in Appendix B. [§ 60-1610(a)(3)] The court, at its discretion, may award joint custody of minor children if it finds that both parents are suitable and it approves of the custody implementation plan submitted by the parents. [§ 60-1610(a)(3)]

*Child Support:* Regardless of the type of custodial arrangement ordered by the court, the court may order either or both parents to pay for the support and education of minor children, considering all relevant factors, without regard to marital misconduct, including factors 1, 4, and 5, listed in Appendix D. All child support payments ordered by the court are to be paid through the clerk of the district court or the court trustee. [§ 60-1610(a)]

*Spousal Support/Alimony:* The court may award to either party an amount that is fair, just, and equitable for a period of time not to exceed 121 months. Upon the expiration of the initial 121 months, the recipient may file a motion for the reinstatement of maintenance. Payments may be reinstated for up to 121 months. Whenever spousal support or alimony is ordered by the court, payments are to be made through the clerk of the district court or the court trustee. [§ 60-1610(b)(2)]

*Enforcement of Support Orders:* The court may order a person obligated to pay child support or maintenance to make an assignment of a part of that person's periodic earnings or trust income to the person entitled to receive the support or maintenance payments. (§ 60-1613) See also the Revised Uniform Reciprocal Enforcement of Support Act of 1968, §§ 23-401 *et seq.*

*Spouse's Name:* Upon the request of a spouse, the court will order the restoration of a former or maiden name. [§ 60-1610(c)]

*Divorce by Affidavit or Summary Judgment:* There is no relevant statutory provision.

*Displaced Homemaker Laws:* The Secretary of Human Resources is authorized to establish as a pilot project one multipurpose services center to provide displaced homemakers with counseling, training, employment skills, and education to enable them to become gainfully employed. (§§ 44-1301 to -1311)

# DOMESTIC VIOLENCE

**STATUTORY PROVISIONS:** Willfully attempting or wantonly causing bodily injury, or willfully placing another in fear of imminent bodily injury by physical threat, or engaging in sexual acts with a minor under 16 years of age is prohibited. (§ 60-3102)

**WHO IS PROTECTED?** The law protects children under 16 and persons who reside or formerly resided together where both parties continue to have legal access to the residence. (§ 60-3102)

**RELIEF AVAILABLE:** A victim of domestic abuse may file with any district court or with the clerk of the court a verified petition alleging that he or she is a victim of domestic violence. (§ 60-3104) Relief includes protective orders, temporary orders, or emergency relief orders. (§§ 60-1607, -3106) Such orders may provide for the exclusive possession of the marital residence by one spouse, suitable alternative housing for the spouse and any minor children, eviction, temporary custody and visitation rights, support payments for the spouse or any minor children, and professional counseling. (§ 60-3107) Violation of an order restraining a person from abusing or molesting the other will subject that person to criminal trespass charges. [§ 21-3721(c)]

**MARITAL RAPE:** A woman may not charge her husband with rape unless the couple is living apart in separate residences or either spouse has filed an action for annulment, separate maintenance, or divorce; or the woman has filed for relief under the Protection from Abuse Act. [§§ 21-3501, -3502 (1984 Supp.)]

**CIVIL LAWSUIT FOR RAPE OR ASSAULT:** There are no cases on point. But in *Fisher v. Toler*, 401 P.2d 1012 (Kan. 1965), the court held that spouses may not sue each other for torts.

**CHILD ABUSE:** Child abuse is willfully torturing, cruelly beating, or inflicting cruel and inhuman corporal punishment upon any child under the age of 18 years. This is a Class E felony. (§ 21-3609)

>    *Notification Requirement:* All medical personnel, certified psychologists, Christian Science practitioners, licensed social workers, teachers and school administrators or other school employees, licensed child care workers or their employers, or law enforcement officers having reason to suspect that a child has been abused or neglected must report the matter to the district court of the county in which the abuse was found or to the Department of Social and Rehabilitation Services. All other persons who have reason to suspect child abuse or neglect may report the matter. (§ 38-717) The district court must promptly notify the Department of Social and Rehabilitation Services. (§ 38-721) The department shall promptly initiate an investigation to determine the accuracy of the report and take immediate action to protect the child and any other child that may be in danger, if there are reasonable grounds to believe that abuse exists. (§ 38-721) Police officers investigating a report of child abuse may take the child into custody where they have reasonable grounds to believe that the child's life or health would be in imminent danger if not taken into custody. [§ 38-721(a)]

# INHERITANCE RIGHTS

**FAILURE TO MAKE A WILL:** The surviving spouse is entitled to the entire estate if the decedent left no children or grandchildren or to one-half of the estate if the decedent left one or more children or grandchildren. (§ 59-504)

**FAILURE TO PROVIDE BY WILL:** There is no relevant statutory provision.

**CHILDREN BORN OUT OF WEDLOCK:** A child born out of wedlock is entitled to inherit from the father where the father has notoriously or in writing recognized his paternity of the child or, where the child's paternity has been determined in the father's lifetime in any proceeding or action in a court of competent jurisdiction. (§§ 59-501, -506)

**HOMESTEAD, PERSONAL, AND FAMILY ALLOWANCES:** The surviving spouse is entitled to 1 acre of land in a city and 160 acres outside the city or to a mobile home as an exempt homestead so long as the surviving spouse and children continue to occupy it as a residence and it was occupied by the decedent and his or her family as a residence at the time of the decedent's death. (§ 59-401) The homestead is not subject to forced partition unless the surviving spouse remarries or until all children reach the age of majority. (§ 59-402) The surviving spouse is also entitled to use, for his or her benefit or for the children's benefit during their minority, clothing, family library, furniture, musical instruments, household goods, car, and provisions and fuel sufficient for 1 year. (§ 59-403) In addition to a reasonable allowance of not less than $750 and not more than $7500 in money, or other personal property at its appraised value, with the exact amount to be determined by the court. This property shall be exempt from payment of all the decedent's debts except liens existing at time of the decedent's death. (§ 59-403) This homestead is not waived where the surviving spouse elects to take under the will unless it clearly appears that provisions were made under the will in lieu of the homestead.

**OPTION TO DISREGARD THE WILL:** The surviving spouse may reject the will and take the share he or she would receive if there were no will, unless he or she consented to the will in writing during the decedent's lifetime. [§§ 59-602(2), -603]

# UNMARRIED COUPLES

**COMMON-LAW MARRIAGE:** Common-law marriage is valid. [§ 23-101; *Fleming v. Fleming*, 559 P.2d 329 (Kan. 1977)] The requirements for a valid common-law marriage include the capacity of both parties to marry, a present marriage agreement between the parties, and the parties presenting themselves as husband and wife to the public. [*Eaton v. Johnston*, 681 P.2d 606 (Kan. 1984)]

**COHABITAL RELATIONSHIPS:** In *Eaton v. Johnson*, 681 P.2d 606 (Kan. 1984), the court held that, either under its statutory authority in § 60-1606 or in the exercise of its equitable power independent of the statute, a court was authorized to make an equitable division of the property accumulated by the parties during cohabitation once the cohabitation ceased.

**CHILDREN**

*Custody:* There is no relevant statutory provision.

*Legitimation Proceedings:* A child born out of wedlock, whose parents marry subsequent to its birth, is legitimate. (§ 23-125) Both parents must appear before a district court judge as soon as practicable after such marriage and execute affidavits attesting to the fact that each is a parent of the child and that they have married subsequent to the child's birth. (§ 23-126) Proof of lawful marriage and of the birth of the child must be presented to the judge. Upon proper proof of the marriage and of the birth of child who had been registered in Kansas as illegitimate, the affidavit will be approved and forwarded to the state registrar of vital statistics. (§ 23-127)

*Paternity Proceedings:* A child whose paternity has not been determined, or any person on behalf of such child, may bring an action to determine the existence of the father-and-child relationship and at any time until 3 years after the child reaches its majority. (1985 Kan. Sess. Laws ch. 114, new § 6, p. 556) In addition, in cases where the Secretary of Social and Rehabilitiation Services receives an assignment of support rights from a person applying for or receiving Aid to Families with Dependent Children, the secretary may bring an action at any time during the child's minority to determine the existence of the father-and-child relationship. (§ 39-755; 1985 Kan. Sess. Laws ch. 114, new § 6, p. 556)

*Obligations of the Putative Father:* Upon a determination of the existence of the parent and child relationship, the court will make provisions for the support and education of the child and for the payment of the necessary medical expenses incident to the birth of the child. The court may order the support and education expenses to be paid by either or both parents for the minor child. When the child reaches 18, the support shall end unless the parents agree by written agreement approved by the court, to continue support payments beyond 18. The judgment must specify the terms of payment and must require that payments be made through the clerk of the district court or the court trustee. (1985 Kan. Sess. Laws ch 114, new § 12, p. 558)

# Education

## STATUTORY PROVISION

Sex discrimination in admission to public schools is prohibited under Kansas Acts against Discrimination. (Kan. Admin. Regs., Civil Rights Rule 21-46-3; § 44-1002)

## AREAS COVERED

The statute is broadly worded to cover any problem of discrimination concerning students or employees. [§ 44-1005(c) as amended by 1984 Kan. Sess. Laws ch. 186, p. 961]

**ENFORCEMENT:** See "Community Life: Public Accommodations."

# Employment

## EQUAL PAY LAWS

It is unlawful to discriminate on the basis of sex in wages paid to employees who perform equal work requiring equal skill, effort, and responsibility under similar working conditions. Wage differentials are not prohibited if based on a seniority system, a merit system, the quantity or quality of production, or any factor other than sex. (§ 44-1205)

**ENFORCEMENT:** A person alleging violation of the equal pay law may file a complaint with the Secretary of Human Resources. A civil action may also be brought in any court of competent jurisdiction within 2 years of the occurrence of the alleged discriminatory act. (§§ 44-1210, 60-513)

## FAIR EMPLOYMENT LAWS

It is unlawful for employers to follow any employment procedure or practice which results in discrimination, segregation, or separation without a valid business motive. [§44-1009(1)] This prohibition does not apply to nonprofit fraternal or social associations or corporations or to an individual employed in domestic service. [§§ 44-1002(b), (c)]

**ENFORCEMENT:** See "Community Life: Public Accommodations."

## GOVERNMENT CONTRACTORS AND SUBCONTRACTORS

Contractors and subcontractors must agree not to discriminate in employment on the basis of sex. In addition, all solicitations and advertisements for employees must include the phrase "equal opportunity employer." (§44-1030)

**ENFORCEMENT:** The Commission on Civil Rights may initiate and conduct compliance reviews of government contractors and subcontractors and upon a finding of any violation, it may initiate and process a complaint. (§§ 44-1032, -1033) Individuals who feel they have been discriminated against may either file a complaint with the Secretary of Human Resources or bring a civil action within 2 years of the occurrence of the alleged discriminatory act. (§§ 44-1210, 60-513)

## STATE EMPLOYEE LAWS

State employees are covered under the Fair Employment Practices Law. [§44-1002(b)] There is a further prohibition against state personnel decisions based on discrimination. (§ 75-2925) Sexual harassment in state employment is specifically prohibited by Exec. Order No. 82-55, effective January 13, 1982.

**ENFORCEMENT:** See "Public Accommodations." Furthermore, the civil service board will hear appeals concerning any demotion, dismissal, or supervision of a permanent employee in the classified service, or concerning any refusal to examine an applicant or certify a person eligible for a job class. [§ 75-2929(d)] In the case of a permanent employee, the appeal must be filed within 30 days after the alleged discrimination. [§75-2949(f)]

## VETERAN'S PREFERENCE

A veteran who has passed any open competitive examination shall have five points added to his or her score; ten points are added to the passing score of veterans with service-connected disabilities of 10 percent or more. (§ 75-2955)

# Community Life

## CREDIT

There is no relevant statutory provision. However, it should be noted that federal law, the Equal Credit Opportunity Act of 1977, 12 C.F.R. § 202, may apply. See also "Housing" in regard to real estate loans.

## HOUSING

It is unlawful for any person to refuse to sell or rent after the making of a bona fide offer; to fail to transmit a bona fide offer; to refuse to negotiate in good faith; to discriminate in the terms, conditions, privileges, or furnishing of services or facilities in connection with a sale or rental; to represent that property is not available for inspection, sale, or rental when it is available; or to discriminate in the use or occupancy of property on the basis of sex. These provisions do not apply to buildings with four or fewer living units in which the owner actually resides in one of the units. (§ 44-101) It is unlawful for any bank, building and loan association, insurance company, person, or firm which makes real estate loans to deny a loan or other financial assistance for the purchase, construction, improvement, repair, or maintenance of real property or to discriminate in the amount, interest rate, duration, or other terms or conditions of the loan or other financial assistance on the basis of sex. (§ 44-1017)

**ENFORCEMENT:** Any aggrieved person may file a verified complaint with the Kansas Commission on Civil Rights within 180 days of the occurrence of the alleged discriminatory practice. The Kansas Commission on Civil Rights may also initiate complaints. (§ 44-1019)

# INSURANCE

Discrimination is prohibited between individuals of the same class and equal expectation of life, in the rates charged for life insurance or annuity contracts, or between individuals of the same class and essentially the same hazard in the amount of premium, policy fees, or rates charged for accident or health insurance, in the benefits payable under these contracts, or in any other term or condition of these contracts. [§40-2404(7a), (7b)]

**ENFORCEMENT:** The Commissioner of Insurance has the power to examine and investigate the conduct of every person engaged in the insurance industry. (§40-2405) When an unfair practice is alleged, the Commissioner of Insurance shall issue and serve a statement of charges and notice of hearing upon the person guilty of unfair practice. If, following the hearing, the charges are proved to be true, the commissioner may issue an order requiring the insurer to cease and desist from engaging in the discriminatory practice. The commissioner may also impose a monetary fine or suspend or revoke the insurer's license if the insurer knew or should have known that he or she was violating the law. (§§ 40-2406, -2407)

# PUBLIC ACCOMMODATIONS

It is unlawful for an owner, operator, lessee, manager, agent, or employee of a place of public accommodation to refuse, deny, or make a distinction, directly or indirectly, in offering its goods, services, facilities, and accommodations to any person on the basis of sex, except where a distinction because of sex is necessary because of the "intrinsic nature" of the accommodation. [§44-1009(c)(1)]

**ENFORCEMENT:** Complaints alleging discrimination in public accommodations may be filed with the Commissioner of Civil Rights within 180 days of the occurrence of the alleged discriminatory practice. The commissioner may also initiate complaints. (§44-1005)

# KENTUCKY

## Home and Family

## MARRIAGE

**AGE OF CONSENT:** A person 18 years of age or older may consent to marry. (§ 402.020)*

**CONSENT REQUIREMENT:** A person under 18 years of age may marry only with the consent of a parent, guardian, or other person legally responsible for him or her. However, in the case of pregnancy, the male and female, or either of them, under 18, may apply to a district court judge for permission to marry. Such permission is given at the judge's discretion. [§ 402.020(4)]

**LICENSE REQUIREMENT:** A license issued by the county clerk is required. (§ 402.080) There is no statutory requirement for a premarital examination. However, every physician examining an applicant for a marriage license may obtain specimens of their blood to be tested for the nonexistence of sickle-cell trait or any other genetically transmitted blood diseases. When both parties are carriers of the trait or disease, genetic counseling may be provided. (§ 402.320) No marriage which has been solemnized is invalid for want of a marriage license if it is consummated with the belief of either or both parties that they have been lawfully married. (§ 402.070) A marriage license is valid for 30 days from the date of issuance. (§ 402.105)

**PROHIBITED MARRIAGES:** No marriages may be contracted between persons who are closer in relationship than second cousins, whether by the whole or half blood. (§ 402.010) Polygamous marriages, bigamous marriages, marriages not solemnized by an authorized person or society, and marriages to persons adjudged mentally disabled by a court of competent jurisdiction are prohibited. (§ 402.020) However, except for polygamous marriages, a marriage valid in the state where contracted is valid in Kentucky. [§ 402.040; *Stevenson v. Gray*, 56 Kentucky (17B. Mon) 193 (1856)] Children born of void marriages are legitimate. (§ 391.100)

## DISSOLUTION OF MARRIAGE

**ANNULMENT:** Factors 19, 32, 33, 36, and 38, listed in Appendix A, are grounds for annulment. (§ 403.120)
   *Residency Requirement:* There is no relevant statutory provision.

**LEGAL SEPARATION:** Appendix A, factor 2, is grounds for legal separation. (§§ 403.050, .140)
   *Residency Requirement:* A party filing for a legal separation must be a resident of the state or a member of the armed services stationed in the state for a period of 180 days before commencement of the action. (§ 403.140)

**DIVORCE**
   *Residency Requirement:* See "Legal Separation."
   *Grounds for Divorce:* Appendix A, factor 2, is the only grounds for divorce. (§ 403.140)

---

*Unless otherwise specified, all citation references are to the Kentucky Revised Statutes (1970).

*Conciliation Requirement:* Where both parties agree or one party does not deny that the marriage is irretrievably broken, no decree shall be entered until the parties have lived apart for 60 days. (Living apart includes living under the same roof without sexual cohabitation.) However, when one party disagrees, the court shall consider relevant factors and the prospect of reconciliation and shall make a finding about whether the marriage is irretrievably broken; or the court may continue the matter in 30 to 60 days, as the court's calendar permits, and may suggest that the parties seek counseling. At the request of the parties or on its own motion, the court may order a conciliation conference and, at the end of such conference, shall make a finding about whether the marriage is irretrievably broken. (§ 403.170)

*Property Distribution:* The court shall assign to the spouses their separate property and shall divide marital property without regard to marital misconduct in just proportions based on all relevant factors including factors 1, 2, 3, 5, and 25, listed in Appendix F. (§ 403.190)

*Child Custody:* The court shall determine sole or joint custody in accordance with the best interests of the child, giving equal consideration to each parent. The court's decision will be based upon factors 5, 10, 11, 12, and 14, listed in Appendix B. (§ 403.270) The abandonment of the family residence by a custodial parent will not be considered when the custodial parent was physically harmed or seriously threatened with physical harm by his or her spouse. (§ 403.270)

*Child Support:* The court may order either or both parents to pay an amount reasonable for the child's support by considering factors 1, 2, 3, 4, and 5, listed in Appendix D, without regard to marital misconduct. (§ 403.210)

*Spousal Support/Alimony:* After considering factors 1, 2, 3, 4, 5, 6, and 14, listed in Appendix E, the court may grant maintenance to either spouse who lacks property to provide for his or her reasonable needs or is unable to fund appropriate employment or to work because of custodial obligations. (§ 403.200)

*Enforcement of Support Orders:* When a parent is delinquent in paying court-ordered child support for at least 32 days, judicial or administrative remedies may be used to enforce support obligations by the person or agency owed such payments. (§ 405.460) In addition, support orders may be enforced by means of execution, wage assignment, contempt of court proceedings, and other means. (§§ 405.460, .470) All real and personal property of either spouse is subject to judicial and administrative enforcement. (§ 405.440) See also the Uniform Reciprocal Enforcement of Support Act, §§ 407.010 *et seq.*

*Spouse's Name:* The court may grant the spouse's request to restore her maiden or former name where there are no children. (§ 403.230)

*Divorce by Affidavit or Summary Judgment:* There is no relevant statutory provision.

*Displaced Homemaker Laws:* Multipurpose service centers have been established to provide the necessary training, counseling, and services to displaced homemakers 40 years and older so that they may enjoy the independence and economic security vital to a productive life. (§§ 195.120 *et seq.*)

# DOMESTIC VIOLENCE

**STATUTORY PROVISIONS:** Inflicting physical injury, serious physical injury, or fear of imminent physical injury or serious physical injury between family members is prohibited. (§ 403.720)

**WHO IS PROTECTED?** Spouses, parents, children, stepchildren, or any other persons related by blood or affinity within the second degree are protected. (§ 403.720)

**RELIEF AVAILABLE:** The victim of domestic violence may receive an emergency protective order restricting the abusing party from further acts of abuse, or an order enjoining a spouse from disposing of or damaging any property, or an order directing him or her to vacate the residence. (§ 403.740) Temporary custody of children, temporary support, counseling for either party, or such relief the court feels will assist in eliminating the violence is also available. When summoned to the scene of domestic violence, a law enforcement officer is to remain with the victim until the victim is out of danger and assist the victim in obtaining medical treatment. (§ 408.785) Abused persons also have access to protective shelters operated by the Cabinet of Human Resources. (§ 209.160)

**MARITAL RAPE:** A woman may not charge her husband with rape. [§§ 510.010(3), (8)]

**CIVIL LAWSUIT FOR RAPE OR ASSAULT:** There is no case on point. However, spouses may sue each other for torts. [*Brown v. Gasser*, 262 S.W.2d 480 (1953); *Layne v. Layne*, 433 S.W.2d 116 (1968); *Annette v. Thompson*, 433 S.W.2d 109 (Ky. 1968)]

**CHILD ABUSE:** Child abuse occurs when a parent, guardian, or other person having custody inflicts or allows to be inflicted physical or mental injury upon the child by other than accidental means or allows the creation of risks of physical or mental injury by other than accidental means. Child abuse also includes abandonment; sexual abuse or exploitation; and inadequate supervision, food, clothing, education, and medical care. However, parents or guardians legitimately practicing their religious beliefs who fail to provide specified medical treatment to a child will not be considered negligent for that reason alone. This exception will not preclude a court from ordering that medical services be provided to the child, where the child's health requires it. [§ 199.011(6)]

> *Notification Requirement:* All health professionals, school personnel, social workers, coroners, medical examiners, child care personnel, peace officers, or other persons who know or have reasonable cause to believe that a child is abused or neglected must report or have reported such abuse or neglect by telephone immediately to the Department of Social Services. If there is reason to believe that the child needs immediate protection, an oral report shall be made to the proper law enforcement officer, who shall promptly report it to the Department of Social Services. The Department of Social Services may request a written report within 48 hours and convey this report to the proper law enforcement agency immediately. (§ 199.335)

# INHERITANCE RIGHTS

**FAILURE TO MAKE A WILL:** The surviving spouse is entitled to the entire estate if the decedent left no other heirs or to nothing but the dower share if the decedent left children, grandchildren, parents, brothers, sisters, nieces, or nephews. (§§ 391.010, .030)

**FAILURE TO PROVIDE BY WILL:** The surviving spouse is entitled to a life interest in one-third of all the lands owned by the decedent during the marriage and to an absolute interest in one-half the personal property owned by the decedent at death. (§ 392.020)

**CHILDREN BORN OUT OF WEDLOCK:** Statutes which barred a child born out of wedlock from inheriting from the father were declared unconstitutional by

*Trimble v. Gordon*, 430 U.S. 762 (1977), which upheld an out-of-wedlock child's right to inherit from the father where there had been a formal adjudication of paternity and the deceased had contributed to the child's support before his death.

**HOMESTEAD, PERSONAL, AND FAMILY ALLOWANCES:** A surviving spouse (or if there is no surviving spouse, the children of the decedent) is entitled to $7500 in money or personal property set aside as a family allowance. The surviving spouse may also petition the court to permit the withdrawal of up to $1000 from the decedent's bank deposits before the time any other property or money is set aside by the court; the money withdrawn is subtracted from the permitted allowance. (§ 391.030) In addition to the personal property exemption, a surviving spouse's interest of up to $7500 in real property that the surviving spouse uses as a permanent residence is exempt from sale under execution, attachment, or judgment, except for the foreclosure of a mortgage given by the owner of the homestead or for the purchase money due on the mortgage. (§ 427.060)

**OPTION TO DISREGARD THE WILL:** Within 6 months after probate, the surviving spouse may reject the will and take his or her dower share; however, the spouse's share of the real property owned by the decedent is reduced to one-third. (§ 392.080)

# REPRODUCTIVE RIGHTS

## ABORTION

*Statutory Provisions:* A woman may perform an abortion upon herself in the first trimester of her pregancy, provided it is done under the advice of a licensed physician. Otherwise, only a licensed physician may perform abortions, once he or she determines the abortion to be necessary in his or her best clinical judgment or upon the certified recommendation of a referring physician. (§§ 311.723, .750) Physicians may perform saline abortions only in the first trimester. Second- and third-trimester abortions may be performed only by duly licensed physicians in duly licensed hospitals to protect the life or health of the pregnant woman. (§§ 311.760, .770, .780) However, where an abortion is performed after viability, all reasonable precautions must be taken to preserve the life and health of the fetus. (§§ 311.710, .780) Publicly owned hospitals or health care facilities may perform abortions only to save the life of the pregnant woman. No public or private hospitals or health-care facilities and no medical professionals may be required to, or be held liable for refusing to, perform or permit the performance of abortions where it is against their moral, religious, or professional principles. (§ 311.800)

*Informed Consent:* The consent of the woman must be informed and freely given. A 2-hour waiting period is required after the pregnant woman is given information about alternatives to abortions unless in the medical judgment of the attending physician there exists a medical emergency. (§§ 311.726, .729) It must include the receipt by the pregnant woman of a copy of her pregnancy test, if done by the physician who is to perform the abortion or his or her agent, at least 2 hours before the abortion. (§ 311.726) The woman must also receive printed materials furnished by the Department of Human Resources advising the pregnant woman of available alternatives to abortion including adoption services. Also included in the materials are the description of the fetus at that particular age and the possibility of the fetus surviving. (§ 311.732)

*Parental Consent:* If a pregnant woman is under 18 and not emancipated or if she has been adjudged an incompetent, the physician must obtain the consent of the pregnant woman and her parents if she is less than 18 or her guardian if she is incompetent. The parent or guardian must consider the pregnant woman's best interests in giving his or her consent. Where only one parent is available, the consent of the remaining parent or of the parent having custody in the case of divorce is sufficient. If there is no available parent, the consent of an adult standing in the place of the parent is sufficient. When one or both parents refuse consent or where the pregnant woman elects not to seek parental consent, she may petition the circuit court of the county in which she resides or in which the abortion will be performed for such consent, which will be granted after a showing that she is sufficiently mature or competent to give her informed consent. Where maturity is lacking, the court may deny consent to abortion where it finds it is not in the pregnant woman's best interest. (§ 211.732)

*Spousal Consent:* Notice to the spouse is required either before or within 30 days after the abortion, where reasonably possible. This provision does not apply where before the abortion a petition for dissolution of the marriage has been filed by either party and served on the respondent, or where a medical emergency exists. In the case of a medical emergency, notice shall be given, where reasonably possible, within 30 days after the abortion. (§ 311.735) This statute is unconstitutional; see Op. Att'y Gen. No. 82.97.

*Health Insurance Regulations:* No health insurance contracts, plans, or policies may provide coverage for elective abortions except by an optional rider for which an additional premium is paid. (§ 304.5-160)

*Reporting Requirements:* Doctors must report all abortions which they performed to the Department of Human Resources within 15 days after each reporting month. The report must contain the age, marital status, and address of the woman; the location of the facility where the abortion was performed; the procedure employed; any resulting complications; the names of the attending and referring doctors; the legal residence of the father, if known; and the length and weight of the fetus. (§§ 213.055, 311.723) In addition, every hospital and facility in which an abortion is performed during any quarter of the year must file a report with the Department of Human Resources showing the latest number of abortions performed and the total number performed in each trimester of pregnancy. [§ 213.055(3)]

*State Funding:* Public funds cannot be used for the purpose of obtaining an abortion or paying for the performance of an abortion. (§ 311.715)

**BIRTH CONTROL:** There is no relevant statutory provision.

**STERILIZATION:** After counseling by the physician requested to perform the sterilization, a nontherapeutic sterilization can be performed 24 hours after the individual requesting it has given her written informed consent; where the individual requesting it is a minor and is unmarried, consent is given by her parents or guardian. (§§ 212.343, .345, .347)

# UNMARRIED COUPLES

**COMMON-LAW MARRIAGE:** Common-law marriages are not valid in Kentucky. However, Kentucky recognizes common-law marriages validly entered into in another state. [*Tarter v. Medley*, 356 W.W.2d. 255 (Ky. Ct. App. 1962)]

**COHABITAL RELATIONSHIPS:** There are no relevant statutory provisions. However, a woman who had lived in a cohabital relationship was denied the right to administer the estate of her deceased partner, a right reserved to lawful spouses.

[*Vaughn v. Hufnagel*, 473 S.W.2d. 124 (Ky. Ct. App.) *cert. denied*, 405 U.S. 1041 (1971)]

### CHILDREN

*Custody:* There is no relevant statutory provision.

*Legitimation Proceedings:* There is no relevant statutory provision.

*Paternity Proceedings:* Upon the complaint of the mother, child, person, or agency substantially contributing to the support of the child, an action may be brought by the county attorney for the purpose of determining a child's paternity. Paternity may also be determined by the district court when either the mother or father submit affidavits in which the mother states the father's name and the father admits paternity or the mother and father testify to such before the district court. (§ 406.021) The mother, child, and alleged father may be ordered to submit to blood tests upon the request of either party or on the court's motion. (§ 406.081) Actions to determine paternity must be brought within 4 years after the birth, miscarriage, or stillbirth of the child, where there is no further cohabitation. Where there is continued cohabitation, the action must be brought within 4 years after cohabitation ceases. (§ 406.031) However, a paternity action may be brought by both natural parents anytime before the child's eighteenth birthday. (§ 406.031)

*Obligations of the Putative Father:* The father of a child born out of wedlock is liable to the same extent as the father of the child born in wedlock, whether or not the child is born alive, for the reasonable expenses of the mother's pregnancy and confinement and for the education, necessary support, and funeral expenses of the child. See the Uniform Act on Paternity, §§ 406.011 *et seq*.

# Education

## STATUTORY PROVISION

There is no relevant statutory provision. However, it should be noted that if federal funds are involved, federal law, Title IX of the Education Amendments of 1972, Pub. L. No. 92-318, 20 U.S.C. §§ 1681–86, may apply.

# Employment

## EQUAL PAY LAWS

An employer who employs two or more employees in each of 20 calendar weeks may not discriminate on the basis of sex by paying any employee at a rate less than the rate paid to an employee of the opposite sex for work requiring comparable skill, effort, and responsibility. Wage differentials are allowed if paid pursuant to established seniority or merit systems which do not discriminate on the basis of sex. (§ 337.423)

**ENFORCEMENT:** An action to recover unpaid wages may be maintained in any court of competent jurisdiction by the Commissioner of Labor or by one or more employees within 6 months of the occurrence of the alleged discriminatory act. (§§ 337.427, .430)

# FAIR EMPLOYMENT LAWS

It is unlawful for an employer of eight or more persons to refuse to hire or otherwise discriminate in terms, privileges, and conditions of employment (§§ 344.030, .040); or for an employment agency to refuse to refer for employment (§ 344.050); or for a labor organization to exclude or expel an applicant or member from such organization (§ 344.060); or for an apprenticeship or training program to discriminate among its applicants on the basis of sex. (§ 344.070)

> **ENFORCEMENT:** Complaints of discrimination may be submitted to the Commissioner on Human Rights within 180 days of the occurrence of the alleged discrimination. (§ 344.200)

# GOVERNMENT CONTRACTORS AND SUBCONTRACTORS

A contractor or subcontractor who is awarded a contract of more than $250,000 and who employs more than eight people must agree not to discriminate against any employee or applicant for employment because of sex. Failure to comply is a material breach of contract. [§§45.570(1), .580; .580(1), (2)]

> **ENFORCEMENT:** The Department of Finance and Administration is charged with the enforcement of this provision. Its decision is subject to judicial review. (§ 45.620)

# STATE EMPLOYEE LAWS

State employees are not covered under the Fair Employment Practices Act. [§ 344.030(1)] However, an employer with more than fifteen employees is prohibited from discriminating on the basis of sex by federal law, Title VII of the Civil Rights Act of 1964, 42 U.S.C. §§ 2000e *et seq.*

> **ENFORCEMENT:** The Commissioner on Human Rights will enforce complaints brought within 180 days of the occurrence of the alleged discriminatory act. (§ 344.200)

# VETERAN'S PREFERENCE

All persons who served in the armed forces during a period of hostilities in World War II, the Korean War, or the Vietnam conflict, who have been honorably discharged, who are resident voters, and who are applicants for any civil service position shall be entitled to a 5 percent increase on their passing score on a civil service exam. (§ 67A.240)

# Community Life

# CREDIT

It is unlawful for financial institutions or their employees to discriminate against an individual on the basis of sex. Financial institutions or their employees are also prohibited from using any unlawful credit practice in the form of application, record keeping, or inquiry in connection with credit applications or from refusing to give full recognition to the income of each spouse where both are to be jointly liable in real estate transactions. (§§ 344.010, .370) It is further unlawful for any person to deny credit; increase charges, fees, or collateral requirements; restrict the amount or use of credit or impose different terms; or attempt to do any of these unlawful acts because of a person's sex. (§§ 344.010, .370, .400)

**ENFORCEMENT:** Upon a complaint filed within 180 days of the occurrence of the alleged discriminatory act, the Commissioner of Human Rights shall investigate and enter into a conciliation agreement with the parties. (§ 344.200) An action may also be maintained in circuit court to enjoin further violation and to recover actual damages, court costs, and reasonable attorney's fees. (§ 344.450) Such a civil action shall be brought within 1 year of the occurrence of the alleged discriminatory act. (§ 413.140)

# HOUSING

It is unlawful for real estate operators, brokers, salespersons, or any of their employees to discriminate against any person in any real estate transaction or to advertise in any way that indicates discrimination on the basis of sex. (§§ 344.360, .362) This section does not apply to the YMCA, YWCA, or single-sex dormitory rental properties, including those in higher education institutions; to landlords who refuse to rent to unmarried couples, or to landlords who choose to rent to one sex where they have no more than ten units in a house in which they reside; or to rooms or rental units where the tenants share a common bath or kitchen facility. (§ 344.362)

**ENFORCEMENT:** See "Credit."

# INSURANCE

No insurer shall fail or refuse to issue or renew insurance of any person because of sex; however, rates determined by valid actuarial tables are valid. (§ 304.085) Discrimination is prohibited between individuals of the same class and equal expectations of life in rates charged for life insurance or annuity contracts or between individuals of the same class and essentially the same hazards in the amount of the premium or rates charged for health insurance, in the benefits payable under these contracts, or in any other terms or conditions of these contracts, except that in determining the class, consideration may be given to the nature of the risk, the plan of insurance, the actual or expected expense of conducting business, or any other relevant factor. (§ 304.12-080)

**ENFORCEMENT:** The Commissioner of Insurance investigates all charges of discriminatory practices in the insurance industry. If, after an investigation such charges are proved true, the commissioner may order the insurer to desist from such practices. The commissioner may also, subsequent to a hearing, bring an action to enjoin and restrain the insurer from engaging further in such discriminatory practices. (§§ 304.12-120, -130)

# PUBLIC ACCOMMODATIONS

It is unlawful to deny any individual the full and equal enjoyment of goods, services, facilities, privileges, advantages and accommodations of restaurants, hotels, or motels because of sex. (§§ 344.130, .145) However, this provision does not apply to private clubs and their facilities and services if they are available only to members and their friends; or to rooming houses with no more than one room for rent and in which the owner resides; or to restrooms, showers, bathhouses, and similar facilities that are distinctly private in nature, or to the YMCA, YWCA, and similar dormitories. (§§ 344.130, .145) It is also unlawful for any person to advertise public accommodations in such a way as either to indicate that their use will be refused or denied a person because of sex or to indicate that persons of a particular sex are unwelcome, unacceptable, or undesirable. (§ 344.140)

**ENFORCEMENT:** See "Credit."

# LOUISIANA

## Home and Family

## MARRIAGE

**AGE OF CONSENT:** A person 21 years or older may consent to marry. (§ 9:282)*

**CONSENT REQUIREMENT:** A minor over 18 but under 21 must obtain the consent of one or both parents or, if they are both dead, of his or her tutor and the oath of two persons 21 years of age or older that the applicants are the ages they represent themselves to be. (§ 9:282; Civ. Code Ann. art. 97, Op. Atty. Gen. No. OO, September 22, 1965) Judges with jurisdiction over the juvenile court may grant permission for underage applicants to marry. (§ 9:208)

**LICENSE REQUIREMENT:** Licenses are issued by the Board of Health and by judges of the city courts in the parish of Orleans and by clerks of the courts in all other parishes. Where the clerk is a party to the marriage, the license is issued by the district judge. (Civ. Code Ann. art 99) Before issuance of such license, both parties to the marriage must file with the license-issuing authority certified copies of their birth certificates and medical certificates, dated within 10 days of the license application, certifying that they do not have a venereal disease. (§§ 9:241, :242) There is a 12-hour waiting period before the marriage can be performed. (§ 9:203) However, the court may waive this waiting period for meritorious reasons. (§ 9:204)

**PROHIBITED MARRIAGES:** Bigamous marriages and marriages between parent and child, brother and sister, aunt and nephew, niece and uncle, and first cousins are prohibited. (Civ. Code Ann. arts. 93, 95) Children born of void marriages are legitimate. [*Cortes v. Fleming*, 267 So. 2d 236 (La. 1972); *Melancon v. Sonnier*, 157 So. 2d 577 (La. 1963)]

## DISSOLUTION OF MARRIAGE

**ANNULMENT:** Factors 19, 33, and 45, listed in Appendix A, are grounds for annulment. (Civ. Code Ann. arts. 91, 93, 110, 116)
   *Residency Requirement:* There is no relevant statutory provision.

**LEGAL SEPARATION:** Factors 4, 5, 15 (and has fled justice), 17, 20, 22 (with 28), 25, 28, 30, 46, 47, and 48, listed in Appendix A, are grounds for legal separation. (Civ. Code Ann. art. 138)
   *Residency Requirement:* Where the grounds for separation have arisen inside the state, there is no relevant statutory provision. However, where the grounds for separation have arisen outside the state, residency of the party seeking the legal separation is required at the time of the filing the action. (Civ. Code Ann. art. 142)

### DIVORCE
   *Residency Requirement:* See "Legal Separation."
   *Grounds for Divorce:* Appendix A, factors 4, 13, and 15, are grounds for immediate divorce, and factor 31 is grounds after a 1-year separation. (Civ. Code Ann. art. 139; § 9:301, :302)

*Unless otherwise specified, all citation references are to West's Louisiana Revised Statutes Annotated (1930).

240

*Conciliation Requirement:*  There is no relevant statutory provision.

*Property Distribution:*  Community property is divided equally between the spouses; separate property is awarded to the owner. (Civ. Code Ann. art. 155) Personal property, including wearing apparel belonging to the petitioning spouse and children in his or her custody, food and eating utensils necessary for their nourishment and any other items necessary for their safety and well-being, will be awarded to the petitioning spouse. (§ 9:307) Either spouse may petition the court to allow him or her the use and occupancy of the family residence pending the partition of the community property. In awarding the family residence to either party, the court considers factors 2, 3, and 27, listed in Appendix F. (§ 9:308)

*Child Custody:*  Custody will be awarded according to the best interest of the child in the following order of preference: to both parents or either parent (without regard to race or sex), to the person or persons with whom the child has been living, or to any other person or persons the court deems suitable and able to provide an adequate and stable environment to the child. There is a rebuttable presumption that joint custody is in the best interests of a minor child. In awarding joint custody, the court will consider factors 3, 4, 6, 7, 8, 9, 10, 11, 12, 13, and 15, listed in Appendix B. (Civ. Code Ann. art. 146) See also the Uniform Child Custody Jurisdiction Act, §§ 13:700 *et seq*.

*Child Support:*  Both parents are obligated to support their minor children. (Civ. Code Ann. art. 158) This obligation does not terminate upon the dissolution of the marriage. [*Lewis v. Lewis*, 404 So. 2d 1230 (La. 1981)]

*Spousal Support/Alimony:*  The spouse without fault and without sufficient means for support may be granted permanent periodic alimony which shall not exceed one-third of his or her ex-spouse's income. The factors considered in granting alimony are 1, 2, 6, 8, 13, 14, 16, and 18, listed in Appendix E. (Civ. Code Ann. art. 160) The court may order support from either party during the separation or divorce proceeding. (Civ. Code Ann. arts. 141, 148)

*Enforcement of Support Orders:*  Support orders are enforced by means of contempt proceedings; assignment of wages; and posting of a bond with the court. (§§ 14:75, 46:236.3A, :236.3C) See also the Uniform Reciprocal Enforcement of Support Act, §§ 13:1641 *et seq*.

*Spouse's Name:*  There is no relevant statutory provision.

*Divorce by Affidavit or Summary Judgment:*  There is no relevant statutory provision.

*Displaced Homemaker Laws:*  The Department of Health and Human Resources may establish multipurpose service programs that provide counseling, training, and employment referrals to displaced homemakers to enable them to contribute to society and maintain the economic security of the family. (§ 46:1994)

# DOMESTIC VIOLENCE

**STATUTORY PROVISION:** Domestic abuse is physical abuse and any offense against the person, excluding negligent injury but including assault, battery, and rape and defamation committed by one family or household member against another. [§§ 14.29 *et seq*., 46:2132(3)]

**WHO IS PROTECTED?** The law protects spouses, former spouses, parents, children, stepparents, stepchildren, foster parents, and foster children. [§ 46:2132(4)]

**RELIEF AVAILABLE:** A victim of domestic violence can obtain temporary restraining orders upon a showing of immediate and present danger of abuse, orders allowing the use and possession of specified community property, orders enjoining the transfer or disposal of community property, and orders assigning the temporary custody of minor children. (§ 46:2135) The court may also grant protective orders, orders for the payment of temporary support, and orders for the provision of suitable housing. The court may order the parties to undergo counseling or professional medical treatment. (§ 46:2136) In addition, under the Protection from Family Violence Act, victims of domestic violence are provided with shelter, emergency psychological support and counseling, emergency medical care, job training, and referral and other social services. (§ 46:2124)

**MARITAL RAPE:** A spouse may charge his or her spouse with rape only if they are legally separated. (§ 14:41)

**CIVIL LAWSUIT FOR RAPE OR ASSAULT:** There is no relevant case. However, spouses may not sue each other unless they are legally separated. (§ 9:291)

**CHILD ABUSE:** Inflicting physical or mental injury on a child or causing the child to deteriorate constitutes child abuse. Child abuse also includes sexual abuse or exploitation and overwork of the child by a person responsible for the child's care to the extent that the child's health, moral, or emotional well-being is endangered. [§ 14:403(B)]

> *Notification Requirement:* Any person who believes that a child's physical or mental health has been or may be affected by abuse shall report such belief to the parish's child welfare unit or agency responsible for the protection of juveniles and, if necessary, to a local or state law enforcement agency. [§ 14:403(c)]

# INHERITANCE RIGHTS

**FAILURE TO MAKE A WILL:** The surviving spouse is entitled to receive all the decedent's share of the community property if the decedent left no parents, children, or grandchildren. If the deceased is survived by his or her parents, the surviving spouse shall receive one-half of the decedent's share of the community property. Where children of the marriage survive, the surviving spouse shall hold during his or her lifetime or until he or she remarries that portion of the decedent's share of the community property that the children would inherit. (Civ. Code Ann. arts. 915, 916)

**FAILURE TO PROVIDE BY WILL:** There is no relevant statutory provision.

**CHILDREN BORN OUT OF WEDLOCK:** A child born out of wedlock is the legitimate heir of the mother. However, such a child can only inherit from the father where it had been acknowledged by the father during his lifetime. [Civ. Code Ann. art. 880; *Succession of Richardson*, 392 So. 2d. 105, *writ denied*, 396 So. 2d 1324 (La. 1981)]

**HOMESTEAD, PERSONAL, AND FAMILY ALLOWANCES:** The surviving spouse or minor children of a deceased owner shall have a homestead exemption of up to $15,000 which shall be exempt from seizure and sale by any process whatsoever. This does not apply to money loaned for the purchase of the homestead; to labor, money, and material furnished for building, repairing, or improving the homestead; or to taxes or assessment. (§ 20:1) If the surviving spouse or minor children are in need, they may receive up to $1000 from the decedent's estate if they do not possess property on their own right valued at $1000. This amount has priority over all estate debts except conventional mortgages, vendors' liens, and expenses incurred in selling property left by the decedent. (Civ. Code Ann. art. 3252)

**OPTION TO DISREGARD THE WILL:** When the surviving spouse is entitled to the marital portion, he or she may receive a periodic allowance, the amount to be determined by the court, during the probate of the will. (Civ. Code Ann. art. 2437) The surviving spouse may elect to take his or her marital portion if the decedent was richer than his or her spouse. (Civ. Code Ann. arts. 2432, 2433) The marital portion is one-quarter of the decedent's inheritable property if he or she died without children; the use of one-quarter, if he or she left three or fewer children; or a child's share if he or she left more than three children. (Civ. Code Ann. art. 2434) The marital portion is deducted from the amount left the surviving spouse under the will. (Civ. Code Ann. art. 2435)

# REPRODUCTIVE RIGHTS
## ABORTION

*Statutory Provisions:* Abortions may only be performed by physicians after an ultrasound test has determined the stage of development of the fetus. All abortions performed after the first trimester of pregnancy must be performed or induced in a licensed hospital. (§ 40:1299.35.2) No abortion shall be performed after viability unless it is necessary to prevent the death or protect the health of the mother. When faced with a choice of methods, the physician must use the one that will best preserve the life and health of the mother and child. After viability, a second physician must be in attendance to take all reasonable precautions to preserve the life and health of the child. (§ 40:1299.35.4)

*Informed Consent:* The written informed consent of the woman is required unless a medical emergency exists. Informed consent consists of a written statement in which the woman acknowledges that she has been informed of her pregnancy, the stage of her pregnancy, the developmental stage of the fetus, the viability of the fetus, the method of abortion to be used, and available alternatives to abortion, including the names of agencies available to assist her during pregnancy and after childbirth. The doctor must also inform the woman of the risks involved with the abortion and provide her with specific oral and written medical instructions to be followed after the abortion. In addition, the physician must give the woman a copy of the signed consent. (§§ 40:1299.35.6, .35.12)

*Parental Consent:* A pregnant minor under 18 years of age and not emancipated must have the written and notarized consent of her parents or guardian that they have been informed of and give consent to the abortion. Where the minor does not have the required consent, a court order may be issued upon a finding that she is sufficiently mature and informed to make the decision to have an abortion on her own. Where the pregnant minor is not sufficiently mature, the court will either order the abortion upon a finding that the abortion is in her best interest or deny the application. Upon such denial, the applicant is entitled to an expedited appeal. (§ 40:1299.35.5) This provision is inapplicable in case of an emergency. The physician must certify the emergency need for the abortion. (§ 40:1299.35.12)

*Spousal Consent:* The informed consent of the husband is required for a minor who has been emancipated by marriage. (§ 40:1299.33)

*Reporting Requirements:* A confidential report, which does not contain the name or address of the abortee, of every abortion performed or induced must be made to the Department of Health and Human Resources by the physician performing the abortion within 30 days of the completion of the postabortion care. (§ 40:1299.35.10)

*State Funding:* Public funds, whether federal, state, or local, may not be used to assist in or provide facilities for an abortion, except where necessary to preserve the life of the mother. (§ 40:1299.34.5)

**BIRTH CONTROL:** By providing for a community action agency, any municipality or parish may provide family planning assistance by all appropriate means in a manner consistent with the individual's moral, philosophical, and religious beliefs and personal and family goals. [§§ 23:65(5), 33:7501(g)]

**STERILIZATION:** There is no relevant statutory provision.

## UNMARRIED COUPLES

**COMMON-LAW MARRIAGE:** Louisiana does not recognize common-law marriages. However, such marriages are given legal effect when validly contracted in another state. [*Liberty Mutual Insurance Co. v. Caesar*, 345 So. 2d 64 (La. 1977)]

**COHABITAL RELATIONSHIPS:** Persons living in cohabital relationship (called *concubinage* in Louisiana) cannot donate immovable property to each other. However, they can donate to each other movable property whose value does not exceed one-tenth the value of their estate. (Civ. Code Ann. art. 1481) However, relevant case law has held that although parties to a cohabital relationship cannot claim property based upon their illegal relationship, they may assert a claim arising out of an independent business transaction where there is strict and conclusive proof that an independent business relationship existed. [*Foshee v. Simkin*; 174 So. 2d 915 (La. 1965)]

### CHILDREN

*Custody:* Custody of a child born out of wedlock who has been formally acknowledged by both parents is awarded in the same manner as custody of a child born in wedlock. (Civ. Code Ann. arts. 146, 245)

*Legitimation Proceedings:* The subsequent marriage of the parents of children born out of wedlock, where the parents have acknowledged them as their children, either formally or informally, renders them legitimate. (Civ. Code Ann. arts. 198, 199) Parents may also legitimate their children by declaring their intentions to do so before a notary public and two witnesses or by the registration of their birth or baptism certificates. (Civ. Code Ann. arts. 200, 203)

*Paternity Proceedings:* The paternity of a child may be proved by a preponderance of the evidence in a civil proceeding instituted by the child or on the child's behalf within 19 years of the birth of the child. Otherwise, such a proceeding may be brought within 1 year of the death of the putative father. (Civ. Code Ann. art. 209)

*Obligations of Putative Father:* Fathers and mothers are obligated to support their children born out of wedlock when such children are in need. (Civ. Code Ann. arts. 240 *et seq.*) Once paternity is established, the father is obligated for the education, support, and maintenance of his child. [Civ. Code Ann.. arts. 179, 180, 227; *In re Tyson*, 306 So. 2d 822 (La. App. 1975)]

# Education

# STATUTORY PROVISION

There is no comprehensive statutory provision. However, students in independent colleges and universities receiving tuition assistance or students awarded state scholarships may not be discriminated against on the basis of sex. [§§ 17:1676, 17:3043.1(E)] Sex discrimination in the fixing of teachers' salaries is prohibited. (Op. Att'y Gen., Sept. 17, 1928, p. 542) Additionally, the Louisiana Constitution, which prohibits unreasonable or arbitrary discrimination in the access of public accommodations, services, and facilities, may operate as a bar to discrimination based on sex or marital status in colleges and universities. (La. Const., art. 1, § 12) Also, it should be noted that if federal funds are involved, Title IX of the Education Amendments of 1972, Pub. L. No. 92-318, 20 U.S.C. §§ 1681–1686, may apply.

## AREAS COVERED

Scholarships, tuition assistance, accommodations, and facilities are covered.

> **ENFORCEMENT:** See "Community Life: Public Accommodations."

# Employment

## EQUAL PAY LAWS

See "Fair Employment Laws."

## FAIR EMPLOYMENT LAWS

The law applies to the state, its political and civil subdivisions, labor unions, employment agencies, and employers of fifteen or more employees. It prohibits the failure or refusal to hire or to refer and the discharge or intentional discrimination against or in favor of individuals with respect to compensation, terms, conditions, or privileges of employment or the intentional segregation or classification of employees in such a way as to deprive them of employment opportunities because of sex. (§ 23:1006) This provision does not apply to any discriminatory act of an employer which is the result of an affirmative action plan; nor does it apply to private educators or religious institutions. (§ 23:1006)

> **ENFORCEMENT:** An employee who is aggrieved may bring an action in the district court for the parish in which the alleged discrimination occurs within 1 year of its occurrence. [§ 23:1006(D); Civ. Code Ann. art. 3492]

## GOVERNMENT CONTRACTORS AND SUBCONTRACTORS

State contracts to architects, engineers, or landscape architects must be awarded without regard to sex. [§§ 38:2310(7), :2315]

> **ENFORCEMENT:** The government has the right to terminate the agreement without liability where charges of sexual discrimination are alleged. [§ 38:2314(A)]

## STATE EMPLOYEE LAWS

See "Fair Employment Laws."

# VETERAN'S PREFERENCE

A five-point preference is accorded honorably discharged veterans in their original appointment, a ten-point preference is accorded disabled veterans, their spouses, unmarried widows, or the unmarried widowed parent of a deceased or totally or permanently disabled veteran. [La. Const. art. 10, § 10(A)(2)]

# Community Life

# CREDIT

It is unlawful for any creditor to refuse to extend credit to any person on the basis of sex or marital status or to require him or her to meet credit qualification standards not required of other persons similarly situated. (§ 9:3583) A creditor must use the same standards in reviewing the applications of men and unmarried women. [Op. Att'y Gen. No. 75-1588 (January 22, 1976)]

> **ENFORCEMENT:** Complaints alleging sexual discrimination in credit may be filed with the Commissioner of Financial Institutions, who may issue cease and desist orders upon finding a violation. The commissioner may also bring suit in a court of competent jurisdiction to restrain and enjoin the creditor from engaging in future discriminatory acts. (§§ 9:3554, :3555)

# HOUSING

It is unlawful for real estate brokers and salespersons, time-share interest salespersons, or any persons who assume to act in any such capacity to refuse to show, sell, or rent any real estate to qualified purchasers or renters because of a person's sex. (§ 37:1455)

> **ENFORCEMENT:** Upon the verified complaint in writing of any person or upon its own motion, the Louisiana Real Estate Commission will investigate charges of alleged discriminatory acts in housing. Persons indicted for violations of the Fair Housing Act of 1968 are automatically investigated by the commissioner. (§ 37:1453)

# INSURANCE

Discrimination is prohibited between individuals of the same class and equal expectation of life in rates charged for life insurance or annuity contracts or between individuals of the same class and essentially the same hazard in the amount of premium, policy fees, or rates charged for accident or health insurance, in the benefits payable under these contracts, or in any other term or condition of these contracts. [§ 22:1214(7)(a), (b)]

> **ENFORCEMENT:** Where discrimination is suspected, the Commissioner of Insurance investigates and holds a hearing. Where discrimination is found, a cease and desist order may be issued. The commissioner may enforce this order by bringing a civil action in the district court for the parish of East Baton Rouge. (§§ 12:1215, :1216, :1217)

# PUBLIC ACCOMMODATIONS

Every person shall be free from discrimination based on sex in access to public areas, public accommodations, and public facilities. (§ 49:146) In addition, the Louisiana Constitution provides that every person shall be free from arbitrary, capricious, and unreasonable discrimination in obtaining access to places of public accommodation. (La. Const. art. 1, § 12)

**ENFORCEMENT:** Anyone denied access to a place of public accommodation on the basis of sex may bring a civil action within 1 year of the occurrence of the alleged discriminatory act for the recovery of damages. (Civ. Code Ann. arts. 2315, 3492)

# MAINE

## Home and Family

## MARRIAGE

**AGE OF CONSENT:** A person 18 years of age or older may consent to marry. (tit. 19, § 62)*

**CONSENT REQUIREMENT:** A child under 18 years of age must have the written consent of his or her parents, guardian, or, in their absence, the judge of probate of the county in which the child resides. In the case of a child under 16 years of age, the written consent of his or her parents, guardian, or court-appointed guardian and of the judge of probate is required. (tit. 19, § 62)

**LICENSE REQUIREMENT:** A valid license issued by the clerk of the town in which each party resides, or of an adjoining town if there is no clerk in their place of residence, is required. In the case of out-of-state residents, the clerk in the town in which they intend to marry shall issue the license. A marriage license is void if not used within 60 days from the date intentions to marry are filed. Intentions to marry must be filed 5 days before the issuance of the license. (tit. 19, § 62)

**PROHIBITED MARRIAGES:** Marriages between parents and children, sisters and brothers, grandparents and grandchildren, aunts and nephews, and nieces and uncles are prohibited. (tit. 19, § 32) Persons who are mentally ill or mentally retarded to the extent that they lack the mental capacity to make decisions about their property or person may not marry. (tit. 19, § 32) Polygamous marriages are void. (tit. 19, § 33) Children born of marriages that have been annulled because of the consanguinity or affinity of the parties are illegitimate. However, children born of marriages annulled because of nonage, mental illness, or retardation are legitimate. (tit. 19, § 633)

## DISSOLUTION OF MARRIAGE

**ANNULMENT:** A marriage may be annulled, when there is doubt about its validity upon the filing of complaint as if for divorce. The grounds for annulment are 3, 19, 26, 33, 34, and 38, listed in Appendix A. (tit. 19, § 632)

*Residency Requirement:* There is no relevant statutory provision.

**LEGAL SEPARATION:** Where a spouse deserts his or her spouse without just cause or the spouses are living apart with just cause for a period of at least 60 days, legal separation will be granted upon the petition of the deserted spouse or his or her guardian or next friend, if the spouse is mentally ill. (tit. 19, § 581)

*Residency Requirement:* There is no relevant statutory provision.

### DIVORCE

*Residency Requirement:* There is no residency requirement if the defendant is a resident of Maine or if the plaintiff is a resident of Maine and either the marriage occurred there or the parties resided there when grounds for divorce occurred; otherwise, the residency requirement is 6 months. (tit. 19, § 691)

---

*Unless otherwise specified, all citation references are to Main Revised Statutes Annotated (1964).

*Grounds for Divorce:* Appendix A, factors 3, 4, 8, 9 (for 7 consecutive years), 12, 17, 22, and 48, are grounds for divorce. [tit. 19, § 691(1)]

*Conciliation Requirement:* Conciliation is mandatory. (tit. 19, § 691)

*Property Distribution:* The court shall set apart each spouse's individual property and divide the marital property in the proportions that it deems fit after considering factors 1, 2, and 3, listed in Appendix F. (tit. 19, § 722-A)

*Child Custody:* Upon granting a divorce, the court may choose one of three types of custody according to the best interests of the child. In the first type, the responsibilities for the various aspects of a child's welfare are divided between the parents. Responsibilities may be divided exclusively or proportionately. Aspects of a child's welfare for which responsibility may be divided include primary physical residence, parent-child contact, support, education, medical and dental care, religious upbringing, travel boundaries and expenses, and any other aspect of parental rights and responsibilities. A parent allocated responsibility for a certain aspect of a child's welfare may be required to inform the other parent of major changes in that aspect. In the second type, parental rights and responsibilities are shared. Most or all aspects of a child's welfare remain the joint responsibility and right of both parents so that both parents retain equal parental rights and responsibilities and both parents must confer and make joint decisions regarding the child's welfare. In the third type, one parent is granted exclusive parental rights and responsibilities with respect to all aspects of a child's welfare, with the possible exception of the right and responsibility for suppport. In addition, factors 2, 4, 6, 8, 9, 11, 13, 14, 17, 23, and 24, listed in Appendix B, will be considered, as well as the parent's capacity and willingness to cooperate, methods for dispute resolution, and the effect on the child of one parent having sole authority over his or her upbringing. (tit. 19, § 752) See also the Uniform Child Custody Jurisdiction Act, tit. 19, §§ 801 *et seq*.

*Child Support:* A court order for child support may run against the father or the mother, in whole or in part, or against both, regardless of the fault of the father or mother in the divorce action. When both parents are ordered to pay child support, the court must specify the amount each parent must pay. An order for child support may include the payment of medical, hospital, and other health care expenses of the child or may require the parent obligated for support to obtain an insurance policy or contract providing coverage of these expenses. The availability of public assistance to the family will not affect the court's decision about the responsibility of a parent to provide child support. [tit. 19, § 752(10)]

*Spousal Support/Alimony:* The court may order either spouse to pay reasonable alimony out of his or her estate and may order the paying spouse to pay a sufficient amount for the defense or prosecution of hearings regarding alimony. The court may also order that as much of the paying spouse's real estate or rents as is necessary be set aside for the other spouse for life, or, instead of alimony, that a specific sum be paid or made payable at the court's direction. The court may alter, amend, or suspend alimony at its discretion, but it may not increase alimony where it is prohibited by the original alimony decree. (tit. 19, § 721)

*Enforcement of Support Orders:* Upon a motion to enforce a support order, the court may hold the defaulting party in contempt of court. (tit. 14, § 252). The court may demand that the defaulting party make installment payments to the party seeking to enforce the support order; or it may decree orders attaching property or orders directing an employer or other payor of earnings to make direct payment to the party seeking to enforce the support order or it may use any other method of enforcement that is available in civil actions. (tit. 14, §§ 3132, 3137; tit. 19, § 774) See also the Revised Uniform Enforcement of Support Act of 1968, tit. 19, §§ 331 *et seq.*

*Spouse's Name:*   A wife may have her name changed, upon her request during an action for divorce or annulment or at any time thereafter. [tit. 19, § 752(11)]

*Displaced Homemaker Laws:*  The Department of Labor provides job counseling, job training, job placement and referral services to displaced homemakers. (tit. 26, § 1601)

# DOMESTIC VIOLENCE

**STATUTORY PROVISION:** Family and household members are prohibited from attempting to cause or causing bodily injury or offensive physical contact or from attempting to place or placing another member in fear of imminent bodily injury. (tit. 19, § 762)

**WHO IS PROTECTED?** Spouses, former spouses, individuals presently or formerly living together as spouses, natural parents of the same child, and adult household members related by blood or marriage are protected. (tit. 19, § 762)

**RELIEF AVAILABLE:** Victims of domestic violence may obtain protection orders, emergency relief orders, and restraining orders; the exclusive possession of the family residence by one party or provision for suitable alternative housing for one party; temporary custody of children and visitation rights; temporary support payments for one party and/or minor children; professional counseling and monetary compensation for loss of earnings, personal injuries, property damage, and reasonable moving expenses. A police officer may, without a warrant, arrest a party for violating a protective order. The police must use the same standards for dealing with incidents of domestic violence as with incidents involving strangers. A police officer must make an arrest if he or she has probable cause to believe that domestic violence has occurred or that a party has violated a protective order. (tit. 19, §§ 761 *et seq.*) The Department of Human Resources is authorized by statute to contract for shelters, counseling, and emergency services for victims of domestic violence. (tit. 22, § 8501)

**MARITAL RAPE:** Spouses who are living together may not charge each other with rape. (tit. 17-A, §§ 251, 252)

**CIVIL LAWSUIT FOR RAPE OR ASSAULT:** There is no relevant statutory provision. However, spouses may not bring a suit against each other for torts committed during the marriage. [*Moulton v. Moulton*, 309 A.2d 224 (Maine 1973)]

**CHILD ABUSE:** It is unlawful for any person responsible for the care of any minor less than 18 years of age to threaten the minor's welfare or health by physical or mental injury or impairment, sexual abuse or exploitation, deprivation of essential needs or neglect. (tit. 22, § 4002)

*Notification Requirement:*  Any medical, dental, or child care personnel, school official, medical examiner, chiropractor, podiatrist, social worker, Christian Science practitioner, teacher, homemaker, home health aide, psychologist, or law enforcement officer who knows or has reasonable cause to suspect a child is, or is about to be, abused or neglected shall report it, or cause a report to be made, immediately to the Department of Human Services. Any person may make a report if he or she knows or has reasonable cause to suspect a child has been or is likely to be abused or neglected. (tit. 22, § 4011)

# INHERITANCE RIGHTS

### FAILURE TO MAKE A WILL:
The surviving spouse is entitled to the entire estate if the decedent left no children or parents; to $50,000 and one-half the estate if the decedent is survived by only parents; to $50,000 plus one-half the estate if there are one or more children or grandchildren, all of whom are also the surviving spouse's; or to one-half the estate if there are one or more children or grandchildren who are not the children or grandchildren of the spouse. (tit. 18-A, § 2-102)

### FAILURE TO PROVIDE BY WILL:
A surviving spouse who married the testator after the will was executed shall receive the same share of the estate he or she would have received if his or her spouse had died without a will, unless it appears that the omission was intentional or the surviving spouse has been otherwise provided for by a transfer that was intended to be in lieu of the provisions under the will. (tit. 18-A, § 2-301)

### CHILDREN BORN OUT OF WEDLOCK:
A child born out of wedlock is the child of the mother and may inherit from her or her kin. However, a child born out of wedlock is the child of the father and may inherit from him only if the natural parents married before or after his or her birth, or the father adopted the child or acknowledged the child in writing before a justice of the peace or a notary public, or paternity has been established by the court before the death of the father, or by clear and convincing evidence after the father's death. Paternity by acknowledgment or adjudication does not entitle the father or his relatives to inherit from the child born out of wedlock unless the father had openly treated the child as his own and had not refused to support the child. (tit. 18-A, § 2-109)

### HOMESTEAD, PERSONAL, AND FAMILY ALLOWANCES:
The surviving spouse or minor children, if there is no surviving spouse, of a decedent domiciled in the state is entitled to a $5000 homestead allowance. The surviving spouse, or minor children, is also entitled to the value of up to $3500 in personal property, including household furnishings, household goods, clothing, fuel, farm produce, or tools. (tit. 18-A, §§ 2-401, -402) These allowances are exempt from, and have priority over all claims against the estate and are in addition to any share passing by will or statutory share or intestate succession. (tit. 18-A, §§ 2-401, -402)

### OPTION TO DISREGARD THE WILL:
If the decedent resided in the state, the surviving spouse may reject the will and take one-third of the augmented estate. If the decedent lived elsewhere, the right to disregard the will and take an elective share is governed by the laws of the state where the decedent lived when he or she died. (tit. 18-A, § 2-201) The augmented estate is the estate after the deduction of funeral and administration expenses, homestead and family allowances, and exemptions and enforceable claims. (tit. 18-A, § 2-202) A decision to take the elective share does not affect the surviving spouse's rights to the homestead allowance and exempt property and family allowances. (tit. 18-A, § 2-206)

# REPRODUCTIVE RIGHTS

## ABORTION

*Statutory Provisions:* All abortions must be performed by a licensed medical or osteopathic physician. Abortions after viability are prohibited except to preserve the life and health of the mother. (tit. 22, § 1598) When an abortion procedure results in a live birth, all reasonable steps must be taken to preserve the life and health of the child. (tit. 22, § 1594) It is a crime for a person who is not a licensed physician or osteopath to perform an abortion on another person or to perform an abortion after viability. (tit. 22, § 1598) Hospitals, health care facilities, or medical personnel are not required to perform or participate in abortions. (tit. 22, § 1591)

*Informed Consent:* The written informed consent of the woman is required prior to the abortion. The physician must certify that the mother gave her consent freely and without coercion. Informed consent includes telling the woman that in the doctor's best judgment she is pregnant and informing her of the length of her pregnancy, the risks associated with her own pregnancy, the abortion techniques to be performed, alternatives to an abortion, and the names of agencies that provide adoption assistance if she so requests. (tit. 22, § 1598)

*Parental Consent:* No consent is required. However, notice of the physician's intent to perform the abortion must be given to one parent or a guardian. Where the physician is unable to give notice to a parent or guardian, it must be given to the Department of Human Services. Actual notice must be given within 24 hours of the abortion. If it cannot be given, written notice must be sent to the last known address of the parent or guardian, or it must be given to the Department of Human Services. This notice requirement is waived when, in the physician's best judgment, the abortion is an emergency. (tit. 22, § 1597)

*Spousal Consent:* There is no relevant statutory provision.

*Mandatory Waiting Period:* An abortion can only be performed 48 hours after the woman has given her physician her written informed consent. (tit. 22, § 1598) This requirement is waived where a medical emergency exists. (tit. 22, §§ 1597, 1598)

*Reporting Requirements:* Each abortion performed and each miscarriage which was attended by a physician must be reported to the Department of Human Services within 10 days following the end of the month in which they occurred. The patient shall not be identified in these reports. (tit. 22, § 1596)

**BIRTH CONTROL:** Family planning services shall be readily and practically available to all persons desiring and needing them. However, nothing shall prevent a physician from refusing to give family planning services for medical, religious, or conscientious reasons. (tit. 22, § 1903) The Department of Human Services may make funds available for family planning to poor families and to all others at a reasonable fee. (tit. 22, § 1906) Any minor who is a parent or married or has the consent of his or her parent or legal guardian may receive family planning services. Minors who may suffer probable health hazards, in a physician's judgment, if such services are not provided may also receive family planning services. (tit. 22, § 1908) No person shall be denied public assistance, public health services, or other public benefits because of his or her refusal to accept family planning services. (tit. 22, § 1907)

**STERILIZATION:** A physician must obtain the informed consent of the person seeking sterilization. In the case of minors, persons under private or public guardianship, persons in state custody, and persons from whom the physician cannot obtain consent, the sterilization procedure can only be perfromed after a hearing is held and a court order is obtained. A court order will be issued upon a determination that the person is competent to give his or her informed consent and that he or she has given it. (tit. 34-B, §§ 7004, 7005) Consent to sterilization may not be a requirement for release from confinement, receiving public assistance, or the exercise of any right, privilege, or freedom. (tit. 34-B, § 7009) A parent, spouse, guardian, or custodian of any person who is unable to give consent may petition the district court to determine if sterilization is in the best interest of the person. (tit. 34-B, § 7010) A determination that sterilization is in the best interest of the person requires a showing of clear and convincing evidence that less drastic methods of contraception do not work or are inappropriate for the person and that sterilization is necessary to preserve the physical and mental health of the person. (tit. 34-B, § 7013)

# UNMARRIED COUPLES

**COMMON-LAW MARRIAGE:**  Common-law marriages are not valid in Maine. [*Pierce v. Secretary of U.S. Department of Health, Education & Welfare*, 254 A.2d 46 (Maine 1969)]

**COHABITAL RELATIONSHIPS:**  There is no case directly on point. However, in an action for partition brought by the woman after the man had moved out, the highest court in Maine ordered the sale and division of the proceeds of the real estate which had been purchased jointly and occupied by the unmarried man and woman. [*Libby v. Lorrain*, 430 A.2d 37 (Maine 1981)]

## CHILDREN

*Custody:*  There is no relevant statutory provision.

*Legitimation Proceedings:*  A child born out of wedlock is the child of the natural parents and is entitled to the same legal rights as the child born in wedlock, except as otherwise provided by statute. (tit. 19, § 220)

*Paternity Proceedings:*  Paternity may be determined upon the complaint of the mother, the child, or the public authority chargeable by law with the support of the child. (tit. 19, § 272) The court on its own or upon the motion of any party may order the mother, the child, or the putative father to undergo blood tests. Refusal to do so resolves the paternity question against the refusing party. (tit. 19, § 277) A negative blood test resolves the issue; however, where the test shows a probability of the alleged father's paternity, the results may be used as evidence at the court's discretion. (tit. 19, § 280) Paternity proceedings may be brought befor the birth of the child or at any time thereafter. (tit. 19, § 271) See the Uniform Act on Paternity, tit. 19, §§ 271 *et seq*.

*Obligations of the Putative Father:*  The putative father of a child from out of wedlock has the same obligations as if the child were born in lawful wedlock for all reasonable expenses of the mother's pregnancy and confinement and for the education and necessary support and financial expenses of the child. (tit. 19, § 271) Once paternity has been established, the father's liability for the support and education of the child is limited to the 6 years prior to commencement of the paternity suit. (tit. 19, §§ 272–273) See also the Uniform Act on Paternity, tit. 19, §§ 271 *et seq*.

# Education

# STATUTORY PROVISIONS

It is unlawful for educational institutions to discriminate on the basis of sex or marital status. (tit. 5, § 4601)

## AREAS COVERED

Areas covered include academic extracurricular research, occupational training, athletic programs, admissions, access to information about the institutions, and financial assistance. (tit. 5, § 4602)

> **ENFORCEMENT:** See "Community Life: Credit."

# Employment

## EQUAL PAY LAWS

It is unlawful to discriminate on the basis of sex in wages paid to employees in the same establishment who perform work requiring comparable skill, effort, and responsibility. Wage differentials are not prohibited if based on a bona fide seniority or merit increase system or difference in shift or time of day worked. (tit. 26, § 628)

> **ENFORCEMENT:** An employee who has been discriminated against in the payment of wages on the basis of sex may bring a civil action for the collection of all unpaid wages within 2 years of the occurrence of the alleged discrimination. In addition to the unpaid wages, the court may award a reasonable rate of interest plus an additional amount equal to twice the amount of such wages and costs of the action, including reasonable attorney's fees. The Department of Labor may also bring the action to collect wages on behalf of the aggrieved employee. (tit. 5, §§ 626-A, 4613)

## FAIR EMPLOYMENT LAWS

It is unlawful for any employer, employment agency, or labor organization to discriminate in hiring, recruitment, selection of apprentices, discharge, discipline, employment referrals, or tenure or in any terms, conditions, or privileges of employment on the basis of sex or marital status. (tit. 5, §§ 4553(4), 4572-A) This prohibition, however, does not apply where a valid merit or seniority system exists or where sex is a bona fide occupational qualification, and it does not apply to not-for-profit religious or fraternal organizations or to persons employing their parents, children, or spouse. (tit. 5, § 4553)

> **ENFORCEMENT:** See "Community Life: Credit."

## GOVERNMENT CONTRACTORS AND SUBCONTRACTORS

Contractors must agree not to discriminate because of sex during the contract period. The law covers upgrading, layoffs or terminations, compensation, and training. [tit. 5, § 784(2)]

> **ENFORCEMENT:** See "Community Life: Credit."

## STATE EMPLOYEE LAWS

State employees are not covered by the Fair Employment Practices Law. However, for employers who employ fifteen or more employees, note that Title VII of the Civil Rights Act of 1964, 42 U.S.C. §§ 2000e *et seq.*, may apply.

# VETERAN'S PREFERENCE

Five points are added to the passing score on a civil service exam of a veteran, or to the surviving unmarried spouse of a veteran, who served at least 90 consecutive days in the armed forces during a war. Ten points are added to the passing score of a veteran who has been honorably discharged or has a service-connected disability of 10 percent or more, or of a surviving spouse, or of a natural parent of a veteran who was killed while on active duty. (tit. 5, § 674)

# Community Life

## CREDIT

It is unlawful for any creditor to refuse to extend credit to any person in any credit transaction on the basis of sex or marital status. (tit. 5, §§ 4595, 4596). This prohibition does not apply where there is discrimination in order to comply with the terms and conditions of a bona fide credit, life, accident, or health insurance plan or where a financial institution, as a condition for extending credit, requires both the husband and wife to sign a note and mortgage. (tit. 5, § 4596)

**ENFORCEMENT:** Any person who believes he or she has been subjected to unlawful discrimination may file a complaint with the Maine Human Rights Commission within 6 months of the occurrence of the alleged unlawful discrimination. (tit. 5, §§ 4611, 4632) In addition, the aggrieved person or the commission may bring a civil action in the superior court within 2 years of the occurrence of the alleged discriminatory act. (tit. 5, § 4613)

## HOUSING

It is unlawful for any owner, lessee, sublessee, managing agent, or other person having the right to sell, rent, lease, or manage a housing accommodation to refuse to show, sell, rent, lease, let, or otherwise deny or withhold any housing accommodation; or to discriminate in the price, terms, conditions, privileges, or in the furnishing of facilities or services in connection with the sale, rental, or lease of any housing accommodation, or to evict or attempt to evict any tenant on the basis of sex. It is unlawful for any real estate broker, salesperson, or agent to fail or refuse to show a housing accommodation, to misrepresent the availability or asking price of a housing accommodation, to fail to transmit a bona fide offer, or to discriminate in any other manner on the basis of sex. It is unlawful for any person to whom application is made for a loan or other form of financial assistance for the acquisition, construction, rehabilitation, repair, or maintenance of any housing accommodation to discriminate in the granting of such financial assistance or in the terms, conditions, or privileges relating to the obtaining or use of any financial assistance on the basis of sex. It is also unlawful to advertise the sale, rental, or lease of housing accommodation in such a way as to indicate any limitation, specification, or discrimination on the basis of sex. (tit. 5, § 4582)

**ENFORCEMENT:** See "Credit."

## INSURANCE

Discrimination is prohibited between individuals of the same class and equal expectation in the rates charged for life insurance or annuity contracts or between individuals of the same class and essentially the same hazard in the amount of premiums, policy fees, or rates charged for health insurance, or in the benefits payable under these contracts, or in any other terms or conditions of these contracts. (tit. 24-A, § 2159)

**ENFORCEMENT:** The Superintendent of the Bureau of Insurance investigates all charges of unlawful practices in the industry. Upon a finding that a person has engaged in any prohibited act or practice, the superintendent shall order such person to desist from such acts or practices. (tit. 24-A, § 2165)

# PUBLIC ACCOMMODATIONS

It is unlawful for any owner, lessee, proprietor, manager, superintendent, agent, or employee of any place of public accommodation, directly or indirectly, to refuse, withhold from, or deny to any person any of the accommodations, advantages, facilities, or privileges of a place of public accommodation or to publish or post any notice that the patronage of an individual is unwelcome or objectionable on the basis of sex. (tit. 5, §§ 4591, 4592)

**ENFORCEMENT:** See "Credit."

# MARYLAND

## Home and Family

## MARRIAGE

**AGE OF CONSENT:** A person 18 years of age or older may consent to marry. (Fam. Law § 2-301)*

**CONSENT REQUIREMENT:** Persons under 16 must have the consent of a parent or guardian and either party must provide the clerk with certified proof from a licensed physician that the woman to be married is pregnant or has given birth to a child. (Fam. Law § 2-302) Persons 16 or 17 years old must have either the consent of a parent or guardian, who must swear that the individual is at least 16 years old, or a medical certificate from a licensed physician stating that the woman to be married is pregnant or has given birth to a child. (Fam. Law § 2-301)

**LICENSE REQUIREMENT:** A license issued by the county clerk is required in order to marry. (Fam. Law §§ 2-401, -402)

**PROHIBITED MARRIAGES:** Marriage between a person and his or her grandparent, sister, brother, aunt, uncle, niece, nephew, son-in-law, daughter-in-law, stepparent, mother-in-law, or father-in-law are prohibited. (Fam. Law § 2-202) Bigamous marriages are also prohibited. (art. 27, § 18) Children born of void or prohibited marriages are legitimate. (Fam. Law § 5-202)

## DISSOLUTION OF MARRIAGE

**ANNULMENT:** Factors 19 and 40, listed in Appendix A, are grounds for annulment. (Md. Rule S76, Vol. 2)

*Residency Requirement:* There is no relevant statutory provision. However, an action for annulment must be filed in the county where the party seeking the annulment resides; or in the county where the spouse from whom the annulment is sought resides, is regularly employed, or has a place of business; or in the county where the marriage ceremony was performed. (Md. Rule S70, Vol. 2)

**LEGAL SEPARATION:** A legal separation may be obtained based upon factors 16, 17, 28 (with 31), listed in Appendix A. [Fam. Law § 7-102; *Atkinson v. Atkinson*, 281 A.2d 407 (Md. 1971)] The court requires the parties to participate in a good-faith effort to achieve reconciliation, and the separation, when granted, may be temporary or permanent. (Fam. Law § 7-102)

*Residency Requirement:* At least one of the parties must have lived in Maryland at least 1 year before filing for a separation. (Fam. Law § 7-101)

### DIVORCE

*Residency Requirement:* See "Legal Separation." In the case of insanity as a ground for divorce, one party must have resided in Maryland for 2 years before filing for the divorce. (Fam. Law § 7-103)

*Grounds for Divorce:* Factors 4, 9 (for no less than 3 years confinement), 16 (for 12 months without interruption), 15 (or misdemeanor with at least a 3-year

*Unless otherwise specified, all reference citations are to the Annotated Code of Maryland (1957).

sentence and after 1 year has been served), 28 (1 year), and 31 (2 years), listed in Appendix A, are grounds for divorce. (Fam. Law § 7-103)

*Conciliation Requirement:* There is no relevant statutory provision.

*Property Distribution:* When the court grants an absolute divorce, it may not transfer the ownership of either personal or real property to either spouse. Upon a determination of ownership it may grant a decree stating each party's ownership interest and order either a division of the property or its sale and the division of the proceeds between the parties. (Fam. Law § 8-202) If there is a dispute about whether certain property is marital property, the court will determine which property is marital property. Marital property includes military pensions as well as other retirement benefits. (Fam. Law § 8-203) After the court determines which property is marital property and what the value of the property is, it may grant a monetary award as an adjustment of the equities and rights of the parties concerning marital property whether or not alimony is awarded, after considering factors 1, 2, 3, 5, 6, 15, 21, 22, and 28, listed in Appendix F. (Fam. Law § 8-205)

*Child Custody:* No parent is presumed to have a superior right to custody. Therefore, custody may be awarded to either parent and joint custody to both parents, even where it is not requested by the parents, in accordance with the best interests of the child. [Fam. Law § 5-203; Op. Att'y Gen. No. 83-024 (June 2, 1983); art. 72A, § 1] Custody may also be granted to a third party. [art. 72A, § 1; *Ross v. Hoffman*, 372 A.2d 582 (Md. 1977)] See also the Uniform Child Custody Jurisdiction Act, Fam. Law § 12-101.

*Child Support:* There are no factors set out for a determination of the amount of child support. The court may, however, award child support retroactively to the filing date of the request for child support. (Fam. Law § 12-101) A child support decree shall last until the child is 21 years old, where the order was issued before July 1, 1973, unless an action has been commenced to amend, terminate, modify or vacate the provisions of the order. [Op. Att'y Gen. No. 59 (1974)]

*Spousal Support/Alimony:* The court may award alimony to either party during a divorce, alimony, or annulment proceeding. (Fam. Law § 11-102) The factors that are considered in determining the amount and duration of alimony are 2, 3, 4, 5, 6, 8, 10, 11, 13, 14, and 20, listed in Appendix E. (Fam. Law § 11-106)

*Enforcement of Support Orders:* Support orders may be enforced by bringing a contempt proceeding which may be brought within 3 years of the date the payment became due. (Fam. Law § 10-102) The Child Support Enforcement Administration of the Department of Human Resources may locate absent parents; determine their ability to pay support; accept an assignment of any right, title, or interest in child support from a party owed the support; or prosecute and maintain any legal or equitable action available in order to collect support payments. (Fam. Law § 10-108; art. 88A, § 48) The Child Support Enforcement Administration may also act as a payee or as a collection agent; make settlements of arrearages in an amount less than the total amount due; and intercept state income tax refunds. (Fam. Law §§ 10-108, -112, -113) In addition, child support can be deducted and withheld from unemployment insurance benefits (art. 95A, § 5A) and, if the party owing a duty of support is in arrears for more than 30 days, the spouse, child, or support enforcement agency may petition the court to impose a lien on the earnings of the party owing support. (Fam. Law § 10-120) See also the Uniform Revised Enforcement of Support Act of 1968, Fam. Law §§ 10-301 *et seq.*

*Spouse's Name:* Upon granting a divorce, a court may restore a woman to her former or birth name if the purpose is not illegal, fraudulent, or immoral. (Fam. Law § 7-105)

*Divorce by Affidavit or Summary Judgment:* Such divorces are not permitted in any case. (Cts. & Jud. Proc. § 3-409)

*Displaced Homemaker Laws:* A multipurpose center has been established to assist displaced homemakers in becoming gainfully employed, providing counseling, training, job placement, and health and educational services. (Fam. Law §§ 4-605 to -607)

# DOMESTIC VIOLENCE

**STATUTORY PROVISION:** It is unlawful for a household member to cause serious bodily harm to another household member, or to place him or her in fear of imminent serious bodily harm, or to abuse a child sexually. (Fam. Law § 4-501)

**WHO IS PROTECTED?** Spouses, parents, children, or blood relatives who live together are protected. (Fam. Law § 4-501)

**RELIEF AVAILABLE:** Temporary orders of protection ordering the alleged abuser to stop the abuse or to vacate the home immediately, granting temporary possession of the home to the victim for 5 days and temporary custody of minor household members, and ordering all household members to participate in professionally supervised counseling are available. (Fam. Law § 4-505) Under Maryland's battered spouse program, the spouse and minor children may receive temporary shelter or help in obtaining shelter, counseling, information, referral, and rehabilitation from the Department of Human Services. (Fam. Law §§ 4-513, -515) A battered spouse may also seek the assistance of a law enforcement officer in removing his or her personal effects and those of children in his or her care from the home. (art. 27, § 11F)

**MARITAL RAPE:** A person may not be prosecuted for the rape of his or her spouse unless the parties are legally separated. (art. 27, § 464D)

**CIVIL LAWSUIT FOR RAPE OR ASSAULT:** There is no relevant statutory provision. However, in *Lusby v. Lusby*, 390 A.2d 77 (Md. Ct. Spec. App. 1978), the court held that spouses could sue each other for intentional outrageous conduct.

**CHILD ABUSE:** It is unlawful for a parent or any person having permanent or temporary care, custody, or responsibility for the supervision of a child under 18 to physically injure the child by means of cruel and inhuman treatment or to commit a malicious act or sexual abuse whether or not injury results. (art. 27, § 35A; Fam. Law § 5-901)

*Notification Requirement:* All health practitioners, police officers, educators, social workers and child care institution workers who contact, examine, attend or treat a child and who have reason to believe that the child has been abused shall notify the Department of Social Services that has jurisdiction in the county where the alleged abused child lives or where the abuse is alleged to have taken place. (Fam. Law § 5-901 to -904)

# INHERITANCE RIGHTS

**FAILURE TO MAKE A WILL:** The surviving spouse is entitled to the entire estate where there is no surviving child, grandchild, or parent; to the first $15,000 plus one-half the residue if there is a surviving parent but no surviving child or grandchild; to the first $15,000 plus one-half the residue if there is no surviving minor child but there is a surviving child or grandchild; or to one-half the estate if there is a surviving minor child. (Est. & Trusts § 3-102)

**FAILURE TO PROVIDE BY WILL:** There is no relevant statutory provision.

**CHILDREN BORN OUT OF WEDLOCK:** A child born out of wedlock is the natural heir of its mother and her kin. (Est. & Trusts § 1-208) However, such a child can only inherit from the father if he has been adjudicated the father in a proceeding brought for that purpose or if he has been judicially ordered to support the child. [*Dawson v. Eversberg*, 262 A.2d (Md. 1970)]

**HOMESTEAD, PERSONAL, AND FAMILY ALLOWANCES:** There is no relevant statutory provision. However, the surviving spouse is entitled to receive an allowance of $2000 for his or her personal use and an additional $1000 for each unmarried child of the decedent under 18 years old. This allowance is exempt from the Maryland inheritance tax. [Est. & Trusts § 3-201(a), (b)]

**OPTION TO DISREGARD THE WILL:** The surviving spouse may reject the will and take one-third of the net estate if the decedent left children or grandchildren or one-half the net estate if the decedent left no children or grandchildren. (Est. & Trusts § 3-203)

# REPRODUCTIVE RIGHTS
## ABORTION

*Statutory Provisions:* Abortions must be performed by a licensed physician in an accredited hospital. Abortions may be performed only if the pregnancy is likely to result in the death of the mother; or there is substantial risk that continuation of the pregnancy will gravely impair the physical or mental health of the mother; or there is substantial risk of a child with grave and permanent physical deformity and mental retardation being born; or the pregnancy was the result of a rape (which must be substantiated by the state's Attorney of Baltimore City or the county in which it occurred); or the fetus is no more than 26 weeks old (except where it is dead and the mother's life is in danger and there has been authorization by the hospital abortion review authority). (Health Gen. § 20-208)

*Informed Consent:* The written informed consent of the woman is required, unless the abortion is needed to save her life. Before performing an abortion the physician must advise the woman of services available to help her carry the pregnancy to term and to raise and support the child, including information on adoption and social service agencies. (Health Gen. § 20-211)

*Parental Consent:* A minor who is married or the mother of a child may consent to an abortion. (Health Gen. § 20-102) A physician may not perform an abortion on an unmarried minor without first notifying the parent or guardian of the minor, unless the minor does not live with the parent or guardian and a reasonable effort to give notice was unsuccessful or if, in the physician's professional judgment, notice will lead to physical or emotional abuse. (Health Gen. § 20-103)

*Spousal Consent:* There is no relevant statutory provision.

*Reporting Requirements:* All therapeutic abortions must be reported by the director of the hospital to the Joint Commission on Hospital Administration and the state Board of Health and Mental Hygiene. (Health Gen. § 20-208)

**BIRTH CONTROL:** Contraceptives or contraceptive devices may not be sold or offered for sale by way of vending machines, whether advertised as contraceptives or prophylactics. (art. 27, § 41)

**STERILIZATION:** The refusal of an individual to submit to or give consent for sterilization (or abortion) may not be grounds for the loss of any privileges to which an individual is entitled or a precondition to the receipt of any public benefits. (Health Gen. § 20-214) A minor may not give consent to sterilization. [Health Gen. § 20-102(c)(5)] The court may authorize the guardian of an incompetent minor to consent to sterilization where clear and convincing evidence shows that sterilization is in the best interests of the child. [*Wentzer v. Montgomery General Hospital*, 447 A.2d 1244 (Md. 1982), *cert. denied* 103 S. Ct. 790 (1983)]

## UNMARRIED COUPLES

**COMMON-LAW MARRIAGE:** Common-law marriages are not valid. [*Henderson v. Henderson*, 87 A.2d 403 (1952)] However, a common-law marriage, when valid where contracted, is recognized in Maryland. [*Goldin v. Goldin*, 426 A.2d 410 (Md. App. 1981)]

**COHABITAL RELATIONSHIPS:** There is no relevant statutory provision. However, a case on point held that contracts made by the parties to a cohabital relationship are enforceable so long as the contract does not stand upon the relationship. [*Donovan v. Scuderi*, 443 A.2d 121 (Md. App. 1982)]

**CHILDREN**

*Custody:* There is no relevant statutory provision. However, custody may be awarded to either parent, and neither parent is presumed to have a superior right to custody. (Fam. Law § 5-203)

*Legitimation Proceedings:* The child born out of wedlock is the child of the mother and shall be considered the child of the father only if he has been judicially determined to be the father in a paternity proceeding, or he has acknowledged himself to be the father in writing, or he has openly and notoriously recognized the child as his own, or he has subsequently married the mother and has acknowledged himself to be the father, either in writing or orally. (Est. & Trusts § 1-208)

*Paternity Proceedings:* A paternity proceeding may be brought during the pregnancy of the mother or any time thereafter. (Fam. Law § 5-1006)

*Obligations of the Putative Father:* Upon a determination of paternity the court may order either parent to pay all or part of child support; the mother's medical and hospital expenses for pregnancy, confinement, and recovery; and the funeral expenses of the child. The father may be ordered to pay all or part of the child's medical expenses and counsel fees. (Fam. Law § 5-1033)

# Education

## STATUTORY PROVISION

There is no relevant statutory provision. Maryland's constitution does, however, provide for equality of rights regardless of sex. (Md. Const. art. 46) Sex may not be a factor when appointing, assigning, compensating, or transferring public school teachers, except where sex is a bona fide occupational qualification. (Educ. § 6-105) Note also that if federal funds are involved, federal law, Title IX of the Education Amendments of 1972, Pub. L. No. 92-318, 20 U.S.C. §§ 1681–1986, may apply.

## AREAS COVERED

Areas covered include employment, assignment compensation, and transfer of teachers. (Educ. §§ 4-107, -109; 6-105)

> **ENFORCEMENT:** The Superintendent of Schools and the Board of Education enforce rules and regulations pertaining to education. (Educ. § 2-203)

# Employment

## EQUAL PAY LAWS

It is unlawful for an employer to discriminate on the basis of sex in wages paid to employees in the same establishment who perform work requiring equal skill, effort, and responsibility. Wage differentials are not prohibited, however, if based on a seniority or merit system, different skills or ability, different duties or services performed regularly, or different shifts or time of day worked. (art. 100, § 55A)

> **ENFORCEMENT:** Employees may bring an action in any court of competent jurisdiction on their own behalf or on behalf of others within 3 years after the alleged wage discrimination. (art. 100, § 55D) Furthermore, the Commissioner of Labor and Industry may use such informal methods as conferences, conciliation and persuasion, and supervision of the wage payments in order to eliminate unlawful pay practices. (art. 100, § 55C)

## FAIR EMPLOYMENT LAWS

It is unlawful for the state of Maryland, its political and civil subdivisions, or employers of fifteen or more employees to discriminate in hiring, discharge, compensation, terms, and conditions of employment or to limit, segregate, or classify employees so as to deprive them of employment opportunities or to adversely affect their employment status on the basis of sex or marital status. This provision also prohibits employment agencies and labor organizations from discriminating on the basis of sex or marital status. (art. 49B, §§ 15, 16) The Fair Employment Act does not apply to situations where sex is a bona fide occupational qualification; to elected and appointed officials and their personal staff; and to religious schools and organizations and bona fide private clubs. (art. 49B, §§ 15, 16)

> **ENFORCEMENT:** An aggrieved person may file a complaint with the Commissioner of Human Relations within 6 months of the occurrence of a discriminatory act. The complaint must be in writing and under oath. (art. 49B, § 9)

## GOVERNMENT CONTRACTORS AND SUBCONTRACTORS

No contract may be awarded to any contractor unless it contains provisions requiring that the contractor not discriminate in any manner (including sexual harassment) against employees or applicants for employment because of sex. Except for subcontracts for commercial supplies and raw materials, all subcontracts must contain similar provisions. (art.

21, § 3-406; Exec. Order No. 01.01.1986.04) Any organizations receiving state financial assistance must include antidiscrimination pledges in their bylaws or constitutions. (Exec. Order No. 01.01.1986.04)

**ENFORCEMENT:** Any person with information concerning unfair labor practices may inform the Board of Public Works and it shall investigate the charges and invoke the applicable remedy where unfair labor practices are found. (art. 21, § 3-406) Complaints against state-aid recipients must be made to the Commissioner of Human Relations. (Exec. Order No. 01.01.1986.04)

## STATE EMPLOYEE LAWS

See "Fair Employment Laws." State employees are also protected by Exec. Order No. 01.01.1986.04, which prohibits discrimination on the basis of sex or marital status (including sexual harassment).

**ENFORCEMENT:** Complaints should be made to the Secretary of Personnel. (Exec. Order No. 01.01.1986.04)

## VETERAN'S PREFERENCE

Veterans who served in the armed forces for a period of 181 days, or were released before that period because of a service-connected disability, and who have been honorably discharged or who have received a certificate of satisfactory completion of service, and who are bona fide residents of Maryland for 5 years or more before the application shall have a special credit of five points added to their passing civil service examination scores. Disabled veterans, their spouses, and the unmarried surviving spouses of deceased veterans may have ten points added to their passing scores. (art. 64A, § 18)

# Community Life

## CREDIT

It is unlawful for an extender of credit to discriminate in granting credit to anyone on the basis of sex or marital status. (Com. Law § 12-305) It is also unlawful to refuse to consider the income of both spouses when either or both apply for a joint account; to refuse to consider alimony or child support as a source of income where it is verifiable as to the amount, length of time, and regularity of receipt; to refuse to issue separate accounts to married couples where each party would be creditworthy if unmarried; to request a credit rating of the other spouse if the applicant is creditworthy and is not applying for a joint account; to refuse to recognize the legal name of any married person; and to request information about birth control practices in evaluating a credit application. (Com. Law § 12-705)

**ENFORCEMENT:** Complaints may be filed with the Commissioner of Consumer Credit; upon a finding of discriminatory practice, a cease and desist order will be issued. (Com. Law § 12-703) In addition, an aggrieved person may bring a civil action for actual damages. The court may award punitive damages of up to $10,000 plus the costs of the action and attorney's fee. The action must be brought within 1 year of the date of the occurrence of the violation. (Com. Law § 12-707) In the case of banks, this provision is enforced by the state bank commissioner. (Com. Law §§ 12-706, -707)

# HOUSING

It is unlawful for any person to refuse to sell, rent, or lease any dwelling on the basis of sex or marital status or to represent that a dwelling is not available for inspection, sale, or rental when it is available. It is also unlawful for any person to refuse to consider both applicants' income when a married couple seeks to buy or lease a dwelling; to refuse to consider court-awarded alimony or child support as a valid source of income; or to request or consider information about birth control practices in evaluating prospective buyers or lessees of a dwelling. These provisions do not apply to dwellings occupied exclusively by members of one sex. Discrimination on the basis of sex or marital status is permitted in the rental of rooms within a dwelling in which the owner resides or in the rental of apartments in a five-unit dwelling in which the owner resides. (art. 49B, § 20) It is unlawful for any financial institution or any person regularly engaged in the business of making mortgages or loans for the purchase, construction, or improvement of dwellings to deny a loan or to discriminate in the fixing of the down payment, interest rate, duration, or other term or condition of a loan on the basis of sex or marital status. (art. 49B, § 22)

**ENFORCEMENT:** An aggrieved person may file a complaint with the Commissioner of Human Relations within 6 months of the occurrence of a discriminatory act. The complaint must be in writing and under oath. (art. 49B, § 9)

# INSURANCE

Except where justified by actuarial tables, no insurer may discriminate on the basis of sex between persons of the same class and equal life expectancy in rates for annuity or life insurance, or between persons of the same class and potentially the same hazards in the amount of premium, policy fees, or rates charged for health insurance or in any terms and conditions of these policies. (art. 48A, §§ 226, 234A; art. 48B, § 223) Temporary disability caused or contributed to by pregnancy or childbirth may be provided for by group or blanket health insurance. (art. 48A, § 477P)

**ENFORCEMENT:** The Commissioner of Insurance may institute suits or other legal proceedings where there is reason to believe that an insurer is involved in discriminatory practices. (art. 48A, § 25)

# PUBLIC ACCOMMODATIONS

It is unlawful for an owner, operator, agent, or employee of a place of public accommodation to refuse or deny any person any of the accommodations, advantages, facilities, or privileges of a place of public accommodation on the basis of sex or marital status. These provisions do not apply to private clubs not open to the public or to facilities that are uniquely private and personal in nature and designed to accommodate members of one sex only. (art. 49B, § 5)

**ENFORCEMENT:** See "Housing."

# MASSACHUSETTS

## Home and Family

## MARRIAGE

**AGE OF CONSENT:** Persons 18 years or older may give consent to marry. (ch. 207, § 7)*

**CONSENT REQUIREMENT:** A minor may marry with the consent of both parents or the surviving parent, or if only one parent resides in the commonwealth, that parent. Notice of the proceeding will be sent to the parent residing outside of the commonwealth. (ch. 207, §§ 25, 26)

**LICENSE REQUIREMENT:** Persons wishing to marry must obtain a certificate permitting the marriage from the clerk or registrar of any city or town in the commonwealth. The certificate is issued between 3 and 60 days after filing a notice of intention to marry. (ch. 207, § 28) The certificate will be issued only when each party has provided a medical certificate from a doctor who has conducted a test for syphilis not more than 30 days before the filing of the notice of intention to marry or not more than 60 days before the issuance of the certificate. A medical certificate certifying that the female has been protected against rubella or is informed about the dangers of not being protected is also required. (This provision does not apply where the female cannot conceive.) The medical certificates can be waived where the death of either party is imminent, where the female is in the advanced stage of pregnancy, or where a waiver has been requested by a member of the clergy or a physician. (ch. 207, § 28A)

**PROHIBITED MARRIAGES:** No person may marry his or her parent, grandparent, child, grandchild, sibling, stepparent, grandparent's spouse, grandchild's spouse, spouse's parent, spouse's grandparent, spouse's child, spouse's grandchild, or parent's sibling. (ch. 207, §§ 1, 2) A marriage contracted where either party has a living spouse is void. (ch. 207, § 4) An insane or feebleminded person committed to an institution or under the supervision of the Department of Mental Health cannot marry. (ch. 207, § 5) A marriage contracted in good faith, where the original spouse is wrongfully presumed dead or divorced, is valid, provided a legal divorce is then secured from the original spouse. (ch. 207, § 6) A marriage solemnized in Massachusetts but which is prohibited by reason of either incest or bigamy is void without a judgment of divorce or other legal process. (ch. 207, § 8) Children born of incestuous marriages are illegitimate. (ch. 207, § 15) However, children born of marriages declared void by reason of the nonage, insanity, or idiocy of either party are legitimate. (ch. 207, § 16) Children born of bigamous marriages contracted in good faith are legitimate. (ch. 207, § 17)

## DISSOLUTION OF MARRIAGE

**ANNULMENT:** Where the validity of a marriage is doubted, either party may institute an action for annulling or affirming the marriage. The action is instituted in

---

*Unless otherwise specified, all citation references are to the Massachusetts General Laws Annotated (West 1932).

265

the same manner as divorce, and all provisions relevant to divorce apply. (ch. 207, § 14)

*Residency Requirement:* If the parties were married in the commonwealth, there is no residency requirement. If they were married outside the commonwealth, they must have resided in the commonwealth either for the 5 years preceding commencement of the action or both when the action was commenced and at the time of the annulment. (§207 14)

**LEGAL SEPARATION:** If a spouse fails without cause to provide support, deserts, or gives the other spouse justifiable cause to live apart, the probate court may require the spouse to support the other spouse and children living apart. No restraint may be imposed on the spouse living apart. (ch. 207, § 32) Separate maintenance may similarly be ordered during a divorce action. (ch. 208, § 1)

*Residency Requirement:* See "Divorce."

## DIVORCE

*Residency Requirement:* Where the cause of the divorce occurred in the state, one party must be a bona fide resident of the state; otherwise, 1 year of residence is required where the cause of the divorce occurred outside the state. (ch. 208, § 4 and 5)

*Grounds for Divorce:* Factors 2, 3, 4, 8, 12 (for 1 year before filing the complaint), 17, and 48, listed in Appendix A, are grounds for divorce. (ch. 208, §§ 1, 1A, 1B)

*Conciliation Requirement:* There is no relevant statutory provision.

*Property Distribution:* The court may assign all or part of the estate of either spouse on the basis of factors 1, 5, 6, 7, 8, 9, 10, 11, and 30, listed in Appendix F. (ch. 208, § 34)

*Child Custody:* Upon a judgment for divorce, the court may make such judgment as it considers expedient relative to the care, custody, and maintenance of the minor children of the parties; and may determine with which of the parents the children or any of them shall remain, or may award their custody to some third person if it seems expedient or for the benefit of the children; and afterward may, upon the action of either parent or of a next friend, revise such judgment or make a new judgment, as the circumstances of the parents and the children may require. Joint custody is permitted, if the parties agree, unless the court specifically finds that joint custody will not be in the children's best interests. (ch. 208, § 28)

*Child Support:* The court may make an appropriate order for the maintenance, support (including insurance where necessary), and education of any child up to 21 years of age who lives in the parent's home and is dependent upon the parent for maintenance. (ch. 208, § 28)

*Spousal Support/Alimony:* The court may render a judgment requiring that alimony be paid to either party. To determine the amount of alimony, the court will consider factors 1, 5, 6, 7, 8, 9, 10, 11, and 30, listed in Appendix E. (ch. 208, § 34) The court may also require either party to pay to the other party the costs of maintaining and defending the action, including insurance, if necessary. (ch. 208, § 17) Fault is not considered in awarding alimony. (ch. 208, § 1A)

*Enforcement of Support Orders:* The court may enforce support orders in the same manner as it enforces judgments in equity. (ch. 208, § 35) As part of an order of support the court may require sufficient security for its payment. The judgment must also include an order directing the party owing the support to assign a portion of his or her salary, wages, earnings, commissions or other periodic income to the party owed the support or any other party designated by the court. (ch. 208, § 36) As a last resort, an order of trustee process may be placed on disposable and future earnings of the spouse. (ch. 208, § 36A) Intercept of unemployment compensation, payable to a party owing child support obligations, is also available. (§ 151A 29) The probate and family court provides child support collection services. A fee not greater than $25 may be charged to the requesting parent for these services in accordance with the Child Support Enforcement Act of 1984, 42 U.S.C. §§ 654 *et seq*. (§ 262 40A) See also the Uniform Reciprocal Enforcement of Support Act, ch. 273A §§ 1 *et seq*.

*Spouse's Name:* Upon granting a divorce, the court may allow the woman to resume her maiden name or the name of a former spouse. (ch. 208, § 23)

*Divorce by Affidavit or Summary Judgment:* There is no relevant statutory provision.

*Displaced Homemaker Laws:* The Bay State Skills Corporation has authorized the chairperson of a statewide advisory council to establish five multipurpose service centers designed to meet the demographic and geographic needs of displaced home-makers. The centers are to provide job counseling, training, and placement; prevocational training and educational services; outreach and information services with respect to government employment, education, health, legal, and unemployment assistance programs, and a clearinghouse providing resource libraries. (ch. 401, [§§ 7A *et seq*.)

# DOMESTIC VIOLENCE

**STATUTORY PROVISION:** It is unlawful for one household member to attempt to cause physical harm to another household member, to place another household member in fear of imminent serious physical harm, or to cause another household member to engage in involuntary sexual relations by force, threat of force, or duress. (ch. 209A, § 1)

**WHO IS PROTECTED?** Spouses, former spouses, minor children, and household members or their blood relative are protected. (ch. 209A, § 1)

**RELIEF AVAILABLE:** Persons suffering abuse from family members may file a complaint in court for orders of protection including orders to refrain from further abuse and to vacate the household for up to 1 year. Orders may also be issued for temporary custody of minor children; for monetary compensation for loss of earnings; for support; for losses incurred as a result of injuries sustained; for the payment of medical expenses, moving expenses, and attorney's fees. An action commenced under the civil abuse prevention statute does not preclude any other civil or criminal remedies. (ch. 209A, § 3)

**MARITAL RAPE:** The statute abandons the common-law spousal exclusion, so that a husband can be legally prosecuted for raping his wife. [ch. 265, § 223; *Commonwealth v. Chretien*, 417 N.E.2d 1203 (Mass. 1981)]

**CIVIL LAWSUIT FOR RAPE OR ASSAULT:** Spouses may not sue each other except in cases of breach of contract between the spouses. (ch. 209, §§ 2, 6) However spouses may sue each other for injuries sustained in automobile accidents. [*Lewis v. Lewis*, 351 N.E.2d 526 (Mass. 1976)]

**CHILD ABUSE:** Child abuse is defined as abuse by family or household members who cause or attempt to cause physical harm, or who engage in involuntary sexual relations by force, threat of force, or duress. (ch. 209A, § 1) Assault of a child under 16 with intent to commit rape is a crime punishable by imprisonment for life or a term of years. (ch. 265, § 24B)

*Notification Requirement:* All physicians, health care professionals, public or private school teachers and school personnel, child care providers, social workers, foster parents, and peace officers who have reasonable cause to believe a child under 18 is abused as a result of physical abuse, sexual abuse, neglect, malnutrition, drug addiction, or dependency must make an immediate oral report of this abuse to the Department of Social Services and a written report within 48 hours of the oral report. Failure to make such a report is punishable by a fine of up to $1000. (ch. 119, § 51A)

# INHERITANCE RIGHTS

**FAILURE TO MAKE A WILL:** After payment of estate debts, if there are kin but no children and if the estate has less than $50,000 in assets, the surviving spouse is entitled to the entire estate; otherwise, the surviving spouse will take $50,000 and half of each the remaining personal and real property. If there are children, the survivor gets one-half of each the personal and real property. If there are no children and no kin, the survivor receives the whole. (ch. 190, § 1)

**FAILURE TO PROVIDE BY WILL:** The surviving spouse is entitled to one-third of the personal and one-third of the real property if the deceased left children, or to $25,000 and one-half of the remaining personal and one-half of the remaining real property if the deceased left children. If there are no kin or children, the surviving spouse will receive $25,000 and one-half of the personal and one-half of the real property. (ch. 191, § 15)

**CHILDREN BORN OUT OF WEDLOCK:** A child born out of wedlock is the natural heir of the mother and her kin. Such a child can inherit from the father if the parents intermarried or if the father acknowledged paternity, or if, during the father's lifetime or after his death, the decedent had been adjudged to be the father of the child. (ch. 190, § 7)

**HOMESTEAD, PERSONAL, AND FAMILY ALLOWANCES:** The surviving spouse and the children are entitled to keep the clothes and jewelry that belong to them. If property must be sold to pay estate debts, then the surviving spouse may remain in the house of the deceased spouse, but for no more than 6 months afterward without being charged rent. (ch. 196, § 1) The probate court may also allow such parts of the decedent's personal property as necessaries to the surviving spouse and the family under his or her care, or if there is no surviving spouse, to the deceased's minor children, not exceeding $100 to any child, and also such provisions and other articles as are necessary for the reasonable sustenance of the family and the use of the house and furniture for 6 months. (ch. 196, § 2) Otherwise, the homestead is allowed to the surviving spouse and children until the youngest unmarried child reaches 18 and until the remarriage or death of the surviving spouse. The right, title, and interest to the homestead are subject to the laws relating to devise, descent, dower, and sale for the payment of estate debts and legacies. (ch. 188, § 3)

**OPTION TO DISREGARD THE WILL:** Within 6 months after probate of the will, the surviving spouse may reject the will and take $25,000 and one-half the balance of the estate if the decedent left no other heirs; $25,000 and a life income in one-half the balance of the estate if the decedent left children or grandchildren;

or $25,000 and a life income in one-half the balance if the decedent left other heirs but no children. (ch. 191, § 15)

# REPRODUCTIVE RIGHTS

## ABORTION

*Statutory Provisions:* All abortions must be performed by licensed physicians. (ch. 112, §§ 12L, 12M) Pregnancies of fewer than 24 weeks can only be terminated if the physician, in his or her best medical judgment, believes the abortion necessary under all attendant circumstances. (ch. 112, § 12L) Pregnancies of 24 weeks or more can only be terminated where the abortion is necessary to prevent impairment of the physical or mental health of the woman. (ch. 112, § 12M)

*Informed Consent:* A physician must obtain the written informed consent of the woman before performing an abortion. Informed consent exists after the physician has provided the woman with the applicable form issued by the Commissioner of Public Health describing the stage of the development of the fetus, the type of procedure that will be used to perform the abortion, the possible complications associated with the particular procedure and with the performance of an abortion, the availability of alternatives to an abortion, and, finally, a statement that refusal to undergo an abortion does not constitute grounds for denial of public assistance. (ch. 112, § 12S)

*Parental Consent:* Where the unmarried pregnant woman is under 18, consent of both the woman and her parents is required. A judge of the superior court department of the trial court may, after a hearing, permit an abortion if the unmarried woman under 18 refuses to seek parental consent or if such consent is refused. (ch. 112, § 12S)

*Spousal Consent:* There is no relevant statutory provision.

*Health Insurance Regulations:* Group life and accidental death and dismemberment insurance policies provided to state employees by the state may provide abortion coverage only where an abortion is necessary to prevent the death of the woman. (ch. 32A, § 4)

*Reporting Requirements:* The physician performing the abortion must file a written report of all abortions performed with the Commissioner of Public Health within 30 days of performing an abortion. (ch. 112, § 12R)

*State Funding:* State funds may not be used to fund abortions unless the attending physician has certified in writing that the abortion is necessary to prevent the death of the woman. (ch. 29, § 20B; ch. 32B, § 3A) This provision was held to be a violation of the Massachusetts Constitution in *Moe v. Secretary of Administration and Finance*, 417 N.E.2d 387 (Mass. 1981).

**BIRTH CONTROL:** Registered physicians may prescribe birth control methods to any person. [ch. 272, § 21A; *Eisenstadt v. Baird*, 405 U.S. 438 (1972)]

**STERILIZATION:** Voluntary sterilization procedures cannot be performed, except in an emergency, without the knowledgeable consent, in writing, of the individual seeking to be sterilized. (ch. 112, § 12W)

# UNMARRIED COUPLES

**COMMON-LAW MARRIAGE:** Common-law marriages are not valid. (ch. 207, § 14)

**COHABITAL RELATIONSHIPS:** Massachussetts has a statute which makes it a criminal offense for unmarried couples to cohabit. (ch. 272, § 16) This law has, therefore, severely limited the ability of former cohabitants to legally divide property which they acquired jointly during their period of cohabitation.

## CHILDREN

*Custody:* The court may make a determination of custody according to the child's welfare. (ch. 273, § 14)

*Legitimation Proceedings:* A child born out of wedlock is legitimized by the intermarriage of the parents. (ch. 273, § 17)

*Paternity Proceedings:* Paternity proceedings are brought in the superior court in the county where the alleged father or mother of the child resides, or if in the district court, in the court in the judicial district where the alleged father or mother resides, during the child's minority. If the alleged father pleads or is found to be guilty, or if he pleads *nolo contendere*, an order will be entered adjudging him to be the father of the child. Such an order will not be entered against one pleading not guilty, against his objection, until the child is born or the mother is 6 months pregnant. [ch. 273, § 12; *Commonwealth v. Gruttner*, 432 N.E.2d 518 (Mass. 1982)] On the motion of the alleged father, the court will order the parties to submit to blood tests. Such tests are only admissible in evidence where definite exclusion of the alleged father as the child's father has been established. Refusal of any party to comply with the court's order is admissible evidence. (ch. 273, § 12A)

# Education

## STATUTORY PROVISION

No one will be prevented from attending the public school of any town on account of sex. (ch. 76, § 5) Educational institutions may not, on account of sex, exclude or limit or otherwise discriminate against any person seeking admission to a course of study leading to a degree or graduate degree or so discriminate against any such student in benefits, privileges, and placement services. [ch. 151C, § 1(d)] Rights to vocational education are likewise protected. (ch. 151C, § 2A) No student may be expelled or disciplined because of marriage or pregnancy. (ch. 71, § 84)

**ENFORCEMENT:** See "Credit."

# Employment

## EQUAL PAY LAWS

No employer may discriminate in any way in the payment of wages between the sexes or pay any person in his or her employ salary or wage rates less than the rates paid to employees of the opposite sex for work of like or comparable character or work on like or comparable operations except in the case of seniority. (ch. 149, § 105A)

**ENFORCEMENT:** A person alleging an unlawful discriminatory practice may bring a civil action within 1 year of the occurrence of the alleged discriminatory practice for the recovery of the unpaid wages and an additional equal amount as liquidated damages. The judgment will also include reasonable attorney's fees and costs of the action. (ch. 149, § 105A) The employer may also be punished by a fine of not more than $100 if the employer in any manner discriminates against an employee on account of filing an action. (ch. 149, § 105A)

# FAIR EMPLOYMENT LAWS

The law applies to Massachusetts, its political and civil subdivisions, employers of six or more persons, labor organizations, and employment agencies. (ch. 151B, § 1) It prohibits the failure to hire or recruit; the discharge, limitation, segregation, or classification; the expulsion or exclusion from membership in a labor union; or the failure of an employment agency to recruit or refer an individual for employment on the basis of sex. The provisions of the law do not apply where sex is a bona fide occupational qualification or where a bona fide seniority or merit system or employee benefit plan such as a retirement pension or insurance plan exists which is not a subterfuge to evade the law. (ch. 151B, § 4)

**ENFORCEMENT:** See "Community Life: Credit."

# GOVERNMENT CONTRACTORS AND SUBCONTRACTORS

There is no relevant statutory provision. However the Governor's Code of Fair Practices § 4.1, Exec. Order No. 74, amended by Exec. Order No. 116, requires that government contractors and subcontractors must agree not to discriminate against protected classes in employment. (ch. 272, § 98B)

**ENFORCEMENT:** See "Community Life: Credit."

# VETERAN'S PREFERENCE

Veterans are given preference in public employment over all other persons. (ch. 41, § 112) The order of preference for appointment to any position in official service is (1) disabled veterans, (2) veterans, and (3) widows or widowed mothers of veterans killed in action. (ch. 31, § 26)

# Community Life

# CREDIT

It is unlawful to deny credit or adversely affect a person's credit standing on the basis of sex or marital status. [ch. 151B, § 14(14)] Furthermore, an individual is not required to use a particular name based on marital status, if generally known by another name, for any purpose including the extension of credit. [ch. 151B, § 14(15)]

**ENFORCEMENT:** Persons claiming to be aggrieved by an unlawful discriminatory practice may by themselves or by their attorney file a verified complaint in writing with the Massachusetts Commission against Discrimination within 6 months of the occurrence of the alleged discriminatory act. (ch. 151B, § 5) A civil action for damages and/or injunctive relief may also be brought in the superior or probate court for the county in which the alleged discriminatory practice occurred within 90 days after filing a complaint with the commission. The petitioner must notify the commission of the filing of the action. Once notified, the commission will dismiss the complaint without prejudice, and the petitioner will be barred from subsequently bringing a complaint on the same matter before the commission. An aggrieved person may also seek temporary injunctive relief in the superior or probate court to prevent irreparable injury during the pendency of, or before filing, a complaint with the commission. (ch. 151, § B 9)

# HOUSING

It is unlawful to discriminate on the basis of sex in the rental or sale of real property. [ch. 151B, § 4(6)]

**ENFORCEMENT:** See "Credit."

# INSURANCE

No insurance company or savings or insurance bank may issue accident or sickness insurance, disability insurance, or policies of life or endowment insurance or refuse to issue such policy or limit coverage solely on the basis of sex. (ch. 175, § 25A)

**ENFORCEMENT:** See "Credit."

# PUBLIC ACCOMMODATIONS

All persons are entitled to the full and equal accommodations, advantages, facilities, and privileges of any place of public accommodation, resort, or amusement subject only to the conditions and limitations established by law and applicable alike to all persons. Discriminatory treatment and admissions policies based on sex are prohibited. (ch. 272, § 98)

**ENFORCEMENT:** See "Credit." In addition, violation may be punished by a fine of not more than $2500 or imprisonment for not more than 1 year, or both, and civil damages may be awarded where such damages exceed $300.

# MICHIGAN

## Home and Family

## MARRIAGE

**AGE OF CONSENT:** A person 18 years of age or older may consent to marry. (§ 551.103)*

**CONSENT REQUIREMENT:** A person aged 16 or 17 years old may marry with the consent of a parent or guardian. (§ 551.103) In addition, a county probate judge may without publicity marry persons below marriageable age if the license application is accompanied by a written request of all the parents or guardians of the underage party or parties. (§ 551.201)

**LICENSE REQUIREMENT:** In order to obtain a license to marry, the parties must file with the county clerk a physician's health certificate and an affidavit attesting that they are legally competent to marry. The license is valid for 33 days after issuance. A license fee of $20 must be paid. At the request of the county clerk, a party may be required to submit a birth certificate or other proof of age. (§§ 551.103, 333.241)

**PROHIBITED MARRIAGES:** Bigamous marriages are prohibited. No person may marry his or her parent, grandparent, child, grandchild, stepparent, stepchild, grandparent's or grandchild's former spouse, niece, nephew, uncle, aunt, sibling, or first cousin. No person may marry a mentally incompetent person. (§§ 551.3 to .6)

## DISSOLUTION OF MARRIAGE

**ANNULMENT:** Factors 19, 34, and 38, listed in Appendix A, are grounds for annulment. Prohibited marriages are void without the necessity of legal process. A marriage performed while either of the parties was under the age of legal consent, where consent was obtained by force or fraud, is void unless the parties have subsequently voluntarily cohabited after attaining the age of legal consent. Children born of a void marriage are deemed legitimate. (§§ 552.1 to .3)

*Residency Requirement:* There is no relevant statutory provision.

**LEGAL SEPARATION:** An action for separate maintenance may be brought on the grounds of irretrievable breakdown of the marriage. (§ 552.7)

*Residency Requirement:* There is no relevant statutory provision.

**DIVORCE**

*Residency Requirement:* A party filing for divorce must have been a resident of the state for 180 days and a resident of the county in which the complaint is filed for 10 days. (§ 552.9)

*Grounds for Divorce:* An action for divorce may be brought when the marriage is irretrievably broken. (§ 552.6)

*Conciliation Requirement:* There is no relevant statutory provision.

*Property Distribution:* The court may make such distribution of the parties' property as it deems just and reasonable. (§ 552.19) Cases have held that the

*Unless otherwise specified, all citation references are to the Michigan Compiled Laws Annotated (1948).

factors to be considered include factors 1, 5, 19, 20, and 28, listed in Appendix F, along with the source of the property, the cause of the divorce, and each party's overall financial circumstances. [*Ripley v. Ripley*, 315 N.W.2d 576, 112 Mich. App. 219 (1982); *McAllister v. McAllister*, 300 N.W.2d 629, 101 Mich. App. 543 (1980)] A pension fund which has a reasonably ascertainable present value is a marital asset to be considered in making an equitable division of property. See *Ripley v. Ripley*.

*Child Custody:* The court may make such order regarding the custody of any minor children as it deems just and proper and in accordance with their best interests. Factors 1, 3, 4, 6, 7, 8, 9, 11, 12, and 23, listed in Appendix B. (§§ 552.16, 722.23, .25). The court may award joint custody. (§ 722.26a)

*Child Support:* The court may order child support as it deems just and proper. (§ 552.16) It may require either parent to pay such allowance as may be deemed proper for the support of each child until each child shall have attained the age of 18, and it may, in case of exceptional circumstances, require payment of such allowance for any child after he or she attains that age. [§ 552.17(a)]

*Spousal Support/Alimony:* The court may require either party to pay alimony for the suitable maintenance of the adverse party, to pay such sums as shall be deemed proper and necessary to conserve any real or personal property owned by either or both of the parties, and to pay any sums necessary to enable the adverse party to carry on or defend the action during its pendency. It may award costs against either party and award execution of same, or it may direct such costs to be paid out of any property sequestered, or in the power of the court, or in the hands of the receiver. An award of alimony may be terminated by the court on the date the party receiving alimony remarries, unless an agreement to the contrary is stated in the divorce decree. (§ 552.13)

*Enforcement of Support Orders:* Upon granting a divorce, and as part of its decree, the court may require the husband to file a bond, with one or more sureties, as a guarantee for the payment of child support. (§ 552.16) Where an allowance for the support and maintenance of minor children is awarded by the court, such an allowance constitutes the imposition of a lien upon the real and personal property of the parent owing support, and in case of delinquency in payment, the court may order the sale of such property to satisfy the court-ordered support payments. (§§ 552.27, .333) Wage and income withholding is available to enforce support obligations. §§ 551.601 *et seq.* The nonpayment of court-ordered support is punishable by a fine and/or imprisonment. (§ 552.151). See also the Uniform Reciprocal Enforcement of Support Act, §§ 780.151 *et seq.*

*Spouse's Name:* A court granting a divorce may, at the request of the woman, restore her birth name or her legal surname before the marriage was terminated, or allow her to adopt another surname, so long as there is no fraudulent intent. (§ 552.391)

*Divorce by Affidavit or Summary Judgment:* There is no relevant statutory provision.

*Displaced Homemaker Laws:* The Fitzgerald Elliot Displaced Homemakers Act provides for multipurpose service centers to offer necessary training, counseling, and education to displaced homemakers. The purpose of the services provided is to enable the displaced homemaker to become gainfully employed.(§§ 451.121 *et seq.*)

# DOMESTIC VIOLENCE

**STATUTORY PROVISION:** Domestic violence means a violent physical attack or fear of such an attack. (§ 400.1501)

**WHO IS PROTECTED?** Those protected are spouses, former spouses, any adults or emancipated minors assaulted by an adult person of the opposite sex with whom the assaulted person cohabits or formerly cohabited and with whom the assaulted person has or had a consensual sexual relationship. (§ 400.1501)

**RELIEF AVAILABLE:** A victim of domestic violence may petition a court for an order restraining or enjoining the abusing party from entering the premises; from assaulting, molesting, or wounding a named person; and from removing minor children from the person having legal custody except as otherwise authorized by a court-ordered custody or visitation order. Failure to comply with such an order is contempt of court, punishable by imprisonment for up to 90 days and a fine of up to $500. (§ 600.2950) A decree of divorce, annulment, or separate maintenance may contain these provisions and penalties for its violation. (§ 552.14) A person may be arrested without a warrant when a peace officer has reason to believe that he or she is violating such a protective order or is otherwise committing violence against a past or present spouse or cohabitant. (§§ 764.15a, .15b) A victim of domestic violence also has recourse to the criminal assault statutes. [§§ 750.81, .81(a)] A domestic violence treatment board within the Department of Social Services is empowered to coordinate, monitor, and fund programs for the prevention of domestic violence and for the provision of services to its victims, including shelters for victims and their dependent children; shelters are to provide such services as counseling, emergency health care, legal assistance, financial assistance, housing assistance, transportation assistance, and child care. (§§ 400.1501 *et seq.*)

**MARITAL RAPE:** A person may be charged with rape of a spouse only if the parties are living apart and one of them has filed for divorce or separate maintenance. (§ 750.520l)

**CIVIL LAWSUIT FOR RAPE OR ASSAULT:** Under Michigan common law, a victim of rape may recover damages in a civil suit. (*Mich. Law & Practice*, Rape, § 15)

**CHILD ABUSE:** Any parent, guardian, or other person who cruelly or unlawfully punishes a child under his or her protection; who willfully, negligently, or unlawfully deprives a child of necessities; who abandons a child under the age of 16; who habitually causes or permits the health of a child under 16 to be harmed or endangered; who causes or permits a child to engage in any occupation that will likely endanger his or her health or morals; who habitually permits a child to beg in public places or consort with reputed prostitutes or thieves; or who by vicious training depraves the morals of a child is guilty of a felony. (§ 750.136)

> *Notification Requirement:* All medical professionals, social workers, school personnel, law enforcement officers, and regulated child care providers who have reasonable cause to suspect child abuse or neglect must immediately report such suspicion to the Department of Social Services. A hospital may detain a child, if there is suspicion of child abuse or neglect and the attending physician determines that release would endanger the child's health or welfare. (§§ 722.623, .626)

# INHERITANCE RIGHTS

**FAILURE TO MAKE A WILL:** The surviving spouse inherits the entire estate if the decedent left no surviving issue or parents. If the decedent left no surviving issue but was survived by at least one parent, the surviving spouse inherits the first $60,000 and half of the balance of the estate. If there are surviving issue, all of whom are also the issue of the surviving spouse, the surviving spouse inherits the first $60,000 and half of the balance of the estate. If there are surviving issue, at least one of whom is not also the issue of the surviving spouse, the surviving spouse inherits half of the estate. (§ 700.105) Alternatively, a woman may elect to take her dower right of one-third of her deceased husband's lands for her life.

**FAILURE TO PROVIDE BY WILL:** There is no relevant statutory provision.

**CHILDREN BORN OUT OF WEDLOCK:** A child born out of wedlock is the heir of each of the natural parents, regardless of the parents' relationship to each other. A man is considered the natural father of a child even though he is not married to the child's mother if (1) the man and the mother have jointly acknowledged his paternity, (2) the man and the mother have joined in a written request resulting in correction of the child's birth certificate to reflect the man's paternity, or (3) the man and the child have had a mutually acknowledged relationship of father and child which began before the child reached the age of 18 and continued until the death of either. (§§ 700.110, .111)

**HOMESTEAD, PERSONAL, AND FAMILY ALLOWANCES:** The surviving spouse is entitled to a homestead allowance of $10,000. If there is no surviving spouse, each minor child of the decedent is entitled to receive a homestead allowance in the amount of $10,000 divided by the number of minor children of the decedent. (§ 700.285) The surviving spouse (or surviving minor children jointly, if there is no surviving spouse) is also entitled to receive up to $3500 worth of household furniture, appliances, and personal effects. If such exempt property has a value of less than $3500 the surviving spouse (or minor children) is entitled to receive other assets of the estate up to a value of $3500. In addition, the surviving spouse and dependent legal children are entitled to a reasonable family allowance from the estate for their maintenance during the settlement of the estate or for 1 year, whichever period is shorter. (§ 700.287) The surviving spouse may remain in the dwelling house of the decedent for 1 year after the decedent's death or until the surviving spouse's share of the estate is assigned to him or her, whichever period is shorter. During this period, the surviving spouse shall not be chargeable with rent, taxes, water bills, repairs (except those necessitated by the surviving spouse's own act or omission), insurance premiums, or payments of principal or interest due under a mortgage or land-sale contract. (§ 700.288)

**OPTION TO DISREGARD THE WILL:** The surviving spouse of a decedent who has left a will may elect to take half of the share that would have passed to the spouse had the decedent died without a will or, if a woman, take her dower right to one-third of her deceased husband's lands for her life. (§§ 558.1 *et seq.*)

# REPRODUCTIVE RIGHTS

## ABORTION

*Statutory Provisions:* Existing statutory law makes performance of an abortion a felony, unless necessary to preserve the life of the woman. (§ 750.14) The Michigan Supreme Court has found the statute constitutional by reading into the statute all exceptions required by U.S. Supreme Court decisions. [*People v. Bricker*, 208 N.W.2d 172 (Mich. 1973)

*Consent Requirement:* There is no relevant statutory provision.

*Reporting Requirements:* There is no relevant statutory provision.

## BIRTH CONTROL

*Sale and Distribution of Contraceptives:* The United States Court of Appeals for the Sixth Circuit has held that a publicly operated family planning center does not violate the constitutional rights of parents by furnishing contraceptives to minor children without notification to or consent of the parents. [*Doe v. Irwin*, 615 F.2d 1162, *cert. denied*, 449 U.S. 829 (1980)]

**Family Planning Programs:** The state health commissioner and local health boards and departments are authorized to inform indigent women of the availability of family planning services but may not urge women to use or not to use such services. The Department of Mental Health is authorized to inform any person receiving its mental health services of the availability of family planning services and, upon request, to provide family planning education and information. [§ 400.14(b)] Local school boards may offer a program in sex education which includes birth control information. But no birth control drug or device may be distributed through the public schools. Sex education may be offered only on an elective basis, and no pupil may be enrolled in a class discussing birth control unless his or her parents have received advance notice of the content of the course, an opportunity to review the course materials, and notice of their right to have the pupil excused from the class. (§§ 380.1507, .1508)

**STERILIZATION:** There is no relevant statutory provision.

# UNMARRIED COUPLES

**COMMON-LAW MARRIAGE:** Common-law marriages are not valid if entered into after January 1, 1957. (§ 551.27) But Michigan does recognize as valid common-law marriages entered into in accordance with the laws of states which do allow common-law marriage. [*Matter of Brack's Estate*, 329 N.W.2d 432 (Mich. 1982)]

**COHABITAL RELATIONSHIPS:** Any man and woman not married to each other who cohabit are guilty of a misdemeanor. (§ 750.335) Nonetheless, an express agreement between cohabitants to divide money and property which they accumulate during their period of cohabitation is enforceable so long as the agreement was independent of their meretricious relationship. [*Tyranski v. Piggins*, 205 N.W.2d 595 (Mich. 1973)]

## CHILDREN

*Custody:* If the putative father appears at a hearing to terminate his parental rights and requests custody of the child, the court shall inquire into his fitness and his ability to properly care for the child and shall determine whether the best interests of the child will be served by granting custody to him. If the court finds that it would not be in the best interests of the child to grant custody to the putative father, the court shall terminate his rights to the child. If the putatuve father has established a custodial relationship with the child or has provided support or care for the mother during pregnancy or for either mother or child after the child's birth during the 90 days before notice of the hearing was served upon him, the rights of the putative father shall not be terminated except where the putative father has either failed or neglected to support the child for a period of 2 years or has failed to visit, contact, or communicate with the child for 2 years. (§§ 7120.39, .51)

*Legitimation Proceedings:* A child born out of wedlock is legitimated if, before the child's birth, the man claiming under oath to be the father files a verified notice of intent to claim paternity with the court in any county of the state. After receipt of the notice, the court transmits it to the vital records division of the Department of Public Health. A man filing such a notice is presumed to be the child's father, and the notice creates a rebuttable presumption as to paternity of the child for purposes of dependency and neglect proceedings. (§ 710.33)

*Paternity Proceedings:* An action to establish paternity may be brought by the mother, the putative father, or the Department of Social Services. Such an action may be brought at any time during pregnancy or within 6 years of the child's birth. If the putative father has made any support payments within the first 6 years of the child's life, an action may be brought within 6 years of the last such payment. Any time during which the defendant was out of the state shall not be counted toward the statutory 6 years. The court shall, on motion of either party or on its own motion, order tissue-typing tests on the mother, the father, and the child, the results of which shall be admissible at trial. (§§ 722.711 *et seq.*)

*Obligations of the Putative Father:* When the putative father's paternity has been established or admitted, the court shall issue an order of filiation declaring paternity and requiring the father to make specified payments for the child's support and education; for the necessary expenses incurred by or for the mother in connection with her confinement; for the support of the child before the order of filiation; and for such expenses in connection with the pregnancy of the mother or the paternity proceedings as the court deems proper. (§ 722.712)

# Education

## STATUTORY PROVISION

Educational institutions fall within the legal definition of places of public accommodation which are forbidden to discriminate on the basis of sex or marital status. (§§ 37.2301, .2302) In addition, discrimination by a public or private educational institution on the basis of sex is prohibited. The prohibition against discrimination on the basis of sex does not apply to private single-sex educational institutions. But single-sex public schools or their departments are prohibited. (§§ 37.2401, .2402; 380.1146)

## AREAS COVERED

Areas covered include admission, expulsion, and all services, activities, and programs; all noncontact interscholastic sports; and pregnancy. (§§ 37.2402; 380.1289, .1301)

**ENFORCEMENT:** See "Housing."

# Employment

## EQUAL PAY LAWS

It is unlawful for any employer of two or more employees to pay employees of one sex at a rate less than that paid to employees of the opposite sex for work which requires equal skill, effort, and responsibility and which is performed under similar working conditions. The law does not apply where the wage differentials occur as a result of a seniority or merit system, a system based on quantity or quality of production, or any factor other than sex. (§ 408.397)

**ENFORCEMENT:** An aggrieved employee may bring a civil action or file a complaint. The civil action must be brought within 3 years of the discriminatory act for the amount by which the employee was underpaid and an equal additional amount as liquidated damages, along with costs and reasonable attorney's fees. The complaint must be filed with the director of the Department of Labor, who, upon finding that there is reasonable cause to believe that a violation has occurred, may seek voluntary compliance by the employer. If voluntary compliance cannot be obtained, the director may bring a civil action for the same remedies enumerated above. (§ 408.393)

# FAIR EMPLOYMENT LAWS

It is unlawful for the state, its political and civil subdivision, or any employer, labor organization, or employment agency to discriminate on the basis of sex, marital status, or other protected characteristics. Prohibited discrimination includes failure to hire or recruit; discharge; the limitation, segregation, or classification of an employee or applicant that in any way tends to deprive him or her of an employment opportunity or otherwise affects his or her status; the refusal by an employment agency to procure, refer, recruit, or place for employment; the expulsion or exclusion from membership by a labor union; and publication of any notice, advertisement, or sign indicating a preference for a particular sex. Discrimination on the basis of sex includes sexual harassment when such harassment is made, implicitly or explicitly, a term or condition of employment; when submission to or rejection of such harassment is a factor in the making of decisions affecting an individual's employment; or when such harassment has the purpose or effect of substantially interfering with an individual's employment; or of creating an intimidating, hostile, or offensive work environment. The law does not apply where sex is a bona fide occupational qualification. (§§ 37.2103, .2201 *et seq.*)

**ENFORCEMENT:** See "Community Life: Housing."

# GOVERNMENT CONTRACTORS AND SUBCONTRACTORS

A contract to which the state or an agency or political subdivision thereof is a party must contain a covenant by the contractor and any subcontractors not to discriminate in employment on the basis of sex, marital status, or other protected characteristics. (§ 37.2209)

**ENFORCEMENT:** See "Community Life: Housing." In addition, violation of the required nondiscrimination covenant may be regarded as a material breach of the contract, creating in the state or the agency or political subdivision of the state the power of termination. (§ 37.2209)

# STATE EMPLOYEE LAWS

The state and all its agencies and political subdivisions are included among the employers who may not discriminate on the basis of sex, marital status, and other protected characteristics. (§§ 37.2103 *et seq.*)

**ENFORCEMENT:** See "Community Life: Housing."

# VETERAN'S PREFERENCE

Honorably discharged veterans are to be preferred for employment by any public department and on any public works project of the state and any county or municipal subdivision thereof, provided that the applicant has been a resident of the state for at least 2 years and a resident of the county where the job is located for at least 1 year, is of good moral character, and has any other requisite qualifications. No veteran in any public department or on any public work, except high-ranking political appointees, may be removed, suspended, or transferred without his or her consent, except for official misconduct, neglect of duty, extortion, conviction of intoxication or of a felony, or incompetency (after a hearing following written notice of the charges). (§§ 35.401 *et seq.*)

# Community Life

## CREDIT

It is unlawful to discriminate on the basis of sex, marital status, or other protected characteristics in the granting of credit or a loan or in the rating of a person's creditworthiness. This prohibition does not apply to nonprofit corporations whose members share the same protected characteristics or blend of such characteristics and grants credit or loans only to their members. (§ 750.147a)

> **ENFORCEMENT:** A violation of this law is a misdemeanor punishable by a fine of up to $1000. A party violating the law is also liable to the injured party in a civil action for $200 or actual damage, whichever is greater. Damages in a class action are limited to $200 per injured party. The prevailing party in a civil action is entitled to recover court costs and reasonable attorney's fees. (§ 750.147a)

## HOUSING

It is unlawful for persons engaged in real estate transactions to discriminate on the basis of sex, marital status, or other protected characteristics in the sale or rental of housing or other real estate. This prohibition does not apply to the rental of housing accommodations in a building of two housing units where one unit is occupied by the lessor or a member of the lessor's immediate family; nor does it apply to the rental of a housing unit for 1 year or less by an owner or lessor who has occupied it for at least 3 months immediately preceding the rental in question and maintains it as his or her legal residence while temporarily vacating. (§§ 37.2501 *et seq.*)

> **ENFORCEMENT:** Persons who feel aggrieved by a discriminatory practice may file a written, verified complaint with the Department of Civil Rights, which will receive, initiate, conciliate, adjust, dispose of, issue charges, and hold hearings on the complaint and approve or disapprove plans to correct past discriminatory practices. (§ 37.2102) Alternatively, persons alleging unlawful discriminatory practices may bring a civil action for appropriate injunctive relief or damages or both and reasonable attorney's fees. (§ 37.2801) The court may also award all or a portion of the costs of litigation and witness fees. (§ 37.2802) The action must be brought within 3 years of the occurrence of the alleged discriminatory act. [§ 600.5805(8)]

## INSURANCE

Prohibited unfair insurance practices include the refusal to issue or the limiting of the amount of insurance available to any person on the basis of sex, marital status, and other protected characteristics. Charging a different rate for the same coverage on the basis of sex, marital status, and other protected characteristics is not an unfair practice (1) if the rate differential is based on sound actuarial principles and a reasonable classification system and is related to the actual and credible loss statistics, or reasonably anticipated experience in the case of new coverages, or (2) if the rate has been approved by the state insurance commissioner. (§ 500.2027)

**ENFORCEMENT:** The Bureau of Insurance investigates all charges of unfair practice in the insurance industry. If after a hearing the bureau determines that one or more unfair practices have occurred, the commissioner may impose fines, order refunds of any overcharges, and, if the violator knowingly and persistently committed unfair practices, may suspend or revoke the violator's license or certificate of authority. (§§ 500.2028 *et seq.*)

# PUBLIC ACCOMMODATIONS

It is unlawful to deny any individual the full and equal enjoyment of the goods, services, facilities, privileges, advantages, or accommodations of a place of public accommodation or public service on the basis of sex, marital status, or other protected characteristics or to indicate by any notice, sign, or advertisement that any person will be denied such equal enjoyment or that any person's patronage is unwelcome on the basis of sex, marital status, or other protected characteristics. These prohibitions do not apply to a private club or establishment not in fact open to the public, except to the extent that the goods, services, facilities, privileges, advantages, or accommodations of the private club or establishment are made available to the customers or patrons of another establishment that is a place of public accommodation or holds a state liquor license. (§§ 37.2301 *et seq.*)

**ENFORCEMENT:** See "Housing."

# MINNESOTA

## Home and Family

## MARRIAGE

**AGE OF CONSENT:** Every person who is 18 years or older may enter into a valid marriage. (§ 517.02)*

**CONSENT REQUIREMENT:** A person who is under 18 but at least 16 years of age may marry with parental consent and after the judge of the juvenile court in which the person resides has approved the application for a marriage license. (§ 517.02)

**LICENSE REQUIREMENT:** Applications for marriage must state the parties' full names, addresses, ages, and address after marriage if either party has previously been married. [§ 517.05(1a)] Applications should be filed with the clerk of county district court. (§ 517.07) The license is valid for 6 months from the date of issuance [§ 517.08(1b)]

**PROHIBITED MARRIAGES:** Marriages between a person and his or her ancestor, descendant, brother, sister, uncle, aunt, first cousin, nephew, or niece are prohibited as incestuous, unless permitted by customs of aborigine cultures. [§ 517.03(b), (c)] Bigamous marriages are prohibited. [§ 517.03(a)]

## DISSOLUTION OF MARRIAGE

**ANNULMENT:** Factors 32, 33, 34, and 36, listed in Appendix A, are grounds for annulment.

*Residency Requirement:* There is no relevant statutory provision.

**LEGAL SEPARATION:** A legal separation will be granted if the court finds that the parties need a legal separation. (§ 518.06)

*Residency Requirement:* One of the parties must have resided in or been a domiciliary of the state for not less than 6 months before action is commenced. (§ 518.07)

### DIVORCE

*Residency Requirement:* See "Legal Separation."

*Grounds for Divorce:* If the marriage has been irrevocably broken, the parties may file for a divorce. (§ 518.06)

*Conciliation Requirement:* There is no relevant statutory provision.

*Property Distribution:* Marital property is divided equitably between the parties without regard to fault. In making the division, the court will consider factors 1, 3, 5, 6, 7, 8, 9, 10, 11, 15, and 20, listed in Appendix F. (§ 518.58)

*Child Custody:* If child custody is to be awarded to only one parent, it will be awarded according to the best interests of the child. The child's cultural background, and factors 3, 4, 6, 8, 10, 11, 12, 14, 15, 17, 23, and 24, listed in Appendix B, are considered. (§ 518.17) The Minnesota Supreme Court held in *Pikula v. Piklua*, 374 S.W.2d 705 (Minn. 1985) that when both parents seek custody of a child

---

*Unless otherwise specified, all citation references are to the Minnesota Statutes Annotated (West 1946).

too young to express a preference, custody should be awarded to the "primary caretaker." If joint custody is sought, the court will consider dispute resolution methods and the effect of one parent having custody, as well as the factors listed above and factor 1, listed in Appendix C. [§ 518.17(2)]

*Child Support:* In determining the amount of child support due, the court will consider factors 1, 2, 3, 4, and 5, listed in Appendix D. [§ 518.17(4)]

*Spousal Support/Alimony:* The court may award maintenance to either party based on consideration of the sacrifices a homemaker has made in terms of earnings, employment, experience, and opportunities, and factors 1, 2, 3, 4, 5, 6, 10, 11, 13, and 14, listed in Appendix E. (§ 518.552)

*Enforcement of Support Orders:* Support orders may be enforced by means of appointing a trustee or attaching the salary of the nonpaying spouse. (§§ 518.61, .611) Failure to provide support for more than 90 days constitutes a felony punishable by up to 5 years in prison [§ 609.375(2)]

*Spouse's Name:* The court shall consent to a request by either party to a name change, unless intent to defraud or mislead is found. (§ 518.27)

*Divorce by Affidavit or Summary Judgment:* There is no relevant statutory provision.

*Displaced Homemaker Laws:* There is no relevant statutory provision.

# DOMESTIC VIOLENCE

**STATUTORY PROVISION:** It is prohibited to abuse a family or household member, inflict physical harm, place another in fear of immediate physical harm, or inflict criminal sexual conduct or intrafamilial sexual abuse on a minor. [§ 518B.01(2b)]

**WHO IS PROTECTED?** A spouse, former spouse, parents, children, blood relatives, present and past cohabitants, and persons who have had a child together are protected. [§ 518B.01(2b)]

**RELIEF AVAILABLE:** A victim of domestic abuse may obtain the following relief: a restraining order, an order barring the abuser from entering the petitioner's residence; temporary custody or child visitation orders; an order granting temporary spousal or child support and withholding income of the abuser; counseling or other social services; an order directing the abuser to obtain treatment; and a directive to the police to protect the petitioner. [§ 518B.01(6)] Police officers may arrest the abuser without a warrant if probable cause exists to believe that domestic violence has occurred. (§§ 629.341, .72)

**MARITAL RAPE:** A woman may not charge her spouse with rape unless the couple is living apart and a petition for separation or divorce has been filed. (§ 609.349)

**CIVIL LAWSUIT FOR RAPE OR ASSAULT:** There is no statutory or court decision directly on this point. However, in *Beaudette v. Frana*, 285 Minn. 366, 173 N.W.2d 416 (1969), the court held that one spouse can sue another for injuries if they were caused by "plainly excessive" conduct or constituted a "gross abuse of normal privilege."

**CHILD ABUSE:** See "Statutory Provisions." Also the criminal code makes it a crime for an adult to sexually abuse a minor family member. (§§ 609.341 *et seq.*)

*Notification Requirement:* All medical, professional, social services, hospital personnel, education, and law enforcement employees must report suspected cases of child abuse to the local welfare agency, police department, or county sheriff. The local welfare agency must investigate all reported cases and seek authority to remove the child if necessary. (§ 626.556)

# INHERITANCE RIGHTS

**FAILURE TO MAKE A WILL:** The surviving spouse is entitled to the entire estate if the decedent left no other heirs; to one-half of the personal property and real property if the decedent left only one child; to one-third of the real and personal property if the decedent left more than one child. (§ 525.16)

**FAILURE TO PROVIDE BY WILL:** Dower and curtesy have been abolished.

**CHILDREN BORN OUT OF WEDLOCK:** A child born out of wedlock may inherit through the mother as if the mother had been married. The child may inherit from the father only if the father declared himself to be the child's father in writing before a witness or if paternity was established by a court.

**HOMESTEAD, PERSONAL, AND FAMILY ALLOWANCES:** The homestead shall descend directly to the spouse if there are no children. If there are children, the homestead shall descend to the spouse for the duration of the spouse's life. (§ 525.145) The spouse is entitled to clothing, furniture, and household goods up to $6000 and to real personal property up to $3000. During the probate of the will, the spouse is entitled to receive support upon filing a request with the court within 18 months of the death. (§ 525.15)

**OPTION TO DISREGARD THE WILL:** The surviving spouse may disregard the will and take the share she or he would have received had there been no will, except that this share should not exceed one-half of the estate. If the decedent is survived by one or more children or by one or more grandchildren, the spouse's share is limited to one-third of the estate. (§ 525.214)

# REPRODUCTIVE RIGHTS

## ABORTION

*Statutory Provisions:* Abortions are legal if performed by a doctor before the eighteenth week of the gestation period. Abortions are legal after the eighteenth week only if it is necessary to preserve the life of the mother. (§ 145.412) Note that this provision is in conflict with the Supreme Court ruling in *Roe v. Wade*.

*Consent Requirements:* The consent of the woman is required after she has been fully apprised of the procedure and its effects. [§ 145.412(4)]

*Reporting Requirements:* The Commissioner of Health shall establish rules to obtain statistical data on the number of abortions. The death of a woman within 30 days of an abortion must be reported to the Health Commission. (§ 145.413)

**BIRTH CONTROL:** Contraceptives may be sold by qualified health and welfare organizations. (§ 617.251) A person under 18 years of age who is independent from his or her parents may consent to any medical or health services without parental approval. (§ 144.341) A person under 18 may give consent, without the necessity of parental approval, to medical or health services if the person has a child or to diagnosis and treatment of pregnancy and venereal disease. (§§ 144.341 to .343)

**STERILIZATION:** It is a misdemeanor for any employee of a state agency or any employee of a private agency that is funded by the state to coerce a recipient of benefits to undergo sterilization. (§ 145.925)

# UNMARRIED COUPLES

**COMMON-LAW MARRIAGE:** Common-law marriages are valid only if entered into before April 26, 1941. (§ 517.01)

**COHABITAL RELATIONSHIPS:** In *Abbott v. Abbott*, 282 N.W.2d 561 (1979) the court held that the imposition of a support obligation upon a party to a nonmarital relationship would violate public policy. However, in *Carlson v. Olson*, 256 N.W.2d 249 (1977), the court held that it had the power to equally distribute the property acquired during a nonmarital relationship because the couple had lived together for 2 years, raised a child, and held property as joint tenants.

## CHILDREN

*Custody:* The mother of a child born out of wedlock shall have sole custody. A father who acknowledges paternity may petition the court for visitation or custody.

*Legitimation Proceedings:* The parent-child relationship extends equally to every child and to every parent, regardless of marital status. See the Uniform Parentage Act, § 257.42.

*Paternity Proceedings:* A child, the natural mother, or a man presumed to be the father may bring an action to determine the existence of a father-child relationship. The action must be brought within 3 years of the child's birth. [§ 257.57(b)] A child can bring a paternity action until 1 year after she or he reaches the age of 18. (§ 257.58)

*Obligations of the Putative Father:* The court may make provision for the child's support, custody, name, visitation, and other matters in the best interests of the child. In determining the amount of support, the court will consider factors 1, 2, 3, 4, 6, 10, and 11, listed in Appendix E. (§ 257.66)

# Education

# STATUTORY PROVISION

Under the Minnesota Human Rights Act it is unlawful to deny a person the full utilization or benefit of any educational institution because of sex or marital status. It is also unlawful to deny a student admission or to expel or exclude a student because of sex or marital status. [§ 363.03(5)] Sexual harassment is also forbidden. (§ 363.01) Single-sex schools are exempt. [§ 363.02(3)] It is also not a violation to provide separate athletic teams for each sex. [§ 363.02(3)] The Education Law requires that members of both sexes be afforded equal access to athletic programs. (§ 126.21)

# AREAS COVERED

The Minnesota Human Rights Act applies to all public and private colleges, elementary and secondary school, extension courses, kindergartens, nursery schools, and business, nursing, professional, secretarial and vocational schools. [§ 363.01(20)] The Education Law applies to the public school system.

**ENFORCEMENT:** Violations of the Minnesota Human Rights Act are handled by the Minnesota Department of Human Rights. Complaints alleging a violation of the Education Law should be filed with the Board of Education. [§ 126.21(5)]

# Employment

## EQUAL PAY LAWS

It is unlawful to discriminate on the basis of sex in wages paid to employees who perform work requiring equal skill, effort, and responsibility under similar working conditions. Wage differentials based on a seniority system, merit system, or the quantity or quality of production do not violate the act. [§ 181.67(1)]

> **ENFORCEMENT:** Victims of discrimination may file a lawsuit. If successful they will recover the amount of unpaid wages for 1 year before the filing of a complaint. Attorney's fees are also recoverable.

## FAIR EMPLOYMENT LAWS

The Minnesota Human Rights Act prohibits sex discrimination (including sexual harassment) and discrimination based on pregnancy or marital status in hiring, firing, promotion, testing, and other terms and conditions of employment. Labor unions and employment agencies also may not discriminate on the basis of sex. [§ 363.02(1)]

> **ENFORCEMENT:** Complaints should be filed with the Minnesota Department of Human Rights within 300 days of the act of discrimination.

## GOVERNMENT CONTRACTORS AND SUBCONTRACTORS

There is no relevant statutory provision. However, it should be noted that if federal funds are involved, Exec. Order No. 11246, 3 C.F.R. 339, *reprinted* in 42 U.S.C. § 2000e app. at 1232, 41 C.F.R. § 60-1.2, may apply.

## STATE EMPLOYEE LAWS

See "Fair Employment Laws." The Minnesota Human Rights Act applies to state employees. [§ 363.01(7)] State and municipal employees are also covered by the Comparable Worth Law, which requires that equal wages be paid to employees who perform work of comparable value. The law requires that public entities establish equitable compensation rates between female-dominated and male-dominated classes of employees by August 1, 1987. (§ 471.991)

> **ENFORCEMENT:** After August 1, 1987, a woman who receives less money than a man who performs a job of comparable worth may file an action in court. Public employees who are victims of discrimination under the Minnesota Human Rights Act should file a complaint with the state Department of Human Rights within 300 days of the act of discrimination.

## VETERAN'S PREFERENCE

Ten points are added to the passing civil service exam scores of disabled veterans; five points are added to the promotional civil service exam scores of disabled veterans.

Five points are added to the passing civil service exam scores of able-bodied veterans. (§ 43.30)

# Community Life

## CREDIT

Discrimination on the basis of sex in the extension of credit is prohibited. [§ 363.03(8)]

> **ENFORCEMENT:** A person who has been denied credit because of his or her sex may file a complaint with the Minnesota Department of Human Rights within 300 days of the denial. (§ 363.06)

## HOUSING

It is unlawful to refuse to sell, rent, or lease property to a person because of his or her sex. It is also illegal to discriminate in the terms, conditions, or privileges pertaining to housing. Real estate brokers and agents are also barred from sex discrimination. [§ 363.03(2)] Banks and financial institutions may not discriminate on the basis of sex in extending mortgages or other housing financing. [§ 363.03(3)]

> **ENFORCEMENT:** Any person who has been the victim of discrimination in housing should file a complaint within 300 days of the discriminatory act with the Minnesota Department of Human Rights. (§ 363.06)

## INSURANCE

There is no relevant statutory provision.

## PUBLIC ACCOMMODATIONS

It is unlawful for any person to deny the full and equal enjoyment of the goods, services, facilities, privileges, advantages, or accommodations of a public accommodation on the basis of sex. [§ 363.03(3)]

> **ENFORCEMENT:** A complaint should be filed with the Minnesota Department of Human Rights within 300 days of the occurrence. (§ 363.06)

# MISSISSIPPI

## Home and Family

## MARRIAGE

**AGE OF CONSENT:** Males 17 years of age or older and females 15 years of age or older may marry without parental consent. [§ 93-1-5(d)]*

**CONSENT REQUIREMENT:** Parental consent is required if the male is under 17 years of age or the female is under 15 years of age. [§ 93-1-5(d)]

**LICENSE REQUIREMENT:** A license, issued by the circuit court clerk, is required. (§ 93-1-13) An application for a license must be filed with the circuit court clerk, and the parties must wait 3 days, during which time the application remains on file and open to the public, before a marriage license may be issued. [§ 93-1-5(b)] The application may be filed with any circuit court unless the woman is under 21, in which case the application must be filed in the circuit court of her county of residence. [§ 93-1-5(a)] The parties applying for the license must also present a medical certificate stating that the applicants are free from syphilis. [§ 93-1-5(e)]

**PROHIBITED MARRIAGES:** Marriages between a man and his grandmother, mother, or stepmother; between a father and his daughter or legally adopted daughter; between a man and his stepsister (when they have the same father) or aunt (his father's or mother's sister); or between first cousins by blood are declared incestuous and void. Also incestuous and void are marriages between a father and his son's widow; between a man and his wife's daughter or his wife's granddaughter; or between a man and his niece by blood. These provisions apply equally to females. (§ 93-1-1) Bigamous marriages are also prohibited and deemed void. (§ 93-7-1)

## DISSOLUTION OF MARRIAGE

**ANNULMENT:** Factors 3, 10, 19, 32, 33, 35, 36, and 38, listed in Appendix A, are considered grounds for annulment. Also considered is the failure of the parties to comply with the marriage license requirements, provided the parties did not cohabit after the marriage. Suits for annulment based on factors 10, 32, 33, 35, 36, must be brought within 6 months after the particular grounds for annulment are or should be discovered. (§ 93-7-3)

*Residency Requirement:* There is no relevant statutory provision. However, a bill for annulment must be filed in the county where the defendant resides, in the county where the marriage license was issued, or the county where the complainant resides if the defendant is a nonresident. (§ 93-7-9)

**LEGAL SEPARATION:** There is no relevant statutory provision.

**DIVORCE**

*Residency Requirement:* A person filing for divorce must be a resident for 6 months before commencing a suit for divorce. If stationed in the state at the time the couple separates, a member of the armed forces and his or her spouse shall

---

*Unless otherwise specified, all citation references are to the Mississippi Code Annotated (1972).

be considered a resident of the state for purposes of filing for divorce. However, in any case where the proof shows that residence was acquired for the purpose of securing a divorce, the complaint will be dismissed at the cost of the complainant. (§ 93-5-5)

**Grounds for Divorce:** Factors 3, 4, 6, 8, 9 (3 years before divorce petition), 10, 16 (for 1 year), 17, 22, 36, and 38, listed in Appendix A, are grounds for divorce. (§ 93-5-1) No divorce on grounds of irreconcilable differences will be granted if the divorce is contested or denied (unless the contest or denial has been withdrawn by the party asserting it), and unless the court is satisfied that adequate child custody, maintenance, and property distribution arrangements have been made by the parties by a written agreement. (§ 93-5-2) All bills for divorce must be accompanied by an affidavit stating there has been no collusion between the parties. (§ 93-5-7)

**Conciliation Requirement:** There is no relevant statutory provision.

**Property Distribution:** There is no relevant statutory provision.

**Child Custody:** Child custody is awarded by the court as it deems equitable and just and according to the best interests of the child. (§§ 93-5-23, -24) The court may award joint physical and legal custody to one or both parents, physical custody to both parents and legal custody to one parent, legal custody to both parents and physical custody to one parent, or custody to a third party if the court finds that the child's parents have abandoned the child or are otherwise unfit to raise the child. Where both parents agree to joint physical and legal custody, there is a presumption that joint custody is in the best interests of the child. (§ 93-5-24) Joint custody may be awarded upon application by both parties where irreconcilable differences are the grounds for divorce; in other cases, joint custody may be awarded upon the application of one parent. In all cases the award of joint custody is a matter of the discretion of the court. (§ 93-5-24) Finally, in suits for custody in which the court finds that both parties are fit to care for and adequately provide for the child, and the child is 12 years of age or older, the child may choose the parent with whom he or she wishes to live. (§ 93-11-65)

**Child Support:** The court will designate the responsibility for the support of the child as it deems equitable and just. (§ 93-5-23) Where both parents have separate incomes or estates, the court may require each parent to contribute to the support of the child in proportion to the relative financial ability of each parent. (§ 93-11-64) Legally responsible parents who have health insurance coverage may be required to provide additional coverage in favor of the child. (§ 93-11-65)

**Spousal Support/Alimony:** Alimony may be awarded to either spouse as the court deems equitable and just. (§ 93-5-23) The court may review the award of alimony at any time upon a showing of changed circumstances. [*Smith v. Necaise*, 357 So. 2d 931 (Miss. 1978)] Remarriage of the party to whom alimony is owed will terminate the obligation. [*East v. Collins*, 12 So. 2d 133 (Miss. 1943)]

**Enforcement of Support Orders:** Support obligations are enforceable by wages and income withholding; by a judgment in the amount due and owing, which becomes a lien upon all property of the judgment debtor; or by the posting of a bond or other security to ensure future payments. (§§ 93-5-23, -11-65, 11-71, -11-103) The Mississippi Department of Public Welfare will collect and disburse support payments to the party entitled to receive such support. (§ 43-19-31) Federal law provides for the interception of federal income tax refunds to be applied toward support obligations. [26 U.S.C.A. § 6402(c)] Child support obligations may also be withheld from unemployment compensation benefits. (§ 71-5-516) A court's child support order may require the parent to obtain health insurance for the child. (§ 93-5-23) In addition, failure to obey a child support order is punishable by contempt proceedings. (§ 43-23-19) See also the Uniform Reciprocal Enforcement of Support Law, § 93-11-1 *et seq*.

*Spouse's Name:* There is no relevant statutory provision. However, in general any person may petition the court for a legal name change. (§ 93-17-1)

*Divorce by Affidavit or Summary Judgment:* There is no relevant statutory provision.

*Displaced Homemaker Laws:* There is no relevant statutory provision.

# DOMESTIC VIOLENCE

**STATUTORY PROVISION:** Domestic abuse prohibited by statute consists of intentionally, knowingly, or recklessly causing or attempting to cause bodily injury or serious bodily injury with or without a weapon, or placing another in fear of imminent serious bodily injury by physical menace or threat. [§§ 93-21-3(a)(i), (ii)] In addition, criminal sexual conduct committed against a child constitutes domestic abuse. [§ 93-21-3(a)(iii)]

**WHO IS PROTECTED?** Persons, including spouses, former spouses, parents and children, or other persons related by blood or marriage who currently reside or formerly resided in the same household as the abuser are protected. [§ 93-21-3(a), (d)]

**RELIEF AVAILABLE:** A person seeking relief from domestic violence may file a petition in the chancery court to request one or more protective orders. [§ 93-21-9(1)(d)] The court may grant any protective order directing the defendant to refrain from the abuse; grant the possession of the residence to the petitioner and exclude the other spouse; award temporary custody, visitation, and child support; order the defendant to pay the complaining spouse for losses incurred by the abuse, including medical expenses, lost earnings or support, moving expenses, and attorney's fees; order one or both parties to obtain counseling or medical treatment; and prohibit the transfer of mutually owned property by one of the spouses. (§ 93-21-15) Any such orders or any consent agreement to the same effect shall not remain in effect for more than 1 year. (§ 93-21-17) The above orders may also be issued in *ex parte* proceedings when the petitioner alleges that there is immediate and present danger to the petitioner or to minor children. Orders issued on an *ex parte* basis may not remain in effect for longer than 10 days, unless the petitioner asks for an extension of the order, in which case it may be extended for an additional 20 days. (§ 93-21-13) Domestic violence shelters are available in Mississippi. (§§ 93-21-101 *et seq*.) The shelters that receive state funding must provide temporary food and housing; counseling; referrals for community services, legal assistance, and medical care; counseling for the victim and the offender; and information regarding job counseling, housing referrals, and other social services. (§ 93-21-107)

**MARITAL RAPE:** A woman may charge her husband with sexual battery if, at the time of the alleged offense, the parties were living separate and apart. (§ 97-3-99)

**CIVIL LAWSUIT FOR RAPE OR ASSAULT:** Spouses may sue each other, but not for personal injuries inflicted by one upon the other. [§ 93-3-3; *Tobias v. Tobias*, 683 So. 2d 638 (Miss. 1955)]

**CHILD ABUSE:** See "Statutory Provision." A law enforcement officer or an agent of the Department of Public Welfare may take a child into custody without a court order if he or she believes the child is in immediate danger of personal harm; otherwise, a court order is necessary to take a child into custody. (§ 43-21-303) A judge of the youth court may, upon a finding that a child has been the victim of abuse, give legal custody of the child to the Department of Public Welfare or any other private or public organization equipped to educate, care for, and maintain the child (§ 43-21-609); or the judge may order the parent or guardian of the child to stop abusing or neglecting the child. (§ 43-21-617)

> *Notification Requirement:* Any attorney, health care worker, school personnel, social worker, child care giver, minister, or law enforcement officer who has reasonable cause to suspect that a child is neglected or abused is required to report such suspicions to the Department of Public Welfare. (§ 43-21-353)

# INHERITANCE RIGHTS

**FAILURE TO MAKE A WILL:** The surviving spouse is entitled to the entire estate if there are no surviving children or to a share equal to that of each child if there are children or descendants. (§ 91-1-7)

**FAILURE TO PROVIDE BY WILL:** The surviving spouse has the right to renounce the will as if it were a will containing an unsatisfactory provision. See "Option to Disregard the Will." (§ 91-5-27)

**CHILDREN BORN OUT OF WEDLOCK:** A child born out of wedlock may inherit as if legitimate from and through the mother and the mother's kindred. The child may not inherit from or through the natural father unless the natural parents participated in a marriage ceremony before the child's birth, even if the marriage was subsequently declared void; or unless paternity has been adjudicated before the death of the natural father; or unless paternity has been adjudicated after the death of the natural father and the claim against the estate is filed within 1 year of the natural father's death. (§ 91-1-15)

**HOMESTEAD, PERSONAL, AND FAMILY ALLOWANCES:** The surviving spouse and children are entitled to comfortable support from the estate, including money for clothing and tuition, for 1 year. (§ 91-7-135) The family homestead, consisting of the family home and up to 160 acres of land worth up to $30,000 (or proceeds of insurance on the property not exceeding $30,000), passes equally to the surviving spouse and children or grandchildren of the decedent. If the surviving spouse owns a place of residence equal in value to the homestead of the decedent, and if the decedent has children or grandchildren of his or her own from a former marriage but no surviving children from this marriage, the homestead does not pass to the surviving spouse but passes instead to the children or grandchildren of the former marriage. (§§ 85-3-21, -23; 91-1-19 to -23)

**OPTION TO DISREGARD THE WILL:** The surviving spouse may, within 90 days after the probate of the will, reject the will and take the share she or he is entitled to if there had been no will. However the spouse may receive no more than one-half of the estate, even if there are no surviving children or grandchildren. (§ 91-5-23) If the surviving spouse has separate property equal in value to his or her lawful share of the decedent's estate, then he or she may not renounce the will and must accept its provisions. (§ 91-5-29) If the separate property of the surviving spouse is less in value than his or her lawful share of the decedent's estate, then the spouse may accept the difference in value; at a minimum, the surviving spouse may reject the will and take the statutory share if the separate property is less than one-fifth the value of what he or she would have been entitled to take under the right to elect against the will. (§ 91-5-29)

# REPRODUCTIVE RIGHTS
## ABORTION
*Statutory Provisions:* The statute governing abortions currently classifies abortion as a felony, unless it is performed by a physician to save the life of the mother or unless the pregnancy resulted from rape. (§ 97-3-3) However, these provisions were invalidated by the Supreme Court in *Roe v. Wade*, 410 U.S. 113 *reh'g denied*, 410 U.S. 959 (1973), and *Planned Parenthood of Central Missouri v. Danforth*, 428 U.S. 52 (1976), which provide, respectively, that the state may not restrict a woman to exercise her right to an abortion in the first two trimesters of her pregnancy, and that the state may not impose a blanket parental consent requirement as a prerequisite to abortions being performed on minors.

*Parental Consent:* A physician must obtain the written consent of both parents or the legal guardian of an unemancipated minor or, if the parents are divorced, the written consent of the parent with primary custody, before performing an abortion. If the minor's parents are married but only one parent is available, the written consent of the available parent is sufficient. A minor may petition the court in the county in which she resides or in which the abortion is to be performed for a waiver of this consent requirement. The court will waive the consent requirement if it finds that the minor is mature enough to make the decision on her own or that the abortion is in the best interests of the minor. (1986 Miss. Laws, H. B. No. 396 §§ 1 *et seq.*)

**BIRTH CONTROL:** Current statutory provisions authorize the Board of Health to allocate funds for family planning to any organization engaged in supplying contraceptive procedures, supplies, and information. (§41-42-5) The state medicaid program pays for all or part of the cost of contraceptive drugs and devices for eligible poor women. (§ 43-13-117) Under current law, minors may receive contraceptive supplies and information from a physician only if the minor is married; has the consent of his or her parent; or has been referred by another physician, member of the clergy, family planning clinic, school, or any agency or instrumentality of the state or its subdivisions. (§ 41-42-7) Nonetheless, any unemancipated, unmarried minor who is of sufficient intelligence to understand the consequences of a proposed surgical or medical treatment may consent to that treatment. [§ 41-41-3(h)]

**STERILIZATION:** There is no relevant statutory provision.

# UNMARRIED COUPLES
**COMMON-LAW MARRIAGE:** Common-law marriages are invalid if entered into after April 5, 1956. (§ 93-1-15) However, common-law marriages entered into in other states where common-law marriage is valid will be recognized in Mississippi. [*George v. George*, 389 So. 2d 1389 (Miss. 1980)]

**COHABITAL RELATIONSHIPS:** Cohabitation between unmarried persons is a crime punishable by a fine and up to 6 months in prison. (§ 97-29-1) However, in *Chrismond v. Chrismond*, 52 So. 2d 624 (Miss. 1951), the court held that a woman who had lived in the defendant's house, cared for and kept house for him, worked and assisted with him in accumulation of property, and subsequently married the defendant in good faith (although the marriage was invalid because the defendant was already married) was entitled to equitable distribution of the property accumulated by their joint efforts when they lived together.

## CHILDREN

*Custody:* There is no relevant statutory provision.

*Legitimation Proceedings:* A child born out of wedlock is legitimated if the natural parents intermarry and the father acknowledges the child. [§ 93-17-1(2)]

*Paternity Proceedings:* A petition to establish paternity may be brought by the mother or the child. The proceedings may be brought until the child reaches the age of 18. (§§ 43-19-31, -33) The court, upon the child's motion, shall order the mother, the child, and the alleged father to submit to blood tests. (§ 93-9-21) If the finding of the court shows that the defendant is the father of the child, an order of filiation will be entered requiring the father to support the child and provide for the child's education, health insurance, and funeral expenses. (§ 93-9-29)

*Obligations of the Putative Father:* The father of a child born out of wedlock is liable to the same extent as the father of a child born of a lawful marriage, whether or not the child is born alive, for the reasonable expense of the mother's pregnancy and for the support, maintenance, educational, medical, and funeral expenses of the child. (§ 93-9-7)

# Education

## STATUTORY PROVISION

There is no relevant statutory provision. However, it should be noted that if federal funds are involved, Title IX of the Education Amendments of 1972, Pub. L. No. 92-318, 20 U.S.C. §§ 1681–1686, may apply.

# Employment

## EQUAL PAY LAWS

There is no relevant statutory provision. However, it should be noted that the federal Equal Pay Act of 1963, 29 U.S.C. §§ 201 *et seq.*, may apply.

## FAIR EMPLOYMENT LAWS

There is no relevant statutory provision. However, an employer with fifteen or more employees is prohibited from discriminating on the basis of sex by federal law, Title VII of the Civil Rights Act of 1964, 42 U.S.C. §§ 2000e *et seq*.

## GOVERNMENT CONTRACTORS AND SUBCONTRACTORS

There is no relevant statutory provision. However, it should be noted that if federal funds are involved, Exec. Order No. 11246, 3 C.F.R. 339, *reprinted in* 42 U.S.C. § 2000e app. at 1232, 41 C.F.R. § 60-1.2, may apply. See also "Fair Employment Laws."

## STATE EMPLOYEE LAWS

State employees and applicants for state jobs are required to be treated fairly without regard to political affiliation, race, national origin, sex, religious creed, age, or physical disability. (§ 25-9-103, -149)

## VETERAN'S PREFERENCE

Fully qualified veterans are given preference for state jobs; fully qualified disabled veterans are given additional preference. Preferences apply to hiring, promotion, and layoffs. (§ 25-9-303) Civil servants who leave their jobs to participate in the United States Armed Forces shall have preference in reemployment. (§ 21-31-7)

# Community Life

## CREDIT

There is no relevant statutory provision. However, it should be noted that the federal Equal Credit Opportunity Act of 1977, 12 C.F.R. § 202, may apply.

## HOUSING

There is no relevant statutory provision. However, Title VIII of the Civil Rights Act of 1968, 42 U.S.C. §§ 3601–3619, and Exec. Order No. 11060, 3 C.F.R. 652, (1962), *reprinted in* 42 U.S.C. § 1982, as amended by Exec. Order No. 12259, 3 C.F.R. 307 (1981), *reprinted in* 42 U.S.C. § 3608, may apply.

## INSURANCE

Discrimination is prohibited between individuals of the same class and life expectancy in the premium, amounts, or rates charged for policies of life or endowment insurance and in the dividends or other benefits payable under these policies. (§ 83-7-3)

**ENFORCEMENT:** The Commissioner of Insurance has the power to investigate claims of discrimination and to revoke or suspend the license of any company or insurance agent found to be in violation of the prohibition against discrimination. (§ 83-7-3)

## PUBLIC ACCOMMODATIONS

There is no relevant statutory provision.

# MISSOURI

## Home and Family

## MARRIAGE

**AGE OF CONSENT:** A person 18 years of age or older may consent to marry. (§ 451.090)*

**CONSENT REQUIREMENT:** Persons 15 years of age or older but under 18 may not marry without the consent of a parent or guardian, and such consent must be written and sworn to before an officer authorized to administer oaths. (§ 451.090) Persons under 15 years of age may marry only with the consent of the circuit or associate circuit court judge of the county where the license is sought.

**LICENSE REQUIREMENT:** The license will be issued for good cause shown and by reason of such unusual conditions as make the marriage advisable. (§ 451.090) Licenses are valid for 90 days. (§ 451.140)

**PROHIBITED MARRIAGES:** Marriages between parents and children, including grandparents and grandchildren of every degree, between brothers and sisters of the half or the whole blood, between uncles and nieces, aunts and nephews, between first cousins, and between persons who lack capacity to enter into a marriage contract are presumptively void. (§ 451.020) Bigamous marriages are also void. (§ 451.030)

## DISSOLUTION OF MARRIAGE

**ANNULMENT:** There is no relevant statutory provision. However, if factors 19, 34, or 38, listed in Appendix A, are present, the marriage is presumptively void. (§§ 451.020, .030)

*Residency Requirement:* There is no relevant statutory provision.

**LEGAL SEPARATION:** Irretrievable breakdown, which may include factors 4, 5, and 29, listed in Appendix A, is grounds for a legal separation. (§§ 452.305, .320)

*Residency Requirement:* One of the parties filing for a legal separation must be a resident of the state for 90 days before the commencement of the proceeding. (§ 452.305)

**DIVORCE**

*Residency Requirement:* See "Legal Separation."

*Grounds for Divorce:* See "Legal Separation." Irretrievable breakdown of the marriage is grounds for divorce.

*Property Distribution:* The court will award to each spouse his or her separate property. The marital property which is presumed to include all property acquired after the marriage, whether held individually or in co-ownership, will be divided as the court sees fit. Considered by the court in dividing marital property include factors 1, 2, 3, and 29, listed in Appendix F, as well as the conduct of the parties generally during the marriage. The court will also consider the desirability of awarding the family home to the spouse having custody of the children. (§ 452.330)

*Child Custody:* Sole or joint custody will be awarded according to the best interests of the child. Factors 5, 10, 11, 12, 13, and 14, listed in Appendix B, and the

*Unless otherwise specified, all citations are to Vernon's Annotated Missouri Statutes (1949).

child's need for a continuing relationship with both parents and their ability and willingness to perform parental obligations are considered. (§ 452.375)

*Child Support:* The court may order either or both parents to pay child support; however, the father of the child has primary responsibility for the child's support. The court will consider factors 1, 2, 3, 4, and 5, listed in Appendix D, in determining child support. (§ 452.340)

*Spousal Support/Alimony:* Alimony can be awarded to either spouse. For the court to award alimony, the spouse seeking it must show a lack of sufficient property to provide for his or her needs and the inability to support himself or herself. The court may also consider factors 1, 2, 3, 4, 5, 6, 13, 14, and 22, listed in Appendix E, in awarding alimony. (§ 452.335) The court may also award temporary alimony while the marital action is pending. (§ 452.315)

*Enforcement of Support Orders:* A support order may require that the party owing the support provide sufficient security, bond, or other guarantee to secure payment of the obligation. (§ 452.344) The order may also provide that periodic support payments be made to the circuit clerk as trustee for remittance to the person entitled to receive these payments. (§ 452.345) Assignment of wages or income are available to enforce support obligations, as is the imposition of liens on real property. (§§ 454.350, .515) Child support enforcement services are provided by the Department of Health and Human Services. A fee is charged for these services. (§ 454.425) State income tax refunds may be intercepted and remitted to a person owed child support (§ 143.781). Federal law 26 U.S.C.A. 6402(c) provides for intercepted federal income tax refunds to be applied toward support obligations.

*Spouse's Name:* There is no relevant statutory provision.

*Divorce by Affidavit or Summary Judgment:* There is no relevant statutory provision.

*Displaced Homemaker Laws:* There is no relevant statutory provision. However, the Council on Women's Economic Development and Training Act of 1985 provides for programs to be conducted in this area. (§§ 186.005 *et seq.*)

# DOMESTIC VIOLENCE

**STATUTORY PROVISION:** Domestic violence is defined as attempting to cause or causing bodily injury to a family or household member, or placing family or household members in fear of immediate injury. (§ 455.200)

**WHO IS PROTECTED?** Spouses, former spouses, persons related by blood or marriage, cohabitants, and former cohabitants of the opposite sex. (§ 455.200)

**RELIEF AVAILABLE:** A victim of domestic violence can obtain the following relief: a temporary or permanent order of protection restraining the household member from abusing, threatening to abuse, molesting, or disturbing the peace of the petitioner; a temporary or permanent order of protection restraining the household member from entering the dwelling of the petitioner; temporary maintenance; temporary or permanent child custody and child support. (§§ 455.045, .050) In addition, shelters for victims of domestic violence are available and can provide medical, psychological, financial, educational, vocational, child care, and legal services. (§ 455.225) Law enforcement agencies are required to provide the same standard of response to an alleged incident of domestic abuse as they do to any similar incident involving strangers, taking into consideration such factors as whether the abused party has been a prior victim of abuse and whether the abused party was previously granted an order of protection. (§ 455.080)

**MARITAL RAPE:** A woman may charge her husband with rape only if they are living apart pursuant to a judgment of legal separation. (§§ 566.010, .030)

**CIVIL LAWSUIT FOR RAPE OR ASSAULT:** Spouses may not sue each other for torts occurring during the marriage. [*Huff v. LaSieur*, 571 S.W.2d 654 (Mo. App. 1978)]

**CHILD ABUSE:** Abuse of a child under the age of 17 by knowingly inflicting cruel and unusual punishment, or by photographing or filming a child in a prohibited sexual act or in the simulation of a prohibited sexual act is a felony. (§ 568.060)

> *Notification Requirement:* All health care professionals, hospital and clinic personnel, psychologists, mental health professionals, social workers, child care center workers, juvenile officers, teachers, school personnel, and law enforcement officers must report all suspected cases of child abuse to the Division of Family Services. (§ 210.145) A law enforcement officer or physician who has reasonable cause to believe a child is in imminent danger of serious harm or death may retain that child in temporary protective custody for up to 24 hours without a court order. (§ 210.125) The Division of Family Services is required to publicize the existence of a statewide toll-free telephone number which has been established to receive reports of child abuse or neglect. (§ 210.155)

# INHERITANCE RIGHTS

**FAILURE TO MAKE A WILL:** The surviving spouse is entitled to the entire estate if the decedent left no issue or parents; to $20,000 and one-half of the balance of the estate, if there are no surviving issue but one or both parents of the decedent are still living; to $20,000 and one-half of the balance of the estate if there are surviving issue, one or more of whom are not the issue of the surviving spouse. (§ 474.010)

**FAILURE TO PROVIDE BY WILL:** If the testator fails to provide by will for the surviving spouse who married the testator after the execution of the will, the surviving spouse is entitled to a share of the estate equal to that which the surviving spouse would have received had the testator left no will, unless it appears from the will that the omission was intentional or that the testator provided for the surviving spouse outside the will. (§ 474.235)

**CHILDREN BORN OUT OF WEDLOCK:** A child born out of wedlock is the legitimate child of the mother, and each may inherit from the other. A child born out of wedlock is also the child of the father and therefore may inherit from him if the natural parents participated in a marriage ceremony either before or after the child's birth, even though the attempted marriage is void; or if paternity was established by an adjudication before the death of the father, or established after the death of the father by clear and convincing proof. However, where paternity was established, the father may not inherit from the child unless the father had openly treated the child as his and had not refused to support the child. (§ 474.060)

**HOMESTEAD, PERSONAL, AND FAMILY ALLOWANCES:** The surviving spouse is entitled absolutely to the family bible, one family car, all family clothing, household electrical appliances, musical and amusement instruments, furniture, and utensils, regardless of the value of the items. (§ 474.250) He or she is also entitled to a homestead allowance not to exceed 50 percent of the value of the estate (not including exempt property or $7500). The homestead allowance is exempt from all claims against the estate, can be in the form of real estate or personal property, and is offset against the share of the estate to which the surviving spouse is entitled; but the allowance may not be diminished if it is greater than the distributive share. (§ 474.290)

**OPTION TO DISREGARD THE WILL:** The surviving spouse may reject the will and elect to take, in addition to exempt property and a 1-year support allowance, one-half of the estate if the decedent left no lineal descendants, or one-third of the estate if the decedent did leave lineal descendants. (§§ 474.250, .260) The amount taken by the surviving spouse under this provision is subject to claims against the estate, and any homestead allowance made to the surviving spouse will be offset against the share taken under this provision. (§ 474.160)

# REPRODUCTIVE RIGHTS
## ABORTION

*Statutory Provisions:* All abortions must be performed by a physician. (§ 188.020) Abortions may be performed in a clinic, physician's office, or any other facility in which abortions are performed, including a hospital. (§ 188.015) The statutory provision that required every abortion subsequent to the first 12 weeks of pregnancy to be performed in a hospital (§ 188.025) was held unconstitutional by the U.S. Supreme Court in *Planned Parenthood v. Ashcroft*, 462 U.S. 476 (1983). Abortions performed when the fetus is viable are permitted, but only when necessary to preserve the life or health of the woman. (§ 188.030) A physician who performs an abortion which results in the birth of a viable fetus is required to choose a method that will most likely preserve its health and life, unless such method would pose a greater risk to the life or health of the woman; in this case, another method may be used. (§ 188.0309) An abortion of a viable fetus requires the presence of a second physician, other than the physician who is performing the abortion, to take control of, and care for, the fetus if the fetus is born alive. (§ 188.030)

*Informed Consent:* Pregnant women over the age of 18 may terminate their pregnancies by abortion, provided they give their prior, informed, and written consent. (§§ 188.027, .039) Previous consent conditions, such as a 48-hour waiting period between the consent and the abortion, the requirement that the physician inform the woman of the anatomical and physical characteristics of the fetus and of long-term physical and psychological trauma that may result from abortion, and the requirement that the physician tell the woman the probable age in weeks of her unborn child, were held unconstitutional in *Planned Parenthood Association of Kansas City, Missouri, Inc. v. Ashcroft*, 655 F.2d 848 (8th Cir. 1981). However, the physician is required, under current Missouri law, to inform the woman of the particular risks associated with the abortion technique chosen and to advise her of alternatives to abortion. (§ 188.030; *Planned Parenthood v. Ashcroft*)

*Parental Consent:* Abortions may be performed on females under the age of 18 only when the physician who is to perform the abortion has obtained the informed written consent of the pregnant minor and one parent or guardian. (§ 188.028) However, consent of one parent or guardian is not required if the minor is emancipated and has given informed written consent herself, or if the minor has received a court order granting her the right to consent to the abortion and she has consented to it in writing, or if the court has given informed written consent to the abortion and the minor is having the abortion willingly. The right of a minor to self-consent may be granted by a court after the minor or her next friend petitions the court for this right. The petition must contain the age and initials of the minor, the names and addresses of each of her parents or her guardian, and a statement to the effect that the minor is of sound mind and intellectual capacity to consent to the abortion and that she has been fully informed of the risks and consequences of the abortion. Copies of the minor's petition are required to be personally served on the minor's parents, or mailed to the parents if personal service cannot be effected in 2 days. (§ 188.028) These provisions governing the parental consent of minors desiring abortions withstood a constitutional challenge and were upheld by the Supreme Court in *Planned Parenthood v. Ashcroft*, 462 U.S. 476 (1983). As a result, parental consent is still required unless the minor can successfully petition the court to grant the right of self-consent, and any such petition submitted on behalf of the pregnant minor will be sent to her parents or guardians.

*Spousal Consent:* There is no relevant statutory provision.

*Reporting Requirements:* The physician performing the abortion is required to file a report with the state division of health within 45 days from the date of the abortion. A copy of the report must remain part of the woman's medical record at the facility at which the abortion was performed. (§ 188.052) In addition, a tissue sample from every abortion performed must be submitted to a board-eligible or board-certified pathologist for analysis and must be made part of the woman's permanent record at the facility at which the abortion was performed. (§ 188.047)

*State Funding:* Abortions may not be paid for by state welfare medical benefits programs (medicaid) unless the physician performing the abortion certifies in writing to the medicaid agency that the life of the mother would have been endangered had the fetus been carried to term. (§ 208.152)

**BIRTH CONTROL:** The state provides family planning services to poor women through its welfare program; however, abortions are not covered by the state medicaid system unless performed to save the life of the woman. [§ 208.152(14)] Moreover, recipients of birth control pills and other contraceptive devices and other services may be required to pay part of the cost of these services. [§ 208.152(14)]

**STERILIZATION:** There is no relevant statutory provision.

# UNMARRIED COUPLES

**COMMON-LAW MARRIAGE:** Common-law marriages are not valid if entered into after 1921. [§ 451.040(5)] In addition, Missouri courts have held that Missouri will not recognize a common-law marriage between Missouri residents if it was entered into in a state where common-law marriage is recognized. [*Stein v. Stein.*, 641 S.W.2d 856 (Mo. App. 1982)]

**COHABITAL RELATIONSHIPS:** In an action for division of jointly held assets by a woman against a man with whom she had cohabited, the court held that the woman was entitled to partition their farm and to share in the proceeds from its sale where the woman and man had owned the farm as tenants in common and where there was evidence of the woman's contribution to the couple's arrangement by reasons of domestic services she had rendered during their period of cohabitation. [*Brooks v. Kunz*, 597 S.W.2d 183 (Mo. App. 1980)]

**CHILDREN**

*Custody:* There is no relevant statutory provision. However, statutes governing child custody provide that neither parent has a superior right to custody on account of his or her sex. [§ 452.375(3)] Thus, it would appear that child custody laws apply equally to unmarried and married couples. However, unwed fathers may be required to demonstrate concern and the capacity to care for the child before the court will afford the father the equal presumption of fitness afforded to married parents. [*State ex. rel. J.D.S. v. Edwards*, 574 S.W.2d 405 (Mo. Sup. Ct. 1978)]

**Legitimation Proceedings:** If the father and mother intermarry, a child born out of wedlock is rendered legitimate, even if the marriage is void. [§ 474.060(2)] Legitimacy may also be accomplished by an acknowledgment on the part of the father that the child is his by filing an affidavit to that effect or by placing his name on the child's birth certificate. [*State ex. rel. T.A.B. v. Corrigan*, 600 S.W.2d 87 (Mo. App. 1980)]

**Paternity Proceedings:** There is no relevant statutory provision. However, an action to determine paternity may be brought by the mother of the child; paternity must be proven by the one asserting it by a preponderance of the evidence. [*Stegemann v. Fank*, 571 S.W.2d 697 (Mo. App. 1978)] Blood tests may be used only to prove nonparentage, but not to prove parentage. [*Imms v. Clarke*, 654 S.W.2d 281 (Mo. App. 1983)]

**Obligations of the Putative Father:** Once paternity is established, the father is liable for the support of the child, and for past expenses of the mother in caring for the child. [*Mueller v. Jones*, 583 S.W.2d 222 (Mo. App. 1979)]

# Education

## STATUTORY PROVISION

There is no relevant statutory provision. However, the Public Accommodations Act, § 314.020(5), may operate to prohibit sexual discrimination in education. Also, it should be noted that if federal funds are involved, Title IX of the Education Amendments of 1972, Pub. L. No. 92-318, 20 U.S.C. §§ 1681–1686, may apply.

# Employment

## EQUAL PAY LAWS

It is unlawful for an employer to discriminate on the basis of sex by paying female employees less than male employees when both work at the same establishment and perform the same quantity and quality of the same classification of work. Differences in pay are not unlawful when based on seniority, length of service, ability, skill, difference in duties or services performed, difference in the shift or time of day worked, hours of work, restrictions or prohibitions on lifting or moving objects in excess of specified weight, or reasonable factors other than sex. (§ 290.410)

**ENFORCEMENT:** The Industrial Commission of Missouri enforces the equal pay laws. An employee who has been discriminated against may file a complaint with the commission, which will mediate the wage dispute. (§§ 290.420, .430) The employee may also bring a civil action to recover back wages plus costs in the circuit court within 6 months after the date of the alleged violation. (§§ 290.440, .450) However, an employer will not be liable for any back pay due for more than 30 days before the employer's receipt of a written notice of claim from the employee. (§ 290.450)

# FAIR EMPLOYMENT LAWS

Under the Fair Employment Practices Law discrimination in employment on the basis of sex and other characteristics is prohibited. This includes hiring and termination decisions; compensation; and terms, conditions, and privileges of employment based on sex. [§ 296.020(1)] The law applies to the state of Missouri, its political and civil subdivisions, labor organizations, employers of six employees or more, employment agencies, and any person acting in the interest of an employer. The law does not cover corporations and associations owned and operated by religious or sectarian groups. [§ 296.010(2)] Further, it is not an unlawful employment practice to discriminate by applying different standards of pay to employees based on a bona fide seniority or merit system or a system that measures earnings by the differences in quantity or quality of production by employees working in different areas. [§ 296.020(2)] Women may retire at a younger age than men, and differences are also permitted in annuity, death, and survivor benefits between widows and widowers of employees. [§ 296.040(4)]

**ENFORCEMENT:** Any person claiming to be aggrieved by an unlawful employment practice may file a written, verified complaint with the Commission on Human Rights, which is empowered to investigate, hold hearings, and order the employer to cease and desist from the unlawful practice. The complaint must be filed within 180 days of the occurrence of the alleged discriminatory practice. (§ 296.040) The commission may also require the employer to take any affirmative action as in its judgment will effectuate the purposes of the law, including a requirement that the respondent report on its manner of compliance. [§ 296.404(7)]

# GOVERNMENT CONTRACTORS AND SUBCONTRACTORS

Any employer who contracts to provide goods or services to the state must comply with the requirements of the Fair Employment Practices Laws. (Exec. Order, art. 7, issued September 10, 1973)

**ENFORCEMENT:** See "Fair Employment Laws."

# STATE EMPLOYEE LAWS

State employees are covered by the Fair Employment Practices Law. [§ 296.010(21)]

**ENFORCEMENT:** See "Fair Employment Laws."

# VETERAN'S PREFERENCE

Five points are added to passing examination scores of veterans, widows of veterans, and wives of disabled veterans; ten points are added to the passing scores of disabled veterans. (§ 36.220)

# Community Life

## CREDIT

No person, upon proper application, may be refused credit solely on the basis of his or her sex or marital status. However, any creditor may require the signature of both husband and wife on the credit instrument. (§§ 314.100, 408.550)

> **ENFORCEMENT:** People who believe they have been denied credit on the basis of sex may bring an action for damages within 1 year of the occurrence of the alleged discrimination, and if the discrimination was willful, punitive damages not to exceed $1000 may be awarded. (§§ 314.105, .115)

## HOUSING

It is unlawful for any person to refuse to sell or rent a dwelling after the making of a bona fide offer, or to refuse to negotiate the sale or rental of any dwelling on the basis of sex. Further, it is unlawful to discriminate on the basis of sex against any person in the terms or conditions of a sale or rental; to publish any advertisement or notice that indicates any preference or limitation based on sex; or to represent to any person, on the basis of that person's sex, that a dwelling is not available when in fact it is available. (§ 213.105) In addition, it is unlawful for any bank, building and loan association, insurance company, or other commercial real estate loan organization to deny a housing or home improvement loan, or to discriminate in fixing the interest rate for such loans, on the basis of the applicant's sex. (§§ 213.110, 408.575)

> **ENFORCEMENT:** Any person who believes he or she has been or is about to be the victim of a discriminatory housing practice may file a complaint with the Commissioner on Human Rights within 180 days of the occurrence of the alleged discriminatory act. (§ 213.120)

## INSURANCE

Individuals of the same class and life expectancy may not be charged different premium rates for, or be paid different benefits from, a life insurance policy. Such practices constitute unfair discrimination. [§ 375.936(11)] It is also unfairly discriminatory to charge different premiums, rates, and fees to individuals of the same class and essentially the same hazard for accident and health insurance. [§ 375.936(11)]

> **ENFORCEMENT:** The Division of Insurance, Department of Consumer Affairs, examines and investigates all charges of discrimination in the insurance industry. (§ 375.938) A director who believes that discrimination has taken place may conduct hearings and issue an order requiring the insurer to cease and desist from engaging in the practice and may also suspend or revoke the insurer's license. (§§ 375.940, .942)

## PUBLIC ACCOMMODATIONS

All persons are entitled to the free and equal use and enjoyment of any place of public accommodation regardless of sex. (§ 314.010) Exempted from this law are public accommodations owned or operated by religious corporations, associations, or societies who give preference to members of their own religious faith and private clubs. [§§ 314.030(2), .040]

**ENFORCEMENT:** Any person alleging discrimination may file a complaint with the Commission on Human Rights within 90 days of the occurrence of the alleged discriminatory act. The commission may conduct hearings and issue an order requiring cessation of discriminatory practices. (§ 314.060) Willful violation of the public accommodations law constitutes a misdemeanor. (§ 314.080)

# MONTANA

## Home and Family

## MARRIAGE

**AGE OF CONSENT:** A person 18 years of age or older may consent to marry. (§ 40-1-202)*

**CONSENT REQUIREMENT:** The district court may issue a marriage license and marriage certificate form to a party aged 16 or 17 if there is no parent capable of giving consent or if there was consent given by both parents or the parent having the actual care, custody and control of child, and is capable of giving consent. A guardian may also consent. As a condition of the order for issuance of a marriage license, the court must require both parties to participate in a period of marriage counseling. (§ 40-1-213)

**LICENSE REQUIREMENT:** A license issued by the county clerk is required. (§ 40-1-201) The marriage license fee is $30 and shall be issued upon proof that each party to the marriage will have attained the age of 18 at the time the license is effective or will have attained the age of 16 and has obtained the judicial approval required. In addition, a certificate of the results of any medical examination is required. Each female applicant, unless exempted, shall file with the license issuer a medical certificate from a physician, stating that the applicant has been given a standard blood test performed not more than 6 months before the date of issuance of the license. (§ 40-203) A license to marry becomes effective throughout the state of Montana 3 days after the date of issuance, unless the district court orders that the license is effective when issued, and expires 6 months after it becomes effective. (§ 40-1-212)

**PROHIBITED MARRIAGES:** Bigamous marriages and marriages between ancestors and descendants, between brothers and sisters, whether the relationship is by the half or the whole blood, between first cousins, between uncles and nieces or aunts and nephews, whether by half or whole blood are prohibited. If parties to a prohibited marriage cohabit after the removal of the impediment, they will be deemed as lawfully married as of the date of the removal of the impediment. Children born of an annulled marriage are legitimate. (§§ 40-1-401, -402)

## DISSOLUTION OF MARRIAGE

**ANNULMENT:** Factors, 32, 33, 35, 36, and 38, listed in Appendix A, are grounds for annulment. (§§ 40-1-401, -402)

*Residency Requirement:* There is no relevant statutory provision.

**LEGAL SEPARATION:** If the marriage is irretrievably broken, the parties may file for legal separation. (§ 40-4-104)

*Residency Requirement:* One of the parties must be a resident for 90 days. (§ 40-4-104)

### DIVORCE

*Residency Requirement:* See "Legal Separation."

*Grounds for Divorce:* If the marriage is irretrievably broken, the parties may file for divorce. (§ 40-4-104)

*Unless otherwise specified, all citation references are to the Montana Code Annotated (1979).

*Conciliation Requirement:* When there are minor children of a marriage or when one spouse denies that the marriage is irretrievably broken, the court may refer the parties to a pastor or director of any religious denomination to which the parties belong or to a psychiatrist, physician, attorney, social worker or other person who is competent and qualified in personal counseling. (§§ 40-3-111, -724)

*Property Distribution:* The court, without regard to marital misconduct, will finally approve all distribution of property, real and personal, considering factors 1, 5, 6, 7, 8, 9, 10, 11, 14, 16, 20, 21, and 25, listed in Appendix F. (§ 40-4-202)

*Child Custody:* The court determines custody in accordance with the best interests of the child. The court will consider factors 5, 10, 11, 12, and 14, listed in Appendix B. (§ 40-4-212) In making an award to either parent, the court will consider, along with the above factors, which parent is more likely to allow the child frequent and continuing contact with the noncustodial parent. The court may not prefer a parent as custodian because of the parent's sex. (§ 40-4-223) Upon the application of either or both parents for joint custody, the court shall consider whether or not such custody is in the best interests of the minor child. (§ 40-4-224)

*Child Support:* The court may order either or both parents to pay an amount reasonable or necessary for the child's support, without regard to marital misconduct, after considering factors, 1, 2, 3, 4, and 5, listed in Appendix D and the amount received by children under the Aid to Families with Dependent Children program. (§ 4-4-204)

## DIVORCE

*Spousal Support/Alimony:* The court may award support to either party for such amounts and for such periods of time as it deems just. The court will consider factors 1, 2, 3, 4, 5, 6, 13, 14, listed in Appendix E. (§ 40-4-203)

*Enforcement of Support Orders:* Child support orders may be enforced by filing a petition with the district court ordering the deduction of delinquent support payments from income or wage of the person owing the duty of support. (§§ 40-5-301 *et seq.* ) Persons owed a duty of support may request the Department of Revenue to enforce such duty. The department charges a fee for its services. However, the fee may be waived upon a showing of necessity. (§ 40-5-203) See also the Uniform Reciprocal Enforcement of Support Act, §§ 40-5-101 *et seq.*

*Spouse's Name:* Upon request by a wife whose marriage is dissolved or declared invalid, the court shall order her maiden name or a former name restored. (§ 40-4-108)

*Divorce by Affidavit or Summary Judgment:* There is no relevant statutory provision.

*Displaced Homemaker Laws:* It is the intent of the legislature to provide necessary counseling, training, jobs, services, and health care to displaced homemakers so they may achieve independence and economic security vital to a productive life. (§§ 37-7-301, 39-7-310)

# DOMESTIC VIOLENCE

**STATUTORY PROVISION:** There is a grant program established within the Department of Social and Rehabilitation Services for the allocation of grant money to local battered spouses and domestic violence programs. (§ 40-2-401)

**WHO IS PROTECTED?** The Department of Social and Rehabilitation Services is authorized by statute to provide grants to shelters for victims of domestic violence, for counseling victims or their spouses, and to educate the public about domestic violence. Funding is primarily to come from a $9 surcharge on every marriage license issued. (§§ 40-2-401, -405)

**RELIEF AVAILABLE:** Battered persons may apply to the court for an injunction or temporary restraining order to restrain another from causing great or irreparable injury. (§§ 27-19-201, 40-4-106)

**MARITAL RAPE:** A woman who is living with her husband or a cohabitant may not charge her husband or cohabitant with rape; however, a woman who is living apart from her husband may charge him with rape. (§ 45-5-511)

**CIVIL LAWSUIT FOR RAPE OR ASSAULT:** There are no relevant cases. A spouse may sue the other for damages caused by the other's intentional tort. (§ 40-2-109)

**CHILD ABUSE:** A child or its relative may bring an action for abuse of parental authority; if abuse is established, the child may be removed from the home. (§ 40-6-233) All doctors, health care professionals, coroners, school personnel, social workers, child care center personnel, foster parents, and police officers must report all suspected cases of child abuse to the Department of Social and Rehabilitative Services. A prompt and thorough investigation must then be made, and protective services must be provided to an abused child. The court may issue such relief as may be required for the immediate protection of a child, including removing the child from its home or transferring custody to another relative, the department, or a child-placing agency. (§ 41-3-201)

> *Notification Requirement:* Any person, official, or institution required by law to report known or suspected child abuse or neglect or to perform any other act who fails to do so or who prevents another person from reasonably doing so is liable in a civil suit for the damages resulting from such failure. (§ 41-3-207)

# INHERITANCE RIGHTS

**FAILURE TO MAKE A WILL:** The surviving spouse is entitled to the entire estate if the decedent left no children or grandchildren or left children or grandchildren who are also the spouse's children or grandchildren; to one-half the estate if decedent left one child or children of a deceased child who are not also the spouse's child or grandchildren; to one-third the estate if decedent left more than one child or children of more than one deceased child who are not also the spouse's children or grandchildren. (§ 72-2-202)

**FAILURE TO PROVIDE BY WILL:** If a testator fails to provide by will for the surviving spouse who married the testator after the execution of the will, the omitted spouse shall receive the same share of the estate that he or she would have received if the decedent left no will, unless it appears that the omission was intentional or the testator provided for the spouse by transfer outside the will and the intent that the transfer be in lieu of a testamentary provision is shown by statements of the testator or from the amount of the transfer. (§ 72-2-601)

**CHILDREN BORN OUT OF WEDLOCK:** A child born out of wedlock is the natural heir of the mother. Such a child can inherit from the father only if the parent-and-child relationship has been established during the father's lifetime. This relationship comes into being where the father and mother have married or attempted to marry after the child's birth and the father has either acknowledged his paternity in a signed writing filed with the Department of Health and Environmental Sciences or with the district court for the county where he resides; or with his consent he is named the father of the child on the child's birth certificate; or he is obligated to support the child either voluntarily or by court order; or while the child is still a minor, he receives the child into his home and openly treats the child as his own. (§§ 40-6-105, 72-2-503)

**HOMESTEAD, PERSONAL, AND FAMILY ALLOWANCES:** The surviving spouse of a decedent domiciled in Montana is entitled to a homestead allowance of $20,000. The surviving spouse is also entitled to household furniture, cars, furnishings, appliances, and personal effects of the decedent up to $3500. These rights have priority over all claims against the estate and are in addition to any share or benefit passing by will (unless otherwise provided), intestate succession, or statutory share. (§§ 72-2-801, -802)

**OPTION TO DISREGARD THE WILL:** If the decedent was domiciled in Montana, the surviving spouse may elect to take one-third of the decedent's estate; if the decedent was not a Montana domiciliary, the right of the spouse to take the statutory share of property located in Montana is governed by the laws of the state in which the decedent is domiciled at death. If the spouse elects to take the statutory share, he or she need not renounce his or her share under the will through intestate succession. The spouse is entitled to the homestead exemption and family allowance, whether or not he or she elects to take the statutory share. (§§ 72-2-702, -704)

# REPRODUCTIVE RIGHTS
## ABORTION
*Statutory Provisions:* Only a licensed physician can perform abortions. All abortions performed after the first trimester must be performed in a licensed hospital. A postviability abortion can be performed if, in the physician's best medical judgment, the abortion is necessary to preserve the life or health of the mother. In addition, before they can be performed, the physician must certify in writing the facts relied upon in making the judgment, and two other physicians must concur in writing with the judgment that the abortion is necessary to preserve the life of the woman. The timing and procedure used must be such that the viability of the fetus is not intentionally or negligently endangered. (§ 50-20-109) All persons, private hospitals, or health care facilities have the right to refuse to advise concerning, or participate in, abortions on religious or moral grounds. (§ 50-20-111) Whenever a premature infant who is the subject of abortion is born alive and viable, the child becomes a dependent and neglected child unless the termination of the pregnancy is necessary to preserve the life of the woman or unless the woman and the father agreed in writing before the abortion or within 72 hours after its performance to accept the parental rights and responsibilities of the premature infant. (§ 50-20-108)

*Consent Requirements:* No abortion may be performed upon any woman in the absence of informed consent. Informed consent means voluntary consent to an abortion by the woman upon whom the abortion is to be performed only after full disclosure of the size of the fetus, the physical and psychological effects of abortion, and the alternatives to abortion have been given. Informed consent may be a written statement, in a form prescribed by the Department of Health and Environmental Sciences and signed by the physician and the woman upon whom the abortion is to be performed. [§ 50-20-104(3)] Informed consent is not required if a licensed physician certifies the abortion is necessary to preserve the life of the mother. (§ 50-20-106)

*Reporting Requirements:* Every facility in which an abortion is performed within the state shall keep on file upon a special form a statement dated and certified by the physician who performed the abortion setting forth information regarding prior pregnancies, the medical procedure employed to administer the abortion, the gestational age of the fetus, the vital signs of the fetus after abortion, if any, and if viabile, the medical procedures employed to protect and preserve the life and health of the fetus. The physician performing an abortion shall keep pathology reports on file. In addition, the consent forms shall be kept on file. Within 30 days after the abortion, the facility which performed the abortion shall file all the information required with the department. (§ 50-20-110)

**BIRTH CONTROL:** It is unlawful for any person, firm, corporation, partnership, or association to sell, offer for sale, or give away, by means of vending machines, personal or collective distribution, solicitation, or peddling, or in any other manner whatsoever contraceptive drugs or devices, prophylactic rubber goods, or other articles for the prevention of venereal diseases. This does not apply to regularly licensed practioners of medicine or osteopathy, other licensed persons practicing other healing arts, registered pharmacists, or wholesale drug jobbers, or manufacturers who sell to retail stores only. It is unlawful to exhibit or display prophylactics or contraceptives in any show window on the streets or in any public place other than in the place of business of a pharmacist. (§ 45-8-204)

**STERILIZATION:** No private hospital or health care facility shall be required, contrary to their stated religious belief or moral sanctions, to admit any person for the purpose of sterilization or to permit the use of its facilities for this purpose. (§ 50-5-502) All persons shall have the right to refuse to participate in sterilization because of religious beliefs. (§ 50-5-503) It is unlawful to interfere or attempt to interfere with the right of refusal authorized by this provision. (§ 50-5-504)

# UNMARRIED COUPLES

**COMMON-LAW MARRIAGE:** Common-law marriages are valid. (§ 40-1403)

**COHABITAL RELATIONSHIPS:** There is no relevant statutory provision.

**CHILDREN**

*Custody:* The father and mother of an unmarried minor child are equally entitled to the custody, services, and earnings of the child. If either parent is dead or unable or refuses custody, the other is entitled to the custody unless otherwise determined. (§ 40-6-221)

*Legitimation Proceedings:* A child born out of wedlock becomes legitimate by the subsequent marriage of its parents. (§ 40-6-203)

*Paternity Proceedings:* Any interested party may bring an action for the purpose of determining the existence or nonexistence of the father-and-child relationship. (§ 40-6-107) The action must be brought no later than 2 years after the child reaches its majority. (§ 40-6-108) Testimony relating to sexual access to the mother by an unidentified man at any time or by an identified man at a time other than the probable time of conception of child is inadmissible in evidence, unless offered by the mother. (§ 40-6-115)

*Obligations of the Putative Father:* The judgment or order declaring the paternity of a child may contain provisions concerning the duty of support, which may include the furnishing of a bond or other security for the payment of the judgment. The order may also direct the father to pay the reasonable expenses of the mother's pregnancy and confinement. (§ 40-6-129)

# Education

## STATUTORY PROVISION

All persons regardless of their sex are entitled to equal rights and opportunities in the educational institutions of the state. (Mont. Const. art 10, § 37) It is unlawful for an educational institution, which includes public or private elementary or secondary schools, colleges, universities, kindergartens, nursery schools or business, nursing, professional, secretarial, technical, or vocational schools, to discriminate against an individual enrolled as a student or seeking admission as a student. (§ 49-2-307) Sex may be considered in order to correct a previous discriminatory practice, even though the use of quotas to limit or deny educational opportunities on the basis of sex is prohibited. (§ 49-2-403)

## AREAS COVERED

The Montana education equity laws prohibit discrimination in any education, counseling, or national guidance programs or in any apprenticeship or on-the-job training programs in which state or local agencies operate or participate. (§ 49-3-203) In addition, the state university system must instruct men and women on equal terms. (§ 20-25-101)

> **ENFORCEMENT:** A written complaint must be filed with the Commission for Human Rights within 180 days after the alleged unlawful discriminatory practice occurred or was discovered. (§ 49-2-501)

# Employment

## EQUAL PAY LAWS

It is unlawful to pay women in any occupation less compensation than that paid to men for equivalent service or for work in the same industry, establishment, or other place of employment. [§ 39-3-104(1)]

> **ENFORCEMENT:** A person who has been discriminated against in the payment of wages may file a written verified complaint with the Montana Human Rights Commission within 180 days after the alleged unlawful practice occurred or was discovered. (§ 49-2-501)

## FAIR EMPLOYMENT LAWS

The Fair Employment Practices Law applies to employers of one or more employees, labor organizations, and employment agencies. It prohibits an employer from refusing to hire, or from discriminating in the terms, conditions, and privileges of employment on the basis of sex, or a labor organization from excluding or expelling from membership or discriminating in any way against its applicants or members, or an employment agency from refusing to refer an applicant for employment on account of sex. (§ 49-2-310) In addition, Montana guarantees a reasonable maternity leave to public and private employees. (§ 49-2-310) Excepted from this act are not-for-profit fraternal, charitable, and religious associations; situations where the discrimination is a result of a bona fide occupational qualification; persons who were granted special exemptions from the Montana Human Rights Commission; and discrimination which is done for the purpose of correcting a previous discriminatory practice. [§§ 49-2-101(1), -203(1)(d), -401, -403]

**ENFORCEMENT:** An individual who has been discriminated against in violation of the Fair Employment Practices Law may file a written verified complaint with the Montana Human Rights Commission within 180 days after the unlawful practice occurred or was discovered. (§ 49-2-501)

# GOVERNMENT CONTRACTORS AND SUBCONTRACTORS

These are prohibited from discriminating on the basis of sex and other protected characteristics. (§ 49-3-207)

**ENFORCEMENT:** The Montana Human Rights Commission is charged with the enforcement of this provision and will investigate complaints that are filed with the commission within 180 days after the alleged discriminatory practice occurred or was discovered. (§ 49-2-303)

# STATE EMPLOYEE LAWS

Exec. Order No. 24-81 (October 13, 1981) prohibits discrimination in state employment. State employees are protected from discrimination in recruitment, appointment, assignment, training, evaluation, and promotion. [§ 49-3-201(1)] In addition, discrimination in state employment is covered under the comparable worth law. Under this law, the Department of Administration is required to work toward the goal of establishing a standard of equal pay for comparable work by eliminating, in job classifications, the use of judgments and factors that contain inherent biases based on sex, and by comparing, in job classifications, the factors for determining job worth across occupational groups whenever those groups are dominated by males or females. (§ 2-118-208) Sexual harassment in state employment is prohibited by Exec. Order No. 7-82 (August 6, 1982).

**ENFORCEMENT:** See "Community Life: Credit."

# VETERAN'S PREFERENCE

When written or oral examinations are required for employment in the civil service, veterans, disabled veterans, their spouses and surviving spouses, and other dependents shall have ten points added to their passing examination scores. All other veterans, their spouses, surviving spouses, and dependents shall have five points added to their passing scores.

# Community Life

## CREDIT

It is unlawful for a financial institution and persons extending credit to discriminate on the basis of sex or marital status.

**ENFORCEMENT:** A written complaint must be filed with the Human Rights Commission within 180 days after the alleged discriminatory practice occurred or was discovered. (§ 49-2-501)

## HOUSING

It is unlawful for the owner, lessee, manager, or other person having the right to sell, lease, or rent a housing accommodation to refuse to sell, to negotiate, lease, or rent a housing accommodation or to discriminate in a term, condition, or privilege relating to the use, sale, lease, or rental of a housing accommodation, or to make an oral inquiry regarding status on the basis of sex, age, race, color, religion, national origin, or physical or mental handicap. These provisions do not apply to a private residence designed for single-family occupancy in which rooms are rented and in which the owner resides. (§ 49-2-305)

**ENFORCEMENT:** See "Credit."

## INSURANCE

Effective October 1, 1985, it is unlawful for any financial institution or person to discriminate solely on the basis of sex or marital status in the issuance or operation of any type of insurance policy, plan, or coverage or in any pension or retirement plan, program, or coverage, including discrimination in regard to rates or premiums and payments or benefits. (§ 49-2-3) This act does not apply to any insurance policy, plan, coverage, or any pension or retirement plan, program, or coverage in effect before October 1, 1985. Discrimination is also prohibited between individuals of the same class and equal expectation of life in rates charged for life insurance or annuity contracts or between individuals of the same class and essentially the same hazard in the amount of premium, policy fees, or rates charged for disability insurance, in the benefits payable under those contracts. (§ 33-18-206) No insurer may refuse to issue insurance to continue a policy in force or limit the amount of coverage to an individual because of sex or marital status. An insurer may, however, take marital status into account in determining whether a person is eligible for dependent's benefits. (§ 33-18-210)

**ENFORCEMENT:** The Commissioner of Insurance has the power to examine and investigate the affairs of every person engaged in the business of insurance to determine if there are any violators of this provision. (§ 33-18-1002)

## PUBLIC ACCOMMODATIONS

It is unlawful for the owner, lessee, manager, agent, or employee of a public accommodation to refuse, withhold from, or deny any person the services, goods, facilities, advantages, or privileges of a public accommodation or to publish or post a notice that implies that any of the services, goods, facilities, advantages, or privileges of a public accommodation will be refused, withheld from, or denied on the basis of sex, age, race, color, religion, national origin, or physical or mental handicap. (§ 49-2-304)

**ENFORCEMENT:** See "Credit."

# NEBRASKA

## Home and Family

## MARRIAGE

**AGE OF CONSENT:** Any person 17 years or older may consent to marry. (§ 42-102)*

**CONSENT REQUIREMENT:** When either party is a minor, the written consent is required of either one of the parents of such minor, if the parents are living together; the custodial parent, if the parents are living separate and apart; the surviving parent, if one of the parents of such minor is deceased; or the guardian, conservator, or person having the legal and actual custody of such minor. (§ 42-105)

**LICENSE REQUIREMENT:** Persons wishing to marry must obtain a license from a county court. The application for the license must be made at least 2 days before it is issued. Before any county judge issues a license, each applicant must file a certificate stating whether the female applicant has laboratory evidence of immunological response to German measles. The certificate is not required if the applicant is over 50, has had surgical sterilization, or presents laboratory evidence of a prior test declaring her immunity to rubella. (§§ 42-104, -121)

**PROHIBITED MARRIAGES:** Bigamous marriages and marriages with insane or mentally incompetent persons are void and prohibited. Marriages between parents and children, grandparents and grandchildren, brother and sister of the half as well as the whole blood, first cousins of the whole blood, uncle and niece, and aunt and nephew are also void and prohibited. (§ 42-103) Children born into a marriage relationship which may be annulled are legitimate unless otherwise decreed by the court. (§ 42-377)

## DISSOLUTION OF MARRIAGE

**ANNULMENT:** Factors 3, 19, 35, 36, 38, 40, and 43, listed in Appendix A, are grounds for annulment. Annulment actions on behalf of persons under disability may be brought by a parent or adult next friend. (§§ 42-119, -374, -375)

*Residency Requirement:* The petitioner must be an actual resident of the county in which the petition is filed. (§ 42-373)

**LEGAL SEPARATION:** There is no relevant statutory provision.

**DIVORCE**

*Residency Requirement:* No action for dissolution of marriage may be brought unless at least one of the parties has had actual residence in the state, with a bona fide intention of making Nebraska his or her permanent home, for at least 1 year prior to the filing of the petition, or unless the marriage was solemnized in the state and either party had resided in the state from the time of marriage to filing the petition. (§ 42-349)

*Grounds for Divorce:* Factors 2 and 36, listed in Appendix A, are grounds for divorce. (§§ 42-361, -362)

*Unless otherwise specified, all reference citations are to the Revised Statutes of Nebraska (1943).

*Conciliation Requirement:* No decree will be entered unless the court finds that every reasonable effort to effect a reconciliation has been made. Divorce actions, when filed, are subject to transfer to a conciliation court. In counties having no conciliation court the parties may be referred to a qualified marriage counselor or family service agency or other agencies which provide conciliation services if the court finds that there appears to be some reasonable possibility of a reconciliation. (§ 42-360)

*Property Distribution:* The court may divide the parties' property as may be reasonable, considering factors 1, 3, 5, and 25, listed in Appendix F. (§ 42-365)

*Child Custody:* Custody and visitation of minor children are determined according to their best interests. Factors 3, 6, 13, and 14, listed in Appendix B, are considered by the court. (§ 42-364)

*Child Support:* Factor 9, listed in Appendix D, is considered when determining child support. (§ 42-364)

*Spousal Support/Alimony:* The court may order payment of alimony to either party as may be reasonable. Factors 1, 4, and 11, listed in Appendix E, are considered. The court will also consider the ability of the supported party to engage in gainful employment without interfering with the interests of any minor children in his or her custody. (§ 42-365)

*Enforcement of Support Orders:* In any proceeding where a court has ordered payment of temporary or permanent child support, the court may upon application, order the employer to withhold from the parent-employee's disposable earnings such amounts as are necessary to reduce the parent-employee's previous arrearage in child support payments arising from his or her failure to comply fully with an order previously entered to pay child support. Such an order may also provide that the employer withhold amounts necessary to pay future support payments as they become due and may also award attorney's fees in such a proceeding. In addition, the order may prohibit the employer from dismissing, demoting, disciplining, or in any way penalizing the parent-employee on account of the proceeding to collect child support or on account of any order entered by the court in such a proceeding, or on account of the employer's compliance with such an order. (§ 42-364.01) An order to withhold and transmit earnings has priority over any attachment, execution, garnishment, or wage assignment, unless otherwise ordered by the court. (§ 42-364.09) When a parent is 30 days in arrears in the payment of court-ordered child support and also fails to appear before the court to show cause why payment is not being made, a warrant will be issued for his or her arrest. (§ 42-364.13) All judgments for temporary or permanent alimony must direct the payment of these sums to be made to the clerk of the district court for disbursement to the spouse for whom they have been awarded and shall constitute liens upon property and may be enforced or collected by execution. (§§ 42-369, -371) See also the Uniform Reciprocal Enforcement Support Act, §§ 42-701 *et seq.*

*Spouse's Name:* There is no relevant statutory provision.

*Divorce by Affidavit or Summary Judgment:* There is no relevant statutory provision.

*Displaced Homemaker Laws:* In order to enable displaced homemakers to contribute to society and maintain independence and economic security, the Commissioner of Public Welfare shall establish and maintain multipurpose service centers for displaced homemakers. The center shall develop services which shall counsel displaced homemakers with respect to appropriate job opportunities; identify community needs and seek funding for new public sector jobs; provide displaced homemakers with the necessary counseling, training, skills, and referral services to become gainfully employed, healthy, and independent; and refer displaced homemakers to agencies which may provide information and assistance with respect to health care, financial matters, education, nutrition, and legal problems. (§§ 48-1303, -1304)

# DOMESTIC VIOLENCE

**STATUTORY PROVISION:** Attempting to cause or intentionally, knowingly, or recklessly causing bodily injury or serious bodily injury with or without a deadly weapon, or by physical menace placing another in fear of imminent serious bodily injury is prohibited. (§ 42-903)

**WHO IS PROTECTED?** Spouses, cohabitants, and adult members of the same household are protected. (§ 42-903)

**RELIEF AVAILABLE:** Any victims of domestic abuse, including a cohabitant, may obtain a temporary order restraining the abusing party from threatening, assaulting, molesting, or attacking the victim or requiring the abusing person to vacate the family residence. The Department of Public Welfare is required by statute to establish and maintain comprehensive support centers, which are to provide prevention and treatment programs to aid both the families and victims of domestic abuse and the abusers. The department must provide emergency services for up to 72 hours for victims of abuse, including immediate transportation from a victim's home to a hospital or place of safety, immediate medical services or first aid, emergency legal counseling and referral, emergency financial aid, and a safe living environment. The department must also provide support services for up to 30 days for victims of domestic abuse, including relocation, financial security, employment, and alternatives to returning to the abuser. The department must also provide services for children, including emergency services such as housing, food, clothing, transportation to school, and counseling for trauma which occurs as a result of domestic abuse. All law enforcement agencies are required to educate their officers about domestic abuse, train them in procedures which enable them to deal with the problem, and provide them with information about and the services and facilities available to abused family and household members. (§§ 42-924, -907, -909, -910, -927)

**MARITAL RAPE:** There is no relevant statutory provision.

**CIVIL LAWSUIT FOR RAPE OR ASSAULT:** In *Emerson v. Western Seed & Irrigation Co.*, 216 N.W. 297 (Neb. 1927), the court held that a wife could not sue her husband for personal injuries.

**CHILD ABUSE:** A person commits child abuse if he or she knowingly, intentionally, or negligently causes or permits a minor child to be placed in a situation that endangers his or her life or health or cruelly punishes or deprives the child of necessary food, clothing, shelter, or care. (§ 28-707, 1984 Cum. Supp.)

*Notification Requirement:* When any physician, medical institution, nurse, school employee, social worker, or any other person has reasonable cause to believe that a child has been subjected to abuse or neglect, or observes such person being subjected to conditions or circumstances which reasonably would result in abuse or neglect, that person shall report such incident or cause a report to be made to the proper law enforcement agency or to the Department of Public Welfare on the 24-hour statewide toll-free number. Law enforcement agencies receiving any reports of abuse or neglect shall notify the state central registry on the next working day. (§ 28-711, 1984 Cum. Supp.)

# INHERITANCE RIGHTS

**FAILURE TO MAKE A WILL:** The surviving spouse is entitled to the entire estate if there are no surviving children or parents of the decedent; to the first $50,000 plus one-half of the balance of the estate if there are no surviving children but the decedent is survived by a parent or parents; to the first $50,000 plus one-half of the balance of the estate if there are surviving children all of whom are children of the surviving spouse; to one-half of the estate if there are surviving children, one or more of whom are not children of the surviving spouse. (§ 30-2302, 1984 Cum. Supp.)

**FAILURE TO PROVIDE BY WILL:** If a testator fails to provide by will for his or her surviving spouse who married the testator after the execution of the will, the omitted spouse shall receive the same share of the estate that he or she would have received if the decedent had left no will, unless the surviving spouse had waived the right of election before or after the marriage by a written instrument signed by him or her after fair disclosure. (§§ 30-2320, -2316)

**CHILDREN BORN OUT OF WEDLOCK:** A child born out of wedlock is the natural heir of the mother and her kin. Such a child is a child of the father and can inherit from him and his kin if the natural parents married and the marriage was later declared void or the paternity of the child is established by an adjudication before the death of the father or is established thereafter by strict, clear, and convincing proof. However, paternity so established is ineffective to qualify the father or his kindred to inherit from or through his child unless the father had not refused to support or had openly treated the child as his. (§ 30-2309)

**HOMESTEAD, PERSONAL, AND FAMILY ALLOWANCES:** The surviving spouse of a decedent who was domiciled in this state is entitled to a homestead allowance of $7500 which is exempt from and has priority over all claims against the estate except for costs and expenses of administration. (§ 30-2332, 1984 Cum. Supp.) In addition, the surviving spouse of a decedent who was domiciled in the state is entitled from the estate to value not exceeding $5000 in excess of any security interests therein in household furniture, automobiles, furnishings, appliances, and personal effects. (§ 30-2323, 1984 Cum. Supp.) If the decedent was domiciled in the state, the surviving spouse and minor children, whom the decedent was obligated to support and children who were in fact being supported by him or her are entitled to a reasonable allowance in money out of the estate for their maintenance during the period of administration. The allowance may not continue for longer than 1 year if the estate is inadequate to discharge allowed claims. (§ 30-2324)

**OPTION TO DISREGARD THE WILL:** If the decedent was domiciled in Nebraska, the surviving spouse may elect to take a share in any fraction not in excess of one-half of the augmented estate. If the decedent was not domiciled in the state, the surviving spouse's right, if any, to take an elective share in property situated in Nebraska and the amount or extent of such share are governed by the law of the decedent's domicile at death. (§ 30-2313)

# REPRODUCTIVE RIGHTS

## ABORTION

*Statutory Provisions:* All abortions must be performed by a licensed physician. (§ 28-335) No abortion can be performed where, in the sound medical judgment of the attending physician, the unborn child appears to have reached viability, except when the abortion is necessary to preserve the life or health of the woman. (§ 28-329) When a fetus is aborted alive, all reasonable steps, in accordance with the sound medical judgment of the physician, must be employed to preserve its life. (§ 28-331) No physician, medical personnel, or health care facility is required to perform or participate in the performance of an abortion. (§§ 28-337, -338)

*Consent Requirement:* No abortion shall be performed on any woman in the absence of her informed consent, except in emergency situations if her life or health is endangered and she is unable to give her informed consent. (§ 28-327, 1984 Cum. Supp.)

*Reporting Requirements:* Every abortion performed or prescribed in the state shall be reported to the Bureau of Vital Statistics, Department of Health. The abortion reporting form shall contain the age of the pregnant woman, where the abortion was performed, the type of procedure performed, complications, if any, the name of the attending physician, the woman's obstetrical history regarding previous pregnancies, abortions, and live births, the stated reasons the abortion was requested, the state of the woman's legal residence, and whether an emergency situation caused the physician to waive any informed consent requirements. (§ 28-343, 1984 Cum. Supp.)

**BIRTH CONTROL:** It is unlawful to sell, give away, or otherwise dispose of any prophylactics except by persons licensed to do so. Physicians are excepted. (§ 71-1105 reissue of 1981)

**STERILIZATION:** There is no relevant statutory provision.


# UNMARRIED COUPLES

**COMMON-LAW MARRIAGE:** Common-law marriages are not valid. (§ 42-104)

**COHABITAL RELATIONSHIPS:** In *Abramson v. Abramson*, 74 N.W.2d 919 (Neb. 1956), the court dismissed a suit for separate maintenance where the evidence showed that no valid marriage had existed; however, the court stated that the existence of a meretricious relationship would not bar a claim to property acquired during the period of the relationship where the claim is based on general principles of law without respect to marital status.

## CHILDREN
*Custody:* There is no relevant statutory provision.

*Legitimation Proceedings:* A child whose parents marry is legitimate. A man will be considered to have acknowledged paternity if he states in writing that he is the father of the child or performs acts such as furnishing support which reasonably indicate that he is the father of the child. (§ 43-1409)

*Paternity Proceedings:* A civil proceeding to establish the paternity of a child may be instituted in any district court of the district where the child is domiciled or found, by the mother of such child, either during pregnancy or within 4 years after the child's birth or by the guardian or next friend of the child at any time. [§ 43-1411; *Doak v. Milbauer*, 343 N.W.2d 751 (Neb. 1984)]

*Obligations of the Putative Father:* The parents of a child whose paternity is established either by judicial proceedings or by acknowledgment are liable for the child's support to the same extent and in the same manner as the parents of a child born in lawful wedlock are liable. (§ 43-1402)

# Education

## STATUTORY PROVISION

No person is to be deprived of the advantages of the University of Nebraska because of sex. (§ 85-116 reissue of 1981) The Public Accommodations Act may operate to prohibit sex discrimination in public schools as well. (§§ 20-133, -134)

**ENFORCEMENT:** See "Public Accommodations."

# Employment

## EQUAL PAY LAWS

It is unlawful for an employer to discriminate on the basis of sex in wages paid to employees in the same establishment who perform work requiring equal skill, effort, and responsibility under similar working conditions. Wage differential is not prohibited if based on seniority system, merit increase system, quantity or quality of production, or any factor other than sex. (§§ 48-1219, -1221)

**ENFORCEMENT:** Any person claiming to have been discriminated against in his or her wages on the basis of sex may bring a civil action for the recovery of any unpaid wages within 4 years of the occurrence of the discrimination. In addition to any judgment awarded, the court may award the plaintiff costs of the action and reasonable attorney's fees. (§§ 48-1223, -1224) At the request of the complainant, the action may be brought by the Equal Employment Opportunity Commission on his or her behalf. (§ 48-1223)

## FAIR EMPLOYMENT LAWS

The law applies to the state of Nebraska, its civil and political subdivision, employers of fifteen or more employees, labor organizations, and employment agencies. Prohibited practices include discrimination in hire, discharge, compensation, terms, conditions, or privileges of employment; expelling or excluding individuals from a labor organization because of their sex; limiting, advertising, soliciting, segregating, or classifying individuals so as to deprive them of employment opportunities or adversely affect their employee status. [§§ 48-1101, -1102(2), -1104]

**ENFORCEMENT:** Any person claiming to be aggrieved by an unlawful discriminatory practice may file a written charge with the Equal Employment Opportunity Commission within 180 days after the occurrence of the alleged discriminatory act. (§ 48-1118)

# GOVERNMENT CONTRACTORS AND SUBCONTRACTORS

These must agree not to discriminate against protected classes in hire, tenure, terms, conditions, or privileges of employment. (§ 48-1122)

**ENFORCEMENT:** See "Fair Employment Laws."

# STATE EMPLOYEE LAWS

State employees are covered under the Fair Employment Practices Law.

**ENFORCEMENT:** See "Fair Employment Laws."

# VETERAN'S PREFERENCE

In agencies without merit systems, veterans shall be given preference in employment. Veterans who obtain passing scores on all parts or phases of an examination shall have five points added to their passing scores; an additional five points shall be added to the passing score of any disabled veteran. (§§ 48-226, -227) The law does not apply to spouses or unremarried widows or widowers of veterans.

# Community Life

# CREDIT

There is no relevant statutory provision. However, it should be noted that federal law, the Equal Credit Opportunity Act of 1977, 12 C.F.R. § 202, may apply.

# HOUSING

It is unlawful for any person engaged in real estate to refuse to sell or rent after the transaction of a bona fide offer, to refuse to negotiate for the sale or rental of, or otherwise make unavailable or deny, to refuse to show, receive, or transmit an offer for a dwelling to any person because of sex. (§ 20-107) The law does not prevent a religious organization or society from limiting the sale, rental, or occupancy of a dwelling which it owns or operates for other than commercial purposes to persons of the same religion or from giving preference to such persons. Private clubs not open to the public are also exempt from the law's coverage. Also exempt are persons who make available for rental or occupancy fewer than four sleeping rooms in their home. (§ 20-110) It is also unlawful to deny any person access to or membership or participation in any multiple listing service, real estate brokers organization, or other organization or facility relating to the business of selling or renting dwellings or to discriminate against such person in the terms or conditions of such access, membership, or participation on account of sex. (§ 20-109)

**ENFORCEMENT:** Any person who claims to have been injured by a discriminatory housing practice may file a complaint with the Equal Opportunity Commission within 180 days of the occurrence of the alleged discriminatory act. The commission shall investigate the complaint and determine whether probable cause exists to credit the allegations. If probable cause is shown, the commission will try to eliminate or correct the alleged discriminatory housing practice. (§ 20-114) If within 30 days after a complaint is filed the commission has been unable to obtain voluntary compliance, the commission shall commence a civil action in district court on behalf of the complainant within 30 days after its determination that it is unable to obtain voluntary compliance. Alternatively, a complainant may file a civil action in district court on his or her own behalf. Such an action must be commenced within 180 days after the complaint arose. The court may award a successful complainant equitable and affirmative relief, together with costs of the action and reasonable attorney's fees. (§§ 20-117, -118, -119)

# INSURANCE

Discrimination is prohibited between individuals of the same class and equal expectation of life in rates charged for life insurance or annuity contracts or between individuals of the same class or essentially the same hazard in the amount of premium, policy fees, or rates charged for accident or health insurance, in the benefits under these contracts, or in any other term or condition of these contracts. [§ 44-1525(7)]

> **ENFORCEMENT:** Whenever the Director of Insurance shall have reason to believe that a person has engaged or is engaging in a discriminatory practice, the director shall issue and serve upon such person a statement of the charges and a notice of the time of the hearing. The director will make an order requiring the person to stop engaging in the discriminatory practice. (§ 44-1528) Failure to do so may result in the imposition of monetary fines of up to $10,000 for each violation or the suspension or revocation of the insurer's license. (§ 44-1532)

# PUBLIC ACCOMMODATIONS

It is unlawful for any person, directly or indirectly, to refuse, withhold from, or deny any person any of the accommodations, advantages, facilities, services, or privileges of a public accommodation or to segregate any person in a place of public accommodation on the basis of sex. (§ 20-134 reissue of 1983)

> **ENFORCEMENT:** Any person claiming to be aggrieved by an unlawful discriminatory practice may file a complaint with the Equal Opportunity Commission. If the commission determines there is reasonable cause to believe the charge is true, the commission will endeavor to eliminate the unlawful practice by informal methods of conference, conciliation, and persuasion. (§ 20-140 reissue of 1983)

# NEVADA

## Home and Family

## MARRIAGE

**AGE OF CONSENT:** A person 18 years or older may consent to marry. (§ 122.020)*

**CONSENT REQUIREMENT:** Persons at least 16 years of age may marry if they have the consent of either parent or legal guardian. (§ 122.020) Persons younger than 16 may marry only if they have the consent of either parent or legal guardian and authorization of the district court. The court will authorize marriages of persons under 16 in extraordinary circumstances including but not limited to pregnancy. (§ 122.025)

**LICENSE REQUIREMENT:** Persons wishing to marry must obtain a license from the county clerk of any county in the state. Proof of age may be required. (§ 122.040)

**PROHIBITED MARRIAGE:** Incestuous marriages and bigamous marriages are void without the necessity of a decree of divorce or annulment or other legal proceeding. (§ 125.290) Children born of void marriages are legitimate. (§ 125.410)

## DISSOLUTION OF MARRIAGE

**ANNULMENT:** Annulment of marriages contracted, performed, or entered into within the state may be obtained by complaint, under oath, to any district court of the state. (§ 125.360) Factors 24, 35, and 36, listed in Appendix A, are grounds for annulment. (§§ 125.320, .330, .340) A marriage may also be annulled for any cause which is grounds for annulling or declaring a contract void in a court of equity. (§ 125.350)

*Residency Requirement:* There is no residency requirement if the marriage was contracted, performed, or entered into within the state (§§ 125.360, .370); otherwise, the requirement is 6 weeks.

**LEGAL SEPARATION:** A husband and wife may agree to an immediate separation and may make provision for the support of either spouse and the children. (§ 123.080)

*Residency Requirement:* There is no relevant statutory provision.

**DIVORCE**

*Residency Requirement:* Residency of 6 weeks is required to obtain a divorce in Nevada. (§ 125.020)

*Grounds for Divorce:* Grounds for divorce include factors 1 and 31 (for 1 year), listed in Appendix A, and insanity which existed for 2 years before the commencement of the action. (§ 125.010)

*Conciliation Requirement:* There is no relevant statutory provision.

*Property Distribution:* The court will make an equitable disposition of all community property and property held jointly by the spouses on or after July 1,

---

*Unless otherwise specified, all reference citations are to the Nevada Revised Statutes (1957).

1979. Factors considered are 3, 22, 23, and 24, listed in Appendix F. Either party's property is also subject to distribution for the support of the other or the children, as the situation may require. The court may, on its own motion or upon the request of either party, partition the property held by the parties jointly. (§ 125.150)

*Child Custody:* In determining sole or joint custody of a minor child, the sole consideration of the court is the best interests of the child. The factors considered in awarding custody are 6, 10, and 13, listed in Appendix B. (§ 125.480)

*Child Support:* In an action for divorce or permanent support and maintenance, the court may make such preliminary and final orders as it may deem proper for the support of any minor children of the parties. (§ 125.230)

*Spousal Support/Alimony:* The court may award alimony to either party. Payments cease on the death or remarriage of the recipient spouse. (§ 125.150)

*Enforcement of Support Orders:* In order to ensure compliance with an order of support, the court may appoint a receiver, require that security be posted, provide for execution, or order the sale of real or personal property of either spouse as under execution in other cases. (§ 125.240) Specifically, to enforce support obligations owed a minor child, the court may order the parent to assign to the county clerk, the custodial parent, or the state welfare administrator that portion of his or her salary, wages, or commissions due or to become due which will be sufficient to pay the amount ordered by the court for the support, maintenance, and education of the minor child. (§ 31-463) In addition, a portion of unemployment insurance benefits payable to a person owing child support may be deducted in order to meet the support obligations. (§ 612.457) Disobedience of any support order is punishable by contempt. (§ 125.240) See also the Revised Uniform Reciprocal Enforcement of Support Act of 1968, §§ 130.010 *et seq.*

*Spouse's Name:* Upon granting a divorce, the court will change the name of the woman to a former name which she has legally borne, if a just and reasonable cause can be shown. (§ 125.130)

*Divorce by Affidavit or Summary Judgment:* A marriage may be dissolved by summary proceedings when all the following conditions exist at the time the proceeding is commenced: (1) either party resided in the state 6 weeks before suit was brought; (2) the parties have lived separate and apart for 1 year without cohabitation or they are incompatible; (3) there are no minor children born or adopted before or during the marriage, and the wife, to her knowledge, is not pregnant; (4) the parties have executed an agreement setting forth the division of property and the assumption of the community liabilities; (5) the parties waive their rights to spousal support; (6) the parties waive their rights to notice of entry of the decree of divorce, to appeal, to request findings of fact and conclusions of law and to move for a new trial; and (7) the parties want the court to enter a decree of divorce. (§ 125.181)

*Displaced Homemaker Laws:* The state board for vocational education is authorized to establish a center where services are provided for displaced homemakers. (§ 388.630) The center shall provide counseling services, services related to vocational training, and employment placement; educational and counseling services related to health and health care; services related to financial management, publicity, and information about legal assistance and education; and services related to publicity and information about programs of assistance. (§ 388.640)

# DOMESTIC VIOLENCE

**STATUTORY PROVISION:** Attempting to cause or causing bodily injury to a family or household member or placing the family member in fear of imminent physical harm by threat or force is prohibited. (§ 217.400)

**WHO IS PROTECTED?** Spouses, cohabitants, and minor children are protected. (§ 33.020)

**RELIEF AVAILABLE:** Spouses or cohabitants may obtain a temporary order restraining the abuser from threatening or physically injuring the victim or minor child or requiring the abuser to vacate the family residence for a period of up to 30 days. A police officer may arrest an abuser without a warrant if the officer has probable cause to believe that the person to be arrested abused his or her spouse and the officer finds evidence of bodily harm to the spouse. [§ 171.124(f)]

**MARITAL RAPE:** A husband may not be convicted of a sexual assault upon his spouse, unless at the time the sexual assault occurred the couple was living separate and apart and one of them had filed an action for separate maintenance or divorce, the act committed was other than sexual intercourse in its ordinary meaning, or the husband was an accomplice or accessory to the sexual assault by a third person. (§ 200.373)

**CIVIL LAWSUIT FOR RAPE OR ASSAULT:** There are no relevant cases. Spouses may only sue each other for torts arising out of motor vehicle accidents. [*Rupert v. Stienne*, 528 P.2d 1013 (Nev. 1974)]

**CHILD ABUSE:** Any physical or mental injury of a nonaccidental nature, sexual abuse, sexual exploitation, negligent treatment, or maltreatment of a child under the age of 18 by a person who is responsible for the child's welfare, under circumstances which indicate the child's health and welfare are harmed or threatened, is prohibited. (§ 200.5011) Any person who so abuses a child is guilty of a gross misdemeanor unless a more severe penalty is prescribed by law for an act or omission which brings about the abuse, neglect, or danger. (§ 200.508)

> *Notification Requirement:* All persons and health care professionals, attorneys, members of the clergy, social workers, teachers, and school and child care personnel must report all suspected cases of child abuse to the local office of the welfare division of the Department of Human Resources, the police department, a sheriff's office, or the agency authorized by the juvenile court to receive such reports. [§ 200.502(2)]

# INHERITANCE RIGHTS

**FAILURE TO MAKE A WILL:** The surviving spouse is entitled to one-half of all the community property (§§ 123.250, 134.010) in addition to all the decedent's separate property if the decedent left no other heirs; to one-half, if the decedent left one child or children of one deceased child, or parents, siblings, nieces, or nephews; to one-third, if the decedent left more than one child or left one child and the children of one or more deceased children. (§§ 134.040, 050)

**FAILURE TO PROVIDE BY WILL:** If a decedent had married after making a will, the will is revoked as to the surviving spouse, unless provision had been made for the survivor by marriage contract or unless the surviving spouse is mentioned in the will in a provision evidencing the testator's intention not to provide for the surviving spouse. (§ 133.110)

**CHILDREN BORN OUT OF WEDLOCK:** A child born out of wedlock is the natural heir of the mother and her kin. Such a child can inherit from the father and his kin only where the natural parents have married or attempted to marry before the child's birth and the marriage is later declared void; or if the attempted marriage is invalid without a court order, the child is born within 285 days after the termination of cohabitation; or while the child was still a minor, the father received the child into his home and openly held the child out as his own natural child; or the father had acknowledged or admitted his paternity of the child in a writing filed with the state registrar of vital statistics. (§ 126.051)

**HOMESTEAD, PERSONAL, AND FAMILY ALLOWANCES:** If the whole property exempt by law is set apart and is not sufficient for the support of the surviving spouse, child, or children, the court shall make such reasonable allowance out of the estate as is necessary for the maintenance of the family according to their circumstances during the progress of the settlement of the estate which, in the case of an insolvent estate, shall not be longer than 1 year after granting the letters of administration. (§ 146.030) Support payments have priority over all claims except funeral charges, expenses of the decedent's last illness, and administrative expenses. (§ 146.040)

**OPTION TO DISREGARD THE WILL:** Upon the death of either husband or wife, an undivided one-half interest in the community property becomes the property of the surviving spouse in addition to his or her sole separate property. (§ 123.250)

# REPRODUCTIVE RIGHTS
## ABORTION
*Statutory Provisions:* Abortions may be performed only by a physician who is licensed to practice in the state or is in the employ of the government of the United States, within 24 weeks after the commencement of the pregnancy. Abortions may be performed after the twenty-fourth week of pregnancy only if the physician has reasonable cause to believe that an abortion is necessary to preserve the health of the pregnant woman. (§ 422.250)

*Informed Consent:* The attending physician shall accurately and in a manner which is reasonably likely to be understood by the pregnant woman explain that she is pregnant and inform her that a copy of her pregnancy test is available to her; inform her of the number of weeks that have elapsed since conception; explain any known immediate or long-term physical or psychological dangers resulting from abortions, including an increase in the incidence of premature births, tubal pregnancies, and still-births; explain the risks associated with her pregnancy; describe the medical procedure to be used; present alternatives to abortion; explain that if the child is born alive, all reasonable steps will be taken to preserve its life; and present any other material facts which in the physician's professional judgment are necessary to allow the woman to give her informed consent. If the woman doesn't understand English, the form indicating consent must be written in a language understood by her. (§ 442.253)

*Parental Consent:* There is no relevant statutory provision. However, an abortion is not to be performed upon an unmarried and unemancipated woman under 18 years of age unless her parent or guardian is notified at least 24 hours before the

abortion is performed, if it is possible to notify the parent or guardian. (§ 442.255)
*Spousal Consent:* There is no relevant statutory provision. However, if the woman is married, the physician may not perform or induce the abortion without notifying the husband of the impending abortion at least 24 hours before the abortion, if it is possible to do so. Notification to the husband is not required if the parties are legally separated or the woman has secured a judicial declaration of paternity stating that a man other than her husband impregnated her. (§ 442.244)
*Reporting Requirements:* A physician who performs an abortion must maintain a record of it for at least 5 years after it is performed. The record must contain the written consent of the woman; a statement of the information that was provided to the woman; and a description of efforts to give any required notice if the woman is under 18 years of age or is married. (§ 442.256)

**BIRTH CONTROL:** The health division of the Nevada Department of Human Resources, shall provide information on birth control. (§ 442.080) The state welfare division is authorized to conduct a family planning service in any county of the state. Such service may include the dispensing of information and the distribution of literature on birth control methods. (§ 442.235)

**STERILIZATION:** There is no relevant statutory provision.

# UNMARRIED COUPLES

**COMMON-LAW MARRIAGE:** Common-law marriage is not valid if entered into after March 29, 1943. (§ 122.010)

**COHABITAL RELATIONSHIPS:** The Nevada Supreme Court has upheld the right of unmarried former cohabitants who had cohabited for 23 years to seek a division of properties acquired by the parties during the period of their cohabitation. Although the woman failed to prove the existence of an express contract between the parties to pool funds or form a partnership, the existence of an implied contract was inferred by the court based on the purpose, duration, and stability of the relationship and the expectations of the parties. [*Hay v. Hay*, 678 P.2d 672 (Nev. 1984)]

## CHILDREN

*Custody:* Once the parent-and-child relationship has been established, the court may make any provision concerning the custody and guardianship of the child and visitation privileges as are in the child's best interests. (§ 126.161)
*Legitimation Proceedings:* Illegitimate children become legitimate by the subsequent intermarriage of their parents. (§ 122.140)
*Paternity Proceedings:* A child, the natural mother, a man presumed or alleged to be the father, or an interested party may bring an action to determine the paternity of a child born out of wedlock. The action can be brought up until 3 years after the child reaches its majority. (§§ 126.071, .081) The court may, and shall upon the motion of a party, order the parties to the action to submit to one or more blood tests. The results of the tests may be received into evidence. (§ 126.121) Other evidence relating to paternity includes evidence of sexual intercourse between the mother and alleged father at any possible time of conception; an expert opinion concerning the statistical probability of the father's paternity based upon the duration of mother's pregnancy; and medical and anthropological evidence based on tests performed by experts. (§ 126.131)
*Obligations of the Putative Father:* The judgment or order finding paternity may contain provisions concerning the duty of support and the furnishing of a

bond or other security for the payment of the judgment or any other matter in the best interests of the child. The judgment may also direct the father to pay the reasonable expenses of the mother's pregnancy and confinement. (§ 126.161)

# Education

## STATUTORY PROVISION

There is no relevant statutory provision. However, it should be noted that if federal funds are involved, federal law, Title IX of the Education Amendments of 1972, Pub. L. No. 92-318, 20 U.S.C. §§ 1681–1686, may apply. There will be no discrimination in the admission of students to the University of Nevada, on account of sex, race, or color. (§ 396.530)

# Employment

## EQUAL PAY LAWS

It is unlawful for an employer to discriminate on the basis of sex in wages paid to employees in the same establishment who perform work requiring equal skill, effort, and responsibility, under similar working conditions. Wage differentials are not prohibited if based on a bona fide seniority or merit system, the quality or quantity of production, or any factor other than sex. (§ 608.017)

**ENFORCEMENT:** Whenever an employee brings a suit for wages earned but not paid and establishes by decision of the court or by jury verdict that the amount is justly due, and that demand had been made in writing at least 5 days before suit was brought, for a sum not exceeding the amount due, the court will award the plaintiff reasonable attorney's fees, in addition to the amount due for wages plus penalties to be taxed as costs of the suit. (§ 608.140) The action must be commenced within 3 years of the occurrence of the unlawful discriminatory act. [§ 11.190(3)(a)]

## FAIR EMPLOYMENT LAWS

The law applies to the state, its political subdivisions, natural persons, employers of fifteen or more employees, labor organizations, and employment agencies. It makes it an unlawful employment practice for an employer to fail or refuse to hire or to discharge any person, or for a labor organization or employment agency to discriminate against any person with respect to the terms, conditions, or privileges of employment or employment-related services. (§ 613.330) It is not unlawful to hire someone on the basis of that person's sex in those instances where sex is a bona fide occupational qualification reasonably necessary to the normal operation of that particular business or enterprise. [§ 613.350(1)]

**ENFORCEMENT:** Any person injured by an unlawful employment practice may file a complaint to that effect with the Nevada Equal Rights Commission. (§ 613.405) If the commission does not conclude that an unfair employment practice has occurred, the person alleging such a practice may apply to the district court for an order granting or restoring to that person the rights to which he or she is entitled. (§ 613.420) Any such action must be brought within 180 days of the occurrence of the discriminatory act. (§ 613.430)

## GOVERNMENT CONTRACTORS AND SUBCONTRACTORS

It is unlawful for any government contractor or subcontractor to refuse to employ or to discharge from employment any person because of sex or to discriminate against a person with respect to hire, tenure, advancement, compensation or other terms, conditions or privileges of employment because of his or her sex. (§ 338.125)

**ENFORCEMENT:** Any violation of the above provision shall constitute a material breach of contract. [§ 338.125(3)] For contractors or subcontractors who employ fifteen or more persons, see "Fair Employment Laws."

## STATE EMPLOYEE LAWS

See "Fair Employment Laws."

## VETERAN'S PREFERENCE

Five points are added to the civil service examination passing scores of veterans and the widows of veterans, and ten points to the passing scores of disabled veterans; preference may be applied to any open competitive examination but only to one promotional examination. (§ 284.260)

# Community Life

## CREDIT

It is unlawful for any creditor to discriminate against any applicant with respect to any aspect of a credit transaction on the basis of sex or marital status. A creditor must consider the combined income of both spouses in extending credit to a married couple and may not exclude the income of either without just cause. If each spouse separately and voluntarily applies for and obtains separate credit from the same creditor, the credit accounts may not be aggregated or combined for the purpose of determining permissible finance charges or loan ceilings. (§§ 598.100, .110, .120)

**ENFORCEMENT:** Any person who has been discriminated against in credit may file a complaint with the Division of Financial Institutions of the Department of Commerce. (§ 598B.140) Upon receipt of such a complaint, the division will investigate matters alleged to be discriminatory and seek to eliminate or correct the cause of the complaint or discriminatory condition by methods of conference and conciliation. (§ 598B.150) Alternatively, an aggrieved party may apply directly to the district court for relief. If discrimination is found to have occurred, the court may enjoin the creditor from continued violation and award damages to the plaintiff. (§ 598B.170) Any action brought under these statutes must be commenced within 1 year from the date of the occurrence of the violation. (§ 598B.180)

# HOUSING

It is unlawful for any person to refuse to sell, lease, rent, negotiate for the sale or rental, or otherwise make unavailable or deny a dwelling, or to represent that a dwelling when it is available, is not available for inspection, sale, or rental on the basis of sex. (§§ 118.100, 118.105, 207.300) These provisions do not apply to the sale or rental of a single family house by the owner if a real estate broker or salesperson is not used and if discriminatory advertising is not employed, or to the rental of housing in a four-family building in which the owner or a member of the owner's family resides. (§ 118.060)

**ENFORCEMENT:** Any person who claims to have been injured by a discriminatory housing practice or who believes he or she will be irreparably injured by such a practice that is about to occur may file a complaint with the Nevada Equal Rights Commission. (§ 118.110) Any person may commence an action in district court to enforce the statutory provisions prohibiting housing discrimination. If the court determines that the law has been violated by the defendant and that the plaintiff has been injured as a result of the violation, it may enjoin the defendant from continued violation or take such other affirmative action as may be appropriate and may award a prevailing plaintiff actual damages for any economic loss, together with court costs and reasonable attorney's fees. (§ 118.120)

# INSURANCE

Discrimination is prohibited between individuals of the same class and equal expectation of life in rates charged for life insurance or annuity contracts or between individuals of the same class and essentially the same hazard in the amount of premium, policy fees, or rates charged for health insurance, in the benefits payable under these contracts, or in any other term or condition of these contracts. (§ 686A.100) No health, group health, or blanket health insurance policy may contain any exclusion, reduction, or other limitation of coverage relating to complications of pregnancy, unless the provision applies generally to all benefits payable under the policy. (§§ 689A.042, 689B.260)

**ENFORCEMENT:** If the Commissioner of Insurance believes that any person engaged in the insurance business is engaging in a method of competition which is discriminatory or unfair and that proceedings would be in the public interest, the commissioner will, after a hearing of which notice of the charges against such person are given, make a written report of the relevant findings. If such method of competition is not discontinued, the commissioner may cause an action to be instituted in district court to enjoin and restrain such person from engaging in such method, act, or practice. (§ 686A.170)

# PUBLIC ACCOMMODATIONS

It is unlawful to deny, deprive, or withhold the full and equal enjoyment of the goods, services, facilities, privileges, advantages, and accommodations of any place of public accommodation on the basis of race, color, religion, national origin, or physical or visual handicap.

Although the law states that *all* persons are entitled to the equal enjoyment of places of public accommodation, it fails to include sex as a protected characteristic. (§ 651.070)

**ENFORCEMENT:** A person who believes he or she has been denied the full and equal enjoyment of goods, services, facilities, privileges, and advantages may file a complaint with the Nevada Equal Rights Commission. (§ 651.110) The person may also bring a civil action in a court in and for the county in which the discriminatory act occurred or the defendant resides. The plaintiff can recover actual damages for any economic loss plus court costs and reasonable attorney's fees. (§ 651.090) Any action brought pursuant to this law must be commenced within 1 year from the date the act complained of occurred. (§ 651.120)

# NEW HAMPSHIRE

## Home and Family

## MARRIAGE

**AGE OF CONSENT:** A person 18 years of age or older may consent to marry. (§ 457:4)*

**CONSENT REQUIREMENT:** No male under age 14 and no female under age 13 is capable of contracting a valid marriage. Parents may bring a suit to annul the marriage of their minor child who married under 18 years of age. The annulment lies with the discretion of superior court. (§ 457:5) If special cause exists and minors between the ages of 13 and 18 desire to marry, they and their parents may apply in writing to a justice of superior court or to the judge of probate of the county in which one of them resides for permission to marry. (§ 457:6)

**LICENSE REQUIREMENT:** All persons wishing to marry must first file a notice of intention to marry with the town clerk, who will issue to the applicant a certificate of marriage 3 days thereafter. However, before the certificate is issued, the applicants must obtain a report from a licensed physician stating they are free from syphilis or gonorrhea and will not infect others. (§§ 457:17, :22, :26) The certificate, once issued, is valid for 90 days. (§ 457:26)

**PROHIBITED MARRIAGES:** All marriages between a woman and her father, uncle, mother's husband, grandfather, son, husband's son, daughter's husband, brother, grandson, granddaughter's husband, nephew, or cousin are incestuous and void. (§ 457:2) Bigamous marriages are also prohibited. (§ 639:1) Children born of incestuous marriages entered into in New Hampshire are deemed children born out of wedlock. However, if the marriage was entered into and valid in another state, it will be valid in New Hampshire provided the spouses are or become permanent residents of the state. Children born of such marriages are legitimate. (§ 457:3)

## DISSOLUTION OF MARRIAGE

**ANNULMENT:** A petition for annulment may be filed by a parent or guardian of a minor child. Parties under the age of consent at the time of the marriage may petition for an annulment in the Superior Court, unless one of the parties, after arriving at the age of consent, confirmed the marriage. (§ 457:5)

*Residency Requirement:* When the parties are underage, a suit may be maintained for annulment if one of them is a resident of the state. [*Foster v. Foster*, 199 A.367 (N.H. 1938)] In any proceeding for an annulment, for any cause, the court may annul the marriage if it was performed in the state although neither party had ever been a resident of the state. (§ 458:3)

**LEGAL SEPARATION:** Grounds for separation include factors 3 to 5 (not been heard of for 2 years) 6 (sentence of more than 1 year served), 11, 12 (by husband for 2 years), 17, 22, 25, and 31 (wife left without consent for 2 years), listed in

---

*Unless otherwise specified, all reference citations are to New Hampshire Revised Statutes Annotated (1955).

Appendix A, as well as situations when there is mental abuse, when either party has joined a religious society which professes that the relationship of husband and wife is unlawful and refuses to cohabit with the other for 6 consecutive months, or when the wife of any citizen leaves the state and resides elsewhere for 10 consecutive years without her husband's consent and without returning to claim her marriage rights; or when the wife lives in the state and her husband becomes a citizen of a foreign country without supporting the wife. (§§ 458:7, :7a, :26)

*Residency Requirement:* See "Divorce."

## DIVORCE

*Residency Requirement:* The court may only grant a divorce if either or both parties are domiciled in the state when the action is commenced, or where the person bringing the action has been a resident for at least 1 year preceding the action and the cause for the divorce arose in the state. (§§ 458:5, :6)

*Grounds for Divorce:* Factor 13, listed in Appendix A, and all other factors listed in "Legal Separation" are grounds for divorce.

*Conciliation Requirement:* If the court determines that there is a reasonable possibility of reconciliation before a final decree of divorce is entered, it will continue the proceedings and require both parties to submit to marriage counseling. (§§ 458:6, :7)

*Property Distribution:* After the filing of a divorce action, the court may grant a temporary order which prohibits transferring, encumbering, disposing of, or concealing in any way any real or personal property, except as reasonable in the usual course of business or for necessities of life. (§ 458:16) When a decree of divorce becomes final, the court may assign to the wife all or part of her estate and such parts of her former husband's estate as is just. (§ 458:19) The court divides the property equitably, regardless of gender. [*Hanson v. Hanson*, 433 A.2d 1310)]

*Child Custody:* There is a presumption that joint legal custody is in the best interests of the child. Joint legal custody includes all parental rights with the exception of physical custody, which the court will award without any preference to either parent because of the parent's sex. The court will consider factors 5, 13, 18, 21, and 23, listed in Appendix B. (§§ 458:17, :17a)

*Child Support:* Whenever a final decree of divorce is entered, the court may order reasonable provisions as to the support and education of the child. Whenever the custody of the child is awarded to the director of the division of welfare, the court will make an order requiring the town in which the child resides to bear the expenses for the maintenance of the child. (§§ 458:17, :18)

*Spousal Support/Alimony:* See "Property Distribution." The court may order either spouse to pay a sum of money to the other. In cases where there are no children or where children have reached the age of majority, the order will be effective for 3 years, or for 3 years after the youngest child has reached the age of majority. After this time, the order may be renewed for an additional 3-year period if justice requires. (§ 459:19) See also *Buckner v. Buckner*, 415 A.2d 871 (N.H. 1980).

*Enforcement of Support Orders:* In all cases where the court awards maintenance or child support, it may order that the property be sold or money turned over to a trustee for investment and that the income derived from such investment be applied toward the support of the wife or maintenance and education of the minor children. (§ 458:20) The court may also require the person owing a duty of support to post a bond as security for the payment of support obligations. (§ 458:21) See also the Revised Uniform Reciprocal Enforcement of Support Act of 1968, §§ 546:1 *et seq.*

*Spouse's Name:* When a decree of divorce or annulity is made, the court may restore the maiden or former name of the wife. (§ 458:24)

*Divorce by Affidavit or Summary Judgment:* There is no relevant statutory provision.

*Displaced Homemaker Laws:* Centers have been established to offer job counseling, training and referral services, and information and assistance with respect to health care, financial matters, education, nutrition, and legal problems to displaced homemakers. (§§ 275-D:2, :3)

# DOMESTIC VIOLENCE

**STATUTORY PROVISION:** Domestic violence is defined as one or more of the following acts between household members: attempting to cause, purposely or recklessly causing bodily injury with or without a deadly weapon, attempting to or purposely placing another in fear of bodily injury by threats or physical menace, or attempting to engage in sexual relations with another by means of force, threat, or coercion. (§ 173-B:1)

**WHO IS PROTECTED?** Spouses, former spouses, cohabitants, former cohabitants, parents, and other kin who reside with the aggressor other than minor children are protected. (§ 173-B:1)

**RELIEF AVAILABLE:** Victims of domestic violence may file a petition in district or superior court in the county where they reside. There is no filing fee, and the victim may file without legal counsel. Any proceeding under this law will not bar any other available criminal or civil remedy. The court will hold a hearing within 30 days of the filing of a petition or within 10 days after the aggressor receives notice of the suit, whichever occurs later. Upon a showing of abuse, the court may grant protective orders preventing the aggressor from further abusing the victim or entering victim's home; granting temporary custody of minor children to either parent; requiring both parties to submit to counseling; or requiring aggressor to pay the victim for loss of earnings or support, medical expenses, moving expenses, and reasonable attorney's fees. The court may also grant temporary relief as stated above if there is a showing of immediate and present danger of abuse without notice to the aggressor. The victim's whereabouts will not be revealed except by an order of the court and for good cause. (§§ 173-B:3 to :6) A police officer may arrest a person without a warrant if there is probable cause to believe the person has assaulted a family or household member within the past 6 hours. (§ 594:10)

**MARITAL RAPE:** Even though the victim is the aggressor's legal spouse, sexual penetration is a felony when the aggressor uses force or physical violence, when the victim is surprised or physically helpless to resist, when the aggressor uses threats of force or violence against the victim or any other person and the victim believes the aggressor has the ability to carry out the threats in the future, or when the victim is drugged. (§§ 632-A:1, :2, :5)

**CIVIL LAWSUIT FOR RAPE OR ASSAULT:** There are no cases directly on point. However, in *Gilman v. Gilman*, 95 A.657 (N.H. 1915), the court held that spouses may sue each other for torts.

**CHILD ABUSE:** A person is guilty of a crime if he or she knowingly endangers the welfare of a child under 18 years of age; induces a child to engage in conduct that endangers the child's health or safety; intentionally injures the child either physically or mentally; tattoos the child; or forces or solicits a child under 16 to engage in sexual activity for pornographic purposes. (§§ 169-C:3, 639:3, 649-A:2)

*Notification Requirement:* Any medical practitioners, including hospital personnel, engaged in the examination, care, and treatment of persons; all teachers, school officials, law enforcement officials, priests, ministers, or rabbis; or any other persons having reason to suspect that a child has been abused must report this to the Bureau of Child and Family Services, Division of Welfare, Department of Health and Welfare. An oral report made immediately in person or by phone may have to be followed by a written report at the bureau's request. Anyone making a report under this law or who participates in any investigation or judicial proceeding is immune from any liability. (§§ 169-C:29 to :31)

# INHERITANCE RIGHTS

**FAILURE TO MAKE A WILL:** If there are no surviving children or parents of the decedent, the surviving spouse will receive the entire estate; if the decedent is survived by a parent but no children, the spouse receives the first $50,000 plus one-half of the balance of the estate; if there are surviving children, all of whom are the children of the surviving spouse, the spouse receives the first $50,000 plus one-half of the balance of the estate; if there are surviving children one or more of whom are not children of the surviving spouse, the spouse receives one-half of the estate. (§ 561:1)

**FAILURE TO PROVIDE BY WILL:** There is no relevant statutory provision.

**CHILDREN BORN OUT OF WEDLOCK:** A child born of unwed parents will inherit from the mother as if born in lawful wedlock. The child will inherit from the father if the parents marry after the birth of the child, if there is an acknowledgment of paternity or legitimation by the father, if a court decrees the decedent to be the father before his death, if paternity is established after the death of the father, or if the decedent has adopted the child. (§ 561:4)

**HOMESTEAD, PERSONAL, AND FAMILY ALLOWANCES:** The court may make a reasonable allowance to the widow out of the estate for her support, which will be subtracted in whole or in part from her distributive share, whether the deceased died testate or intestate. The surviving spouse may remain in the house of the decedent 40 days after the decedent's death without being charged rent. (§§ 560:1, :2) Every person is entitled to $5000 worth of his or her homestead, which is property owned and occupied as a dwelling by that person. This right lasts for the person's lifetime. The homestead right does not include land upon which the house is situated if the land is not owned by the owner of the house. (§§ 480:1, :3-a)

**OPTION TO DISREGARD THE WILL:** Under this provision, the surviving spouse must waive the homestead right, if any, and any provisions in the will in his or her favor. The survivor will receive the following after the payment of debts and expenses of administration are taken from the estate. If there are surviving children or grandchildren, the spouse receives one-third of the personal property and one-third of the real estate; if there are no children or grandchildren but a surviving parent, sister, or brother, the spouse will receive $10,000 in value of decedents personal property and all real property if it is worth less than $10,000. If the real estate or personal property is worth more than $10,000, the spouse receives $10,000 plus half of any amount remaining. If the decedent left no other heirs, the spouse will receive $10,000 plus $2000 for each full year that the spouses were married, plus half the balance of the estate. (§ 560:10)

# REPRODUCTIVE RIGHTS

**ABORTION:**  There is no relevant statutory provision.

**BIRTH CONTROL:**  When the town clerk issues a certificate of marriage to a couple, a list of family planning agencies and services is provided to them. (§ 457:28-a)

**STERILIZATION:**  No health facility which permits sterilization operations for contraceptive purposes may require the person requesting the operation to meet any special nonmedical qualifications such as age, marital status, and number of children, which are not imposed on people seeking other types of operations in the facilities. However, such a facility may establish requirements relating to the physical or mental condition of the patient and require the attending physician to counsel or advise the patient as to whether sterilization is appropriate. (§ 460:21-a)

# UNMARRIED COUPLES

**COMMON-LAW MARRIAGE:**  Persons cohabiting and acknowledging each other as husband and wife and generally reputed to be such in the community for a period of 3 years and until one of them dies, will be deemed to have been legally married. (§ 457:39)

**COHABITAL RELATIONSHIPS:**  See "Common-Law Marriage."

**CHILDREN**

*Custody:*  There is no relevant statutory provision.

*Legitimation Proceedings:*  When parents of children born out of wedlock enter marriage (or fulfill the cohabital requirement above) and recognize such children as their own, the children are legitimate. (§ 457:42)

*Paternity Proceedings:*  An action to determine paternity must be brought in the superior court within 2 years of the child's birth. A mother, child, or public authority may petition to determine paternity. Upon request of the petitioner, the court will schedule an immediate hearing on the issue be required to post in advance as security for the payment of maternity and other expenses for which he may be liable. The court has continuing jurisdiction to make, modify, or revoke a judgment for future education and necessary support.

*Obligations of the Putative Father:*  If paternity has been determined, the father will be liable for the expenses of pregnancy, confinement, education, or support that was furnished for the child by the mother or by a public or private agency. (§ 168-A:2) The father of a child born of unwed parents is liable to the same extent as the father of a child born in wedlock, whether or not the child was born alive, for the reasonable expense of the mother's pregnancy and confinement and for the education and necessary support of the child. A child born of unwed parents includes a child born to a married woman by a man other than her husband. (§ 168-A:1)

# Education

## STATUTORY PROVISION

The New Hampshire Constitution contains an equal rights provision which may be used to challenge sex discrimination. (N.H. Const. part 1, art. 2) The Commission on the Status of Women is authorized to study and revise statutes relative to women, recommend methods of overcoming discrimination, promote more effective methods for enabling women to develop their skills and continue their education, and secure appropriate recognition of women's accomplishments and contributions to the state. (§ 19-B:4)

# Employment

## EQUAL PAY LAWS

It is unlawful to discriminate on the basis of sex in wages for work requiring equal skill, effort, and responsibilty. Wage variations are permitted, however, if based on seniority, experience, training, skill, ability, difference in duties and services performed (regularly or occasionally), difference in shift, difference in availability for other operations, or if provided by a collective bargaining agreement. (§ 275:37)

**ENFORCEMENT:** The Commissioner of Labor has the power and duty to enforce the provisions of the law. (§ 275:38) An employer who violates the provisions above will be liable to the employee in the amount of unpaid wages and in an additional equal amount of liquidated damages. An action to recover unpaid wages and damages must be brought within 1 year of the occurrence of the discriminatory act in any court with competent jurisdiction. (§§ 275:39, :40)

## FAIR EMPLOYMENT LAWS

The law covers employers of six or more people, the state, its political and civil subdivisions, labor organizations, and employment agencies. (§ 345-A:3) It makes it unlawful for an employer to refuse to hire or to discriminate in compensation, terms, conditions, or privileges of employment on the basis of sex; for a labor organization to exclude or expel its members because of sex; or for an employment agency to refuse to recruit, place, or refer an individual for employment because of the individual's sex. [§§ 354-A:8, -A:8(1)]

**ENFORCEMENT:** A person claiming to be agrieved by an unlawful discriminatory practice must file a complaint with the Commission for Human Rights within 180 days of the occurrence of the alleged discriminatory act. The commission makes a prompt investigation of all charges, and if they are found to be true, it issues an order requiring the respondent to cease and desist from such unlawful discriminatory practices and to take appropriate affirmative action as in the judgment of the commission will effectuate the purpose of the law, including a requirement that the respondent report the manner of compliance to the commission. (§ 354-A:9)

# GOVERNMENT CONTRACTORS AND SUBCONTRACTORS

There is no relevant statutory provision. However, it should be noted that if federal funds are involved, Exec. Order No. 11246, 3 C.F.R. § 339 (1965), *reprinted in* 42 U.S.C. § 2000e app. at 1232, 41 C.F.R. § 60-1.2, may apply.

# STATE EMPLOYEE LAWS

See "Fair Employment Laws."

# VETERAN'S PREFERENCE

Veterans have preference of employment when applying for any job with the state or when another party contracts with the state for a construction project. (§ 283:4) This preference is extended to any unremarried widow of a veteran or any wife of a totally disabled veteran. (§ 283:5) Every political subdivision of the state must reemploy a veteran who has been placed on inactive status or has been discharged if the treasurer is notified that the veteran desires to be reinstituted in his or her prior position with the state. (§ 97:1)

# Community Life

# CREDIT

There is no applicable statutory provision available. However, it should be noted that federal law, the Equal Credit Opportunity Act of 1977, 12 C.F.R. § 202, may apply.

# HOUSING

It is an unlawful discriminatory practice for any owner, managing agent, or any other person having the right to rent or lease a dwelling or commercial structure, or any person in the business of selling or renting dwellings or commercial structures, to refuse to sell, rent, negotiate, or otherwise make unavailable or deny any dwelling or commercial structure to any person. It is unlawful to discriminate because of sex or marital status against any person with reference to the terms, conditions, privileges or provision of services or facilities in connection with the rental or sale of a dwelling or commercial structure; or to represent that a dwelling or commercial structure is not available for inspection, sale, or rental when such dwelling is in fact available. These provisions do not apply to a religious or charitable institution if the structure is owned to promote the religious principles for which the institution was established; to the sale or rental of any single-family home sold or rented by the owner if the owner does not own more than three such homes; to the sale or rental of a three-family home in which the owner or members of his or her family reside; or to the sale or rental of a single-family house by the owner if a broker and discriminatory advertising are not used. [§ 354-A:8(V)]

**ENFORCEMENT:** A person claiming to be aggrieved by an unlawful discriminatory practice must file a complaint with the Commission for Human Rights within 180 days of the occurrence of the alleged discriminatory act. The commission makes a prompt investigation of all charges, and if they are found to be true, it issues an order requiring the respondent to cease and desist from such unlawful discriminatory practices and to take appropriate affirmative action as in the judgment of the commission will effectuate the purpose of the law, including a requirement that the respondent report the manner of compliance to the commission. (§ 354-A:9)

# INSURANCE

Discrimination is prohibited between individuals of the same class and equal life expectancy in rates charged for life insurance or annuity contracts; between individuals of the same class and essentially the same hazard in the amount of premiums, policy fees, or rates charged for health insurance; or between persons as to any provision, term, condition, or benefit included in the contract. It is unlawful to refuse to insure risks solely because of age, race, sex, marital status or lawful occupation (except for life, accident, or health insurance). [§ 417:4(VIII)]

**ENFORCEMENT:** The Commissioner of Insurance has the power to serve notice upon and institute a hearing against any person engaged in the business of insurance whenever the commissioner has reason to believe such a person has engaged in an unfair practice. If after the hearing the charges are proved to be true, the commissioner may suspend, revoke, or refuse to renew that person's license or impose monetary fines for each discriminatory practice found to be in violation of the law. (§§ 417:6 to :11)

# PUBLIC ACCOMMODATIONS

It is unlawful for any owner, lessor, proprietor, manager, or employee to directly or indirectly refuse, withhold from, or deny any person any of the accommodations, advantages, facilities, or privileges of any place of public accomodation or to publish or post a written notice to the effect that the patronage of a person is unwelcome or objectionable on the basis of sex or marital status. [§ 354-A:8(IV)] However, the statute does not prohibit a religious organization from limiting admission or giving preference to persons of the same religion in order to promote the religious principles for which it is established or maintained.

**ENFORCEMENT:** See "Housing."

# NEW JERSEY

## Home and Family

## MARRIAGE

**AGE OF CONSENT:** A person 18 years of age or older may consent to marry. (§ 37:1-6)*

**CONSENT REQUIREMENT:** Persons under 18 years of age may not marry without the consent of their parents or guardian given in the presence of witnesses. Any person under 16 years of age is required to have such consent approved in writing by either a county judge or any juvenile and domestic relations judge. (§ 37:1-6)

**LICENSE REQUIREMENT:** A license must be obtained from the licensing officer of the municipality in which the woman resides; or in which the man resides if the woman is a nonresident; or in which the marriage will take place if both parties are nonresidents. Before the license will be granted, applicants must present a medical certificate stating they are not infected with syphilis. The marriage license is valid for 30 days after the date of issuance. (§§ 37:1-2 to :1-4, :1-13, :1-20)

**PROHIBITED MARRIAGES:** Bigamous marriages and marriages between ancestors and descendants, between sisters and brothers, aunts and nephews, uncles and nieces, whether of the whole or half blood, are prohibited and void. (§§ 2C:24-1, 37:1-1) Children born of void or prohibited marriages are legitimate regardless of the parents' marital status. (§ 9:17-40)

## DISSOLUTION OF MARRIAGE

**ANNULMENT:** Factors 19, 32, 36, and 38, listed in Appendix A, are grounds for annulment. Also any minor under the age of 18 at the time of marriage may nullify the marriage if he or she has not confirmed it after reaching the age of majority; a marriage may also be annulled if it is allowable under the general equity jurisdiction of Superior Court. (§ 2A:34-1)

*Residency Requirement:* Either party must be a bona fide resident of the state at the time the action is commenced. (§ 2A:34-9)

**LEGAL SEPARATION:** A divorce from bed and board or a legal separation will be granted based on factors 4, 6 (18 or more consecutive months), 7, 8 (12 or more consecutive months), 9 (12 or more consecutive months), 16 (24 or more consecutive months), 17, and 28, listed in Appendix A. (§ 2A:24-3)

*Residency Requirement:* There is no relevant statutory provision.

### DIVORCE

*Residency Requirement:* Either party must be a resident of the state when the cause of action arose and must have continued to be one when the action commenced. No action for absolute divorce will be granted on grounds other than adultery unless one of the parties has been a resident of the state for 1 year preceding the commencement of the action. (§ 2A:34-10)

*Unless otherwise specified, all reference citations are to New Jersey Statutes Annotated (West 1937).

338

*Grounds for Divorce:* Factors 4, 6, 7 to 9, 16, 17, and 30, listed in Appendix A, are grounds for divorce. (§ 2A:34-2)

*Conciliation Requirement:* There is no relevant statutory provision.

*Property Distribution:* The court makes an equitable distribution of real and personal property which was legally acquired by either party (except by way of gift, devise, or intestate succession) during the marriage. Factors 2, 4, 5, 6, 8, 11, 13, 15, 17, 18, 21, and 22, listed in Appendix F, will be considered. (§ 2A:34-23) See also *Painter v. Painter*, 320 A.2d 496 (1974).

*Child Custody:* When parents live separately or after a judgment of divorce is final, the court may make an order as to the care, custody, maintenance, and education of the minor child. Although the statute does not specifically authorize an award of joint custody, the New Jersey Supreme Court has endorsed joint custody as an alternative to sole custody in appropriate cases. [*Beck v. Beck*, 432 A.2d 63 (N.J. 1981)] When living separately, the minor child in actual custody of the mother may not be taken by the father forcibly or against the mother's will, unless the court otherwise orders. Pending, or after a divorce, factors 3, 6, and 13, listed in Appendix B, are considered. (§§ 2A:34-23, 9:2-4)

*Child Support:* See "Child Custody."

*Spousal Support/Alimony:* In all actions for divorce or nullity the court may award alimony to either party, considering factors 4, 5, 9, and 10, listed in Appendix E. (§ 2A:34-23)

*Enforcement of Support Orders:* Every order of a court awarding alimony, maintenance, or child support payments must include a notice to the party owing the duty of support that the order may be enforced by an income execution upon the commissions, earnings, salaries, wages, and other current or future income due from the payer's employer or successor employers. (§ 2A:17-56.8) Additionally, every order of support may require the party owing support to post reasonable security for the due observance of the order. Upon neglect or failure to give such reasonable security, the court may award and issue process for the immediate sequestration of the party's personal estate and rents and profits derived from such estate and appoint a receiver to administer the estate and cause any necessary amounts of support due to be paid out of the personal estate, rents and profits. (§ 2A:34-23) See also the Revised Uniform Reciprocal Enforcement of Support Act of 1968, §§ 2A:4-30.24 *et seq*.

*Spouse's Name:* After granting a divorce, the court may allow the wife to resume any name used by her before the marriage and may also order the wife to refrain from using her former husband's surname. (§ 2A:34-21)

*Divorce by Affidavit or Summary Judgment:* There is no relevant statutory provision.

*Displaced Homemaker Laws:* Job counseling, training and placement services, and health and legal referral services are among the displaced homemakers programs under this statute. (§§ 52:27D-43.19, -43.20)

# DOMESTIC VIOLENCE

**STATUTORY PROVISION:** Assault, kidnapping, criminal restraint, false imprisonment, sexual assault, criminal sexual contact, lewdness, criminal mischief, burglary, and harassment of one family member by another is a crime. (§§ 2C:25-2, -3)

**WHO IS PROTECTED?** Cohabitants, spouses, persons who are the parents of one or more children regardless of their marital status or whether they have lived together at any time, or persons 18 years of age or older related by blood and currently residing together. (§ 2C:25-3)

**RELIEF AVAILABLE:** A victim of domestic violence has the right to file a complaint in the juvenile and domestic relations court and/or in criminal court. At the hearing, the court may issue an order prohibiting the attacker from having contact with the victim or victim's family in the place of residence, employment, business, or school; an order excluding the attacker from entering the place of residence; an order determining child support, visitation rights, or custody; an order requiring the attacker to pay the victim monetary compensation for losses suffered as a direct result of the violence; and an order requiring the attacker to receive professional counseling. In emergency situations, a temporary restraining order may be granted to protect the life, health, or welfare of the victim. A hearing will be held within 10 days after such an order is granted. (§§ 2C:25-7, -13)

**MARITAL RAPE:** A woman may charge her husband with rape. [§§ 2C:14-2, -5(b)]

**CIVIL LAWSUIT FOR RAPE OR ASSAULT:** There are no cases directly on point. However, in *Cherry v. Cherry*, 403 A.2d 45, (N.J. 1979) the court held that spouses may sue each other in tort.

**CHILD ABUSE:** Any person who abandons, abuses, or is cruel to a child or who engages in sexual conduct with a child is guilty of a crime. (§§ 2C:24-4, 7:6-3) Any parent, guardian, or custodian of a child who inflicts physical injury by other than accidental means; creates a substantial risk of death, disfigurement, or impairment of physical or emotional health; commits acts of sexual abuse against the child, or fails to provide adequate food, clothing, shelter, medical care, and education is guilty of a crime. (§ 9:6-8.9)

> *Notification Requirement:* Any person having reasonable cause to believe that a child has been subject to child abuse must report it to the Bureau of Children's Services by telephone or other means. The bureau operates a 24-hour emergency telephone service to receive reports. All such reports will be kept confidential and anyone reporting a case of child abuse will be immune from liability. [§§ 9:6-8.10, -8.10(a), -8.12]

# INHERITANCE RIGHTS

**FAILURE TO MAKE A WILL:** The surviving spouse is entitled to the entire estate if decedent has no surviving parent or child. If decedent is survived by a parent but not by any children, the spouse receives the first $50,000 plus one-half of the balance of the estate. If there are surviving children, all of whom are children of the spouse, the spouse receives the first $50,000 plus one-half of the balance of the estate. If there are surviving children, one or more of whom are not the children of the surviving spouse, the spouse receives one-half of the estate. (§ 3B:5-3) When the total value of decedent's estate is less than $10,000, the surviving spouse is entitled to all the real and personal property left by the decedent, and the assets of the estate up to $5000 will be free from all debts of the decedent. (§ 3B:10-3)

**FAILURE TO PROVIDE BY WILL:** If the surviving spouse married the decedent after the will was made and is omitted from it, the spouse will receive the same share of the estate that would have been received if decedent died without a will, unless it appears from the will that the omission was intentional or the decedent provided for the spouse by a transfer outside the will. This section applies to wills executed after September 1, 1978. (§ 3B:5-15)

**CHILDREN BORN OUT OF WEDLOCK:** A child born out of wedlock is the natural heir of its mother and her kin. However, such a child can only inherit from its father if the parents marry or attempt to marry after his or her birth, the child's paternity has been established by adjudication before the death of the father, or paternity is established thereafter by clear and convincing proof, except that the paternity established under this statute will not enable the father or his kin to inherit from or through his out-of-wedlock child unless he had openly treated the child as his and had not refused to support the child. (§ 3B:5-10)

**HOMESTEAD, PERSONAL, AND FAMILY ALLOWANCES:** There is no relevant statutory provision. However, the clothing and personal property up to $5000 of the decedent will be reserved for use of the family against all creditors and before any other distribution. This statute applies provided it does not conflict with the will of the decedent. (§ 3B:16-5)

**OPTION TO DISREGARD THE WILL:** Dower rights of the widow provide she will receive, for the rest of her life, a full equal half of all real property which the decedent owned at any time during their marriage prior to May 28, 1980, if the widow has not given up her right to dower by a duly executed deed. (§ 3B:28-1) In addition, if a married person domiciled in the state dies on or after May 28, 1980, the surviving spouse has a right of election to take one-third of the augmented estate, provided that the decedent and surviving spouse had not been living separately or had not ceased to cohabit as husband and wife. (§ 3B:8-3)

# REPRODUCTIVE RIGHTS

## ABORTION

*Statutory Provisions:* There is no relevant statutory provision. However, the New Jersey Supreme Court has held that the right to choose whether to have an abortion is a fundamental right of all pregnant women. [*Right to Choose v. Byrne*, 450 A.2d 925 (N.J. 1982)] Also, the state may not directly restrict the right of women to seek abortions before the fetus is viable. [*Doe v. Bridgeton Hospital Ass'n Inc.*, 403 A.2d 965 (N.J. 1979)] Only physicians in nonprofit, nonsectarian hospitals are absolutely required to provide abortion services or procedures. (§§ 2A:65A-1, -2)

*Consent Requirements:* There is no relevant statutory provision.

*Reporting Requirements:* The physician must report to the Department of Health all instances where a fetus aborted after 15 weeks has a birth defect. (§ 26:8-40.22)

*State Funding:* Medicaid funds are payable only when the abortion is necessary to save the woman's life. (§ 30:4D-6.1) This provision was ruled unconstitutional in *Right to Choose v. Byrne*, 450 A.2d 925 (N.J. 1982).

**BIRTH CONTROL:** There is no relevant statutory provision. However, no hospital or private institution is required to provide birth control contrary to the dogmatic or moral beliefs of any well-established religious body or denomination. (§ 30:11-9)

**STERILIZATION:** There is no relevant statutory provision. However, no hospital or private institution is required to provide, practice, or permit sterilization procedures contrary to the dogmatic or moral beliefs of any well-established religious body or denomination. (§§ 2A:65A-1, -2, 30:11-9)

# UNMARRIED COUPLES

**COMMON-LAW MARRIAGE:**  Any common-law marriage entered into before December 1, 1939, is valid. (§ 37:1-10)

**COHABITAL RELATIONSHIPS:**  There is no relevant statutory provision. However, in *Kozlowski v. Kozlowski*, 403 A.2d 902 (N.J. 1979), the New Jersey Supreme Court held that agreements, either express or implied, between cohabitants are enforceable as long as they are not based on sexual services or on a promise to marry. In this case a "palimony" award of $55,000 was granted to the woman, which represented the present value of the reasonable future support the man promised to provide. In determining if a palimony award is appropriate, courts will consider the stability and direction of the relationship. [*Crowe v. De Gioia*, 447 A.2d 173 (N.J. 1982)]

## CHILDREN

*Custody:*  The judgment or order in a paternity proceeding under the New Jersey Parentage Act may contain a provision concerning the custody and guardianship of the child. (§ 9:17-53)

*Legitimation Proceedings:*  A child born out of wedlock becomes legitimate when the natural parents marry or attempt to marry, or have entered into a common-law marriage which is valid in the place where it was contracted, as when the paternity of the child has been established by adjudication before the death of the father or by clear and convincing proof. (§ 3B:5-10)

*Paternity Proceedings:*  A child or legal representative of the child, the natural mother, a man alleging himself to be the father, the Division of Public Welfare in the Department of Human Services, the county welfare agency, or any person with a valid interest may bring or defend an action of paternity to determine whether the parent and child relationship exists. No action may be brought more than 5 years after the child reaches the age of majority. All proceedings in any such action are to be decided by the juvenile and domestic relations court which will consider the mother's and alleged father's testimony, medical information relating to the pregnancy, blood and genetic tests, and various other factors. (§§ 9:17-48 to -52)

*Obligations of the Putative Father:*  Once paternity has been established, the court's order will direct the father to pay the reasonable expenses of the mother's pregnancy and confinement, including repayment to an agency which provided public assistance funds for those expenses. A judgment for the child's support may require periodic payments or the purchase of an annuity may be ordered to meet support obligations in lieu of period payments. In determining the amount and period of support, a court will consider factors 1, 7, 9, 10, 12, 16, 17, 20, 23, and 28, listed in Appendix D. (§ 9:17-53)

# Education

# STATUTORY PROVISION

Sex discrimination in admission or in obtaining any advantages, privileges, or courses of study in public elementary, secondary, or vocational schools is prohibited. (§ 18A:36-20) Guidance tests and procedures may not discriminate or stereotype on the basis of sex. [§ 6:4-1.5(g)] Pregnant students may not be excluded from public schools and must be given an opportunity to continue their schoolwork after a voluntary leave without prejudice or penalty. [N.J. Admin. Code (1969) § 6:4-1.5(c)] Sex discrimination is prohibited in trade or business schools, academies, colleges and universities, and any institution under state supervision; however, private single-sex secondary and postsecondary schools are excluded from the provisions of this law. [§§ 10:5-5(1), -12(f)]

## AREAS COVERED

Teachers' wages, compensation, appointment, assignment, promotion, transfer, resignation, and dismissal; athletics; and educational materials and curricula are covered. [§§ 18A:6-6; N.J. Admin. Code (1977) §§ 6:4-1.3, -1.5(e), (f)]

> **ENFORCEMENT:** A person claiming to be aggrieved by unlawful discrimination may file a verified complaint with the Division of Civil Rights within 180 days of the occurrence of the unlawful discrimination or may bring a civil action in superior court without first filing a complaint with the Division of Civil Rights within 6 years of the occurrence of the unlawful discrimination. (§§ 2A:14-1, 10:5-13)

# Employment

## EQUAL PAY LAWS

No employer shall discriminate in any way in the rate or method of payment of wages to any employee because of his or her sex. A differential in pay between employees based on a reasonable factor or factors other than sex shall not constitute discrimination within the meaning of this section. (§ 34:11-56.2)

> **ENFORCEMENT:** The Commissioner of Labor and Industry has authority to enforce the act and may inspect records, make regulations, and impose fines and/or prison sentences. Employees may collect civil damages equal to back pay and an equal amount as liquidated damages, as well as costs and attorney's fees at the court's discretion. (§§ 34:11-56.3, -56.4, -56.5, -56.8)

## FAIR EMPLOYMENT LAWS

The law applies to the state, its political and civil subdivisions, all employers, labor organizations and employment agencies. It prohibits an employer from discriminating in hire, discharge, terms, conditions, or privileges of employment; a labor organization from expelling or excluding from its membership; or an employment agency from limiting, advertising, soliciting, segregating, or classifying employees so as to deprive any individual of employment opportunities because of sex. (§§ 10:5-5, -12) However, this law does not apply where sex is a bona fide occupational qualification or where a bona fide seniority or merit system exists. (§ 10:5-2)

> **ENFORCEMENT:** A person claiming to be aggrieved by unlawful discrimination may file a verified complaint with the Division of Civil Rights within 180 days of the occurrence of the unlawful discrimination or may bring a civil action in the superior court without first filing a complaint with the Division of Civil Rights within 6 years of the occurrence of the unlawful discrimination. (§§ 2A:14-1, 10:5-13)

## GOVERNMENT CONTRACTORS AND SUBCONTRACTORS

Every contract made by or on behalf of the state or any county, municipality, or other political subdivision of the state will contain provisions in which the contractor agrees not to discriminate in the hiring of persons or in securing services or supplies under the contract on the basis of marital status or sex. (§ 10:2-1; N.J. Admin. Code (1969) § 13:6-1.3)

**ENFORCEMENT:** See "Fair Employment Laws."

## STATE EMPLOYEE LAWS

State employees are covered by the Fair Employment Practices Law. [§ 10:5-5(e)] Equal employment opportunity is guaranteed to all state employees and applicants seeking employment with the state. (§ 11:2D-2)

**ENFORCEMENT:** The Division of Equal Employment Opportunity and Affirmative Action will ensure each state agency's compliance with all laws and regulations in areas relating to equal employment opportunity and will seek correction of discriminatory practices and procedures. (§ 11:2D-4) See also "Fair Employment Laws."

## VETERAN'S PREFERENCE

Preference in civil service employment is given to veterans, disabled veterans and their wives, widows who have not remarried, and mothers of soldiers or nurses who died in the service. (§§ 11:27-1.2, -1.3)

# Community Life

## CREDIT

It is unlawful for any person, bank, mortgage company, insurance company, lender, or credit institution to whom application is made for financial assistance to discriminate against any person or group of persons on the basis of marital status or sex in the granting, withholding, extending, modifying or renewing, or in the fixing of rates, terms, conditions, or provisions of any loan. [§ 10:5-12(1)]

**ENFORCEMENT:** Any person claiming to be aggrieved by an unlawful discrimination may file a complaint with the Division of Civil Rights within 180 days of the occurrence of the unlawful discrimination or may bring a civil suit in the superior court without first filing a complaint with the division within 6 years of the occurrence of the unlawful discrimination. (§§ 2A:14-1, 10:5-13)

## HOUSING

All persons have the opportunity to obtain publically assisted housing and other real property without discrimination because of marital status or sex, subject only to conditions and other limitations applicable alike to all persons. This opportunity is recognized and declared to be a civil right. (§ 10:5-4) It is unlawful for any real estate broker or anyone having ownership and the right to sell, lease or sublease any real property to refuse to sell, lease or sublease or to discriminate in the terms, conditions or privileges of the sale, rental, or lease of any real property on the basis of marital status or sex. [§§ 10:5-12(g), (h), (i)]

**ENFORCEMENT:** See "Credit."

# INSURANCE

It is unlawful for an insurer to discriminate against a person or between members of the same class of individuals in the issuance or renewal of any insurance policy or in the fixing of the rates, terms, or conditions in the policy. (§ 17B:30-12)

**ENFORCEMENT:** Individuals claiming to be aggrieved by unlawful discrimination may file a complaint with the Commissioner of Insurance. Whenever the commissioner finds, as a result of a hearing, that there has been a violation of the law, the commissioner will issue a cease and desist order enjoining the insurer from further engaging in the unlawful discrimination or the commissioner may impose monetary penalties of up to $5000 if the insurer knew or should have known that the law was violated. (§ 17B:30-17)

# PUBLIC ACCOMMODATIONS

It is unlawful for any owner, lessee, proprietor, manager, superintendent, or employee of any place of public accommodation to directly or indirectly refuse, withhold, or deny to any person any of the accommodations, facilities or privileges thereof or to discriminate against any person in the furnishing thereof on the basis of sex or marital status. However accommodations reasonably restricted to individuals of one sex are excluded. This exclusion does not apply to restaurants or bars. [§ 10:5-12(f)]

**ENFORCEMENT:** See "Credit."

# NEW MEXICO

## Home and Family

## MARRIAGE

**AGE OF CONSENT:** A person 18 years of age or older may consent to marry. (§ 40-1-5)*

**CONSENT REQUIREMENT:** No person under the age of 18 years may marry without the consent of the parent or guardian. No person under the age of 16 years may marry, with or without the consent of a parent or guardian, unless the female is pregnant and the marriage would not be incestuous. (§§ 40-1-5, -6)

**LICENSE REQUIREMENT:** Each couple desiring to marry in New Mexico shall obtain a license from a county clerk and file it for recording. (§ 40-1-10)

**PROHIBITED MARRIAGES:** Bigamous marriages and all marriages between relations and children, including grandfathers and grandchildren of all degrees, brothers and sisters of the half or the whole blood, and uncles and nieces or aunts and nephews, are void. (§ 40-1-7)

## DISSOLUTION OF MARRIAGE

**ANNULMENT:** Factors 35 and 38, listed in Appendix A, are grounds for annulment. Children born of an annulled marriage are legitimate. (§ 40-1-9)

*Residency Requirement:* The district court has jurisdiction over a divorce proceeding when the party has resided in the state for at least 6 months immediately preceding the date of filing and has a domicile in New Mexico. (§ 40-4-5)

**LEGAL SEPARATION:** Whenever the husband and wife have permanently separated and no longer live or cohabit as husband and wife, either may institute proceedings in the district court for the division of property, disposition of children, or alimony, without asking for or obtaining in the proceedings a dissolution of marriage. (§ 40-4-3)

*Residency Requirement:* See "Annulment."

**DIVORCE**

*Residency Requirement:* See "Annulment."

*Grounds for Divorce:* Factors 1, 4, 5, and 17, listed in Appendix A, are grounds for divorce. (§ 40-4-1)

*Conciliation Requirement:* There is no relevant statutory provision.

*Property Distribution:* New Mexico is a community property state. The court may divide community property as is just and proper, although court decisions hold that community property must be divided equally. The court may award alimony to either party. (§ 40-4-7)

*Child Custody:* Custody is to be determined by the best interest of the child. If the minor is 14 years of age or older, the court shall consider the wishes of the child. (§ 40-4-9) There is a presumption that joint custody is in the best interest

*Unless otherwise specified, all reference citations are to New Mexico Statutes Annotated (1978).

of a child in the initial custody determination. In making an award of joint custody, the court will consider factors 1 and 4 to 7, listed in Appendix C, and whether each parent is willing to accept all the responsibilities of parenting, including a willingness to accept or relinquish care at specified times, whether each parent is able to allow the other to provide care without intrusion, and the suitability of a parenting plan for the implementation of joint custody. (40-4-9.1)

*Child Support:* The court shall make a specific determination of the amount of support to be paid by a parent, considering the financial resources of the parent. (§§ 40-4-7, -11)

*Spousal Support/Alimony:* The court may award alimony to either party as may seem just and proper, taking into account factors 4 to 6, 9, 13, and 14, listed in Appendix E. In addition, the amount of property each party owns is considered. [§ 40-4-7; *Hertz v. Hertz*, 99 N.M. 320, 657 P.2d 1169 (1983)]

*Enforcement of Support Orders:* The Uniform Reciprocal Enforcement of Support Act, §§ 40-6-1 *et seq.*, applies. The purpose of the act is to improve and extend by reciprocal legislation the enforcement of duties of support.

*Spouse's Name:* There is no relevant statutory provision.

*Divorce by Affidavit or Summary Judgment:* There is no relevant statutory provision.

*Displaced Homemaker Laws:* Within the Commission on the Status of Women there is an office to conduct research and planning for programs to meet the needs of displaced homemakers. (§ 28-3-11)

# DOMESTIC VIOLENCE

**STATUTORY PROVISION:** There is no relevant statutory provision which defines domestic violence. However, there is a provision which defines crimes against children and dependents. (§§ 30-6-1, -2)

**WHO IS PROTECTED?** The act applies to the abuse of children under the age of 18 and dependents. (§§ 30-6-1, -2)

**RELIEF AVAILABLE:** If a child is found to be neglected or abused, the court may transfer legal custody of the child to an agency responsible for the care of neglected or abused children, a child-placing agency, or a relative. The court may also permit the child to remain at home subject to whatever conditions and limitations the court deems necessary. (§ 32-1-34)

**MARITAL RAPE:** A woman may charge her husband with rape only if they are living apart or one of them has filed for divorce or separation. [§ 30-9-10(E)]

**CIVIL LAWSUIT FOR RAPE OR ASSAULT:** In *Flores v. Flores*, 506 P.2d 345, 84 N.M. 601 (App. 1973), the court held that a woman could sue her husband for injuries sustained when the husband intentionally wounded her with a knife.

**CHILD ABUSE:** Any person who knowingly, intentionally, or negligently abuses a child by torturing, cruelly confining, or cruelly punishing the child or by placing the child in a situation that may endanger his or her life or health is guilty of a felony. [§ 30-6-1(C)]

*Notification Requirement:* All doctors, residents, interns, nurses, teachers, social workers, police officers, or any other person must report all suspected cases of child abuse to the district attorney, the county social services office of the Department of Human Services, or the probation office of the court. A prompt investigation of all reports must be made. (§ 2-1-15)

# INHERITANCE RIGHTS

**FAILURE TO MAKE A WILL:** The surviving spouse is entitled to all of the separate property if decedent left no children or grandchildren and to one-fourth if decedent left children or grandchildren. (§ 34-2-102)

**FAILURE TO PROVIDE BY WILL:** The surviving spouse who married the testator after the execution of the will, shall receive the same share of the estate that the omitted spouse would have received if the decedent died without a will, unless it appears that the omission was intentional or that decedent provided for the spouse by transfer outside the will. (§ 45-2-301)

**CHILDREN BORN OUT OF WEDLOCK:** There is no relevant statutory provison.

**HOMESTEAD, PERSONAL, AND FAMILY ALLOWANCES:** The surviving spouse is entitled to an exemption of $20,000 in a homestead occupied by the spouse and to an exemption in other real or personal property in the amount of $2000. If the homestead exists, these exemptions are in lieu of the family allowances. (§§ 45-2-401 to -405) The spouse is entitled to a personal property allowance. (§§ 42-9-10, 45-2-405) The spouse is also entitled to household furniture, cars, furnishings, appliances, and personal effects of the decedent up to $3500; this allowance has priority over all claims against the estate and is in addition to any share or benefit passing by will (unless otherwise provided) or intestate succession, but it may not be claimed if the spouse elects to take the homestead exemption. (§§ 45-2-402 to -405)

**OPTION TO DISREGARD THE WILL:** There is no relevant statutory provision.

# REPRODUCTIVE RIGHTS

**ABORTION:** The statutory provisions found in New Mexico were invalidated by *Roe v. Wade*.

**BIRTH CONTROL:** The Family Planning Act ensures that comprehensive family planning services are accessible on a voluntary basis to all who want and need them. (§§ 24-8-1 to -3)

**STERILIZATION:** Any person otherwise capable of consenting to medical treatment need not obtain the consent of his or her spouse for his or her medical sterilization if that person has been abandoned by his or her spouse. (§ 24-9-1)

# UNMARRIED COUPLES

**COMMON-LAW MARRIAGE:** These are not valid. [*Hazelwood v. Hazelwood*, 556 P.2d 345, 89 N.M. 659 (1976)]

**COHABITAL RELATIONSHIPS:** In *Dominquez v. Cruz*, 7 FLR 2025 (N.M. Ct. App. 1980), the court held that an oral agreement between an unmarried couple to pool the property acquired during the period of their cohabitation is enforceable; the court found that the parties intended to own jointly all property acquired during their relationship.

## CHILDREN

*Custody:* There is no relevant statutory provision. However, the father and mother of a child born out of wedlock are jointly and severally liable for the support of a child until the child reaches the age of majority. (§ 40-5-1)

*Legitimation Proceedings:* There is no relevant statutory provision.

*Paternity Proceedings:* New Mexico has adopted the Uniform Parentage Act. (1986 N.M. Laws, Chaps 47, S.B. 119) A man is presumed to be the natural father of a child if he and the child's natural mother are or have been married to each other, or attempted to marry in apparent compliance with law, although the marriage is or could be declared invalid, and the child is born during the marriage or within 300 days after the marriage is terminated; he and the child's mother have attempted to marry each other after the child's birth, even though the marriage is or could be declared invalid, and he has acknowledged his paternity in writing filed with the Bureau of Vital Statistics; he is named as the child's father on the birth certificate with his consent; he is obligated to support the child under a written voluntary promise or by court order; or he openly holds out the child as his natural child and has established a personal, financial, or custodial relationship with the child while the child is a minor. [§ 5A(1)-(5)] Any interested party may bring an action to determine the parent-child relationship (§ 7) An action to determine a parent-child relationship shall be brought no later than 3 years after the child reaches the age of majority. (§ 23)

*Obligations of the Putative Father:* If a parent-child relationship is found, the court may enter an order governing past and future support, custody, and visitation and may direct the father to pay the reasonable expenses of the mother's pregnancy, birth, and confinement. (§ 14C)

# Education

## STATUTORY PROVISION

The New Mexico Constitution contains an equal rights provision which may be used to challenge sex discrimination in education. (N.M. Const. art. 2, § 8) In addition, if federal funds are involved, Title IX of the Education Amendments of 1972, Pub. L. No. 92-318, 20 U.S.C. §§ 1681–1686, may apply.

# Employment

## EQUAL PAY LAWS

See "Fair Employment Laws."

## FAIR EMPLOYMENT LAWS

The New Mexico Human Rights Act prohibits employers of four or more employees, the state of New Mexico, and its political subdivisions from discriminating in employment on the basis of sex, race, age, religion, color, national origin, ancestry, or physical or mental handicap. (§ 28-1-7) The act covers refusing to hire, discharge, promote, demote, or compensate, except where the discrimination occurs as the result of a bona fide occupational qualification. [§ 28-1-7(A)] In addition, religious organizations may hire persons of a particular religion. [§ 28-1-9(B)]

**ENFORCEMENT:** The Human Rights Act is administered by the New Mexico Human Rights Commission.

## GOVERNMENT CONTRACTORS AND SUBCONTRACTORS

There is no relevant statutory provision.

## STATE EMPLOYEE LAWS

See "Fair Employment Laws." In addition, the development of affirmative action plans in state government are mandated by the Exec. Order No. 81-5 (August 10, 1981).

## VETERAN'S PREFERENCE

Veterans who leave work in the public or private sector to serve in the armed forces are given preference for reemployment.

# Community Life

## CREDIT

It is unlawful for any person to whom application is made either for any type of consumer credit assistance or for financial assistance for the acquisition, construction, rehabilitation, repair, or maintenance of any housing accommodation or real property to consider the sex, race, religion, color, national origin, ancestry, or physical or mental handicap of any individual in the granting, withholding, extending, modifying, or renewing, or in the rates, terms, conditions, or provisions of any financial assistance or in the extension of services in connection with the request for financial assistance. [§ 28-1-7(H)]

> **ENFORCEMENT:** At the request of the Commission for Human Rights the attorney general or district attorney shall secure enforcement of the provision. (§ 28-1-12) Any person claiming to be aggrieved by an unlawful discriminatory practice must file a written complaint with the commission within 180 days after the alleged act was committed. (§ 28-1-10)

## INSURANCE

Discrimination is prohibited between individuals of the same class and equal expectation of life in rates charged for life insurance or annuity contracts or between individuals of the same class and essentially the same hazard in the amount of premium, policy fees, or rates charged for accident or health insurance, in the benefits payable under these contracts, or in any other term or condition of these contracts. [§ 9-11-13(G)]

> **ENFORCEMENT:** The New Mexico Superintendent of Insurance may examine and investigate the affairs of every person engaged in the business of insurance in New Mexico to determine whether the provision has been violated. (§ 59-11-14)

# HOUSING

It is unlawful for any person to refuse to sell, rent, assign, lease, sublease, or offer for sale, rental, lease, assignment, or sublease any housing accommodation, to refuse to negotiate for the sale, rental, lease, assignment, or sublease of any housing accommodation, or to discriminate in the terms, conditions, privileges, or provisions or services in connection with the sale, rental, assignment, lease, or sublease of any housing accommodation on the basis of sex, race, religion, color, national origin, ancestry, or physical or mental handicap. [§ 28-1-7(A)] These provisions do not apply to the sale, lease, sublease, or rental of a single family dwelling by the owner if discriminatory advertising is not employed or to the rental of housing in a four-family dwelling in which the owner resides. (§ 28-1-9)

**ENFORCEMENT:** See "Credit."

# PUBLIC ACCOMMODATIONS

It is unlawful for any person in any public accommodation to make a distinction, directly or indirectly, in offering or refusing to offer its services on the basis of sex, race, religion, color, national origin, ancestry, or physical or mental handicap, provided that the physical or mental handicap is unrelated to an individual's ability to acquire or rent and maintain the property or housing accommodation. [§ 28-1-7(F)] These provisions do not apply to public rest rooms, showers, dressing rooms, or sleeping quarters in public institutions, where restriction is based on sex. [§ 28-1-9(D)]

**ENFORCEMENT:** See "Credit."

# NEW YORK

## Home and Family

### MARRIAGE

**AGE OF CONSENT:** A person 18 years of age or older may consent to marry. (Dom. Rel. §§ 2, 7)*

**CONSENT REQUIREMENT:** If either party is at least 16 years old but under 18, he or she may marry with the written and authorized consent of the parent(s) or guardian. A party between the ages of 14 and 16 may marry with the written and authorized consent of a parent(s) or guardian and the written approval and consent of a justice of the court. (Dom. Rel. §§ 15, 15a)

**LICENSE REQUIREMENT:** Persons wishing to marry must obtain a license from the city clerk. Before the license is issued, each party must file a premarital certificate plus the results of a standard serological test from a licensed physician not more than 13 days prior to issuance of the license. (Dom. Rel. § 13a) The license is valid for 60 days. (Dom. Rel. § 13)

**PROHIBITED MARRIAGES:** A marriage is void if it is between ancestors and descendants, brothers and sisters of either the whole or half blood, uncle and niece, or aunt and nephew. (Dom. Rel. § 5) Bigamous marriages are also void. (Dom. Rel. § 6) Children of void marriages are legitimate. (Dom. Rel. § 24)

### DISSOLUTION OF MARRIAGE

**ANNULMENT:** Factors 19, 32, 33, 35, 36, and 40 (for 5 years or more), listed in Appendix A, are grounds for annulment. (Dom. Rel. §§ 6, 7)
  *Residency Requirement:* There is none if the grounds arose in the state and both parties are residents at the time of the suit; 1 year if the parties were married or resided in, or if the grounds arose in, the state; 2 years if one party resides in the state at the time of the action. (Dom. Rel. § 230) Determination of residency will be based upon the location of the party bringing the action. (Dom. Rel. § 231)

**LEGAL SEPARATION:** Grounds for a legal separation include factors 4, 5, 17, and 47, listed in Appendix A, and confinement of a spouse in prison for a period of 3 or more consecutive years after the marriage. (Dom. Rel. § 200)
  *Residency Requirement:* See "Annulment."

### DIVORCE
  *Residency Requirement:* See "Annulment."
  *Grounds for Divorce:* Grounds for divorce include factors 4, 5, 6 (for 3 or more consecutive years), 11, 17, and 48, listed in Appendix A. (Dom. Rel. § 170)
  *Conciliation Requirement:* There is no relevant statutory provision.

---

*Unless otherwise specified, all reference citations are to McKinney's Consolidated Laws of New York Annotated (1960).

***Property Distribution:*** Marital property will be distributed equitably between the parties; separate property will remain such. The court will consider factors 1 to 3, 5, 6, 8, 15, 18, 19, 21, and 25, listed in Appendix F. Also considered are the type of marital property (liquid or nonliquid); the impossibility or difficulty of evaluating an interest in an asset such as a business, profession, or corporation; and the desirability of keeping such an asset intact and free from interference by the other party. (Dom. Rel. § 236, Part B)

***Child Custody:*** The court will determine custody with the best interests of the child in mind. Neither parent is entitled to a preference. (Dom. Rel. § 240) Where it is in the best interests of the child, joint custody may be awarded. [*Perotti v. Perotti*, 355 N.Y.S.2d 68 (Sup. Ct. Queens Co. 1974)]

***Child Support:*** The court may order either or both parents to pay an amount necessary for the support, maintenance, and education of the child in accordance with each parent's respective means. Factors 1, 3, 4, 5, and 24, listed in Appendix D, and the nonmonetary contributions that the parents will make toward the care and well-being of the child are considered. (Dom. Rel. §§ 32, 33, 236, Part B)

***Spousal Support/Alimony:*** Factors 2 to 4, 7, 10 to 12, 13, 14, 17, and 18, listed in Appendix E, are considered. (Dom. Rel. § 236, Part B)

***Enforcement of Support Orders:*** When a party owing support has missed three support payments, an execution for the amounts owed may be issued by either the support collection unit, the sheriff, the clerk of the court, or the attorney of the party owed support. When the debtor is receiving or will receive income (income includes not only wages but interest, dividends, worker's compensation, disability, unemployment insurance, or social security benefits), the execution may be served upon an employer or income payer after notice to the debtor. The employer or income payer must begin deductions from the debtor's income no later than the first pay period 14 days following the service of the execution, and payment must be made within 10 days of the date that the debtor is paid.

The employer or income debtor will be liable to the party owed support for his or her failure to deduct the amounts specified, provided, however, that deduction of the amounts specified by the employer or income payer will not relieve the debtor of the underlying obligation to support. If the employer or income payer fails to make the specified deductions, the party owed support may begin a proceeding against him or her for accrued deductions, together with interest and reasonable attorney's fees. If the debtor is currently supporting a spouse or dependent child other than the creditor, the amount of the deductions to be withheld must not exceed 50 percent of his or her disposable earnings; otherwise, the amount is increased to 60 percent of disposable earnings. An order to the employer to withhold wages has priority over any assignment, levy, or process. Money payable directly by a department of the state or by one of its institutions to a person owing a duty of support may also be withheld. (N.Y.S. Support Enforcement Act of 1985, N.Y. Civ. Prac. Law § 5241, 1985 N.Y. Laws, No. 7, ch. 809, October 1985) Also, upon the application of a creditor and for good cause shown, the court may enter an income deduction order for support enforcement. In determining good cause, the court may take into consideration evidence of the debtor's past financial responsibility, credit references, credit history, and any other matter the court considers relevant in determining the likelihood that payment will be made in accordance with its order. Proof of default establishes a strong case against the debtor which can be overcome only by proof of the debtor's inability to pay. An income deduction order for support enforcement also has priority over other assignment, levy, or process and an employer or income payer is also liable to the creditor for failure to make the specified deduction. (N.Y.S. Support Enforcement Act of 1985, N.Y. Civ. Prac. Law § 5242, 1985 N.Y. Laws, No. 7, ch. 809, October 1985)

An employer may not discharge, lay off, or discipline an employee or refuse to hire a prospective employee because one or more wage assignment or income deductions have been served upon an employer or former employer or because an action or judgment against such employee or prospective employee for nonpayment of support obligations is pending. An employee or prospective employee may institute a civil action for damages for wages lost as a result of the violation of this statute within 90 days of the violation. (N.Y.S. Support Enforcement Act of 1985, N.Y. Civ. Prac. Law § 5252, 1985 N.Y. Laws, No. 7, ch. 809, October 1985)

In addition to enforcement procedures, amendments to the Social Services Law allow the Department of Social Services to credit overpayments of tax to any spouse owed past-due spousal support who applies to the department for such services. (Tax § 171-c; Soc. Serv. § 111-m) This mechanism is also available to enforce child support obligations. (Soc. Serv. § 111-n)

A written undertaking with sufficient surety approved by the court may be required by the court to ensure that a respondent will comply with a support order. (Fam. Ct. Act § 471) The property securing the undertaking may consist of land. In that event, the undertaking must be filed with the county clerk of the county in which the land is located, and this act constitutes the imposition of a lien upon the land. (Fam. Ct. Act § 472) Banks and other fiduciary institutions may be required to report to the court full information regarding any fund deposited with them by a person owing support. (Fam. Ct. Act § 228) Finally, arrest and contempt proceedings are available to a party seeking to enforce a support order. (Fam. Ct. Act §§ 428, 454)See also the Uniform Support of Dependents Law. (Dom. Rel. 30 *et seq*.)

*Spouse's Name:* Upon granting a divorce and upon the request of the wife, the court may restore her maiden or other former surname. (Dom. Rel. § 240a)

*Divorce by Affidavit or Summary Judgment:* A marriage may be summarily dissolved if the parties have lived apart for 1 year or more according to the terms of a separation decree or agreement and satisfactory proof has been submitted that the party seeking the divorce that has substantially performed all the terms and conditions of the decree or agreement. (Dom. Rel. § 170)

*Displaced Homemaker Laws:* The Displaced Homemakers Act authorizes the labor commissioner to develop multipurpose service centers, job counseling, training and placement, assistance, and counseling relating to education, health, family care, financial management, and alcohol and drug addiction, among others. (Lab. § 825)

# DOMESTIC VIOLENCE

**STATUTORY PROVISION:** The Family Court Act prohibits recklessly endangering another person with a substantial risk of imminent death or physical injury, threatening or intimidating another by word or conduct, disorderly conduct, intentionally or recklessly causing or attempting to cause bodily injury, and harassing. (Fam. Ct. Act § 812)

**WHO IS PROTECTED?** Spouses and persons related by consanguinity or affinity are protected. Unmarried cohabitants are not protected by this act; however, an order of protection may be issued as part of a paternity suit or custody proceeding. (Fam. Ct. Act § 812)

**RELIEF AVAILABLE:** A victim of domestic violence may obtain the following relief: if a civil proceeding is commenced, the family court has the authority to issue a temporary order of protection or an order of protection requiring the abuser to stay away from the home, the other spouse, or children, to abstain from abusing the spouse or children, to care for the home, or to permit visitation with the children. A protective order is valid for 1 year. (Fam. Ct. Act §§ 841, 842) If a criminal proceeding is commenced, the criminal court has the authority to issue a temporary order of protection as a condition of pretrial release and an order of protection if the individual is convicted; these orders may require the individual to stay away from the home, school, or place of employment of the spouse, child, relative, or household member or to abstain from further abusive conduct. A criminal proceeding may be commenced by former spouses or unmarried persons who have a child in common. (Crim. Proc. §§ 530.11, .12)

**MARITAL RAPE:** A woman may charge her husband with rape. [*People v. Liberta*, 64 N.Y.S.2d 152 (1984)]

**CIVIL LAWSUIT FOR RAPE OR ASSAULT:** Spouses may sue each other for torts. (Gen. Oblig. § 3:313)

**CHILD ABUSE:** Harm or threatened harm to a child's physical or mental health or welfare by the acts or omissions of the parent or other person responsible for the child's welfare, if the child is under 18, is prohibited. Harm and threatened harm include physical or mental injury inflicted by other than accidental means; sexual offenses against a child; neglect; abandonment; or failure to provide adequate food, clothing, shelter, health care, and education. (Fam. Ct. Act 1012)

> *Notification Requirement:* Any person, official, or institution who has reason to believe that a child has suffered harm as a result of abuse or maltreatment, and who willfully fails to report it, is guilty of a Class A misdemeanor and can also be liable for civil damages caused by the failure to report the suspected abuse. (Soc. Serv. § 420)

# INHERITANCE RIGHTS

**FAILURE TO MAKE A WILL:** If there are no other heirs, the surviving spouse is entitled to the entire estate. If the decedent is survived by a spouse and one child, the spouse is entitled to $4000 in money or personal property and one-half of the estate, with the balance going to the child; if there is more than one child, the spouse is entitled to $4000 and one-third of the estate. If there is a spouse and one or two surviving parents, the spouse is entitled to $25,000 in money or personal property and one-half of the estate, with the balance going to the parent(s). (Est. Powers & Trusts § 4-1.1)

**FAILURE TO PROVIDE BY WILL:** If the testator fails to provide by will for a surviving spouse who married the testator after the execution of the will, the omitted spouse shall receive one-third of the net estate if the decedent is survived by one or more issue and, in all other cases, one-half of the estate unless the omission was the result of an intentional waiver or release of right to election by the surviving spouse. (Est. Powers & Trusts § 5-1.1)

**CHILDREN BORN OUT OF WEDLOCK:** A child born out of wedlock is the natural heir of its mother and her kin. However, such a child can inherit from its father and his kin if, during the father's lifetime, a court of competent jurisdiction made an order of filiation declaring paternity; or if the father had signed an instrument acknowledging paternity, provided the instrument is duly executed and recorded before one or more witnesses and filed 60 days from its making with the putative father registry of the Department of Social Services, and the department, within 7 days of the filing of the instrument, sends notice of such filing to the mother; or if paternity has been established by clear and convincing evidence, and the father has openly and notoriously acknowledged the child as his own. (Est. Powers & Trusts § 4-1.2)

**HOMESTEAD, PERSONAL, AND FAMILY ALLOWANCES:** A surviving spouse and children are entitled to a homestead exemption of $10,000 in a house, cooperative apartment, or condominium apartment occupied by them until the death of the spouse or until the youngest child reaches 21, whichever occurs last. (Civ. Prac. Law and Rules § 5206) The surviving spouse and/or minor children are entitled to utensils, furniture, appliances, fuel, provisions, and clothing of the decedent worth up to $5000; money or other personal property worth up to $1000; and a motor vehicle worth up to $10,000. (Est. Powers & Trusts § 5-3.1)

**OPTION TO DISREGARD THE WILL:** A spouse may not renounce a will if it provides a life income in property which is equal to or greater than the statutory share of one-third the net estate where the decedent is survived by one or more children or grandchildren, or one-half the net estate in all other cases. (Est. Powers & Trusts § 5-1.1) A surviving spouse may choose to release or waive the right of election where the deceased spouse provided for him or her outside the will. [Est. Powers & Trusts § 5-1.1(lf)]

# REPRODUCTIVE RIGHTS

## ABORTION

*Statutory Provisions:* Abortions after the twelfth week must be performed in hospitals on an in-patient basis; after the twentieth week, a second physician must be present in case the fetus is born alive. (Pub. Health § 5164)

*Consent Requirement:* A woman must give her informed consent to an abortion. (Penal § 125-05)

**BIRTH CONTROL:** A person has the right to purchase prescription or nonprescription contraceptives. Nonprescription contraceptives do not have to be purchased from a licensed physician. There is no longer a restriction on the purchase of contraceptives by minors. [*Carey v. Population Services, International*, 431 U.S. 678 (1977); Educ. § 6811]

**STERILIZATION:** A person is legally entitled to a sterilization by a licensed physician, clinic, or other facility offering gynecological services. [Pub. Health § 2308(a)]

# UNMARRIED COUPLES

**COMMON-LAW MARRIAGE:** Common-law marriages contracted on or after April 29, 1933, are not valid in New York. (Dom. Rel. § 11) The state however, will recognize common-law marriages entered into in states which recognize them. [*Merrit v. Chevrolet Tonowanda Div., Gen. Motors Corp.*, 377 N.Y.S.2d 663 (A.D.3d 1975)]

**COHABITAL RELATIONSHIPS:** New York has recognized express agreements, written or oral, between unmarried cohabitants as valid and enforceable as long as illicit sexual relations are not a part of the agreement. [*Morone v. Morone*, 50 N.Y.S.2d 481 (1980)]

## CHILDREN

*Custody:* There is no relevant statutory provision.

*Legitimation Proceedings:* A child born out of wedlock is legitimated if there is a subsequent marriage of the parents after the child is born; or if the parents have entered into a common-law marriage, where such a marriage is recognized; or where the parents lived together before the child's birth and married and the marriage was later declared void. (Dom. Rel. § 24)

*Paternity Proceedings:* An action to determine paternity may be brought by the mother, the alleged father, the child's guardian or next of kin, or by any authorized representative of an incorporated not-for-profit organization, or, if the mother or child is likely to become a public charge, by a public welfare official. (Fam. Ct. Act § 522) The action may be brought during pregnancy or after the birth of the child but cannot be brought after the child reaches 21 years unless paternity has been acknowledged in writing or by furnishing support. (Fam. Ct. Act § 517 as amended, N.Y.S. Sess. Laws, No. 7, ch. 809, October 1985) The court may require the mother, the alleged father and the child to submit to blood tests in order to determine paternity. (Fam. Ct. Act § 532)

*Obligations of the Putative Father:* The parents of a child born out of wedlock are liable for its necessary support and education. (Fam. Ct. Act § 513) However, the liability of the father is not enforceable unless he has acknowledged paternity or has been adjudicated to be the child's father by a court of law. (Dom. Rel. § 33.5) Once paternity is established as part of its order, the court may apportion the costs of the support and education of the child between the parents according to their respective means and responsibilities. (Fam. Ct. Act § 563)

# Education

# STATUTORY PROVISION

In New York the opportunity to obtain an education without discrimination because of sex is a recognized civil right. Discrimination on the basis of sex is prohibited in New York State public elementary and high schools in admission and courses of instruction. Discrimination is also prohibited in coeducational nonpublic schools in curricular or extra-curricular nonathletic programs or activities. (8 Civ. Rights § 100.4) Schools may sponsor single-sex activities provided that similar activities are available to members of the opposite sex. [Exec. § 291(2)] Discrimination based on sex in the determination of salaries paid to public school teachers is prohibited. (Educ. § 3026)

**ENFORCEMENT:** A person who claims to have been discriminated against on the basis of sex may file a complaint within 1 year with the Commissioner of Education. A commissioner who finds discrimination and fails to conciliate the matter will refer the matter to the Board of Regents, and a hearing will be set. (Educ. § 313)

# Employment

## EQUAL PAY LAWS

It is unlawful for an employer to discriminate on the basis of sex in wages paid to employees performing equal work requiring equal skill, effort, and responsibility, under similar working conditions. However, wage differentials are lawful when they are based on a seniority system, a merit system, a system which measures earnings by quantity or quality of production, or any factor other than sex. (Lab. § 194)

**ENFORCEMENT:** Any person who is paid less than the wage to which he or she is entitled may recover in a civil suit the amount of any underpayments together with court costs and attorney's fees. If the conduct by the employer is found to be willful, an additional 25 percent of the total underpayments will be awarded to the complainant. The Commissioner of Labor may also bring such a civil suit. The suit must be brought within 6 years of the occurrence of the violation. (Lab. § 663)

## FAIR EMPLOYMENT LAWS

The Human Rights Law of New York prohibits discrimination in employment on the basis of sex, marital status and other characteristics. It applies to the state of New York, its political and civil subdivisions, employers of four or more employees, employment agencies, and labor organizations. The law prohibits discrimination in hiring, discharge, compensation, terms, privileges, and conditions of employment; the expulsion or exclusion from membership in a labor organization and the refusal to recruit or refer an individual for employment on the basis of sex. It makes it unlawful for an employer to compel a woman who is pregnant to take a leave of absence unless she is prevented from performing her job or occupation as a result of her pregnancy. The law does not apply to a bona fide occupational qualification, religious groups wishing to give preference to persons of certain religions, and employers who take affirmative action to recruit and hire minorities. (Exec. §§ 291, 292, 296)

**ENFORCEMENT:** Any person who has been discriminated against in violation of the Human Rights Act, may within 1 year, alone or with an attorney, file a complaint with the New York State Commission on Human Rights. The commissioner will determine within 180 days if there is probable cause of discriminatory practice. If probable cause is determined, the commissioner will attempt to eliminate the discriminatory practice by conference, conciliation, and persuasion. If probable cause is not found, a person may file a civil suit within 60 days with the appellate division of the New York Supreme Court. (Exec. § 298) If an agreement cannot be reached, a public hearing will be scheduled and the hearing officer's recommendation will be issued within 180 days to the commissioner. If the complainant prevails, the commission is empowered to make an order enjoining the respondent from engaging further in the discriminatory practice and take whatever affirmative action is necessary to ensure compliance with the law. The commission may also require the respondent to remit to the state profits obtained by his or her discriminatory practice and make a report of steps taken in compliance with its order. (Exec. § 297)

## GOVERNMENT CONTRACTORS AND SUBCONTRACTORS

Any employer who has a federal, state, or local government contract is prohibited from discriminating on the basis of sex. Exec. Order No. 21, (August 1, 1983) established an office to oversee and aid businesses owned by women and minorities in obtaining their fair share of state contracts. [Lab. § 220(e)]

**ENFORCEMENT:** If there is an alleged discrimination, a person may file a complaint with the Commissioner of Labor. In the case of a state contract, a complaint should be filed with the state Human Rights Commission. See "Equal Pay Laws" and "Fair Employment Laws."

## STATE EMPLOYEE LAWS

Employment discrimination by both state and local governments based on sex and marital status is prohibited by the New York state and city Human Rights Law. (Exec. § 296)

**ENFORCEMENT:** See "Fair Employment Laws."

## VETERAN'S PREFERENCE

A disabled veteran is awarded ten extra points to passing scores when seeking an appointment and five points when seeking a promotion. Able-bodied veterans are awarded five points when seeking an appointment and two and a half points when seeking a promotion. Preference is also granted to veterans for retention. [Civ. Serv. §§ 85(2)(a), 85(7)] Spouses and widows of veterans are not entitled to preference in the civil service.

# Community Life

## CREDIT

Discrimination on the basis of sex, marital status, pregnancy, and parenthood in credit and financing practices is prohibited. [Exec. § 296(a)]

**ENFORCEMENT:** A person who has been denied credit may request the specific reasons for the denial. [Exec. § 296(a)(4)(G)] A claim of discrimination may be filed with the state Human Rights Commission. See "Employment: Fair Employment Laws." If the commission finds discrimination, the requested credit may be granted and money damages awarded. (Exec. § 297) A complaint may also be filed with the superintendent of banking within 1 year of the occurrence of the alleged discriminatory act. If probable cause for the discrimination is found, the superintendent will attempt to conciliate the matter. If a settlement is not made, a hearing will be set. If the claimant prevails, credit and money damages may be awarded [Exec. §§ 277, 296(a)(7)]

# HOUSING

Discrimination on the basis of sex or marital status in the sale, lease, or rental of housing accommodations, land, or commercial space is prohibited. [Exec. § 296(5)]

**ENFORCEMENT:** See "Fair Employment Laws."

# INSURANCE

Any person or entity is prohibited from refusing to issue or renew or from canceling a policy of insurance on the basis of sex or marital status. (Ins. § 2607)

**ENFORCEMENT:** See "Fair Employment Laws." Complaints may also be filed with the Department of Insurance of New York.

# PUBLIC ACCOMMODATIONS

Discrimination on the basis of sex or marital status in the access to or enjoyment, employment, privilege, or advantage of any public accommodation is prohibited. [Exec. § 296(2)]

**ENFORCEMENT:** See "Fair Employment Laws."

# NORTH CAROLINA

## Home and Family

## MARRIAGE

**AGE OF CONSENT:** A person 18 years or older may consent to marry. (§ 51-2)*

**CONSENT REQUIREMENT:** A person over 16 and under 18, must obtain the written consent of either parent if living with both parents; the consent of the custodial parent if the parents are not living together; or the consent of the person, agency, or institution having legal custody or serving as guardian. An unmarried female between the ages of 12 and 18 who is pregnant or has given birth may marry the putative father of the child provided the parties agree and written consent as set out above has been obtained or the consent of the director of social services has been given. (§ 51-2)

**LICENSE REQUIREMENT:** A license, issued by the registrar of deed of the county where the marriage is intended to take place, is required. In order to get a license, the registrar may require the applicants to produce certified copies of their birth certificates or birth registration cards and a certificate executed within 30 days from the date presented that a regularly licensed physician examined the applicants. The license is valid for 60 days from the date issued. (§§ 51-8, -9, -16)

**PROHIBITED MARRIAGES:** Bigamous marriages are void, as are marriages between any two persons nearer of kin than first cousins; double first cousins; a male under 16 and any female. Also prohibited are marriages in which one or both parties are physically impotent or incapable of contracting marriage from lack of will or under-standing. (§ 51-3) Children born of void or avoidable marriages are legitimate. (§ 50-11.1)

## DISSOLUTION OF MARRIAGE

**ANNULMENT:** Factors 19, 32, 35, 36, and 38, listed in Appendix A, are grounds for an annulment. (§ 51-3)
   *Residency Requirement:* There is no relevant statutory provision.

**LEGAL SEPARATION:** Grounds for separation include factors 5, 8, 17 (with 20), and 18, listed in Appendix A, and maliciously turning a spouse out of doors. (§ 50-7)
   *Residency Requirement:* There is no relevant statutory provision.

**DIVORCE**
   *Residency Requirement:* A party filing for a divorce must be a resident of the state for at least 6 months before filing the complaint. If the complainant is a nonresi-

---

*Unless otherwise specified, all reference citations are to the General Statutes of North Carolina (1943).

dent of the state, the action is brought in the defendant's county of residence. (§ 50-8)

*Grounds for Divorce:* Grounds are factors 9 (3 years), 31 (1 year), and 40 (examined for 3 years), listed in Appendix A. (§§ 50-5.1, -6)

*Conciliation Requirement:* There is no relevant statutory provision.

*Property Distribution:* Marital property means all real and personal property presently owned or acquired by either or both spouses during the marriage and before the date of the separation. The court will make an equal division of this property by using its net value unless it determines that such a division is not equitable. Factors considered include the liquid or nonliquid character of the property, the difficulty of evaluating any component asset or interest in a business or profession, and the desirability of returning such asset free from any claim by the other party, and 1, 3 to 6, 12, 15, 17, 19, 20, and 25, listed in Appendix F, are considered. If the court determines that equitable distribution is impractical, it will make a distributive award in order to achieve equity. (§ 50-20)

*Child Custody:* Custody will be determined according to the interests and welfare of the child. If it is clearly in the child's best interests, custody may be given to two or more persons, agencies, organizations, or institutions for certain periods of time. [§ 50-13.2(b)]

*Child Support:* The mother and father are primarily responsible for the support of a minor child. In awarding child support, the court will consider the needs of the child and the parent's ability to pay. (§ 50-13.4)

*Spousal Support/Alimony:* A court may award alimony to the dependent spouse, whether husband or wife. Factors 3, 8, 10, and 14, listed in Appendix E, are considered. Alimony is not payable to an adulterous spouse. (§§ 50-16.5, -16.6)

*Enforcement of Support Orders:* Upon the motion of either spouse or upon its own motion, the court may order that support payments be made to the clerk of the court for remittance to the party entitled to such payments. If the party owing a duty of support fails to make such payments and is in arrears, the clerk shall notify him or her by mail prior to initiating civil contempt procedures for the enforcement of its order. (§ 50-13.9) As to the enforcement of orders of alimony, the court may require the spouse owing the duty of support to secure the payment of alimony by means of a bond, mortgage, or deed of trust, or any other means ordinarily used to secure an obligation to pay money or transfer property, or by requiring him or her to execute an assignment of wages, salary, or other income due or to become due. (§ 50-16.7) See also the Uniform Reciprocal Enforcement of Support Act, §§ 52A-1 *et seq*.

*Spouse's Name:* A woman may, at any time after the marriage has been dissolved, resume the use of her maiden name or the name of a prior deceased husband or a combination of both. She can petition the court for this in her divorce complaint or make an application to the clerk of the court of the county where she resides. (§ 50-12)

*Divorce by Affidavit or Summary Judgment:* There is no relevant statutory provision.

*Displaced Homemaker Laws:* A center for displaced homemakers, established by the Council on the Status of Women, provides the necessary counseling, training, services, skills, and education to enable them to secure gainful employment as necessary for their health, safety and well-being. The center also provides job counseling, training and placement services; health, education, and financial management; and educational and informational services. (§§ 143B-394.5, -394.8)

# DOMESTIC VIOLENCE

**STATUTORY PROVISION:** Attempting to cause bodily injury or intentionally causing bodily injury or placing another person in fear of imminent serious bodily injury by the threat of force is prohibited. (§ 50B-1)

**WHO IS PROTECTED?** Spouses, former spouses, cohabitants, and former cohabitants of the opposite sex are protected. (§ 50B-1)

**RELIEF AVAILABLE:** A victim of domestic violence may seek relief by filing a civil action alleging the acts of domestic violence. The victim may additionally obtain emergency relief necessary for self-protection or to protect minor children from immediate and present danger. Such relief includes orders directing a party to refrain from further acts of violence, granting the victim possession of the residence and excluding the other spouse from the residence, awarding temporary custody of minor children and visitation rights, ordering the eviction of a party from the household, ordering a party to make payments for the support of the other, ordering one party to refrain from harassing or interfering with the other, and awarding attorney's fees and costs to either party. (§ 50B-3) A victim of domestic violence may also seek the assistance of a police officer who is authorized to take whatever steps are reasonably necessary to protect the complainant from harm and is also authorized to advise him or her of medical care, counseling, and other services and escort the complainant to a shelter or hospital when necessary. (§ 50B-5)

**MARITAL RAPE:** A woman cannot charge her husband with rape unless at the time of the act the parties are living separate and apart pursuant to a written agreement or judicial decree. (§ 14-27.8)

**CIVIL LAWSUIT FOR RAPE OR ASSAULT:** A husband and wife may sue each other for torts. (§ 52.5)

**CHILD ABUSE:** It is a misdemeanor for any parent of a child under 16 years old or for any person responsible for the care or supervision of a child to inflict or allow physical injury to be inflicted on the child. Also, a person who commits, permits, or encourages any act of prostitution with or by a juvenile or commits or allows the commission of a sexual act upon a juvenile is guilty of child abuse. (§§ 14-318.2, -318.4)

> *Notification Requirement:* Any person or institution who has cause to suspect that a juvenile is abused or neglected shall report it to the Department of Social Services orally, by telephone, or in writing. The local law enforcement agency may also be notified. The Director of Social Services investigates and determines if immediate removal of the child from the home is warranted. If removal is necessary, a protective services worker may assume temporary custody of the child. Any physician or medical facility administrator has the right to temporary physical custody of a child for up to 12 hours if that administrator determines that the child should remain for medical treatment or that it is unsafe to return the child to the parents, guardian, or caretaker. (§§ 7A-543, -544, -548, -549, -647, 115C-400)

# INHERITANCE RIGHTS

**FAILURE TO MAKE A WILL:** With regard to real property, if there are no other heirs, the surviving spouse receives all of the estate. If the decedent is survived by one lineal descendant or one or more parents, the surviving spouse receives one-half of the estate. If there are two or more lineal descendants, the surviving spouse receives one-third of the estate. As to personal property, if there are no heirs, the surviving spouse receives the entire estate. If one or more parents survive and the net personal property does not exceed $25,000 in value, the surviving spouse receives all; if it exceeds $25,000, then the surviving spouse receives the first $25,000 and one-half of the balance. If two or more children or lineal descendants survive and the net value of the personal property does not exceed $15,000, the surviving spouse receives all; if it exceeds $15,000, then he or she receives $15,000 and one-third of the balance. If there is one child or one lineal descendant and the value does not exceed $15,000, then the surviving spouse receives all; if it exceeds $15,000, then he or she receives the first $15,000 and one-half of the balance. In lieu of the share provided for by statute, the surviving spouse can take a life estate in one-third the value of all the real property owned by the decedent. (§§ 29-14, -30)

**FAILURE TO PROVIDE BY WILL:** There is no relevant statutory provision.

**CHILDREN BORN OUT OF WEDLOCK:** A child born out of wedlock is the natural heir of the mother and her kin. The child can inherit from the father if the father acknowledged himself as such during his own and the child's lifetime in a written instrument executed and acknowledged before a notary public, judge, or magistrate and filed during his own and the child's lifetime in the office of the clerk of the superior court of the county where either he or the child resides. (§ 29-19)

**HOMESTEAD, PERSONAL, AND FAMILY ALLOWANCES:** Every surviving spouse, unless forfeiting this right, gets an allowance out of the personal property of the deceased of $5000 for his or her support for 1 year after the death of the spouse. This allowance can be charged against the surviving spouse's share. If the decedent dies possessed of a homestead and leaves a surviving spouse but no minor children, the homestead is exempt from the decedent's debts, and the rents and profits derived from the homestead accrue to the benefit of the surviving spouse until remarriage unless the survivor is the owner of a separate homestead. The homestead is exempt from payment of any debt during the minority of the owner's children. The exemption ends when the spouse remarries or the children reach their majority. When a parent dies leaving a child under 18, a child who is less than 22 years old and a full-time student, or a child under 21 who is mentally incompetent or totally disabled, the child gets $1000 for support for the next year, less the value of any articles the child consumed since the death of the parent. This allowance is in addition to the child's share of the estate. (§§ 30-15, -17; N.C. Const. art. 10, § 2)

**OPTION TO DISREGARD THE WILL:** The surviving spouse can reject the will where the aggregate value of its provisions when added to the value of the property or interest in the property passing in any manner outside the will is less than the intestate share, or less than one-half the amount provided in the Intestate Succession Act where the surviving spouse is a second or successive spouse and the testator has surviving him or her lineal descendants by a former marriage and no lineal descendants by the second or successive marriage. The effect of this is that the spouse will take the same share as if the deceased had died intestate. (§§ 30-2, -3)

# REPRODUCTIVE RIGHTS

## ABORTION

*Statutory Provisions:* Abortions can be performed only during the first 20 weeks of pregnancy by a physician licensed to practice medicine in a North Carolina hospital or by a clinic certified by the Department of Human Resources to be a suitable facility for the performance of abortions. An abortion can be performed after 20 weeks only if there is a substantial risk that continuing the pregnancy would threaten the life or gravely impair the health of the woman. Otherwise performing an abortion is a felony. (§§ 14-44, -45, -45.1)

*Consent Requirements:*  There is no relevant statutory provision.

*Reporting Requirements:*  The Department of Human Resources collects annually representative samplings of statistical summary reports concerning the medical and demographic characteristics of abortions performed by hospitals and clinics. (§ 14-45.1)

**BIRTH CONTROL:**  There is no relevant statutory provision.

**STERILIZATION:**  No physician or surgeon licensed by the state may perform a sterilization procedure on any person 18 years or older or under the age of 18, if legally married, unless the request for the procedure is made in writing and provided that prior to or at the time the request is made, a full and reasonable medical explanation is given by the physician or surgeon to the person making the request of the meaning and consequences of the procedure and provided further that the operation is performed in a hospital or clinic licensed by the state. (§ 90-271)

# UNMARRIED COUPLES

**COMMON-LAW MARRIAGE:**  Common-law marriages are not valid. (§ 51-1)

**COHABITAL RELATIONSHIPS:**  Cohabitation without marriage is a misdemeanor. (§ 14-184) However, the North Carolina Court of Appeals allowed a woman to recover $12,000 for the value of the services the woman had rendered her former cohabitant during the course of their relationship. [*McAulliffe v. Wilson*, 254 S.E.2d 547 (N.C. 1979)]

## CHILDREN

*Custody:*  Once the paternity of a child has been established, the rights of the father, with regard to custody, are the same as those existing when the child is born in lawful wedlock. (§ 49-15)

*Legitimation Proceedings:*  The putative father of a child born out of wedlock can, by a verified written petition filed in a special proceeding in the superior court of the county in which he resides or in the superior court of the county in which the child resides, ask that the child be declared legitimate. If it appears to the court that the petitioner is the father of the child, it will declare and pronounce the child legitimated. (§ 49-10) A new birth certificate will be issued and the child's surname changed. (§ 49-13) A child is also legitimated when the mother and reputed father marry any time after its birth. (§ 49-12)

*Paternity Proceedings:*  The mother or the child or their personal representative, the father or the director of social services when the child is likely to become a public charge, may bring a civil action to determine the paternity of a child born out of wedlock. The action may be brought at any time prior to the child's eighteenth birthday. If the action is brought more than 3 years after the birth of the child, paternity cannot be established in a contested case without evidence from a blood-grouping test or evidence that the putative father has declined an opportunity for such testing. (§§ 49-14, -16)

*Obligations of the Putative Father:*  Once paternity is established, the proper amount of support is determined in the same manner as for a child born in lawful wedlock. The court has considerable discretion, but the welfare of the child is the primary consideration. The court may also make an action directing the father to pay for the medical expenses incident to the mother's pregnancy and confinement. (§ 49-15)

# Education

## STATUTORY PROVISION

There is no relevant statutory provision. However, it should be noted that if federal funds are involved, Title IX of the Education Amendments of 1972, Pub. L. No. 92-318, 20 U.S.C. §§ 1681–1686, may apply.

# Employment

## EQUAL PAY LAWS

There is no relevant statutory provision. However, it should be noted that the Equal Pay Act of 1963, 29 U.S.C. §§ 201 *et seq.*, may apply.

## FAIR EMPLOYMENT LAWS

It is the public policy of the state to protect and safeguard the right and opportunity of all persons to seek, obtain and hold employment without discrimination on account of sex by employers with fifteen or more employees. (§ 143-422.2)

> **ENFORCEMENT:** Complaints to the Equal Employment Opportunity Commission are brought to the attention of the Human Relations Council in the Department of Administration which is to effect an amicable resolution of the charges of discrimination. (§ 143-422.3)

## GOVERNMENT CONTRACTORS AND SUBCONTRACTORS

There is no relevant statutory provision. However, it should be noted that if federal funds are involved, Exec. Order No. 11246, 3 C.F.R. 339 (1965), *reprinted in* 42 U.S.C. § 2000e app. at 1232, 41 C.F.R. § 60-12, may apply.

## STATE EMPLOYEE LAWS

All departments, agencies, and local political subdivisions of the state shall give equal employment opportunity and equal compensation without regard to sex to their employees, except where specific requirements constitute bona fide occupational qualifications necessary to proper and efficient administration. (§ 126-16)

> **ENFORCEMENT:** Complaints should be made to the Office of State Personnel under the administration and supervision of a state personnel director. (§ 126-4)

# VETERAN'S PREFERENCE

A ten-point preference rating is awarded to all qualified veterans in their civil service examination passing scores. This also applies to the widows of veterans and the wives of disabled veterans. In promotional examinations, a preference rating of one point per year, not to exceed five points, for time spent in the service is given. (§ 128-15)

# Community Life

## CREDIT

It is unlawful for an extender of credit to deny a married or unmarried woman credit in her own name if her uncommingled earnings, separate property or other assets are such that a man in her position would receive the credit requested. A credit reporting agency must, when requested by a married person, identify the separate credit histories of the spouses. (§§ 25B-1, -2)

> **ENFORCEMENT:** A person denied credit may bring a civil action to receive actual damages and reasonable attorney's fees in the court's discretion. (§ 25B-3) The action must be brought within 3 years of the occurrence of the discrimination. (§ 1-52)

## HOUSING

It is unlawful for any person engaged in the business of real estate to discriminate on the basis of a person's sex in the terms, conditions, or privileges of a real estate transaction; to refuse to receive or transmit a bona fide offer to engage in a transaction; to represent that real property is not available for inspection, sale, or lease when in fact it is available; or to print, circulate, or publish discriminatory advertisements. (§ 41A-4) This prohibition does not apply to the rental of a room or rooms in a private house if the owner or a member of the owner's family resides in the house. (§ 41A-6) It is also unlawful for a financial institution to whom application for a loan or financial assistance is made to discriminate on the basis of sex or to use applications or keep records with the specific intent to limit or discriminate because of sex. (§ 41A-4)

> **ENFORCEMENT:** A person claiming to have been discriminated against in housing may file a complaint with the Human Relations Council within 180 days of the occurrence of the alleged discriminatory act. The council will seek to eliminate or correct the discriminatory housing practice by informal conference, conciliation, or persuasion. If the council fails to resolve the complaint within 180 days of its receipt, the council may, upon request, issue a right-to-sue letter to the complainant. The civil action must be brought within 180 days after the filing of the complaint with the council. The court may award injunctive relief and may award to the plaintiff actual and punitive damages, court costs, and reasonable attorney's fees. (§§ 41A-7, -9)

## INSURANCE

It is unlawful for an insurance company or its agents or brokers to discriminate in favor of any person because of sex. Life insurance companies may not discriminate between insured of the same class and equal expectation of life. No insurer may base private passenger automobile or motorcycle rates in whole or in part, directly or indirectly, on sex. (§§ 58-30.3, -44.3, -198)

**ENFORCEMENT:** The Commissioner of Insurance investigates all charges of alleged discriminatory practices in the insurance industry and may revoke an insurer's license for specified periods of time if the charges are proved to be true. (§ 58-44.4)

# PUBLIC ACCOMMODATIONS

There is no relevant statutory provision.

# NORTH DAKOTA

## Home and Family

## MARRIAGE

**AGE OF CONSENT:** A person 18 years of age or older may consent to marry. (§ 14-03-02)*

**CONSENT REQUIREMENT:** Persons between the ages of 16 and 18 need parental or guardian consent to marry. Persons under 16 years of age may not marry under any circumstances. (§ 14-03-02)

**LICENSE REQUIREMENT:** Persons wishing to marry must apply to a county judge for the marriage license. The judge shall require the applicants to furnish an affidavit of some disinterested and credible person that the parties are over 18; if they are under 18, a certificate of parental or guardian consent signed under oath before a notary public is required. The judge shall also require an affidavit showing whether either party has ever been divorced, is not a habitual criminal, is under a duty to pay child support or alimony. The applicants must also furnish a physician's certificate showing that neither party is afflicted with syphilis or any other contagious venereal disease. The judge may examine and question witnesses as to the legality of any contemplated marriage. The license is valid for 60 days. (§§ 14-03-17, -19)

**PROHIBITED MARRIAGES:** Marriages between persons who are intoxicated or under the influence of drugs; marriage by an institutionalized severely retarded woman under 45 or a man of any age, unless he marries a woman over the age of 45; and marriages between parent and child, grandparent and grandchild, brother and sister of the half and whole blood, and first cousins of the half and whole blood are prohibited. (§§ 14-03-03, -07, -18) Children of void marriages are legitimate. (§ 14-04-03)

## DISSOLUTION OF MARRIAGE

**ANNULMENT:** A marriage may be annulled by action in district court. Grounds for annulment include factors 19, 32, 33 (unless afterward with full knowledge of the facts, the party cohabited with the other as husband or wife), 34 (unless after coming to reason the party freely cohabited with the other as husband or wife), 35 (unless after attaining legal age, the party freely cohabited with the other as husband or wife), and 38, listed in Appendix A. (§ 14-04-01)

*Residency Requirement:* There is no relevant statutory provision.

**LEGAL SEPARATION:** Grounds for separation include factors 4, 9 (for a period of 5 years), 15, 16, 17, 21, 22, and 25, listed in Appendix A. (§§ 14-05-03, -06-01)

*Residency Requirement:* The plaintiff in the action must be a resident in good faith for 6 months preceding the entry of the decree of separation. (§ 14-06-06)

**DIVORCE**

*Residency Requirement:* The plaintiff must be a resident in good faith for 6 months preceding the entry of the divorce decree. (§ 14-05-17)

*Unless otherwise noted, all reference to citations are to North Dakota Century Code (1943).

*Grounds for Divorce:* See "Legal Separation."

*Conciliation Requirement:* All actions for divorce or separation may not be filed unless family court jurisdiction has been waived or a petition has been filed in the district court clerk's office about the controversy. The court may set time a for a hearing and refer the parties to a family court counselor in an attempt to reconcile the spouses. From the time of the filing of the petition and lasting for 90 days, neither spouse can file for divorce or separation. (§§ 27-05.1-06, -10, -18)

*Property Distribution:* The court will make an equitable distribution of the real and personal property of the parties as is just and proper. It may also compel either party to provide for the maintenance of the children of the marriage and to make suitable allowances for the other party's support for life or a shorter period. Factors affecting property distribution are 1 to 3, 5, 6, 8, 15, 18, 22, and 29, in Appendix F. [§§ 14-05-24, -06-03; *Rhode v. Rhode*, 154 N.W.2d 385 (N.D. 1967)]

*Child Custody:* The custody of an unmarried minor child is awarded to the person, agency, organization, or institution which will promote the best interests and welfare of the child. The court will consider factors 1, 3, 4, 6 to 8, 11, 12, 17, and 23, listed in Appendix B. (§§ 14-09-06.1, -06.2)

*Child Support:* Parents have a mutual duty to support their children. The court determines the amount of child support by taking into account the net income of the parties, other resources available, and the circumstances that might be considered in reducing the amount of support on the basis of hardship. (§§ 14-09-08, -09.7)

*Spousal Support/Alimony:* See "Property Distribution."

*Enforcement of Support Orders:* In any action where a court orders child support or alimony, the order must provide that these payments be made to the clerk of the court as trustee for remittance to the spouse or child or to the public agency providing such support. Failure to timely remit support payment is punishable by contempt. (§ 14-08-07) In addition, judgments containing child support provisions must include a provision directing the party owing the support to assign a part of his or her salary to the clerk of the court in an amount sufficient to meet the support payments. Such wage assignments have priority over any attachment, garnishment, or wage assignment for purposes other than child support. (§ 14-09-09.1) See also the Revised Uniform Reciprocal Enforcement of Support Act of 1968, §§ 14-12.1 *et seq.*

*Spouse's Name:* While a decree of divorce does not automatically restore the wife's maiden surname, such relief may be requested and granted in divorce proceedings. [*Meadows v. Meadows*, 312 N.W.2d 464 (N.D. 1981)]

*Divorce by Affidavit or Summary Judgment:* There is no relevant statutory provision.

*Displaced Homemaker Laws:* Service centers, staffed by qualified displaced homemakers and others trained to meet the needs of displaced homemakers, are available for personal and employment counseling, interpersonal skill building, job readiness, job search and job training information, and community referral services. Each center has an outreach component capable of delivering the full range of services to groups of displaced homemakers in rural communities. Other services that may be available are peer counseling, skill updating and development, health counseling and referral clinics, and money management courses supplying information about assistance programs such as supplemental social security, veteran's administrative benefits, welfare, and food stamps. (§§ 14-06.1-02, -03, -05)

# DOMESTIC VIOLENCE

**STATUTORY PROVISION:** Any act or threatened act which results in, or threatens to result in, bodily injury is prohibited. (§§ 14-07.1-01, -07.2-02)

**WHO IS PROTECTED?** The act protects spouses, former spouses, parents, children, persons related by blood, persons presently residing together or who have resided together in the past, persons who have a child in common regardless of marital status, or any other person if the court determines that the relationship between that person and the alleged person is sufficient to warrant the issuance of an adult abuse protection order. (§ 14-07.1-02)

**RELIEF AVAILABLE:** When a victim of domestic violence alleges an immediate and present danger of abuse, based upon the occurrence of a recent incident of actual abuse or threat of abuse, the court may grant him or her a temporary order of protection, restraining any party from threatening, molesting or injuring any other person; excluding a party from the residence or from an adult abuse care facility; awarding temporary custody or establishing temporary visitation rights with regard to minor children; recommending or requiring either or both parties to undergo counseling; requiring payment of support to a party and minor children; or paying reasonable attorney's fees and costs. (§ 14-07.1-03) In addition, a peace officer may make an arrest without a warrant if a protection order has been violated or the officer has reason to believe that the alleged abuser has, within the preceding 4 hours, assaulted a spouse or family member, although the assault did not take place in the officer's presence. (§ 14.07.1-06) Violation of a protection order is a misdemeanor and constitutes criminal contempt of court. (§ 14-07.1-06)

**MARITAL RAPE:** A woman may not charge her husband with marital rape unless the spouses are living apart under a decree of judicial separation, a temporary or permanent adult abuse protection order, or an interim order issued in connection with a divorce or separation action. (§ 121-20-01)

**CIVIL LAWSUIT FOR RAPE OR ASSAULT:** There is no relevant statutory provision.

**CHILD ABUSE:** It is unlawful for a parent, guardian, or custodian to cruelly abuse or willfully neglect or refuse to provide subsistence, education, or other necessary care for the health, morals, or well-being of a child. (§ 14-09-22)

*Notification Requirement:* Any health care professional, medical examiner or coroner, religious practitioner of the healing arts, school personnel, social worker, day care center or any other child care worker, or law enforcement officer having knowledge of or reasonable cause to suspect that a child coming before him or her is abused or neglected shall report the circumstances to the division of community services of the Department of Human Services. A physician who knows or suspects abuse may keep a child in the custody of a hospital or medical facility for 96 hours. The physician must notify the juvenile court and try to notify whoever is responsible for the child. Any person required to report who willfully fails to do so is guilty of a misdemeanor. (§§ 50-25.1-03, -04, -07, -13)

# INHERITANCE RIGHTS

**FAILURE TO MAKE A WILL:** If there is no surviving issue or parent of the decedent, the spouse receives the entire estate. If the decedent is survived by parents, the spouse receives $50,000 plus one-half of the balance of the estate. If the decedent is survived by issue, also of the spouse, the spouse's share is $50,000 plus one-half of the balance of the estate. If the decedent is survived by issue not of the spouse, the spouse receives one-half of the estate. (§ 30.1-04-02)

**FAILURE TO PROVIDE BY WILL:** If a testator fails to provide for a spouse who married the testator after the execution of the will, the omitted spouse shall receive the same share as if the decedent left no will, unless it appears from the will that the omission was intentional or the testator provided for transfer of property to the spouse outside the will. (§ 30.1-06-01)

**CHILDREN BORN OUT OF WEDLOCK:** A child born out of wedlock is the natural heir of the mother and her kin. However, such a child can only inherit from the father if the father and child relationship was established during the father's lifetime; if the father and mother married or attempted to marry and the father acknowledged his paternity of the child in writing filed with the Department of Health; if with his consent, he is named the child's father on the child's birth certificate; if he is obligated to support the child voluntarily or by a court order; or if while the child is still a minor, he receives the child into his home and openly holds out the child as his natural child. (§ 14-17-04)

**HOMESTEAD, PERSONAL, AND FAMILY ALLOWANCES:** The surviving spouse is entitled to receive from the estate not more than $5000 in household furniture, automobiles, furnishings, appliances, and personal effects. If there is no surviving spouse, the children are jointly entitled to the same amount. This right has priority over all claims against the estate and is, in addition to any share or benefit passing by will, intestate succession or statutory share. If the decedent was domiciled in North Dakota, the surviving spouse and minor children who were being supported by the decedent are entitled to a reasonable allowance in money out of the estate during the administration of the will for up to 1 year if the estate is inadequate to discharge its debt. The surviving spouse may occupy the homestead for life or until he or she remarries. (§§ 30-16-02, 30.1-07-01, -07-02, 34-01-12, 47-18-01)

**OPTION TO DISREGARD THE WILL:** The surviving spouse has a right of election to take one-half of the augmented estate if the decedent was domiciled in North Dakota. The augmented estate means the value of the estate minus funeral and administrative expenses, homestead and family allowances, estate debts, the added value of property transferred by the decedent, and the value of property owned by the surviving spouse and derived from the decedent. (30.1-05-02)

# REPRODUCTIVE RIGHTS

## ABORTION

*Statutory Provisions:* An abortion is to be performed by a licensed physician only. After the first 12 weeks of pregnancy but prior to viability, no abortion is to be performed outside a licensed hospital. After viability, an abortion can be performed only in a hospital and only if, in the judgment of the physician, it is necessary to preserve the woman's life or if, in the physician's opinion, continuing the pregnancy will impose a substantial risk of grave impairment to the physical or mental health of the woman. The physician has to certify this in writing and have the concurrence of two other licensed physicians who have examined the patient. An abortion of a viable child can be performed only when there is in attendance another physician who will take control and provide immediate care for the viable child born as a result of the abortion. (§§ 14-02.1-04, -02.1-05)

*Informed Consent:* No physician can perform an abortion unless prior to the abortion, the physician certifies in writing that the woman gave informed consent fully and without coercion and was given information as to the age of the fetus, anatomical and physiological features at the time of the abortion, physical dangers, psychological trauma, particular risks of her abortion, alternatives to abortion, and the extent to which the physician is legally obligated to preserve the life and health of the viable unborn fetus during and after the abortion. The woman must be given this information between 2 and 30 days prior to the abortion. The woman's age and marital status must be certified to in writing. (§ 14-02.1-03)

*Parental Consent:* No person can perform an abortion upon a woman under 18 unless she is married and has given her informed consent; the attending physician has obtained the written consent of the minor woman and that of her parents, custodial parent or legal guardian; or the abortion has been authorized by the juvenile court. A minor under 18 or her next friend can apply to the juvenile court for permission to obtain an abortion without parental authority. The judge will determine if the minor is sufficiently mature and well-informed to make the decision without the required consent. In the event of an adverse determination, the minor pregnant woman is entitled to an expedited appeal. All such proceedings are kept confidential. (§ 14-02.1-03.1)

*Spousal Consent:* There are no relevant statutory provisions.

*Reporting Requirements:* All abortion facilities and hospitals where abortions are performed must keep records for up to 7 years. The medical records are kept confidential and are used only by the Department of Health for gathering statistical data and complying with state law. An individual abortion report for each abortion performed must be completed by the attending physician and is to be submitted to the Department of Health within 30 days from date of abortion. A copy of the abortion report is made part of each patient's medical record. The Department of Health is responsible for collecting all the data and reporting any violations to the attorney general. (§ 14-02.1-07)

*State Funding:* No state or federal funds are to be used to pay for the performance or for promoting the performance of abortions unless the abortion is necessary to prevent the death of the woman. (§ 14-02.3-01)

*Health Insurance Regulations:* No health insurance contracts, plans, or policies delivered or issued in the state shall provide coverage for abortions except by an optional rider for which an additional premium is paid, except where the performance of the abortion is necessary to prevent the death of the woman. (§ 14-02.3-03)

**BIRTH CONTROL:** There is no relevant statutory provision.

**STERILIZATION:** There is no relevant statutory provision.

# UNMARRIED COUPLES

**COMMON-LAW MARRIAGE:** Common-law marriages are not valid in North Dakota. (§ 14-03-01)

**COHABITAL RELATIONSHIPS:** There is no relevant statutory provision.

**CHILDREN**

*Custody:* When the maternity and paternity of a child born out of wedlock is positively established, the parents have equal rights to custody and such custody is determined according to the best interests of the child. (§ 14-09-05)

*Legitimation Proceedings:* A child born out of wedlock is legitimated if the father adopts him or her or publicly acknowledges the minor as his child, receiving the minor into the home, with the consent of his wife, if married, and otherwise treating the minor as if born in lawful wedlock or if he subsequently marries the mother. (§§ 14-09-02, -15-20)

*Paternity Proceedings:* A child, the natural mother, or their personal representative, an interested party, a man presumed to be the father, or the authorities charged with the support of the child may bring an action any time for the purpose of declaring the existence of the father-and-child relationship. However, an action brought by or on behalf of a child whose paternity has not been determined is not barred until 3 years after the child reaches majority. (§§ 14-17-05, -06) The court may require the parties to undergo blood tests. Evidence of paternity includes sexual intercourse at the time, blood tests, expert's opinion on the statistical probability of the alleged father's paternity, and medical or other anthropological evidence. (§§ 14-17-10, -11)

*Obligations of the Putative Father:* Upon a determination of paternity the court may order custody and guardianship, visitation privileges, the furnishing of a bond or other security for the payment of a judgment of support or any other matter that is in the best interests of the child. The father may also be directed to pay reasonable expenses of the mother's pregnancy and confinement. The judgment may be paid in a lump sum, periodically, or by the purchase of an annuity. (§ 14-17-14)

# Education

## STATUTORY PROVISION

There is no relevant statutory provision. However, it should be noted that if federal funds are involved, federal law, Title IX of the Education Amendments of 1972, Pub. L. No. 92-318, 20 U.S.C. §§ 1681–1686, may apply.

# Employment

## EQUAL PAY LAWS

No employer shall discriminate between the sexes by paying wages to any employee in any occupation at a rate less than the rate at which he or she pays an employee of the opposite sex for comparable work which requires the same skill, effort, and responsibility. (§ 34-06.1-03)

**ENFORCEMENT:** An employee who has been discriminated against in the payment of wages because of sex may bring a civil action within 2 years of the violation for the recovery of those wages. The court may award, in addition to the unpaid wages, an additional equal amount as liquidated damages, if the violation was willful, and reasonable attorney's fees; or the Commissioner of Labor may bring the action on behalf of aggrieved persons to collect claims for unpaid wages. (§§ 34-06.1-04 to -06)

# FAIR EMPLOYMENT LAWS

The law applies to the state, its political and civil subdivisions, persons employing ten or more full time employees, labor organizations, and employment agencies. It prohibits an employer from refusing to hire or discriminate in the terms, privileges, and conditions of employment; an employment agency from refusing to refer for employment; and a labor organization from denying full and equal membership rights or expelling or suspending its members because of sex. (§§ 14-02.4-03 to -06)

**ENFORCEMENT:** An aggrieved party may bring a civil action in the district court within 3 years from the date the alleged discrimination occurred. The court may enjoin the respondent from further acts of discrimination, issue an injunction, and give equitable relief and back pay limited to no more than 2 years from date of filing of the charge. If the Department of Labor receives a complaint of discriminatory employment practices, it has 60 days to negotiate a settlement agreement. (§§ 14-02.4-19 to -21)

# GOVERNMENT CONTRACTORS AND SUBCONTRACTORS

There is no relevant statutory provision. However, it should be noted that if federal funds are involved, federal law, Exec. Order No. 11246, 3 C.F.R. 339 (1965), 42 U.S.C. § 2000e app. at 1232, 41 C.F.R. § 60-1.2, may apply.

**ENFORCEMENT:** There is no relevant statutory provision.

# STATE EMPLOYEE LAWS

State employees are covered by the Fair Employment Practices Law. In addition, discrimination in the civil service is prohibited. All promotions and appointments in the state classified service are to be made without regard to sex. (§§ 54-44.3-22, -44.3-01)

**ENFORCEMENT:** Any person who intentionally violates any provision shall be guilty of an infraction and upon conviction shall be ineligible for 1 year for appointment or employment in the classified service. (§§ 37-19.1-03, 54-44.3-26)

# VETERAN'S PREFERENCE

The unremarried spouse of a veteran who died while in the service or later from a service-connected cause is entitled to employment or appointment preference. The spouse of a disabled veteran who has a service-connected disability is entitled to employment or appointment preference. Veterans who are North Dakota residents are entitled to preference over all other applicants in employment or appointments by governmental agencies. In addition, five points are added to the civil service examination passing scores of veterans, and ten points are added to disabled veterans' passing scores. (§§ 37-19.1-02, 43-07-02)

# Community Life

## CREDIT

It is unlawful for a person to deny credit, increase charges or fees for securing credit; restrict the amount or use of credit extended, or impose different terms or conditions with respect to the credit extended to a person because of sex. (§ 14-02.4-17)

> **ENFORCEMENT:** An action may be brought in the district court within 3 years of the alleged discriminatory act. The court may enjoin the respondent from engaging in the practice or grant a temporary or permanent injunction, equitable relief, or attorney's fees. (§§ 14-02.4-19, -02.4-20)

## HOUSING

It is unlawful for an owner of housing or real property's agent to refuse to transfer an interest to a person; to discriminate against a person in terms, conditions, privileges, of the transfer of the interest; or to indicate or publicize that the transfer of an interest is unwelcome, objectionable, not accepted, or not solicited because of a person's sex. (§§ 14-02.4-12, -02.4-13)

> **ENFORCEMENT:** See "Credit." The action must be brought within 180 days of the alleged wrongdoing. (§§ 14-02.4-19, -02.4-20)

## INSURANCE

Unfair methods of competition or unfair or deceptive acts or practices including unfair discrimination between individuals of the same class and equal expectation of life and of essentially the same hazard are prohibited. (§ 26.1-04-03)

> **ENFORCEMENT:** The Commissioner of Insurance investigates all charges of alleged discrimination practices in the insurance industry. Upon a finding of a violation, the commissioner either can order the respondent to cease and desist, or impose monetary penalties, or revoke or suspend the offender's license. (§ 26.1-04-13)

## PUBLIC ACCOMMODATIONS

It is unlawful for a person engaged in providing a public accommodation to refuse access to the use of any benefit from services and facilities or to give unequal treatment to persons with respect to the availability, terms, conditions, or price of the services and facilities provided. It is also discriminatory to advertise or indicate or publicize that patrons of a particular sex are not acceptable. (§§ 12.1-14-04, 14-02.4-14, -02.4-16)

> **ENFORCEMENT:** See "Housing."

# OHIO

## Home and Family

## MARRIAGE

**AGE OF CONSENT:** Males 18 years old and females 16 years old may consent to marry. (§ 3101.01)*

**CONSENT REQUIREMENT:** A minor may marry with the consent of his or her parents or guardian or anyone who has been awarded permanent custody of the minor by a juvenile court. However, parental consent is not required if a parent resides in a foreign country, has neglected or abused a minor for 1 year or more, is incompetent, is an inmate of a state mental or penal institution, or has been deprived of custody. (§ 3101.01)

**LICENSE REQUIREMENT:** An application for a marriage license is issued by the probate court within the county where either applicant resides or, if neither is a resident of the state, where the marriage is expected to be solemnized. Both parties must personally apply for the license unless a judge is satisfied upon an affidavit of an active and reputable physician that one of the parties is unable to appear in court. In such a case a license may be issued upon the application and oath of the other party; but the person unable to appear in court must file an affidavit giving the information required for the issuance of a license. If either applicant is under the age of 18, the judge may require them to state that they have received marriage counseling satisfactory to the court. (§ 3101.05) A license will not be issued when either party is under the influence of liquor or a controlled substance or is infected with a communicable form of syphilis. (§ 3101.06) The license, once issued, is valid for 60 days. (§ 3101.07)

**PROHIBITED MARRIAGES:** Bigamous marriages and marriages between parties nearer of kin than second cousins are prohibited. (§ 3101.01) Children born of void or prohibited marriages are legitimate. [*Abelt v. Zeman*, 173 N.E.2d 907 (Ohio 1961)]

## DISSOLUTION OF MARRIAGE

**ANNULMENT:** Factors 14, 19, 33, 34, and 35, listed in Appendix A, are grounds for annulment. (§ 3105.31)

*Residency Requirement:* The plaintiff must reside in the state for at least 6 months immediately before filing the complaint. (§ 3105.03)

**LEGAL SEPARATION:** There is no relevant statutory provision. However, when the spouses are living separate and apart, they may bring a suit for alimony which will be granted upon a finding of ill treatment and any of factors 4 to 6, 25, and 48, listed in Appendix A. (§ 3105.17)

**DIVORCE**

*Residency Requirement:* See "Annulment."

*Grounds for Divorce:* Grounds for divorce include factors 3, 4, 6, 9 (4 years), 16 (1 year), 17, 19, 25, 31 (2 years), and 48, listed in Appendix A. In addition,

*Unless otherwise specified, all reference citations are to Ohio Revised Code Annotated (1953).

a final divorce decree obtained outside the state which does not release the other party from the obligations of the marriage inside this state is grounds for divorce. (§ 3105.01)

*Conciliation Requirement:* Upon the motion of either party to a divorce, annulment, or alimony, or upon its own motion, the court may order the parties to undergo conciliation for a period of time not exceeding 90 days. The order will set forth the conciliation procedure and name the conciliator. (§ 3105.091)

*Property Distribution:* There is no specific statute providing for the equitable distribution of the parties' property. However, an equitable division of property is allowed pursuant to an award of alimony after considering factors 1, 5, 6, 9, 11, 13, 14, 18, 19, and 25, listed in Appendix E, and the property brought to the marriage by either party. (§ 3105.18)

*Child Custody:* The court may grant the care, custody, and control of the children to either parent or to the parents jointly in accordance with the best interests of the child. The court will consider factors 6, 10, 11, 12, 14, and 21, listed in Appendix B. Joint custody may be awarded upon a motion of both parties and the filing of a plan for joint custody. All the factors listed above are considered in this determination. (§ 3109.04)

*Child Support:* The court may order either or both parents to support their children, without regard to marital misconduct. In determining the amount reasonable or necessary for support, including the medical needs of the child, the court will consider factors 1, 3, 4, and 5, listed in Appendix D. [§ 3109.05]

*Spousal Support/Alimony:* The court may award alimony to either party as it deems reasonable, in real or personal property, in a lump sum, or by periodic installments. See "Property Distribution" for factors considered. (§ 3105.18)

*Enforcement of Support Orders:* In any action where support is ordered and it appears that the person owing the support has failed to make payments, the court, on its own motion, or on the motion of an interested party, may order an employer or the Bureau of Worker's Compensation to withhold the amount owed from the personal earnings or benefits of the person owing the support. If the person is neither employed nor receiving worker's compensation benefits, the court may order a financial institution to deduct from the person's account a specified amount for support or order the person to enter a bond with the court. (§ 3113.21) See also the Revised Uniform Reciprocal Enforcement of Support Act of 1968, §§ 3115.01.01 *et seq.*

*Spouse's Name:* When a divorce is granted, or when a marriage is declared void or is annulled, the court may restore a person's former or birth name, if the person so desires. (§§ 3105.16, .34)

*Divorce by Affidavit or Summary Judgment:* There is no relevant statutory provision.

*Displaced Homemaker Laws:* Multipurpose service centers provide education, training, employment, health care, and counseling services to displaced homemakers 27 years of age and older to enable them to become gainfully employed and to maintain productive and independent lives. (§§ 3354.19 to 24)

# DOMESTIC VIOLENCE

**STATUTORY PROVISION:** Any act that attempts to cause or recklessly causes bodily injury, that places another person, by the threat of force, in fear of imminent serious physical harm, or that results in child abuse is prohibited. (§§ 2919.25, 3113.31)

**WHO IS PROTECTED?** The act applies to family or household members who reside together or have resided together and includes spouses, former spouses, parents, children, or other persons related by consanguinity or affinity to spouses. (§§ 2919.25, 3113.31)

**RELIEF AVAILABLE:** A victim of domestic violence may seek relief for himself or herself, or any parent or adult household member may seek relief on behalf of any other family or household member by commencing a civil or criminal action. If a civil action is commenced, the court may grant any protection order after a hearing or may oppose any consent agreement. The order or agreement may direct the respondent to refrain from further engaging in acts of abuse; grant possession of the residence or household to the petitioner or other family member; order the abuser to vacate the premises; award temporary custody of or establish temporary visitation rights with regard to minor children; require the respondent to maintain support; require any or all of the parties involved to seek counseling; require the abuser to refrain from entering the residence, school, business, or place of employment of the petitioner or other family or household member; or grant other relief the court considers fair and equitable. (§ 3113.31) If a criminal action is commenced, the court may issue a temporary protection order as a pretrial condition of release of the alleged offender. Violation of an order is a crime. If a person is found guilty of domestic violence, the court may place the abuser on probation conditioned upon his or her participation in a clinically appropriate treatment program. (§§ 2919, 2925, 2926, 2933.16) A police officer may arrest a person without a warrant if there is reasonable ground to believe that an offense of violence has occurred; a written statement by a victim of domestic violence constitutes reasonable cause. (§ 2935.03) All new police officers must receive at least 15 hours of training in handling domestic violence problems. (§ 109.77)

**MARITAL RAPE:** A woman may charge her husband with rape where the parties have entered into a written separation agreement; when an action for divorce, annulment, or dissolution of marriage is pending; or after the effective date of a judgment for alimony. [§ 2907.01(L)]

**CIVIL LAWSUIT FOR RAPE OR ASSAULT:** There are no cases directly on point. However, in *Green v. Green*, 446 N.E.2d 837 (Ohio 1982), the court held that a woman could sue her husband for injuries inflicted upon her by his intentional tortious acts.

**CHILD ABUSE:** It is unlawful for a parent, guardian, or custodian of a child under 18 or a handicapped child under 21 to create a substantial risk to the health or safety of the child by torture, extensive corporal punishment, or unreasonable and excessive restraint, sexual exploitation, or abuse or by allowing, encouraging, or forcing the child to submit to or engage in prostitution. (§§ 2919.22; 2151.031) A police or court officer may remove a child from his or her home without a court order if the officer has reasonable grounds to believe the child to be in immediate danger and that the child's removal is necessary. If a court determines that a child has been abused or neglected, it may permit the child to stay with the parents, guardian, or custodian or grant temporary or permanent legal custody of the child to the Department of Public Welfare, a child placement agency, a child care institution, or a relative. (§§ 2151.31, .353)

  *Notification Requirement:* All attorneys, health care professionals, coroners, child care employees, teachers, school personnel, and social workers must report all suspected cases of child abuse and neglect of children under 18 or handicapped children under 21 to the Children's Services Board, the Department of Human Services, or to a police officer. (§ 2151.421)

# INHERITANCE RIGHTS

**FAILURE TO MAKE A WILL:** The surviving spouse is entitled to the entire estate if there are no children or grandchildren; to the first $30,000 and one-half of the balance if the decedent left one child or lineal descendants who are also the surviving spouse's child or lineal descendants; to $10,000 and one-half of the balance if the decedent left one child or lineal descendants who are not also the surviving spouse's child or lineal descendants; to the first $30,000 and one-third of the balance if the decedent left more than one child or the children of more than one deceased child who are also the surviving spouse's children or grandchildren; to $10,000 and one-third of the balance if the decedent left more than one child or the children of more than one deceased child who are not also the spouse's children or grandchildren. (§ 2105.06) The surviving spouse may also elect to receive as part of his or her share of the intestate estate the decedent's entire interest in the marital home. (§ 2105.062)

**FAILURE TO PROVIDE BY WILL:** The dower share has been abolished except as to any real property which was transferred or encumbered by the decedent during the marriage without the surviving spouse's consent. The surviving spouse is entitled to a life estate in one-third of all this property. However, instead of the dower interest, the surviving spouse may elect to take a share of the decedent's estate that he or she would have been entitled to had the decedent died without having made a will. (§ 2103.02)

**CHILDREN BORN OUT OF WEDLOCK:** Statutes which barred children born out of wedlock from inheriting from their fathers were declared unconstitutional by *Trimble v. Gordon*, 430 U.S. 762 (1977), which held that a child born out of wedlock could inherit from his or her father provided that during his lifetime the father had acknowledged his paternity of the child and had supported the child.

**HOMESTEAD, PERSONAL, AND FAMILY ALLOWANCES:** The surviving spouse or minor children are entitled to receive in money or property the sum of $5000 as an allowance for support. When the decedent is a nonresident leaving property in the state, the surviving spouse or minor children may apply for a setoff of allowance from the property. The amount set off will not exceed the amount usually allowed in the state. (§§ 2117, 2123) A surviving spouse may remain in the decedent's mansion house rent free for 1 year, except that the house may be sold within the year to satisfy the decedent's debts, in which case the spouse is entitled to receive compensation in an amount equal to the fair rental value for the unexpired period. Both this amount and the allowance made to the surviving spouse or children have priority over all the decedent's debts. (§§ 2117.24, .25)

**OPTION TO DISREGARD THE WILL:** The surviving spouse may elect to disregard the will and take the share he or she would have received if the decedent had died without a will, after the will has been probated, but not later than 1 month after the service of the citation to elect. If the spouse elects to disregard the will and the value of the property that he or she is entitled to is equal to or greater than the value of the mansion house, the survivor is also entitled to elect, as part of his or her share of the intestate estate, the decedent's entire interest in the mansion house which is equal to its appraised value less all liens existing at the time of the decedent's death. However, the spouse may never take more than one-half of the net estate (even if the decedent left no heirs) or more than one-third of the net estate if decedent left two or more children or their children. When the surviving spouse succeeds to the decedent's entire estate, it is presumed that the spouse elects to take under the will. No citation will be issued or election required unless a contrary intention is manifested. (§ 2107.39)

# REPRODUCTIVE RIGHTS
## ABORTION

*Statutory Provisions:* An abortion may be performed by a licensed physician or surgeon only. (§ 4732.41)

*Informed Consent:* An abortion can be performed only upon obtaining the informed consent of the woman. (§ 2919.12)

*Parental Consent:* An unmarried pregnant minor's consent must be accompanied by the informed consent of a parent, custodian, or guardian. Violation of this provision is a misdemeanor and may involve civil compensatory and exemplary damages. (§ 2919.12)

*Spousal Consent:* There is no relevant statutory provision.

*Reporting Requirements:* The Public Health Council is directed to adopt rules for reporting forms and pathological reports; the rules may be enforced by temporary or permanent injunctions. (§ 3701.341)

*State Funding:* The use of state or local public funds to subsidize any abortion not necessary to save the woman's life or her physical or mental health, as certified in writing by the physician, is prohibited. (§ 5011.55)

**BIRTH CONTROL:** Mothers receiving Aid to Families with Dependent Children may be referred to any private or public agency, doctor, clinic, or organization where they can receive family planning information. The county administration may procure for such mothers any pills or devices needed or desired. (§ 5107.10)

**STERILIZATION:** The law governing voluntary sterilization has the same requirements as laws governing other surgical procedures.

# UNMARRIED COUPLES

**COMMON-LAW MARRIAGE:** Common-law marriages are valid. [*Fahrer v. Fahrer*, 304 N.E.2d 411 (1973)] Proof of cohabitation and reputation of the parties as husband and wife is evidence of such a marriage. (§ 3105.12)

**COHABITAL RELATIONSHIPS:** There is no case directly on point.

## CHILDREN

*Custody:* Once paternity is established, the father may petition for custody of the child in a separate proceeding. (§ 3111.13)

*Legitimation Proceedings:* The natural father of a child may file an application in the probate court of the county in which he or the child resides or was born, acknowledging that the child is his. If such an application is filed, and upon the mother's consent, or if she is deceased, incompetent, or has surrendered custody, upon the consent of the person or agency having custody, the probate court may, if satisfied that the applicant is the natural father and that the establishment of the relationship is in the best interests of the child, find that the child is the applicant's child as though born to him in lawful wedlock. (§ 2105.18)

*Paternity Proceedings:* A civil action may be brought by the child, the mother, a man alleged or alleging himself to be the father, or the personal representative of any of the above within 5 years after the child reaches the age of 18. [§§ 3111.04(A); .05(B)] The court, upon its own motion or upon the motion of any party, may order the involved parties to submit to genetic tests. [§ 3111.09(A), .09(B)] Once paternity has been established, the court may order payment for the child's support and the father may petition for custody or visitation rights. [§ 3111.13(A)]

*Obligations of the Putative Father:* Once custody has been established, the court may direct the father to pay all or part of the reasonable expenses of the mother's pregnancy and confinement, order the payment of support for the child, and make provisions for visitation privileges or any other matter in the best interests of the child. In its determination of support, the court will consider all relevant facts, including factors 1, 5, 9, 12, 17, 18, 20, 23, 24, and 28, listed in Appendix D, and the needs and earning ability of the child. [§ 3111.13(A)]

# Education

## STATUTORY PROVISION

There are no relevant statutory provisions. However, it should be noted that if federal funds are involved, Title IX of the Education Amendments of 1972, Pub. L. No. 92-318, 20 U.S.C. §§ 1681–1686, may apply.

# Employment

## EQUAL PAY LAWS

It is unlawful for an employee to discriminate on the basis of sex in wages paid to employees performing equal work requiring equal skill, effort, and responsibility under similar working conditions except if the differential in pay is based on a seniority or merit system, quantity or quality of product, and any factor other than sex. (§ 4111.17)

**ENFORCEMENT:** Any employee discriminated against may sue in any court of competent jurisdiction to recover twice the amount unlawfully withheld from the date the violation began, costs of the action and attorney's fees. The Director of Industrial Relations may sue on the employee's behalf. Any action arising out of a violation must be commenced within 1 year after the date of the violation. (§ 4111.17)

## FAIR EMPLOYMENT LAWS

The Fair Employment Parctices Law applies to the state, its political and civil subdivisions, employers of four or more persons, labor organizations, and employment agencies. It prohibits employers from refusing to hire, discharging without cause, or discriminating in any of the terms, conditions, and privileges of employment on the basis of sex; labor organizations or apprentice training programs from limiting or classifying or refusing to refer for employment any individual on the basis of sex. [§ 4112.02(A)] Discrimination on the basis of pregnancy is included. [§ 4112.01(B)] However, the law does not apply to domestic servants or religious groups and educational institutions operated, controlled, or supervised by a religious organization who may employ persons of particular religions or denominations. [§§ 4112.01(A)(3), .02(L)]

**ENFORCEMENT:** See "Community Life: Credit."

# GOVERNMENT CONTRACTORS AND SUBCONTRACTORS

Every contractor for the construction, alteration, or repair of any public building or other public work must agree not to discriminate in hiring, or intimidate any person hired, on the basis of sex. (§§ 125.111, 153.59)

**ENFORCEMENT:** The Department of Administrative Services will ensure no capital money is appropriated for projects that do not provide affirmative action programs for the employment and effective utilization of disadvantaged persons whose disadvantage may arise from sex. (§ 153.59) All contracts provide that the contractor forfeit $25 for each person who is discriminated against or intimidated in violation of the terms of the contract or that the contract be canceled or terminated and all money to become due be forfeited if a second or subsequent violation of the terms of the contract occurs. (§ 153.60)

# STATE EMPLOYEE LAWS

State employees are covered by the Fair Employment Practice's Law. [§ 4112.01 (A)(2)]

**ENFORCEMENT:** See "Community Life: Credit."

# VETERAN'S PREFERENCE

Veterans are entitled to preference in original appointments to any competitive positions in the state civil service. (§ 124.27) They will have an additional 20 percent credit added to their passing scores on classified service examinations. (§ 124.23) Veterans receive preference over nonveterans with the same scores. [§ 124.26(A)]

# Community Life

# CREDIT

It is unlawful for an institution extending credit to discriminate against any applicant for credit by refusing to grant or renew credit; by refusing to consider the sources of income of an applicant or disregarding or ignoring the applicant's income; by imposing special requirements or conditions; or by failing to maintain, upon the individual's request, a separate account for each individual to whom credit is extended on the basis of sex or marital status. [§ 4112.021(B)]

**ENFORCEMENT:** Aggrieved individuals may file a civil action in the court of common pleas within 180 days of the occurrence of the alleged violation. Relief granted by the court may include a permanent or temporary injunction, a temporary restraining order, or an award of actual and punitive damages not less than $100, as well as attorney's fees and court costs. [§ 4112.021(D)] In addition, the Civil Rights Commission is authorized to receive, investigate, hold hearings on, and pass orders upon, any written charges made under oath and filed within 6 months of the occurrence of the alleged discriminatory act, and to issue cease and desist orders enjoining any person from engaging in further discriminatory acts. (§ 4112.05)

# HOUSING

It is unlawful to discriminate against any individual on the basis of sex or marital status by refusing to sell, assign, rent, lease, sublease, finance, or otherwise deny or withhold available housing accommodations; by refusing to lend money or withholding financing for the acquisition, construction, or rehabilitation of housing; by printing, publishing, or circulating any statement indicating a preference or limitation; or by denying any person access to membership or participation in any multiple listing service, real estate broker's organization, or other organization related to the sale or rental of housing accommodations. [§ 4112.02(H)]

> **ENFORCEMENT:** Aggrieved private persons may file a civil action in a court of common place within 180 days of the occurrence of the alleged discrimination. If the court finds that a discriminatory practice has occurred or is about to occur, it may enjoin the respondent or order affirmative action. It may also grant injunctions or restraining orders and may award the plaintiff actual damages. The court must notify the Civil Rights Commission of its findings of discrimination within 15 days of the finding. (§ 4112.051)

# INSURANCE

It is unlawful to discriminate against an individual on the basis of sex or marital status by refusing to issue or by canceling or declining to renew any insurance policy under these contracts; by discriminating between individuals of the same class and equal expectation of life in the rates, terms, or conditions of life insurance or annuity contracts or in the dividends or benefits payable thereunder; by discriminating between individuals of the same class and essentially the same hazard in the amount of premium, policy fees or rates charged for any other type of insurance, in the benefits payable or in any other terms or conditions of these contracts. It is an unfair practice to refuse to issue disability insurance solely because the applicant's principal occupation is that of managing a household or to refuse to make maternity benefits available to a policyholder if such benefits are offered under any individual or group sickness and accident insurance policy. (§§ 3901.21(F), (L), (M), (N), (O)]

> **ENFORCEMENT:** The Superintendent of Insurance may conduct hearings to determine whether violations have occurred, upon the written application of an aggrieved party. A superintendent who determines that a violation has occurred may issue a cease and desist order, suspend or revoke a license to engage in the business of insurance, and/or order that an insurance company or agency not employ the offending party, or permit him or her to serve as a director, consultant, or in any other capacity for as long as the superintendent thinks appropriate. If an order of the superintendent has been violated, a civil action or proceeding may be initiated which may result in the imposition of monetary fines on the offending party. (§ 3901.22)

# PUBLIC ACCOMMODATIONS

It is unlawful for any proprietor or employee, keeper, or manager of a place of public accommodation to deny any person the full access, enjoyment, advantages or privileges of that facility on the basis of sex. [§ 4112.02(G)]

> **ENFORCEMENT:** See "Credit."

# OKLAHOMA

## Home and Family

## MARRIAGE

**AGE OF CONSENT:** An unmarried person 18 years of age or older may consent to marriage with a person of the opposite sex. (tit. 43, § 3)*

**CONSENT REQUIREMENT:** A person under 18 years of age can marry with the express consent and authority of a parent or guardian. Every person under 16 years of age is expressly prohibited to marry, unless the court authorizes the marriage in settlement of suits for seduction or paternity or unless the unmarried female is pregnant or has given birth to a child. However, the court will not authorize the marriage of males or females under 16 years of age when the unmarried female is pregnant, unless at least one parent, guardian or custodian of each minor has had an opportunity to be heard and object to the marriage. (tit. 43, § 3)

**LICENSE REQUIREMENT:** A marriage license issued by a judge or the clerk of the district court is required. The license is issued upon written application, signed, and sworn to in person before the judge or clerk by both parties to be married and upon the filing of a certificate or affidavit from a physician licensed by the state, stating that each party has been given a standard serological examination not more than 30 days prior to the application date and that neither party is infected with a communicable stage of syphilis. If one or both parties is under the legal age, the application must be on file in the clerk's office for at least 72 hours. The license issued is valid in any county within the state for 30 days. (tit. 43, §§ 5, 32, 36)

**PROHIBITED MARRIAGES:** Incestuous and prohibited marriages include marriages between ancestors and descendants of any degree; stepfather and stepdaughter or stepmother and stepson; uncle and niece or aunt and nephew, except in cases where such relationship is only by marriage; siblings of the half or whole blood; and first cousins. However, any marriage of first cousins performed lawfully in another state is valid and binding. (tit. 43, § 2) Bigamous marriages are also prohibited. (tit. 12, § 1280) The children of void marriages are legitimate. (tit. 84, § 215)

## DISSOLUTION OF MARRIAGE

**ANNULMENT:** Factors 19 (remarriage within 6 months of a divorce), 35, and 36, listed in Appendix A, are grounds for annulment. [tit. 12, §§ 1281(b), 1283]

*Residency Requirement:* There is no relevant statutory requirement.

**LEGAL SEPARATION:** There is no relevant statutory provision. However a spouse may bring an action for separate maintenance as if for divorce. (tit. 12, § 1284)

*Residency Requirement:* There is no relevant statutory requirement.

**DIVORCE**

*Residency Requirement:* Either party in a divorce action must have been an actual resident in good faith for 6 months. (tit. 12, § 1272)

*Unless otherwise noted, all reference citations are to Oklahoma Statutes Annotated (West 1910).

*Grounds for Divorce:* Factors 1, 3 to 5 (1 year), 6, 9 (5 years), 17, 24, 25, and 48, listed in Appendix A, are grounds for divorce. In addition, a final divorce decree obtained outside the state which does not release the other party from the obligations of the marriage inside this state is grounds for divorce. (tit. 12, § 1271)

*Conciliation Requirement:* There is no relevant statutory provision.

*Property Distribution:* When a divorce is granted, the court will return to each spouse the property owned by him or her before marriage and the undisposed of property acquired by either spouse in his or her own right during the marriage to the appropriate spouse. The court will divide all real and personal property acquired jointly during marriage, however held, in a manner that appears just and reasonable. This may be accomplished by a division in kind or by setting apart the property to one spouse and requiring that spouse to pay to the other a fair amount in compensation. A portion of the property may also be set aside from one spouse to the other for the support of any minor children who reside with that spouse. (tit. 12, § 1278) In any case where the divorce is based upon the misconduct of both parties, where the divorce is refused or where alimony is granted without a divorce, the court may equitably divide and dispose of the property, however held, as may be just, taking into consideration the way in which the property is held and the time and manner of its acquisition. (tit. 12, § 1275)

*Child Custody:* In awarding the custody of a minor, unmarried child, the court considers the preference and what happens to be in the best interests of the physical, mental and moral welfare of the child. Either sole or joint custody will be granted. (tit. 12, §§ 1275.4, 1277.1)

*Child Support:* Any child is entitled to support by its parents until the age of 18. Any dependent child regularly and continuously attending high school is entitled to support by the parents through the age of 18. (tit. 12, § 1277) The custodial parent must give the child support and education suitable to the parents' circumstances. If the support and education which the custodial parent is able to give are inadequate, the other parent must assist to the extent of his or her ability. (tit. 10, § 3) When a divorce is granted, the court may set apart a portion of the separate estate of one spouse to the other spouse for the support of the children when custody is with that other spouse. (tit. 12, § 1278)

*Spousal Support/Alimony:* A wife or husband may obtain alimony from the other without a divorce, in an action brought for that purpose in the district court for any of the causes for which a divorce may be granted. (tit. 12, § 1284) When a divorce is granted, either spouse may be allowed alimony out of the real and personal property of the other as the court thinks reasonable, having due regard for the value of such property. Alimony may be allowed from real or personal property or both, or in the form of a money judgment, payable either in a lump sum or in installments as the court deems just and equitable. (tit. 12, § 1278) Upon the death or remarriage of the recipient, the payments for support, if not already accrued, will terminate unless the recipient can make a proper showing for any amount past due or for some amount which is still needed within 90 days of death or remarriage. The order for support is not a lien against the real property of the obligated party unless the court's order specifically so provides. The voluntary cohabitation of a former spouse with a member of the opposite sex is a ground to modify an order for alimony. The court may in such a case reduce or terminate the support payments upon proof of changed circumstances. (tit. 12, §§ 1278, 1284, 1289)

*Enforcement of Support Orders:* Support orders may be enforced as an indirect contempt of court. (tit. 12, § 1276.2) They may additionally be enforced by attaching the property of the party owing support, thereby enjoining its sale or disposition and setting it aside for the use of the parties to whom support is owed. (tit. 12, §§ 1276, 1278) See also the Revised Uniform Reciprocal Enforcement of Support Act of 1968, tit. 12, §§ 1600.1 *et seq.*

*Spouse's Name:* When a divorce is granted, the wife, if she so desires, will be restored to her maiden or former name. (tit. 12, § 1278)

*Divorce by Affidavit or Summary Judgment:* There is no relevant statutory provision.

*Displaced Homemaker Laws:* These provide for the necessary counseling, training, jobs, services, and support programs to displaced homemakers so that they may enjoy the independence and economic security vital to a productive life. (tit. 70, § 14-113)

# DOMESTIC VIOLENCE

**STATUTORY PROVISION:** Causing or attempting to cause serious physical harm or threatening another with imminent serious physical harm, between family and household members is prohibited. (tit. 22, § 40)

**WHO IS PROTECTED?** Spouses, former spouses, parents, children, persons otherwise related by blood or marriage, or persons living in the same household. This includes the elderly and handicapped. (tit. 22, §§ 40 *et seq.* )

**RELIEF AVAILABLE:** A victim of domestic abuse, or any adult household member on behalf of any other minor or incompetent family or household member, may obtain an emergency restraining order from the district court of the county in which the victim resides. The order may provide that the abuser not abuse or injure the victim, assault, molest, harass, threaten or otherwise interfere with the victim, and leave the residence. A protective order may also include a provision for attorney's fees and court costs. Any relief granted will be for a fixed period not to exceed 1 year. However, this period may be extended or modified upon the motion of either party as deemed necessary by the court. (tit. 22, §§ 60.3, .4) Violation of either type of order is a misdemeanor. All orders have statewide validity. (tit. 22, §§ 60.6, .7)

**MARITAL RAPE:** A male or female may charge his or her spouse with rape if force or violence is used or threatened under any of the following circumstances: a petition for divorce or legal separation is pending or has been granted, a petition for a protective order is pending or the victim and perpetrator are living separate and apart from each other. [Tit. 21, § 1111(B)] A spouse may also be charged with rape where the victim submits to sexual intercourse under the belief that the person committing the act is a spouse and such belief is induced by artifice, pretense or concealment practiced by that person in collusion with the spouse with intent to induce such belief. [tit. 21, § 1111(A)(6)] A spouse may also be charged with rape by instrumentality. (tit. 21, § 1111.1)

**CIVIL LAWSUIT FOR RAPE OR ASSAULT:** There is no case law directly on point. However, spouses may maintain tort actions against each other. [*White v. White*, 618 P.2d 921 (Okla. 1980)]

**CHILD ABUSE:** Harm or threatened harm to a child under 18 by nonaccidental physical or mental injury, sexual abuse, negligent treatment, or maltreatment, including the failure to provide adequate food, clothing, or shelter when done by a person responsible for a child's health and welfare is prohibited. (tit. 21, § 845) Any parent or other person who willfully or maliciously injures, tortures, or uses unreasonable force upon a child under 18 or who causes, procures, or permits any of these acts to be done is guilty of a crime. This does not, however, prohibit a parent, teacher, or other person from using ordinary force as a means of discipline. (tit. 21, §§ 843, 844) Any parent or legal custodian who willfully omits, without any lawful excuse, the performance of any duty imposed upon him or her to furnish necessary food, clothing, shelter, or medical attention for the child is guilty of a crime. A court may assume custody of a child and order whatever action may be necessary. (tit. 21, § 852) The intentional and knowing commission of lewd or indecent proposals or acts to children under 16 years by persons over 18 who are at least 3 years older than the victim is also a crime. (Tit. 21, § 1123)

*Notification Requirement:* All health care professionals, assistants, or registered nurses examining, attending, or treating the victim of what appears to be criminally injurious conduct and every other person having reason to believe that a child under 18 has had physical injuries inflicted upon him or her by other than accidental means, where the injuries appear to have been caused as a result of physical abuse or neglect, must report the matter promptly by telephone to the nearest appropriate law enforcement agency in the county where the abuse or neglect occurred. (tit. 21, §§ 846, 846.1) Any person making such report will have immunity from any civil or criminal liability that might otherwise be incurred or imposed. (tit. 21, § 847)

# INHERITANCE RIGHTS

**FAILURE TO MAKE A WILL:** As of July 1, 1985, the surviving spouse is entitled to the entire estate if there is no surviving issue, parents, or siblings; to all the property acquired by the joint industry of the spouses during their marriage and to an undivided one-third interest in the remaining estate if there is no surviving issue but the decedent is survived by parents or siblings; to an undivided one-half interest in all property of the estate, whether acquired by the joint industry of the spouses during marriage or otherwise, if there are surviving issue, all of whom are also issue of the surviving spouse; to an undivided one-half interest in property acquired by the joint industry of the spouses during their marriage and to an undivided equal part in the remaining estate with each of the living children of the decedent and the lawful issue of any deceased child by right of representation if there are surviving issue, one or more of whom are not also issue of the surviving spouse. [tit. 84, § 213(B)]

**FAILURE TO PROVIDE BY WILL:** Every estate in property may be disposed of by will, except that a written antenuptial agreement prevails over a will. However, no spouse can bequeath or devise away from the other spouse so much of his or her estate that the other spouse will receive less than an undivided one-half interest in the property acquired by the joint industry of the spouses during the marriage. (tit. 84, § 44)

**CHILDREN BORN OUT OF WEDLOCK:** A child born out of wedlock may inherit from and through the mother and her kindred. The child may inherit from or through the father and his kindred only if the father signed an acknowledgment in the presence of a witness that he is the child's father; or the father and mother intermarried after the child's birth and after the marriage the father acknowledged the child as his own or adopted him into his family; or the father publicly acknowledged the child as his own, receiving him or her into his family, with the consent of his wife, if he's married, and otherwise treating the child as legitimate; or the father was judicially determined to be such in a paternity proceeding before a court of competent jurisdiction. The children of all annulled marriages or marriages dissolved by divorce are considered legitimate. (tit. 84, § 215)

**HOMESTEAD, PERSONAL, AND FAMILY ALLOWANCES:** A spouse may bequeath the homestead to the other spouse. [tit. 84, § 44(B)(1)] Upon the death of either spouse, the survivor may continue to possess and occupy the whole homestead, and upon the death of both parents the children may continue to possess and occupy the whole homestead until the youngest child becomes of age. In addition, all family pictures; a pew or other seating in a house of worship; a lot or lots in any burial ground; the family Bible, all schoolbooks used by the family, and all other books used as part of the family library not exceeding $100; all the descendants' apparel and clothing; supplies and fuel necessary for one year; all household and kitchen furniture, including stoves, beds, and bedding will be immediately delivered to the surviving spouse and children and are not to be considered assets, nor are they subject to the payment of any prior debts of the decedent. If this amount is insufficient for the support of the surviving spouse and children or if there is no personal property to be set apart and there is other property in the decedent's estate, the court, at its discretion, may make a reasonable allowance out of the property as is necessary for the maintenance of the family during the settlement of the estate. In the case of an insolvent estate, this period must not exceed 1 year after the granting of letters testamentary or of administration. Any allowances made by the court must be paid in preference to all charges except funeral and administration expenses. However, when the widow has an independent income from her own property equal to the amount given above, the whole property set apart must go to the minor children, except the homestead. (tit. 58, §§ 311, 313, 314, 315, 318) If the decedent died intestate, the surviving spouse is entitled to the decedent's car. (tit. 84, § 232)

**OPTION TO DISREGARD THE WILL:** As of July 1, 1985 the surviving spouse may reject the will and take the undivided one-half interest in the property acquired by their joint industry during the marriage. The surviving spouse must make the election in writing and file it in the district court in which the decedent's estate is being administered. Such a right is a personal one which may only be exercised during the surviving spouse's lifetime. (tit. 84, § 44) Annulment of the marriage or a divorce after the making of a will results in revocation of all provisions in favor of the testator's spouse. (tit. 84, § 114)

# REPRODUCTIVE RIGHTS
## ABORTION

*Statutory Provisions:* Only a physician licensed to practice in the state may perform or induce an abortion. Violation of this section is a crime. [tit. 63, § 1-731(B)] However, no abortions can be performed if an unborn child has become viable unless the abortion is necessary to prevent the death of the pregnant woman or to prevent impairment to her health. [tit. 63, § 1-732(A)] A woman may perform an abortion upon herself only under the supervision of a duly licensed physician. (tit. 63, § 1-733) Abortions permitted by law may be performed only in hospitals, which includes general hospitals, public health centers, and related facilities such as laboratories, outpatient departments, nurses' homes and training facilities, and central service facilities operated in connection with hospitals, which meet the standard set by the Department of Health. [Tit. 63, §§ 1-737, -710(a)]

*Informed Consent:* There is no relevant statutory provision.

*Parental Consent:* The minor's consent statute specifically excludes abortion from the services for which minors may give self-consent, although it does permit minors to consent to abortion counseling services. (tit. 63, §§ 2601, 2602)

*Spousal Consent:* There is no relevant statutory provision.

*Reporting Requirements:* Any physician who performs or induces an abortion must complete a form provided by the Department of Health. The form must include all medical facts pertinent to the abortion and must allow the physician and the woman to volunteer other personal facts for statistical public health purposes. (tit. 63, § 1-738) Hospitals and other health facilities that perform abortions must keep in their permanent files for at least 7 years all certifications and records pertaining to abortions. (tit. 63, § 1-739)

**BIRTH CONTROL:** The Department of Health has established family planning centers which operate as part of county, district, cooperative, or city services or in cooperation with nongovernmental agencies or organizations. These centers furnish educational materials and information regarding planned parenthood, including advice as to contraceptive practices, and are authorized to perform clinical activities including medical examination, insertion of contraceptive devices, and prescription of drugs and devices to eligible people. The centers are required to be under the direction of a licensed physician. (tit. 63, §§ 2071, 2072, 2074) Family planning and services are available to recipients of public assistance from the Department of Public Welfare. (tit. 56, § 28.1)

**STERILIZATION:** There is no statute governing voluntary sterilization of competent persons by licensed physicians; the laws applicable to such procedures are the same as for other surgical procedures. The provision establishing family planning centers does not state whether voluntary sterilizations are included in the services available. (tit. 63, § 2073) However, there is a provision which authorizes the Department of Health to pay for voluntary sterilizations performed on male public assistance recipients under 65 by licensed physicians or surgeons. (tit. 56, § 200.1) The minor's consent statute specifically excludes sterilization from the health services a minor may consent to. [tit. 63, § 2601(c)]

# UNMARRIED COUPLES

**COMMON-LAW MARRIAGE:** There is no relevant statutory provision. In *Matter of Bouse's Estate*, 583 P.2d 514 (Okla. 1978), the court held that an actual and mutual agreement to enter into matrimonial relations, permanent and exclusive of all others, between parties capable of making such a contract, and consummated by their cohabitation as husband and wife or their open mutual assumption of marital duties and obligations established a common-law marriage.

**COHABITAL RELATIONSHIPS:** There is no relevant statutory provision.

**CHILDREN**

*Custody:* The mother of a child born out of wedlock is entitled to the child's custody, services, and earnings. (tit. 10, § 6)

*Legitimation Proceedings:* A child born before wedlock becomes legitimate by the subsequent marriage of the parents. (tit. 10, § 2) The father of such a child, by publicly acknowledging the child as his own, receiving the child into his family as such, with the consent of his wife, if he's married, and otherwise treating the child as if he or she were legitimate, thereby adopts it as such. The child is thereafter legitimate for all purposes from the time of its birth and obtains the status of a child adopted by regular court procedure. (tit. 12, § 55)

*Paternity Proceedings:* Whenever a woman gives birth to a child born out of wedlock, a complaint to the district court may be made by any person charging the alleged father with the child's paternity. The proceeding may be brought in any county where the mother of the child resides. If the mother is dead at the time that the action is brought, it must be brought in the county where the mother resided and in the name of the state against the alleged father and must be commenced within 3 years after the child's birth. (tit. 10, §§ 71, 82)

*Obligations of the Putative Father:* If paternity is established, the father will be charged with the maintenance of the child including support and education, the reasonable expenses of the mother during pregnancy, confinement and recovery, and the costs of the suit. An action to enforce these obligations may be brought by the mother or guardian, the public authority chargeable with the support, or the child within 3 years from the time the alleged father last contributed to the child's support and education. The father will be held in contempt for disobeying an order to pay support. The father's obligation to pay ends if the child is adopted. (tit. 10, §§ 78, 83, 84)

# Education

## STATUTORY PROVISION

The statute prohibits only discrimination in the granting of state tuition aid. (tit. 70, § 626.5) However, it should be noted that, in the absence of a comprehensive state law governing discrimination in higher education, if federal funds are involved, federal law, Title IX of the Education Amendments of 1972, Pub. L. No. 92-318, 20 U.S.C. §§ 1681–1686, may apply.

**ENFORCEMENT:** The state Regents for Higher Education administer provisions against discrimination in the granting of state aid. (tit. 70, § 626.3)

# Employment

## EQUAL PAY LAWS

Employers may not willfully discriminate on the basis of sex in wages paid to employees for work requiring comparable skill, effort, and responsibility. However, a wage differential is not prohibited if based on a seniority system, a merit system, quantity or quality of production, or any factors other than sex. (tit. 40, § 198.1)

**ENFORCEMENT:** Violations may be reported to the Commissioner of Labor, who will investigate the charges and, in his or her discretion, initiate court proceedings for the enforcement of penalties. (tit. 40, § 198.2)

## FAIR EMPLOYMENT LAWS

The law covers the state, any of its governmental entities and agencies, employers of fifteen or more employees, labor organizations, and employment agencies. (tit. 25, §§

1201, 1301) It prohibits an employer from discriminating in hiring, discharge, or terms, conditions, or privileges of employment; a labor organization from expelling or excluding from its membership; or an employment agency from limiting, advertising, soliciting, segregating, or classifying employees so as to deprive any individual of employment opportunities because of sex. (tit. 25, §§ 1302 to 1304) The law's prohibitions do not apply where sex is a bona fide occupational qualification or where a bona fide seniority or merit system exists. Nor is it unlawful for an employer to differentiate on the basis of sex in employee annuities or death and survivors' benefits between widows and widowers of employees. (tit. 25, § 1311)

**ENFORCEMENT:** A person claiming to be aggrieved by a discriminatory practice may, by his or her attorney, the attorney general, or a legal services organization, file a complaint with the Commission of Human Rights within 180 days of the occurrence of the alleged discriminatory practice. The commission is empowered to receive, investigate, conciliate, hold hearings, and pass upon complaints alleging discrimination. Within 30 days after the commission has issued its finding, it may petition the district court for an order of enforcement. The court may grant affirmative relief, issue restraining orders, and restrain further violations of the commissioner's order. (tit. 25, §§ 1501 to 1507)

## GOVERNMENT CONTRACTORS AND SUBCONTRACTORS

They are covered under the Fair Employment Practices Law.

**ENFORCEMENT:** See "Fair Employment Laws."

## STATE EMPLOYEE LAWS

State employees are covered under the Fair Employment Practices Law. [tit. 25, §§ 1201(5), 1301(1)]

**ENFORCEMENT:** See "Fair Employment Laws."

## VETERAN'S PREFERENCE

The employment of veterans in competitive and noncompetitive jobs is preferred in the merit system. Accordingly, for disabled veterans, ten points are added to the passing grade achieved in the examination. For nondisabled veterans and for surviving spouses of veterans, five points are added to the passing grade achieved. Preference is also given in register ranks. Accordingly, five points are added to the final passing grade of veterans, spouses, unmarried surviving spouses or dependent parents; ten points are added to the final passing grade of disabled veterans and their spouses, unmarried surviving spouses, or dependent parents. (tit. 74, § 840.15)

# Community Life

## CREDIT

It is unlawful for an extender of credit to discriminate in the extension of credit in consumer credit sales, consumer leases, and consumer loans on the basis of sex or marital status. (tit. 14A, § 1-109)

**ENFORCEMENT:** There is no private right of action for violations of this statute. The Department of Consumer Credit is authorized to enforce this provision. (tit. 14A, § 1-109)

# HOUSING

There is no relevant statutory provision. However, federal law, Title VIII of the Civil Rights Act of 1968, 42 U.S.C. §§ 3601–3619, and Exec. Order No. 11063, 3 C.F.R. 652 (1962), *reprinted in* 42 U.S.C. § 1982, as amended by Exec. Order No. 12259, 3 C.F.R. 307 (1981), *reprinted in* 42 U.S.C. § 3608, may apply.

# INSURANCE

Discrimination is prohibited between individuals of the same class and equal expectation of life in rates charged for life insurance, annuity contracts, dividends, and other benefits payable; or between individuals of the same class and of essentially the same hazard in the amount of premium, policy fees, rates charged for accident or health insurance, benefits payable under these contracts, or any other term or condition of these contracts. Discrimination is also prohibited between risk and exposure factors, or expense elements, in the terms, conditions, rates, or premiums of any other type of insurance contract. [tit. 36, § 1204(7)]

**ENFORCEMENT:** The Commissioner of Insurance examines and investigates all charges of prohibited practices in the insurance industry. If alleged charges of unlawful practices are found to be true, the commissioner may issue a cease and desist order enjoining an insurer from further violating the law. (tit. 36, § 1207) If the cease and desist order is violated, the commissioner may impose fines of up to $1000 for its violation. (tit. 36, § 1211)

# PUBLIC ACCOMMODATIONS

As of November 1985, the relevant statutory provision did not prohibit discriminatory practices in the access, use and enjoyment of public facilities on the basis of sex or marital status. (tit. 25, § 1402)

# OREGON

## Home and Family

## MARRIAGE

**AGE OF CONSENT:** Persons at least 17 years of age may contract to marry. (§ 106.010)*

**CONSENT REQUIREMENT:** Persons under 18 may marry with the written consent of the parents or guardian. A license may be granted to persons under 18 years of age if either party has no parent or guardian living in the state and either party to the marriage has resided in the county 6 months prior to filing the application. (§ 106.060)

**LICENSE REQUIREMENT:** Parties wishing to marry must obtain a marriage license from the county clerk. Before the license is issued, the applicants must file with the county clerk an affidavit by some person other than the applicants stating whether the applicants are under 18 and, if so, that they have complied with the consent requirement. The license is effective 3 days after its issuance and is valid for 30 days thereafter. The waiting period may be waived with court permission. (§§ 106.050, .060, .077)

**PROHIBITED MARRIAGES:** Bigamous marriages and marriages between first cousins or any nearer relative of the whole or half blood are prohibited. (§ 106.020) Children of void marriages are legitimate. (§ 106.190)

## DISSOLUTION OF MARRIAGE

**ANNULMENT:** Factors 19, 33, 35, 36, 37, and 38, listed in Appendix A, are grounds for annulment without regard to fault. However, the court will accept evidence of misconduct where child custody is an issue or where such a showing is necessary to prove irreconcilable differences. (§§ 106.020, 107.005, .015, .036)

*Residency Requirement:* If the marriage was not solemnized in the state, at least one party must be a resident of or domiciled in the state at the time suit is commenced and continuously for a period of 6 months prior to the suit. (§ 107.075)

**LEGAL SEPARATION:** Factors 2 and 22, listed in Appendix A, are grounds for legal separation. The parties may enter into a separation agreement to live apart for at least 1 year. (§ 107.025)

*Residency Requirement:* At least one of the parties must be a resident of the state at the time the suit is commenced. [§ 107.075(3)]

### DIVORCE

*Residency Requirement:* See "Annulment."

*Grounds for Divorce:* Factors 2, 22, 33, 35, and 36, listed in Appendix A, are grounds for divorce without regard to fault. Misconduct will be considered only where child custody is at issue or where such a showing is necessary to prove irreconcilable differences. (§§ 107.025, .025)

*Conciliation Requirement:* Whenever any domestic relations suit is commenced in a circuit court exercising conciliation jurisdiction and providing conciliation ser-

*Unless specified otherwise, all reference citations are to the Oregon Revised Statutes (1953).

vices, the court may, in its discretion, or upon motion of either party, exercise conciliation jurisdiction over the controversy and over the parties and all persons having any relation to the controversy. If, within 45 days after the court commences to exercise conciliation jurisdiction, a reconciliation or a settlement of the controversy has not been effected, the domestic relations suit will proceed as if the court had not exercised conciliation jurisdiction. (§§ 107.540, .550)

*Property Distribution:* The court will make a just and equitable distribution of all property, real and personal, held by the parties. In making its decision, the court considers factors 1, 19, and 21, listed in Appendix F. There is a rebuttable presumption that both spouses have contributed equally to the acquisition of property during the marriage whether such property is jointly or separately held. The court will not consider fault in determining property distribution but will take into account costs and sale of assets as well as taxes and liens on all property. (§§ 107.036, .105)

*Child Custody:* Whenever the court grants a decree of dissolution or separation it has the power to decide the issue of child custody prior to all other issues. The court encourages, where practicable, joint parental custody, joint responsibility for the welfare of the child and extensive contact between the minor children and the parents. [§ 107.105(b)] In determining the best interests of the child, the court considers factors 7, 8, 13, 14, and 15, listed in Appendix B, as well as the parents' interests and attitude toward the child. [§§ 107.105, .137)]

*Child Support:* In its decree of child support, the court determines the amount of the support after a consideration of the economic needs of the child and the amount to be paid by the parents in proportion to their respective ability to pay, in addition to factors 3, 4, 18, 22, 23, 24, and 25, listed in Appendix D. [§ 107.105(c)] Child support will not be provided for minors who become self-supporting, are emancipated or married, or have ceased to attend school. [§ 107.105(b)] If the court so orders, a trustee will be appointed to manage and control real and personal property allocated for the children's welfare. [§ 107.105(f)]

*Spousal Support/Alimony:* The court may order support and alimony as it deems just and equitable. In making its determination it considers factors 2, 3, 4, 8, 10 to 16, 18, and 19, listed in Appendix E, and any life insurance premiums on the life of a party ordered to pay support and costs of health care to a party. [§ 107.105(d)] If the court finds the party receiving support has not made a reasonable effort during the previous 10 years to become self-supporting, support will be terminated. (§ 107.412)

*Enforcement of Support Orders:* Upon the delinquency of any support payments and upon the application of the party to whom support is owed, or of the district attorney or Support Enforcement Division of the Department of Justice, the court shall issue an order directing any employer, trustee, or conservator of the party owing a duty of support to withhold and pay over either to the clerk of the court out of which the order is issued or to the spouse or child, by deposit into a bank account, out of money due or to become due him or her at each pay period, an amount to be paid for support. As part of its order of spousal or child support, the court may order the party owing the duty of support to maintain any existing insurance policies on his or her life and in which the dependent spouse is named as beneficiary. If the party ordered to pay support or a share of a pension or retirement plan has no life insurance policy naming as beneficiary the party ordered to receive the support, or if an existing plan is inadequate to cover the obligation, the court may order the party owing the obligation to purchase a life insurance policy naming as beneficiary the party receiving the support, to pay the premiums, and to keep the policy in force until the obligation ends. (§ 107.820) The court may also require that the party owing the duty of support post a bond, security, or other guarantee to secure his or her support obligation. (§ 23-865) Contempt proceedings are also available to enforce support obligations. (§ 23-800) See also the Revised Uniform Reciprocal Enforcement of Support Act of 1968, §§ 110.005 *et seq.* In addition, delinquent spousal and child support payments may be collected through execution of pension and retirement benefits. (§§ 237.170, .201) Child support may be collected by withholding all or a portion of unemployment insurance benefits. (§ 657.780)

*Spouse's Name:* The parties may retain their own names during the marriage and may resume their prior names after a divorce. [§§ 106.220, 107.105(g)]

*Divorce by Affidavit or Summary Judgment:* A court may grant a motion for immediate divorce upon a showing of emergency and necessity to protect the rights or interest of any party. (§ 107.065)

*Displaced Homemaker Laws:* The Director of Human Resources has been authorized to establish multipurpose service programs to be staffed to the maximum extent feasible by displaced homemakers. Services to be provided by these programs include job placement and career counseling services, job training, health and financial management services, information and referral services. (§ 411.905)

# DOMESTIC VIOLENCE

**STATUTORY PROVISION:** Intentionally, knowingly, or recklessly causing bodily injury, placing another in fear of imminent serious bodily injury, or causing another to engage in involuntary sexual intercourse by force, threat, or duress is prohibited. (§ 107.705)

**WHO IS PROTECTED?** Spouses, former spouses, adults related by blood or marriage, cohabitants and former cohabitants, who cohabited with each other within 1 year preceding the filing of a petition for relief are protected. (§ 107.705)

**RELIEF AVAILABLE:** A petition may be filed with the circuit court. The court may award temporary custody or visitation rights of children; require a party to move away from the family residence; require either party from molesting, interfering with, or menacing the other or minor children; and order either party to pay attorney's fees. Moreover, the court may accept a consent agreement to cease abuse. A court order is valid for 1 year. Violation of an order is punishable as contempt. The Director of Human Resources is authorized to fund shelters and create programs for victims of domestic violence in order to prevent, identify, and treat family abuse. (§§ 107.700, .716; 184.885, .890)

**MARITAL RAPE:** A woman may charge her husband with rape. (§ 163.305)

**CIVIL LAWSUIT FOR RAPE OR ASSAULT:** Spouses may sue each other for intentional torts. [*Davis v. Bostick*, 580 P.2d 544 (Or. 1978)]

**CHILD ABUSE:** There is no specific statute prohibiting child abuse. However, statutes prohibiting abandonment and neglect (§ 163.535), assault (§§ 163.160, .165, .175, .185), and sexual abuse [§§ 163.415(b), .425(1)(a)(A)] may be relevant.

*Notification Requirement:* All health care professionals, school personnel, government employees, police officers, clergy, social workers, child care providers, attorneys, and all other persons must report all suspected cases of child abuse to the Children's Services Division or the police. An investigation must immediately be made to determine the nature and cause of the abuse. (§§ 418.740 *et seq.*)

# INHERITANCE RIGHTS

**FAILURE TO MAKE A WILL:** The surviving spouse is entitled to the entire estate if the decedent left no children or grandchildren or to one-half, if the decedent left children or grandchildren. (§ 112.025)

**FAILURE TO PROVIDE BY WILL:** A spouse may take an elective share of one-fourth or the value of the net estate. (§ 114.105)

**CHILDREN BORN OUT OF WEDLOCK:** When a purported father of a child born out of wedlock dies without having made a will, his paternity of the child must have been established or acknowledged in writing before the child may claim part of his estate as a rightful descendant. (§§ 109.060; 112.105)

**HOMESTEAD, PERSONAL, AND FAMILY ALLOWANCES:** A surviving spouse is entitled to a homestead exemption of up to $15,000, consisting of up to one city block, or up to 160 acres elsewhere. (§§ 23.240, .250) The surviving spouse and dependent children are entitled to reasonable support during the administration of the estate; temporary support may be allowed until a hearing for support is held. Support may consist of personal property, real property, and/or periodic payments of money payable for up to 2 years, except that if the estate is insolvent, payments of money must not continue for more than 1 year. (§§ 114.015, .035, .055, .065) The surviving spouse and/or dependent children may also occupy the decedent's home for 1 year after the decedent's death. (§ 114.005)

**OPTION TO DISREGARD THE WILL:** If the decedent was domiciled in Oregon, the surviving spouse may reject the will and take one-fourth of the value of net estate, which will be reduced by the value of property given by the decedent outright; the present value of legal life estates; the present value of the right of the surviving spouse to income or an annuity, or a right of withdrawal from any property transferred in trust by the will that is capable of valuation with reasonable certainty. (§ 114.105)

# REPRODUCTIVE RIGHTS

## ABORTION

*Statutory Provisions:* There is no relevant statutory provision. No hospital, physician or medical staff member is required to participate in an abortion. (§§ 435.475, .485)

*Reporting Requirements:* Hospitals and physicians must report all abortions within 5 days of their performance to the Vital Statistics Unit. (§ 435.496)

**BIRTH CONTROL:** A physician may provide birth control services to any person without regard to age. (§ 109.640) The Department of Human Resources shall offer family planning and birth control services within the limits of available funds. (§ 435.205) Any person may refuse these services without affecting his or her right to receive further public assistance. (§ 435.215) Any employee of the Adult Family Services Division may refuse to offer these services to the extent that such a duty is contrary to his or her personal or religious beliefs. (§ 435.225)

**STERILIZATION:** A person may be sterilized by appropriate means upon his or her request and upon the advice of a licensed physician. No physician may be held liable for performing a sterilization without obtaining the consent of the spouse of the person who was sterilized. The Department of Human Resources may conduct free clinics to perform sterilizations for men seeking to be sterilized. (§§ 435.205, .305)

# UNMARRIED COUPLES

**COMMON-LAW MARRIAGE:**  Common-law marriage is not valid. [§ 106.010; *Matter of Ullmarth's Estate*, 556 P.2d 990 (Or. 1976)]

**COHABITAL RELATIONSHIPS:**  There is no relevant statutory provision. In *Latham v. Latham* 547 P.2d 144 (Or. 1976), the court held that express agreements between unmarried cohabitants which contemplate all the burdens and amenities of married life are valid and enforceable. Such a living arrangement entitles either party to receive one-half of all the property accumulated during the relationship. The court will examine the intent of the parties to determine what they expressly or implicitly agreed when they commenced the relationship. [*Beal v. Beal*, 577 P.2d 507 (Or. 1978)]

## CHILDREN

*Custody:*  If the paternity of a child born out of wedlock is established, the parent with physical custody at the time of filing the petition has sole legal custody until a court specifically orders otherwise. (§ 109.175) Either parent may initiate a civil proceeding to determine custody or support of the child. Unmarried parents have the same rights and responsibilities concerning the child as married parents. (§§ 109.060, .103)

*Legitimation Proceedings:*  A child born out of wedlock is legitimated upon the marriage of the mother and the reputed father. The child may then take the father's name. A new birth certificate may also be issued. (§ 432.425)

*Paternity Proceedings:*  An action to establish paternity may be brought by the child, the mother, the alleged father, a state agency, or a guardian. (§ 109.125) The action may be brought any time. (§ 109.135) The court may order the parties to submit to blood tests if necessary for the determination of paternity. If any party refuses, the court may resolve the question of paternity against such party or enforce its order. (§ 109.252)

*Obligations of the Putative Father:*  The legal rights and obligations between a person and his or her descendants are the same for all people, whether or not the parents have been married. (§ 109.060) If paternity has been established, the court may order the father to pay an appropriate sum for past and future support of the child during the child's minority, while the child is attending school, and the reasonable and necessary expenses incurred in prenatal, birth, and postnatal care. (§ 109.155)

# Education

# STATUTORY PROVISION

Intentional or unintentional differential treatment based on sex is prohibited in any public elementary, secondary, or community college program or service, school, or interschool activity or in any higher education program or service, school, or interschool activity receiving state funds. (§ 659.150)

# AREAS COVERED

Areas covered include admission and instruction; teacher's compensation; interscholastic and intramural athletics; educational materials and curricula. [§§ 179.750, 336.082, 342.970(1), 345.240; Or. Admin. R. §§ 580-15-040, -15-085, -21-046(6), -43-116(8), 581-11-060, -11-100 to -103, -11-106, -21-046(4), -43-116(7)]

> **ENFORCEMENT:** Any person alleging discrimination in any of the covered areas of education may file a petition with the Commissioner of the Bureau of Labor and Industries, who will hold a hearing. If discrimination is determined to exist, the school's license may be revoked or suspended. (§ 345.20) If discriminatory hiring practices are found to exist, the Supervisor of Public Instruction may issue sanctions including withholding all of or part of state funding. (§ 659.155)

# Employment

# EQUAL PAY LAWS

It is unlawful for an employer to discriminate on the basis of sex in wages paid for work of comparable character, the performance of which requires comparable skills. Wage differentials are permitted if based on a seniority or merit system or factors other than sex. (§ 652.220) The statute does not apply to the state civil service system or to federal employees. (§ 652.210)

> **ENFORCEMENT:** Any employee who has been subject to discriminatory wage rates has a cause of action against an employer for 1 year preceding the claim for payment of the unpaid wages, liquidated damages, and reasonable attorney's fees. (§ 652.230)

# FAIR EMPLOYMENT LAWS

No employer, state or private, labor organization, or employment agency may refuse to hire or employ, bar or discharge from employment; discriminate in compensation, terms, conditions, or privileges of employment; exclude or expel from membership; or refuse to recruit or refer any individual for employment because of that individual's sex, marital status, or family relationship. [§§ 659.010(6), .030(1)(a); Or. Admin. R. §§ 839-06-200 to -255] Discrimination because of sex includes pregnancy, childbirth, and related medical conditions. (§ 659.029) Exceptions to the law are situations where sex is a bona fide occupational qualification, or where bona fide seniority or employee benefit plans such as retirement, pension, or insurance plans exist. (§ 659.028)

> **ENFORCEMENT:** Complaints may be filed with the Commissioner of the Bureau of Labor and Industries. The attorney general or the commissioner may also file complaints in the case of suspected violations. The commissioner will conduct an investigation and, where there is substantial evidence of violation, engage in conciliation to eliminate the unlawful practice. Hearings may be conducted if these measures fail, and orders and judgments for damages may be issued. Parties may also file civil suits where no conciliation agreement is obtained. (§§ 659.040, .050, .060, .070, .095)

# GOVERNMENT CONTRACTORS AND SUBCONTRACTORS

There are no statutory provisions.

## STATE EMPLOYEE LAWS

State employees are covered under the Fair Employment Practices Law. [§ 659.010(6)] In addition, the state has a program of affirmative action to promote employment opportunities regardless of sex or marital status. (§ 243.305) It is also the state's declared policy to attempt to achieve an equitable relationship between the comparable value of work and compensation. (§ 240.190)

**ENFORCEMENT:** See "Fair Employment Laws."

## VETERAN'S PREFERENCE

Five points are added to the passing grades of veterans in civil service examinations, ten points to the passing grades of disabled veterans. (§ 408.230)

# Community Life

## CREDIT

There is no relevant statutory provision. However, it should be noted that federal law, the Equal Credit Opportunity Act of 1977, 12 C.F.R. § 202, may apply.

## HOUSING

It is unlawful for any person to refuse to sell, lease, or rent any real property; to expel a purchaser from any real property; to discriminate in the price, terms, conditions, privileges, or furnishing of any facilities or services in connection with the sale, rental, lease, or occupancy of real property; or to attempt to discourage the sale, rental, or lease of any real property on the basis of sex or marital status. These provisions do not apply to limitations based on sex where unrelated persons of the opposite sex must use common bath or bedroom facilities. (§ 659.033)

**ENFORCEMENT:** Any person claiming to be aggrieved by a discriminatory practice may file a written, verified complaint with the Bureau of Labor and Industries within 1 year of the occurrence of the alleged discriminatory act. (§ 659.045) If within 1 year of the filing of the complaint the commissioner has been unable to resolve the issue, he or she must notify the complainant of such failure, and within 90 days of mailing such notice, the complainant may file a civil suit for injunctive and any other equitable relief the court deems fair. The court may also award a successful complainant court costs and reasonable attorney's fees. (§§ 659.095, .121)

## INSURANCE

Discrimination is prohibited between individuals of the same class and equal life expectancy or between risks of essentially the same degree of hazard in the availability of rates, benefits, or any other term of the insurance contract. [§ 746.015(1)] Insurance rates may not be excessive, inadequate or unfairly discriminatory. [§ 737.310(1)]

**ENFORCEMENT:** If the Commissioner of the Bureau of Labor and Industries believes an insurance company has willfully discriminated, notice will be given to the insurer to correct the situation within 10 days. If the insurer does not comply, a hearing will be held. If a violation is found, the court will order the discriminatory practice to cease. If the insurer continues the unlawful conduct, the commissioner may then revoke or suspend the certificate of authority to insure. [§§ 746.015(4), (5)]

# PUBLIC ACCOMMODATIONS

All persons are entitled to the full and equal advantages, facilities, and privileges of any place of public accommodation without any distinction, discrimination, or restriction on the basis of sex or marital status. It is unlawful for any person to publish or display any notice that any of the accommodations, advantages, facilities, services, or privileges of a public accommodation will be refused, withheld from, or denied to, any person on the basis of sex or marital status. These provisions do not apply to private clubs. (§§ 30.670, .675; 659.037)

> **ENFORCEMENT:** Any person discriminated against may bring a civil action to recover compensatory and punitive damages from the operator, manager, or employees of such a place. Reasonable attorney's fees are also awarded. (§ 30.680)

# PENNSYLVANIA

## Home and Family

## MARRIAGE

**AGE OF CONSENT:** A person 18 years or older may consent to marry. [tit. 48, § 1-5(c)]*

**CONSENT REQUIREMENT:** A person under 18 years of age may marry with the consent of a parent or guardian. [tit. 48, § 1-5(c)] Persons under 16 years of age may marry only upon a decision rendered by the orphans' court. [tit. 48, § 1-5(b)]

**LICENSE REQUIREMENT:** Persons wishing to marry must obtain a license issued by the orphans' court of any county. (tit. 48, § 1-2) A syphilis test is required. [tit. 48, § 1-5(a)] There is a 3-day waiting period after applying for the license except in an emergency or extraordinary circumstances. (tit. 48, § 1-4) The license is valid for 60 days. (tit. 48, § 1-11)

**PROHIBITED MARRIAGES:** Bigamous marriages are void. [*Commw. ex rel. Alexander v. Alexander*, 289 A.2d 83 (Pa. 1971)] Marriages to an ancestor, descendant, brother, sister, uncle, aunt, niece, nephew, first cousin, the spouse of one's parent or child, or the child or grandchild of one's spouse; marriage to an insane person unless a judge of the orphans' court decides the marriage is in the best interest of the parties and the public; and marriage to a person infected with communicable syphilis are all prohibited. [tit. 48, § 1-5(a), (d), (g), (i)]

## DISSOLUTION OF MARRIAGE

**ANNULMENT:** Factors 3, 19, 33, 35, 36 (60-day limit for filing action for temporary incapacity), and 38, listed in Appendix A, and a marriage entered into when either of the parties was under the influence of intoxicating drugs or liquor, are grounds for annulment. Either party may bring an action for annulment in a court of competent jurisdiction. (tit. 23, §§ 203, 204, 205)

*Residency Requirement:* At least one party to the annulment must have resided in the state for a minimum of 6 months prior to filing the complaint. (tit. 23, § 302)

**LEGAL SEPARATION:** Any adequate reason at law is sufficient to justify a husband and wife living apart. [*Commw. ex rel. Ross v. Ross* 213 A.2d 135 (Pa. 1965)] A husband and wife may also enter into a binding separation agreement if made upon reasonable terms and carried into effect by both parties in good faith. [Scott's Estate A. 214, 147 (Pa. 1892) (tit. 18, § 4322)]

*Residency Requirement:* There is no relevant statutory provision.

**DIVORCE**

*Residency Requirement:* The party filing for divorce must be a resident for at least 6 months before filing the complaint. (tit. 23, § 302)

---

*Unless otherwise specified, all references are to Purdon's Pennsylvania Statutes Annotated (1930).

***Grounds for Divorce:*** Factors 2 (with 31), 4, 6 (2 or more years), 9 (3 years), 16, 17 (with 20), and 18, listed in Appendix A, are grounds for divorce. (tit. 23, § 201)

***Conciliation Requirement:*** If the court determines there is a reasonable prospect of reconciliation, it shall require the parties to seek counseling for a period of not less than 90 days and not more than 120, unless the parties agree. The court shall require up to three counseling sessions where either party so requests. If no reconciliation is reached at the end of the period and one party states the marriage is irretrievably broken, the court may grant a divorce. [tit. 23, §§ 201(c), 202]

***Property Distribution:*** The court will divide the marital property equitably between the parties without regard to marital misconduct after considering factors 1, 2, 3, 5, 6, 7, 8 (including retirement and any other benefits), 9, 10, 11, 13, 15, 16, 19, 20, and 29, as well as any contributions toward the education, training, or increased earning power of the other party. All nonmarital property will be restored to the respective parties. [tit. 23, §§ 401(d), (e)]

***Child Custody:*** In making an order for custody to either parent, the court shall consider, among other factors, which parent is more likely to encourage, permit, and allow frequent and continuing contact, including physical access, between the noncustodial parent and the child or children. The court shall issue sole custody when it is in the best interests of the child or children. The court may also award shared custody when it is in the best interests of the child or children. It may require the parents to attend counseling sessions and may consider the recommendations of the counselors before awarding sole or shared custody. These counseling sessions may include but shall not be limited to discussions of the responsibilities and decision-making arrangements involved in both sole and shared custody and the suitability of each arrangement to each or both parents' capabilities. Additionally, the court, in its discretion, may require the parents to submit a plan for the implementation of any custody order. Upon the request of either party or the court, the local Domestic Relations Office or other party or agency approved by the court shall assist in the formulation and implementation of the plan. (tit. 23, §§ 1004 *et seq.*) The court may order a physical examination of all persons to aid in the determination of the child's best interests. (tit. 23, §§ 1001 *et seq.*; tit. 42, Rule of Civil Procedures, Rule 1915.8) See also the Uniform Child Custody Jurisdiction Act of 1968, tit. 42, § 5341.

***Child Support:*** Child support is the equal responsibility of both parents and both are obligated to contribute to the support of their children in accordance with their respective abilities to pay. [*Roberts v. Beckin* 461 A.2d 630 (Pa. 1983)]

***Spousal Support/Alimony:*** The court may allow an award of rehabilitative alimony as it deems reasonable only if it finds that the party seeking alimony lacks sufficient property to provide for his or her needs and is unable to be self-supporting through appropriate employment. In determining the alimony award, the court considers the parties' sources of income, including benefits, expectancies and inheritances, assets and liabilities, and property brought into the marriage by either party. Factors 1, 2, 3, 4, 5, 6, 7, 8, 9, 10, 11, 13, 14, 17, 19, and 22, listed in Appendix E, will also be considered. The court shall limit the duration of the order to allow the party seeking alimony to obtain appropriate employment. A change of circumstances may modify the order. Remarriage terminates the award. [tit. 23, §§ 501(a), (b), (c), (e)]

***Enforcement of Support Orders:*** When so ordered by the court, support payments are made to the domestic relations section of the court and are then distributed to the party entitled to receive such support. When a party is 30 days in arrears, the court may enter judgment; authorize the taking of goods and chattels and the collection of rents and profits of real estate; attach up to 50 percent of wages, salary, and commissions; award interest on unpaid installments; require security to ensure future payments; issue attachment proceedings; or initiate civil contempt proceedings that may result in imprisonment for up to 6 months. (tit. 23, §§ 503, 504; tit. 42, Rule of Civil Procedures, Rule 1910.21 to .23) If a party owing support is about to leave the court's jurisdiction, the court may direct that party to give security with one or more sureties to assure the performance of a support order. (tit. 42, Rule of Civil Procedures, Rule 1910.14; tit. 42, § 6707) The court may also appoint a temporary receiver to ensure that the party owing support does not dispose of his or her property. (tit. 42, Rule of Civil Procedures, Rule 1910.25) The court may impose a lien or charge upon marital property as security for the payment of alimony or other award. It may also direct the continued maintenance and beneficiary designations of existing life insurance policies. [tit. 23, §§ 401(g), (i)] Child support obligations may be paid out of unemployment compensation benefits received by the party owing support. (tit. 43, § 63.1) See also the Revised Uniform Reciprocal Enforcement of Support Act of 1968, tit. 62, §§ 2043-1 *et seq*.

*Spouse's Name:* Any woman whose marriage has been annulled or who has been divorced may retake her prior name. A written notice showing such intention must be filed in the office of the prothonotary in the court where the decree of divorce or annulment was entered. (tit. 23, § 702)

*Divorce by Affidavit or Summary Judgment:* There is no relevant statutory provision.

*Displaced Homemaker Laws:* There is no relevant statutory provision.

# DOMESTIC VIOLENCE

**STATUTORY PROVISION:** The Protection from Abuse Act of 1976 prohibits abuse between family and household members who reside together and who intentionally, knowingly, or recklessly injure each other, with or without a deadly weapon, or place another in fear of imminent serious bodily injury, or sexually abuse minors. (tit. 35, §§ 10181 *et seq*.) Police officers have the same right of arrest without a warrant in cases of criminal assault, involuntary manslaughter, and reckless endangerment of another person where the victim is the defendant's spouse or present or former cohabitant. [tit. 18, § 2711(a)] Police officers must notify victims of domestic violence of the availability of a shelter and of their remedies under the Protection from Abuse Act. [tit. 18, § 2711(d)]

**WHO IS PROTECTED?** The act protects spouses, cohabitants, parents, children, and other persons related by blood or marriage. (tit. 35, § 10182)

**RELIEF AVAILABLE:** Victims of domestic abuse may obtain restraining orders granting the exclusive possession of the residence or household to one party, provision of suitable alternative housing (if both parties agree), temporary custody of and visitation rights to minor children, or support payments for a spouse and/or minor children. The duration of a protective order is 1 year. Support orders are valid for 2 weeks. Emergency relief may be granted for a maximum of 72 hours. Any person may seek relief for himself or herself or on behalf of minors by filing a petition alleging abuse with the court. Violation of an order is punishable as indirect criminal contempt. (tit.

35, §§ 10184 to 10186, 10188) The Department of Public Welfare has been authorized to fund domestic violence centers and rape crisis centers to assist victims of domestic abuse and sexual assault. (tit. 62, §§ 1201 *et seq*.)

**MARITAL RAPE:** A woman may sue her husband for rape only if they are living apart or they have entered into a written separation agreement. A woman cohabiting with a man may not charge him with rape. However, a woman may charge her husband with spousal sexual assault. The occurrence of the assault must be reported within 90 days. (tit. 18, §§ 3103, 3128)

**CIVIL LAWSUIT FOR RAPE OR ASSAULT:** Spouses may not sue each other for torts while they are married to each other. [*Policino v. Ehrlich*, 345 A.2d 224 (Pa. 1975)]

**CHILD ABUSE:** Endangering the welfare of a child by violating a duty of care, protection, and support is a crime. (tit. 18, § 4304) Serious mental or physical injury not explained by available medical history, or sexual abuse, or physical neglect may also constitute abuse. (tit. 11, § 2203)

> *Notification Requirement:* All health care professionals, hospital personnel, teachers, school administrators, social workers, child care personnel, mental health professionals, police officers, and all other persons who have reason to suspect child abuse must report it to the Child Protective Service of the county public welfare agency. A doctor or hospital administrator may take a child into custody without a court order for 24 hours if protective custody is immediately necessary. (tit. 11, §§ 2203, 2204) See also the Child Protective Services Act No. 1985-33 (January 1, 1986), Pa. Legis. Serv., Session of 1985, Acts 1985-26 to 1985-59, No. 3, 1985.

# INHERITANCE RIGHTS

**FAILURE TO MAKE A WILL:** The surviving spouse is entitled to the entire estate if the decedent left no other heirs; to $30,000 and one-half the balance, if the decedent left parents or children or grandchildren who are also the spouse's children or grandchildren; to one-half the estate, if the decedent left one or more children or grandchildren who are not also the spouse's children or grandchildren. (tit. 20, § 2102)

**FAILURE TO PROVIDE BY WILL:** A surviving spouse has a right to an elective share of one-third of all of the decedent's property. Such property includes property passing from the decedent by will or intestacy; income from property conveyed by the decedent during the marriage to the extent that the decedent at the time of death had the use of the property or an interest in or power to withdraw the income from such property; property conveyed by the decedent during his lifetime to the extent that the decedent at the time of his death had a power to revoke the conveyance or to consume, invade, or dispose of the principal for his own benefit; property conveyed by the decedent during the marriage to himself and another or others with right of survivorship to the extent of any interest in the property that the decedent had the power at the time of his death unilaterally to convey absolutely or in fee; survivorship rights conveyed to a beneficiary of an annuity contract; and property conveyed by the decedent during the marriage and within 1 year of his death to the extent that the aggregate amount so conveyed to each donee exceeds $3000, valued at the time of conveyance. (tit. 20, § 2203)

**CHILDREN BORN OUT OF WEDLOCK:** A child born out of wedlock may inherit through the mother and her kin and from the father only if paternity is established. However, if the parents of the child marry, the child is considered legitimate and may inherit from both. (tit. 20, § 2514) A child born out of wedlock may share in the inheritance unless specifically indicated to the contrary. [*Estates of Dulles* 431 A.2d 208 (Pa. 1981)]

**HOMESTEAD, PERSONAL, AND FAMILY ALLOWANCES:** The surviving spouse of a decedent living in Pennsylvania may retain or claim real and/or personal property valued up to $2000. The surviving spouse may also receive from the decedent's employer wages or employee benefits due the deceased up to $3500. (tit. 20, §§ 3101, 3121)

**OPTION TO DISREGARD THE WILL:** See "Failure to Provide by Will."

# REPRODUCTIVE RIGHTS

## ABORTION

*Statutory Provisions:* The Abortion Control Act of 1974 recognizes a woman's fundamental right of privacy, and balances legitimate state interest and interests of pregnant women. An abortion may only be performed by a physician. The act also protects the rights of conscience of persons who choose not to obtain, receive, subsidize, accept, or provide abortions. The intentional, knowing, or reckless performance or inducement of an abortion of a viable fetus is a third degree felony. (tit. 18, §§ 3201, 3202) A number of provisions of the act, including ones requiring two physicians to attend the abortion and requiring a physician to choose the method of abortion most likely to save the fetus's life unless the risk to the mother is significantly greater [tit. 18, §§ 3210(b), (c)], were declared unconstitutional in *American College of Obstetricians and Gynecologists (ACOG) v. Thornburgh*, 737 F.2d 283 (3rd Cir. 1985). This case is currently on appeal to the Supreme Court.

*Informed Consent:* A woman over the age of 18 may give her informed consent to an abortion. Currently, the law states that the following information must be provided to the woman 24 hours before the abortion: name of physician, possibility of unforeseeable physical and psychological effects, risks and dangers involved, the probable gestational age of the fetus, and medical risks involved. The requirements that the counseling be provided 24 hours in advance and that the woman be counseled about risks were held unconstitutional in *ACOG v. Thornburgh*. The woman must also be informed of available prenatal, neonatal, and child care assistance. [tit. 18, §§ 3205(a)(1), (2)]

*Parental Consent:* A woman under the age of 18 may give her consent if she has graduated from high school or has been married. Otherwise a pregnant woman who is under 18 or incompetent requires the consent of one of her parents or a guardian. The parents or guardian will be furnished with the information stated in "Informed Consent." If the parents or guardian refuse consent, the court of common pleas where the pregnant woman resides may give consent. (tit. 18, §§ 3205, 3206; tit. 35, §§ 10101 to 10105)

*Spousal Consent:* There is no relevant statutory provision.

*Reporting Requirements:* Currently, the law states that a detailed report of each abortion, excluding the patient's name, must be made to the Department of Health. The report is completed by the hospital or licensed facility. Tissue is to be examined to determine pregnancy, pregnancy termination, and possible viability of the fetus.

Annual statistics must be prepared. Each hospital or facility must report the number of abortions and the trimesters in which they are performed. Reports of maternal deaths and complications must also be submitted. (tit. 18, § 3214) These requirements were held unconstitutional in *ACOG v. Thornburgh*.

**BIRTH CONTROL:**  There is no relevant statutory provision.

**STERILIZATION:**  Pennsylvania does not require spousal consent for voluntary sterilization. [Op. Atty. Gen. No. 75-40 (Nov. 5, 1975)] A physician or staff member is not liable for refusing to perform a sterilization. Furthermore, under the Conscience Act of 1973, public hospitals must provide staff and facilities for sterilizations and abortions. (tit. 43, § 955.2)

# UNMARRIED COUPLES

**COMMON-LAW MARRIAGE:**  Common-law marriage is valid in Pennsylvania. The elements of a common-law marriage are a reputation of husband and wife, constant cohabitation, and an express agreement of intent to marry in the present tense. Additionally, parties to a common-law marriage, by virtue of their status as spouses, may make claims to property even without an agreement. (tit. 48, § 1-23) See also *Knauer v. Knauer* 470 A.2d 553 (Pa. Super. 1983).

**COHABITAL RELATIONSHIPS:**  Persons cohabitating may not claim alimony or property. Cohabitation may be used as proof of common-law marriage if no other proof is available. If there is no contract for union to constitute a common-law marriage, persons cohabitating are free to contract in other areas. [tit. 23, § 507; *In re Estate of Rees*, 489 A.2d 327 (Pa. 1984)]

**CHILDREN**

*Custody:*  There is no relevant statutory provision. However, as with children born in lawful wedlock, the best interests of the child born out of wedlock govern the custody award. [*Commw. v. Rozanski*, 213 A.2d 155 (1976)]

*Legitimation Proceedings:*  The marriage of the natural parents legitimates a child born out of wedlock. (tit. 20, § 2107)

*Paternity Proceedings:*  A civil action to establish paternity may be brought at any time until the child reaches his or her eighteenth birthday. (tit. 23, § 4343) Paternity can also be established if the father acknowledges his paternity in writing. (tit. 23, § 8302) Where paternity is in dispute, a court may, without a jury, decide the matter unless a jury is demanded by either party. (tit. 42, § 6704; tit. 42, Rule of Civil Procedures, Rule 1910.15)

*Obligations of the Putative Father:*  A father of a child born out of wedlock has the same rights and duties as he would toward a child born in lawful wedlock. (tit. 23, § 8302)

# Education

# STATUTORY PROVISION

The Pennsylvania Constitution contains an equal rights provision which has been interpreted to prohibit sex discrimination in education. (Pa. Const. art 1, § 28) The state also prohibits discrimination in employment, compensation, tenure, terms, conditions, or privileges of employment on the basis of sex. [tit. 22, Pa. Admin. Code § 32.3(1)] Moreover, it is illegal to prohibit competition between males and females in sports, even if separate teams exist. [*Packel v. Pennsylvania Interscholastic Athletic Association*, 334. A.2d 839 (Pa. Commw. 1975)]

## AREAS COVERED

Sex discrimination is prohibited in admission to or facilities of state-aided, -owned, or -licensed postsecondary schools or secretarial, business, trade, or vocational schools of secondary or postsecondary level. (tit. 24, §§ 5002 *et seq.*) Discrimination on the basis of sex is prohibited in the state educational system and in all educational institutions under the supervision of the commonwealth. (tit. 43, §§ 954 *et seq.*) All community colleges and state-related or state-aided higher-education institutions are required to provide written assurances to the state Board of Education that there is no sex discrimination in admissions, programs, activities, and facilities. [tit. 22, Pa. Admin. Code § 32.3(2)]

> **ENFORCEMENT:** Any aggrieved person, or his or her representative, who alleges discrimination may file a verified complaint with the Human Relations Commission within 6 months after the unfair practice has occurred. (tit. 24, § 5007)

# Employment

## EQUAL PAY LAWS

It is unlawful for any employer to discriminate on the basis of sex in wages paid to employees in the same establishment who perform work requiring equal skill, effort, and responsibility under similar working conditions. Wage differentials are not prohibited, however, if they are based on a seniority system or merit system; the quantity or quality of production; or any factor other than sex. (tit. 43, § 336.3)

> **ENFORCEMENT:** Any employee who has been discriminated against on the basis of sex in wages paid may bring an action within 2 years to recover such wages, in addition to liquidated damages, in any court of competent jurisdiction. Alternatively, an employee may ask the Secretary of Labor and Industry to bring action to collect the claim. (tit. 43, § 336.6)

## FAIR EMPLOYMENT LAWS

The law applies to the commonwealth of Pennsylvania, its political and civil subdivisions, employers of four or more persons, labor organizations, and employment agencies. (tit. 43, §§ 954, 955) The law prohibits the limiting, segregating, or classifying persons on the basis of sex; the refusal by an employment agency to recruit, refer, or place an individual on account of sex; the expulsion or exclusion of an individual from a labor organization on account of sex; or the publication of any notice, advertisement, or sign which indicates preference for a particular sex. (tit. 43, § 955) Religious, fraternal, and charitable organizations employing four or more persons are covered by the law. [tit. 43, § 954(b)]

> **ENFORCEMENT:** A person claiming to be aggrieved by a discriminatory practice may file a complaint with the Human Relations Commission within 90 days of the occurrence of the alleged discriminatory practice. If the charges of discrimination are

proven, the commission may issue a cease and desist order and may direct the respondent to take such affirmative action as in the commission's judgment will effectuate the purpose of the law, including a requirement for report of the manner of compliance chosen by the respondent. (tit. 43, § 959) Alternatively, a complainant may bring a civil action in the court of common pleas, if the commission dismisses the complaint or has failed to conciliate the dispute within 1 year after the complaint was filed with the commission. The court shall enjoin the respondent from engaging in the complained-of discriminatory practice and order affirmative action or any other appropriate legal or equitable relief. (tit. 43, § 962)

## GOVERNMENT CONTRACTORS AND SUBCONTRACTORS

Administrative guidelines for contract compliance require contractors to agree not to discriminate in employment on the basis of sex. (tit. 16, Pa. Admin. Code § 49.101) Also a contractor or subcontractor who employs four or more employees is subject to the Fair Employment Practices Law. (tit. 43, § 954) If federal funds are involved, federal law, Exec. Order No. 11246, 3 C.F.R. 339 (1965), *reprinted in* 42 U.S.C. § 2000e, app. at 1232, 41 C.F.R. § 60-1.2, may apply.

**ENFORCEMENT:** See "Fair Employment Laws."

## STATE EMPLOYEE LAWS

State employees are covered under the Fair Employment Practices Law. [tit. 43, § 954(b)] In addition, Exec. Orders No. 1979-15 and 1975-5 have ordered state affirmative action plans to include women and racial and ethnic minorities and prohibit discrimination in state employment based on sexual orientation.

## VETERAN'S PREFERENCE

Ten points are added to veterans' passing grades on competitive examinations for initial appointments. [tit. 51, § 7103(a)] Spouses of deceased or disabled veterans are entitled to the same bonus. (tit. 51, § 7108)

# Community Life

## CREDIT

There is no relevant statutory provision. However, it should be noted that federal law, the Equal Credit Opportunity Act of 1977, 12 C.F.R. § 202, may apply.

## HOUSING

It is unlawful for any person to refuse to sell, lease, finance, or otherwise deny or withhold housing or to discriminate in the terms, conditions, or furnishing of facilities, services, or privileges in connection with the selling, leasing, ownership, occupancy, or use of any housing on the basis of sex. It is unlawful for any person to refuse to lend money or otherwise withhold financing or to discriminate in the terms or conditions of any loan for the acquisition, construction, rehabilitation, repair, or maintenance of any housing on the basis of sex. These provisions do not apply to the rental of housing in a two-family dwelling in which the owner or lessee resides or to the rental of rooms in a landlord-occupied rooming house with a common entrance. [tit. 43, §§ 954(j), (k), 955(h), (j)]

**ENFORCEMENT:** See "Employment: Fair Employment Laws."

# INSURANCE

Discrimination is prohibited between individuals of the same class and essentially the same hazard with regard to underwriting standards and practices or eligibility requirement on the basis of sex, marital status, family size or occupation, or place of residence. Discrimination is also prohibited between individuals of the same class and equal expectation of life in the rates charged for life insurance or annuity contracts or between individuals of the same class and essentially the same hazard in the amount of premium, policy, fees, or rates charged for any contract of insurance, in the benefits payable under these contracts, or in any term or condition of these contracts. [tit. 40, § 1171.5(7)] Sex-based auto insurance rates are discriminatory and prohibited. [*Hartford Accident & Indemnity Co. v. Insurance Commissioner*, 505 Pa. 571, 482 A.2d 542 (1984)]

**ENFORCEMENT:** The Commissioner of Insurance examines and investigates the affairs of every person engaged in the business of insurance in the state. Upon receiving a complaint of a discriminatory practice, the commission will hold a hearing, and, if the charges are proven to be true, the commission may issue an order requiring the insurer to cease and desist from engaging in such practice or may suspend or revoke the person's license. Failure to comply with the commission's order may result in an action for injunction by the commission for civil penalties. (tit. 40, §§ 1171.7 *et seq.*)

# PUBLIC ACCOMMODATIONS

It is unlawful for any person to refuse, withhold from, or deny, either directly or indirectly, any of the accommodations, advantages, facilities, or privileges of a place of public accommodation, resort, or amusement or to publish or post a written notice that the patronage of a person is unwelcome or objectionable on the basis of sex. [tit. 43, § 955(i)]

**ENFORCEMENT:** See "Housing."

# RHODE ISLAND

## Home and Family

## MARRIAGE

**AGE OF CONSENT:** A person 18 years of age or older may consent to marry. (§ 15-2-11)*

**CONSENT REQUIREMENT:** If a female is under 16 years old and a male is under 18 years old, they may marry only with the consent of the Director of Public Welfare. Females between the ages of 16 and 18 may marry only with parental consent. (§ 15-2-11)

**LICENSE REQUIREMENT:** A marriage license must be obtained from the clerk of the town or city in which the female resides; the town or city in which the male resides, if the female is a nonresident of this state; or the city or town in which the proposed marriage is to be performed, if both parties are nonresidents of this state. Persons who have previously been married are required to present a copy of their divorce decree to the town clerk. (§ 15-2-1) Before a license is issued, each applicant must file a certificate from a licensed physician. (§ 15-2-3) The license is valid for 90 days. (§ 15-2-8)

**PROHIBITED MARRIAGES:** Marriage is prohibited if either party has a living spouse. Any marriage where either spouse is an idiot or a lunatic at the time of such marriage is void. Marriages between parents and children, including grandparents and grandchildren of every degree; between sisters and brothers of the half or the whole blood; between uncles and nieces or aunts and nephews; between first cousins; and between stepparents or parents and their children's spouses, including stepgrandparents or grandparents and their grandchildren's spouses, are prohibited and void. Marriages are also void if either spouse is civilly dead or if, from his or her absence or other circumstances, a spouse may be presumed to be actually dead. (§§ 15-1-1, -1-2, -1-5, 15-5-1) Children born of void marriages are legitimate. (§ 15-1-6)

## DISSOLUTION OF MARRIAGE

**ANNULMENT:** Factor 19 is a ground for annulment. See *Lynch v. Lynch*, 83 A. 83 (R.I. 1912).

*Residency Requirement:* There is no relevant statutory provision.

**LEGAL SEPARATION:** Divorce from bed and board or a legal separation will be granted based on factors 3, 4, 5 (and presumed dead), 8, 9, 14, 16 (for 5 years or less, within court's discretion), 17, 19, 26, 34, 38, and 48, listed in Appendix A. Note that factor 48 only requires the husband to provide support. (§§ 15-5-1, -2, -5)

*Residency Requirement:* The party seeking the legal separation must have resided in the state for such a period of time as the court deems proper. (§ 15-5-9)

### DIVORCE

*Residency Requirement:* Plaintiff and defendant both must have been a resident of Rhode Island for 1 year prior to the filing of the complaint. (§ 15-5-12)

*Unless otherwise specified, all reference citations are to the General Laws of Rhode Island (1956).

*Grounds for Divorce:* See "Legal Separation."

*Conciliation Requirement:* There is no relevant statutory provision.

*Property Distribution:* The court may assign to either spouse a portion of the estate of the other. Factors 1, 5, and 29, listed in Appendix F, are used to determine the nature and value of the property to be so assigned. The court may not assign property or any part of the property to one party if the other party had owned it prior to the marriage or if it had been transferred to one party by inheritance before, during, or after the term of the marriage. (§ 15-5-16.1)

*Child Custody:* The court, in awarding child custody, provides a reasonable right of visitation to the noncustodial parent, except where doing so would be harmful to the child. (§ 15-5-16) Although there is no statutory provision for determining custody, the courts have awarded custody of minor children to that parent who, according to the court, will most suitably serve the best interests of the children. See *Petition of Loudin*, 219 A.2d 915 (1966). But generally, the mother, if fit, should have custody of young children, especially girls. See *Loebenberg v. Loebenberg*, 127 A.2d 500. (1956)

*Child Support:* The court may order either or both parents to pay an amount reasonable or necessary for the support of the children after considering factors 1 to 5, listed in Appendix D. (§ 15-5-16.2)

*Spousal Support/Alimony:* Alimony may be awarded to either party during the marriage or after a divorce or legal separation. In determining the amount of alimony to be paid, the court considers factors 4, 8, 9, 13, 14, 15, and 16, listed in Appendix E. (§ 15-5-16)

*Enforcement of Support Orders:* The court may punish a party in violation of a support order by attaching that party's wages or sequestrating his or her tangible property. The assignment of wages will take effect when the violating party has failed to make a support payment in full within 14 days of the due date or, if the court finds that the violating party has a history of nonsupport. If the court decides this party is likely to default on the timely support orders, with respect to child support only, the court shall order the assignment to take effect immediately. (§§ 15-5-16.2, -24) The court may also order that arrearages be withheld from the present and future income or earnings of the party owing a duty of support to either a spouse or child. (§ 15-5-25)

*Spouse's Name:* Any divorced woman may request a name change even if there are children born of the prior marriage. (§ 15-5-7)

*Divorce by Affidavit or Summary Judgment:* There is no relevant statutory provision.

*Displaced Homemaker Laws:* The statute establishes, within the Department of Community Affairs, a displaced homemaker center to provide counseling, training, and referral services to help homemakers become gainfully employed and financially independent. (§§ 42-44-46 *et seq.*)

# DOMESTIC VIOLENCE

**STATUTORY PROVISION:** Domestic assault, whether committed upon a spouse or cohabitant, is prohibited. (§ 11-5-9)

**WHO IS PROTECTED?** Spouses and cohabitants are protected. (§ 11-5-9)

**RELIEF AVAILABLE:** A victim of domestic assault may call the police to arrest the attacker without a warrant, provided the assault occurred within 24 hours. The victim also has the right to file a criminal complaint alleging domestic assault or threats of domestic assault; demand that the officer drive the victim to the nearest hospital if medical treatment is needed; and demand that the officer remain at the scene for his or her protection until the victim and any children can leave or are safe. Spouses' rights include petitioning for orders restraining the attacker from abusing them or minor children; awarding the exclusive use of the domicile; awarding custody of minor children; directing the attacker to pay alimony and/or child support if the attacker has a legal obligation to give support; and directing the attacker to pay attorney's fees. In addition, the victim has the right, whether or not he or she is married to the attacker, to request that the court issue a peace bond prohibiting the attacker from further abusing the victim. (§ 11-5-9)

**MARITAL RAPE:** A person may charge a spouse with rape only if the assailant has been living apart from him or her pursuant to a court order and a complaint for divorce has been filed, a restraining order against the attacker has been filed, the parties have been actually living apart, a decision pending entry of the final judgment of divorce has been entered. (§ 11-37-2.1)

**CIVIL LAWSUIT FOR RAPE OR ASSAULT:** There is no case directly on point.

**CHILD ABUSE:** Abuse of a child by anyone who inflicts physical injuries on the child, including injuries which don't cause permanent disfigurement, is a crime. Sexual abuse by a person over the age of 18 or of a minor under 13 or over 13 but under 16 is a crime. Gross and habitual cruelty to a child by a parent or legal guardian is a crime. (§§ 11-9-5, -5.3, 11-37-4, -6)

> *Notification Requirement:* Any person who has reasonable cause to suspect that a child has been abused must make a report to the Department for Children and their Families within 24 hours. The department must immediately investigate all reports. Doctors must telephone and write to the department or a law enforcement agency immediately if they suspect a patient is an abused or neglected child. The department must forward reports of child abuse to the child advocate. (§§ 40-11-3, -6, -6.1, -7)

# INHERITANCE RIGHTS

**FAILURE TO MAKE A WILL:** The surviving spouse is entitled to all the decedent's real property if the decedent left no children, parents, siblings, or other heirs; to a life interest in all real estate if the decedent left no children or grandchildren. In addition, if the decedent left no children or grandchildren the court may grant the spouse absolute ownership of real property worth up to $25,000 if not required to pay the decedent's debts. The surviving spouse is entitled to receive personal property valued at $50,000 (after the payments of debts) and one-half of the balance of the estate if decedent left no children or grandchildren. If the decedent died leaving children or grandchildren, the spouse receives one-half of the personal estate. (§§ 33-1-1, -5, -6, -10)

**FAILURE TO PROVIDE BY WILL:** Whenever any person dies and leaves a spouse surviving, that spouse is entitled to a life estate in all real property owned by decedent at death, subject to any encumbrances existing at such death. (§ 33-25-2)

**CHILDREN BORN OUT OF WEDLOCK:** A child born out of wedlock may inherit, as if born in lawful wedlock, on the part of its mother. Such a child may inherit from its father if the parents lawfully marry each other and acknowledge the child as their own. (§ 33-1-8)

**HOMESTEAD, PERSONAL, AND FAMILY ALLOWANCES:** There are no provisions for a homestead exemption. However, the widow and minor children are entitled to keep their clothing. The widow may be given such household goods, supplies, and other personal property of the decedent, as the court deems necessary. (§ 33-10-1)

**OPTION TO DISREGARD THE WILL:** The surviving spouse may reject the provisions of the will bequeathing real property and take a life interest in all real property owned by the decedent at death within 6 months after the probate of the will. (§ 33-25-4)

# REPRODUCTIVE RIGHTS

## ABORTION

*Statutory Provisions:* The abortion statutes do not prescribe when or where abortions can be performed. However, there is a presumption that only physicians and surgeons may perform abortions since they are required to obtain the required consent and make the required disclosures prior to performing abortions (§§ 23-4.7-3, -6) and the law imposes certain liabilities for their willful violation of these statutes. (§ 23-4.7-7)

*Informed Consent:* A woman's written consent is required before an abortion is performed. The consent form must be provided by the doctor or facility and must contain the woman's agreement that the doctor is her agent and an acknowledgment that she has been told that she is pregnant and she has been given an explanation of the medical nature of an abortion, including the age of the fetus at the time of the expected abortion, the present gestational age of the fetus, the medical and/or surgical procedures involved, and all known material risks. (§§ 23-4.7-2, -3, -5)

*Parental Consent:* If the pregnant woman is less than 18 years old and is not married, an abortion will not be performed until she and one of her parents consent; until a judge determines that she is mature and capable of giving informed consent; or until the judge decides that the abortion would be in her best interests. (§ 23-4.7-6)

*Spousal Consent:* There is no relevant statutory provision. However the woman's physician must notify her husband of the proposed abortion, if reasonably possible, before the abortion is performed. (§ 23-4.8-2)

*Health Insurance Regulations:* No health insurance contract, plan, or policies delivered or issued for delivery in the state shall provide coverage for induced abortions (except where the life of the mother would be endangered if the fetus were carried to term or where the pregnancy resulted from rape or incest) except by an optional rider for which there must be paid an additional premium. (§ 27-18-28) This prohibition applies to insurance coverage provided to employees of the state, its cities, and its towns, but it does not pertain to insurance coverage for complications arising as the result of an abortion. (§ 3612-2.1)

**BIRTH CONTROL:** There is no relevant statutory provision.

**STERILIZATION:** It is a felony to perform or aid and abet in the performance of a sterilization procedure on any person under the age of 18, unless the sterilization is unavoidable or incidental to some other medical treatment or procedure required to preserve the life or health of the person. (§ 11-9-17)

# UNMARRIED COUPLES

**COMMON-LAW MARRIAGE:** Common-law marriages are valid. [*Souza v. O'Hara*, 395 A.2d 1060 (1978)]

**COHABITAL RELATIONSHIPS:** There is no relevant statutory provision.

## CHILDREN

*Custody:* There is no relevant statutory provision.

*Legitimation Proceedings:* Any child whose parents marry and acknowledge him or her as their child becomes legitimate. (§ 33-1-8)

*Paternity Proceedings:* The mother, child, or the public authority chargeable by law with the support of the child may bring suit to determine paternity. A paternity action may not be brought later than 4 years from the birth of a child who has no presumed father. An action brought by or on behalf of a child whose paternity has not been determined, but may have been presumed, is not barred until 4 years after the child's majority. The court may order blood tests. (§§ 15-8-2, -11)

*Obligations of the Putative Father:* The father of a child born out of wedlock is liable to the same extent as the father of a child born in lawful wedlock, whether or not the child is born alive, for the reasonable expenses of the mother's pregnancy and confinement; the child's education, necessary support; the maintenance, medical, and funeral expenses of the child; and reasonable counsel fees for the prosecution of the paternity proceedings. (§ 15-8-1) These liabilities may be enforced by the mother, the child, or the public authority which has furnished the reasonable expenses of pregnancy, confinement, education, necessary support or funeral expenses. (§§ 15-8-2, -9, -18)

# Education

## STATUTORY PROVISION

There is no relevant statutory provision. However, it should be noted that if federal funds are involved, federal law, Title IX of the Education Amendments of 1972, Pub. L. No. 92-318, 20 U.S.C. §§ 1681–1686, may apply.

# Employment

## EQUAL PAY LAWS

It is unlawful for an employer to discriminate on the basis of sex in wages paid to employees performing work requiring comparable skill, effort, and responsibility. However, wage differentials are permitted if such differentials are based on seniority, experience, training, skill, or ability; difference in duties performed, either regularly or occasionally; difference in the time of day worked; difference in availability for other operations; or any other reasonable differentiation except difference in sex. This law does not apply to domestic help and employees of social clubs or fraternal, charitable, educational, religious, scientific, or literary associations. (§§ 28-6-17, -18)

**ENFORCEMENT:** A party who has been discriminated against on the basis of sex in the payment of wages may bring a civil action for the unpaid wages and an additional equal amount of liquidated damages. The action must be brought within 1 year after the alleged discriminatory practice occurred. (§§ 28-5-18, -6-20, -21)

# FAIR EMPLOYMENT LAWS

The law applies to the state and all its political subdivisions, employers of four or more employees, labor organizations, and employment agencies. It makes it unlawful for an employer to refuse to hire or discriminate in compensation, terms, tenure, conditions, or privileges of employment on the basis of sex; for a labor organization to exclude or expel its members because of sex; or for an employment agency to refuse to recruit, place, or refer an individual for employment because of the individual's sex. This law does not cover domestic servants or an individual employed by his or her parent, child, or spouse. In addition, religious groups may hire persons of a particular religion. [§§ 28-5-5, -6(B), -7]

**ENFORCEMENT:** The Rhode Island Commission for Human Rights is authorized to eliminate any unlawful employment practices through informal methods of persuasion or, it may order the employer complained against to cease and desist from such unlawful employment practices. Any complaint must be issued within 1 year after the alleged unfair employment practices were committed. In addition, an aggrieved person may ask the commission for a right to sue in state court after 120 days but before 2 years have elapsed from the date of filing a charge with the commission, if the commission has been unable to secure a settlement or conciliation agreement and has not commenced a hearing on the complaint. (§§ 28-5-18, -24, -24.1)

# GOVERNMENT CONTRACTORS AND SUBCONTRACTORS

There is no relevant statutory provision. However, it should be noted that if federal funds are involved, federal law, Exec. Order No. 11246, 3 C.F.R. 339 (1965), *reprinted in* 42 U.S.C. § 2000e app. at 1232, 41 C.F.R. § 60-1.2, may apply.

# STATE EMPLOYEE LAWS

See "Fair Employment Laws."

# VETERAN'S PREFERENCE

Veterans are given a preference over nonveterans in public employment. (§ 30-21-8) The statute expressly applies to males. (§ 30-21-11)

# Community Life

## CREDIT

It is unlawful for any financial institution or any other credit-granting commercial institution to discriminate in the granting or extension of any form of loan or credit, or in the privilege or capacity to obtain any form of loan or credit, on the basis of sex or marital status. (§ 34-37-4.1)

**ENFORCEMENT:** The Rhode Island Commission for Human Rights may conduct an investigation, on the complaint of a person or on its own initiative, to determine whether a prohibited discriminatory practice has occurred. If it is probable that discriminatory practices have occurred, then the commission may initiate proceedings appropriate to resolve the issue. In addition, an aggrieved party may bring a civil action within 1 year after the issuance of an order by the commissioner and, if the alleged discriminatory practices are proved to be true, may be awarded actual and punitive damages, the costs of the action, and reasonable attorney's fees. (§ 34-37-5)

## HOUSING

It is unlawful for any person having the right to sell, rent, lease, or manage a housing accommodation to refuse to sell, rent, lease, let, or deny any housing accommodation on the basis of sex or marital status, or to advertise of such housing accommodation which indicates any discrimination based on sex or marital status. It is unlawful for any person to whom application is made for a loan in connection with a housing accommodation to discriminate in the terms, conditions, or privileges relating to the obtaining or use of any financial assistance on the basis of sex and marital status. (§ 34-37-4)

**ENFORCEMENT:** See "Credit."

## INSURANCE

Unfair discrimination between individuals of the same class and equal expectation of life in the rates charged for life insurance or annuity contracts or between individuals of the same class and essentially the same hazard in the amount of premium, policy fees, rates charged for accident or health insurance, or benefits payable under these contracts is prohibited. [§ 27-29-4(7)]

**ENFORCEMENT:** Upon receipt of a complaint alleging an unfair discriminatory practice, the Commissioner of Insurance has the authority to investigate the charges alleged in the complaint through a hearing which must take place within 10 days after the party is notified. If the complaint is proved true, the commissioner may order the insurer complained against to cease and desist from engaging in the discriminatory practice. (§§ 27-29-5, -6)

## PUBLIC ACCOMMODATIONS

It is unlawful for any owner, lessee, proprietor, manager, superintendent, agent, or employee of any place of public accommodation, resort, or amusement, directly or indirectly, to refuse, withhold from, or deny any person any of the accommodations, advantages, facilities, or privileges of a public accommodation, or to publish or post a written notice that the patronage of a person is unwelcome or objectionable on the basis of sex. These provisions do not apply to separate restrooms, bath houses, and dressing rooms for males and females. (§§ 11-24-2, -3.1)

**ENFORCEMENT:** The Rhode Island Commission for Human Rights may investigate a complaint if it determines that it is probable that discriminatory practices have occurred. It may eliminate such practices by informal methods of conferences or by an order to cease and desist from such practices. (§§ 11-24-4, 28-5-13, -16, -36)

# SOUTH CAROLINA

## Home and Family

## MARRIAGE

**AGE OF CONSENT:** A person over the age of 18 may consent to marry. (§ 20-1-250)* Proof of age is required of all applicants over 18 but under 25. (§ 20-1-270)

**CONSENT REQUIREMENT:** Parental or guardian consent is required when the woman is between the ages of 14 and 18 and the man is between the ages of 16 and 18. (§ 20-1-250) Consent of one of the female's parents or of the Superintendent of the Department of Social Services is required for the marriage of a female and male under 18, who could otherwise enter into a marital contract, when the female is pregnant or has given birth to a child and the male is the putative father. (§ 20-1-300)

**LICENSE REQUIREMENT:** A license is required for all persons wishing to marry. A written application must be filed with the probate judge (in Darlington and Georgetown counties, with the clerk of the court) at least 24 hours before the marriage license is issued. (§§ 20-1-210, -220)

**PROHIBITED MARRIAGES:** No person may marry his or her parent, grandparent, child, grandchild, sibling, grandparent's spouse, child's spouse, grandchild's spouse, spouse's parent, spouse's grandparent, stepchild, stepgrandchild, sibling's child, or parent's sibling. Bigamous marriages are void, except when a spouse who is presumed to be dead for 7 years is found to be living. (§§ 20-1-10; -80) Children born of void marriages are legitimate. (§ 20-1-90)

## DISSOLUTION OF MARRIAGE

**ANNULMENT:** Factors 14, 19, 36, and 38, listed in Appendix A, are grounds for annulment. (§§ 20-1-10, -80, -530)

*Residency Requirement:* In an action for annulment, the plaintiff may serve the complaint on the judge when the defendant is a nonresident or has left the state, or may serve the complaint by publication if the marriage was contracted outside the state when the plaintiff was a resident at the time of marriage or has been a resident for at least 1 year prior to the action for annulment. (§ 20-1-550)

**LEGAL SEPARATION:** There is no relevant statutory provision.

**DIVORCE**

*Residency Requirement:* Either party wishing to file for a divorce must have resided in the state for at least 1 year before starting the divorce action. However, if both parties are residents when the action is commenced, the person filing must only have resided in the state for 3 months before starting the action. (§ 20-3-30)

*Grounds for Divorce:* Factors 4, 8, 11, 16 (1 year), and 31 (1 year), listed in Appendix A, are grounds for divorce. (§ 20-3-10)

*Unless otherwise specified, all reference citations are to the Code of Laws of South Carolina (1976).

*Conciliation Requirement:* When the parties to a divorce are referred to a master or special referee, the referee must make an earnest effort to bring about a reconciliation of the parties. In such cases, no divorce may be granted unless the special referee has certified as to this attempt at reconciliation unless the judge has attempted to do so without success. (§ 20-3-90)

*Property Distribution:* There is no statute governing the division of marital property. However, the court may decide all the legal and equitable rights of the parties to the real and personal property acquired during the marriage. [*Jones v. Jones*, 314 S.E.2d 33 (S.C. 1984)]

*Child Custody:* The court may consider the circumstances of the parties, the nature of the case, and the best spiritual as well as other interests of the children which may be fit, equitable, and just in determining custody and support. (§ 20-3-160)

*Child Support:* See "Child Custody."

*Spousal Support/Alimony:* The court may award alimony to either spouse considering factors 4, 8, 9, 11, 13, 14, and 22, listed in Appendix E. See *Powers v. Powers*, 254 S.E.2d 289 (S.C. 1979). Alimony will not be granted to an adulterous spouse. (§ 20-3-130)

*Enforcement of Support Orders:* The court may require a party owing a duty of support to make support payments either to the parties owed the support or through the clerk of the court. It may also require such a party to give security by a written undertaking that such persons will be paid and may provide that failure to make the payments is punishable by contempt. (§ 20-7-420) A party who fails to make court-ordered support payments may be subject to arrest or probation. [§§ 20-7-420(23), -870] Additionally, upon notification from the support enforcement division of the Department of Social Services that a taxpayer is at least 60 days in arrears in his or her support payments, and the amount due is more than $25, the Tax Commission will transfer to the Department of Social Services the amount of past-due support. (§ 127-2240) See also the Revised Uniform Reciprocal Enforcement of Support Act of 1968, §§ 20-7-960 *et seq*.

*Spouse's Name:* After granting a divorce, the court may allow a wife to resume her maiden name or the name of any former husband. (§ 20-3-180)

*Divorce by Affidavit or Summary Judgment:* There is no relevant statutory provision.

*Displaced Homemaker Laws:* There is no relevant statutory provision.

# DOMESTIC VIOLENCE

**STATUTORY PROVISION:** Physical harm, the threat of physical harm, or any sexual criminal offense committed against family or household members is prohibited. (§ 20-4-20)

**WHO IS PROTECTED?** Spouses, former spouses, parents, children, or persons related by consanguinity or affinity within the second degree are protected. (§ 20-4-20)

**RELIEF AVAILABLE:** The court may restrain or enjoin either party from harming, interfering with, or molesting the other when a divorce is pending. However, in the case of domestic abuse during a marriage, the victim of domestic abuse may file a verified petition for an order of protection which must state the specific time, place, details of the abuse, and other facts upon which the relief is sought. A protective order may provide several forms of relief, including awarding temporary custody, with visitation rights, of minor children; directing the abuser to pay temporary support to the petitioner and minor children; prohibiting the transfer, encumbrance, or destruction of marital property; providing for temporary possession of the personal property of the parties; and awarding costs and attorney's fees to either party. Violation of a protective order is a criminal offense punishable by 30 days in jail or a fine of $200; it may also constitute contempt of court punishable by up to 1 year in jail and/or a fine not to exceed $500. (§ 20-4-60) Victims of domestic abuse also have recourse to the criminal domestic violence statute. Unlike its civil counterpart, this statute extends its protection to cohabitants and former cohabitants. (§ 1625-20) Any person who violates this statute will be guilty of a misdemeanor and upon conviction will be imprisoned for not more than 30 days or fined not more than $200. (§ 16-25-30) A police officer may arrest, without a warrant, a person who the officer suspects to have committed an act of domestic abuse or violated an order of protection. (§ 16-25-70)

**MARITAL RAPE:** A woman may charge her husband with rape only if they are living apart under a court order. (§ 16-3-658)

**CIVIL LAWSUIT FOR RAPE OR ASSAULT:** In *Prosser v. Prosser*, 102 S.E. 787 (S.C. 1920), the court held that a wife could sue her husband for willfully injuring her.

**CHILD ABUSE:** It is unlawful for a person responsible for a child's welfare to harm or threaten the child's physical or mental health or welfare or to abandon, cruelly ill-treat, commit, or allow a sexual offense to be committed against the child. (§§ 20-7-50, -70, -80, -490)

> *Notification Requirement:* Any health care or mental health professional, religious healer, schoolteacher, counselor, social worker, child care worker, police officer, or judge having reason to believe that a child's physical or mental health has been abused or neglected is required to report such abuse or neglect, either orally or in writing, to the Department of Social Services. (§ 20-7-510)

# INHERITANCE RIGHTS

**FAILURE TO MAKE A WILL:** The surviving spouse is entitled to the entire estate if the decedent left no heirs; to one-half if the decedent left one child or parents, siblings, nieces, or nephews; to one-third if the decedent left more than one child. (§ 21-3-20)

**FAILURE TO PROVIDE BY WILL:** There is no relevant statutory provision. However, the courts have held that if the property of the decedent is undisposed of by will or otherwise, the surviving spouse is entitled to one-half of any property left by the decedent. See *Busby v. Busby*, 140 S.E. 801 (S.C. 1927).

**CHILDREN BORN OUT OF WEDLOCK:** A child born out of wedlock is the natural heir of the mother and her kin. (§ 21-3-30) However, such a child can inherit from the father only if the father has acknowledged his paternity and supported the child before his death. [*Trimble v. Gordon*, 430 U.S. 762 (1977)]

**HOMESTEAD, PERSONAL, AND FAMILY ALLOWANCES:** The surviving spouse and children are entitled to a homestead exemption of land up to $1000 in value. (§§ 15-4-10, -100) If the land's value exceeds $1000 and cannot be divided without injury, the party claiming the homestead exemption must pay the amount above the $1000 limit within 60 days of notice. Personal property of up to $300 in value, consisting of clothes and tools, is exempt from creditors. Also exempt is the personal property of up to $500 belonging to the head of any family residing in the state, as well as the personal property of any person residing in the household. (§§ 15-41-50, -310)

**OPTION TO DISREGARD THE WILL:** There is no relevant statutory provision. A wife may either elect to take her intestate share or her dower share; dower may be either a one-third life estate in her deceased husband's lands or a one-sixth interest in fee simple. [§§ 21-3-70, -5-710, -5-910; *Estate of Kennedy v. U.S.*, 302 F. Supp. 343 (D.C.S.C. 1969)]

# REPRODUCTIVE RIGHTS
## ABORTION

*Statutory Provisions:* All abortions require the prior consent of the woman and must be performed by physicians licensed by the state. Second-trimester abortions must be performed in a hospital or clinic certified by the Department of Health and Environmental Control. Third-trimester abortions can only be performed in a certified hospital and only if the attending physician and one consulting physician certify in writing to the hospital in which the abortion is to be performed that the abortion is necessary, based on their best medical judgment, to preserve the life or health of the woman. (§ 44-41-20) However, the District Court of South Carolina has held that the part of the statute requiring that a physician consult another physician before performing an abortion is unconstitutional. [*Floyd v. Anders*, 440 F. Supp. 535 (D.C.S.C. 1977)] No private or governmental hospitals or clinics, doctors, nurses, technicians, or other employees of a medical facility are required to perform abortions or assist in their performance. (§§ 44-41-40, -50)

*Informed Consent:* The pregnant woman must consent in every case except when there is a medical emergency or where she is mentally incompetent.

*Parental Consent:* If the woman is under 16 years old and unmarried, parental consent or consent of her legal guardian is necessary. This requirement has been declared unconstitutional. [*Floyd V. Anders*, 440 F. Supp. 535 (D.C.S.C. 1977)]

*Spousal Consent:* If a woman is married and in her third trimester of pregnancy, both her and her husband's consent are required before an abortion can be performed. (§ 44-41-30) However, this requirement has been declared unconstitutional. [*Floyd v. Anders*, 440 F. Supp. 535 (D.C.S.C. 1977)]

*Reporting Requirements:* Doctors must report abortions on a standard form to the Department of Health and Environmental Control. Reports must be received within 7 days of the performance of the abortion. The name of the patient is not to be disclosed on the form. (§ 44-41-60)

**BIRTH CONTROL:** All persons authorized to issue a marriage license must, at the time of issuance, provide applicants with family planning information supplied by the Board of Health. (§ 20-1-240)

**STERILIZATION:** There is no relevant statutory provision. However, under current law in South Carolina it is unclear whether spousal consent is required before a competent consenting adult can be voluntarily sterilized. [Op. Atty. Gen. 77-110 (1977)]

# UNMARRIED COUPLES
**COMMON-LAW MARRIAGE:** Common-law marriages are valid. [§ 20-1-360; *Johnson v. Johnson*, 112 S.E.2d 647 (S.C. 1960)]

**COHABITAL RELATIONSHIPS:** A South Carolina court has held that a contract based on past cohabitation might be enforceable, but a contract based either totally or in part on future cohabitation is void. [*Grant v. Butt*, 17 S.E.2d 689 (S.C. 1941)]

## CHILDREN

*Custody:* Unless the court provides otherwise, or unless the mother has relinquished the right, the custody of a child born out of wedlock rests solely with the natural mother. If paternity of the child has been acknowledged, the father may petition for custody in a separate proceeding before the court. [§ 20-7-953(B)]

*Legitimation Proceedings:* The child of a couple living together in anticipation of marriage is legitimate. A child is also legitimated if the parents intermarry after its birth. (§§ 20-1-40, -50, -60)

*Paternity Proceedings:* The child, the mother, the alleged father, or a person or agency in whose care the child has been placed may initiate a paternity action at any time before the child reaches 18. The court may order blood tests if necessary to make a determination of paternity. (§§ 20-7-952, -954)

*Obligations of the Putative Father:* If the court finds that the putative father is the natural father of the child, it may require him to support the child. The court may also grant other relief requested by the parties which it deems reasonable. (§ 20-7-957)

# Education

## STATUTORY PROVISION

There is no relevant statutory provision. However, it should be noted that if federal funds are involved, federal law, Title IX of the Education Amendments of 1972, Pub. L. No. 92-318, 20 U.S.C. §§ 1681–1686, may apply.

# Employment

## EQUAL PAY LAWS

An employer may not discriminate against an individual in the terms of compensation. [§ 1-1380(a)(1)]

**ENFORCEMENT:** The state Human Affairs Commission investigates and attempts to resolve all charges of alleged discriminatory practices by conference, conciliation, or persuasion with the complainant and respondent. [§ 1-13-90(c)(3)] If a charge brought by a complainant is dismissed by the commission or if within 180 days of filing such a charge, the commission has not filed an action or entered into a conciliation agreement, the complainant may bring an action in equity against the respondent in circuit court. The action must be brought within 1 year of the occurrence of the alleged discriminatory act, or within 90 days of the date the complainant's charge is dismissed by the commission, whichever occurs earlier. This period may be extended by written consent of the respondent. [§ 1-13-90(d)(6)]

## FAIR EMPLOYMENT LAWS

The law applies to the state, its political subdivisions, employers of fifteen or more employees, labor organizations, and employment agencies. It makes unlawful the failure or refusal to hire; discrimination in discharge, compensation, terms, conditions, or privileges of employment; expulsion or exclusion of an individual from membership in a labor organization; refusal to recruit or refer an individual for employment on the basis of sex; or indication of a preference for a particular sex in advertisements for employment. The law does not apply where sex is a bona fide occupational qualification, nor does it apply to Indian tribes, bona fide private membership clubs, public officials and their non-civil service staffs, to discrimination occurring where a bona fide seniority or merit system exists, or to religious groups. (§§ 1-13-30, -80)

**ENFORCEMENT:** See "Equal Pay Laws."

## GOVERNMENT CONTRACTORS AND SUBCONTRACTORS

There is no relevant statutory provision. However, it should be noted that if federal funds are involved, Exec. Order No. 11246, 3 C.F.R. 339 (1965), *reprinted in* 42 U.S.C. § 2000e app. at 1232, 41 C.F.R. § 60-1.2, may apply.

## STATE EMPLOYEE LAWS

State employees are covered under the Fair Employment Practices Law. [§ 1-13-30(d)] The state personnel division is required to make all appointments in the state civil service without regard to sex. [§ 8-11-230(3)]

**ENFORCEMENT:** See "Equal Pay Laws."

## VETERAN'S PREFERENCE

Veterans have preference for appointment and employment in the public service. (§ 1-1-550)

# Community Life

## CREDIT

There is no relevant statutory provision. However, it should be noted that federal law, the Equal Credit Opportunity Act of 1977, 12 C.F.R. § 202, may apply.

## HOUSING

There is no relevant statutory provision. However, federal law, Title VIII of the Civil Rights Act of 1968, 42 U.S.C. §§ 3601–3619, and Exec. Order No. 11063, 3 C.F.R. 652 (1962), *reprinted in* 42 U.S.C. § 1982, as amended by Exec. Order No. 12259, 3 C.F.R. 307 (1981), *reprinted in* 42 U.S.C. § 3608, may apply.

# INSURANCE

Discrimination is prohibited between individuals of the same class and equal expectation of life in the rates charged for life insurance or annuity contracts; between individuals of the same class and essentially the same hazards in the amount of premium, policy fees, or rates charged for disability insurance, in the benefits payable under these contracts; or in any other term or condition of these contracts. (§ 38-55-120) Discrimination is also prohibited between insured of the same class and risk involving the same hazard in the premiums, rates, benefits, dividends, or any other term or condition of any other type of insurance contract. (§ 38-9-80) Life insurance companies may give women lower rates based on their more favorable life expectancy. (§ 38-9-100)

**ENFORCEMENT:** If after a hearing, a person is found to have engaged in any prohibited act or practice, the Commissioner of Insurance shall issue an order requiring such person to cease and desist from engaging in such act or practice or an order suspending or revoking the insurer's license or authority to do business or shall impose a monetary fine of up to $500 for each offending act or practice. (§ 38-55-200) The insurer may also be found guilty of a misdemeanor by a court of law and, upon conviction, be subject to imprisonment. (§ 38-9-90)

# PUBLIC ACCOMMODATIONS

There is no relevant statutory provision.

# SOUTH DAKOTA

## Home and Family

## MARRIAGE

**AGE OF CONSENT:** A person 18 years of age or older may consent to marry. (§ 25-1-9)*

**CONSENT REQUIREMENT:** A person under the age of 18 may marry with the written consent of the parent or guardian. (§ 25-1-13) A woman who is pregnant or has given birth to a child may marry at any age without parental consent. (§ 25-1-12)

**LICENSE REQUIREMENT:** A marriage license must be obtained from the county treasurer for a $25 fee. The license is valid for 20 days from the date of issuance. (§§ 25-1-10, -24)

**PROHIBITED MARRIAGES:** Marriages between parents and children, ancestors and descendants of every degree, brothers and sisters, half-brothers and half-sisters, uncles and nieces, aunts and nephews, and cousins of the half as well as of the whole blood are null and void. (§ 25-1-6) Marriage with a stepchild is null and void. (§ 25-1-7) Bigamous marriages are also void. (§ 25-1-8) Children of void marriages are legitimate. (§ 25-5-2)

## DISSOLUTION OF MARRIAGE

**ANNULMENT:** Factors 19, 32, 33, 34, and 35, listed in Appendix A, are grounds for annulment. (§§ 25-3-1, -9)

*Residency Requirement:* There is no relevant statutory provision.

**LEGAL SEPARATION:** Factors 2 and 23, listed in Appendix A, together constitute the ground for legal separation. (§ 25-4-17.2)

### DIVORCE

*Residency Requirement:* The person filing for divorce or separate maintenance must, at the time the action is commenced, be a resident or a member of the armed services stationed in the state, and the residence or military presence must be maintained until the decree is entered. (§ 25-4-30)

*Grounds for Divorce:* Factors 4, 9 (discretionary grounds, 5 years), 15 to 17, 21, 25, and 29, listed in Appendix A, are grounds for divorce. (§§ 25-4-2, -18)

*Conciliation Requirement:* There is no relevant statutory provision.

*Property Distribution:* The court divides equitably the property belonging to either husband or wife or both. (§ 25-4-44) Fault is not considered, except as it may be relevant to the acquisition of property during the marriage. (§ 25-4-45.1) Factors 1, 2, 5, 6, and 18, listed in Appendix F, and the value of the property and the income-producing capacity of the parties' assets will be considered by the courts in making an equitable property division. [*Clement v. Clement*, 292 N.W.2d 799 (S.D. 1980)]

---

*Unless otherwise spevidied, all reference citations are to South Dakota Codified Laws (1967).

*Child Custody:* During or after a divorce or annulment action, the court may give such direction for the custody, care, and education of the children as may seem necessary and proper and may at any time vacate or modify the same. (§§ 25-3-11, -4-25) Fault is not taken into account except as it may be relevant to the fitness of either parent in awarding the custody of children. (§ 25-4-45.1) Appendix B, factor 5, while not controlling, may be considered by a trial judge in determining custody matters. [*Hansen v. Hansen*, 327 N.W.2d 47 (S.D. 1982)]

*Child Support:* The parents of a child are jointly and severally obligated for the necessary maintenance, education, and support of the child in accordance with their respective means. (§ 25-7-7) While a divorce action is pending, the court may in its discretion require one spouse to pay any money necessary to support the children. (§ 25-4-38) During or after an action for annulment or divorce, the court may give such direction for the custody, care, and education of the children as may seem necessary and proper and may at any time vacate and modify the same. (§§ 25-3-11, -4-45) In the absence of a court order, the Department of Social Services shall adopt a scale based on factors 5, 9, 10, 16, and 20, listed in Appendix D, the deduction of expenses in determining net income, the amount of public assistance the child is eligible to receive under the full standard of need, and a determination that the child for whom support is sought benefits from the income and resources of the owing parent on an equitable basis in comparison with any other child of that parent. (§ 25-7A-9) Further, child support should be a reasonable amount suitable to the children's circumstances and situation in life and their parents' financial means and ability to pay. [*Park v. Park*, 309 N.W.2d 827 (S.D. 1981)]

*Spousal Support/Alimony:* Upon divorce, the court may award a suitable allowance to either party for life or for a shorter period, as it deems just, taking into account the circumstances of the parties. It may modify its orders from time to time. (§ 25-4-41) While a divorce action is pending, the court may, in its discretion, require one spouse to support the other. (§ 25-4-38) Factors 4, 5, 6, 8, 13, 14, and 22 (fault), listed in Appendix E, and the social standing of the parties may be considered by the court. [*Hanks v. Hanks*, 296 N.W.2d 523 (S.D. 1980)]

*Enforcement of Support Orders:* For failure to obey the support order of a court, the court can direct the parent to assign part of his or her salary or wages as will be sufficient to meet the child support obligation. (§§ 25-7-31 to -36) In addition, the Department of Social Services may issue an order to withhold and deliver any personal property, including earnings belonging to a parent in arrears on a support obligation, due to a spouse or children. (§ 25-7A-12) The court may require a spouse to give reasonable security for making payments. (§ 25-4-42) The Department of Social Services may also enforce spouse and child support obligations. (§§ 28-7-17.1, -17.2) See also the Revised Uniform Reciprocal Enforcement of Support Act of 1968, §§ 25-9A-1 *et seq*.

*Spouse's Name:* Upon a divorce decree, the court may, in its discretion or upon application by either party, restore to the woman her maiden name or her prior legal name. (§ 25-4-47)

*Divorce by Affidavit or Summary Judgment:* There is no relevant statutory provision.

*Displaced Homemaker Laws:* South Dakota has established a multipurpose service center for displaced homemakers which provides job counseling and training; health care education; legal counseling; and information and referrals regarding academic education, financial management, taxes, and loans. (§§ 60-6B-1 to -10)

# DOMESTIC VIOLENCE

**STATUTORY PROVISION:** Statutes prohibit physical harm, bodily injury, attempts to cause physical harm or bodily injury, or the infliction of fear of imminent physical harm or bodily injury between family or household members. (§ 25-10-1)

**WHO IS PROTECTED?** The statute protects spouses; former spouses; persons related by blood, adoption, or law; or persons living in the same household. (§ 25-10-1)

**RELIEF AVAILABLE:** Pending a full hearing, the abused party may petition the court for a protection order restraining a party from committing further abuse; excluding the abusive party from the victim's residence; awarding temporary custody, visitation, or support of minor children; recommending counseling; or ordering any other necessary relief. (§§ 25-10-1 to -14)

**MARITAL RAPE:** A woman may charge her husband with rape only when the spouses are no longer cohabitating or are legally separated. The complaint for spousal rape must be made to a law enforcement officer within 90 days of the occurrence of the rape. (§ 22-22-1.1)

**CIVIL LAWSUIT FOR RAPE OR ASSAULT:** In *Scotvald v. Scotvald*, 298 N.W. 266 (S.D. 1941), the court held that one spouse could sue another for damages for personal torts committed by one against the other.

**CHILD ABUSE:** Any person who abuses, exposes, tortures, torments, or cruelly punishes a minor is guilty of a felony. (§ 26-10-1) Reports of child abuse must be immediately investigated. (§§ 26-10-10 to -12.1) Child abuse is a ground for taking a child into protective custody and terminating parental rights. (§§ 25-5-16, 26-8-19.1, -35.1, -35.2, -35.3, -36)

> *Notification Requirement:* All medical practitioners, hospital and school personnel, child welfare providers, law enforcement officers and coroners must report child abuse cases as provided by law. Any person who intentionally fails to make a report required of him or her is guilty of a misdemeanor. (§§ 26-10-10 to -12.1)

# INHERITANCE RIGHTS

**FAILURE TO MAKE A WILL:** The surviving spouse is entitled to the decedent's entire estate if there are no children, no parents, and no brothers or sisters. (§ 29-1-8) If only one child, or the issue of one child, survives, then the estate is divided equally. If more than one child or descendant survives, then the spouse receives one-third of the estate with the remainder going to the children or descendants. (§ 29-1-5) If the decedent left no children, then the spouse is entitled to $100,000 and one-half the balance above $100,000 if there are surviving parents, brothers, or sisters. (§ 29-1-6)

**FAILURE TO PROVIDE BY WILL:** A surviving spouse may exercise the right to an elective share which must not exceed one-third of the decedent's augmented estate or $100,000, whichever is greater. The court awards the elective share so as to be equitable according to the circumstances. (§§ 30-5A-1 to -8)

**CHILDREN BORN OUT OF WEDLOCK:** Every child born out of wedlock is an heir of the mother's estate but is an heir of the father's estate only if the father had acknowledged his paternity of the child in writing. (§ 29-1-15)

**HOMESTEAD, PERSONAL, AND FAMILY ALLOWANCES:** The surviving spouse and children are entitled to the homestead, which may consist of a house, mobile home, and real property that constituted the decedent's homestead at the time of death. (§§ 30-20-1, -4, 43-31-2) The homestead exemption may be subject to creditors' liens if the estate is insolvent and the court so orders. (§§ 30-20-7, -8, -9, 43-31-1) The spouse and children are entitled to all family pictures, burial lots, a religious pew, the family bible and other books worth up to $100, clothing, provisions on hand or growing, and all household and kitchen furniture. (§ 30-20-16) The spouse or children are also allowed money or personal property worth up to $1500. If the estate consists entirely of personal property and the decedent left no will, the family is entitled to money or property up to $2500. (§ 30-20-18)

**OPTION TO DISREGARD THE WILL:** The surviving spouse has a right to an elective share of the decedent's augmented estate. See "Failure to Provide by Will."

## REPRODUCTIVE RIGHTS:

## ABORTION

*Statutory Provisions:* An abortion may be performed during the first 12 weeks of pregnancy. The decision to perform an abortion during that period must be left to the women's attending physician. (§ 34-23A-3) An abortion may be performed through the twenty-fourth week of pregnancy by a physician only in a licensed hospital or the licensed physician's medical clinic or office which has blood supplies available. (§§ 34-23A-4, -6) An abortion may be performed after the twenty-fourth week of pregnancy only in a hospital and only if it is necessary to preserve the life or health of the mother. (§ 34-23A-5) Any person who performs, procures, or advises an abortion other than those legally authorized (as described above) is guilty of a felony. (§§ 22-17-5, 34-23A-2)

*Informed Consent* The woman must give her written consent to having the abortion. If the woman refuses to sign the prescribed written statement of informed consent, her physician may read it to her and sign it. (§ 34-23A-7)

*Parental Consent:* An unmarried minor must have her parents' consent. (§ 34-23A-10.1)

*Spousal Consent:* A married minor must have her husband's consent. (§§ 34-23A-7, -10.2) However, in *Planned Parenthood of Central Missouri v. Danforth*, 428 U.S. 52 (1976), the United States Supreme Court held that permitting a woman's husband or parents to veto her abortion decision violated the Constitution.

*Reporting Requirements:* Any facility or physician must report to the Department of Health Information the total number of abortions performed, the method of abortion used in each operation, complete pathology reports, numbers of maternal deaths due directly or indirectly to the abortions, and reports of all follow-up care, including reports of complications resulting from the abortion. No report shall include the name of any woman receiving an abortion. (§ 34-23A-19) Whenever an abortion procedure results in a live birth, a birth certificate must be issued. (§ 34-23A-16)

*State Funding:* No funds of the state or any state agency or political subdivision and no federal funds passing through the state treasury or any agency of the state or its political subdivisions may be spent in connection with any abortion that is not necessary to preserve the life of the person on whom the abortion is performed. (§ 28-6-4.5)

**BIRTH CONTROL:** There is no relevant statutory provision.

**STERILIZATION:** There is no statutory provision. Sterilization is dealt with as any other surgical procedure.

# UNMARRIED COUPLES

**COMMON-LAW MARRIAGE:** With the exception of a lawful marriage consented to and subsequently consummated prior to July 1, 1959, a common-law marriage is not valid. (§§ 25-1-1, -29) The court upheld the common-law marriage of a couple who were married, divorced, and then resumed their relationship in 1978 without a second ceremony. [*In re Estate of Miller*, 243 N.W.2d 788 (S.D. 1976)]

**COHABITAL RELATIONSHIPS:** There is no relevant statutory provision. Although a cohabital relationship does not give rise to marital or property rights, one party may acquire an interest in property accumulated in the other's name during the relationship if acquired through the joint efforts or contributions of the parties with the intention that both share its benefits and the extent of each party's interest is proportional to the contributions of money or effort made by the party. [*Beuck v. Howe*, 23 N.W.2d 744 (S.D. 1946)]

## CHILDREN

*Custody:* The mother of a child born out of wedlock is entitled to the child's custody, services, and earnings. In a paternity action, the court may award custody to either parent, considering the best interests of the child. (§ 25-5-10) See also "Divorce: Child Custody."

*Legitimation Proceedings:* A child born before wedlock becomes legitimate by the subsequent marriage of its parents. (§ 25-5-5)

*Paternity Proceedings:* An action to determine the paternity of a child born out of wedlock may be brought during the mother's pregnancy or after the birth of the child. (§ 25-8-12)

*Obligations of the Putative Father:* Once paternity has been determined, the court will make an order for the support and custody of the child. The order of support will be for annual amounts, equal or varying, and the payments will be made as the court directs. The court may require the father to give reasonable security for the payment of support. (§ 25-8-7) The father is also liable for the expenses of the mother's pregnancy and confinement. (§ 25-8-3) The mother may recover a reasonable share of child support furnished for a period not to exceed 6 years prior to bringing the paternity action. (§ 25-8-5)

# Education

# STATUTORY PROVISION

It is an unfair or discriminatory practice for any educational institution to discriminate on the basis of sex; to exclude, expel, limit, or otherwise discriminate against an individual seeking admission or already enrolled; or to use a written or oral inquiry or application form for admission which elicits discriminatory information. The law does not apply to religious institutions. (§ 20-13-22)

# AREAS COVERED

The provisions which prohibit discrimination on the basis of sex do not apply to the following when conducted for any educational, social, or recreational purpose: voluntary youth service organizations, nationally chartered veterans associations; mother-daughter or father-son activities, social fraternities or sororities, and any officers or members affiliated with the above mentioned programs. (§ 20-13-22.1) Segregation by sex of athletic activities offered by an educational institution does not constitute discrimination on the basis of sex if the opportunity to participate in athletic activities offered by the educational institution is substantially equal for both sexes. (§ 20-13-22)

**ENFORCEMENT:** See "Community Life: Housing."

# Employment

## EQUAL PAY LAWS

It is unlawful for an employer to discriminate on the basis of sex in wages paid to employees for work requiring comparable skill, effort, and responsibility but not for work requiring physical strength. (§ 60-12-15)

**ENFORCEMENT:** An employer who violates the provisions of the equal pay law is liable to an employee in the amount of his or her unpaid wages. An action to recover unpaid wages may be brought in a court of competent jurisdiction within 2 years of the occurrence of the unlawful act. The court may also award reasonable attorney's fees and costs to be paid by the defendant. (§§ 60-12-18, -20) See also "Community Life: Housing."

## FAIR EMPLOYMENT LAWS

It is unlawful for any person, employer, employment agency, labor organization, the state, or its political subdivision and agencies to fail or refuse to hire, to discharge, or to accord adverse or unequal treatment to any person or employee with respect to application, hiring, training, apprenticeship, tenure, promotion, upgrading, compensation, layoff, or any term or condition of employment on the basis of sex. (§§ 20-13-1, -10 to -12) Sex differentiation is permitted when based on seniority, job description, ability, test, merit, or executive training systems, provided that such differences are not the result of an intention to discriminate. (§§ 20-13-15 to -17)

**ENFORCEMENT:** See "Community Life: Housing."

## GOVERNMENT CONTRACTORS AND SUBCONTRACTORS

There is no relevant statutory provision.

## STATE EMPLOYEE LAWS

State employees are covered under the fair employment laws. [§ 20-13-1(4), (5)] Sexual harassment in state employment is prohibited by Exec. Order No. 81-08, (June 18, 1981)

**ENFORCEMENT:** See "Community Life: Housing."

# VETERAN'S PREFERENCE

Veterans are preferred for public appointment, employment, and promotion, provided they possess the qualifications and business capacity necessary to discharge the duties of the position involved. A disabled veteran is given preference over a nondisabled veteran. (§ 3-3-1) The unmarried spouse of a veteran who died while in service or later died from a service connected cause is entitled to the same preferences given to veterans provided he or she is qualified. (§§ 3-3-7, -8)

# Community Life

## CREDIT

There is no relevant statutory provision. However, it should be noted that federal law, the Equal Credit Opportunity Act of 1977, 12 C.F.R. § 202, may apply.

## HOUSING

It is an unfair or discriminatory practice for an owner, his or her agent, a real estate broker or salesperson, attorney, auctioneer, or any person acting under court order, deed of trust, or will to refuse to sell, rent, lease, assign, sublease, or transfer any real property or housing accommodation to any person because of sex; to discriminate in the terms, conditions, or privileges of the transfer; or to indicate a preference in advertisements for the transfer of real property or accommodations. The law does not apply to owner-occupied dwellings containing two or fewer families. (§ 20-13-20) It is also an unfair or discriminatory practice for any person, bank, mortgage company, insurance company, or other financial institution or lender to discriminate in the extension of financial assistance on the basis of sex. (§ 20-13-21)

> **ENFORCEMENT:** A person aggrieved by a discriminatory practice may file a written charge with the Division of Human Rights within 180 days after the alleged discriminatory or unfair practice occurred. The division conducts investigations of alleged discriminatory practices and attempts to eliminate them by education and conciliation. (§ 20-13-7) If, after a hearing, the division finds that a discriminatory or unfair practice has occurred, it shall order the respondent to cease and desist from engaging further in the discriminatory act or practice and to take affirmative actions to effectuate the purposes of the human rights law. (§§ 20-13-28 to -51)

## INSURANCE

Insurance rates shall not be excessive, inadequate, or unfairly discriminatory. (§ 58-24-5) It is a misdemeanor to refuse to issue or to renew an automobile insurance policy solely because of marital status. (§ 58-11-55) It is a misdemeanor to make or permit any unfair discrimination between individuals of the same class regarding life insurance, annuities, and health insurance. (§§ 58-33-12, -13) For insurance contracts delivered or amended after July 1, 1980, sex or marital status discrimination is prohibited. However, an insurer may take marital status into account to define persons eligible for dependents benefits. (§§ 58-33-13.1, -13.2)

**ENFORCEMENT:** The Division of Insurance shall institute such suits or other legal proceedings as may be required for the enforcement of any provisions of the insurance laws. (§ 58-4-5) If the director believes, on the basis of substantial evidence, that a provision has been or is about to be violated, the director may issue a temporary cease and desist order pending a hearing. (§ 58-4-7) If, after a hearing, the director finds that an insurer is engaging in a prohibited act or practice, the director may order the person to permanently cease and desist from the acts or practices. (§ 58-33-40) A person damaged by certain unlawful discriminatory acts may also bring a civil action for the recovery of damages and reasonable attorney's fees. (§ 58-33-46.1)

# PUBLIC ACCOMMODATIONS

It is an unfair or discriminatory practice for any person engaged in the provision of public accommodations to refuse access to such accommodations, its services, and its facilities to any person on the basis of sex. (§ 20-13-23) The definition of public accommodations does not include private clubs except during any periods when the club caters or offers services, facilities, or goods to the general public. [§ 20-13-1(12)]

**ENFORCEMENT:** See "Housing."

# TENNESSEE

## Home and Family

## MARRIAGE

**AGE OF CONSENT:** A person 18 years or older may consent to marry. (§ 36-3-108)*

**CONSENT REQUIREMENT:** A person 16 or 17 years of age may marry with parental, next of kin, or guardian consent, sworn under oath. (§ 36-3-106)

**LICENSE REQUIREMENT:** Persons wishing to marry must obtain a license from the clerk of the county where the woman resides or where the marriage ceremony is to be performed. [§ 36-3-104(3)] The license is valid for 30 days thereafter. (§ 36-3-103) A premarital physical examination is required before a marriage license is issued. [§ 36-3104(2)] However, this requirement is waived if the woman is pregnant at the time of the application. (§ 36-3-208)

**PROHIBITED MARRIAGES:** Bigamous marriages are prohibited. (§ 36-3-102) Marriages to a parent, child, grandparent, or grandchild (in any degree) are prohibited. So, too, are marriages to siblings, uncles and aunts, descendants of a spouse, or descendants of a parent's spouse. (§ 36-3-101)

## DISSOLUTION OF MARRIAGE

**ANNULMENT:** There is no relevant statutory provision, but factors 14, 19, 25, 34, and 38, listed in Appendix A, are grounds for annulment in case law.

**LEGAL SEPARATION:** A legal separation (and separate maintenance for the wife) may be obtained upon a finding by a court that either spouse is guilty of such cruel and inhuman treatment to the other that cohabitation is unsafe or improper, that the husband has made the wife's condition intolerable with personal indignities, or the husband has abandoned the wife or forced her to leave the marital home without providing for her. (§ 36-4-102)

*Residency Requirement:* There is no relevant statutory provision.

### DIVORCE

*Residency Requirement:* A party seeking a divorce must have been a resident of the state during the period in which the alleged acts were committed, or if the acts were committed out of state, either party must have resided in the state for 6 months prior to the commencement of the action. (§ 36-4-104)

*Grounds for Divorce:* Refusing to move to Tennessee with a spouse and willfully absenting oneself from the new residence for 2 years are grounds for divorce, as are factors 3, 4, 6, 8, 10, 15, 16 (1 year), 19, 20, 22, 27, and 31 (3 years and no minor children), listed in Appendix A. (§ 36-4-101) See also "Legal Separation."

*Conciliation Requirement:* The court may stay the divorce proceedings, upon written request of both the husband and wife, in order that they may attempt a reconciliation. (§ 36-4-126)

---

*Unless otherwise specified, all reference citations are to the Tennessee Code Annotated (1956).

*Property Distribution:* Marital property (but not separate property) is distributed by the court in equitable proportions without regard to fault. Tangible and intangible contributions made by one party to the education, training, or increased earning power of the other, as well as factors 1 to 6, 9 to 12, 15, 17, and 18, listed in Appendix F, are considered. (§ 36-4-121)

*Child Custody:* Custody is awarded according to the best interests of the child. The child's preference will be considered. (§ § 36-6-101, -102)

*Child Support:* The court may order either or both natural or adoptive parents to provide suitable support. If a father gets custody, the mother cannot be required to contribute to the support of minor children. In making the award the court will consider factors 1, 3, 4, 5, 9, 12, and 25, listed in Appendix D, and monetary and nonmonetary contributions to the child's well-being. (§ 36-5-101)

*Spousal Support/Alimony:* The court may award maintenance to either spouse wherever appropriate, with the intention that, if possible, it should be rehabilitative and temporary. The court considers the value of separate property and divided marital property and factors 1 to 4, 8 to 12, 15, 16, and 22 (including relative fault where appropriate), listed in Appendix E. (§ 36-5-101)

*Enforcement of Support Orders:* When a person owing a duty of support fails to pay alimony or child support, the court may order him or her to post a bond or give sufficient personal surety to secure past, present, and future payments. The court may enforce its orders by sequestering the rents and profits of his or her real estate or personal estate, if any, and appoint a receiver who will pass these on to the former spouse and the children. Persons owed a duty of support may enforce the provisions of a court order, recover judgment for defaults in the payments, and obtain execution in addition to reasonable attorney's fees incurred in enforcing the support order. (§ 36-5-103) A person failing to comply with a support order may also be punished by imprisonment for up to 6 months. (§ 36-5-104) See also the Intercounty Enforcement of Support Act of 1985, §§ 36-5-307 *et seq.*, and the Uniform Reciprocal Enforcement of Support Act of 1950, §§ 36-5-201 *et seq.*

*Spouse's Name:* There is no relevant statutory provision.

*Divorce by Affidavit or Summary Judgment:* There is no relevant statutory provision.

*Displaced Homemaker Laws:* There is no relevant statutory provision.

# DOMESTIC VIOLENCE

**STATUTORY PROVISION:** Threatened or actual infliction (or attempted infliction) of physical injury is prohibited. (§ 36-3-602)

**WHO IS PROTECTED?** The statute is intended to protect a person from his or her legally married spouse at the time of application. Relief may also be sought against persons living as spouses, persons related by blood or marriage, and other adults living in the same household. (§ 36-3-602)

**RELIEF AVAILABLE:** Protection orders may be applied for. In an emergency where immediate danger of abuse can be shown, an order which will last up to 10 days may be issued without a hearing. Following this, successive orders for 120 days may be applied for at a hearing. (§ 36-3-610) A police officer may arrest a person for violation of an order without a warrant. (§ 36-3-611)

**MARITAL RAPE:** A woman may charge her husband with rape only if they are living apart and one of them has filed for divorce or separation. (§ 39-2-610)

**CIVIL LAWSUIT FOR RAPE OR ASSAULT:** There is no relevant statutory provision. However, in *Wooley v. Pather* 432 S.W.2d 882 (Tenn. 1968), the court held that spouses may not sue each other for torts committed during the marriage.

**CHILD ABUSE:** Intentional physical injury to a child and failure to provide for a child's welfare and health are prohibited. (§ 39-4-401)

> *Notification Requirement:* Any person who reasonably believes that a child is being abused must report this immediately to a judge of the juvenile court, the county Department of Human Services, or the police. Any person who knowingly fails to report an incidence of child abuse is guilty of a misdemeanor and may be fined. (§ 37-1-412)

# INHERITANCE RIGHTS

**FAILURE TO MAKE A WILL:** If the decedent is survived by children or grandchildren, the surviving spouse is entitled to receive one-third of all property or a share equal to that left each child, if that is greater. If the decedent is not survived by children or grandchildren, the surviving spouse is entitled to receive the entire estate. (§ 31-2-104)

**FAILURE TO PROVIDE BY WILL:** There is no relevant statutory provision.

**CHILDREN BORN OUT OF WEDLOCK:** A child born out of wedlock may inherit from the mother and her kin. Such a child may inherit through the father where paternity is proved during the father's lifetime or after his death before rights of inheritance vest or where the father had married the mother and acknowledged the child as his own. (§ 31-2-105)

**HOMESTEAD, PERSONAL, AND FAMILY ALLOWANCES:** The surviving spouse is entitled to occupy and use for life the homestead owned by the decedent at death. (§ 31-1-104) The spouse is also entitled to the family bible and other books, the family car, all the deceased's clothing, and all household electrical appliances, musical instruments, furniture, utensils, and implements. (§ 30-2-101) A surviving spouse or a spouse dissenting from a will is also entitled to receive reasonable support for 1 year. (§ 30-2-102) The spouse may receive from the decedent's employer any salary due, up to $500; this money must be deducted from the family allowance or homestead exemption. (§ 30-2-103)

**OPTION TO DISREGARD THE WILL:** A surviving spouse may reject the will and take one-half of the decedent's net estate. (§ 31-4101)

# REPRODUCTIVE RIGHTS

## ABORTION

> *Statutory Provisions:* All abortions must be performed by licensed physicians (and in a licensed hospital, if performed during the second trimester). Any person except a licensed physician operating to save the life or health of the woman, who intentionally performs an abortion after the end of the second trimester of the pregnancy, commits a criminal offense. (§ 39-4-201) When the abortion results in a live birth, the doctor performing the abortion must take all necessary steps to preserve the child's life and health. (§ 39-4-206) If the infant dies owing to a willful failure by the doctor or any person in attendance to take such care, such person will be guilty of a felony. (§ 39-4-206) No hospital or doctor can be required to perform an abortion. (§ 39-4-204)

*Residency Requirement:* The pregnant woman must be a resident of Tennessee. (§ 39-4-201)

*Informed Consent:* The informed written consent of the woman, given after a 2-day consideration period, is required, unless the abortion is necessary to preserve her life. (§ 39-4-202)

*Parental Consent:* The parents or legal guardians of an unemancipated minor under the age of 18 must be given 2 days' notice of the abortion, unless the physician determines that the abortion is necessary earlier to preserve the life or health of the minor. (§ 39-4-202)

*Spousal Consent:* There is no relevant statutory provision.

*Reporting Requirements:* Physicians performing abortions must record each operation and make a report to the Commissioner of Public Health. Records are confidential and not accessible to the public. (§ 39-4-202)

*State Funding:* Public funds may not be used for abortions except in pregnancies resulting from incest or certifiable rape, or where the fetus is severely deformed or abnormal, or the woman's physical or mental health would be permanently impaired if the fetus is carried to term. (1985 General Appropriations Act, Acts of 1985, ch. 467, § 14, Item 15)

**BIRTH CONTROL:** It is the state policy that contraceptives should be readily and practicably available to all. (§ 68-34-104) Contraceptive supplies and information are to be made available to all persons eligible for free medical supplies and to others who cannot obtain them cheaply, at a cost to be determined by the Commissioner of Public Health. (§ 68-34-104) Minors may be given birth control supplies and information on request. (§ 68-34-107)

**STERILIZATION:** Upon written request, a licensed physician may perform a vasectomy or hysterectomy on a person over 18, or on a person under 18 who is legally married. (§ 68-34-108)

# UNMARRIED COUPLES

**COMMON-LAW MARRIAGE:** Common-law marriages are not valid. [*Troxel v. Jones*, 322 S.W.2d 251 (Tenn. 1958)]

**COHABITAL RELATIONSHIPS:** Cohabitation violates public policy. The courts have held that express or implied contracts between cohabitants are not valid or enforceable. [*Roach v. Buttons*, 6 F.L.R. 2355 (Tenn. Ch. Ct. Feb. 29, 1980)]

## CHILDREN

*Custody:* As part of its order, or upon the request of the father in a paternity proceeding, and if it is in the best interests of the child, the court may award custody to the father, provided that he had not denied his paternity of the child and consents to the child assuming his surname. (§ 36-2-108)

*Legitimation Proceedings:* Children born out of wedlock are legitimate if their parents intermarry and the father recognizes the child as his, or if a circuit, juvenile or probate court legitimates the child upon application by the natural father. (§§ 36-2-201, -207)

*Paternity Proceedings:* The mother, her personal representative or the Department of Human Services may bring a paternity action before or after the birth of the child until 1 year beyond the child's age of majority. (§ 36-2-103) The court may order all parties to undergo blood tests. (§ 36-2-107)

*Obligations of the Putative Father:* The father is liable to pay for the expenses of the mother's pregnancy and confinement, the necessary support and education of the child until the child reaches the age of 18, and for the child's funeral expenses. (§ 36-2-108)

# Education

## STATUTORY PROVISION

Sex discrimination in awards of student assistance under Tennessee state programs is prohibited. [§ 49-4-301(2)] With regard to higher education, it should be noted that if federal funds are involved, federal law, Title IX of the Education Amendments of 1972, Pub. L. No. 92-318, 20 U.S.C. §§ 1681–1686, may apply.

**ENFORCEMENT:** The Tennessee Student Assistance Corporation administers awards in accordance with §§ 49-4-203, -204, -301(2).

# Employment

## EQUAL PAY LAWS

It is unlawful for an employer to discriminate on the basis of sex in wages paid to employees in the same establishment who perform work requiring comparable skill, effort, and responsibility under similar working conditions. However, wage differentials are not prohibited if based on a bona fide seniority or merit system, the quantity or quality of production, or any factor other than sex. (§ 50-2-202)

**ENFORCEMENT:** The Commissioner of Labor has the power to administer the law and to use informal methods to eliminate unfair pay practices. (§ 50-2-203) A civil action for unpaid wages, and for additional damages if the violation is willful, may be brought by an employee in any court of competent jurisdiction within 2 years of the occurrence of the alleged discriminatory act. (§§ 50-2-204, -205)

## FAIR EMPLOYMENT LAWS

The law applies to the state, its political and civil subdivisions, employers of eight or more employees, labor organizations, and employment agencies. (§ 4-21-102) It is unlawful to discriminate on the basis of sex in the hire, discharge, compensation, and terms, conditions or privileges of employment; in limiting, segregating, or classifying an individual in any way which would deprive him or her of employment opportunities; or in refusing to recruit or refer a person for employment on the basis of sex. (§ 4-21-105) However, the law does not apply where sex is a good faith occupational qualification. (§§ 4-21-109, -110, -125) The statute does not apply to domestic servants. (§ 4-21-105) Sex discrimination in apprenticeship and training programs is also prohibited. (§ 4-21-108)

**ENFORCEMENT:** See "Community Life: Housing"

# GOVERNMENT CONTRACTORS AND SUBCONTRACTORS

Government contractors must agree not to discriminate against employees or applicants for employment on account of their sex with regard to promotion, rates of pay, transfers, recruitment, terminations, layoffs, training, and apprenticeship programs. [Exec. Order No. 17 (January 14, 1972)] See also "Fair Employment Laws."

**ENFORCEMENT:** See "Community Life: Housing."

# STATE EMPLOYEE LAWS

See "Fair Employment Laws."

# VETERAN'S PREFERENCE

Five points are added to the civil service examination passing scores of veterans. Ten points are added to the passing scores of disabled veterans, their spouses, and their unremarried widowed spouses. (§ 8-30-306)

# Community Life

# CREDIT

It is unlawful for any lending institution or credit card issuer to discriminate between equally qualified individuals solely on account of marital status. (§ 47-17-102)

**ENFORCEMENT:** Any creditor or credit card issuer who discriminates against any individual may be fined between $100 and $1000 if an individual brings an action, or up to $10,000 if a class action is brought. The action must be brought within 1 year of the occurrence of the alleged discrimination. Costs of the action and attorney's fees are also recoverable. (§§ 47-17-104, -105)

# HOUSING

It is unlawful for any person engaging in a real estate transaction to discriminate on the basis of sex. (§ 4-21-127)

**ENFORCEMENT:** Any person claiming to be aggrieved by a discriminatory practice may file a complaint with the Commission for Human Development within 180 days of the occurrence of the alleged discriminatory act. (§ 4-21-11) In addition the person also has a civil cause of action in chancery court to enjoin further violations and to recover actual damages, together with the costs of the lawsuit and reasonable attorney's fees. (§ 4-21-124) This action must be commenced within 1 year of the occurrence of the alleged discriminatory act. (§ 28-3-104)

# INSURANCE

It is unlawful for an insurer to discriminate between individuals of the same class and equal expectation of life in rates charged for life insurance or annuity contracts or between individuals of the same class and essentially the same hazard in the amount of premium, policy fees, or rates charged for accident or health insurance; in the benefits payable under these contracts; or in any other term or condition of these contracts. (§ 56-8-107)

**ENFORCEMENT:** The Commissioner of Insurance has the power to examine and investigate insurance practices in order to determine their fairness or unfairness. (§ 56-8-105) The commissioner may hold hearings and issue orders requiring the insurer to cease and desist from engaging in the discriminatory practice. (§§ 58-8-106, -107)

# PUBLIC ACCOMMODATIONS

No person may deny an individual the full and equal enjoyment of the goods, services, facilities, privileges, advantages, and accommodations of a place of public accommodation, resort, or amusement on the basis of sex. (§ 4-21-111)

**ENFORCEMENT:** See "Housing."

# TEXAS

## Home and Family

## MARRIAGE

**AGE OF CONSENT:** A person 18 years or older may consent to marry. (Fam. § 1.51)*

**CONSENT REQUIREMENT:** A male or female 16 or 17 years of age may marry with the written consent of a parent or guardian. (Fam. § 1.51)

**LICENSE REQUIREMENT:** Persons wishing to marry must first obtain a license from the county clerk. (Fam. § 1.01) A premarital medical examination is required; a medical examination certificate must be submitted with the application for the license. (Fam. § 1.21) The marriage license is valid for the 21 days immediately following the date of the medical examination. (Fam. § 1.81)

**PROHIBITED MARRIAGES:** A person may not marry an ancestor or descendant by blood or adoption, a brother or sister of the whole or half blood or by adoption, or a parent's brother or sister of the whole or half blood. (Fam. § 2.21) Bigamous marriages are void. (Fam. § 2.22)

## DISSOLUTION OF MARRIAGE

**ANNULMENT:** Grounds for annulment include one party divorcing another party 30 days before the wedding without informing his or her new spouse. Factors 32, 33, 35, and 36 (mental incompetence or under influence of alcohol or narcotics), listed in Appendix A, are also grounds for annulment. (Fam. §§ 2.41 to .46)

   *Residency Requirement:* The parties must have married in the state or one must be domiciled in the state. (Fam. § 3.25)

**LEGAL SEPARATION:** There is no relevant statutory provision.

**DIVORCE**

   *Residency Requirement:* One of the parties must have been domiciled in the state for 6 months prior to the divorce application, and reside in the county where it is filed for 90 days before the application. (Fam. § 3.21)

   *Grounds for Divorce:* Factors 2, 4, 5, 9 (3 years), 15, 17, and 31 (3 years), listed in Appendix A, are grounds for divorce. (Fam. §§ 3.01 to .07)

   *Conciliation Requirement:* The court is authorized to order both parties to see a marriage counselor if one of the parties requests this. If the counselor's report to the court shows a reasonable expectation of the parties' reconciliation, the court may order further counseling for up to 60 days. If no reconciliation has taken place, the divorce proceedings will continue. (Fam. § 3.54)

   *Property Distribution:* The court will divide all the jointly owned property of the parties in a just and right manner. Separately owned property will generally be restored to its owner. (Fam. § 3.63)

   *Child Custody:* Custody will be determined in the best interests of the child. The qualifications of the parents, without regard to sex, will be taken into account

*Unless otherwise specified all reference citations are to Texas Codes Annotated (Vernon 1984).

in deciding who should be "managing conservator." (Fam. § 14.01 and annotations; § 36.02)

*Child Support:* The court may order either or both parents to make periodic payments, a lump-sum payment, or both for the support of the child until the child is 18, or older if the child is mentally or physically handicapped. (Fam. § 14.05)

*Spousal Support/Alimony:* The statutes and public policy of the state of Texas do not sanction alimony for the wife after the judgment for divorce has been entered. [*Brunell v. Brunell* 494 S.W.2d 621 (Civ. App. 1973)]

*Enforcement of Support Orders:* Child support orders may be enforced by contempt proceedings, or the person owed the support may bring an action for a debt judgment, which can be enforced like any other judgment. The penalties for continuing nonpayment include imprisonment. (Fam. § 14.09) In addition, child support obligations may be deducted from the unemployment insurance benefits payable to a party owing a duty of support and through garnishment of wages for personal services. [Lab art. 5221b-13(d); Tex. Const. art. 16, § 28]

*Spouse's Name:* The court may change the name of either party on request in the decree for divorce or annulment. (Fam. § 3.64)

*Divorce by Affidavit or Summary Judgment:* There is no relevant statutory provision.

*Displaced Homemaker Laws:* The Texas Employment Commission is authorized to establish a special-assistance job counseling program for displaced homemakers. The counseling shall consider and build upon the skills and experiences of a homemaker and shall prepare the person through employment counseling to reenter the paid workforce and develop job skills. The program shall assist displaced homemakers in obtaining training and education and place such persons in suitable employment. [Lab art. 5221g]

# DOMESTIC VIOLENCE

**STATUTORY PROVISION:** Knowingly or recklessly causing one's spouse bodily injury or threatening one's spouse with imminent bodily injury is an offense. (Penal § 22.01)

**WHO IS PROTECTED?** Spouses, former spouses, cohabitants, former cohabitants, and relatives are protected. (Fam. § 71.01)

**RELIEF AVAILABLE:** A police officer who is informed that one spouse has threatened to injure the other spouse has a duty to prevent the threatened or potential injury, using whatever measures or amount of force necessary. (Crim. Proc. §§ 6.05, .06) Protected persons may also obtain protective or temporary protective orders, unless a divorce suit has already been filed and is pending, in which case protective orders are not available. (Fam. §§ 71.04, .06, .15) Other available relief includes restraining orders, exclusive possession of the residence by one party, temporary custody of minor children and visitation rights, support payments for a spouse or minor children, and professional counseling. (Fam. § 71.11) Protective orders last 1 year; temporary orders last 20 days, but they may be extended for additional 20-day periods. (Fam. §§ 71.13, .15) Violation of an order is punishable as contempt of court and may also be a criminal offense. (Fam. § 71.16) The Department of Human Resources contracts with nonprofit organizations to set up shelters for victims of family violence which provide 24-hour emergency medical care and transportation, psychological counseling, and legal assistance to victims of domestic violence and their families. (Hum. Res. §§ 51.002 *et seq.*)

**MARITAL RAPE:** A woman may charge her husband with rape only when they live separate and apart or there is an action pending between them for dissolution of the marriage or for separate maintenance. [Penal § 22.011(c)(2)]

**CIVIL LAWSUIT FOR RAPE OR ASSAULT:** In *Dousbach v. Ofield* 488 S.W.2d 494 (Tex. 1972), the court held that family members could not sue each other for negligent or intentional torts.

**CHILD ABUSE:** A person who knowingly or recklessly causes bodily injury to a child under 16 is guilty of the crime of child abuse. (Penal § 22.04)
> *Notification Requirement:* Any person who has cause to believe that a child has been abused must report this to the police, the Department of Human Resources, or a court-designated child protection agency. All reports must be promptly and thoroughly investigated. (Fam. §§ 34.01, .02, .05)

# INHERITANCE RIGHTS

**FAILURE TO MAKE A WILL:** The surviving spouse is entitled to the entire community property estate if the decedent left no descendants or to one-half of the decedent's share of their joint property if the decedent left a child or grandchild. If the decedent had title to any property other than the community estate, the surviving spouse is entitled to all of the personal property if the decedent left no children or grandchildren, but must share one-half of any real property with the decedent's parents, siblings, or nieces or nephews, if any. If the decedent left a child or grandchild, the surviving spouse takes one-third of the personal property and a life interest in one-third of the real property. (Prob. § 38)

**FAILURE TO PROVIDE BY WILL:** Texas is a community property state. The surviving spouse owns one-half of the community property as owner, not heir, whatever the will provides. (Prob. § 45)

**CHILDREN BORN OUT OF WEDLOCK:** Children born out of wedlock may inherit from their mothers. They may inherit from their fathers if they have been legitimated by court decree or if the father made a statement of paternity. (Prob. § 42)

**HOMESTEAD, PERSONAL, AND FAMILY ALLOWANCES:** The surviving spouse is entitled to occupy and use the decedent's homestead during his or her life. A homestead consists of up to 200 acres for a family, 100 acres for a single person in a rural area, or one or more lots of up to 1 acre in an urban area. (Prob. § 283; Prop. § 41.001) The surviving spouse is entitled to have set aside up to $15,000 of the decedent's personal property for his or her use or up to $30,000 for a family. Personal property includes home furnishings, provisions, tools, clothing, sports equipment, guns, cars, and livestock. Instead of this personal property, the surviving spouse may receive allowances of up to $1000 in cash. (Prop. §§ 42.001, .002; Prob. § 273)

**OPTION TO DISREGARD THE WILL:** There is no relevant statutory provision.

# REPRODUCTIVE RIGHTS
## ABORTION

*Statutory Provisions:* Abortions may be performed only by physicians. First-trimester abortions need not be performed in hospitals, although facilities performing later abortions may be regulated by the state in the interest of the woman's health. [Op. Atty. Gen. No. H-369 (1974)] It is an offense punishable with imprisonment to destroy a fetus in the process of being born if it would otherwise have been born alive. (Civ. art. 4512.5) A child born alive after an abortion has the rights of any other living child, and a representative of the Texas Department of Human Resources may assume custody on filing an emergency order petition certifying that there is immediate danger to the child. No physicians, nurses, hospital employees, or private hospitals who object to participating in an abortion may be required to do so. (Civ. art. 4512.7)

*Consent Requirement:* There is no relevant statutory provision.

**BIRTH CONTROL:** Registered pharmacists may sell contraceptives to the public. [Civ. art. 4504(a)] There are no other relevant statutory provisions.

**STERILIZATION:** There is no relevant statutory provision.

# UNMARRIED COUPLES

**COMMON-LAW MARRIAGE:** Common-law marriages are valid. (Fam. § 1.71) Common-law marriage may be proved by the fact that the parties agreed to be married and then lived together in the state as husband and wife, representing that they were married, or by a declaration of informal marriage sworn before the county clerk. (Fam. §§ 1.91, .92)

**COHABITAL RELATIONSHIPS:** A cohabitant may recover for property purchased by his or her services or efforts during the cohabitation period, if he or she has proof of the contributions made toward its purchase without relying on the illegal agreement to cohabit. [*McClelland v. Cowden* 175 F.2d 601, (5th Cir. 1949); *Hyman v. Hyman* 275 S.W.2d (Tex. 1954)]

## CHILDREN

*Custody:* An unmarried father who has not been designated father of the child has no custodial rights. [*House of Holy Infancy v. Kasha* 397 S.W.2d 208 (Tex. 1965)]

*Legitimation Proceedings:* The father or mother of the child or the Texas Department of Human Resources may file a petition for a decree designating the father as the father of the child born out of wedlock. A statement of paternity by the father must be attached, and the mother must consent, unless the court waives this consent in the best interests of the child. (Fam. § 13.21) A child may also be legitimated by the subsequent marriage of its parents. (Fam. § 12.02)

*Paternity Proceedings:* An action to determine paternity of a child born out of wedlock must be brought on or before the second anniversary of the day the child becomes an adult. (Fam. § 13.01) Both parents and the child may be ordered to undergo blood tests. (Fam. § 13.02) On a finding of the court that the alleged father is the father of the child, the court issues an order designating the alleged father as father of the child. (Fam. § 13.08)

*Obligations of the Putative Father:* Before the father is designated father of the child, he has no rights or obligations toward the child. However, once he is a designated parent, he has the same rights, privileges, duties, and powers as the mother, including the right to custody and the duty to support. (Fam. §§ 12.04, 13.09, 13.23)

# Education

## STATUTORY PROVISION

The Texas Guaranteed Student Loan Corporation may not discriminate against an eligible student in making a loan or loan guarantee on the basis of sex. (Educ. § 57.50) Appointments to the Board of Education must be made without regard to the sex of appointees. (Educ. § 11.22) The Texas Constitution also contains an equal rights provision which prohibits generally denial or abridgment of equality under the law because of sex. It should be noted that if federal funds are involved, federal law, Title IX of the Education Amendments of 1972, Pub. L. No. 92-318, 20 U.S.C. §§ 1681–1686, may apply.

**ENFORCEMENT:** There is no relevant statutory provision.

# Employment

## EQUAL PAY LAWS

It is unlawful for an employer to discriminate in wages on the basis of sex for the same kind, grade, and quantity of work in public service. (Civ. art. 6825) See also "Fair Employment Laws."

## FAIR EMPLOYMENT LAWS

The law applies to employers of fifteen or more employees, the state, its political and civil subdivisions, labor organizations, and employment agencies. It prohibits discrimination on the basis of sex in hire, discharge, compensation, or any other terms, conditions, or privileges of employment. It also prohibits limiting, segregating, or classifying an employee on the basis of sex in a way that would deprive him or her of employment opportunities and discriminating in admission for or participation in training programs. [Civ. art. 5221(k), §§ 2.01, 5.01 *et seq.*] However, this prohibition does not apply where sex is a bona fide occupational qualification; or where a valid merit or seniority system exists; or to public schools where an affirmative action plan designed to end discriminatory school practices exists; or where employees in different locations are treated differently if that difference is not based on sex. The law does not apply to religious organizations or where a person is employed by his or her parent, spouse, or child. [Civ. art. 5221(k), §§ 5.05 to .07]

**ENFORCEMENT:** The Texas Commission on Human Rights receives, investigates, conciliates, and passes on complaints of unfair employment practices. Local commissions set up by political subdivisions have the same powers and may also file civil actions if the state commission has referred the complaint and if conciliation has been ineffective. [Civ. art. 5221(k), §§ 3.02, 4.03] A complaint must be filed within 180 days of the occurrence of the alleged discriminatory practice and must be in writing under oath or affirmation. [Civ. art. 5221(k), § 6.01]

## GOVERNMENT CONTRACTORS AND SUBCONTRACTORS

There is no relevant statutory provision. However, see "Fair Employment Laws." It should also be noted that if federal funds are involved, federal law, Exec. Order No. 11246, 3 C.F.R. 339 (1965), *reprinted in* 42 U.S.C. § 2000e app. at 1232, 41 C.F.R. § 60-1.2, may apply.

## STATE EMPLOYEE LAWS

See "Fair Employment Laws."

## VETERAN'S PREFERENCE

Veterans, both male and female, and their widows and orphans who have lived in Texas for at least 5 years are entitled to preference in appointment and employment over other equally qualified applicants. [Civ. art. 4413(31)]

# Community Life

## CREDIT

It is unlawful to deny an individual credit or loans in his or her name or to restrict or limit the credit or loan granted solely on the basis of sex. (Civ. art 5069-2.07)

**ENFORCEMENT:** The Consumer Credit Commissioner enforces the fair credit provision. Upon receipt of a written complaint the commissioner has the authority to conduct an investigation and hold hearings. The commissioner has wide powers to subpoena any information necessary and may issue orders demanding that any violation ceases and may seek injunctions to that effect in any district court. (Civ. arts. 5069-2.02A, -2.03)

## HOUSING

There is no relevant statutory provision. However, federal law, Title VIII of the Civil Rights Act of 1968, 42 U.S.C. §§ 3601–3619, and Exec. Order No. 11063, 3 C.F.R. 652 (1962), *reprinted in* 42 U.S.C. § 1982, as amended by Exec. Order No. 12259, 3 C.F.R. 307 (1981), *reprinted in* 42 U.S.C. § 3608, may apply.

# INSURANCE

It is unlawful for any insurer to discriminate between individuals of the same class and equal expectation of life in the rates charged for or terms and conditions of any contract or life insurance. It is also unlawful to discriminate between individuals of the same class and of essentially the same hazard in the amount of premium, policy fees, or rates charged for accident or health insurance, in the benefits payable under these contracts, or in any other term or condition of these contracts. [Ins. § 21.21 4(7)]

**ENFORCEMENT:** The Board of Insurance Commissioners investigates unfair discriminatory practices and may call hearings, issue cease and desist orders, ask the attorney general to seek an injunction, or bring a class action where discriminatory practices are found. (Ins. art. 21.21, §§ 6, 7, 15, 17) Individuals may also bring actions for injunctive and compensatory relief. (Ins. art 21.21, § 16)

# PUBLIC ACCOMMODATIONS

There is no relevant statutory provision.

# UTAH

## Home and Family

## MARRIAGE

**AGE OF CONSENT:** A person 18 years of age or older may consent to marry. (§30-1-9)*

**CONSENT REQUIREMENT:** A person under 18 but over 14 years of age may marry with the consent of his or her father, mother, or guardian, given in person to the court clerk, or in writing, signed and acknowledged before a person authorized to administer oaths. (§ 30-1-9)

**LICENSE REQUIREMENT:** A license issued by the county clerk is required. The license is valid for 30 days from issuance and must be returned to the clerk within 30 days after the ceremony, with a marriage certificate, by the person who solemnized the marriage. If the county clerk does not know the parties personally, one of them must swear and file an affidavit showing that there is no lawful reason to stop the marriage. (§§ 30-1-7, -10, -11)

**PROHIBITED MARRIAGES:** Marriages between parents and children, ancestors and descendants of every degree, brothers and sisters of the half or the whole blood, uncles and nieces, aunts and nephews, or first cousins or between any persons related to each other by five removes or fewer are void. (§ 30-1-1) Marriage to a person with communicable syphilis or gonorrhea, to a person of the same sex, or to a person under 16 years of age if consent is not obtained is prohibited. Bigamous marriages and remarriages before a divorce is absolute are also prohibited and void. (§ 30-1-2) Marriages which are not solemnized by ministers or priests of any denomination, justices of the peace, city mayors, judges or the county clerk, are void, unless the parties assumed that the person solemnizing had authority. (§§ 30-1-2, -6) Children born of void marriages are legitimate. (§ 30-1.17.2)

## DISSOLUTION OF MARRIAGE

**ANNULMENT:** Prohibited marriages may be annulled at common law. Factors 10, 14, 32, 33, and 36, listed in Appendix A, are among the grounds for annulment. (§ 30-1.17.1)

*Residency Requirement:* There is no relevant statutory provision.

**LEGAL SEPARATION:** Factors 16, 31, and 48, listed in Appendix A, are grounds for an order of separate maintenance. (§ 30-4-1)

*Residency Requirement:* The deserting spouse must either be a resident of the state or own property in the state in which the deserted spouse resides. (§ 30-4-1)

**DIVORCE**

*Residency Requirement:* A party filing for divorce must have been a resident of the state and of the county where the action is filed or stationed in the state under military orders for at least 3 months. (§ 30-3-1)

*Grounds for Divorce:* Factors 3, 4, 13, 15, 16 (1 year), 17, 21, 25, and 40, listed in Appendix A, are grounds for divorce. (§ 30-3-1)

*Unless otherwise specified, all reference citations are to the Utah Code Annotated (1953).

448

*Conciliation Requirement:* If one or both parties files a petition for conciliation, the court may refer the parties to domestic relations counselors for a conciliation conference. Use of the counseling service does not mean that the aggrieved party condones the behavior of his or her spouse that provided the original grounds for the divorce. (§§ 30-3-15.2, -16.2, -18)

*Property Distribution:* The court will divide the property equitably. (§ 30-3-5)

*Child Custody:* Before the divorce, where a husband or wife has abandoned his or her spouse, that spouse is entitled to custody of the minor children unless a court directs otherwise. (§ 30-2-10) The divorce court will consider the best interests of the child and the past conduct and moral standards of each of the parties. The child's preference will be taken into account, but is not controlling. (§ 30-3-10) In determining visitation rights of the other parent and grandparents, the welfare of the child will be considered. (§ 30-3-5)

*Child Support:* The court will make an equitable order relating to the children. (§ 30-3-5) Support may be ordered up to age 21. (§ 15-2-1) The court must order either or both parents to pay reasonable and necessary medical and dental expenses and to buy appropriate health insurance for the children. (§ 30-3-5) The court may also order the noncustodial parent to pay for all or some child care expenses or to provide day care while the custodial parent works or undergoes training. (§ 30-3-5)

*Spousal Support/Alimony:* The court may include in the divorce decree an equitable order relating to the parties. (§ 30-3-5) An order that a party pay alimony to a former spouse automatically terminates upon the latter's remarriage or upon proof by the paying party that the former spouse is living with a person of the opposite sex and having sexual relations with that person. [§ 30-3-5; *Kusteson v. Kusteson*, 619 P.2d 1387 (1980)] The court may order alimony and money to pay for participation in the suit, to be paid before the divorce is final. (§ 30-3-3)

*Enforcement of Support Orders:* Any order for child support or support of a former spouse with whom a child of the marriage lives will include a provision for withholding income as a means of collecting child support. (§§ 30-3-5.1, 78-45d-2) Unless orders provide otherwise, one-half of the support and alimony payments is due by the fifth day of each month, and the remaining half is due by the twentieth day of that month. (§ 30-3-10.5) An order of support may be enforced by the Department of Social Services (where the department has contracted to collect support) by means of wage assignments, garnishment, and other methods. Child support obligations may be deducted and withheld from any unemployment compensation payable to an individual who owes such obligations. (§§ 35-4-18, 78-45b-2, -3, -4) See also the Revised Uniform Reciprocal Enforcement of Support Act of 1968, §§ 77-31-1 *et seq.*

*Spouse's Name:* There is no relevant statutory provision.

*Divorce by Affidavit or Summary Judgment:* There is no relevant statutory provision.

*Displaced Homemaker Laws:* Under 1986 Utah Laws H.B. No. 110, the Board for Vocational Education shall establish a program for the education, training, and transitional counseling of displaced homemakers. [§§ 53-16-27(1) to (10)]

# DOMESTIC VIOLENCE

**STATUTORY PROVISION:** The act prohibits intentionally or knowingly causing or attempting to cause physical harm to adult family members. (§ 30-6-1) Intentionally placing another in fear of imminent physical harm is also prohibited. (§ 30-6-1)

**WHO IS PROTECTED?** Spouses, cohabitants, former spouses and cohabitants, and adults residing or having resided at the same residence are protected. (§ 30-6-1)

**RELIEF AVAILABLE:** A victim of domestic violence can obtain a protective order, which may include an order that the defendant refrain from abusing the plaintiff, immediately vacate and refrain from entering the plaintiff's dwelling, or any court order the court deems appropriate. (§ 30-6-6) Violation of the order is a misdemeanor. (§ 76-5-108) The court must hear the case within 10 days of the filing of the complaint. (§ 30-6-5) Meanwhile, an *ex parte* protective order may be issued. After the hearing, the protective order will last up to 60 days. (§ 30-6-5) Police officers informed of the existence of an order must use all reasonable means to enforce it, including immediately arresting the offender and taking him or her into physical custody. (§ 30-6-8) Domestic violence is also a criminal offense. (§§ 77-36-1 *et seq*.) A court order may restrict the defendant's contact with the victim and require the defendant to participate in therapy. The defendant may be ordered to pay for therapy for the victim. (§ 77-36-5)

**MARITAL RAPE:** Marital rape is not an offense unless the parties are living apart pursuant to a court order. (§§ 76-5-402, -407)

**CIVIL LAWSUIT FOR RAPE OR ASSAULT:** Spouses may sue each other for the infliction of intentional injuries. [*Stoker v. Stoker*, 616 P.2d 590 (Utah 1980)]

**CHILD ABUSE:** The act prohibits serious physical injury and physical injury inflicted intentionally, recklessly, or with criminal negligence on a child of 17 years or less by any person. Physical injury includes failure to thrive, malnutrition, and any physical condition which imperils a child's health and welfare. (§ 76-5-109)

> *Notification Requirement:* Any person who has reason to believe that a child of 18 or younger has been or will be subjected to incest, molestation, sexual exploitation, or sexual abuse or has been or will be physically abused or neglected must immediately notify the nearest peace officer, law enforcement agency, or office of the Division of Family Services of the Department of Social Services. (§§ 78-3b-2, -3) Failure to report is a misdemeanor. (§ 78-3b-10) The division must make a thorough investigation promptly. (§ 78-3b-8) A doctor or hospital may take a child into protective custody for 72 hours without parental consent or a court order if there is reason to believe that the child's life or safety will be in danger otherwise. (§ 78-3b-9)

# INHERITANCE RIGHTS

**FAILURE TO MAKE A WILL:** The surviving spouse is entitled to the entire estate if the decedent left no heirs or surviving parents; to the first $100,000 and half the balance of the estate if the decedent and spouse have living children or grandchildren; to half the estate if the decedent left one or more children or grandchildren who are not also the spouse's children or grandchildren. (§ 75-2-102)

**FAILURE TO PROVIDE BY WILL:** If a testator fails to provide by will for his or her surviving spouse who married the testator after the execution of the will, the omitted spouse will receive the same share of the estate as if the decedent left no will, unless it appears that the omission was intentional or the testator provided for the spouse by transfer outside the will and statements of the testator support the intent that the transfer was to be in lieu of a provision in the will. (§ 75-2-301)

**CHILDREN BORN OUT OF WEDLOCK:** A child born out of wedlock is the legitimate heir of the mother and her kin. Such child may only inherit from the father and his kin if the parents participated in a marriage ceremony before or after the child's birth, even though the attempted marriage is void, or if the paternity is established by an adjudication during the father's lifetime or after the father's death, by clear and convincing proof. The father and his kindred may not inherit from the child unless the father openly treated the child as his and did not refuse support. (§ 75-2-109)

**HOMESTEAD, PERSONAL, AND FAMILY ALLOWANCES:** A surviving spouse domiciled in Utah is entitled to a homestead allowance of $6000. If there is no surviving spouse, any minor and dependent children may divide the homestead allowance of $6000 equally among themselves. The homestead allowance is exempt from, and has priority over, all claims against the estate except those for reasonable funeral expenses. The surviving spouse, or the surviving children if no spouse survives, is entitled to household furniture, cars, furnishings, appliances, and personal effects of the decedent up to a value of $3500. (§ 75-2-402) The homestead and personal allowances are in addition to any share passing to the surviving spouse or minor or dependent children by will, by intestate succession, or by way of elective share. The surviving spouse, minor children, and children supported by the decedent are also entitled to a reasonable allowance in money out of the estate for their maintenance during the period of administration. (§ 75-2-403) This allowance is exempt from, and has priority over, all claims except those for reasonable funeral expenses and the homestead allowance. (§ 75-2-403)

**OPTION TO DISREGARD THE WILL:** If the decedent was domiciled in Utah, the surviving spouse may reject the will and take one-third of the estate, specially defined for the purpose. If the decedent was domiciled elsewhere, the right of the surviving spouse to take a share of property located in Utah is governed by the laws of the state in which the decedent was domiciled at death. (§ 75-2-201) See also "Homestead, Personal, and Family Allowance."

# REPRODUCTIVE RIGHTS
## ABORTION

*Statutory Provisions:* It is a felony to perform, supply means for, or perform an abortion, except as permitted by law. (§ 76-7-314) After the first trimester all abortions must be performed by a physician and in a hospital, except in a serious medical emergency. (76-7-302) In all cases, the physician must concur on the basis of his or her best clinical judgment, taking into consideration the woman's physical, emotional, and psychological health and safety, her age, and familiar situation. (§§ 76-7-303, -304) Where a fetus may be viable outside the womb, an abortion may be performed only if it is necessary to save the life of the pregnant woman or to prevent serious and permanent damage to her health. (76-7-315) Also, the physician must use a procedure that gives the fetus the best chance to survive and must not use any procedure designed to kill or injure the unborn child, unless it is necessary to save the woman's life or prevent serious and permanent damage to her health. (§ 76-7-307) The physician must also, consistent with the preservation of the woman's life or the prevention of damage to her health, use all his or her skills to keep the fetus alive if it has any reasonable chance of survival. (§ 76-7-308) Experimentation on live fetuses is prohibited, but they may be tested for genetic defects.

(§ 76-7-310) Violation of the provisions of §§ 76-7-307, -308, and -310 is a felony. No physician or employee of a hospital in which an abortion has been authorized who states an objection to abortion on moral or religious grounds shall be required to participate in the abortion procedures or be discriminated against because of this. No private or denominational hospital shall be required to perform an abortion. (§ 76-7-306)

*Residency Requirement:* There is no relevant statutory provision.

*Informed Consent:* No abortion may be performed unless a voluntary and informed written consent is obtained by the attending physician from the woman. The consent will not be considered voluntary and informed (except in a serious medical emergency) unless the attending physician has given the woman the names of two licensed adoption agencies and told her of the services they perform and of the legality of nonagency adoption. She must also be told the details of the developments of the fetus, the procedure to be used, the foreseeable complications and risks, the nature of the postoperative recuperation, and any other factors the physician deems relevant. (§§ 76-7-305, -315) Upon the woman's request, she will be given published materials by the Department of Health giving the same advice. (§ 76-7-305.5) Every abortion facility must notify each patient as to the availability of these materials unless the attending physician certifies in writing that exceptional circumstances exist and that disclosure of the materials is likely to cause severe detriment to the patient's health. (§ 76-7-305.5)

*Parental Consent:* The attending physician should notify, if possible and except in a serious medical emergency, the parents or guardian of the woman upon whom the abortion is to be performed, if she is a minor. (§ 76-7-304)

*Spousal Consent:* The attending physician should notify, if possible and except in a serious medical emergency, the husband of the woman if she is married. (§ 76-7-315)

*State Funding:* No public funds shall be used to provide abortion services to an unmarried, unemancipated minor who is not a member of the armed forces of the United States, without the prior written consent of the minor's parent or guardian. (§§ 76-7-321, -322) Public funding for support entities providing contraceptive services to minors is similarly restricted. (§ 76-7-323)

*Reporting Requirements:* Within 10 days after the abortion, the attending physician must supply the following confidential and privileged information to the Department of Health: the age of the woman; her marital status and county of residence; the number of previous abortions performed on her; the hospital or facility where performed; the weight of the aborted fetus; the pathological description of the fetus, the given menstrual age of the fetus, the measurements, if possible to ascertain, and the medical procedure used. (§ 76-7-313) The Department of Health will also compile and report annually, preserving physician and patient anonymity, of the total amount of informed consent material distributed, the number of women who had abortions without receiving the material, the number of physicians stating that exceptional circumstances applied to their patient, and any other information pertaining to protecting the informed consent of women seeking abortions. (§ 76-7-305.5)

**BIRTH CONTROL:** No public funds shall be used to provide contraceptive services to an unmarried minor without the prior written consent of the minor's parents. (§ 76-7-322) No public funds may be given to support entities which provide contraceptive services to an unmarried minor without the prior written consent of the minor's parent or guardian. (§ 76-7-322) Any person providing an unmarried minor with contraceptives shall notify, wherever possible, the minor's parents or guardian of the service requested by the minor. (§ 76-7-325)

**STERILIZATION:** It is lawful for a physician to sterilize a person 18 years of age or older who has the capacity to give informed consent. (§ 64-10-2) It is unlawful to sterilize a person under 18 years of age unless the person is married or otherwise emancipated and the physician, through careful examination and counseling, ensures that the person is capable of giving informed consent, or a petition for an order authorizing sterilization is filed by the minor, the parent, guardian, custodian, or other interested party and the court grants the petition. (§§ 64-10-3, -7, -8)

## UNMARRIED COUPLES

**COMMON-LAW MARRIAGE:** Utah does not recognize common-law marriages. [*Hendrich v. Anderson*, 191 F.2d 242 (10th Cir. 1951)]

**COHABITAL RELATIONSHIPS:** In *Edgar v. Wagner* 572 P.2d 405 (Utah 1977), the court permitted a woman who had married a man, knowing that he was already married, to recover a portion of the value of a house in which the couple lived; the couple were joint tenants. The court also upheld a monetary award to the woman which represented the value of the services the woman had performed for the man in helping him run his business.

### CHILDREN
*Custody:* There is no relevant statutory provision.

*Legitimation Proceedings:* A child born out of wedlock is legitimated upon the marriage of the natural parents to each other or when the child's parentage has been established by a court of competent jurisdiction or by legal adoption. (§ 26-2-10)

*Paternity Proceedings:* The mother, child, or public authority chargeable with the support of the child may bring an action to establish paternity. (§ 78-45a-2) The trial may not take place until after the birth or miscarriage of the child. (§ 78-45a-6) The court may order the mother, child, and alleged father to submit to blood tests. (§ 78-45a-7)

*Obligations of the Putative Father:* The father of a child born out of wedlock is liable to the same extent as the father of a legitimate child for the reasonable expense of the mother's pregnancy and confinement, and for the education, necessary support, and funeral expenses of the child. (§ 78-45a-1) The father's liability for past education and necessary support are limited to a period of 4 years next preceding the commencement of an action. (§ 78-45a-3)

# Employment

## EQUAL PAY LAWS

The state or any political subdivision or board, commission, department, institution, school district, trust or agent thereof, or any other person employing fifteen or more employees for at least 20 weeks a year may not pay differing wages or salaries to employees having substantially equal experience, responsibilities, and competency for the particular job. This does not apply to increases in pay governed by a uniform seniority plan which is applicable to all employees on a substantially proportional basis, nor to rates of pay agreed between employer and employee to protect social security payments for benefit. (§ 34-35-6)

> **ENFORCEMENT:** A person aggrieved by a discriminatory act may file a verified complaint with the Commissioner of Industry within 180 days of the occurrence of the alleged discriminatory act. (§ 34-35.7.1) The commissioner's final order is subject to judicial review. (§ 34-35-8)

## FAIR EMPLOYMENT LAWS

See "Equal Pay Laws." Employers, labor organizations, and employment agencies may not discriminate because of sex in hire, promotion, discharge, demotion, termination, compensation, membership, recruitment, referral, terms, privileges, and conditions of employment against any person otherwise qualified. (§ 34-35-6) Retaliation against an employee because he or she has opposed any such prohibited practice or participated in any way in any proceeding, investigation, or hearing relating to such a practice is also prohibited. (§ 34-35-6)

> **ENFORCEMENT:** See "Equal Pay Laws."

## GOVERNMENT CONTRACTORS AND SUBCONTRACTORS

See "Fair Employment Laws." These are applicable if there are fifteen or more employees. In addition, if federal funds are involved, federal law, Exec. Order No. 11246, 3 C.F.R. 339 (1965), *reprinted in* 42 U.S.C. § 2000e app. at 1232, 41 C.F.R. § 60-1.2, may apply.

## STATE EMPLOYEE LAWS

State employees are covered by the fair employment law.

## VETERAN'S PREFERENCE

Honorably discharged veterans and the unremarried surviving spouses of such veterans, who have served in the armed forces during a period of conflict, war, or other national emergencies, and any unremarried surviving spouse of such honorably displaced veterans are preferred for appointment or employment and any work in which the state, and its political or civil subdivisions are engaged, either directly or by contract, if they possess qualifications for that employment and if the honorably discharged veterans are residents of the state. (§ 34-30-11)

# Community Life

## CREDIT

It is unlawful for any business establishment (regulated by the state) to deny full and equal accommodations, advantages, facilities, privileges, goods and services to any person on the basis of sex. (§§ 13-7-2, -3)

**ENFORCEMENT:** Violation of the act constitutes a public nuisance which may be enjoined. The attorney general will investigate and seek to conciliate any compliant made to him or her. Failing conciliation, the attorney general may seek an injunction. Any person whose rights are violated may bring a civil action for damages. (§ 13-7-4)

# HOUSING

There is no relevant statutory provision. However, federal law, Title VIII of the Civil Rights Act of 1968, the Fair Housing Act, 42 U.S.C. §§ 3601–3619, and Exec. Order No. 11063, 3 C.F.R. 652 (1962), *reprinted in* 42 U.S.C. § 1982 app. at 1217-17, as amended by Exec. Order No. 12259, 3 C.F.R. 307 (1981), *reprinted in* 42 U.S.C. § 3608 app. at 816–818, may apply.

# INSURANCE

See "Credit."

# PUBLIC ACCOMMODATIONS

All persons are entitled to full and equal accommodations, advantages, facilities, privileges, goods, and services in all business establishments and in all places of public accommodation and by all enterprises regulated by the state, without discrimination on the basis of sex. (§ 13-7-3) Religious organizations are exempt. (§ 13-7-3)

**ENFORCEMENT:** See "Credit."

# VERMONT

## Home and Family

## MARRIAGE

**AGE OF CONSENT:** A person 18 years of age or older may consent to marry. (tit. 18, § 173)*

**CONSENT REQUIREMENT:** Persons under 18 may marry with written parental or guardian consent. Persons under 16 need the above-mentioned consent in addition to a certificate from a probate, district, or superior judge certifying that the public good requires the license to be issued. No person under 14 may marry. (tit. 18, § 5142)

**LICENSE REQUIREMENT:** Persons wishing to marry must obtain a license from a town clerk. At least one of the parties to the proposed marriage must sign the certifying application as to the accuracy of the facts supplied by the applicants. The license shall be issued by the clerk of the town where either the bride or groom resides or, if neither is a resident of the state, by a town clerk in the county where the marriage is to be solemnized. (tit. 18, § 5131)

**PROHIBITED MARRIAGES:** Men and women are prohibited from marrying their parents, grandparents, children, siblings, siblings' children, aunts, and uncles. (tit. 15, §§ 1, 2) All marriages which are void because of incest or bigamy do not require a decree of divorce or other legal process to declare their nullity. (tit. 15, § 511)

## DISSOLUTION OF MARRIAGE

**ANNULMENT:** Factors 19, 32, 33, 35, 36, and 38, listed in Appendix A, and one partner being a minor under 16 are grounds for annulment. (tit. 15, §§ 511, 512)

>*Residency Requirement:* Either party must reside within the state for a period of 6 months or more. Temporary absence from the state because of illness, employment without the state, service as a member of the armed forces of the United States, or other legitimate and bona fide cause shall not affect the 6-month period, provided the person has otherwise retained residence in this state. (tit. 15, § 592)

**LEGAL SEPARATION:** A legal separation forever or for a limited time may be granted based upon factors 4, 6, (for life or 3 years or more), 16 (for 7 years), 17 (intolerable severity), 31 (6 months), 40, and 48, listed in Appendix A. (tit. 15, §§ 551, 555)

**DIVORCE**

>*Residency Requirement:* An action for divorce may be brought if either party to the marriage has resided within the state for a period of 6 months or more. In addition, either party must reside in the state 1 year before the date of the final hearing. Temporary absence from the state because of illness, employment outside the state, service as a member of the armed forces, or other legitimate and bona fide cause, shall not affect the 6-month or 1-year period. (tit. 15, § 592)

*Unless otherwise noted, all reference citations are to Vermont Statutes Annotated (1959).

*Grounds for Divorce:* See "Legal Separation."

*Conciliation Requirement:* If one of the parties has denied under oath that the parties have lived apart for the requisite period of time or has alleged that reconciliation is probable, the court shall consider all relevant factors, including the circumstances that gave rise to the filing of the petition and the prospect of reconciliation, and shall make a finding as to whether the parties have lived apart for the requisite period and whether a reconciliation is reasonably probable. Or the court may continue the matter for a further hearing not fewer than 30 or more than 60 days later and may suggest that the parties seek counseling. (tit. 15, § 552)

*Property Distribution:* Upon the petition of either party, the court shall settle the rights of the parties to their property by including in its judgment provisions which equitably divide and assign the property. All property owned by either or both of the parties, however and whenever acquired, shall be subject to the jurisdiction of the court. Title to the property, whether in the names of the husband, the wife, both parties, or a nominee, shall be immaterial, except where equitable distribution can be made without disturbing separate property. The court will consider the contribution by one spouse to the education, training, or increased earning power of the other, and factors 1, 2, 5 to 11, and 21 to 25, listed in Appendix F. (tit. 15, § 751)

*Child Custody:* In awarding custody of minor child, the court shall be guided by the best interests of the child and may consider all relevant factors, including factors 10 to 14, listed in Appendix B. Neither parent is presumed to have a superior right to custody. (tit. 15, § 652)

*Child Support:* The court may order either or both parents to pay child support, taking into account factors 1 to 5 and 25, and increases in the cost of living, listed in Appendix D. (tit. 15, § 651)

*Spousal Support/Alimony:* A court may order either spouse to make maintenance payments to the other, either rehabilitative or permanent in nature, considering factors 2 to 6, 13, 14, and 26, listed in Appendix E, and the lack of sufficient income, property, or both, including property apportioned according to the terms of the property settlement and inflation with relation to the cost of living. (tit. 15, § 752)

*Enforcement of Support Orders:* A petitioner to whom a support order has been issued may request a wage assignment if the respondent's delinquency in connection with such order is greater than one-twelfth of the respondent's annual support obligation. (tit. 15, § 782) In addition, when part of the estate of either spouse, or a sum of money, is awarded to the spouse having custody of minor children, instead of ordering these to be delivered to the custodial spouse, the court may order it delivered or paid to one or more trustees appointed by the court. The trustees shall invest the same and apply the income to the support and maintenance of the custodial spouse and minor children as the court directs and shall pay the principal to them in such proportions and at such times as it shall order. (tit. 15, § 756) The court may require that sufficient security be given for the payment of support obligations. (tit. 15, § 757) The court may also assign insurance benefits to a spouse or children and may require the spouse who is required to make the assignment to execute a blanket assignment, giving notice of the assignment to the insurer. (tit. 15, § 762) The violation of support orders is enforceable by contempt proceedings. (tit. 15, § 603) Interception of unemployment compensation benefits is available to meet child support obligations. [tit. 21, § 1367(a)] See also the Revised Uniform Reciprocal Enforcement of Support Act of 1968, tit. 15, §§ 385 *et seq.*

*Spouse's Name:* Upon the granting of a divorce, a woman may resume her maiden name or the name of the former husband, unless good cause is shown why her name should not be changed. (tit. 15, § 558)

*Divorce by Affidavit or Summary Judgment:* There is no relevant statutory provision.

*Displaced Homemaker Laws:* There is no relevant statutory provision.

# DOMESTIC VIOLENCE

**STATUTORY PROVISION:** Abuse is defined as an attempt to cause or causing physical harm, placing another in fear of imminent serious physical harm, or abuse to children by family or household members. (tit. 15,§ 1101)

**WHO IS PROTECTED?** The law protects spouses, former spouses, persons of the opposite sex living as spouses now or in the past, or persons 60 years of age or older living in the same house and related by blood or marriage and children. (tit. 15, § 1101)

**RELIEF AVAILABLE:** A victim of domestic violence can obtain orders or protection from the court. Such orders may restrain the defendant from abusing the plaintiff or from entering the residence, award sole possession to the plaintiff, or award temporary custody of minors to plaintiff. (tit. 15, § 1104) Law enforcement officers are required to enforce court orders of protection by making an arrest, by assisting the recipient of an order granting sole possession of the residence to obtain such possession, and by assisting him or her to obtain sole custody of the children if the defendant refuses to release them. (tit. 15, § 1108)

**MARITAL RAPE:** Effective May 1985, a woman may charge her husband with rape. (tit. 13, § 3252)

**CIVIL LAWSUIT FOR RAPE OR ASSAULT:** Spouses may sue each other for injuries arising out of motor vehicle accidents. [tit. 15, § 61; *Greenwood V. Richard*, 300 A.2d 637 (Vt. 1973)]

**CHILD ABUSE:** The act protects children whose health and welfare may be adversely affected through abuse or neglect. An abused or neglected child means a child whose physical or mental welfare is harmed or threatened by the acts or omissions of his or her parents or other people responsible for the child's welfare. (tit. 33, § 681)

> *Notification Requirement:* All health care professionals, dentists, psychologists, school personnel, day care workers, mental health professionals, social workers, probation officers, police officers and any other persons must report child abuse to the Commissioner of Social and Rehabilitation Services. Any person who violates this shall be fined not more than $500. (tit. 33, §§ 683, 684)

# INHERITANCE RIGHTS

**FAILURE TO MAKE A WILL:** The surviving spouse is entitled to the entire estate if decedent left no heirs; to $25,000 and one-half of the balance if decedent left heirs but no children or grandchildren; to one-half or one-third of the real property and at least one-third of decedent's personal property if decedent left a child or grandchild. (tit. 14, §§ 551, 401)

**FAILURE TO PROVIDE BY WILL:** If the testator fails to provide by will for the surviving spouse the survivor is entitled to what would have been received if the testator had died without making a will. (tit. 14, § 551)

**CHILDREN BORN OUT OF WEDLOCK:** An illegitimate child shall inherit from or through the mother as if born in lawful wedlock. An illegitimate child shall inherit from or through the father as if born in lawful wedlock if the father has been declared the putative father of the child or if the father has openly and notoriously claimed the child to be his own. (tit. 14, § 553)

**HOMESTEAD, PERSONAL, AND FAMILY ALLOWANCES:** Surviving spouse is entitled to decedent's homestead; homestead consists of land and buildings worth not more than $30,000. (tit. 27, §§ 101, 105) If decedent left no will and no children or grandchildren, surviving spouse who resided with decedent until his or her death may be given all household goods, furnishings, and furniture belonging in and to decedent's household. (tit. 14, § 3403) The surviving spouse and/or minor children may be granted reasonable allowance for support out of the decedent's personal estate or the income from the decedent's real or personal property during settlement of the estate; if the estate is insolvent, support payments must not continue for more than 8 months. (tit. 14, § 404)

**OPTION TO DISREGARD THE WILL:** Surviving spouse may reject the will and take a one-half or one-third share in real property. (tit. 14, § 461)

# REPRODUCTIVE RIGHTS

## ABORTION

*Statutory Provisions:* Existing statute, tit. 13, § 101, which makes the performance of all abortions a crime punishable by imprisonment, was declared unconstitutional by both the Vermont Supreme Court in *Beecham V. Leahy*, 287 A.2d 836 (Vt. 1972) and the United States Supreme Court in *Roe V. Wade*, 410 U.S. 113 (1973).

**BIRTH CONTROL:** There is no relevant statutory provision.

**STERILIZATION:** There is no relevant statutory provision.

# UNMARRIED COUPLES

**COMMON-LAW MARRIAGE:** Common-law marriages are not valid. [*Stahl v. Stahl*, 385 A.2d 1091 (Vt. 1970)]

**COHABITAL RELATIONSHIPS:** In *Steward v. Waterman*, 123 A. 524 (Vt. 1924), the court held that where a woman knowingly and voluntarily lives in an illicit relationship with a man, she cannot recover on the basis of an express contract to pay for her services if the contract is made in contemplation of the illicit relationship; however, if the contract is not so made, the mere existence of the relationship does not make the contract illegal.

## CHILDREN

*Custody:* The mother of a child born out of wedlock is the guardian of such child until another is appointed. (tit. 14, § 2644)

*Legitimation Proceedings:* When the parents of a child born out of wedlock intermarry, the child is legitimated and becomes capable of inheriting, if recognized by the father as his child. (tit. 14, § 554)

*Paternity Proceedings:* An action to establish parentage, in cases where parentage has not been previously determined either by an action or by adoption, may be brought by a child who has reached the age of majority; the personal representative of a minor child; a person alleged or alleging himself or herself to be the natural parent of a child or that person's personal representative if the child is a minor, incompetent, or has died; or the Department of Social Welfare chargeable with the support of the child at the time the action is commenced. An action to establish parentage may be brought at any time after birth, but no later than 3 years after the child reaches majority. (tit. 15, § 302)

*Obligations of the Putative Father:* In an action to determine parentage, the court may include in its order provisions relating to the obligations of parentage, including future child support, visitation, and custody. (tit. 15, § 306)

# Education

## STATUTORY PROVISION

There is no relevant statutory provision. However, it should be noted that if federal funds are involved, federal law, Title IX of the Education Amendments of 1972, Pub. L. No. 92-318, 20 U.S.C. §§ 1681–1686, may apply.

# Employment

## EQUAL PAY LAWS

There is no relevant statutory provision. However, equal pay is required by the fair employment laws. [tit. 21, § 495(1)] In addition, tit. 21, § 495(e) provides for restitution of wages. It should also be noted that federal law, the Equal Pay Act of 1963, 29 U.S.C. §§ 201 *et seq.* may apply.

## FAIR EMPLOYMENT LAWS

The state of Vermont, its political and civil subdivisions, and all employers, labor organizations, and employment agencies are prohibited from discriminating in employment on the basis of sex. The exception to this prohibition is when discrimination occurs as a bona fide occupational qualification or bona fide seniority system or employee benefit plan exists. (tit. 21, § 495)

**ENFORCEMENT:** See "Fair Employment Laws." The attorney general or a state's attorney may enforce this provision by restraining prohibited acts, seeking civil penalties, obtaining assurances of discontinuance, and conducting civil investigations. A person aggrieved by a discriminatory practice may bring an action in superior court seeking damages or equitable relief, including restraint of the prohibited acts, restitution of wages, costs, reasonable attorney's fees, and other appropriate relief. (tit. 21, § 495b)

## GOVERNMENT CONTRACTORS AND SUBCONTRACTORS

The state of Vermont and all of its contracting agencies must agree to comply with the provisions of the fair employment laws. (tit. 21, § 495a)

**ENFORCEMENT:** See "Fair Employment Laws."

# STATE EMPLOYEE LAWS
State employees are covered under the fair employment laws. [tit. 21, § 459d(1)]

**ENFORCEMENT:** See "Fair Employment Laws."

# VETERAN'S PREFERENCE
Preference in state employment is given to veterans, particularly disabled veterans, and their wives, and unremarried widows, in appointment, employment, and retention. (tit. 20, § 1543)

# Community Life

# CREDIT
It is unlawful for a bank or financial institution to discriminate against an applicant for a loan, mortgage, or bank credit card on the basis of sex or marital status. (tit. 8, § 1211) Nothing in this section shall be taken to prohibit the establishment of separate credit card accounts for a husband and wife. [tit. 8, § 1302(3)]

**ENFORCEMENT:** Any person, partnership, association, or corporation or its officers or employees who are found to have engaged in discriminatory credit practices may be either fined not more that $1000 or imprisoned for not more than 1 year or both. [tit. 8, § 1306; tit. 9, § 50(c)]

# HOUSING
It is unlawful to discriminate in the sale, lease, or other transfer of title, occupancy, or possession of real estate on the basis of race, religious creed, color, or national origin. This law does not include sex as a protected characteristic, nor does it apply to the rental of housing in a two-family dwelling in which the owner or members of the owner's family resides or to the rental of not more than four rooms in a housing accommodation in which the owner or members of the owner's family resides. (tit. 13, § 1452)

**ENFORCEMENT:** A person aggrieved by a discriminatory act may file a written, verified charge with the Vermont Human Rights Commission within 6 months of the occurrence of the alleged discriminatory act. [tit. 13, §§ 1463(b) *et seq.*]

# INSURANCE
Discrimination is prohibited against an applicant or an insured on the basis of sex or marital status with regard to underwriting standards and practices, eligibility requirements, or rates. Discrimination is also prohibited between individuals of the same class and equal risk in rates charged for any contract of insurance, in the benefits payable under a contract, or in any other term or condition of a contract. [tit. 8, § 4724(7)]

**ENFORCEMENT:** The Commissioner of Banking and Insurance examines and investigates any person engaged in the business of insurance. Upon finding a violation, the commissioner may impose fines or either suspend or revoke the insurer's license. (tit. 8, § 4726)

# PUBLIC ACCOMMODATIONS

It is unlawful for any owner, operator, agent, or employee of a place of public accommodation to refuse, withhold from, or deny any person any of the accommodations, advantages, facilities, and privileges of a public accommodation on the basis of race, creed, color, national origin, or blindness. An owner or operator of a place of public accommodation shall not prohibit a blind or deaf person accompanied by a guide dog from entering the public accommodation. (tit. 13, § 1451)

**ENFORCEMENT:** See "Housing."

# VIRGINIA

## Home and Family

## MARRIAGE

**AGE OF CONSENT:** A person who is 18 years or older may consent to marry. (§ 20-49)*

**CONSENT REQUIREMENT:** Persons between the ages of 16 and 18 may marry with parental or guardian consent or, when parental or guardian consent cannot be obtained because the parties are orphans or have been abandoned, with the consent of the judge of the circuit court of the county or city where either party resides. (§ 20-49) In case of pregnancy, when either party is under 16 or where the woman has been pregnant within 9 months of having undergone a medical examination verifying the pregnancy, the clerk of the county where the female resides may issue a marriage license to the underage parties provided they obtain the consent of either a parent or guardian. (§ 20-43)

**LICENSE REQUIREMENT:** The license for a marriage shall be issued by the clerk of the circuit court of the county or city in which the either of the parties resides. (§ 20-14) The license is valid for 60 days from the date of issuance. (§ 20-14.1) Persons empowered to issue marriage licenses shall, at the time of issuing the license, provide the applicants with information concerning genetic disorders and a list of family planning clinics located in the county or city of the issuing office. (§ 20-14.2)

**PROHIBITED MARRIAGES:** Bigamous marriages are absolutely void. (§§ 20-38.1, -43) Marriages between an ancestor and a descendant, a brother and a sister, an uncle and a niece, or an aunt and a nephew, whether the relationship is by the half or the whole blood, are prohibited. (§ 20-38.1) Marriages between parties under the age of 18 contracted without the required consent and marriages in which one party lacks the capacity to consent to marriage because of mental infirmity are void. (§ 20-45.1) Marriages between persons of the same sex are also prohibited. (§ 20-45.2)

## DISSOLUTION OF MARRIAGE

**ANNULMENT:** Factors 3, 10, 15 (before the marriage and without the knowledge of the other party), 19, 33, 35, 36, and 38, as listed in Appendix A, are grounds for annulment. Also, if either party had been a prostitute before the marriage and without the knowledge of the other, or if the man fathered a child born to a woman other than his wife within 10 months after the solemnization of the marriage, the marriage may be annulled. (§ 20-89.1)

>*Residency Requirement:* One of the parties must be domiciled in or have been an actual bona fide resident of the state for at least 6 months preceding the commencement of the suit. (§ 20-97)

**LEGAL SEPARATION:** A legal separation may be granted on the grounds of cruelty, reasonable apprehension of bodily injury, willful desertion, or abandonment. (§ 20-95)

*Unless otherwise specified, all references are to the Code of Virginia (1950).

*Residency Requirement:* See "Annulment."

# DIVORCE

*Residency Requirement:* See "Annulment."

*Grounds for Divorce:* Factors 4 (including homosexual acts), 5, 6 (with 15), 16, and 31 (1 year), listed in Appendix A, and where the parties have entered into a separation agreement, there are no minor children and they have lived separate and apart without cohabitation and continuously for 6 months. (§ 20-91)

*Conciliation Requirement:* There is no relevant statutory provision.

*Property Distribution:* Upon decreeing the dissolution of a marriage, the court may equitably divide marital property only and may make a lump sum or periodic monetary award to adjust the equities. The court shall have no authority to order the conveyance of separate property or marital property not titled in the names of both parties; however, in the final decree of divorce, it may partition marital property which is titled in the names of both parties or retain jurisdiction for the purpose of such partition. The party against whom a monetary award is made may satisfy the award, in whole or in part, by conveyance of property, subject to the approval of the court. The court may also direct payment of a percentage of pension, profit sharing or retirement benefits, whether vested or nonvested, payable in a lump sum or over a period of time and only as such benefits are payable. The court shall determine the amount of the monetary award without regard to maintenance and support awarded for either party or support for the minor children of both parties and shall, after or at the time of such determination and upon motion of either party, consider whether an order for support and maintenance of a spouse or children shall be entered or, if previously entered, whether such order shall be modified or vacated. Factors 1, 5, 6, 12, 15, 17, 19, 22, and 28, listed in Appendix F, are considered by the court, as well as the character of all marital property and contributions of each party to the well-being of the family. (§ 20-107.3)

*Child Custody:* In awarding custody of the children, the court shall give primary consideration to their welfare and, as between the parents, shall make no presumption or inference of law in favor of either. The court shall consider factors 2, 3, 7, 12, 13, 16, and 23, listed in Appendix B, and the age of each parent and the role played and to be played by each in the care of the child. The court shall also make a decree concerning visitation rights of the noncustodial parent and of grandparents, stepparents, or other family members. (§ 20-107.2)

*Child Support:* In determining the amount of child support to be awarded the court shall consider factors 1, 3, 4, 9, 12, and 25, listed in Appendix D, as well as the division of marital property, the contributions of the parties to the family's well-being, and the education of the parents and their ability to secure education and training. [§ 20-107.2(2)]

*Spousal Support/Alimony:* Upon the dissolution of a marriage, the court, in its discretion, may decree that maintenance and support of a spouse be made in periodic payments, in a lump sum award, or both. Factors 2, 3, 4, 6, 8, 9, 10, 11, 12, 13, 14, and 19, listed in Appendix E, and the property interests of the parties are considered. The parties may stipulate that maintenance and support awards shall cease upon the death or remarriage of the recipient spouse. Permanent maintenance and support will not be awarded to a spouse divorced on the grounds of adultery, conviction of a felony, cruelty, reasonable apprehension of bodily injury, willful desertion, or abandonment. (§§ 20-95, -107.1)

*Enforcement of Support Orders:* As part of its order directing a person to pay child or spousal support, a court may order that person's employer to deduct from his or her earnings any amount of current support due and an amount to be applied to arrearages, if any. (§§ 20-79.1, 63.250-3) A support order may also require the giving of a recognizance, with or without surety, in order to assure compliance with its provisions. (§ 20-11.4) If the party refuses to give the recognizance or upon conviction of the party for contempt of court in failing to comply with the court's order, the court may commit the party to a state correctional institution, work house, city farm or work squad, or the state convict road force at hard labor for a period not exceeding 12 months. Also, when a person owing a duty of support fails to provide court-ordered child or spousal support, upon the petition of the party owed support the court may transfer the matter to the juvenile and domestic relations district court for enforcement. [§ 20-79(c)] Unemployment compensation and state income tax refunds may be intercepted as a means of enforcing support obligations. (§§ 58.1-20 *et seq.*, 60.1-52.6) The Department of Social Services is authorized to enforce support obligations. (§ 63.1-287) See also the Revised Uniform Reciprocal Enforcement of Support Act of 1968, §§ 20-88.12 *et seq*.

*Spouse's Name:* Upon decreeing a divorce the court shall, on motion of a party who changed his or her name by reason of the marriage, restore such party's former name. (§ 20-121.4)

*Divorce by Affidavit or Summary Judgment:* There is no relevant statutory provision.

*Displaced Homemaker Laws:* There is no relevant statutory provision.

# DOMESTIC VIOLENCE

**STATUTORY PROVISION:** Any act of violence, including forceful detention, which results in a physical injury and which is committed by a person against another person to whom such a person is married or has been married is prohibited. (§ 63.1-316)

**WHO IS PROTECTED?** The statute extends its protection to spouses and former spouses. (§ 63.1-316)

**RELIEF AVAILABLE:** The statute does not contain any provisions for relief. However, it is presumed that in the absence of specific relief within the statute, a battered spouse could resort to relief provided for analogous crimes under criminal law. Virginia has designated the Department of Welfare as the state agency responsible for funding domestic abuse shelters, and for providing 24-hour crisis intervention hotlines, self-help groups, and counseling services to combat spouse abuse. (§§ 63.1-315 *et seq.*)

**MARITAL RAPE:** In *Weishaupt v. Commonwealth*, 315 S.E.2d 847 (Va. 1984), the court held that a wife can unilaterally revoke her implied consent to marital sex where she has made manifest her intent to terminate the marital relationship by living separate and apart from her husband, refraining from voluntary sexual intercourse with him, and, in light of all the circumstances, conducting herself in a manner that establishes a *de facto* end to the marriage. And, once the implied consent is revoked, even though the parties have not divorced, the husband can be found guilty of raping his wife. (§ 18.2-61)

**CIVIL LAWSUIT FOR RAPE OR ASSAULT:** In *Smith v. Kauffman*, 133 S.E.2d 190 (Va. 1971), the court held that spouses may not sue each other for personal injuries.

**CHILD ABUSE:** Creating, inflicting, or allowing the infliction of physical or mental injury upon a child under 18 by other than accidental means, neglecting or refusing to provide necessary care, abandoning a child, or committing or allowing to be committed any act of sexual exploitation or any sexual act upon a child by a parent or person responsible for the care of such child is prohibited. (§ 63.1-248.2)

*Notification Requirement:* All persons and all health care professionals, social workers, probation officers, teachers, school personnel, child care providers, hospital personnel, and police officers must report all suspected cases of child abuse to the local department of public welfare or social services. The department must immediately investigate these reports and petition the court for removal of a child from its home if deemed necessary. A doctor, protective service worker of the local department, or the police may take a child into custody for 72 hours without a court order if the child's life or health is in imminent danger and a court order is not immediately obtainable. (§§ 63.1-248.1 *et seq.*)

# INHERITANCE RIGHTS

**FAILURE TO MAKE A WILL:** The surviving spouse is entitled to the decedent's entire real and personal estate if the decedent left no children or grandchildren; to his or her dower share in real property and a one-third share of the decedent's personal estate if the decedent left children or grandchildren. (§§ 64.1-1, -11)

**FAILURE TO PROVIDE BY WILL:** The surviving spouse is entitled to one-third of all the lands owned by the deceased spouse during the marriage. (§§ 64.1-19, -19.1)

**CHILDREN BORN OUT OF WEDLOCK:** A child born out of wedlock is the child of the mother and can inherit from her and her kin. The child is a child of the father and can inherit from him and his kin if the parents intermarried or paternity has been established. Paternity is established if the father cohabited with the mother during all the 10 months immediately before the child was born; or he is named the father in the child's birth certificate; or he allowed the child to use his surname; or he claimed the child as his on a tax return or other document filed and signed with any federal, state, or local agency; or he admitted in open court that he was the child's father; or he voluntarily admitted paternity in a signed writing, under oath. However, when paternity is established pursuant to the above, the father and his kin may not inherit from or through the child unless he has openly treated the child as his and had not refused to support the child. No claim of succession based upon the relationship between a child born out of wedlock and a parent of such a child will be recognized in the settlement of any decedent's estate, unless an affidavit by such child or by someone acting for such child, alleging such parenthood, has been filed within 1 year of the date of the death of the parent in the clerk's office of the circuit court of the jurisdiction wherein the property affected by such claim is located and an action seeking adjudication of parenthood is also filed. (§§ 64.1-5.1, -5.2)

**HOMESTEAD, PERSONAL, AND FAMILY ALLOWANCES:** The surviving spouse may remain in the decedent's mansion house rent-free until dower is assigned. (§ 64.1-33) The survivor is also entitled to claim the decedent's homestead exemption in land up to $5000 until he or she dies or remarries. A surviving spouse who takes the dower share will lose the homestead exemption. (§§ 34-4, -10, -12) The surviving spouse and minor children are also entitled to the family Bible, wedding and engagement rings, family pictures, family library, burial lot, clothing, furniture, pets, utensils, appliances, tools, and provisions. (§§ 64.1-127, 34-26)

**OPTION TO DISREGARD THE WILL:** The surviving spouse may reject the will and take his or her dower share of the real property plus one-half of the personal estate if the decedent left no children or grandchildren or one-third the personal estate if the decedent left children or grandchildren. (§§ 64.1-13, -16, -19, -29)

# REPRODUCTIVE RIGHTS
## ABORTION
*Statutory Provisions:* All abortions must be performed by physicians licensed by the Virginia State Board of Medicine. (§ 18.2-72) Second-trimester abortions must be performed in licensed hospitals. [§ 18.2-73; *Simopoulos v. Virginia*, 103 S. Ct. 2532 (1983)] Abortions in the third trimester can be performed only if the performing physician and two consulting physicians certify and enter in the woman's medical record that, in their medical opinion and based upon their best clinical judgment, the continuation of the pregnancy is likely to result in the death of the woman or substantially and irremediably impair her mental or physical health. Measures for life support for the aborted fetus must be available and utilized if there is any clearly visible evidence of its viability. (§ 18.2-74) No medical facility, employee, or physician is required to assist in or perform abortions. (§ 18.2-75)

*Consent Requirement:* The physician must obtain the woman's informed consent prior to performing an abortion. If the woman is an adjudicated incompetent, the physician must obtain the permission, in writing, of her parent, guardian, or committee. (§ 18.2-76)

*Reporting Requirements:* All fetal deaths occurring as a result of abortions must be reported to the Registrar of Vital Records within 3 days of the performance of the abortion. (§ 32.1-264)

*State Funding:* The Board of Health is authorized to fund abortions for women who otherwise meet the financial eligibility criteria of the state medical assistance plan only in cases where a physician who is trained and qualified to perform such tests certifies in writing, after appropriate tests have been performed, that he or she believes the fetus will be born with a gross and totally incapacitating physical or mental deformity. (§ 32.1-92.2)

**BIRTH CONTROL:** The Board of Mental Health and Retardation must establish family planning clinics in state hospitals to advise, counsel, and educate patients regarding birth control. Each hospital must conduct a minimum of one family planning session every 3 months. Attendance is voluntary. (§ 37.1-23.1) A person who issues a marriage license must distribute to the applicant birth control information and a list of family planning clinics located in the city or the county of the issuing office. (§ 20-14.2) The Department of Corrections must also distribute birth control information and a list of family planning clinics to an inmate before his or her release from prison. (§ 53-94.1)

**STERILIZATION:** When the request is made in writing, a licensed physician may sterilize any person over 18 years old who has the capacity to give informed consent. A full, reasonable, and comprehensive explanation as to the consequences of such an operation and to alternative methods of contraception must be given by the physician to the person requesting the operation. For persons who have not previously become natural or adoptive parents, there is a 30-day waiting period from the date of the written request. (§ 54-325.9)

# UNMARRIED COUPLES
**COMMON-LAW MARRIAGE:** Common-law marriage is not valid in Virginia. (§ 20-13)

**COHABITAL RELATIONSHIPS:** In *Cord v. Gibb*, 254 S.E.2d 71 (Va. 1979), the court held that a woman could not be denied the right to take the state bar examination because she cohabited with a man to whom she was not married. Moreover, the United States District Court for the Eastern District of Virginia recently declared unconstitutional, as a deprivation of the right of privacy, a Virginia statute which made it a crime for unmarried persons to cohabit. [*Doe v. Duling*, 603 F. Supp. 960 (E.D.Va. 1985)] The invalidation of this statute should henceforth enable former cohabitants to come forward and assert their rights to divide property which they acquired during the period of their cohabitation.

## CHILDREN
*Custody:* There is no relevant statutory provision.
*Legitimation Proceedings:* A child born out of wedlock is legitimated if the parents marry each other after the child's birth. (§ 20-31.1)
*Paternity Proceedings:* Paternity is established if the father cohabited with the mother during all the 10 months immediately before the child was born; if he is named the father in the child's birth certificate; if he allowed the child to use his surname; if he claimed the child as his on a tax return or other document filed and signed with any federal, state or local agency; or he admitted in open court that he was the child's father; or if he voluntarily admitted paternity in a signed writing, under oath. (§ 64.1-5.1) As part of a paternity proceeding, the court may order the parties to submit to blood tests and the results will be admitted in evidence. (§ 20-61.2)
*Obligations of the Putative Father:* Whenever a man admits before a court that he is the father of a child or the court finds the man has voluntarily admitted paternity in writing or is shown by other evidence beyond a reasonable doubt to be the father, the court may enter and enforce a judgment for the support, maintenance, and education of the child as if he or she were born in wedlock. (§ 20-61.1)

# Education

## STATUTORY PROVISION

There is no relevant statutory provision. However, the Virginia Constitution prohibits governmental discrimination on the basis of sex. (Va. Const. art 1, § 11) This prohibition applies to the educational system. Also, it should be noted that if federal funds are involved, federal law, Title IX of the Education Amendments of 1972, Pub. L. No. 92-318, 20 U.S.C. §§ 1681–1686, may apply.

# Employment

## EQUAL PAY LAWS

It is unlawful for an employer to discriminate on the basis of sex in wages paid to employees in the same establishment who perform work requiring equal skill, effort, and responsibility under similar working conditions. Wage differentials are not prohibited, however, if based on a seniority or merit system, quantity or quality of production, or any factor other than sex. (§ 40.1-28.6)

**ENFORCEMENT:** An employee whose wages have been unlawfully withheld may bring a civil action to recover damages to the extent of two times the amount of the wages withheld. The action must be brought within 2 years of the occurrence of the violation. (§ 40.1-28.6)

# FAIR EMPLOYMENT LAWS

There is no relevant statutory provision. However, an employer with fifteen or more employees is subject to the federal antidiscrimination law, Title VII of the Civil Rights Act of 1964, 42 U.S.C. §§ 2000e *et seq*.

# GOVERNMENT CONTRACTORS AND SUBCONTRACTORS

Any employer who contracts to provide goods and services to the state must agree not to discriminate on the basis of sex if the contract is over $10,000. However, sex may be a bona fide occupational qualification. (§ 2.1-376)

**ENFORCEMENT:** There is no relevant statutory provision. However, if federal funds are involved, federal law, Exec. Order No. 11246, 3 C.F.R. 339 (1965), *reprinted in* 42 U.S.C. § 2000e, app. at 1232, 41 C.F.R. § 60-1.2, may apply.

# STATE EMPLOYEE LAWS

The state and its political and civil subdivisions are subject to the federal antidiscrimination law, Title VII of the Civil Rights Act of 1964, 42 U.S.C. §§ 2000e *et seq*., where fifteen or more persons are employed. The legislature has declared a policy of nondiscrimination in employment for the state and its agencies but has not enacted any provisions to enforce the policy. (§§ 2.1-116.10 *et seq*.) Moreover, Exec. Order No. 1-82 (January 1, 1982) requires that state appointing officials take affirmative steps that emphasize the recruitment of qualified women, minorities, the handicapped, and older workers.

# VETERAN'S PREFERENCE

In competitive examinations a 5 percent bonus is added to the passing scores of veterans, and a 10 percent bonus is added to the passing scores of disabled veterans. (§ 2.1-112)

# Community Life

# CREDIT

It is unlawful for any creditor to discriminate against any applicant with respect to any aspect of a credit transaction on the basis of sex or marital status, or because all or part of the applicant's income derives from any public assistance. [§ 59.1-21.21:1(a)]

**ENFORCEMENT:** A person alleging discrimination in credit may bring a civil action in any court of competent jurisdiction within 2 years of the occurrence of the alleged discriminatory act for the recovery of actual damages, costs of the action, and reasonable attorney's fees. The court may also grant such equitable and declaratory relief as is necessary to enforce the statute and may also award punitive damages of up to $10,000. (§ 59.1-21.23)

# HOUSING

It is unlawful for any person having the right to sell, lease, rent, negotiate for sale or rental, or otherwise make unavailable or deny a dwelling; to discriminate in the terms, conditions, or privileges of a real estate transaction; or to represent that any dwelling is not available for inspection, sale, or rental when it is available on the basis of sex or parenthood. These provisions do not apply to the sale or rental of a single-family dwelling by the owner if a real estate broker or salesperson is not used or if discriminatory advertising is not employed; to the rental of housing in a four-family dwelling in which the owner resides; to private clubs; or to single-sex residences in educational institutions, hospitals, nursing homes, or religious or correctional institutions. (§§ 36-87 to -93) It is unlawful for any bank, savings and loan association, credit union, insurance company, or other person regularly engaged in the business of making mortgages or other loans for the purchase, construction, improvement, repair, or maintenance of dwellings to deny a loan or to discriminate in the fixing of the down payment, interest rate, duration, or other terms or conditions of a loan on the basis of sex. [§ 36-90(a)]

**ENFORCEMENT:** The Virginia Real Estate Commission has the power to receive complaints and conduct investigations of any violation provided a complaint is filed with the commission within 180 days after the alleged discriminatory housing practice occurred. A person adversely affected by a discriminatory practice may institute an action for injunctive relief and money damages against the person responsible for such discriminatory practice in the circuit court of the county or city where the practice occurred. The court may award a prevailing plaintiff court costs and reasonable attorney's fees, in addition to actual damages suffered. (§ 36-94)

# INSURANCE

Discrimination is prohibited between individuals of the same class and equal expectation of life in rates charged for life insurance or annuity contracts or between individuals of the same class and essentially the same hazard in the amount of premium, policy fees, or rates charged for accident or health insurance; in the benefits payable under these contracts; or in any other term or condition of these contracts. (§ 38.1-52.7)

**ENFORCEMENT:** The state Corporation Commission examines and investigates the affairs of all persons engaged in the business of insurance. Upon receiving a complaint alleging a discriminatory practice, the commission holds a hearing on the complaint. If the charges are found to be true, the commission may issue a cease and desist order, impose fines, or suspend or revoke the insurer's license. (§§ 38.1-53 to -55)

# PUBLIC ACCOMMODATIONS

There is no relevant statutory provision.

# WASHINGTON

## Home and Family

## MARRIAGE

**AGE OF CONSENT:** A person 18 years of age or older may consent to marry. Upon a showing of necessity, this age requirement may be waived by a superior court judge of the county in which one of the parties resides. (§ 26.04.010)*

**CONSENT REQUIREMENT:** Persons 17 years of age may marry with written parental or guardian consent, in the form of an affidavit sworn to and subscribed before a person authorized to administer oaths. (§ 26.04.210)

**LICENSE REQUIREMENT:** Persons wishing to marry must obtain a license from the county auditor of the county where they intend to marry. (§§ 26.04.140, .150) Before issuing the license, the county auditor will require the applicants to make and file an affidavit showing that they are not afflicted with any contagious venereal disease. (§ 26.04.210)

**PROHIBITED MARRIAGES:** Marriages between persons under 17 years of age are void. (§ 26.04.010) Bigamous marriages and marriages between parties closer than second cousins, whether of the whole or half blood, are prohibited. Marriages between a man and his father's sister, mother's sister, daughter, sister, son's daughter, daughter's daughter, brother's daughter or sister's daughter and marriages between a woman and her father's mother, mother's brother, son, brother, son's son, daughter's son, brother's son, or sister's son are prohibited. (§ 26.04.020) Children of void marriages are legitimate. [§ 26.09.040(5)]

## DISSOLUTION OF MARRIAGE

**ANNULMENT:** The grounds for annulment include factors 19, 35, 36, and 38, listed in Appendix A, and failure to ratify the marriage by voluntary cohabitation after attaining the age or capacity to consent or after cessation or discovery of force or duress. [§ 26.09.040(4)]

*Residency Requirement:* At least one of the parties must be a resident of the state or a member of the armed forces stationed in the state. [§ 26.09.040(1)]

**LEGAL SEPARATION:** If the marriage is irretrievably broken, the parties may file for a legal separation. (§ 26.09.030)

*Residency Requirement:* A party who is a resident of the state or is a member of the armed forces stationed in the state may petition the court for a legal separation. Ninety days must have elapsed since the petition was filed and from the date when service of summons was made before the court will act on the petition. (§ 26.09.030)

### DIVORCE

*Residency Requirement:* See "Legal Separation."

*Grounds for Divorce:* If the marriage is irretrievably broken, the parties may file for divorce. (§ 26.09.030)

---

*Unless otherwise specified, all reference citations are to the Revised Code of Washington Annotated (1961).

*Conciliation Requirement:* The court, at the request of either party or on its own motion, may transfer the case to family court, refer the parties to a counseling service of their choice and request a report from the counseling service within 60 days of the referral, or continue the matter for not more than 60 days for a hearing. [§ 26.09.030(3)(b)]

*Property Distribution:* In a proceeding for dissolution of a marriage, legal separation or annulment, the court will, without regard to marital misconduct, make such disposition of the property and the liabilities of the parties, either community or separate, in a just and equitable manner after considering factors 2, 3, 5, and 25, listed in Appendix F, the nature and extent of the community property and the desirability of awarding the family home and the right of occupancy for reasonable periods to the custodial parent. (§ 26.09.080)

*Child Custody:* The court shall determine custody in accordance with the best interests of the child and factors 5, 10, 11, 12, 14, and 15, listed in Appendix B. (§ 26.09.190)

*Child Support:* In a proceeding for dissolution of a marriage, legal separation, annulment, maintenance or child support, after considering all relevant factors, but without regard to marital misconduct, the court may order either or both parents owing a duty of support to any child of the marriage dependent upon either or both spouses to pay an amount reasonable or necessary for the child's support. (§ 26.09.100)

*Spousal Support/Alimony:* The court may award maintenance to either spouse without regard to marital misconduct. Factors 2, 3, 4, 5, 6, 9, 13, 14, and 18, listed in Appendix E, are considered. (§ 26.09.090)

*Enforcement of Support Orders:* In order to ensure compliance with its support order, the court may require that support payments be made to either the clerk of the court or to the Department of Social and Health Services. (§ 26.09.120) Or the court may order the party owing the support to assign part of his or her periodic earnings or trust income to the person or agency entitled to receive the support. (§ 26.09.130) Child support obligations are payable from unemployment compensation when a party applying for such discloses that he or she owes such support. (§ 50.40.050) Every court order establishing a child support obligation must state that if a support payment is more than 15 days past due, and the amount is equal to or greater than the support payable for 1 month, the person owed the support may seek a mandatory wage assignment without giving prior notice to the delinquent party. (§§ 26.09.140, .18.060) The court may also, in its discretion and as part of a support order, require the person obligated to pay support for a minor child to post a bond or other security with the court in an amount equal to the support due for a 2-year period. (§ 26.18.150) A person's homestead is subject to execution or forced sale to satisfy a court order establishing child support or spousal maintenance obligations. (§ 6.12.100) In addition, contempt and any other civil or criminal enforcement proceedings are available to enforce support orders. (§§ 26.18.025, .050) Costs and attorney's fees may be awarded a party for maintaining or defending a proceeding to enforce support obligations. (§ 26.09. 140) A party entitled to support who so desires, may request the Department of Social and Health Services to enforce support obligations. The fee for this service, is chargeable to the party owing the support. (§ 74.20.040) See also the Revised Uniform Reciprocal Enforcement of Support Act of 1968, §§ 26.21.010 *et seq.*

*Spouse's Name:* When a marriage is dissolved or declared invalid, if either party so requests, the court shall order the wife to assume her former name, for just and reasonable cause. (§ 26.09.150)

*Divorce by Affidavit or Summary Judgment:* There is no relevant statutory provision.

*Displaced Homemaker Laws:* Effective January 6, 1986, the council for post-secondary education has been authorized to contract with public or private nonprofit organizations to establish multipurpose service centers for the benefit of displaced homemakers. The centers are to provide job counseling and health counseling, including referral to existing health programs; financial management and educational services; legal counseling and referral; outreach and information services with respect to federal and state employment; education; and public assistance and unemployment assistance which the council determines would be of interest and benefit to displaced homemakers. (§§ 28B.04.020 *et seq.*)

# DOMESTIC VIOLENCE

**STATUTORY PROVISION:** It is prohibited to inflict or threaten to inflict physical harm or bodily injury or to assault, family or household members. Sexual assault of one family or household member by another is also prohibited. (§ 26.50.010)

**WHO IS PROTECTED?** Spouses, former spouses, adult persons related by blood or marriage, cohabitants, former cohabitants, and persons who have a child in common, regardless of whether they have been married or have lived together at any time, are protected. (§ 26.50.010)

**RELIEF AVAILABLE:** A victim of domestic violence may petition the court for an order of protection which will provide that the abuser refrain from committing further acts of violence and exclude the abuser from the residence; award temporary custody of minor children and establish temporary visitation rights; order the abuser to participate in counseling or obtain necessary treatment; and determine any other necessary relief. (§§ 26.50.030, .050) An *ex parte* temporary order of protection may also be sought by a victim of domestic violence where the petition alleges that irreparable injury could result from domestic violence. (§ 26.50.070) Additionally, victims of domestic violence have recourse to the criminal domestic violence statute which protects family and household members from assault, reckless endangerment, coercion, burglary, criminal trespass, malicious mischief, kidnapping, unlawful imprisonment, rape, and the violation of the provisions of a protective order. (§ 10.99.020) The Department of Social and Health Services has been authorized by the legislature to contract with nonprofit groups with experience and expertise in the field of domestic violence to establish, fund, and evaluate shelters for the use of the victims of domestic violence. (§§ 70.123.010 *et seq.*)

**MARITAL RAPE:** A woman may charge her husband with rape in the first and second degree, but not in the third degree. (§§ 9A.44.040, .050, .060)

**CIVIL LAWSUIT FOR RAPE OR ASSAULT:** In *Freehe v. Freehe*, 500 P.2d 771 (Wash. 1972), the court held that spouses may sue each other for torts.

**CHILD ABUSE:** Injury to, sexual abuse or sexual exploitation of, or negligent treatment or maltreatment of a child by any person under circumstances which indicate that the child's health, welfare, and safety is harmed is prohibited. [§ 26.44.020(12)]

*Notification Requirement:* Health care professionals, school personnel, social workers, pharmacists, employees of the Department of Social and Health Services, and all other persons must report all suspected cases of child abuse to the Department of Social and Health Services or the police. (§§ 26.44.030 *et seq.*)

# INHERITANCE RIGHTS

**FAILURE TO MAKE A WILL:** The surviving spouse is entitled to all the decedent's share of the net community estate. The survivor is also entitled to one-half of the net separate estate if the decedent left children or grandchildren or to three-fourths of the net separate estate if there is no surviving issue but the decedent is survived by his or her parents or siblings. The surviving spouse is entitled to the entire separate estate if the decedent left no other heirs. (§ 11.04.015)

**FAILURE TO PROVIDE BY WILL:** Upon the death of a spouse, the surviving spouse is entitled to a one-half share of the parties' community property, and the other half is subject to testamentary disposition by the decedent. (§ 11.02.070)

**CHILDREN BORN OUT OF WEDLOCK:** Illegitimacy does not affect the right to inherit by, from, or through any person once the father and child relationship has been established. (§ 11.04.081) This relationship is established if, after the child's birth, the parents marry or attempt to marry and the marriage is later declared void, and the father has acknowledged his paternity in a writing filed with the registrar of vital statistics; or, with his consent, he is named as the child's father on the child's birth certificate, or he is obligated to support the child under a written voluntary promise or by court order; or, while the child is still a minor he receives the child in his home and openly holds out the child as his own; or he acknowledges his paternity in a writing filed with the registrar of vital statistics who shall promptly inform the mother of the filing of the acknowledgment and the mother does not dispute the father's paternity within a reasonable time thereafter. (§ 26.26.040)

**HOMESTEAD, PERSONAL, AND FAMILY ALLOWANCES:** The surviving spouse is entitled to a homestead worth up to $25,000, either out of the community or separate property. (§ 11.52.010) In addition to the homestead, the court may award to the surviving spouse a reasonable amount of cash out of the estate as may be necessary for the maintenance of the family according to their circumstances, during the settlement of the estate. The allowance has preference over all estate debts except funeral charges, expenses of last illness and expenses of administering the estate. (§ 11.52.040)

**OPTION TO DISREGARD THE WILL:** A surviving spouse may disclaim or renounce, in whole or in part, any interest passing to him or her under the deceased spouse's will by means of a written community property agreement entered into prior to the decedent's death. [§ 11.86.020; *Norris v. Norris*, 605 P.2d 1296 (Wash. 1980)]

# REPRODUCTIVE RIGHTS

## ABORTION

*Statutory Provisions:* Abortions can be performed only by licensed physicians. (§ 9.02.060) First-trimester abortions must be performed in a hospital accredited by the state. There is a 90-day residency requirement before an abortion can be performed in the state. (§ 9.02.070) These requirements have been rendered unconstitutional by the United States Supreme Court. No hospital, physician, or hospital employee may be required to perform or participate in abortions. (§ 9.02.080)

*Consent Requirements:* The woman's prior consent and, if married and residing with her husband or unmarried and under 18, the prior consent of her husband or legal guardian is required. These requirements have been rendered unconstitutional by the United States Supreme Court.

*State Funding:* The state is not required to fund medically necessary abortions for which reimbursement is no longer available. [*Harris v. McRae*, 448 U.S. 297 (1980)]

**BIRTH CONTROL:** Medical assistance to eligible medicaid recipients may include physician's service, which shall include prescribed medication and instruction on birth control devices. (§ 74.09.520)

**STERILIZATION:** There is no relevant statutory provision.

# UNMARRIED COUPLES

**COMMON-LAW MARRIAGE:** Common-law marriages are not valid. (§ 26.04.070)

**COHABITAL RELATIONSHIPS:** In *Creassman v. Boyle*, 196 P.2d 835 (Wash. 1948), the court stated that property acquired by a man and a woman not married to each other, but cohabiting as husband and wife, is not community property, and, in the absence of a trust relation, belongs to the one in whose name legal title rests. However, later decisions have employed theories of implied partnership and constructive trusts in order to permit cohabitants of long-term, stable, nonmarital relationships to divide the property which they acquired during the course of their cohabitation. [*In re Estate of Thornton*, 499 P.2d 864 (Wash. 1972); *Omer v. Omer*, 523 P.2d 957 (Wash. 1974)]

**CHILDREN**

*Custody:* The judgment and order of the court determining the existence or nonexistence of the parent-child relationship will provide for custody, guardianship of, and visitation privileges with the child in accordance with its best interests. (§ 26.26.130)

*Legitimation Proceedings:* A child born out of wedlock is legitimated once the father-child relationship has been established. This relationship is established if after the child's birth, the parents marry or attempt to marry and the marriage is later declared void; the father has acknowledged his paternity in writing filed with the registrar of vital statistics; with his consent, he is named as the child's father on the child's birth certificate; he is obligated to support the child under a written voluntary promise or by court order; while the child is still under the age of majority, he receives it into his home and openly holds out the child as his own; or he acknowledges his paternity in a writing filed with the registrar of vital statistics who shall promptly inform the mother of the filing of the acknowledgment and the mother does not dispute the father's paternity within a reasonable time thereafter. (§ 26.26.040)

*Paternity Proceedings:* A paternity action may be brought by the mother, the child, the alleged father, the state, or any interested party at any time. Within a reasonable time, a man presumed to be the father may bring an action to establish he is not the father. (§ 26.26.060) The court may require the parties to submit to blood tests. (§ 26.26.100)

*Obligations of the Putative Father:* Once paternity is established, the court may make an order concerning current, future, and past support, custody of the child, and visitation privileges. The court may limit the father's liability for past support to the proportion of expenses already incurred, provided that the court does not limit the right of nonparties (such as the state) to seek reimbursement for support furnished. The judgment may order the father to pay the reasonable expenses of the mother's pregnancy and confinement. (§ 26.26.130) The court may not order payment for support provided or expenses incurred more than 5 years before the suit was brought. This 5-year period shall not include any time during which the father had concealed himself or avoided the jurisdiction of the court. (§ 26.26.134)

# Education

## STATUTORY PROVISION

The Washington Constitution contains an equal rights amendment which has been held to create a fundamental right to public school education free from sex discrimination. [Wash. Const. art 31, § 1; *Darrin v. Gould*, 540 P.2d 882 (Wash. Sup. Ct. 1975)] The state constitution also requires that all children be provided an education without distinction or preference on account of sex. (Wash. Const. art 9, § 1) Sex discrimination in public elementary and secondary schools is prohibited, including discrimination in access to classes (except sex education and gym classes which can be sex segregated), counseling and guidance services, recreational and athletic activities, and textbook and instructional materials. (§§ 28A.85.010, .020)

## AREAS COVERED

Areas covered include employment of public school personnel and athletics. (§§ 28A.85.020, .58.125, 28B.50.020) The rule prohibiting girls from playing on boys' football teams was held to be unconstitutional under the state equal rights amendment. See *Darrin v. Gould*. The Office of the Superintendent of Public School Instruction must develop regulations and guidelines to eliminate sex discrimination in textbooks and instructional materials. (§ 28A.85.020)

**ENFORCEMENT:** The Office of the Superintendent of Public School Instruction is required to monitor, enforce, and obtain compliance with the statutory provisions. Furthermore any aggrieved person has a right of action in superior court for civil damages. (§§ 28A.85.030, .040, .050)

# Employment

## EQUAL PAY LAWS

It is unlawful for an employer to discriminate in the payment of wages between sexes or to pay any female less than is paid to males similarly employed. (§ 49.12.175)

**ENFORCEMENT:** A person alleging unlawful discrimination may file a complaint with the State Human Rights Commission within 6 months after the alleged discrimination. (§ 49.60.230)

## FAIR EMPLOYMENT LAWS

The law applies to the state of Washington, its political and civil subdivisions, employers of eight or more employees, labor organizations and employment agencies. (§ 49.60.040) It prohibits discriminating in hire, discharge, compensation, terms, or conditions of employment; expelling or excluding an individual from membership in a labor organization; refusing to recruit or refer an individual for employment on account of the individuals' sex; or indicating a preference for a particular sex in employment advertisements. (§ 49.60.180) Exceptions to this provision are situations where sex is a bona fide occupational qualification, where an employer maintains sex-segregated washrooms and lockers, and where the employment of domestic servants is involved. [§§ 49.60.040, .180(1), .180(3)]

**ENFORCEMENT:** See "Equal Pay Laws."

## GOVERNMENT CONTRACTORS AND SUBCONTRACTORS

There is no relevant statutory provision. However, it should be noted that if such persons employ eight or more employees, they are subject to the Fair Employment Practices Law. In addition, if federal funds are involved, federal law, Exec. Order No. 11246, 3 C.F.R. 339 (1965), *reprinted in* 42 U.S.C. § 2000e app. at 1232, 41 C.F.R. § 60-1.2, may apply.

## STATE EMPLOYEE LAWS

State employees are covered under the Fair Employment Practices Law. Discrimination in public employment based on sex is further prohibited by executive order, issued August 2, 1966. Affirmative action in public employment for women and minorities is required by Exec. Order No. 79-08 (October 15, 1979). The state's comparable worth law, effective August 23, 1983, requires that salary changes be fully achieved not later than June 30, 1993. (§ 41.06.155)

**ENFORCEMENT:** See "Equal Pay Laws."

## VETERAN'S PREFERENCE

Veterans, their surviving spouses, and the wives of disabled veterans qualify for preference in public employment. (§ 73.16.010) Percentage bonuses are added to the passing scores achieved on competitive examinations, depending on the applicant's status regarding receipt of veteran's retirement payments. (§ 41.04.010) Veterans are also entitled to reemployment upon return from the service and to seniority and other accrued benefits. (§§ 73.16.033, .051)

# Community Life

## CREDIT

It is unlawful for any person in connection with any credit transaction to deny credit, to increase the charges, fees, or collateral required to secure credit, to restrict the amount or use of credit, or, with respect to the credit extended, to impose different terms or conditions on the basis of sex or marital status. It is also unlawful to use the sex or marital status of an applicant for credit to determine the credit worthiness of the applicant. (§§ 49.60.175, .176)

> **ENFORCEMENT:** Any person claiming to be aggrieved by an alleged unfair practice may, personally or by her or his attorney, file a verified complaint with the state Human Rights Commission within 6 months of the occurrence of the alleged discrimination. (§ 49.60.230)

# INSURANCE

It is unlawful for any person or entity engaged in the business of insurance to cancel, fail, or refuse to issue or renew a portion of insurance to any person on the basis of sex or marital status. It is also unlawful to restrict, modify, exclude, increase, or reduce the amount of benefits payable or any term, rate, condition, or type of coverage on the basis of sex or marital status. However, distinctions based on sex or marital status are permitted if substantiated by actuarial statistics. (§§ 48.30.300, 49.60.178)

> **ENFORCEMENT:** See "Credit."

# HOUSING

It is unlawful for any person to refuse to engage in or negotiate for a real estate transaction, to refuse to receive or transmit a bona fide offer, to discriminate in the terms, conditions, privileges, or furnishings or facilities or supplies in connection with a real estate transaction; to represent that real property is not available for inspection, sale, rental, or lease when it is available; or to expel a person from the occupancy of real estate on the basis of sex or marital status. It is also unlawful to discriminate in the course of negotiating, executing, or financing a real estate transaction or in negotiating or executing any item or service related to a real transaction, such as insurance, mortgage insurance, or loan guarantee. These provisions do not apply to limitations based on sex or marital or family status by educational institutions or dormitories, residence halls, or other student housing. (§ 49.60.222)

> **ENFORCEMENT:** See "Credit."

# PUBLIC ACCOMMODATIONS

It is unlawful for any person, directly or indirectly, to make any distinction, restriction, or discrimination; to require any person to pay a higher sum than the uniform rates charged other persons; or to refuse or withhold from any person the admission or patronage of any place of public resort, accommodation, assemblage, or amusement on the basis of sex. (§ 49.60.215)

> **ENFORCEMENT:** See "Credit."

# WEST VIRGINIA

## Home and Family

## MARRIAGE

**AGE OF CONSENT:** Persons 18 years or older may consent to marry. (§48-1-1)*

**CONSENT REQUIREMENT:** Persons under 18 may marry with the written consent of a parent or legal guardian having custody of the minor at the time the application for a marriage license is made. No person under the age of 16 may be issued a license except upon order of the circuit judge and with the consent of a parent or guardian. (§ 48-1-1)

**LICENSE REQUIREMENT:** Persons wishing to marry must obtain a license from the clerk of the county commission in which either party usually resides. Where both parties are nonresidents of the state, the license will be issued by the clerk of the county commission in which the application is made. Before any license is issued, each applicant must file a certificate from a physician duly licensed by the state, stating that the named party is not infected with syphilis. (§ 48-1-6) In cases of emergency or extraordinary circumstances, a judge of any court of record may waive the requirement of a physician's certificate and may direct the clerk of the court to issue the license. [§ 48-1-6(c)] The license is valid for 60 days upon its issuance. (§ 48-1-10)

**PROHIBITED MARRIAGES:** Men and women are prohibited from marrying their parents, grandparents, siblings, children, grandchildren, half-siblings, aunts, uncles, nieces, nephews, first cousins, and double cousins but not if the relationship was created by adoption. (§§ 48-1-2, -3) Children of void marriages are legitimate. (§ 42-1-7)

## DISSOLUTION OF MARRIAGE

**ANNULMENT:** If the husband was "notoriously licentious" before the marriage without the wife's knowledge, this constitutes grounds for an annulment. Factors 3, 10 (or had been a prostitute), 19, 27 (conviction prior to marriage), 34, 35, 38, and 41, listed in Appendix A, are also grounds for annulment. (§ 48-2-2)

*Residency Requirement:* One of the parties to the marriage must be a bona fide resident of the state. (§ 48-2-6)

**LEGAL SEPARATION:** An action for separate maintenance may be brought by either spouse for abandonment, desertion, and failure to provide suitable support. The court may grant the petitioning spouse alimony and separate maintenance, may prohibit the other spouse from imposing any restraint on the petitioner's personal liberty, and may free the petitioner's real and personal property from the possession, control, or any interest of the other spouse. (§ 48-2-28)

**DIVORCE**

*Residency Requirement:* One of the parties must have been a bona fide resident of the state at the commencement of the action if the ground for the divorce is

---

*Unless otherwise specified, all reference ciatations are to the West Virginia Code (1966).

adultery, whether it arose in or out of the state. If the defendant is a nonresident of this state, the action cannot be brought unless the plaintiff is an actual bona fide resident of the state for at least 1 year preceding the commencement of the action. If the cause for divorce is other than adultery, one of the parties must, at the time the cause of action arose, or since that time, have become an actual bona fide resident of the state for at least 1 year preceding the commencement of the action. (§ 48-2-7)

*Grounds for Divorce:* Grounds for divorce include factors 4, 5 (for 6 months), 8, 9 (for 3 years), 11 (of a child or party), 15, 17 (including false accusations of adultery or homosexuality), 21 (of a child or party), 22, 25, and 31 (for 1 year), listed in Appendix A. (§ 48-2-4)

*Conciliation Requirement:* There is no relevant statutory provision.

*Property Distribution:* In the absence of a valid prenuptial agreement and upon every judgment of annulment, divorce, or separation, the court shall presume that the marital property is to be divided equally between the parties but may alter this distribution, without regard to any attribution of fault to either party, considering factors 1, 2, 8, 15, and 29, listed in Appendix F. Among other factors considered are the value of the labor performed in a family business or in the actual maintenance or improvement of tangible marital property or in the management or investment of assets which are marital property; the contribution of one spouse toward the education or training of the other which has increased the income-earning ability of the other spouse and the foregoing by either party of employment; or other income-earning activity through an understanding of the parties or at the insistence of the other party. (§ 48-2-32)

*Child Custody:* The court may grant custody and make determinations regarding visitation rights, both in and out of the residence of the custodial parent or other person or persons having custody either on a temporary basis while the action is before the court or on a long-term basis. There is a presumption in favor of the parent who is the "primary caretaker." [*Garska v. McCoy*, 278 S.E.2d 357 (W.Va. 1981)] In addition, the court may grant reasonable visitation rights to the grandparents of the minor children upon application, if the grandparents are related to the child through a party whose whereabouts are unknown or who did not answer or otherwise appear and defend the cause of action. (§ 48-2-15) The Child Advocate Office (CAO) has primary responsibility for enforcing custody and visitation orders and may make reports and recommendations to the court (§§ 48A-2-2, -3-2). The CAO will provide mediation facilities in the event of a dispute between the parties, and if informal discussions do not resolve the problem, the CAO will apply a "visitation adjustment policy" approved by the chief circuit judge or commence contempt proceedings which may lead to a county jail sentence for the parent at fault. (§§ 48A-3-5, -5-7)

*Child Support:* The court may require either party to pay child support in the form of periodic installments. The order may require either party to provide health insurance coverage for the other party and the minor children, either directly or in the form of additional alimony, to be paid in periodic installments on a temporary basis while the action is before the court or on a long-term basis. The court may also grant to one of the parties, on either a temporary or a long-term basis, the exclusive use and occupancy of the marital home, together with all or a portion of the household goods, furniture, and furnishings reasonably necessary for such use and occupancy. Such use and occupancy shall be for a definite period, ending at a specific time set forth in the order and subject to modification upon the petition of either party, and shall be limited to those situations where such use and occupancy is reasonably necessary to accommodate the rearing of the minor children. The court may require payments to third parties in the form of home loan installments, land contract payments, rents, payments for utility services, property taxes, insurance coverage, or other expenses or charges reasonably necessary for the use and occupancy of the marital domicile. (§§ 48-2-13, -2-15)

*Spousal Support/Alimony:* The court may require either party to pay alimony in the form of periodic installments, a lump sum, or both for the maintenance of the other party on a temporary basis while the action is before the court or on a long-term basis. Payments of alimony are to be made from a party's employment income and other recurring earnings, but the court may, upon specific findings set forth in the order, order the party to make alimony payments from the corpus of his or her separate estate. An award of such relief shall not be disproportionate to a party's ability to pay, as disclosed by the evidence before the court. The exclusive use and possession of motor vehicles may also be granted. However, in determining whether alimony or what amount is to be awarded, the court shall consider and compare the fault or misconduct of either or both of the parties and the effect of such fault or misconduct as a contributing factor to the deterioration of the marital relationship. Alimony shall not be awarded in any case where both parties prove grounds for divorce and are denied a divorce, nor shall an award of alimony be made to an adulterous party, to a party who has been convicted of a felony subsequent to the marriage, or to a party who had abandoned or deserted his or her spouse for 6 months. In addition, the court will consider factors 1, 2, 4 (and actual period of cohabitation as husband and wife), 8 to 10, 12 to 14, 16, 18, and 19, listed in Appendix E, as well as the cost of education of minor children and of health care for each party and minor children, the distribution of marital property, and any legal obligations of the parties to support themselves and others. (§§ 48-2-13, -2-15, -2-17)

*Enforcement of Support Orders:* The CAO is responsible for all support enforcement. (§ 48A-2-2) By October 1, 1987, the director of the CAO will establish child support guidelines to be followed by the courts which will link the child's standard of living as far as possible to that which he or she would have enjoyed if the parties were still living together. The individual incomes of the parties will be examined, and the CAO may make reports and recommendations to the court as to the level of child support. (§§ 48A-2-8, -3-3) Every order for child or spousal support will include a provision for automatic withholding from the party owing support income if arrearages in support occur, without further court action if monthly payments are more than 30 days in arrears, weekly payments are more than 28 days in arrears, or the payer requests automatic withholding. (§ 48-2-15a)

Support obligations have priority over all other court-ordered attachments of income. (§§ 38-7-42, 46A-2-130) The CAO may make legislative rules whereby past-due support can be deducted from federal and state tax refunds, unemployment compensation benefits and worker's compensation benefits, once an affidavit of accrued support has been filed at court. (§§ 48A-2-15, -2-16, -2-17, -2-18, -5-2) The CAO may order liens on real and personal property and may institute contempt proceedings that may result in county jail sentences. (§§ 48A-5-4, -5-5) Modification of support may be sought in defense (§ 48A-5-2) The CAO will maintain a parent locator office and will cooperate with other states in locating parents owing support and securing compliance with orders (§§ 48A-2-10, -2-11, -7-1 *et seq.*) See also the Revised Uniform Reciprocal Enforcement of Support Act of 1968, §§ 48-9-1 *et seq.*

*Spouse's Name:* If requested to do so by the wife, the court may allow her to resume her maiden name, or the name of a former husband if she has any living minor child or children by her marriage to such a former husband. (§ 48-2-23)

*Divorce by Affidavit or Summary Judgment:* There is no relevant statutory provision.

*Displaced Homemaker Laws:* There is no relevant statutory provision.

# DOMESTIC VIOLENCE

**STATUTORY PROVISION:** Attempting to cause or intentionally, knowingly, or recklessly causing bodily injury with or without a dangerous or deadly weapon; placing by physical menace another in fear of imminent serious bodily injury; or sexually abusing a person under the age of 18 is prohibited. [§ 48-2A-2(a)]

**WHO IS PROTECTED?** Spouses, persons living as spouses, persons who formerly resided as spouses, parents, children, and children or other persons related by consanguinity or affinity are all protected. [§ 48-2A-2(b)]

**RELIEF AVAILABLE:** The court may grant any protective order it deems necessary to bring about a cessation of abuse. Relief may include an order restraining the defendant from further abusing the victim or minor children; granting exclusive possession of the residence to the complainant; requiring provision of suitable alternative housing to a spouse or minor children; and providing temporary custody and visitation rights and temporary support and maintenance for the abused party for 30 days. Violation of an order is punishable as contempt of court. (§ 48-2A-6)

**MARITAL RAPE:** Spouses and cohabitants may not charge each other with rape. (§ 61-8B-1) However, a spouse may be charged with sexual assault.

**CIVIL LAWSUIT FOR RAPE OR ASSAULT:** In *Coffindaffer v. Coffindaffer*, 244 S.E.2d 338 (W. Va. 1978), the court held that spouses may sue each other for torts.

**CHILD ABUSE:** Intentionally inflicting, attempting to inflict, or allowing physical injury or substantial emotional injury upon a child by a parent or guardian where such acts endanger the present physical or mental health of the child or infliction, or attempting to inflict or knowingly allowing to be inflicted sexual abuse upon the child is prohibited. (§ 49-1-3)

*Notification Requirement:* All doctors, dentists, mental health professionals, teachers, school personnel, social workers, child care workers, police officers, and all other persons must report all suspected cases of child abuse to the Child Protective Service, which must commence an investigation within 24 hours and initiate appropriate legal proceedings to protect a child found to be abused. (§§ 49-6A-2, -9)

# INHERITANCE RIGHTS

**FAILURE TO MAKE A WILL:** The surviving spouse is entitled to the entire real and personal estate if the decedent left no children or grandchildren; to his or her dower share in the decedent's real property and to one-third of the decedent's personal property if the decedent left children or grandchildren. (§§ 42-1-1, -2)

**FAILURE TO PROVIDE BY WILL:** The surviving spouse is entitled to a life interest in one-third of all land owned by the decedent during the marriage. (§ 43-1-1) When a divorce is granted, all rights to dower are barred. (§ 48-2-20)

**CHILDREN BORN OUT OF WEDLOCK:** The statute provides that a child born out of wedlock may inherit only from the mother. (§ 42-1-5) However, the West Virginia Supreme Court of Appeals has held that the West Virginia Constitution, art. 3, § 17, prohibits limiting a child born out of wedlock to inheriting solely from its mother's intestate estate. [*Adkins v. McEldowney*, 280 S.E.2d 231 (W. Va. 1981)] See also *Trimble v. Gordon*, 430 U.S. 762 (1977), which held that a child born out of wedlock could inherit from the father provided the father had acknowledged paternity and had supported the child.

**HOMESTEAD, PERSONAL, AND FAMILY ALLOWANCES:** The surviving spouse may remain in the mansion house rent-free until dower is assigned and is entitled to receive one-third of the rents and profits from any other real estate which is subject to a spouse's dower right. (§ 43-1-10) The head of a household owing a homestead is entitled to exemption of up to $5000. (§ 38-9-1) Subject to the rights of the decedent's creditors, the surviving spouse and minor children are entitled to remain in the mansion house until the youngest child reaches 21; dower will not be assigned until that time. (§ 43-1-11) The surviving spouse of a decedent domiciled in West Virginia is also entitled to personal property of decedent worth up to $1000. (§ 38-8-10)

**OPTION TO DISREGARD THE WILL:** The surviving spouse may reject the will and take the share he or she would have received if decedent left no will; however, the survivor may not take more than what would have been received if the decedent left children or grandchildren, whether or not decedent left children or grandchildren. (§ 42-3-1)

# REPRODUCTIVE RIGHTS

## ABORTION

*Statutory Provisions:* Abortions may be performed only by licensed physicians. (§ 16-2F-3) No physician or any other person is required to perform or assist in the performance of abortions. (§ 16-2F-7)

*Informed Consent:* There is no relevant statutory provision.

*Parental Consent:* Before performing an abortion upon an unemancipated minor, the physician must give one of her parents or her legal guardian actual notice, in person or by telephone, of the impending abortion. If a parent or guardian cannot be found and notified after a reasonable effort to do so, the physician must give them constructive notice (by certified mail to their last known address) at least 48 hours before performing the abortion. The physician must advise the unemancipated minor of her right to petition the circuit court for a waiver of the notification. However, the notice requirement may be waived by a duly acknowledged writing signed by the parent or guardian of the minor. Parental notification may also be waived by a physician other than the one who is to perform the abortion if the former finds that the minor is mature enough to make the abortion decision independently or that notification would not be in the minor's best interests provided that the physician requesting the waiver is not associated either professionally or financially with the physician proposing to perform the abortion. (§§ 16-2F-3, -4) The notification requirement does not apply where there exists an emergency which constitutes an immediate threat or grave risk to the life or health of the pregnant minor. (§ 16-2F-5)

*Spousal Consent:* There is no relevant statutory provision.

*Reporting Requirements:* All physicians performing abortions upon unemancipated minors must report such abortions to the Department of Health. The report must include the age; educational level; number of previous pregnancies, live births, and abortions; complications, if any; reason for the waiver of notification if the notice was waived; and the place where the abortion was performed. (§ 16-2F-6)

**BIRTH CONTROL:** The Department of Health is authorized to provide printed material, guidance, advice, financial assistance, appliances, devices, drugs, approved methods, and medicines to local boards of health requesting the same for use in the operation of family planning and child spacing clinics to the extent of funds appropriated by the legislature and any federal funds made available for such purpose. (§§ 16-28-1 *et seq.*)

**STERILIZATION:** It is lawful for any licensed physician to perform a sterilization procedure when requested in writing by any person other than a minor, mentally incompetent person, or any other person suffering from any similar disability which would affect his or her ability to enter into a valid contractual agreement. At the time the written request is received, the physician must give the person a full and reasonable medical explanation as to the meaning and consequences of sterilization. Sterilization of women shall take place only in a hospital or other licensed health facility authorized to perform similar operations. A hospital or its employees may refuse, without being subject to equal sanctions or penalties, to participate in or perform sterilization procedures. (§ 16-11-1)

# UNMARRIED COUPLES

**COMMON-LAW MARRIAGE:** Common-law marriages are not valid. [§ 48-1-5; *State v. Bragg*, 163 S.E.2d 685 (W. Va. 1968)]

**COHABITAL RELATIONSHIPS:** There are no relevant cases on point.

**CHILDREN**

*Custody:* There is no relevant statutory provision.

*Legitimation Proceedings:* A child born out of wedlock is legitimated when its parents intermarry. (§ 42-1-6)

*Paternity Proceedings:* The CAO will represent the plaintiff in a civil action in circuit court to establish paternity. (§§ 48A-6-1, -6-5) The plaintiff may be unmarried or married (if the defendant is not her husband and the plaintiff lived apart from her husband for 1 year before the birth). Anyone with custody, the child's guardian or next friend if the child is a minor, or the child may also bring suit. The action must be brought before the child is 18 (or 21, if the child is the plaintiff). Blood and tissue tests may be required. Once paternity is established, support may be ordered. (§§ 48A-6-1, -6-2, -6-3, -6-4)

*Obligations of the Putative Father:* If the court finds by clear and convincing evidence that the defendant is the father of the child, it will order the defendant to provide support based on his income, assets, earning ability, and other obligations and the needs, other income, and circumstances relevant to the needs of the child. (§§ 48-7-3, -4)

# Education

# STATUTORY PROVISION

There is no relevant statutory provision. However, sex discrimination in public educational institutions may be subject to challenge under the state public accommodations act.

[§§ 5-11-3(j), -9] It should also be noted that if federal funds are involved, federal law Title IX of the Education Amendments of 1972, Pub. L. No. 92-318, 20 U.S.C §§ 1681–1686, may apply.

**ENFORCEMENT:** See "Community Life: Housing."

# Employment

## EQUAL PAY LAWS

It is unlawful for an employer to discriminate on the basis of sex in wages paid to employees for work of comparable character, the performance of which requires comparable skills effort, and responsibility. Wage differentials are not prohibited, however, if based on a bona fide seniority or merit system or factors other than sex. (§ 21-5B-3)

**ENFORCEMENT:** See "Community Life: Housing."

## FAIR EMPLOYMENT LAWS

The state of West Virginia, its political subdivisions, employers of twelve or more employees, labor organizations, and employment agencies are prohibited from discriminating with respect to compensation, hire, tenure, terms, conditions, or privileges of employment on the basis of sex. (§§ 5-11-3 to 9) Exceptions to the prohibition are situations where sex is a bona fide occupational qualification or discrimination occurring as a result of the existence of a bona fide pension, retirement, insurance, or welfare benefit plan. [§ 5-11-3(e)]

**ENFORCEMENT:** See "Community Life: Housing."

## GOVERNMENT CONTRACTORS AND SUBCONTRACTORS

There is no relevant statutory provision. However, it should be noted that if federal funds are involved, federal law, Exec. Order No. 11246, 3 C.F.R. 339 (1965), *reprinted in* 42 U.S.C. § 2000e app. at 1232, 41 C.F.R. § 60-1.2, may apply.

## STATE EMPLOYEE LAWS

See "Fair Employment Laws."

## VETERAN'S PREFERENCE

Five points are added to the civil service examination passing scores of veterans, and ten points are added to the passing scores of disabled veterans. [§ 29-6-10(3)]

# Community Life

## CREDIT

There is no relevant statutory provision. However, it should be noted that federal law, the Equal Credit Opportunity Act of 1977, 12 C.F.R. § 202, may apply.

# HOUSING

It is unlawful for the owner, lessee, sublessee, assignee, or any other person having the right of ownership or possession or the right to sell, rent, lease, assign, or sublease any housing accommodation or real property to refuse to sell, rent, lease, assign, sublease, or otherwise deny or withhold any housing accommodation or real property, or to discriminate in the terms, conditions, or privileges in connection with the sale, rental, or lease of any housing accommodation or real property on the basis of sex or marital status. These provisions do not apply to the rental or lease of housing to the members of one sex where the facilities are suitable for only one sex. [§ 5-11-9(g)] It is unlawful for any person or financial institution or enterprise to whom application is made for financial assistance for the purchase, acquisition, construction, rehabilitation, repair, or maintenance of any housing accommodation or real property to discriminate in the granting, extending, modifying, renewing, or the fixing of rates, terms, conditions, or provisions of financial assistance on the basis of sex. [§ 5-11-9(n)]

**ENFORCEMENT:** Any individual claiming to be aggrieved by an alleged unlawful discriminatory practice may file a written, signed complaint with the West Virginia Commission on Human Rights within 90 days of the occurrence of the alleged act of discrimination. (§ 5-11-10) An aggrieved party may also institute an action against a respondent in the county where the respondent resides or transacts business at any time within 90 days after being given notice of a right to sue by the commission. Filing of such a suit terminates any proceedings pending before the commission. A prevailing party is entitled to affirmative, legal or equitable relief, costs of the action, plus reasonable attorney and witness fees. (§ 5-11-13)

# INSURANCE

Discrimination is prohibited between individuals of the same class and equal expectation of life in rates charged for life insurance or annuity contracts or between individuals of the same class and essentially the same hazard in the amount of premium, policy fees, or rates charged for accident or health insurance, in the benefits payable under these contracts, or in any other term or condition of these contracts. Discrimination is also prohibited between insured or subjects of insurance having substantially similar insuring, risk, and exposure factors or exposure elements, in the terms, conditions, rates or premiums of any other type of insurance contract. (§§ 33-11-4, -7)

**ENFORCEMENT:** The West Virginia Commissioner of Insurance investigates the affairs of any person engaged in the insurance business. If, following an investigation, charges of unlawful discrimination are proven true, the commissioner may issue a cease and desist order, enjoining the insurer from engaging in further discriminatory acts. Violation of a cease and desist order is punishable by a fine or the revocation or suspension of the insurer's license. (§§ 33-11-6 to -9)

# PUBLIC ACCOMMODATIONS

It is unlawful for any owner, lessee, proprietor, manager, superintendent, agent or employee of a place of public accommodation, directly or indirectly, to refuse, withhold from or deny any person any of the accommodations, advantages, facilities, privileges, or services of a place of public accommodation, or to publish or post a written notice that the patronage of an individual is unwelcome or objectionable on the basis of sex. [§ 5-11-9(f)]

**ENFORCEMENT:** See "Housing."

# WISCONSIN

## Home and Family

## MARRIAGE

**AGE OF CONSENT:** A person 18 years of age or older may consent to marry. (§ 765.02)*

**CONSENT REQUIREMENT:** If a person is between the ages of 16 and 18 years, a marriage license may be issued with the written consent of parent, guardian, or custodian. If there is no parent, guardian, or custodian or if the custodian is a state agency or department, the written consent may be obtained from the court, after notice to the agency or department. [§ 765.02(2)]

**LICENSE REQUIREMENT:** A marriage license must be obtained from the county clerk of the county in which one of the parties has resided for at least 30 days immediately prior to making the application. If both parties are nonresidents of the state, the marriage license may be obtained from the county clerk of the county where the marriage ceremony is to be performed. (§ 765.05) The license is valid for 30 days after issuance. [§ 765.12(2)] The fee for a license is $24.50. (§765.15)

**PROHIBITED MARRIAGES:** Bigamous marriages are prohibited, as are marriages between persons who are nearer of kin than second cousins. However, a marriage between first cousins where the female is 55 or where either party, at the time of the application for a marriage license, submits an affidavit signed by a physician stating that either party is permanently sterile is not unlawful. A divorced person may not marry again until 6 months after the judgment of divorce was granted. (§ 765.03)

**MARITAL PROPERTY:** Comprehensive new legislation, effective January 1, 1986, substantially alters the rights of each spouse to the couple's property and creates a form of community property known as marital property. Among other provisions, the legislation provides that all property of spouses, including income of either one, is marital property, except property brought into the marriage, property acquired by one spouse by gift or inheritance, and certain other categories of property; all property of spouses is presumed to be marital property; each spouse has a present undivided one-half interest in each item of marital property; a spouse may rely on the marital property to obtain credit; there are limitations on gifts by one spouse of marital property to a third party; and a spouse may seek court remedies, including an accounting, if the other spouse breaches the requirement to act in good faith in matters involving marital property. Life insurance and pension plans are subject to special rules. Generally, property acquired during marriage but before January 1, 1986, is not treated as marital property while the marriage continues and while both spouses live, but such property will be treated as marital property when one spouse dies or the marriage ends. Certain of the new law's provisions may be altered by a written marital property agreement between the spouses. (§§ 766.01 to .97)

*Unless otherwise specified, all reference citations are to West's Wisconsin Statutes Annotated (1957).

# DISSOLUTION OF MARRIAGE

**ANNULMENT:** Factors 19, 32, 33, 35, 36, and 38, listed in Appendix A, are grounds for annulment. (§ 767.03)

> *Residency Requirement:* One of the parties must have been a resident of the county in which the action is brought for not less that 30 days preceding the commencement of the action, or else the marriage must have been contracted within the state winin 1 year prior to the commencement of the action. [§ 767.05(lm)]

**LEGAL SEPARATION:** Appendix A, factor 2, is the basis for a judgment of legal separation. (§ 767.07)

> *Residency Requirement:* See "Annulment."

## DIVORCE

> *Residency Requirement:* One of the parties must have been a resident of the county in which the action is brought for at least 30 days preceding the commencement of the action. [§ 767.05(lm)]

> *Grounds for Divorce:* See "Legal Separation."

> *Conciliation Requirement:* In every action for annulment, divorce, or legal separation, the family court shall inform the parties of the availability of counseling and referral services offered by the family court or the Department of Family Conciliation. In actions for divorce or legal separation, the family court shall require the petitioner, and the respondent if personally served within the state, to participate in counseling. (§ 767.081)

> *Property Distribution:* There is a presumption that all property, other than property inherited by either party, received by either party as a gift, or paid for by either party with funds acquired by inheritance or gift, is to be divided equally between the parties. The court may alter the equal distribution without regard to fault if the circumstances warrant. It may even consider the division of inherited or gift property in order to prevent a hardship on the other spouse or the children of the marriage. Factors 1, 2, 5 to 10, 12 to 15, 16, 18, 19, 21, and 25, listed in Appendix F, will be considered. The court will also consider whether equity requires reimbursement of one spouse by the other because of certain transactions during the marriage. (§ 767.255) After dissolution of marriage, each former spouse owns a one-half interest in the former marital property as a tenant in common, unless otherwise provided in a decree or agreement. (§ 766.75)

> *Child Custody:* Custody is to be determined according to the best interests of the child and is awarded to either parent without regard to sex. Joint legal custody may also be awarded. The court may consider factors 5, 10 to 14, 21, and 23, listed in Appendix B, as well as the availability of public or private child care services and the desirability of awarding custody to a relative instead of the parties. (§ 767.24)

> *Child Support:* The court may order either or both parents to pay an amount reasonable or necessary for child support and shall specifically assign responsibility for payment of health care expenses. The amount may be expressed by the court as a percentage of parental income or as a fixed sum. In ordering child support, the court must consider the guidelines for the determination of child support established by the Department of Health and Social Services and factors 1, 3 to 5, 12, and 22 to 25, listed in Appendix D. Alternatively, the court may order either or both parents to pay an amount determined by using the percentage standard adopted by the Department of Health and Social Services. (§ 767.25) The court may make an order of family support in place of separate child support and maintenance. (§ 767.261)

*Spousal Support/Alimony:* The court may award maintenance to either party, for a limited or indefinite length of time, by considering the division of property and factors 2, 4, 6, 8, 10, 11, 12, 13, 14, and 16 to 20, listed in Appendix E. (§ 767.26) The court may grant temporary support and costs of a suit to either party during the pendency of the action. (§ 767.23) It may also make an order of family support in place of separate child support and maintenance. (§ 767.261)

*Enforcement of Support Orders:* Any support order constitutes an assignment to the clerk of court of commissions, earnings, salaries, wages, pension benefits, and certain other benefits in an amount sufficient to meet the support payments. The enforcement statutes authorize employers of persons owing a duty of support to withhold a portion of these persons' wages as is necessary to meet support obligations, when so ordered by a court. [§§ 767.265, .395(5)(a)] All orders or judgments providing for temporary or permanent maintenance or child support must direct that payments be made to the clerk of court. (§ 767.29) The court may treat support obligations as a charge upon specific real estate of the party liable for the payments, or it may require that party to give sufficient security for their payment. Enforcement remedies also include execution of the order or judgment, contempt of court, money judgment for past due payments, satisfaction of judgments, and garnishment. (§ 767.30) See also the Revised Uniform Reciprocal Enforcement of Support Act of 1968, §§ 52.10 *et seq*.

*Spouse's Name:* Upon divorce, the court shall grant the request of either spouse to resume a former legal surname. (§ 767.20)

*Divorce by Affidavit or Summary Judgment:* There is no relevant statutory provision.

*Displaced Homemaker Laws:* The Board of Vocational, Technical and Adult Education administers grants to provide services such as counseling and outreach to displaced homemakers. (§ 38.04)

# DOMESTIC VIOLENCE

**STATUTORY PROVISION:** The intentional infliction of physical pain or injury, intentional physical impairment, sexual assault, or the threat to engage in any of the above is prohibited. (§ 813.12)

**WHO IS PROTECTED?** Spouses, children, parents, persons related by consanguinity, cohabitants and former cohabitants are protected. [§ 813.12(1)]

**RELIEF AVAILABLE:** A victim of domestic violence has the right to commence an action by serving a petition on the abuser and filing a copy of the petition in court. After a hearing, the judge or family court commissioner may issue an injunction ordering the abuser to avoid the place or places where the petitioner is living and to avoid contacting the victim or causing any person other than the victim's or abuser's attorney to contact the victim. After the petition has been filed, the judge or family court commissioner may also grant a temporary restraining order. An abuser who violates an injunction or temporary restraining order is subject to arrest. The knowing violation of a temporary restraining order or injunction is punishable by a fine of up to $1000 or imprisonment of up to 9 months or both. (§ 813.12)

**MARITAL RAPE:** A wife may charge her husband with rape. [§§ 766.97(3), 940.225(6)]

**CIVIL LAWSUIT FOR RAPE OR ASSAULT:** Spouses may sue each other for torts. [*Zelinger v. State Sand & Gravel Co.*, 156 N.W.2d 466 (Wis. 1968)]

**CHILD ABUSE:** Torturing or subjecting a child under 16 to cruel maltreatment is a felony. (§ 940.201) It is also a felony for a parent, legal guardian, or other person having temporary or permanent control of a child under 18 to knowingly permit another to subject the child to sexual exploitation. (§ 940.203)

> *Notification Requirement:* Health care professionals, social or public assistance workers, school personnel, child care workers, community service workers, physical, occupational, or speech therapists, and police officers are required to report suspected cases of child abuse or neglect which they observe in the course of their professional duties to a county child welfare agency, a sheriff, or a city police department. (§ 48.981)

# INHERITANCE RIGHTS

**FAILURE TO MAKE A WILL:** Effective January 1, 1986, the surviving spouse is entitled to the entire estate if the decedent left no surviving descendants, or if the surviving descendants are all descended from the surviving spouse as well as the decedent; if there are any surviving descendants who are descended from the decedent but not from the surviving spouse, the surviving spouse is entitled to one-half of that portion of the decedent's net estate not disposed of by will and consisting of property other than marital property and other than the surviving spouse's elective share. (§ 852.01) The surviving spouse automatically retains an undivided one-half interest in each item of marital property. (§ 861.01)

**FAILURE TO PROVIDE BY WILL:** The right of the surviving spouse to take one-third of the net probate estate, reduced by any property given outright to the spouse by the will, was repealed, effective January 1, 1986. (§ 861.05) Effective January 1, 1986, the following rules apply. Upon the death of a spouse, the surviving spouse automatically retains an undivided one-half interest in each item of marital property. (§ 861.01) The surviving spouse may elect not more than a one-half interest in any items of deferred marital property owned by the decedent and includable in the decedent's probate estate, reduced by any amount used to satisfy debts. (§ 861.02) Deferred marital property is all property acquired during the marriage but before January 1, 1986, which would have been marital property if it had been acquired after January 1, 1986. (§ 851.055) Also, the surviving spouse may elect not more than one-half of certain property transferred by the decedent before death. (§§ 861.03, .05) The election must be made in writing and must be filed with the court within 6 months after the decedent's death, except that the 6-month period is subject to extension. (§ 861.11)

**CHILDREN BORN OUT OF WEDLOCK:** A nonmarital child or the child's issue is entitled to take in the same manner as a marital child by intestate succession from and through the mother, and from and through the father if the father has either been adjudicated to be the father in a paternity proceeding, has admitted in open court that he is the father, or has acknowledged himself to be the father in a signed writing. A father may inherit from a nonmarital child who died without a will only if the father has been adjudicated to be the father in a paternity proceeding. (§ 852.05)

**HOMESTEAD, PERSONAL, AND FAMILY ALLOWANCES:** If the estate of a decedent who left no will includes an interest in a home, the decedent's interest passes to the surviving spouse as a part of his or her statutory share. (§ 852.09) A homestead acquired by two spouses after January 1, 1986, automatically passes to the surviving spouse if no contrary intent is expressed on the instrument of transfer.

(§ 766.605) In addition to the homestead, the surviving spouse is also entitled to the decedent's clothing, jewelry, car, household furnishings and appliances, and other personal property worth up to $1000. (§ 861.33) Upon the surviving spouse's request, the court may set aside property worth up to $10,000 for him or her if the court determines that this property is reasonably necessary for support of the spouse and it appears that the estate is insufficient to pay all the claims against it and still leave the spouse with such an amount of property in addition to the spouse's elections and allowances. This sum is exempt from creditors' claims and is applied to the spouse's share of the estate. (§ 861.41) The surviving spouse and/or minor children of the decedent may be granted a reasonable allowance for their support and education during the administration of the estate; the initial order of support may not exceed 1 year, but it may be extended for additional periods not to exceed 1 year at a time. (§ 861.31) Also, where necessary, the court may order an allowance for the later support and education of the decedent's minor children or for the support of the spouse. (§ 861.35)

**OPTION TO DISREGARD THE WILL:** See "Failure to Provide by Will."

# REPRODUCTIVE RIGHTS
## ABORTION

*Statutory Provisions:* The statute makes most abortions a crime. (§ 940.04) However, this statute has been held to be unconstitutional. [*Larkin v. McCann*, 398 F. Supp. 1351 (E.D. Wis. 1974)] An abortion performed after viability of the fetus is a felony unless necessary to preserve the life or health of the woman, performed in a hospital by a physician, and performed using the abortion method most likely to preserve the life and health of the fetus (unless this would increase the risk to the woman). (§ 940.15) Women obtaining abortions are not subject to criminal penalties for illegal abortions. (§ 940.13)

*Informed Consent:* The pregnant woman must be provided with accurate information on whether she is pregnant, the length of her pregnancy, the availability of birth control information, the availability of assistance during pregnancy and after the birth if she chooses not to have an abortion, and any particular risks associated with the woman's pregnancy and the abortion technique to be used. In the absence of an emergency, the patient must sign a written statement of consent after receiving the required information.

*Parental Consent:* If the pregnant woman is a minor, she must be informed about the availability of assistance from a county agency in notifying her parent or guardian and she must be given a copy of the hospital, clinic, or facility's written policy regarding parental notification. The policy must require that personnel of the hospital, clinic, or facility strongly encourage the minor to consult her parents or guardian regarding the abortion, or if there is a valid reason for the minor not to do so, the personnel must encourage her to notify another family member, close family friend, school counselor, social worker, or other appropriate person. No hospital, clinic, or facility or their personnel may notify a parent or guardian without the minor's written consent. (§ 146.78)

*Spousal Consent:* There is no relevant statutory provision.

*State Funding:* No state funds, or any federal funds passing through the state treasury, may be spent for the performance of an abortion except where the performing physician certifies that the abortion is necessary to save the life of the woman;

the pregnancy was the result of sexual assault or incest and the crime was reported to law enforcement authorities; or the abortion is directly and medically necessary to prevent grave, long-lasting damage to the woman's physical health. [§§ 20.297, 59.07(136), 66.04(m)]

**BIRTH CONTROL:** The public health department is authorized to provide family planning counseling services and the dissemination of information relating to family planning, as well as to refer individuals to licensed physicians or local health agencies for consultation, examination, medical treatment, and prescription for family planning purposes. The request of any person for family planning or the refusal to accept such services shall in no way affect that person's right to receive public assistance, public health services, or any other public service. An employee of an agency providing family planning services is permitted to refuse to offer such services if doing so is contrary to his or her personal beliefs. (§ 146.80) It is illegal to sell contraceptives by vending machines. (§ 450.11)

**STERILIZATION:** There is no relevant statutory provision. No licensed nurse or physician is liable for any civil damages resulting from his or her refusal to perform sterilization or abortion, if the refusal is based on religious or moral precepts. [§§ 441.06(6), 448.03(5)]

# UNMARRIED COUPLES

**COMMON-LAW MARRIAGE:** Common-law marriages are not recognized by the state. (§§ 765.16, .21)

**COHABITAL RELATIONSHIPS:** A Wisconsin court has held that although a woman who had cohabited with a man could not invoke the property division provisions of the state's divorce law, under general principles of equity she was not barred from seeking a division of the property accumulated during the course of the relationship in order to prevent the unjust enrichment of the other party. [*Doyle v. Giddley*, 3 F.L.R. 2730 (Wis. Cty. Ct. September 8, 1977)]

## CHILDREN

*Custody:* The mother of a child born out of wedlock has legal custody of the child unless the court grants legal custody to another person or an agency. (§ 48.435) A judgment or order in a paternity proceeding may include a provision concerning the custody and guardianship of the child and visitation privileges. (§ 767.51)

*Legitimation Proceedings:* If the parents of a nonmarital child subsequently marry each other, the child becomes legitimate. (§ 767.60)

*Paternity Proceedings:* The child, the mother, the presumed father, the man alleged or alleging himself to be the father, their personal representative, the legal or physical custodian of the child, or the state may bring an action to determine paternity. Certain government attorneys may represent the person bringing a paternity action with that person's consent. (§ 767.45) The court may, on its own motion, or upon the request of a party, require the parties to undergo blood tests if necessary to make a determination of paternity. (§ 767.48) The action must be begun within 19 years after the birth of the child. (§ 893.88)

*Obligations of the Putative Father:* The judgment or order of paternity may direct the father to pay or contribute to the reasonable expenses of the mother's pregnancy and confinement. The judgment or order may include provisions for the child's support and must specifically assign responsibility for payment of the child's medical expenses. The father's liability for past support is limited to support for the period after the bringing of the action. In ordering child support, the court must consider the guidelines for the determination of child support established by the Department of Health and Social Services and factors 1, 5, 9, 12, 15, 16, 18, 20, 23, and 24, listed in Appendix D. Alternatively, the court may order either or both parents to pay an amount determined by using the percentage standard adopted by the Department of Health and Social Services. (§ 767.51)

# Education

## STATUTORY PROVISION

No child may be excluded from or discriminated against in admission to any public school or in obtaining the advantages, privileges, and courses of study of a public school on account of sex. (§ 101.225)

**ENFORCEMENT:** The Department of Industry, Labor and Human Relations may receive and investigate discrimination complaints. The department may attempt to eliminate discrimination by conference, conciliation, or persuasion, and it may hold hearings. [§§ 101.223(4), 111.39]

# Employment

## EQUAL PAY LAWS

Discriminating against any individual in compensation paid for equal or substantially similar work on the basis of sex, where sex is not a bona fide occupational qualification, is forbidden. [§ 111.36(1)(a)]

## FAIR EMPLOYMENT LAWS

The state of Wisconsin, state agencies, labor organizations, employment agencies, licensing agencies, and all employers of at least one person, are generally prohibited from discrimination based on sex or marital status. Acts undertaken on a discriminatory basis which are forbidden are: refusing to hire, admit, or license any individual; barring or terminating from employment or labor organization membership any individual; discriminating against any individual in promotion, compensation, or in terms, conditions, or privileges of employment or labor organization membership; or using a statement, advertisement, application form, or inquiry which implies or expresses any discrimination or intent to discriminate. Discrimination on the basis of sex includes sexual harassment, discrimination on the basis of pregnancy or related medical conditions, and discrimination on the basis of sexual orientation. (§§ 111.31 to .36)

**ENFORCEMENT:** The Department of Industry, Labor and Human Relations administers the fair employment laws. It will investigate charges of discrimination upon the filing of a complaint within 300 days after the alleged discrimination occurred. If probable cause exists that discrimination has occurred, the department may try to eliminate the discrimination by conference, conciliation, or persuasion. If it is unsuccessful, a hearing may be held before a department hearing examiner. After the hearing, the examiner may grant affirmative relief, including back pay for up to 2 years prior to the filing of a complaint.

## GOVERNMENT CONTRACTORS AND SUBCONTRACTORS

Contracting agencies of the state must include in all contracts a provision requiring the contractor not to discriminate on the basis of sex or sexual orientation in their employment practices, training, or apprenticeship programs, and requiring the contractor to take affirmative action except with respect to sexual orientation. (§ 16.765)

**ENFORCEMENT:** The Department of Administration receives complaints of alleged violations of the antidiscrimination provisions in state contracts. Upon receipt of a complaint, it investigates and determines whether a violation has actually occurred. The Department of Administration may delegate this authority to the contracting state agency for processing in accordance with the department's procedures. If a violation is found, the contractor will be directed to take immediate steps to prevent further violations of this section and to report its corrective action to the state agency involved. If further violations occur, the contractor will be placed on the ineligible list for state contracts or the contracting agency may terminate the contract. In addition to the above remedy, the department refers any individual complaints of discrimination which are subject to investigation under the fair employment laws to the Department of Industry, Labor and Human Relations.

## STATE EMPLOYEE LAWS

State employees are covered under the fair employment laws. [§ 111.32(6)(a)] In addition, state civil service employees are protected from discrimination in recruitment, application, examination, or hiring because of sex or sexual orientation. (§ 230.18)

**ENFORCEMENT:** See "Fair Employment Laws."

## VETERAN'S PREFERENCE

Preference is given to certain qualifying veterans for competitive civil service employment. [§ 230.16(7)] The preference does not extend to spouses or widows of veterans.

# Community Life

## CREDIT

It is unlawful for an extender of credit to discriminate in the area of credit and financing practices on the basis of sex or marital status. (§ 138.20)

**ENFORCEMENT:** Any person violating this action may be fined not more than $1000. Each individual who is discriminated against constitutes a separate violation. (§ 138.20)

# HOUSING

It is unlawful for any person engaged in real estate transactions or their financing to discriminate against an individual on the basis of sex, the sex or marital status of the head of the household, sexual orientation or lawful source of income in the purchase, lease, rental or financing of a house or residence. These provisions expressly apply to the sale or rental of owner-occupied single family residences. (§§ 101.22, 66.432)

**ENFORCEMENT:** The Department of Industry, Labor and Human Relations is charged with the enforcement of this law. The department may investigate written complaints filed within 300 days after the alleged discrimination occurred. The department may also independently test and investigate violations and file complaints. If the department finds probable cause to believe that housing discrimination has occurred, it may attempt to eliminate the discrimination by conference, conciliation, and persuasion. In addition, a person alleging housing discrimination may bring a civil action in the circuit court and seek appropriate relief, including punitive damages. (§ 101.22)

# INSURANCE

No insurer may unfairly discriminate among policy holders by charging different premiums or by offering different terms of coverage except on the basis of classifications related to the nature and degree of the risk or the expenses involved. [§ 628.34(3)]

**ENFORCEMENT:** The Commissioner of Insurance has the power and authority to administer and enforce the insurance code's nondiscrimination requirements. (§ 601.41) The commissioner is empowered to conduct investigations and hearings. (§ 601.61) The county district attorney has the duty to prosecute criminal actions, including misdemeanors. (§ 59.47)

# PUBLIC ACCOMMODATIONS

It is illegal to give preferential treatment to some classes of persons in providing services or facilities in any public place of accommodation or amusement because of sex, race, color, creed, sexual orientation, national origin, or ancestry. The law does not apply to bona fide private, nonprofit organizations or institutions. In addition, no person, club, or organization may refuse to rent, charge a higher price than the regular rate, or give preferential treatment because of sex or sexual orientation, regarding the use of any private facilities commonly rented to the public. (§ 942.04)

**ENFORCEMENT:** The Division of Equal Rights of the Department of Industry, Labor and Human Relations, may investigate complaints filed with the department within 300 days after the alleged discrimination occurred. The department may seek conciliation in any case where it believes discrimination occurred. (§ 101.222) Also, discriminating in a public place of accommodation or amusement is a misdemeanor which may be prosecuted by the county district attorney. (§§ 59.47, 942.04) In addition, the person discriminated against may bring a civil lawsuit. [§ 942.04(6)]

# WYOMING

## Home and Family

## MARRIAGE

**AGE OF CONSENT:** A person 16 or over may contract to marry. (§ 20-1-102)*

**CONSENT REQUIREMENT:** A marriage between persons under 16 years is prohibited and voidable unless before contracting to the marriage a judge approves the marriage and authorizes the county clerk to issue a license. When either party is a minor, no license shall be granted without the verbal consent, if present, and written consent if absent, of the father, mother, guardian, or person having the care and control of the minor. (§ 20-1-102)

**LICENSE REQUIREMENT:** A license from the county clerk is required. Upon receipt of the application, the county clerk shall ascertain, by the testimony of a competent witness and the applicant, the names, residences, and ages of the parties and whether there is any legal impedament to the marriage. (§ 20-1-103) Before a marriage license is issued, a health certificate dated within 30 days before the date of the application for the license must be produced, showing the applicants to be free from any venereal disease in a communicable stage. If the woman is about to give birth or if the death of one or both parties is imminent, a physician may submit a statement to the county clerk, in lieu of the certificate, stating that samples have been taken from the applicant and have been forwarded to the Department of Health and Social Servies. (§ 20-1-104) Should the clerk refuse to issue a license because of the applicants' failure to comply with any of the requirements for its issuance, application can be made to a judge of the district court who will order the clerk to issue the license. If either applicant is under 16 years of age, the parents or guardian may apply to any judge of a court of record in the county of residence of the minor for an order authorizing the issuance of the marriage license. (§ 20-1-105)

**PROHIBITED MARRIAGES:** Bigamous marriages, marriages involving mental incompetents, and marriages between parties who stand in relation to each other of parent and child, grandparent and grandchild, brother and sister of the half or whole blood, uncle and niece, aunt and nephew, or first cousins are prohibited. Also prohibited are marriages between persons below the age of consent who failed to get the required consent. (§ 20-2-101) Children born of void marriages are legitimate. (§ 20-2-117)

## DISSOLUTION OF MARRIAGE

**ANNULMENT:** Factors 19, 35, 36, and 38, listed in Appendix A, are grounds for annulment. (§ 20-2-101)

  *Residency Requirement:* There is no relevant statutory provision.

**LEGAL SEPARATION:** If there are irreconcilable differences in the marital relationship, the parties may file for legal separation. (§ 20-2-106)`

  *Residency Requirement:* No divorce or judicial separation shall be granted unless the plaintiff has resided in this state for 60 days immediately preceding the time

---

*Unless otherwise specified, all reference citations are to Wyoming Statutes Annotated (1977).

of filing the complaint or the marriage was solemnized in this state and the plaintiff has resided in this state for the time of the marriage until the filing of the complaint. (§ 20-2-107)

# DIVORCE

*Residency Requirement:* See "Legal Separation."

*Grounds for Divorce:* Factors 9 (for 2 years) and 22, listed in Appendix A, are grounds for divorce. (§ 20-2-104, -105)

*Conciliation Requirement:* There is no relevant statutory provision.

*Property Distribution:* In granting a divorce, the court shall make such disposition of the property of the parties as appears just and equitable and will consider factors 3, 15, 22, 23, and 24, listed in Appendix F. (§ 20-2-114)

*Child Custody:* In granting a divorce or annulment, the court will award custody in accordance with the best interests of the children. The court will consider the relative competency of both parents and will make its award to either parent without regard to gender of the parent. If there are children of a marriage annulled on grounds of force or fraud, the court will award custody to the innocent party. (§ 20-2-113)

*Child Support:* When a provision is made for the children, the court may order any amount set apart payable to a trustee or trustees appointed by the court, who will invest this sum and apply the income derived from it to the support of the children as the court directs. (§ 20-2-115)

*Spousal Support/Alimony:* In granting a divorce the court may decree to the wife reasonable alimony out of the estate of the other having regard for the payer's ability to pay and may order that so much of the real estate or rents and profits derived from it as is necessary be assigned and set out to either party for life, or may decree a specific sum to the wife. (§ 20-2-114) The controlling element in awarding alimony is always the spouse's (husband's) ability to pay. [*Hendrickson v. Hendrickson*, 583 P.2d 1265 (Wyo. 1970)]

*Enforcement of Support Orders:* The parent of a child or any interested party furnishing physical care or support to the child may commence a civil action against the person responsible for the child's support to recover expenses incurred. The petition must be filed in the district court of the county where the defendant resides, is found, or has assets subject to attachment or execution. (§ 14-2-204) The court may order that any property or money due a party who has been adjudged delinquent in meeting child support obligations be applied toward the satisfaction of a judgment. (§ 1-17-411) An individual filing a new claim for unemployment insurance benefits must disclose whether he or she owes child support obligations. Where such obligations are owed, the employment security commission will deduct from the benefits payable any amount determined by and submitted to the commission by the state or local child support enforcement agency. (§ 27-3-305) In addition, the Division of Public Assistance and Social Services of the Department of Health and Social Services enforces support obligations owed to any person who resides in the state by seeking to collect arrears in child support through the Internal Revenue Service when all other means have been exhausted. [§§ 20-6.105(ii), .106] See also the Revised Uniform Reciprocal Enforcement of Support Act of 1968, §§ 20-4-101 *et seq*.

*Spouse's Name:* There is no relevant statutory provision.

*Divorce by Affidavit or Summary Judgment:* There is no relevant statutory provision.

*Displaced Homemaker Laws:* There is no relevant statutory provision.

# DOMESTIC VIOLENCE

**STATUTORY PROVISION:** Physical abuse, the threat of physical abuse, or an act which unreasonably restrains the personal liberty of any household member by any other household member is prohibited. (§ 35-21-101)

**WHO IS PROTECTED?** Spouses, cohabitants, former spouses, parents, adult children, and other adults sharing a common household. (§ 35-21-101)

**RELIEF AVAILABLE:** A victim of domestic violence can obtain orders of protection from the court. Such order may grant sole possession of the residence of household to the petitioner; award temporary custody of any children; prohibit the respondent from abducting, removing, or concealing any child in the custody of the petitioner; restrain the respondent from disposing of petitioner's property or the joint property of the parties; and order injunctive relief. (§ 35-21-105) In addition, a victim of domestic violence may request the assistance of a law enforcement officer who may take whatever steps are necessary to protect the victim from further abuse. The officer may provide information on the availability of shelter, medical care, and counseling; escort the victim to a place of shelter or to a medical facility; accompany the victim to the residence to remove personal clothing and effects of the victim and children in victim's care; and arrest the abusing household member when appropriate. (§ 35-21-107)

**MARITAL RAPE:** A woman may charge her husband with rape only if a decree of judicial separation or restraining order has been granted. (§ 6-2-307)

**CIVIL LAWSUIT FOR RAPE OR ASSAULT:** Spouses may not sue each other for torts. [*Allstate Ins. Co. v. Wyoming Ins. Dept.*, 672 P.2d 810 (Wyo. 1984)]

**CHILD ABUSE:** Inflicting or causing physical or mental injury, harm, or imminent danger to the physical or mental health or welfare of a child other than by accidental means, including abandonment, excessive or unreasonable corporal punishment, malnutrition, or substantial risk by reason of intentional neglect, and the commission or allowing the commission of a sexual offense against a child is prohibited. (§ 14-3-202)

> *Notification Requirement:* Any person who has reasonable cause to believe that a child has been abused or neglected must immediately report this to the child protective agency or the police. The agency must initiate an investigation within 24 hours of the report and must initiate legal proceedings if the best interest of the child require it. (§§ 14-3-204, -205, -208)

# INHERITANCE RIGHTS

**FAILURE TO MAKE A WILL:** The surviving spouse is entitled to the entire estate if decedent left no other heirs; to one-half if decedent left children or grandchildren; and to $20,000 and three-fourths the balance if decedent left parents, brothers, sisters, nieces, or nephews. [§ 2-4-101(a)]

**FAILURE TO PROVIDE BY WILL:** If a married person domiciled in this state deprives the surviving spouse of more than the elective share, the surviving spouse has a right to one-half of the property if there are no surviving issue of the decedent or one-fourth if the surviving spouse is not the parent of any surviving issue of the decedent. (§ 2-5-101)

**CHILDREN BORN OUT OF WEDLOCK:** A child born out of wedlock is the child of the mother. However, such a child can inherit from the father if that relationship is established by any of the following means: after the child's birth, the father and mother marry or attempt to marry each other, even though the attempted marriage is or could be declared void, and he has acknowledged paternity in a writing filed with the Office of Vital Records Services; or with his consent, he is named as the child's father on the child's birth certificate; or he is obligated to support the child under a written voluntary promise or by court order; or, while the child is under the age of majority, he receives the child into his home and openly holds out the child as his own. (§ 14-2-101)

**HOMESTEAD, PERSONAL, AND FAMILY ALLOWANCES:** The surviving spouse and minor children are entitled to the decedent's homestead having a value of $30,000. [§§ 2-7-501(b), -504, -508] The widow and children may be granted reasonable support during the administration of the estate. (§ 2-7-502) The spouse and children are also entitled to remain in possession of the homestead, their clothing and the decedent's household furniture during administration of the estate. (§ 2-7-501)

**OPTION TO DISREGARD THE WILL:** If the decedent was domiciled in Wyoming, the surviving spouse may reject the will and take one-half of the estate if the decedent left no children or grandchildren or left children or grandchildren who are also the spouse's children or grandchildren, or one-fourth of the estate if the decedent left children or grandchildren who are not also the spouse's children or grandchildren. (§ 2-5-101)

# REPRODUCTIVE RIGHTS
## ABORTION
*Statutory Provisions:* Abortions can be performed by licensed physicians. (§ 35-6-111) No abortion can be performed after the fetus has reached viability except when, according to appropriate medical judgment, it is necessary to preserve the woman from an imminent peril that substantially endangers her life or health. (§ 35-6-102) The commonly accepted means of care must be employed in the treatment of any fetus aborted alive. (§ 35-6-104) No person or private medical institution or facility is required to perform or assist in the performance of abortions. (§§ 35-6-105, -106)

*Consent Requirements:* There is no relevant statutory provision.

*Reporting Requirements:* Physicians must report all abortions that they perform to the Office of Vital Records Services on a reporting form designed by the state. The report includes information on the age of the woman; the type of procedure performed; the occurrence of complications, if any; a summary of the woman's obstetrical history; the physical characteristics of the aborted embryo or fetus; and the type of facility where the abortion was performed. The idenity of any individual participating in the abortion is not to be revealed. (§ 35-6-107)

**BIRTH CONTROL:** The Department of Public Health and Public Welfare is authorized to provide and pay for family planning services. The refusal of any person to accept family planning and birth control services shall in no way affect the right of such person to receive public assistance or other public benefit. The right to refuse family planning must be explained both orally and in writing. All family planning services provided by the Department of Public Health and Public Assistance, including literature and interviews shall be in the language which the person understands. (§§ 35-14-101 to -106)

**STERILIZATION:** There is no relevant statutory provision.

# UNMARRIED COUPLES

**COMMON-LAW MARRIAGE:** Common-law marriages are not recognized by the state. [*In re Roberts' Estate*, 133 P.2d 492 (Wyo. 1943)]

**COHABITAL RELATIONSHIPS:** In *Kinnison v. Kinnison*, 627 P.2d 594 (Wyo. 1981), the Wyoming Supreme Court allowed a woman who had lived in a nonmarital relationship to recover $15,000 on the basis of an oral contract between the couple. The woman based her claims on the theory of unjust enrichment arising out of her labors in the home and in maintaining and managing the household during the couple's unmarried years together.

## CHILDREN

*Custody:* Once the existence of the parent-child relationship has been established, the court may make any provision for the custody and guardianship of a child born out of wedlock. (§ 14-2-113)

*Legitimation Proceedings:* A child born out of wedlock is legitimated if, after the child's birth, the father and mother marry or attempt to marry each other and the father has acknowledged his paternity of the child in a writing filed with the state office of vital records services; or if he is named, with his consent, as the father on the child's birth certificate; or if he is obligated to support the child under a written voluntary promise or by court order; or if he receives the child into his home and openly holds the child out as his own while the child is still a minor. (§ 14-2-101)

*Paternity Proceedings:* An action to determine the paternity of a child born out of wedlock may be brought by the child, the natural mother, the presumed father, an interested party, or the Department of Health and Social Services. (§§ 14-2-104, -105) The action can be brought at any time during the child's minority up until 3 years after the child reaches the age of majority. (§ 14-2-105)

*Obligations of the Putative Father:* Once paternity is established, the court may make an order requiring the father to support the child. The judgment may also order the father to pay the reasonable expenses of the mother's pregnancy and confinement, attorney's fees, and costs of the action. (§§ 14-2-113, -114)

# Education

## STATUTORY PROVISION

The Wyoming Constitution contains an equal rights provision prohibiting sex dsicrimination. (Wyo. Const. art. 1, § 3) It should be noted that, with regard to higher education, if federal funds are involved, federal law, Title IX of the Education Amendments of 1972, Pub. L. No. 92-318, 20 U.S.C. §§ 1681–1686 may apply.

# Employment

## EQUAL PAY LAWS

It is unlawful for an employer to pay any female in any occupation a salary or hourly wage rate less than that paid to a male employed by the same employer for work requiring comparable skill, effort, and responsibility. (§ 27-4-302)

**ENFORCEMENT:** An employer who discriminates against an employee in wages because of the employee's sex is liable to the employee for all the unpaid wages and an additional equal amount as liquidated damages. A civil action may be brought in a court of competent jurisdiction for the recovery of unpaid wages and damages. Alternatively, at the request of an employee, the Commissioner of Labor may take an assignment of such unpaid wages and may bring any legal action necessary to collect the claim, including liquidated damages. (§ 27-4-303) See also "Fair Employment Laws."

# FAIR EMPLOYMENT LAWS

The law applies to the state of Wyoming, its political subdivisions, and employers of two or more employees, labor organizations, and employment agencies. It prohibits an employer from refusing to hire, discharging, promoting, demoting, or discriminating in matters of compensation against any person otherwise qualified on the basis of sex. The law also prohibits an employment agency or labor organization from discriminating because of sex in matters of employment or membership against any person otherwise qualified. The law does not cover religious organizations or associations, and bona fide seniority or merit systems or benefit plans. [§§ 27-9-102(b), -105]

**ENFORCEMENT:** A person claiming to be aggrieved by a discriminatory employment practice may by himself or herself or by an attorney file a written complaint with the Fair Employment Commission within 90 days of the occurrence of the alleged discriminatory practice. If, after a hearing, the commission finds the charges to be true, the commission will issue a cease and desist order and order the discriminating party to take an affirmative step as in its judgment will effectuate the purpose of the law. (§ 27-9-106)

# GOVERNMENT CONTRACTORS AND SUBCONTRACTORS

There is no relevant statutory provision. However, Exec. Order No. 1976-6 (November 15, 1976) requires all state contractors (and their subcontractors) not to discriminate on the basis of protected characteristics. Also, if federal funds are involved, federal law, Exec. Order No. 11246, 3 C.F.R. 339 (1965), *reprinted in* 42 U.S.C. § 2000e app. at 1232, 41 C.F.R. § 60-1.2, may apply.

# STATE EMPLOYEE LAWS

See "Fair Employment Laws."

# VETERAN'S PREFERENCE

Five points are added to the civil service examination passing scores of veterans, and ten points are added to the passing scores of disabled veterans. Veterans and their widows have general preference in state employment. [§§ 19-6-102(a), (c)]

# Community Life

# CREDIT

There is no relevant statutory provision. However, it should be noted that federal law, the Equal Credit Opportunity Act of 1977, 12 C.F.R. § 202, may apply.

# HOUSING

There is no relevant statutory provision. However, federal law, Title VIII of the Civil Rights Act of 1968, the Fair Housing Act, 42 U.S.C. §§ 3601–3619, and Exec. Order No. 11063, 3 C.F.R. 652 (1962), *reprinted in* 42 U.S.C. § 1982 app. at 1217-17, as amended by Exec. Order No. 12259, 3 C.F.R. 307 (1981), *reprinted in* 42 U.S.C. § 3608 app. at 816–818, may apply.

# INSURANCE

Discrimination is prohibited between individuals of the same class and equal expectation of life in rates charged for life insurance or annuity contracts or between individuals of the same class and of essentially the same hazard in the amount of premium, policy fees, or rates charged to disability insurance, in the benefits payable under these contracts, or in any other terms or conditions of these contracts. (§ 26-13-109)

> **ENFORCEMENT:** If after a hearing the Commissioner of Insurance finds that a person conducting an insurance business in the state has engaged in a prohibited act or practice, the commissioner shall order the person to cease and desist from engaging in the prohibited act or practice. (§ 26-13-115) If the prohibited act or practice is not discontinued, the commissioner may, through the attorney general, bring an action to enjoin and restrain the person engaging in the prohibited act or practice. (§ 26-13-116)

# PUBLIC ACCOMMODATIONS

It is unlawful to deny any person of good deportment the full and equal enjoyment, advantages, facilities, and priviliges of any public accommodation on the basis of sex. (§ 6-9-101)

> **ENFORCEMENT:** Any violation of this section is a misdemeanor punishable by imprisonment in the county jail for not more than 6 months and/or a fine of not more than $750. [§ 6-9-101(2)]

# APPENDIX A

## DIVORCE OR ANNULMENT

1   Incompatibility

2   Irretrievable breakdown

3   Impotence

4   Adultery

5   Abandonment

6   Imprisonment

7   Unnatural sexual behavior before or after marriage

8   Alcoholism and/or drug addiction

9   Confinement for incurable insanity

10   Wife pregnant by another at time of marriage without husband's knowledge

11   Physical abuse or reasonable apprehension of abuse

12   Desertion without support

13   Legal separation

14   Failure to consummate marriage

15   Conviction of a felony

16   Willful desertion

17   Cruel and inhuman treatment

18   Personal indignities

19   Bigamy

20   Endangering the life of the spouse

21   Willful neglect

22   Irreconcilable difference

23   Living apart because of incompatibility

24   Fraud

25   Habitual intemperance

26   Life imprisonment

27   Commission and/or conviction of an infamous crime

28   Voluntary separation

29   Separation caused by misconduct

30   Separation caused by mental illness

31   Living separate and apart without cohabitation

32   Lacks physical capacity to consummate marriage

33   Consent obtained by fraud, duress, or force

34   Party is of unsound mind

35   Minor married without lawful consent

36   Party lacked mental capacity to consent (including temporary incapacity resulting from drug or alcohol use)

37   One or both entered into marriage as a jest or dare

38   Incest

39   Conviction for offense involving moral turpitude

40   Incurable mental illness

41   One party suffers from loathsome disease unknown to the other

42   One party has infected the other with a communicable disease

43   Failure to perform a marital duty or obligation

44   Incompatibility by reason of mental illness or mental incapacity

45   Mistake in person or of fact

46   Sentence to death, imprisonment, or hard labor

47   Public defamation

48   Nonsupport whereby the party is able to provide support but grossly, wantonly, or cruelly refuses or neglects to provide suitable maintenance for the complaining spouse

# APPENDIX B

## CHILD CUSTODY

1   Moral character and prudence of the parents

2   Age and sex of the child

3   Physical, emotional, mental, religious, and social needs of the child

4   Capability and desire of each parent to meet the child's needs

5   Preference of the child

6   Preference of the child, if the child is of sufficient age and capacity

7   The love and affection existing between the child and each parent

8   Length of time the child has lived in a stable, satisfactory environment and the desirability of maintaining continuity

9   Desire and ability of each parent to allow an open and loving frequent relationship between the child and the other parent

10   Wishes of the parents

11   The child's adjustment to his or her home, school, and community

12   The mental and physical health of all individuals involved

13   No preference to be given because of parents' sex

14   Relationship of child with parents, siblings, and significant others

15   Conduct of proposed guardian to be considered only as it bears on his or her relationship with the child

16   The material needs of the child

17   The stability of the home environment likely to be offered by each parent

18   The education of the child

19   The advantages of keeping the child in the community where the child resides

20   The optional time for the child to spend with each parent

21   Any findings or recommendations of a neutral mediator

22   A history of violence between the parents

23   Other factors

24   The need to promote continuity and stability in the life of the child

# APPENDIX C

## JOINT OR SHARED CUSTODY

1 The ability of the parents to cooperate and make decisions jointly

2 The ability of the parties to encourage the sharing of love, affection, and contact between the child and the other party

3 Whether the past pattern of involvement of the parties with the child reflects a system of values and mutual support which indicate the parties' ability as joint custodians to provide a positive and nourishing relationship with the child

4 The physical proximity of the parties to each other as this relates to the practical considerations of where the child will reside

5 Whether an award of joint custody will promote more frequent or continuing contact between the child and each of the parties

6 The love, affection, and other emotional ties existing between the parents and the child

7 The capacity and disposition of the parents to provide the child with food, clothing, medical care or other remedial care recognized and permitted under the laws of this state in lieu of medcial care, and other material needs

8 The length of time the child has lived in a stable, satisfactory environment and the desirability of maintaining continuity

9 The permanence, as a family unit, of the existing or proposed custodial home

10 The fitness and suitability of the parents

11 The mental and physical health of the parents

12 The home, school, and community record of the child

13 The reasonable preference of the child, if the court deems the child to be of sufficient intelligence, understanding, and experience to express a preference

14 The nature of the physical and emotional environment in the home of each of the persons awarded joint custody

15 Any other factor considered relevant

16 The willingness and ability of the persons awarded joint custody to communicate and cooperate in advancing the child's welfare

17 The wishes of the child

18 The child has established a close and beneficial realtionship with both of the persons awarded joint custody

19 Both parents have actively cared for the child before and since the separation

20 One or both parents agree to, or are opposed to, joint custody

# APPENDIX D

## CHILD SUPPORT

1  The financial resources of the child
2  The financial resources of the custodial parent
3  The standard of living the child would have enjoyed if the marriage had not been dissolved
4  The physical and emotional conditions and educational needs of the child
5  The financial resources, needs, and obligations of both the noncustodial and the custodial parent
6  The excessive or abnormal expenditures, destruction, concealment, or fraudulent disposition of community, joint tenancy, and other property held in common
7  The age, health, and station of the parents
8  The occupation of each parent
9  The earning capacity of each parent
10  The amount and sources of income of each parent
11  The estate, vocational skills, and employability of each parent
12  The age, health, or station of the child
13  The child's occupation
14  The vocational skills of the child
15  The employability of the child
16  The estate and needs of the child
17  The standard of living and circumstances of each parent
18  The relative financial means of the parents
19  The need and capacity of the child for education, including higher education
20  The responsibility of the parents for the support of others
21  The value of services contributed by the custodial parent
22  The desirability of the parent having either sole custody or physical care of the child remaining in the home as a full-time parent
23  The cost of day care to the parent having custody or physical care of the child if that parent works outside the home, or the value of the child care services performed by that parent if the parent remains in the home
24  Tax consequences to each party
25  Other relevant factors

# APPENDIX E

## SPOUSAL SUPPORT OR ALIMONY

1  Is the custodian of a child whose condition or circumstances makes it appropriate for the spouse not to seek outside employment

2  The time necessary to acquire sufficient education and training to enable the spouse to find appropriate employment, and that party's future earning capacity

3  The standard of living established during the marriage

4  The duration of the marriage

5  The ability of the spouse from whom support is sought to meet his or her needs while meeting those of the spouse seeking support

6  Financial resources of the party seeking maintenance, including marital property apportioned to such party and such party's ability to meet his or her needs independently

7  The excessive or abnormal expenditures, the destruction, concealment, or fraudulent disposition of community, joint tenancy, and other property held in common

8  The comparative financial resources of the spouses, including their comparative earning abilities in the labor market

9  The needs and/or obligations of each party

10  Any other factors that the court deems just and equitable

11  The contribution of each party to the marriage, including but not limited to services rendered in homemaking, child care, education, and career building of the other party

12  The tax consequences to each spouse

13  The age of the parties

14  The physical and emotional conditions of the parties

15  The usual occupation of the parties during the marriage

16  Vocational skills and employability of the party seeking support and maintenance

17  Probable duration of the need of the party seeking support and maintenance

18  Custodial and child support responsibilities

19  The educational level of each party at the time of the marriage and at the time the action is commenced

20  Any mutual agreement between the parties concerning financial or service contributions by one party with the expectation of future reciprocation or compensation by the other

21  Any premarital agreements

22  The conduct of the parties during the marriage

# APPENDIX F

## PROPERTY DISTRIBUTION

1  The contribution of each spouse to the acquisition of the marital property, including the contribution of each spouse as homemaker

2  The value of each spouse's personal property

3  The economic circumstances of each spouse at the time the division of property is to become effective

4  Any increase or decrease in the value of the separate property of the spouse during the marriage or the depletion of the separate property for marital purposes

5  Length of the marriage

6  Age, health, and station in life of the parties

7  The occupation of the parties

8  The amount and sources of income of the parties

9  Vocational skills of the parties

10  Employability of the parties

11  Estate, liabilities, and needs of each party and opportunity of each for further acquisition of capital assets and income

12  The federal income tax consequences of the court's division of the property

13  Standard of living established during the marriage

14  Time necessary for a party to acquire sufficient education to enable the party to find appropriate employment

15  Any other factor necessary to do equity and justice between parties

16  Any premarital agreement

17  Liabilities of each spouse

18  The present and potential earning capability of each party

19  Retirement benefits, including but not limited to social security, civil service, military, and railroad retirement benefits

20  Prior marriage of each spouse

21  Whether the property award is in lieu of or in addition to alimony

22  How and by whom the property was acquired

23  The merits of each party

24  Burdens imposed upon either party for the benefit of the children

25   Custodial provisions for the children

26   Family ties and obligations

27   Needs of the children

28   The circumstances that contributed to the estrangment of the parties

29   The conduct of the parties during the marriage as it relates to the disposition of their property

# APPENDIX G

## REGIONAL OFFICES FOR CIVIL RIGHTS

*Region I: CT, ME, MA, NH, RI, VT*
Regional Director
Office for Civil Rights, Region I
Department of Education, Room 222
J. W. McCormack P.O. and Courthouse
Boston, MA 02109
Telephone: (617) 223-1154

*Region II: NJ, NY, PR, VI*
Regional Director
Office for Civil Rights, Region II
Department of Education
26 Federal Plaza, Room 33-130
New York, NY 10278
Telephone: (212) 264-4633

*Region III: DE, DC, MD, VA, PA, WV*
Regional Director
Office For Civil Rights, Region III
Department of Education
Gateway Building, 3535 Market Street
Post Office Box 13716
Philadelphia, PA 19104
Telephone: (215) 596-6772

*Region IV: AL, FL, GA, KY, MS, NC, SC, TN*
Regional Director
Office for Civil Rights, Region IV
Department of Education
101 Marietta Street NW, 27th Floor
Atlanta, GA 30323
Telephone: (404) 221-2954

*Region V: IL, IN, MI, MN, OH, WI*
Regional Director
Office for Civil Rights, Region V
Department of Education
300 South Wacker Drive, 18th Floor
Chicago, IL 60606
Telephone: (312) 886-3456

*Region VI: AR, LA, NM, OK, TX*
Regional Director
Office for Civil Rights, Region VI
Department of Education
1200 Main Tower Building, Room 1935
Dallas, TX 75202
Telephone: (214) 767-3951

*Region VII: IA, KS, MO, NE*
Regional Director
Office for Civil Rights, Region VII
Department of Education
324 E 11th Street, 24th Floor
Kansas City, MO 64106
Telephone: (816) 374-2223

*Region VIII: CO, MT, ND, SD, UT, WY*
Regional Director
Office for Civil Rights, Region VIII
Department of Education
Federal Office Building
1961 Stout Street, Room 1185
Denver, CO 80294
Telephone: (303) 844-5695

*Region IX: AZ, CA, NV, HI*
Acting Regional Director
Office for Civil Rights, Region IX
Department of Education
1275 Market Street, 14th Floor
San Francisco, CA 94103
Telephone: (415) 556-9894

*Region X: AK, ID, OR, WA*
Regional Director
Office for Civil Rights, Region X
Department of Education
2901 Third Avenue
Seattle, WA 98101
Telephone: (206) 442-1635

# CHAPTER NOTES

## CHAPTER 2

1 Graham Spanier, "Married and Unmarried Cohabitation in the United States, 1980," *Journal of Marriage and the Family*, vol. 45, no. 2, May 1983, pp. 277–288.

2 *Marvin v. Marvin* (I), 557 P.2d 106 (en banc) (Cal. 1976); *Marvin v. Marvin* (II), 5 Fam. L. Rptr. 3077 (1979); *Marvin v. Marvin* (III) 122 Cal. App. 3d 871 (176 Cal. 555, 1981).

3 *Weinberg v. Weinberg*, 6 FLR 2280 (BNA) (N.Y. Fam. Ct., Rensselaer Cty., 1980).

4 *Conley v. Richardson*, unreported decision.

5 Katherine Bouton, "Women and Divorce," *New York Magazine*, October 8, 1984, p. 37.

6 "First-Year Report of the New Jersey Supreme Court Task Force on Women in the Courts," Supreme Court of New Jersey, 1984.

7 *Real Women, Real Lives: Marriage, Divorce, Widowhood*, Governor's Commission on the Status of Women, Madison, Wisc., 1978, p. 54.

8 Carol H. Lefcourt, *Women and the Law*, Clark Boardman, New York, 1984, sec. 6.03, pp. 6–7.

9 "State Divorce Laws Chart and Summary Sheet: Introduction," *Family Law Reporter*, Bureau of National Affairs, Washington, D.C., 1984, p. 3.

10 See, for example, Kentucky Revised Statutes, §§ 406.011 and 406.021 (1970).

11 *Griswold v. Connecticut*, 381 U.S. 479 (1965).

12 *Eisenstadt v. Baird*, 405 U.S. 438 (1972).

13 *Carey v. Population Services International*, 431 U.S. 678 (1977).

14 *Roe v. Wade*, 410 U.S. 113, *reh. den.* 410 U.S. 959 (1973).

15 *Planned Parenthood v. Danforth*, 428 U.S. 52 (1976).

16 *Bellotti v. Baird*, 443 U.S. 622, *reh. den.* _____ U.S. _____, 100 S.Ct. 185 (1979).

17 *H.L. v. Matheson*, 450 U.S. 398 (1981).

18 *City of Akron v. Akron Center for Reproductive Health*, 462 U.S. 416 (1983).

19 Ibid.; see also *Planned Parenthood Association v. Ashcroft*, 462 U.S. 476 (1983).

20 *Beal v. Doe*, 432 U.S. 438 (1977); *Maher v. Roe*, 432 U.S. 464 (1977).

21 *Harris v. McRae*, 448 U.S. 297, *reh. den.* 448 U.S. 917 (1980).

22 Richard Grossboll, "Sterilization Abuse: Current State of the Law and Remedies for Abuse," *10 Golden Gate Law Review*, 1980, pp. 1188–1189.

23 W. Blackstone Comm. 445 (7th ed. 1775); *Bradley v. State*, 2 Miss. (Walker) 156–158 (Miss. Sup. Ct. 1824).

24 Susan Schecter, *Women and Male Violence: The Visions and Struggles of the Battered Women's Movement*, South End Press, Boston, 1982.

25 Susan Deller Ross and Ann Barcher, *The Rights of Women: The Basic ACLU Guide to a Woman's Rights*, rev. ed., Bantam, New York, 1983.

26 *Real Women, Real Lives*, op. cit., p. 41.

27 Simone de Beauvoir, *The Second Sex*, Bantam, New York, 1970, pp. 541–542.

# CHAPTER 3

1 Caroline Bird, *Born Female*, Simon & Schuster, New York, 1969, p. 20.

2 *Grove City College v. Bell*, _____ U.S. _____, 104 S.Ct. _____ (1984).

3 Nancy Duff Campbell, Marcia D. Greenberger, Margaret A. Kohn, and Shirley J. Wilcher, *Sex Discrimination in Education: Legal Rights and Remedies*, vol. 1, National Women's Law Center, Washington, D.C., 1983, pp. 2–46.

4 Ibid. The case referred to is *O'Connor v. Board of Education*, 645 F.2d 578 (7th Cir.), *cert. denied* 454 U.S. 1084 (1981).

5 *North Haven Board of Education v. Bell*, 456 U.S. 512 (1982).

6 *Cleveland Board of Education v. La Fleur*, 414 U.S. 632 (1974).

7 *De La Cruz v. Tormey*, 582 F.2d 45 (1978), *cert. den.* 441 U.S. 965 (1979).

8 "Statement of the National Coalition for Women and Girls in Education: Recommendations on H.R. 4164, the Vocational Technical Education Act of 1983," testimony presented in Washington, D.C., November 3, 1983, p. 3.

9 Sally Reed, "The Reform Movement Still Surging," *The New York Times Fall Survey of Education*, November 11, 1984, p. 33.

# CHAPTER 4

1 J. P. Smith and M. P. Ward, *Women's Wages and Work in the Twentieth Century*, Rand Corporation, Santa Monica, Calif., 1984, p. xviii.

2 *Weeks v. Southern Bell*, 408 F.2d 228 (5th Cir. 1969).

3 Smith and Ward, *Women's Wages*, op. cit.

4 *County of Washington v. Gunther*, 452 U.S. 161 (1981).

5 *AFSCME v. State of Washington*, 578 F. Supp. 846 (1983); rev'd, 770 F.2d 1401 (9th Cir. 1985).

6 Cited in Jolene Saunders, "Law: Sexual Harassment," *Working Woman Magazine*, February 1984, p. 43.

7 Following is an alphabetical listing of the states with the exceptions to the employment-at-will doctrine they recognize:

| | | |
|---|---|---|
| Alabama ......... implied contract | Maryland ......... public policy tort | Ohio ............ implied contract; |
| Alaska ........... implied contract | Massachusetts ............. implied | no public policy tort |
| Arizona .......... implied contract | covenant | Oklahoma ........ implied contract |
| Arkansas ......... implied contract | Michigan ......... implied contract | Oregon .......... implied contract |
| California ............... covenant | Minnesota ........ implied contract | Pennsylvania ....... implied contract |
| of good faith | Missouri .......... implied contract | S. Carolina ........ public policy tort |
| Connecticut ...... public policy tort | Montana ........ implied covenant | S. Dakota ........ implied contract |
| District of Columbia ........ implied | Nebraska ........ implied contract; | Tennessee ........ public policy tort |
| contract; no public policy tort | no public policy tort | Texas ............ implied contract |
| Hawaii ........... public policy tort | Nevada .......... implied contract | Virginia ........... implied contract |
| Idaho ........... public policy tort | New Hampshire .... public policy tort | Washington ........ implied contract |
| Illinois ........... implied contract | New Jersey ....... implied contract | W. Virginia ........ public policy tort |
| Indiana ................... implied | New Mexico ....... implied contract | Wisconsin ........ implied contract; |
| covenant | New York ........ implied contract; | contract action permitted |
| Kansas .......... public policy tort | no public policy tort | based on public policy violations |
| Kentucky ......... implied contract | N. Carolina ....... public policy tort | but not tort action |
| Maine ........... implied contract | N. Dakota ....... implied covenant | Wyoming ......... implied contract |

8   William Serrin, "Experts Say Job Bias Against Women Persists," *The New York Times*, November 25, 1984, p. A1.

# CHAPTER 5

1   Boston Women's Health Book Collective, *The New Our Bodies, Ourselves*, Simon & Schuster, New York, 1984, p. 102.

2   Cited in Diana E. H. Russell, *Rape in Marriage*, Macmillan, New York, 1982, p. 17.

3   *Coker v. Georgia*, 433 U.S. 84 (1977).

4   *Miller v. California*, 413 U.S. 15 (1973).

5   Mary Kay Blakely, "Is One Woman's Sexuality Another Woman's Pornography?" *Ms.*, April 1985, p. 37.

6   *American Booksellers Assoc. v. Hudnut*, 54 U.S.L.W. 3560 (1986).

7   See "Women and Combat: A Comparison of the Services' Laws and Policies," *WEAL Facts*, Women's Equity Action League, Washington, D.C., 1985.

8   *Rostker v. Goldberg*, 453 U.S. 57 (1981).

9   District of Columbia Code, § 1-2515 (1967).

10  Maine Revised Statutes Annotated, tit. 5, § 4582 (1964).

11  Linda Greenhouse, "Court Says States Can Force Jaycees to Admit Women," *The New York Times*, July 4, 1984, pp. A1, B5.

12  Ruth Sivard, *Women: A World Survey*, World Priorities Press, P.O. Box 25140, Washington, DC 20007.

13  *Forward-Looking Strategies of Implementation for the Advancement of Women and Concrete Measures to Overcome Obstacles to the Achievement of the Goals and Objectives of the United Nations Decade for Women for the Period 1986 to the Year 2000: Equality, Development, Peace*, U.N Document A/CONF 116/PC/24, United Nations General Assembly, New York, May 1985.

14  Ibid., pp. 14–15.

15  Ethel Klein, *Gender Politics: From Consciousness to Mass Politics*, Harvard University Press, Cambridge, Mass., 1984, p. 172.

# SELECTED READINGS

## GENERAL REFERENCE

Adler, Mortimer J., and Charles Van Doren (eds.): *Great Treasury of Western Thought*, Bowker, New York, 1977.

Barron, Cynthia: "Rape Trauma Syndrome," *Harvard Women's Law Journal*, vol. 7, no. 1, Spring 1984, p. 301.

Berger, Margaret A.: *Litigation on behalf of Women*, Ford Foundation, New York, 1980.

Bird, Caroline, and Sara Welles Briller: *Born Female*, Pocket Books, New York, 1969.

Boston Women's Health Book Collective: *The New Our Bodies, Ourselves*, Simon & Schuster, New York, 1984.

Cary, Eve, and Kathleen Willert Peratis: *Woman and the Law*, National Textbook Company, Skokie, Ill., 1981.

De Beauvoir, Simone: *The Second Sex*, Bantam, New York, 1952.

Epstein, Cynthia Fuchs: *Women in Law*, Basic, New York, 1981.

Gimlin, Hoyt (ed.): *Editorial Research Reports on the Women's Movement Agenda for the 80's*, Congressional Quarterly, Washington, D.C., 1981.

Gold, Maxine (ed.): *Women Making History*, Commission on the Status of Women, New York, 1985.

Gornick, Vivian, and Barbara K. Moran (eds.): *Woman in Sexist Society: Studies in Power and Powerlessness*, New American Library, New York, 1972.

Hewlett, Sylvia Ann: *A Lesser Life: The Myth of Women's Liberation in America*, William Morrow, New York, 1986.

ISIS Women's International Information and Communication Service: *Women in Development: A Resource Guide for Organization and Action*, New Society Publishers, Philadelphia, 1984.

Lefcourt, Carol H. (ed.): *Women and the Law*, Clark Boardman, New York, 1984.

Morgan, Robin (ed.): *Sisterhood Is Global: The International Women's Movement Anthology*, Anchor Press/Doubleday, New York, 1984.

"NOW Legal Defense and Education Fund 1983–1984 Report," NOWLDEF, New York, 1983.

"NOW Legal Defense and Education Fund Report 2000," NOWLDEF, New York, 1985.

Readers Digest Editors: *Family Legal Guide: A Complete Encyclopedia of Law for the Layman*, Random House, New York, 1981.

Ross, Susan Deller, and Ann Barcher: *The Rights of Women: The Basic ACLU Guide to a Woman's Rights*, rev. ed., Bantam, New York, 1983.

*Social Indicators of Equality for Minorities and Women*, U.S. Commission on Civil Rights, Washington, D.C., August 1978.

*Sourcebook: Tenth National Conference on Women and the Law*, University of Texas School of Law, Austin, Tex., 1979.

*Sourcebook: Fourteenth National Conference on Women and the Law*, Georgetown University Law Center, Washington, D.C., 1983.

Zavitz, Carol, and Hans Kleipool: "International Guide to Women's Periodicals and Resources 1981/82," *Resources for Feminist Research*, vol. 10, no. 4, 1981–1982, pp. 33–95.

# THE LEGAL PROCESS

Levi, Edward H.: *An Introduction to Legal Reasoning*, University of Chicago Press, Chicago, 1948.

Pound, Roscoe: *An Introduction to the Philosophy of Law*, Yale University Press, New Haven, 1959.

# HOME AND FAMILY

Avner, Judith, and Susan Herman: *Divorce Mediation: A Guide for Women*, NOW Legal Defense and Education Fund, New York, 1984.

Bouton, Katherine: "Women and Divorce," *New York Magazine*, October 8, 1984, pp. 34–41.

Brody, Jane E.: "Hope Grows for Vigorous Old Age," *The New York Times*, October 2, 1984, pp. C1, C10.

Brown, Mark Richardson: "Whose Life (Insurance) Is It Anyway? Life Insurance and Divorce in America," *Journal of Family Law*, vol. 22, 1983–1984, pp. 95–128.

Brozan, Nadine: "Complex Problems of Teen-Age Pregnancy," *The New York Times*, March 2, 1985, p. 48.

Collins, Glenn: "Remarriage: Bigger Ready-Made Families," *The New York Times*, May 13, 1985, p. B5.

*Daedalus*, vol. 106, no. 2, Spring 1977, entire issue.

Dodson, Diane, and Robert Horowitz: "Child Support Enforcement Amendments of 1984: New Tools for Enforcement," *Family Law Reporter*, Monograph 5, Bureau of National Affairs, Washington, D.C., 1984.

Dullea, Georgia: "Turning to Mediation to Settle a Divorce," *The New York Times*, October 8, 1984, p. C12.

Ehrenreich, Barbara: "Hers: Is Abortion Really a Moral Dilemma?" *The New York Times*, November 16, 1984, p. A20.

Gallen, Richard, Judith Kaplan, and Joseph Bianco: *The Unmarried Couple's Legal Handbook*, Dell, New York, 1981.

Goodman, Walter: "New Reproduction Techniques Redefine Parenthood," *The New York Times*, November 16, 1984, p. A21.

Gordon, Michael (ed.): *The American Family in Social and Historical Perspective*, 2d. ed., St. Martin's, New York, 1978.

Green, William: "Parents, Judges and A Minor's Abortion Decision: Third-Party Participation and the Evolution of a Judicial Alternative," *Akron Law Review*, vol. 17, no. 1, Summer 1983, pp. 87–110.

Grosboll, Dick: "Sterilization Abuse: Current State of the Law and Remedies for Abuse," *Golden Gate Law Review*, vol. 10, 1980, pp. 1147–1189.

Hauserman, Nancy R., and Carol C Fethke: "Military Pensions as Divisible Assets: The Uniformed Services Former S⌐ ⌐uses' Protection Act," *Journal of Legislation*, vol. 11, no. 27, 1984, pp. 27–55.

Hoffman, Jan: "By Her Husband's Hand," *The Village Voice*, August 13, 1985, p. 16.

Howell, John Cotton: *The Citizen's Legal Guide to No-Fault Divorce*, Prentice-Hall, Englewood Cliffs, N.J., 1979.

"House Adopts Bill to Enforce Child Support," *The New York Times*, August 8, 1984, p. A12.

Klemesrud, Judy: "Number of Single-Parent Adoptions Grows," *The New York Times*, November 19, 1984, p. C13.

Kolko, S. Joel (ed.): *Family Law Handbook*, Bureau of National Affairs, Washington, D.C., 1985.

Loeb, Leonard: "Introduction to the Standards of Practice for Family Mediators," *Family Law Quarterly*, vol. 17, no. 4, Winter 1984, pp. 451–453.

Margolick, David: "Legal Rights of Embryos," *The New York Times*, June 27, 1984, p. 12.

————: " 'Marital Rape: Law's Critics Join an Appeal," *The New York Times*, December 18, 1984, p. B1.

————: "Top State Court Rules Husbands Can Be Charged in Rape of Wives," *The New York Times*, December 21, 1984, pp. A1, A32.

Marks, Lynn A.: "Some Problems with Using Mediation in Child Sexual Abuse Cases," paper presented at the Conference on Women and Mediation, New York University Law School, New York, January 21–22, 1984.

McCoy, Elin: "Grandparents Seek Rights to Visit With a Grandchild," *The New York Times*, October 8, 1984, p. C12.

"National Assembly on the Future of the Family: A Report," NOW Legal Defense and Education Fund, New York, 1979.

"New Laws Recognizing Marital Rape as a Crime," *The New York Times*, December 29, 1984, p. B5.

Nichols, Margaret J.: "Issues to Consider Regarding Mediation of Custody Disputes," paper presented at the Conference on Women and Mediation, New York University Law School, New York, January 21–22, 1984.

Nordheimer, Jon: "Florida Bombing Case Offers Glimpse of Abortion Conflict," *The New York Times*, January 18, 1985, p. A12.

Pear, Robert: "Study Challenges Pension Proposal," *The New York Times*, December 30, 1984, p. A1.

Pearson, Jessica, and Nancy Thoennes: "Mediating and Litigating Custody Disputes," *Family Law Quarterly*, vol. 17, no. 4, Winter 1984, pp. 497–517.

*Real Women, Real Lives: Marriage, Divorce, Widowhood*, Governor's Commission on the Status of Women, Madison, Wisc., 1978.

"Report of the New York Task Force on Women in the Courts," State of New York Unified Court System, Office of Court Administration, March 1986.

*The Retirement Equity Act of 1984 Fact Sheet*, Pension Rights Center, Washington, D.C., 1984.

Simone, Joseph: "New Act Changes Rules Affecting Women's Pensions," *New York Law Journal*, September 17, 1984, p. 1.

"Special Section on the 1984 Tax Reform Act," *Fairshare: The Monthly Letter of Divorce, Alimony and Division of Marital Property*, vol. 4, no. 9, 1984, pp. 3–9.

"Statement of the NOW Legal Defense and Education Fund and the National Center on Women and Family Law before the Subcommittee on Select Education, Committee on Education and Labor, U.S. House of Representatives, on Non-Payment of Child Support," testimony presented in Washington, D.C., September 12, 1983.

"Testimony of the NOW Legal Defense and Education Fund before the Senate Finance Committee on the Retirement Equity Act of 1983 (S. 19) and the Economic Equity Act of 1983 (S. 888)," testimony presented in Washington, D.C., June 21, 1983.

"Testimony of the NOW Legal Defense and Education Fund Relating to the Problems of Older Women Submitted to the House Select Committee on Aging," testimony presented in Washington, D.C., June 26, 1983.

Troyan, William M.: "Pension Evaluation and Equitable Distribution," *Family Law Reporter*, Monograph 1, Bureau of National Affairs, Washington, D.C., 1983.

————: "Divorce and the Valuation of a Disability Pension," *Family Law Reporter*, Monograph 4, Bureau of National Affairs, Washington, D.C., 1984.

Webb, Marilyn: "The Joys and Sorrows of Joint Custody" *New York Magazine*, November 5, 1984, p. 38.

Weitzman, Lenore: "The Economic Consequences of Divorce: An Empirical Study of Property, Alimony, and Child Support Awards," *Family Law Reporter*, Monograph 8, Bureau of National Affairs, Washington, D.C., 1982.

# EDUCATION

Campbell, Nancy Duff, Marcia D. Greenberger, Margaret A. Kohn, and Shirley J. Wilcher: *Sex Discrimination in Education: Legal Rights and Remedies*, National Women's Law Center, Washington, D.C., 1983.

"Feminism in the Academy," *Academe*, September-October 1983, pp. 11–37.

Fiske, Edward B.: "Technology Gaining a Place in Liberal Arts Curriculum," *The New York Times*, April 29, 1984, pp. A1, A20.

————: "Vocational Schools: Problems amid Innovations," *The New York Times*, July 5, 1984, p. B2.

————: "States Gain Wider Influence on School Policy," *The New York Times*, December 4, 1984, pp. A1, A40.

*Grove City College v. Bell: Fact Sheet:* National Coalition for Women and Girls in Education, Washington, D.C., 1983.

Johnson, Laurie Olsen (ed.): *Nonsexist Curricular Materials for Elementary Schools*, The Feminist Press, New York, 1974.

Project on Equal Education Rights: "A Clash of Ideologies: The Reagan Administration Versus the Women's Educational Equity Act," NOW Legal Defense and Education Fund, New York, 1983.

————: "Cracking the Glass Slipper: PEER's Guide to Ending Sex Bias in Your Schools," NOW Legal Defense and Education Fund, New York, 1978.

————: "Selected Excerpts from State Laws for Sex Equity in Education," NOW Legal Defense and Education Fund, New York, 1983.

Rippa, S. Alexander (ed.): *Educational Ideas in America: A Documentary History*, David McKay, New York, 1969.

Schneider, William: "The Public Schools: A Consumer Report," *American Educator*, vol. 8, no. 1, Spring 1984, pp. 1217.

"Statement of Dr. Leslie Wolfe, Former Director, Women's Educational Equity Act Program, Department of Education, before the Committee on Education and Labor, Subcommittee on Elementary, Secondary, and Vocational Education and Committee on Post Office and Civil Service, Subcommittee on Investigations, U.S. House of Representatives," testimony presented in Washington, D.C., September 27, 1983.

"Statement of the National Coalition for Women and Girls in Education: Recommendations on H.R. 4164, the Vocational Technical Education Act of 1983, before the Subcommittee on Elementary, Secondary, and Vocational Education, Committee on Education and Labor, U.S. House of Representatives," testimony presented in Washington, D.C., November 3, 1983.

# EMPLOYMENT

Beck, Joan: "Working Couples Not About to Get Social Security Break," *Fort Lauderdale News/Sun-Sentinel*, January 9, 1985, p. 11A.

Brozan, Nadine: "Disabled Women Meet Role Models," *The New York Times*, November 28, 1984, pp. C1, C11.

*1984 Guidebook to Fair Employment Practices*, Commerce Clearing House, Chicago, Ill., 1983.

Dullea, Georgia: "Women Win the Prize of Law Partnership," *The New York Times*, February 25, 1985, p. B5.

English, Carey: "Bright Job Prospects for the Class of 1985," *U.S. News & World Report*, December 17, 1984, pp. 64–65.

————: "Why It's Harder to Fire Workers These Days," *U.S. News & World Report*, June 4, 1984.

Gross, Jane: "Against the Odds: A Woman's Ascent on Wall Street," *The New York Times Magazine*, January 6, 1985, p. 16.

Hacker, Andrew: "Women vs. Men in the Workforce," *The New York Times Magazine*, December 9, 1984, pp. 124–129.

Hunter, Marjorie: "Hypocrisy of In-House Job Bias," *The New York Times*, January 23, 1985.

Jacoby, Susan: "How 40,000 Women Feel About Their Jobs," *McCall's*, January 1985, p. 69.

Johnson, Sharon: "Women and Long Workdays," *The New York Times*, June 25, 1984, p. B9.

Lewin, Tamar: "Maternity Leave: Is It Leave, Indeed?" *The New York Times*, July 22, 1984, pp. F1, F23.

Lewin, Tamar: "Women in Board Rooms Are Still the Exception," *The New York Times*, pp. C1, C8.

Marshall, Ray: *Work and Women in the 1980's: A Perspective on Basic Trends Affecting Women's Jobs and Job Opportunities*, Women's Research and Education Institute, Congressional Caucus for Women's Issues, Washington, D.C., 1983.

Noble, Kenneth B.: "Comparable Worth among Differing Jobs: How It's Figured," *The New York Times*, February 27, 1985, p. C7.

Russell, Diana E. H.: *Sexual Exploitation: Rape, Child Sexual Abuse and Workplace Harassment*, Sage, Beverly Hills, Calif., 1984.

Salmans, Sandra: "Mentors, Managers and Mary Cunningham," *The New York Times*, June 24, 1984, p. F15.

Saunders, Jolene: "Law: Sexual Harassment," *Working Woman Magazine*, February 1984, pp. 40–44.

Serrin, William: "Experts Say Job Bias against Women Persists," *The New York Times*, November 25, 1984, pp. A1, 32L.

Smith, James, and Michael P. Ward: *Women's Wages and Work in the Twentieth Century*, The Rand Corporation, Santa Monica, Calif., 1984.

Storrie, Kathleen, and Pearl Dykstra: "Bibliography on Sexual Harassment," *Resources for Feminist Research*, vol. 10, no. 4, 1981–1982, pp. 25–32.

Szinovacz, Maximiliane: *Women's Retirement: Policy Implications of Recent Research*, Beverly Hills, Calif., Sage, 1982.

*Time for a Change: 1983 Handbook on Women Workers*, Women's Bureau, U.S. Department of Labor, Washington, D.C., 1983.

"U.N. Chief to Hear Women's Job Complaints," *The New York Times*, November 25, 1984, p. 6L.

"Women in Clerical Jobs Band Together to Learn 9-to-5 Rights," *The New York Times*, February 17, 1985, p. C9.

"World of Work: Company Maternity Leave Policies," *Working Woman Magazine*, February 1984, pp. 79–84.

# WOMEN IN THE COMMUNITY

Abzug, Bella, and Mim Kelber: "Despite the Reagan Sweep, a Gender Gap Remains," *The New York Times*, November 23, 1984, p. A35.

Atwill, Janet: "Single Parents in the Military," *WEAL Facts*, Women's Equity Action League, Washington, D.C., 1983.

"Battered Women's Victories," *Clearinghouse Review*, January 1984, pp. 1020–1022.

Becraft, Carolyn, and Jennifer Dew: "Benefits for Former Spouses of Active-Duty Military Personnel," *WEAL Facts*, Women's Equity Action League, Washington, D.C., 1984.

——— and Susan Scheer: "Benefits for Former Spouses of Retired Military Personnel," *WEAL Facts*, Women's Equity Action League, Washington, D.C., 1984.

Blakely, Mary Kay: "Is One Woman's Sexuality Another Woman's Pornography?" *Ms.*, April 1985, p. 37.

Blakely, Susan Smith: "Credit Opportunity for Women: The ECOA and Its Effects," *Wisconsin Law Review*, vol. 6, 1981, pp. 655–697.

Boffey, Philip M.: "Women Lose a Round in Club Battle," *The New York Times*, January 24, 1985, p. A22.

Bolotin, Susan: "People Are Talking About . . . Politics '85 . . . ," *Vogue*, February 1985, p. 88.

Card, Emily: *Staying Solvent: A Comprehensive Guide to Equal Credit for Women*, Holt, Rinehart & Winston, New York, 1985.

Carney, Robert Mark, and Brian D. Williams: "Premenstrual Syndrome: A Criminal Defense," *Notre Dame Lawyer*, vol. 59, no. 253, 1983, pp. 253–269.

"City Agrees to Provide a Nursery in Women's Jail on Rikers Island," *The New York Times*, September 25, 1984, p. B2.

Cutts, Karen: "Women Investors: How to Avoid Being Patronized, Intimidated and Short-Changed," *Money Maker Magazine*, February-March 1984, pp. 14–18.

"Debate Persists on Rights and Smut," *The New York Times*, November 21, 1984, p. A17.

*Decade for Women Information Resources for 1985*, a six-part series prepared by the International Women's Tribune Center, 777 United Nations Plaza, New York, NY 10017.

Dowd, Maureen, "Reassessing Women's Political Role," *The New York Times Magazine*, December 30, 1984, p. 18.

Dullea, Georgia: "Institute on Women Created," *The New York Times*, November 19, 1984, p. C13.

Ehrenreich, Barbara: "A Feminist's View of the New Man," *The New York Times Magazine*, May 20, 1984, p. 36.

Fein, Esther B.: "The Choice: Women Officers Decide to Stay In or Leave," *The New York Times Magazine*, May 5, 1985, p. 32.

Ferry, Michael, Nina Balsam, and Ruth Przybeck: "Litigation of the Necessaries Doctrine: Funding for Battered Women's Shelters," *Clearinghouse Review*, March 1984, pp. 1193–1202.

*Forward-Looking Strategies of Implementation for the Advancement of Women and Concrete Measures to Overcome Obstacles to the Achievement of the Goals and Objectives of the United Nations Decade for Women for the Period 1986 to the Year 2000: Equality, Development, Peace*, U.N. Document A/CONF. 116/PC/24, United Nations General Assembly, New York, May 1985.

Franklin, Ben A.: "Judge Penalizes Burning Tree Club," *The New York Times*, September 14, 1984, pp. A1, A22.

Friedan, Betty: "How To Get the Women's Movement Moving Again," *The New York Times Magazine*, November 3, 1985, p. 26.

————: "Women on the Firing Line," *The New York Times Magazine*, October 28, 1984, p. 24.

Friendly, Jonathan: "Case of Rape Tests Privacy Law," *The New York Times*, June 3, 1984, pp. B1, B28.

Gusssow, Mel: "Women Playwrights: New Voices in the Theater," *The New York Times Magazine*, May 1, 1983, p. 22.

Hopson, Janet, and Anne Rosenfeld: "PMS: Puzzling Monthly Symptoms," *Psychology Today*, August 1984, pp. 30–35.

*Implementing Your State Equal Rights Amendment: An Action Manual*, NOW Legal Defense and Education Fund and Women's Law Project, New York, 1984.

*Inequality of Sacrifice: The Impact of the Reagan Budget on Women*, 1985 update, published by the Coalition on Women and the Budget, National Women's Law Center, 1751 N Street NW, Washington, DC 20036, 1985.

Kaufman, Stephen R.: "Comment on Banning 'Actuarially Sound' Discrimination: The Proposed Nondiscrimination in Insurance Act," *Harvard Journal on Legislation*, vol. 20, 1983, pp. 631–645.

Klein, Ethel: *Gender Politics: From Consciousness to Mass Politics*, Harvard University Press, Cambridge, Mass., 1984.

"Long Delayed Rape Case Raises Issues of Women's Press Rights," *Dallas Times Herald*, February 5, 1984, p. A13.

Maloney, Lawrence D., Maureen Walsh, Richard L. DeLouise: "Welfare in America: Is It A Flop?" *U.S. News & World Report*, December 24, 1984, pp. 38–43.

Maslin, Janet: "Men and Women in Film: A War Zone Update," *The New York Times*, "Arts and Leisure," August 26, 1984, p. 1.

Matheson, John H.: "The Equal Credit Opportunity Act: A Functional Failure," *Harvard Journal on Legislation*, vol. 21, 1984, pp. 371–403.

"Montana Debates Sex-Blind Insurance Law," *The New York Times*, February 17, 1985, p. 33.

*Myths and Facts about Battered Women*, National Coalition Against Domestic Violence, 1500 Massachusetts Avenue NW, Washington, DC 20005, 1983.

Mulligan, Nora: "Premenstrual Syndrome," *Harvard Women's Law Journal*, vol. 6, no. 1, 1983, pp. 219–227.

"A New Approach to Raising $$$ for Shelters: Sue the Batterer," *Marriage and Divorce Today Newsletter*, July 23, 1984, p.2.

"NOW Sues Over Sex-Based Insurance Rates," *The New York Times*, August 17, 1984, p. A15.

Perlez, Jane: "Ferraro The Campaigner," *The New York Times Magazine*, September 30, 1984, p. 22.

————: "Women, Power and Politics," *The New York Times Magazine*, June 24, 1984, p. 22.

*Piecing It Together: Feminism and Nonviolence*, Feminism and Nonviolence Study Group, 2 College Close, Buckleigh, Westward Ho, Devon EX 39 1 BL, England, in cooperation with the War Resisters International, 55 Dawes Street, London SE 17, 1 EL, England, 1983.

"Public Opinion: The Role of Women in the Military," *WEAL Facts*, Women's Equity Action League, Washington, D.C., 1984.

"Recruitment Statistics and Policies: Women in the Active Armed Services," *WEAL Facts*, Women's Equity Action League, Washington, D.C., 1985.

Rich, Frank: "Theater's Gender Gap Is a Chasm," *The New York Times*, "Arts and Leisure," September 30, 1984, p. 1.

Schoen, Rodric B.: "The Texas Equal Rights Amendment after the First Decade: Judicial Developments 1978–1982," *Houston Law Review*, vol. 20, no. 1321, 1983, pp. 1978–1982.

Schwartz, Susan: "An Argument for the Elimination of the Resistance Requirement from the Definition of Forcible Rape," *Loyola of Los Angeles Law Review*, vol. 16, 1983, pp. 567–602.

Shreve, Anita: "The Working Mother As Role Model," *The New York Times Magazine*, September 9, 1984, p. 39.

Steele, Theo: "New Leadership in the Public Interest," NOW Legal Defense and Education Fund, New York, 1981.

"Testimony before the Subcommittee on Civil and Constitutional Rights of the Judiciary Committee of the House of Representatives," testimony presented by Carolyn Becraft, Women's Equity Action League, National Information Center on Women and the Military, Washington, D.C., October 26, 1983.

"Testimony before the Subcommittee on Civil and Constitutional Rights of the Judiciary Committee of the House of Representatives," testimony presented by Jeanne Paquette Atkins, Women's Equity Action League, National Information Center on Women and the Military, in Washington, D.C., October 26, 1983.

Third-World Forum on Women, Law and Development: *Interim Report and Recommendations*, based on Women, Law and Development seminars, Nairobi, Kenya, July 12–18, 1985 (OEF International, 2101 L Street NW, Washington, DC 20037).

"The War against Pornography," *Newsweek*, March 18, 1985, pp. 58–67.

"Women—A New Superpower," *Ms.*, March 1985, pp. 41–74.

"Women and Combat: A Comparison of the Services' Laws and Policies," *WEAL Facts*, Women's Equity Action League, Washington, D.C., 1985.

"Women in Government," *Barnard Alumnae Magazine*, Winter 1985, pp. 2–13.

"Women of the Year," *Ms.*, January 1985, entire issue.

"Women: Problems and Possibilities," *Lifeline*, vol. 3, no. 1, Winter 1984, entire issue.